As the Romans Did

As the Romans Did

A Source Book in Roman Social History

Jo-Ann Shelton

New York   Oxford
Oxford University Press
1988

Oxford University Press

Oxford   New York   Toronto
Delhi   Bombay   Calcutta   Madras   Karachi
Petaling Jaya   Singapore   Hong Kong   Tokyo
Nairobi   Dar es Salaam   Cape Town
Melbourne   Auckland

and associated companies in
Beirut   Berlin   Ibadan   Nicosia

Published by Oxford University Press, Inc.,
200 Madison Avenue, New York, New York 10016

Library of Congress Cataloging-in-Publication Data
Shelton, Jo-Ann.
As the Romans did.
Bibliography: p.   Includes index. 1. Rome—Social conditions.   2. Social structure—
Rome.   3. Rome—Social life and customs.   4. Social history—To 500.   I. Title.
HN10.R7S45   1987   306'.945'632   87–1582
ISBN 0–19–504176–3   ISBN 0–19–504177–1   pbk.

1 3 5 7 9 8 6 4 2

Printed in the United States of America
on acid-free paper

For my parents,
Max and Helen Shelton

Causa fuit pater his.
(Horace, *Satire* 1.6.71)

Preface

The civilization of the ancient Romans has influenced almost every aspect of our own modern society. On countless occasions we still do as the Romans did. Yet many of us envisage these lively, dynamic, and talkative people as marble statues standing grimly silent in museum hallways. It is the purpose of this book to allow the ancient Romans to step forward and talk to us about themselves. Sociologists gather data about the modern world from personal interviews; social historians must rely for "personal interviews" on the written words of people who lived in the past. This book is an anthology of translations into English of materials written in Latin and Greek about two thousand years ago. It is designed to offer people interested in Roman social history the opportunity to examine at first hand literary source material from the ancient world. These materials include personal letters, legal documents, graffiti, poems, farming manuals, recipes, medical texts, business contracts, and funerary inscriptions. The words were written, engraved, or painted on papyrus, metal, stone, wax, plaster, or clay, and they provide a variety of data.

Our data about the ancient Roman world are paradoxically both incomplete and yet overwhelming. The documents which survive are myriad in number because they accumulated during a thousand years of human history; yet their survival was largely a matter of chance. There exist today, for example, only a few of all the letters written on papyrus in the Roman period, and these are not necessarily the letters a historian would have chosen for preservation. Chance has saved for us some documents which are relatively uninformative, while destroying countless others that might have been very enlightening. Most of the documents, moreover, were never intended by their writers to be informative to subsequent generations, any more than we expect our own personal letters, business contracts, or shopping lists to be of historical value. Gaps exist therefore in our knowledge of the ancient Romans. And since this book contains only a small selection of the extant documents which in turn represent only a small number of the total documents written during the Roman period, it cannot claim to give the reader a complete picture of the lives of the Romans. The passages, however, have been carefully chosen so as to provide data which will enable the reader to gain an accurate perspective on many, diverse aspects of life in the ancient Roman world.

The terms *ancient Roman world* and *Roman civilization* resist a single or simple definition. Civilization is never a static phenomenon. And the number of people who participated in the achievements of the Roman world increased even as the borders of the Roman Empire expanded. The people who lived in the farm village on the hills above the mouth of the Tiber River gradually but relentlessly extended their power and influence throughout Italy, and then throughout Europe and the entire Mediterranean world, until their village, Rome, evolved into a cosmopolitan city which was the mistress of a vast empire. For a thousand years, the inhabitants of Rome dominated the people they encountered. They "Romanized" them and extended to them not only their language, laws, and engineering skills but finally even their citizenship; in A.D. 212, all free persons living within the borders of the Roman Empire became Roman citizens. Henceforth a native of Britain, Syria, or Spain, for example, could declare, "I am a Roman citizen." During these thousand years, the people of Rome introduced their customs and practices to others but were in turn themselves influenced and changed by contact with different societies. The eastern provinces, such as Achaia (Greece) and Egypt, exerted on the people of Rome and of Italy (who became Roman citizens in 88 B.C.) a greater cultural influence, to be sure, than did the western provinces, such as Africa and Gaul (France). But no province failed to leave an impression. The term *ancient Roman world,* therefore, can apply to the city of Rome specifically or to the vast geographic area which the Romans came to dominate. And the term *Roman civilization* can denote the traditional customs, attitudes, and institutions of the inhabitants of Rome, or it can denote a process of cultural evolution and adaptation occurring over a period of many centuries. Our information about life in the ancient Roman world, in its broad sense, thus comes from many different places and time periods. There are passages in this book written by people living in and commenting on life in the city of Rome, but there are also passages written by Roman citizens living in Roman provinces and even by non–Roman citizens living under Roman rule. Some passages were written in the third century B.C. and some in the fourth century A.D. All offer valid data about life in the ancient Roman world, but the reader should keep in mind the distinctions between "Rome" and "the Roman Empire," and between "an inhabitant of Rome" and "a Roman citizen." The introduction to each of the passages in this book provides information about when, and often where, the passage was written.

Archeology has uncovered physical evidence from all classes of society—the pottery of both the rich and the poor, for example, the jewelry of both men and women, the skeletons of both free persons and slaves. The majority of our literary evidence, however, was written by and about wealthy, politically active, upper-class men who lived in the city of Rome. Rarely do we find literary evidence written by women, slaves, or poor free men. It is easy, therefore, to construct from the literary sources a distorted view of the Roman world and to imagine all Romans as plump politicians in white togas, lounging about the Forum discussing affairs of state. One function of this book is to provide information which illuminates the lives of people of all classes and demonstrates the diversity of the Roman world.

It is fascinating to note the similarities—and they are many—between us and the ancient Romans, but there are considerable differences as well. Modern Western society is urban and affluent; we take for granted a standard of living which people in many other areas of the world would consider luxurious. The majority of ancient Romans were poor, compared to us, and many lived at subsistence level. Our own society is also quite mobile. Many of us travel away from the community in which we were born; as we move, we tend to lose touch with our cultural heritage. Most people in the ancient world, however, remained in the same community as their fathers and forefathers. Today we are not only physically but also socially mobile; we live in a society which is essentially classless, and it is sometimes difficult for us to understand what it means to live in a society like that of ancient

Rome, with rigid class distinctions and little social mobility. We are, in addition, so accustomed to excellent medical care, and to good health and an abundance of nutritious food, that we may forget that in the ancient Roman world many people died very young, many lived with considerable pain, and many were hungry. These realities of ancient life, frequently neglected in political histories, have received attention in the pages of this book.

The passages in this book are arranged topically. However, because one passage may include information about more than one topic, readers are advised about the relevance of each passage to other topics by cross-references in the footnotes. The index will also assist the reader in locating information about a specific topic. Appendix I contains short biographies of all authors translated and the Latin titles of their works, as well as brief explanations of the nature of epigraphical, papyrological, and legal sources. Appendix II gives handy information on Roman money. The time chart (Appendix III) is intended to help readers establish the chronological context of events mentioned; similarly, the maps will help readers locate sites relevant to the book. The bibliography includes a select list of books in English which offer further information about the topics of this book.

I wish to thank Professor David Traill, of the University of California at Davis, for reading the manuscript and offering many valuable comments. I also wish to thank for their help in the preparation of the manuscript Douglas Domingo-Foraste, Elizabeth Frech, Randi Glick, Robert Gurval, and Charles Rheinschmidt. The maps were prepared by Joseph Scepan and the plans by D. J. McLaren. And last, though certainly not least, I wish to thank my husband, Daniel Higgins, for all his support and encouragement.

Santa Barbara   J. S.
September 1987

Contents

Introduction   3

The Roman Ideal   3
    1. Horatius at the Bridge   3

I. The Structure of Roman Society   6

Class Structure   6
    2. Aristocracy   10
    3, 4. Definitions of Justice and Law   11
    5, 6. Discrimination in Assigning Penalties   12
Patronage   13
    7. Patrician and Plebeian   14
    8. Patrons and Clients in Republican Rome   14
    9. Patrons and Clients in Imperial Rome   15
    10. Seeking a Handout   16
    11. Patrons and Patrons   16
    12. Rude Patrons   17
    13. No Free Lunches (or Dinners)   17

II. Families   18

Fathers   18
    14. Patria Potestas   18
    15. Horace's Father   18
    16. Cicero's Grief   19
Mothers   20
    17. The Ideal   21
    18. Memory of a Warm Moment   21
    19. A Mother's Concern   22
    20. An Ungrateful Son   23
Brothers and Sisters   23
    21, 22. Affection   23
Producing a Family   24
    23. Fertility   24
    24. Miscarriage   24
    25. Infant Death   25
    26. Birth Announcements   25
Birth Control   26
    27, 28. Contraception   26
    29, 30. Abortion   27
    31, 32. Exposure   27
Encouraging Fertility   28
    33–35. The Legislation of Augustus   28
Adoption   29

36. An Adoption Agreement   29
37. Giving Away One's Child   30
Raising Children   31
38. Filial Obedience   31
39. Spoiled Brats   31
40. Advice about Parental Severity   32
41. Nurses   32
42. Paedagogues   33
43. A Persistent Paedagogue   33
Guardians   34
44. Appointing Guardians   34
Orphans   34
45. An Appeal for Help   34
Welfare Assistance   35
46. Public Assistance   35
47. Private Charity   36

III. Marriage   37

The Age of Marriage Partners   37
48. Child Brides   37
Arranged Marriages   38
49. Matchmakers   38
Weddings   40
50. A Wedding Song   40
51. A Marriage Contract   44
Wives   44
52. The Duties of a Wife   44
53. A Perfect Marriage   45
54. Pliny's Wife   45
55. Calpurnia   46
56. Love for a Wife   46
57. A Good Wife   47
Husbands   47
58. Battered Wives   47
59. Love for a Husband   48
In-Laws   48
60. In-Law Interference   48
Divorce   49
61. A Divorce Agreement   49
Adultery   50
62. Where to Meet   50
63. Deceiving One's Husband   51
64. Poems to a Mistress   52
65. Another Perspective   53
66. Laws to Control Adultery   54
67. Augustus's Own Behavior   55

IV. Housing and City Life   59

Single-Family Houses in the City   59
68. Designs for City Houses   59
Apartments   63
69. Complaints from an Apartment Dweller   63
70. A Dingy Apartment   63
71. A Landlord's Problems   63

House Prices 64
  72. The High Cost of Living in Rome 64
Rental Advertisements 64
  73, 74. Shops and Apartments for Rent 64
Homeowner's Insurance 65
  75. Fire Insurance 65
The Benefits of City Life 65
  76. Aqueducts 65
  77. Roads, Sewers, and the Campus Martius 67
  78. Toilets 68
  79, 80. Roads 68
The Problems of City Life 69
  81. Crowds, Traffic, and Muggers 69
  82. Noise 71
  83. Theft 71
  84. Burglary 72
  85. Urban Alienation 72
Housing in Rural Areas 72
  86. Farm Houses 72
  87. Vacation Villas 76

V. Domestic and Personal Concerns 81

Meals 81
  88. A Peasant's Dinner 82
  89. A Modest Dinner 83
  90. A Dinner Invitation 84
  91. A Rejected Host 84
  92. Recipe for Fish Sauce 85
  93. Numidian Chicken 86
  94. Rabbit with Fruit Sauce 87
  95. Liver Sausage 87
  96. Anchovy Delight without the Anchovies 87
  97. Sweet and Sour Pork 87
Illness 88
  98. Dysentery 88
  99. Asthma 89
Medical Treatments 90
  100. Jaundice 90
  101. Broken Bones 90
  102. Strains and Bruises 90
Doctors 91
  103. Medical Training 91
  104, 105. Change of Profession 91
  106. Distrust of Doctors 92
  107. Midwives 92
Life Expectancy 93
  108. Lutatia Secundina 94
  109. Magnilla 94
  110. Mercurius 94
Death 94
  111. Cicero's Grief 94
  112. Condolences 95
Funerary Laws and Funerals 97
  113. Funerary Laws 97
  114. Curses on Graverobbers 98
  115. Funerals 98

116. A Funeral Club   99
117. Final Words: An Epitaph   101
Personal Messages   102
118–120. The Walls of Pompeii   102

VI. Education   104

The Roman Ideal   104
121. A Traditional Education   104
A Child's Early Years   105
122. The Role of the Parents   105
Teachers and Schools   106
123. Private Tutors   106
124. Orbilius, the Schoolteacher   107
125. A Schoolteacher's Hours   108
126. A Schoolteacher's Salary   109
127. Incentives for Learning   110
128. Book Awards   110
129. An Endowment for a School   111
130. A Letter Home   112
The Litterator   113
131. A Day in the Life of a Schoolboy   113
132. Morals and Memorization   114
133. An Arithmetic Lesson   115
134. Enough Education for the Average Man   115
Vocational Training   115
135. Apprenticeship to a Weaver   115
The Grammaticus   116
136. Curriculum   116
The Rhetor   117
137. The Good Old Days   118
138, 139. Classroom Exercises   119
140. Pity the Teacher   121
141. Criticism of the Rhetor's Exercises   121
142. Criticism of the "New Style"   122
143. The Ideal Orator   123
A Year Abroad   125
144. Studying in Athens   125

VII. Occupations   127

The Day's Activities   127
145. Dividing Up the Day   127
146. City Life   128
Working for a Living   129
147. Scorn for the Working Class   129
148. Tradesmen and Craftsmen   130
149. Workers   131
150. Pride of Workmanship   132
151. Temporary Employment   133
152. Wage and Price Control   133
153. The Grain Dole   136
Business and Investments   137
154. The Roman Attitude toward Profit   138
155. Traders   139
156. Rome, the World Trade Center   139

157. Moneylending 140
158. Loan Companies 141
159. War Bonds 142
160. Cato's Financial Activities 143
161. A Real Estate Speculator 144
162. A Government Construction Contract 146
163. A Government Contract for Military Provisions 146
164. Contract Fraud 148
165, 166. Government Contracts for Tax Collection 148
167. Moneylending in the Provinces 149
168. Kingmakers 150
Activities of the Senatorial Class 151
169. Pliny's Activities 151
Agriculture 152
170. An Attempt at Land Reform 154
171. Tillers of the Fields 158
172. Tenant Farmers 159
173. Sharecroppers 160
174. A Farmer's Life 161
175. Shepherds 163
176. Harassment of Shepherds 164
177. Farmers and Heroes 164
178. Retreat from Reality 165
179. The Romantic Vision 166
180. The Country Mouse and the City Mouse 167

VIII. Slaves 168

Buying a Slave 168
181. A Contract for the Sale of a Slave 168
Renting a Slave 169
182. A Contract for the Rental of a Slave 169
Slaves in the City and on the Farm 170
183. Choosing Slaves for the Farm 171
184. Farm Slaves and a Frugal Owner 172
185. Managing Your Slaves 174
Slaves in the Mines 175
186. Spanish Silver Mines 175
Slaves in a Mill 176
187. A Flour Mill 176
Cruelty to Slaves 176
188. Flogging 176
189. Sadism 177
190. Brutality 177
191. Cruel Laws 178
Running Away 180
192, 193. Slave Collars 180
194. A Search for a Fugitive Slave 180
Slave Revolts 181
195. Revolt within the Household 181
196. A Widespread Revolt 182
Humane Treatment 184
197. Sympathy 184
198. A Stoic View of Slavery 185
199. Laws to Curb Cruelty 188
200. Hadrian's Legislation 188
201. Reiteration 188

202. Humane Interpretation of the Laws   189
203. Slave Families   189

IX. Freedmen   190

Reasons for Manumission   191
204, 205. Recognition of Talent and Intelligence   192
206. Freeing Possible Witnesses   193
207. Adoption   193
208. Marriage   194
209. Criticism of the Manumission Process   194
Roman Attitudes toward Freedmen   195
210. The Stereotype of the Wealthy Freedman   196
211. Resentment   199
212. Prejudice against Foreigners   200
Freedmen and the Job Market   201
213. Construction Work   201
214. Herald   201
215. Teacher   201
216. Slaughterer   202
217. Maid   202
Freedmen and Their Patrons   202
218. Marcus Aurelius Zosimus   203
219. Another Kind Patron   203
220. Selective Kindness   203
Private and Social Life   204
221. A Life Story   204
222. Friendship between Freedmen   204
223. Mother and Daughter   205
224. Buying Respectability   205

X. Government and Politics   206

The Assemblies   206
225. The Comitia   208
226. Comitia and Concilium: Some Differences   208
227. Lex and Plebiscitum   209
228. Contio   209
Magistrates   210
229. The Functions of the Magistrates   211
230. The Titles of the Magistrates   212
231. The Development of the Magistracies   213
232. The Duties of the Consuls   214
233. The Responsibilities of a Magistrate   215
234. Friends in Power   217
235. Abuse of Power   218
Political Campaigns   218
236. Planning a Campaign   219
237. Campaign Literature   224
The Senate   225
238. The Senate in the Republican Period   225
239. The Senate and the People   228
240. The Senate and the Equestrians   230
Government in the Early Imperial Period   231
241. The Powers of Augustus   231
242. The Prefect of the City   235

243, 244. Careers in the Government   236
        245. The End of Popular Elections   237
246, 247. Freedom of Speech   238
        248. The Emperor and the Senate   240
249, 250. The Benefits of Imperial Rule   241
Legislation   242
        251. The Roman Science   244
        252. Sources of Legislation   244
253–255. Categories   245
        256. Definitions   247
257–263. Equity   247
        264. The Force of Custom   248

XI. The Roman Army   249

The Army during the Republican Period   249
        265. The Army before Marius's Reforms   250
        266. A Good Republican Soldier   256
        267. A Triumph   257
The Army during the Imperial Period   259
        268. Reasons for the Army's Success   259
        269. Enlistment   262
        270. Training   262
        271. A Letter Home   264
        272. A Letter of Recommendation   265
        273. How to Advance Quickly   265
        274. A Mutiny   266
275, 276. The Height of Recruits   268
        277. Avoiding the Draft   268

XII. The Provinces   270

Provincial Administration   270
        278. The Publican Problem   272
        279. Cicero as Governor   273
        280. The Noble Brutus   274
        281. A Most Unscrupulous Governor   277
        282. Hatred of Roman Rule   287
        283. The Benefits of Roman Rule   289

XIII. Women in Roman Society   290

Childhood   290
        284. Little Women   290
        285. Single Women   291
Life Expectancy   292
        286. A Brief Life   292
        287. Death in Childbirth   292
Praiseworthy Behavior   293
        288. An Outstanding Example of *Pietas*   293
        289. Emotional Control   296
        290. Loyalty   296
Unacceptable Behavior   298
        291. Scandalous Conduct   298
        292. Women and Politics   299
        293. Women and Education   300

294. Women and Luxuries 301
295. Women and Theatrical Performances 302
Hysteria 302
296. Symptoms 303
297. Causes and Cures 304
Cosmetics 305
298. For the Skin He Loves to Touch 305
299. The Dangers of Hair Dyes 305
Working Women 306
300. A Dressmaker 306
301. A Hairdresser 306
302. A Fishmonger 307

XIV. Leisure and Entertainment 308

Leisure Activities 308
303, 304. The Pleasures of Life 309
305. Gambling and Gaming 309
306. Athletic Activities 310
Baths 311
307. The Good Old Days 311
308. Living above a Public Bath Building 314
309. The Design of a Bath Building 314
Dinner Parties 315
310. Fishing for a Dinner Invitation 316
311. An Early Dinner Guest 316
312. A Thrifty Man 317
313. Roman Doggy Bags 317
314. A Shameless Guest 317
315. A Napkin Thief 318
316. A Rude Host 319
317. House of the Moralist 319
Recitations 319
318. The Persistent Poet 320
319. The Popularity of Recitations 321
320. A Recitation at Pliny's House 322
Hunting and Literary Studies 323
321. Pliny's Hunting Expedition 323
322. A Day in the Country 324
Travel 325
323. Along the Appian Way 326
324. Hotel Sign 329
325. Hotel Bars 329
326. Hotel Prostitutes 329
327. Homesickness 330
328. Loneliness 330
329. No Trespassing 330
330. The Ancient Jet Set 331
Spectacles 331
331. Caesar's Games 333
332. Nero's Games 334
333. Political Wisdom 335
334. The Road to Decadence 336
Theater Events 339
335. The Problems of a Playwright 339
336. Pantomime 341
Amphitheater Events 342

337, 338. Advertising Amphitheater Events   344
         339. Fight Statistics   345
         340. Fans   345
         341. An Unsympathetic Point of View   345
         342. A More Enlightened View   346
         343. Rounding Up the Animals   347
         344. The Harmful Results of Spectacles   348
         345. Escaping the Tortures of the Arena   349
    Circus Events   350
         346. A Driver's Winning Techniques   351
         347. A Day at the Races   352
         348. Fanatical Fans   354
         349. A Successful Driver   355
         350. Cursing One's Opponent   357
         351. A Young Driver   357
         352. A Family of Drivers   358
         353. A Famous Driver   359

XV. Religion and Philosophy   360

The Gods of the State Religion   361
         354. Deities of the Environment   362
         355. A River Spirit   363
         356. Propitiating a Woodland Spirit   364
         357. A Multitude of Deities   365
         358. Naming the Deities   366
         359. The Greek Influence   367
         360. Importing Gods   368
         361. Welcoming the Gods of Your Enemy   369
         362. New Identities for Roman Deities   370
         363. Personal Devotion   370
    Ritual   371
         364. Formalism   373
         365. Conservatism   373
         366. Prayer   375
         367. Vow   376
    368, 369. Divination: Augury and Auspicium   377
         370. Divination: Extispicium   378
         371. The Sibylline Books   379
         372. Festivals   380
         373. Ambarvalia   381
         374. Robigalia   382
         375. Lupercalia   383
         376. Saturnalia   384
         377. Saturnalia Gifts   385
    Officers of the State Religion   386
         378. Pontifices   386
    379, 380. Vestal Virgins   387
    Deification   389
         381. Tiberius and the City of Gythium   389
         382. Requests for Emperor-Worship   390
         383. Tiberius's Resistance to Emperor-Worship   390
    The Permanence of the State Religion   391
         384. Neglect of the State Cult   391
         385. Resistance to Intolerance   392
    Religions from the East   394
         386. Turning to Other Religions   395

Bacchus   396
    387. Suppression of the Bacchanalia   396
    388. The Decree of the Senate   399
Cybele, Magna Mater   401
    389. Bringing the Goddess to Rome   401
    390. A Religious Procession   402
Isis   403
    391. Worship of the Goddess   403
    392. Christian Skepticism   408
Judaism   409
    393. Tolerance   409
    394. Persecution   410
    395. Compromise   410
Christianity   411
    396. The Promises of Christianity   411
    397. First Christians in Rome   412
    398. An Early Instance of Persecution   412
    399. Imperial Advice about Dealing with Christians   414
    400. Christian Reaction to Trajan's Rescriptum   416
    401. Accusations against the Christians   417
    402. A Christian's Reply to the Accusations   418
    403. Martyrs   420
    404. Toleration   421
    405. Christian Intolerance   422
Syncretism   422
    406. A Roman Virtue   422
Magic and Superstition   423
    407. Superstitions   424
    408. The Potency of Words   424
    409. The Potency of Objects   425
    410. The Potency of Rituals   425
    411. Curse Tablets   426
Epicureanism   426
    412. The Reasons for Studying Philosophy   427
    413. The First Principle   428
    414. The Second Principle   428
    415. Proof of the Existence of Atoms   429
    416. Void   430
    417. Life and Death   430
Stoicism   431
    418. The Promise of Philosophy   431
    419. Stoic Definition of Happiness   432
    420. Fate and Free Will   433
    421. Emotions   433
    422. The Invulnerability of the Wise Man   434
    423. Death as True Freedom   434
    424. Training and Preparation   435
    425. Self-Discipline and Steadfastness   436

Maps   439
Appendix I: Sources   446
Appendix II: Roman Money   459
Appendix III: Important Dates and Events   460
Bibliography   464
Index   475

Illustrations

Figure 1. The House of the Surgeon at Pompeii   60
Figure 2. The House of Pansa   60
Figure 3. Plan of a Farm Villa   74
Figure 4. Reconstructed Plan of Pliny's Villa at Laurentum   77
Figure 5. Plan of the Stabian Baths at Pompeii   313

Genealogy Chart 1. The Julio-Claudians   56
Genealogy Chart 2. The Families of Scipio Africanus
                    and Tiberius Gracchus   157
Genealogy Chart 3. The Helvidii   297

Map 1. Plan of Rome in the Imperial Period   439
Map 2. Central Italy   440
Map 3. Italy and Sicily   441
Map 4. Greece and Asia Minor   442
Map 5. The Roman Empire at Its Greatest Extent   444

As the Romans Did

The study of history is beneficial and profitable for the following reasons. You behold the lessons of every historical event as clearly as if they were displayed on a stone monument. From these you may choose for yourself and for your own community what to imitate. From these you may decide what to avoid as shameful in cause or shameful in result. . . . No state was ever greater than Rome, none was more pious or richer in fine examples; there has been no state where greed and luxury entered so late in its development, or where thrift and a modest standard of living were given such great respect.

LIVY, *A History of Rome* 1. Preface. 10 and 11.

Introduction

Ancient Roman society developed in a tiny farm village on the banks of the Tiber River, about fifteen miles from the Mediterranean coast. Over a period of a thousand years this village evolved into a very large[1] and cosmopolitan city which was the mistress of a vast empire. The citizens of Rome had advanced relentlessly to establish control over areas bordering their own, and eventually they came to dominate the peoples of Europe and the entire Mediterranean world. They sometimes introduced, sometimes imposed on these peoples many of their customs and practices so that a gradual Romanization of the western world occurred. In Britain, North Africa, Syria, and elsewhere, people began to embrace various aspects of Roman society as their own. As the Romans extended their influence, they also extended their citizenship, and finally, in A.D. 212, they took the remarkable action of granting Roman citizenship to every free person within the borders of the Roman Empire. Now a free person born in Egypt or in Spain, in Britain, in Greece, or in Syria, could declare, "I am a Roman citizen."

Cultural influence was never, of course, a one-way street. Romans traveling to distant parts of the Empire learned many new practices, and in the city of Rome itself foreigners from diverse areas of the world introduced their customs to the Romans. One of the most remarkable aspects of the ancient Roman character was its ability to absorb elements of other cultures and to adapt them to its own. This process of adaptation and absorption, occurring over many centuries, made Roman society complex and multifarious. Yet the people who made Rome great were essentially conservative; they cherished the traditions of their ancestors and passed them on to each successive generation. Thus, throughout the long period of Rome's greatness, there always remained in Roman society a solid core of convictions and beliefs which had endured from the time when Rome was a village; and it was the preservation of this core which gave to Roman society its stability, cohesiveness, and continuity.

THE ROMAN IDEAL

Horatius at the Bridge

All people make virtues out of necessities, for life would otherwise be unbearable. We glorify the very patterns of behavior which we need for survival. The ancient

---

[1] The population of Rome in the second century A.D. was about one million. The population of Europe declined sharply during the Dark Ages, and by A.D. 1600 only two European cities—Paris and Naples—had populations over 200,000. Not until A.D. 1800 did the population of London exceed one million, and then it was by far Europe's largest city.

3

Romans were no exception. Since Rome began as an agricultural community, the qualities necessary to a successful farmer became esteemed as virtues: diligence, determination, austerity, gravity, discipline, and self-sufficiency. Centuries passed, and the farm village evolved into an imperial capital, but the descendants of the early rugged farmers preserved their ancestors' notion of "the Roman virtues," the qualities to which Rome owed its successes. The Romans thus created for themselves a "national self-image" or a "national character," and they perceived of the ideal Roman as being stern, diligent, and self-sufficient.[2] This perception did not, of course, always match the realities of a particular situation; there were certainly lazy Romans and frivolous Romans. But Romans of all periods nonetheless retained a notion of how a Roman was expected to act, and this undoubtedly influenced their general outlook.

The legends of Rome's early heroes articulate this national self-image, and they are instructive because they indicate to us how the Romans perceived of themselves. The passage translated below tells the story of Horatius Cocles. Horatius was portrayed as the farmer-soldier, the Roman ideal, the man whose main interest was farming but who would fight bravely to defend his own property and that of his fellow citizens.[3] He embodied the characteristics which the Romans prized most highly: dogged determination and an unflinching devotion to duty. It is impossible to understand Roman society without being acquainted with this concept of duty, which the Romans called *pietas*. *Pietas* pervaded every sphere of life, for a Roman was expected to be devoted and dutiful to his family, friends, fellow citizens, country, and gods.

In studying the Roman national character, it is interesting to contrast Greek heroes such as Ulysses, who prevails because he is quick-witted, agile, and aggressive, with a Roman hero like Horatius, who defeats the enemy because he is persistent, stands his ground, and offers a strong defense.[4] And, above all, Horatius is willing to sacrifice his own life to save the city of Rome.

1   Livy,[5] *A History of Rome* 2.10

When the enemy[6] approached, everyone left his fields[7] and headed for the city, which they surrounded with troops. Some parts were protected by the city walls, others by the Tiber River, which served as a barrier. However, the pile bridge almost provided the enemy with access to the city, had it not been for one man, Horatius Cocles. The city of Rome was fortunate to have this strong bulwark on that day. By chance, he had been posted as a guard at the bridge when the enemy captured the Janiculum[8] in a

---

[2] The American self-image is remarkably similar.

[3] References to other farmer-soldier heroes appear in selection 177.

[4] Of all the Homeric heroes, only Ajax resembles Horatius, particularly in *Iliad* 11.556 ff., where he moves as slowly and as obstinately as a donkey who is being chased out of a grain field by boys with sticks. Although Ajax's strength was respected by the Greeks, he was not as attractive to them as Ulysses or Achilles, who were much "flashier." The Romans, on the other hand, would admire Ajax but be suspicious of crafty Ulysses or of Achilles, who would put personal glory before communal safety.

[5] Brief biographies of all authors cited are found in Appendix I.

[6] *the enemy:* the Etruscans. This battle is reported to have taken place in 508 B.C.

[7] *fields:* i.e., which they were farming. The ideal Roman is a farmer-soldier.

[8] *Janiculum:* a hill situated across the Tiber from Rome; see map 1.

sudden attack. He saw them running quickly down the hill toward the bridge. . . . He warned and ordered the Romans who were fleeing before the enemy to destroy the bridge with iron implements, fire, or any instrument at their disposal. He said that he would bear the onset of the enemy, at least as far as it could be withstood by one human body. Then he strode to the entrance of the bridge . . . and astonished the enemy with his amazing audacity. A sense of shame held two other men on the bridge with him, Spurius Larcius and Titus Herminius, both distinguished for their family background and their deeds. With them, Horatius endured the first rush and the stormiest part of the battle. But when only a little bit of the bridge remained and when the men who were cutting it down were calling them back, he forced the other two to retreat to safety. Then, looking around at the Etruscan noblemen with savage, defiant eyes, he first challenged them individually to combat, and then chided them as a group, saying they were slaves of haughty kings and, having lost their own freedom, had come to undermine the freedom of others. The Etruscans hesitated for a moment, each looking at the other, each expecting someone else to start the fight. Finally shame moved them to action; they raised a shout and from every side flung their javelins at their one opponent. But all their weapons stuck in the shield which he used to protect himself, and, obstinate as ever, he stood fixed on the bridge, feet planted wide apart. The Etruscans tried to dislodge him by a charge, but right at that moment two sounds shattered the air: the crash of the falling bridge and the cheer of the Romans excited by the completion of the task. Sudden fear checked the charge of the Etruscans. Then Horatius Cocles cried out, "Father Tiber,[9] I piously invoke you. Receive these arms and this soldier into your kindly waters." Having prayed, he jumped with all his armor and arms into the Tiber and swam safely to his friends despite the barrage of Etruscan missiles, having dared a deed which has gained more fame than credence among posterity.

The state was grateful for such amazing valor; a statue of Horatius was erected, and he was given as much farmland as he could plow around in one day. And amidst these public honors, private displays of gratitude were also apparent, for each citizen, even in this time of distress, bestowed on him some gift proportionate each to his own means, some even depriving themselves of their own provisions.

[9] *Father Tiber:* The Tiber River is personified as a father who will care about his son, Horatius, and receive him with "kindly waters," i.e., not cause his drowning. For more on personifications of the Tiber River, see selection 355.

I

The Structure of Roman Society

CLASS STRUCTURE

Roman society was extremely class-conscious. Three major factors determined the class structure: (1) wealth (or lack of it), (2) freedom (or lack of it), and (3) Roman citizenship (or lack of it). The stratification of ancient Roman society involved much more than snobbish discrimination or a tacit understanding by members of one social group to exclude other people from its company. In ancient Rome social divisions were sustained by laws, and one group might be denied political and legal privileges allowed to another group. For example, until 88 B.C. people dwelling within Italy but outside of Rome had for centuries lived under the domination of Roman citizens and fought alongside the Roman army, but they had been denied the rights of Roman citizenship. They could not vote in Roman elections, they could not participate in the government which ruled them, they could not marry into Roman families, and they were subject to execution for capital offenses.[1] In 90 B.C. the Italians went to war to protest this inequity,[2] and in 89 B.C. the government of Rome yielded to their demands: full Roman citizenship was extended to all free people in Italy. Three hundred years later Roman citizenship was extended to all free people within the borders of the Empire.[3]

This final enfranchisement erased the distinctions between Roman citizen and noncitizen within the Empire. Distinctions based on wealth and freedom, however, persisted. With respect to freedom, for example, three categories existed in Roman society: (1) slaves, (2) freedmen (ex-slaves), and (3) free men. Later chapters will deal with the position of slaves and freedmen.

Among free men who were Roman citizens status was based primarily on wealth. During the period of the monarchy,[4] members of the wealthier families in

[1] Roman citizens could not be executed for capital offenses. It was therefore vital for someone charged with such an offense to be able to declare, "I am a Roman citizen." See note 301 in Chapter XV about St. Paul's declaration of Roman citizenship.

[2] This war is called the Social War, or War with the Allies; the Latin word for "ally" is *socius*.

[3] In A.D. 212.

[4] The legendary date for the founding of Rome is 753 B.C., and the legendary first king was Romulus. The legendary date for the expulsion of the monarchy is 509 B.C. The last king of Rome was Tarquinius Superbus (Tarquin the Arrogant), an Etruscan.

the community served as the king's advisors,[5] and, since they acted as the elders or "fathers" of the state, they were called patricians.[6] The rest of the families in the state were called plebeian.[7] Specific families, therefore, were patrician and could be distinguished from plebeian families by their names. Claudius and Julius, for example, are patrician family names; Clodius and Licinius are plebeian family names. Patrician rank was therefore inherited, and it was never possible for a plebeian to become a patrician, except by adoption.[8] The patrician families formed Rome's earliest aristocracy, and they jealously guarded their own power in the state by establishing rigid limitations on the social and political movements of the plebeians, who formed the majority.

Although the monarchy was expelled from Rome in 509 B.C. and the republic was established, the patricians retained their control of the state. Plebeians were not allowed to hold public office, to become members of the Senate, or to serve as priests. Moreover, plebeians and patricians were not allowed to intermarry. In the fifth century B.C. the plebeians began to agitate for more political power and legal rights, and by 287 B.C. the plebeian families had obtained parity with the patrician families, in theory at least. Since political campaigns were expensive and since most officials received no remuneration for their services, few plebeian families could afford to become politically active even if they now had the right to do so. A small number of plebeian families, however, did achieve political prominence, and by the middle republican period a new aristocracy or, more accurately, an expanded aristocracy had developed which was composed of both the patrician families and the plebeian families who now controlled Rome's wealth and government.[9] These people were often called *nobiles* ("nobles"). Yet, although the composition of the aristocracy had been modified, nevertheless the same rigid social stratification remained: a wealthy powerful few versus a multitude of poor.

The main sources of wealth for most aristocratic families in the early republican period were land ownership and the sale of products from agricultural land. These families seldom worked the land themselves; the farming was done by slaves, indentured servants, hired free men, or sharecroppers. The landowner lived in the city and visited his property occasionally.[10] Traditionally the men of Rome's wealthiest families occupied their time with unpaid public service; they served as legal advisors, judges, magistrates, diplomats, military officers, priests, and senators. The young men of these families aspired to membership in the Roman Senate, which controlled both the domestic and foreign affairs of Rome, and thus the

---

[5] These families may have been native Roman, but it is also possible that they were, like Rome's last kings, Etruscan. The Etruscans dominated Rome during the sixth century B.C. and may have imposed on the native Roman society an Etruscan aristocracy, as William and the Normans imposed a Norman aristocracy on the native Anglo-Saxon society after the battle of Hastings. Within a few generations, of course, the distinction between Etruscan and native Roman would have been forgotten and replaced in people's minds with the distinction between Roman upper-class and Roman lower-class.

[6] *patrician:* Latin *patricius;* Latin *pater* = "father."

[7] *plebeian:* Latin *plebeius;* Latin *plebs* = "multitude."

[8] However, by the end of the republican period, when only about fifteen patrician families still existed, Caesar and Augustus employed a policy of creating new patrician families by decree (see Dio Cassius, *Roman History* 52.42.5).

[9] In the late republican period, therefore, *plebeian* might mean (1) a member of a family with a plebeian name, whether rich or poor, or (2) a commoner, not of the senatorial class.

[10] More information about farmworkers and landowners is given in Chapter VII.

affairs of the whole Empire. Once admitted into the Senate, a man was a member for life, and he and his family were said to belong to the senatorial class or order.[11] Since only a limited number of men had the time and money to pursue senatorial careers, a handful of families controlled Rome and the Empire for generation after generation.

During the early republican period Roman society could be divided into "the many" (the poor, the common people) and "the few" (the wealthy aristocrats, the senatorial families, who dominated every aspect of Roman society). Military expansion and wars overseas in the third and second centuries B.C., however, created new opportunities for trade, shipping, business, and banking, and also a new type of upper class. Some wealthy men chose to devote themselves to business matters rather than public service. Although they may have been born into senatorial families, they did not themselves pursue senatorial careers. These men were called *equites* ("equestrians"),[12] probably because they had done their military service in the cavalry.[13] (Only wealthy young men could afford to be cavalrymen because of the high costs of purchasing and maintaining horses.) *Equites* who embarked on political careers when their eligibility for military service ended were then called *senatores* ("senators"). However, *equites* who were not interested in a senatorial career after military service continued to be called *equites* even though they were no longer attached to the cavalry. The term *eques* thus became a designation for a wealthy man who was not a Roman senator.[14]

By the second century B.C., however, a sharper distinction began to emerge between the wealthy political families and the wealthy nonpolitical families. Overseas expansion had produced an increase in the number of "public contracts," let out by the Senate for road construction, building construction, mine operation, army provisions, and tax collection. Individual businessmen or groups of businessmen would bid on these contracts, and the Senate would choose the bidder it felt would do the best job for the best price. Men who held public contracts were called publicans.[15] It may seem strange to us that the government would hire a private company to collect taxes, but this practice was common in the ancient world. Members of the Senate were not allowed to bid on these government contracts, obviously to prevent conflicts of interest.[16] And since they were expected to devote their time and energy to government and community service (for which they received no salary), they were expected *not* to occupy themselves with trade, busi-

[11] *senatorial order:* Latin *ordo* = "class," "rank." Members of the senatorial order were expected to maintain a net worth of at least 800,000 sesterces, later raised to 1 million sesterces (*sesterce:* a silver coin; see Appendix II).

[12] The Latin word for "horseman" or "equestrian" is *eques* (plural *equites*); the Latin word for "horse" is *equus*. The word *eques* is sometimes translated as "knight."

[13] In the republican period Roman male citizens were eligible for a military draft; see Chapter XI.

[14] An *eques* was not necessarily apolitical. Some equestrians ran for local offices in their hometowns. Generally, however, equestrian families did not pursue the highest public offices of Rome. There were always exceptions, of course; Cicero, who was elected to Rome's highest public office, the consulship, came from an equestrian family which had been active in the local politics of the town of Arpinum. Moreover, equestrians who did not themselves run for office had considerable political influence because of their wealth.

[15] *publican:* Latin *publicanus* = "dealing with public revenues."

[16] Once a man became a member of the Roman Senate, he remained a member for life.

ness, and industry.[17] Of course, members of the Senate were only hindered slightly, not prevented totally, by these legal and social restrictions from engaging in non-agricultural business and trade. They simply hired agents to handle their commercial enterprises, and they became silent partners in contract and banking transactions.[18] Many, if not all, senators would in public solemnly denounce the world of business as dirty and undignified but would in private thank the gods for the success of their most recent investments. Still, there were other men, often the brothers or cousins of senators, who declined to run for public office and who therefore engaged openly in moneymaking. Thus the term *equestrian* evolved to become a designation for a wealthy man actively involved in business and commerce. In turn, it became increasingly more difficult for such a man to embark on a political career in Rome because political positions were the jealously guarded monopoly of the old senatorial families.[19]

The first formal delineation between the senatorial order and the equestrian order appeared in 122 B.C. when senators in the jury system were replaced with equestrians. This action suggests that a method already existed of differentiating members of the senatorial and the equestrian orders. About 100 B.C. a regulation was passed whereby a man could be officially enrolled in the equestrian order if he met a property qualification of 400,000 sesterces. This was considerably less than the 800,000 sesterces required for admission to the senatorial order but was still substantially more money than the average family would ever have.[20]

Members of the equestrian order played a prominent role in the expansion and maintenance of the Roman Empire, and this role increased during the imperial period.[21] As successive emperors sought to reduce the power of the senatorial order by denying its members public offices, they appointed equestrians to high-ranking financial, administrative, and military positions.

The senatorial and equestrian orders formed the upper classes of Roman society. Far beneath them were the lower classes. The gap between rich and poor was so wide that scant opportunity existed for social mobility. Most people remained in the class into which they were born and seemed, moreover, resigned to the inequities of their rigidly structured society. The term *middle class* does not appear in this text because it invites an identification with the modern American middle class, an identification which proves false. The modern American middle class has a high standard of living and represents a large segment of the population and a wide variety of occupations. In ancient Rome, however, the majority of the population had a low standard of living, and many occupations which would today place one in the middle class would have put one in the lower class in Rome. Just as there were varying degrees of wealth among the upper classes, so too there were certainly varying degrees of want among the lower classes. Some families lived at

[17] In fact, a law passed in 218 B.C. forbade senators to own cargo ships.

[18] On the use of agents, see selection 280.

[19] For example, there were only 300 seats in the Roman Senate, and they were held for life.

[20] On the relative values of Roman money, see Appendix II.

[21] The imperial period began in 27 B.C., when Augustus assumed absolute authority in the Roman state and became the first emperor. The preceding period was the republican period, extending from 509 B.C. (the expulsion of the monarchy) to 27 B.C. During the republican period the Roman Empire was ruled by the aristocracy of senatorial families.

bare subsistence level; others lived simply but comfortably. Few families, however, enjoyed the affluence of the modern American middle class.[22]

Aristocracy

The wealthy members of Roman society were convinced that they were superior to the poor in every way—intelligence, talent, and ethical conduct, as well as wealth. Although Rome was called a republic,[23] it was in practice ruled by an aristocracy formed of the senatorial families. Cicero and his fellow senators believed that aristocracy was the best form of government, as long as *they* were the aristocrats, of course.[24] In the passage translated here, Cicero, writing in the first century B.C., discusses the advantages of aristocracy over either monarchy or democracy. Notice that he considers the common people of Roman society ignorant and rash.

2 Cicero, *About the Republic* 1.34.52–53

What situation can be more splendid than the government of the state by excellence and virtue?[25] When the man who rules others is not himself a slave to any base emotions, when he himself cherishes all those things in which he instructs and to which he beckons his fellow citizens, then he does not impose on the people laws which he does not himself obey, but rather offers to his fellow citizens his own life as a model of lawful behavior. If a single individual could accomplish all these things satisfactorily, we would have no need of more than one ruler. Or if all the citizens as a whole could see the best course of action and agree upon it, no one would prefer a small group of rulers. However, the difficulty of devising policy has caused the transfer of power from a king to a group, and the ignorance and rashness of the masses have caused its transfer from the many to the few.[26] Thus, between the weakness of a single

[22] Some scholars consider the equestrian order to have been the middle class of Roman society. Only a small percentage of the population, however, was equestrian; today, on the other hand, the middle class forms the bulk of the population.

[23] *republic:* Latin *res publica* = "the public matter."

[24] In 44 B.C., when Julius Caesar, himself a senator, declared himself dictator for life, his declaration horrified Senate members who knew that his assumption of absolute control meant the end, not of a democracy, but of the aristocracy. They therefore assassinated him in order to preserve the aristocracy and their positions in it. Similarly, the opposition to Augustus (Caesar's grandnephew and Rome's first emperor) came from disgruntled senators who wanted an aristocracy, not a monarchy.

[25] The Latin word for "excellence and virtue" is *virtus*. The corresponding Greek word is *arete*, and cognate with this word is *aristoi*, "the most excellent men," "the best." *Aristocracy* (*kratos* = "power," "rule") therefore means "rule by the best men." Obviously there will always be some disagreement about just which men are the best, although the men in power, the aristocrats, undoubtedly define themselves as best. Democracy means "rule by the people" (Greek *demos* = "common people"), and monarchy means "rule by one man" (Greek *monos* = "one man," and *arche* = "reign," "rule").

[26] It is certainly true that, as policymaking for the Empire became ever more complicated, the people were forced to give the Senate greater authority and control. (It is also true today that the ordinary person, who does not have the time and experience to understand complicated issues of domestic economy or foreign policy, must rely heavily on government "experts" for advice.)

ruler and the rashness of the masses, the aristocrats have occupied a middle position, and there is no position more moderate than theirs.[27] When such men watch over the state, the citizens must necessarily be very happy and blessed, since they are free of anxiety and care and have entrusted their security to others whose duty it is to guard this security and never to act in such a way that the people think their best interests are being neglected by their rulers. Indeed, equality under the law, a right which free people cherish, cannot in fact be maintained, for although the people themselves are unrestricted and unrestrained, they give, for example, many positions of honor to many men, and thus create a great hierarchy of men and honors.[28] And therefore what we now call equality is really very inequitable. On the other hand, if equal honor and rank are held by the highest and the lowest men (for both groups must exist in every state), this so-called equality is also very inequitable. However, this latter type of inequity cannot occur in those states which are ruled by their "best" citizens.

Definitions of Justice and Law

In the previous passage, Cicero stated that "equality under the law [was] a right which free people cherish." And Roman legal theory accepted this proposition as a basic premise in its definitions of justice and law.

3 Cicero, *About the Republic* 3.22.33

True Law is, in fact, unerring Reason, consistent with Nature, applicable to all, unchanging and eternal, which demands that people fulfill their obligations, which deters and prohibits them from wrongdoing. . . . There will not be one law at Rome, another at Athens, or one law now and another later. Rather, all people, at all time, will be bound by one everlasting and immutable law.

The following passage is taken from *The Digest of Laws,* a codification of the Roman laws commissioned by Justinian (emperor A.D. 527–565).[29]

---

[27] Aristocracy is thus seen as the middle ground between "rule by one" and "rule by many (the people)." Cicero supports an oligarchy, "rule by a few" (Greek *oligoi* = "a few men" + *arche*), provided the few are virtuous and excellent. It would be interesting to know how many senators of Cicero's day would fit his definition of "excellent."

[28] *honors:* The Latin word *honor* has two meanings: (1) political office (such as the consulship) to which one is elected by the people, or (2) public esteem. The two meanings are, of course, related. The common people "honor" the senatorial class and show their esteem by electing them to political offices or "honors." And men who occupy these unpaid public "honors" deserve the esteem or "honor" of the multitude. Cicero did not believe that all men are created equal. He believed that some men had greater talent and were therefore chosen by their fellow citizens as leaders. The hierarchy of "ruling class" and "ruled" is therefore, according to Cicero, a natural situation. Cicero opposes a concept of equality which gives equal amounts of political power to each and every man because then the basest men have as much power as the best men. Cicero assumes that it is the morally best men who run for and are elected to public office. In fact, however, in ancient Rome it was the wealthiest men, morally good or bad, who entered politics.

[29] For more on *The Digest,* and on the Roman legal writer Ulpian, see Appendix I.

4   *The Digest of Laws* 1.1.10 (Ulpian)

Justice is the constant and unceasing determination to grant to every man his legal
rights. The precepts of the law are these: live honestly, injure no one, grant to each
man his rights.

Discrimination in Assigning Penalties

Although Roman jurists strove to formulate a definition of justice which would be
valid for all times and all peoples, in practice the Roman legal system, which was
controlled, of course, by the upper class, reinforced the distinctions between the
classes in Roman society.[30] For example, penalties differed for Roman citizens and
noncitizens,[31] for slaves and free men, and even, among free men, for rich and
poor. In the early third century A.D., about the same time that Roman citizenship
was extended to all free people in the Empire, the citizen body was formally divided, for purposes of criminal jurisdiction, into two classes: the *honestiores,* which
included members of the senatorial and equestrian orders, local officials, and army
officers; and the *humiliores,* every other free citizen.[32] Punishments for *humiliores*
were much more severe than for *honestiores.* The upper classes, which made and
enforced the laws, justified this differentiation by arguing that the rich did more
for the state—since they supplied it with magistrates, jurists, army officers, provincial administrators, and so on, and since they risked their money undertaking state
contracts—and that the rich therefore deserved a separate scale of punishments.
This attitude of superiority explains the apparent discrepancy between Roman
theories of justice and the actual laws. This discrepancy can be observed in the
passages translated below.

5   *FIRA* 2, p. 405 (Paulus, *Opinions* 5.19–19a)

Those who break into a temple at night in order to pillage or plunder it are thrown
to wild animals.[33] But if they steal some minor object from the temple during the day,
if they are *honestiores* they are exiled;[34] if they are *humiliores* they are condemned to
the mines.[35]
    In the case of people accused of violating sepulchers, if they actually drag out the
bodies or remove the bones, if they are *humiliores* they are punished with the ultimate

[30] Cicero asserts that "equality under the law . . . cannot in fact be maintained."

[31] On the differing punishments for capital offenses, see note 1 of this chapter.

[32] *honestiores:* literally "more honorable," "more distinguished." *humiliores:* literally
"more humble," "more insignificant."

[33] *thrown to wild animals:* made to fight wild animals, such as lions or bears, in an amphitheater event; see Chapter XIV.

[34] Exile (Latin *deportatio*) meant banishment to a specified remote area (often a small
island) and loss of Roman citizenship.

[35] Condemnation to the mines meant being sent to work at a government mine. Although
not considered a form of execution, it was in reality a death sentence because mineworkers
died quickly of exhaustion; see selection 186.

torture;[36] if they are *honestiores* they are exiled to an island. For other violations, *honestiores* are expelled[37] and *humiliores* are condemned to the mines.

6   *FIRA* 2, p. 407 (Paulus, *Opinions* 5.22.1–2)

People who plot sedition and riot or who stir up the masses are, according to the nature of their social rank, either crucified, or thrown to wild animals, or exiled to an island. Those who dig up or plough up boundary markers, or who cut down boundary trees: (1) if they are slaves acting on their own, they are condemned to the mines; (2) if they are *humiliores,* they are sentenced to work on public construction projects; (3) if they are *honestiores,* they are fined one-third of their property and expelled to an island or driven into exile.

PATRONAGE

The family was the basic unit of Roman society, and the undisputed head of the family was the *pater,* the father. It was his duty to protect the welfare of those inferior to him—his wife and his children—and it was their duty, in turn, to show him total obedience and deference. The Latin word most often used to express this family relationship is *pietas.*[38] The state was the largest unit of Roman society, but the Romans had traditionally viewed membership in the state (the "public matter")[39] as similar to membership in an extended family. As if to emphasize this analogy, the heads of the state, who were the aristocratic senators, were called *patres* ("fathers"). It was considered their duty to devote their time, energy, and money to the welfare of those inferior to them—the lower-class masses—and to provide public services without pay, but they demanded in return gratitude, submission, and veneration. In the imperial period the head of the state was the emperor, who was called the *pater patriae* ("father of the fatherland"). Once again, *pietas* is the word which best describes the ideal relationship between the rulers and the ruled in the Roman state. In practice, of course, the relationship was seldom ideal. The senatorial *patres* frequently put their own welfare ahead of that of the common people and viewed the masses as troublesome children, as naive, uneducated, immature, and inferior beings who needed constant guidance. This arrogant and scornful attitude is quite evident in Cicero's discussion of aristocracy which appears above.

Another type of paternalistic relationship existed in Roman society. An individual might ask someone better educated and more powerful than himself for

[36] *ultimate torture:* Latin *summum supplicium.* This meant a painful death by crucifixion or burning. In the republican period Roman citizens could not be executed for capital offenses (see note 1 of this chapter), although they might be condemned to the mines. By the second century A.D., however, execution was allowed for *humiliores.* Thus *humiliores,* though Roman citizens, were in this respect treated the same as noncitizens.

[37] Expulsion (Latin *relegatio*) meant banishment but no loss of citizenship.

[38] On *pietas,* see the introduction to selection 1.

[39] *the public matter:* Latin *respublica.*

advice and protection. In return, he became a retainer and provided various services for his protector. The retainer was called a *cliens* ("client"), and his protector was called a *patronus* ("patron"). The upper class and the lower class were thus bound to one another in relationships which emphasized deference and obsequiousness on the part of many toward a few. The patronage system was one of the most deep-rooted and pervasive aspects of ancient Roman society. It has endured into modern Italian society where a *padrone* or "godfather" offers protection and assistance to those less wealthy and powerful than himself, and in turn acquires a "clientele" of loyal supporters.

Patrician and Plebeian

In the period of the monarchy, patrons were members of the patrician families.[40] The following passage describes the various duties of both the patrician patrons and their plebeian clients. The establishment of the patronage system was attributed by Roman historians to Romulus, the legendary founder and first king of Rome. In actual fact, we cannot ascertain the precise origins of the patronage system in Rome.

7   *FIRA* 1, p. 4 (Dionysius of Halicarnassus 2.9–10)

After Romulus had distinguished the more powerful members of society from the less powerful, he then set up laws and established what things were to be done by each of the two groups. The patricians were to serve as priests and magistrates, lawyers and judges. The plebeians were to till the land, herd livestock, and work for wages as craftsmen, tradesmen, and laborers. Romulus entrusted the plebeians to the protection of the patricians, but permitted each plebeian to choose for his patron any patrician whom he himself wished. This system is called patronage.

Romulus then established these rules about patronage. It was the duty of the patricians to explain the laws to their clients, to bring suits on their behalf if they were wronged or injured, and to defend them against prosecutors. . . .

It was unlawful and unholy for patricians and clients to bring suit against one another, to testify against one another in court, or to vote against the other. If anyone was convicted of some such misdeed, he was guilty under the law of treason and could be executed.

Patrons and Clients in Republican Rome

By the middle of the republican period, not only patricians were patrons. As some plebeian families gained power and wealth, they were in a position to become patrons. Most patrons were of senatorial rank and devoted their lives to the advancement of their own political careers. They provided free legal and business assistance to their clients but, in return, expected their clients to work for their

---

[40] The words *patron* and *patrician* both evolved from the same root as the word *pater,* "father."

political campaigns, to vote for them,[41] and to appear with them in public as faithful retainers.[42] A man surrounded by many clients was considered more successful than a man accompanied by only a few. In this passage Tacitus, a writer of the early imperial period, describes a scene from Rome in the republican period.

8   Tacitus, *A Dialogue on Orators* 39.4

Today's speaker needs applause and shouts of approval, or even a theatrical stage as it were. The speakers of former times normally encountered an appreciative audience every day, when throngs of distinguished men packed the Forum, when their clients came to offer support, as did delegations from other parts of Italy,[43] when the people of Rome felt that they had a personal interest in the verdict of many cases.

Patrons and Clients in Imperial Rome

The patronage system had originated as a relationship between free citizens. However, slaves who were given their freedom became clients of their former owners, who became their patrons. By the early imperial period many clients were not native Romans and did not view the patron-client relationship in the same way as a native Roman might. Many retained a servile posture toward their former owners. In particular, freedmen who had been born and raised in the East—Greece and Asia Minor—before their enslavement frequently viewed the role of client as that of sycophant. In the imperial period, moreover, the opportunities for political campaigning were severely curtailed, and clients, who had once fulfilled their obligations to their patrons by supporting their campaigns, now sought other ways of maintaining the relationship. The term *client* was sometimes synonymous with *flatterer* or *parasite*. Clients flocked to a patron's house in the morning to salute him.[44] They clustered around him all day, fawning and currying favor, hoping not for legal assistance as much as for a gift, an allowance, an invitation to dinner, or an inheritance. In the passage translated here, Seneca, writing in the first century A.D., laments the changes which have occurred in the patronage system.

9   Seneca the Younger, *Letters* 19.4

Clients, you say? Not one of them waits upon you, but rather what he can get out of you. Once upon a time, clients sought a politically powerful friend; now they seek

[41] In the previous passage, it was pronounced unlawful for a patron or a client "to vote against the other."

[42] In selection 236, Cicero's brother states that a candidate's clients must accompany him from his house to the Forum every day. If they are unable to attend him, they must send a substitute.

[43] For the behavior of clients living outside Rome, see selection 129.

[44] The salute (Latin *salutatio,* from the verb *salutare* = "to greet, salute, pay respects") was a formal reception held usually in the morning. Clients gathered at the home of their patron to bid him good morning. See selection 129.

loot. If a lonely old man changes his will, his morning visitor goes to someone else's door.

Seeking a Handout

In this passage from Martial, a poet of the early imperial period, we recognize both a greedy client and an arrogant patron.

10   Martial, *Epigrams* 6.88

Yesterday, Caecilianus, when I came to bid you "Good Morning," I accidentally greeted you by name and forgot to call you "My Lord." How much did this liberty cost me? You knocked a dollar off my allowance.[45]

Patrons and Patrons

The *salutatio,* or "morning salute," was a ritual which acknowledged publicly and regularly the patron's superiority and the client's deference and obsequiousness. A less important man of the upper class would have a small following of his own clients but would in turn attach himself as a client to a more important man of the upper class; that is, he would be patron to his clients but a client to his patron, and in the latter relationship he would be expected to attend the morning salute. His own clients, then, would not find him at home when they came to pay their respects.

11   Martial, *Epigrams* 5.22

If I didn't wish and didn't deserve to see you "at home" this morning, Paulus—well, then, may I live even farther from your Esquiline home than I do.[46] As it is, I live on the Quirinal, near the temples of Flora and Jupiter.[47] I must ascend the steep path, up the hill from the Subura, and the filthy pavement of the slick steps. I can scarcely break through the long droves of mules and the marble blocks being hauled at the end of many cable ropes.[48] Then, at the end of these thousand labors, something even more annoying happens: Paulus, your doorman tells me, who am thoroughly exhausted, that you are not "at home." This is the outcome of my futile exertion and drenched little toga. I've decided it's just not worth that much to see Paulus in the morning. A dutiful client always has cruel patrons. From now on, you can't be "my lord" unless you stay in bed.[49]

---

[45] *dollar:* The Latin reads "100 quadrantes." The quadrans was a very small Roman coin, worth about as much as our penny; see Appendix II.

[46] *Esquiline, Quirinal:* two of Rome's seven hills; see map 1.

[47] *Flora:* goddess of flowers. *Jupiter:* father of all the gods, lord of heaven.

[48] On the dangers of walking in Rome, see selection 81.

[49] *in bed:* i.e., where I can greet you.

Rude Patrons

12   Seneca the Younger, *An Essay about the Brevity of Life* 14.4

How many patrons are there who drive away their clients by staying in bed when they call, or ignoring their presence, or being rude? How many are there who rush off on a pretense of urgent business after keeping the poor client waiting for a long time? How many avoid going through an atrium[50] packed with clients and escape through a secret back door, as if it were not ruder to avoid a client than to turn him away? How many, still hung-over and half-asleep from last night's drinking, will yawn disdainfully at men who have interrupted their own sleep in order to wait upon his awakening, and will mumble a greeting through half-open lips, and will need to be reminded a thousand times of the client's name?

No Free Lunches (or Dinners)

The poet Juvenal lived at the end of the first century A.D. The client-patron relationship in his time was frequently a tedious social chore or, even worse, a degrading form of charity.

13   Juvenal, *Satires* 5.12–22, 24, 25, 67–71

First of all, remember this: when you are invited to dinner, you are being repaid in full for all your earlier services. Food is your payment for serving as a client to the great. Your master, I mean patron, records these infrequent dinner invitations under "debts discharged." And thus every two months or so, when he feels like using a normally neglected client to fill up an empty spot on the lowest couch,[51] he says: "Come and join us." Your greatest wish is fulfilled! What more can you ask for? This is your reward for cutting short your sleep and rushing out with your shoe laces untied, worrying about whether everyone else in the crowd of clients has already done the rounds before dawn. . . .

Ah, and what a dinner you get! The wine is so bad that even new wool won't absorb it. . . . The bread is so hard you can barely break it, a mouldy crust of petrified dough that you can't bite into without cracking your teeth. Of course, the master of the house is served soft, white bread made from the finest flour.

[50] *atrium:* main reception area of a Roman home.
[51] *the lowest couch:* the couch farthest away from the host. Some Romans reclined on couches during dinner.

II

Families

FATHERS

Patria Potestas

Roman fathers enjoyed absolute legal control over the lives of their children. This control was called the *patria potestas* ("the father's power"). A Roman father[1] had the legal right to expose a newborn child; he arranged marriages for his children and could force them to divorce spouses they loved;[2] he could disown a child, sell a child into slavery, or even kill a child whose behavior displeased him.[3] As late as 63 B.C. a senator named Aulus Fulvius had his adult son executed because he was involved in a plot to overthrow the government.[4] Of course, how strictly or severely an individual father might wield this power would depend very much on his personality and temperament. Arranged marriages were common in Roman society, but the execution of an adult son by his father was rare. The Romans believed that the *patria potestas* had been defined by Romulus, the legendary founder of the city, but we cannot ascertain the precise origins of the practice.

14   *FIRA* 1, p. 8 (Dionysius of Halicarnassus 2.26–27)

Romulus granted to the Roman father absolute power over his son, and this power was valid until the father's death, whether he decided to imprison him, or whip him, to put him in chains and make him work on a farm, or even to kill him. Romulus even allowed the Roman father to sell his son into slavery.

Horace's Father

Although the Roman father might legally abuse and tyrannize his children, most fathers were in reality concerned about the well-being of their offspring. In this

---

[1] *paterfamilias:* the eldest father in the family; he might be the grandfather.

[2] See selection 67.

[3] The themes of many rhetorical school debates were based on "the father's power"; see selection 139.

[4] For more on this plot, see selection 291.

passage a son describes his father's loving concern for him. The author, Horace, was one of Rome's greatest lyric poets.

15   Horace, *Satires* 1.6.65–92

If my character is flawed by a few minor faults, but is otherwise decent and moral, if you can point out only a few scattered blemishes on an otherwise immaculate surface, if no one can accuse me of greed or of sordidness or of profligacy, if I live a virtuous life, free of defilement (pardon, for a moment, my self-praise), and if I am to my friends a good friend, my father deserves all the credit. For although he was a poor man, with only an infertile plot of land, he was not content to send me to Flavius's school[5] which the burly sons of burly centurions[6] attended, carrying their book-bags and writing tablets[7] slung over their left shoulders and paying their few pennies on the Ides.[8] My father had the courage to take his boy to Rome, to have him taught the same skills which any equestrian or senator[9] would have his sons taught. If anyone had seen my clothing or the slaves that attended me, as is the custom in a large city, he would have thought that my expenses were being paid for from an ancestral estate. But my paedagogus,[10] my absolutely incorruptible guardian, was my father who accompanied me to school. Need I say more? He kept me pure, which is the highest level of virtue, not only from every vice, but even from any insinuation of vice. He didn't make these sacrifices because he worried that someone might criticize him if I became a crier[11] or, like him, a money-collector; nor would I have complained if he hadn't taken me to Rome. But as it is now, he deserves from me unstinting gratitude and praise. I could never be ashamed of such a father, nor do I feel any need, as many people do, to apologize for being a freedman's son.[12]

Cicero's Grief

Roman fathers greeted the birth of a boy infant with more joy than the birth of a girl infant. Indeed girl infants were sometimes unwanted and therefore exposed.[13]

[5] *Flavius's school:* the local school in Venusia, a small town east of Naples (Neapolis), where Horace was born; see map 2. Schools were privately operated and schoolowners/teachers such as Flavius were poorly paid (see selections 124 and 126).

[6] *centurions:* officers in the Roman army; see selection 265. Venusia had been settled by military veterans, and there were consequently quite a few centurions in the town. (They may have viewed Horace, the son of an ex-slave, with as much scorn as he viewed them.)

[7] *writing tablets:* waxed tablets on which letters and words were scratched with a sharp-pointed instrument (see selection 132).

[8] *Ides:* teachers' fees were paid monthly. "Ides" was the name given to the fifteenth day of March, May, July, and October and the thirteenth day of all other months.

[9] *equestrian or senator:* see the introduction to Chapter I.

[10] *paedagogus:* a slave who was the companion and chaperone of a young child; see selections 42 and 43.

[11] *crier:* Latin *praeco* = "someone who cries out in public," "a professional loudmouth," a man hired to make announcements, address large groups of people, etc. Most people could not read and therefore depended on heralds for public information of the type now placed in newspapers. For an example of a crier or herald at work, see selection 194. *Praeco* can also mean "auctioneer."

[12] *freedman:* an ex-slave (a slave who has been freed).

[13] See selections 31 and 32.

Daughters who were allowed to live were often married at a very tender age to men chosen by their fathers. It was not uncommon for girls to be engaged at twelve and married at thirteen,[14] and few were asked their opinions about prospective bridegrooms. Yet it would be wrong to conclude that Roman fathers did not love their daughters. Cicero, for example, was very fond of his daughter Tullia and consequently greatly distressed, as this passage indicates, when she died.[15] Tullia had been married three times. Her first husband died and left her a widow (she was probably still a teenager), and she was separated from her second and third husbands by divorce. The first two marriages were evidently arranged by her father, Cicero. While Cicero was in exile, she herself chose her third husband. Her choice did not please Cicero, who complained bitterly about his son-in-law; ultimately this marriage, too, was unhappy. In February of 45 B.C. Tullia died, at about thirty years of age, from complications arising from childbirth. Three months after her death Cicero was still deeply grieved as we learn from this letter to his friend Atticus.

16   Cicero, *Letters to Atticus* 12.46

I think I can master my grief and go from Lanuvium to my villa in Tusculum.[16] For I must give up my property there forever (since my sorrow will remain, although it may become better concealed), or else realize that it doesn't matter whether I go there now or in ten years. Certainly the house there could not possibly remind me of her any more than do already the thoughts which consume me constantly, day and night. You will probably ask, "Is there no consolation in books?" In this case, I am afraid they are actually a hindrance. Without books, I might perhaps have been tougher; but an educated mind is neither insensitive nor callous.

MOTHERS

We know, unfortunately, very little about the relationship between mothers and their children. When Roman writers do describe their mothers, they generally present us with an idealized portrait of a Roman *matrona,* a woman who is virtuous, strong, self-sacrificing, and devoted to the education and political advancement of her family. But we seldom hear of real warmth in the mother-child relationship. Roman writers, when they mention their mothers at all (which is rare), seem to worship them from a distance. There are various explanations for this apparent lack of warmth. Since many women died young, often in childbirth, their children may never have known them. A man might be married two or three times,

---

[14] See selection 56.

[15] See also Pliny's description of Fundanus's grief at the untimely death of his daughter (selection 284).

[16] Lanuvium, Tusculum: towns southeast of Rome. See map 2.

and his children would thus be raised by stepmothers. In cases of divorce, moreover, children remained with their father, not their mother, and they might not see her again.[17] In addition, many upper-class Roman children were raised by nurses or nannies and might therefore feel more love toward the nurses who had fed, bathed, and clothed them than toward their mothers. Yet surely many Romans loved their mothers dearly, and perhaps it was strictly literary convention which led them to describe their mothers in terms of generalized virtues rather than to recall personal and highly individual memories of maternal warmth.

The Ideal

In this passage from his *Biography of Agricola*,[18] Tacitus describes the relationship between Agricola and his mother, Julia Procilla, "a woman of exceptional moral integrity" who devoted herself to her son's education, moral guidance, and political advancement.

17 Tacitus, *A Biography of Agricola* 4.2–4

The mother of Agricola was Julia Procilla, a woman of exceptional moral integrity. He spent his boyhood and adolescence close by her side being gently trained in every aspect of honorable achievement. He was sheltered from the enticements of immorality not only by his virtuous and upright nature, but also because, as a young boy, he had as his residence and as a model for behavior Massilia,[19] a town which provided a mixture and blend of Greek refinement and provincial frugality. I remember that he himself said that he had, in his early youth, been more absorbed with philosophy than was proper for a Roman and a senator until his mother's good sense brought under control his ardent and passionate nature.

Memory of a Warm Moment

Marcus Aurelius was emperor of the Roman world from A.D. 161 to 180, but he is also known as a Stoic philosopher[20] and the author of the *Meditations*. In this letter to his friend Fronto[21] (written between A.D. 144 and 145) he gives us a rare insight into the type of warm, relaxed relationship a Roman son might have with his mother.

17 See selection 284: "She comforted her sister and father." There is no mention of the girl's mother, who is perhaps dead or perhaps separated from her children by divorce.

18 *Agricola:* Gnaeus Julius Agricola (A.D. 40–93) was governor of Britain about A.D. 78–84. He was Tacitus's father-in-law.

19 *Massilia:* modern-day Marseilles, on the south coast of France. It had been established as a colony by the Greeks around 600 B.C.

20 On Stoicism, see selections 418–425.

21 Fronto was Marcus Aurelius's teacher and about twenty years older than he. Selections 176 and 322 are also addressed to Fronto.

18   Marcus Aurelius, *Fronto's Letters* 4.6

We are all well.[22] I slept in a little this morning because I have a slight cold. . . . After lunch we spent some time picking grapes; we worked up a good sweat, but had fun shouting jokes to one another, and, as some poet has said, "we left a few clusters (too high to reach) as survivors of the vintage." Later in the afternoon we returned home. I did a little scholarly research, but not very well. Then I had a long chat with my dear mother who came in and sat on the edge of my bed. I asked her, "What do you think my friend Fronto is doing right now?" And she asked me, "What do you think my friend Gratia[23] is doing?" And then I asked, "What do you think sweet little Gratia[24] is doing?" While we were chatting away and gossiping and playfully arguing about which of us two loved which of you three best, the gong sounded to let us know that my father had gone to take his bath.

A Mother's Concern

Private correspondence was written on papyrus sheets. Since papyrus is a perishable material, almost all letters written 2000 years ago no longer exist.[25] In dry desert regions of Egypt, however, archeologists have discovered some remarkably well-preserved papyrus documents. Egypt became a Roman province in 30 B.C., and many of the documents found there were written during Egypt's Roman period. The letter translated here was written in Egypt in the third century A.D. on the back of a piece of papyrus which had already been used once and then sold as scrap paper. In this letter to her son a mother expresses anxious concern about an injury he has received.

19   *BGU* 380

Late yesterday I went to your employer Serapion and asked him about your health. He told me that you had hurt your foot on a piece of sharp wood. I was very worried that you could walk about only slowly and with difficulty. And I told Serapion that I would travel with him to see you; but he said, "Don't worry so much!" But if you know that you are not well, write to me, and I will come down[26] to you with any traveling companion I can find. Don't forget to write, son, about your health, for you know the anxiety a mother experiences about her child.

Your children send love and greetings.[27]

[22] Marcus was staying at his parents' home.
[23] *Gratia* (the Elder): wife of Fronto.
[24] *Gratia* (the Younger): Fronto's young daughter.
[25] The letters of famous Roman writers such as Cicero, Seneca, and Pliny were written on papyrus but copied after their deaths onto more durable materials such as vellum. Further copies were made by hand during the Middle Ages, until the invention of the printing press made multiple copies easy to obtain. The papyrus originals perished long ago, of course. On papyrus sources see Appendix I.
[26] *come down:* i.e., the Nile River. The man is working out of town. Compare selection 31.
[27] The children seem to be living with their grandmother while their father works out of town. We know nothing about the children's mother.

An Ungrateful Son

Mothers did not have the legal control over their children that fathers did (the *patria potestas*). Indeed, when her husband died a widow might find herself at the mercy of her children unless she had inherited enough money to remain independent. In this letter from second-century A.D. Egypt, Sempronius reprimands his brother Maximus for Maximus's harsh treatment of their mother, who apparently lived with the latter.

20   *Sammelbuch* 6263 (*Select Papyri* 121)

I hope you are well. I have been told that you are not looking after our dear mother very well. Please, sweetest brother, don't cause her any grief. And if our other brothers talk back to her, you should slap them. For you should act like a father now. I know that you can be kind to her without my writing; please don't be offended by my writing and reprimanding you. We ought to revere as a goddess the mother who has given us birth, especially a mother as good and virtuous as ours. I have written you these things, my brother, because I know the sweetness of dear parents. Write and tell me how you are.

BROTHERS AND SISTERS

Affection

The following passages are epitaphs which indicate a warm relationship between brothers and sisters. Other passages in this book also provide evidence of the affection which many siblings had for one another.[28]

This first epitaph was found at Naples, the second at Rome.

21   *CIL* 10.3003 (*ILS* 8002)

A sister provided this memorial for her well-deserving brother Tertius who lived about thirty-one years.

22   *CIL* 6.21874

Publius Malius Firminus lived twenty-four years, three months, and twenty-seven days.
Publius Malius Maximus provided this memorial for his well-deserving brother.

[28] Consider, for example, the relationship between Turia and her sister (selection 288), or Marcus Cicero's concern about the welfare of his brother Quintus Cicero, in selection 60.

PRODUCING A FAMILY

Fertility

Most Romans believed that the function of marriage was to produce a family, and newlyweds were enjoined to have children as soon as possible.[29] One woman so strongly felt that it was her wifely duty to give her husband children that she suggested a divorce when she remained barren.[30] Girls were married in their early teens and expected to bear one child after another.[31] Since the infant mortality rate was very high, however, families were generally moderate rather than large in size. Cornelia,[32] for example, bore twelve children, but only three lived to adulthood. Women embarrassed or distressed by their lack of fertility might seek help from a doctor. Medical writers record various recommendations for increasing the chances of conception, a few of which are translated here. The author of the first passage, Soranus, was a Greek doctor who practiced in Rome around A.D. 100.

23   Soranus, *Gynecology* 1.34.1, 1.36.1–2

Since women are married for the sake of bearing children and heirs, and not for pleasure and enjoyment, it is totally absurd to inquire about the quality or rank of their family line or about the abundance of their wealth, but not to inquire about their ability to conceive children. . . .

Just as every season is not suitable for sowing seed on the ground for the purpose of bringing forth fruit, so too among humans not every time is suitable for the conception of seed ejaculated during intercourse. Therefore, in order that the desired outcome may be attained through the proper timing of intercourse, it is useful to discuss here the problem of proper timing. The best time for intercourse resulting in conception is when menstruation is ending and abating, when the urge and desire for intercourse are present, when the body is neither hungry nor too full and heavy from drunkenness and indigestion, after the body has been refreshed and a light snack has been eaten, and when a pleasant state of body and mind exists.

Miscarriage

In this letter to his wife's grandfather, Pliny the Younger reports the sad news that his wife has had a miscarriage. Miscarriage is always a trauma, but perhaps particularly so in circumstances where there is family pressure to produce heirs and

---

[29] See Catullus's wedding hymn (selection 50); also Pliny the Younger's "letter of recommendation" (selection 49).

[30] See selection 288.

[31] Many died in childbirth; see selection 287.

[32] *Cornelia:* the mother of Tiberius and Gaius Gracchus, well-known political figures of the second century B.C.; see selection 170 and also genealogy chart 2.

where the woman believes that her main function in life is to bear many sons. Consider Soranus on hysteria: "In the majority of cases, the illness (hysteria) is preceded by repeated miscarriage."[33]

24 Pliny the Younger, *Letters* 8.10

Because you are so very anxious for us to produce a great-grandson for you, you will be very sad to hear that your granddaughter has had a miscarriage. She's a young girl and didn't even realize that she was pregnant; consequently she failed to take certain precautions necessary for pregnant women, and she did things she should not have. She has paid for her ignorance, and her lesson has been costly: she was herself gravely ill. And so, although you must be distressed that you have, in your old age, been deprived of a firmly established line of descendants, still you should thank the gods because they denied to you a great-grandson at the present time only in order to save your granddaughter's life. They will surely grant us children; although this pregnancy was not successful, it gives us confidence that we are capable of having children.

I am now offering you the same words of advice and encouragement which I use for myself. For you could not desire great-grandchildren more fervently than I desire children. I think that political careers will be easy for them, since they will be descended from both me and you, and I will bequeath to them a well-known name and a long line of famous ancestors. May they only be born and change our grief to joy.[34]

Infant Deaths

25 *CIL* 6.19159 (*ILS* 8005)

Quintus Haterius Ephebus and Julia Zosime provided this memorial[35] for their most unfortunate daughter Hateria Superba who lived one year, six months, twenty-five days.

Birth Announcements

Happy parents sometimes announced the joyous occasion of a child's birth by painting a message on a house wall. The following birth announcements were found on walls in Pompeii, a town buried by the eruption of Mount Vesuvius in A.D. 79.

26 *CIL* 4.294, 8149

Our daughter was born early in the evening on Saturday, August 2.

Announcing the birth of Cornelius Sabinus!

[33] See selection 297.
[34] Pliny and his wife unfortunately remained childless.
[35] *this memorial:* i.e., epitaph. The inscription was found at Rome. There is also carved on the stone an image of a young girl.

BIRTH CONTROL

Not everyone in the Roman world wanted a family, and some people wanted to
limit the size of their family. Various methods of birth control were used by the
Romans, some of which are mentioned here.

Contraception

Some recommended methods of contraception would obviously have been more
successful than others. The first passage was written by a medical doctor, the second by a scholar who compiled an encyclopedia of natural science. See Appendix
I for more information about both authors.

27   Soranus, *Gynecology* 1.60.4, 1.61.1–3

It is safer to prevent conception from occurring than to destroy the fetus through
abortion. . . . Therefore one must avoid intercourse at those times which we said
were favorable for conception.[36] . . . It also helps, in preventing conception, to smear
the entrance to the uterus with old olive oil or honey or sap from a cedar or balsam
tree, alone or mixed with white lead. . . . One might also add a clump of finespun
wool. . . . Things such as these, which are astringent, cause clogging and have a cool-
ing effect, cause the entrance of the uterus to close before the time of coitus, and do
not allow the sperm to pass through.

28   Pliny the Elder,[37] *Natural History* 29.27.85

There is a third type of spider, called a hairy spider, which has a very large head. If
this is cut open, one finds inside, it is said, two small worms. If these are tied on to
women with a strip of deerhide, they will not conceive, or so says Caecilius in his
notebooks. This contraceptive retains its effectiveness for one year. I think it proper
for me to mention contraception only because some women are so fertile and have
so many children that they need a respite.

[36] See selection 23.

[37] The author of the book *Natural History,* from which this passage is taken, is Pliny the
Elder, the uncle of Pliny the Younger, who wrote selection 24. Pliny the Elder died during
the eruption of Mount Vesuvius in A.D. 79 which buried Pompeii and Herculaneum, two towns
in the Bay of Naples area.

Abortion

29 Soranus, *Gynecology* 1.64.1–2, 1.65.1–7

In order to dislodge the embryo, the woman should take strenuous walks and be shaken up by draft animals. She should also make violent leaps in the air and lift objects which are too heavy for her. . . . If this is ineffective, she should be placed in a mixture, which has first been boiled and purified, of linseed, fenugreek, mallow, marsh-mallow, and wormwood. She should use poultices of the same substances and be treated with infusions of old olive oil, alone or mixed with rue, honey, iris, or wormwood. . . .

A woman who intends to have an abortion must, for two or three days beforehand, take long baths and eat little food. She is then bled, and a large quantity of blood removed from her. . . . After the bleeding, she must be shaken up by draft animals. . . . Or one may insert an abortive suppository . . . such as equal quantities of myrtle, snowdrop seed, and bitter lupines mixed with water. . . . One must be careful not to insert substances too overpowering or to separate and dislodge the embryo with a sharp-edged or sharp-pointed object, for you run the risk of injuring adjacent areas. After the abortion, treat the patient as if for inflammation.

Ovid addressed this poem to his girlfriend, Corinna. He deplored the fact that she would have an abortion simply to avoid "stretch marks." We should, however, not forget that many women chose to have abortions because they believed that they could not afford a child.

30 Ovid, *Love Affairs* 2.14.5–10, 19, 20, 27, 28, 35–40

That woman who was the first to rip a frail fetus out of her womb deserved to die from that butchery herself. And will you prepare to make a similar slaughter just so that your stomach will be free of wrinkles? If this vicious practice had found favor among the mothers of the good old days, the human race would have become extinct. . . . If your own mother had tried to do what you are now planning, you yourself would have perished. . . . Why do you give poisons to your unborn child? . . . No tigress in the Armenian forest does this, no lioness dares to destroy her own cubs. But frail young girls do! They don't, however, escape punishment, for she who destroys the children in her womb often dies herself. Yes, she herself dies, and is carried to the funeral pyre, and everyone who sees her pyre shouts, "She deserved it."

Exposure

If the birth of an unwanted child was not prevented by contraception or abortion, the parents still had one further method available to them to limit the size of their family: they could expose the newborn infant, that is, leave it to die from starvation and other natural causes. Infants were exposed for various reasons. Sick or deformed infants were usually exposed. Girl infants were exposed more often than boy infants because girls were a financial burden; they could not work to support themselves, and they needed dowries. Healthy boy infants might be exposed to avoid the costs of raising them or to prevent the family property from being split many ways.

This letter, found at Oxyrhynchus, was written in Egypt in 1 B.C. by a man named Hilarion to his wife, Alis.

31   *Oxyrhynchus Papyri 744 (Select Papyri 105)*

I send you my warmest greetings. I want you to know that we are still in Alexandria.[38] And please don't worry if all the others come home but I remain in Alexandria. I beg you and entreat you to take care of the child and, if I receive my pay soon, I will send it up to you. If you have the baby before I return, if it is a boy, let it live; if it is a girl, expose it. You sent a message with Aphrodisias, "Don't forget me." How can I forget you? I beg you, then, not to worry.

This passage is taken from the mythological story of Iphis. When Iphis was born her mother concealed the fact that she was a girl infant in order to save her life. (Her mother continued to dress Iphis as a boy. Later the gods changed Iphis into a boy so that he/she could marry a girl.)

32   Ovid, *Metamorphoses* 9.669–684, 704–706

Ligdus was a freeborn man, but from a lower-class family. He was a poor man, but moral and honorable. He told his pregnant wife, when she was approaching labor, "I pray for two things—that you may have an easy labor, and that you may bear a male child. For a daughter is too burdensome, and we just don't have the money. I hate to say this, but if you should bear a girl—I say this with great reluctance, so please forgive me—if you should bear a girl, we'll have to kill her."

He spoke the words, and they both wept, he who had given the order and she who must carry it out. And Telethusa begged her husband over and over again to change his mind, but in vain. His mind was made up. . . .

She went into labor and gave birth to a girl. But the father didn't know this. And the mother lied, and raised her daughter as a boy.

ENCOURAGING FERTILITY

The Legislation of Augustus

Augustus, who was emperor from 27 B.C. to A.D. 14, was concerned about the declining birth rate, particularly among the members of the upper class. He therefore promoted legislation which was intended to encourage people to have large

---

[38] Hilarion works in Alexandria; his family lives in Oxyrhynchus, more than 200 miles up the Nile ("I will send it *up* to you"). Like the man in selection 19, Hilarion works out of town and sends money home to his family.

families, and the Julian Laws were passed in 18 B.C. These laws apparently had little effect, and Augustus once again promoted similar legislation. The Papia-Poppaean Laws were passed in A.D. 9. These laws, too, were unsuccessful. Indeed, Papius and Poppaeus, the two consuls after whom the laws were named, were both bachelors!

33 *ADA*, pp. 174, 184, 187

In the seventh section of the Julian Law priority is given not to the consul who is older, but to the consul who has more children than his colleague. . . .

Bachelors are forbidden by the Julian Law to receive inheritances and legacies. . . .

The Julian Law allowed a woman to be exempt from marriage for one year after the death of her husband, for six months after a divorce. The Papia-Poppaean Law allowed two years after a husband's death and eighteen months after a divorce.

34 Dio Cassius, *Roman History* 54.16.1–2

Augustus placed heavier penalties on unmarried men and on women without husbands. On the other hand, he offered rewards for marriage and for having children. And since there were, among the upper class, far more males than females,[39] he allowed all upper-class men who wished, except senators, to marry freedwomen,[40] and he ordered their children to be considered legitimate.

35 Tacitus, *Annals* 3.25

Toward the end of his life, Augustus passed the Papia-Poppaean Law, which supplemented the earlier Julian Laws, to encourage the enforcement of penalties for celibacy and to enrich the Treasury. However, even with this new law, marriages and births did not increase substantially. Childlessness offered too many advantages.

ADOPTION

A couple who were unable to have children, or who had been careful to limit the size of their family, and then lost their sons through illness or accident, might wish to adopt someone who could inherit the family name and property.

An Adoption Agreement

This agreement was drawn up in A.D. 335. The papyrus was discovered at Oxyrhynchus, Egypt.

---

[39] It is not clear why there were more men than women. Perhaps deaths in childbirth and exposure of girl infants provide partial explanation.

[40] *freedwomen:* ex-slaves.

36   *P. Oxy.* 1206 (*Select Papyri* 10)

Aurelius Heracles and Aurelia Isarion, both of the city of Oxyrhynchus, acknowledge
that we have given to you, Aurelius Horion, for adoption, our son, Patermouthis, who
is two years old.

I, Horion, acknowledge that I hold and consider him as my true son with regard
to maintaining for him the rights of succession to my estate. It shall not be lawful for
me to cast aside or reduce him to slavery because he is well-born and the son of well-
born and free parents.

It shall not be lawful for us, Heracles and Isarion, to reclaim the child from you,
Horion, because we have once and for all given him over to you for adoption.

It shall not be lawful for anyone to transgress hereafter the terms of this agreement because we have consented to and agreed upon these terms.

This adoption agreement, written in duplicate so that each party may have a copy,
is valid; we have had the opportunity to question one another and we have now reached
this agreement.

Giving Away One's Child

Grinding poverty sometimes forced people to give away their children, however
much they loved them.[41] This official document of relinquishment, found at
Oxyrhynchus, was written in A.D. 554. The girl mentioned in this document is
apparently being adopted by a family, as was the young boy in the previous passage. Sometimes, however, parents were forced to sell to slave-dealers children
whom they could not support.

37   *P. Oxy.* 1895 (*Select Papyri* 11)

I, Aurelia Herais. . . .[42] My husband died and I was left, to toil and suffer for my
daughter by him, to provide her with the barest necessities of life. And now I no longer
have the means to feed her. . . . She is now about nine years old. I have requested
that you receive her from me as your daughter, and I acknowledge that I have handed
her over to you from now and forever as your legal daughter so that you may provide
her with the necessities of life and fill the position of parents to a daughter. And I
acknowledge that I have no power henceforth to reclaim her from you. If I do so,
I agree to pay you for all the expenses of raising her. . . .

This agreement, written in one copy only, is valid. I have been questioned carefully and I have given my consent.

[41] In selection 218, a grateful freedman thanks his patron for providing financial assistance which enabled him to keep his children.
[42] There is a gap here in the papyrus.

RAISING CHILDREN

Literary sources tell us very little about the daily activities of Roman children. Much more helpful in this respect are pictorial sources, such as wall-paintings and mosaics, which depict children at play with one another, with toys, and with animals. Although we know that childhood in the Roman world was a period of briefer duration than it is today (girls might be married at twelve, boys at sixteen),[43] yet we should nonetheless assume that Roman children did not differ substantially from modern children in their enjoyments and needs: toys, playmates, games, food (especially sweets), and the love and attention of their parents.

Filial Obedience

Roman parents expected absolute obedience from their children.[44]

38   Seneca the Younger, *An Essay about Kindness* 3.38.2

Even the power of rhetoric and the subtlety of the mind cannot fully express how great an achievement it is, how praiseworthy and how eternally memorable, to be able to say: "I obeyed my parents; I deferred to their authority, whether it was fair or unfair or even harsh; I showed myself compliant and submissive. In only one respect was I unyielding: in refusing to let them do me more kindnesses than I did them."

Spoiled Brats

The Romans thought that strict discipline in the home prepared children for the harsh realities of adult life. Seneca, the author of the previous passage, discussed in another essay the problems of the spoiled child.

39   Seneca the Younger, *An Essay about Anger* 2.21.1–6

It is of the utmost importance that children be raised in the correct manner even if this means harsh discipline. We must be careful not to allow them to have fits of anger, but we must also be careful not to stifle their individual personalities. . . . Unlimited freedom creates an intractable personality, total repression produces an abject personality. Praise lifts the spirit and makes a child self-confident, but too much praise makes him insolent and bad-tempered. We must therefore steer a middle course when raising

---

[43] Boys of the lower class would be out working well before they reached their sixteenth birthday; see selection 135.

[44] The *patria potestas* allowed a father to punish a disobedient child severely; see selections 14 and 139.

a child, sometimes checking him back, sometimes spurring him on. . . . Don't let him whine and pester you for treats; give rewards only for good deeds or for promised good behavior. When he is thrust into competition with children of his own age, don't let him sulk or become angry. . . . When he wins or does something laudable, he should be praised, but not allowed to become excessively elated, for joy leads to exultation, and exultation leads to a swollen head and an inflated opinion of oneself. We should allow a certain amount of leisure, but never let this develop into idleness and sloth, and never let the child become accustomed to a soft and easy life. . . . For the child who has been denied nothing, whose tears an anxious mother always dried, who always had his own way with the paedagogue[45]—this child will be unable to cope with the harsh realities of life.

Advice about Parental Severity

In the letter translated here, Pliny advises his friend to remember that "boys will be boys."

40   Pliny the Younger, *Letters* 9.12

A certain man was rebuking his son because he had bought horses and dogs which were a little too expensive. After the son had left the room, I said to the father, "Hey, have you never done anything which your father could criticize? Did I say 'have you done'? Do you not now sometimes do things which your son, if he suddenly became your father (and you became his son), could criticize with equal severity? Aren't all men led astray by some weakness? One man indulges himself in one way, another man in another way."

I was reminded by this example of excessive severity to write to you, as one friend to another, lest you on some occasion treat your son too harshly and strictly. Remember that he is a boy, and that you were once a boy, and perform your duty as a father always remembering that you are a human being and the father of a human being.

Nurses

Upper-class infants and children were frequently placed in the care of slaves and freedwomen who nursed them and cared for them. In this passage from his textbook on *The Elements of Oratory,* Quintilian, a writer of the first century A.D., indicates that some children spent more time with their nurses than with their mothers.

41   Quintilian, *The Elements of Oratory* 1.1.4–5

Above all, make sure that the infant's nurse speaks correctly. . . . Of course, she should without doubt be chosen on the basis of good moral character, but still make sure that she speaks correctly as well. The child will hear his nurse first, and will learn

[45] *paedagogue:* see selections 42 and 43.

to speak by imitating her words. And by nature we remember best those things which we learned when our minds were youngest.

Paedagogues

Paedagogues[46] were male slaves who looked after young children. They played with them, took them on outings, taught them table manners, and generally baby-sat. When the child was old enough to attend school, the paedagogue escorted him to and from school,[47] as well as to and from baths, the theater, and social functions. The paedagogue might possibly, though certainly not always, be responsible for teaching the child some simple reading and writing.

42   Cicero, *An Essay about Friendship* 20.74

In general, decisions about friendships should not be made until we have developed maturity of age and strength of mind. . . . Otherwise our nurses and our paedagogues, on the principle that they have known us longest, will claim the largest share of our affections. They must not, of course, be neglected, but they must be regarded in a different manner from how we regard the friends we have made as adults.

A Persistent Paedagogue

One function of the paedagogue was to protect the innocent child from the corrupting influences of society. Some paedagogues found it difficult to relinquish this role of guardian of morals once their charges had grown up. In the poem translated below, Martial complains that his former paedagogue, Charidemus, was still trying to monitor his behavior.

43   Martial, *Epigrams* 11.39

You rocked my cradle, Charidemus, and were my guardian and constant companion when I was a boy. Now my beard dirties the barber's towel with shavings, and my girlfriend complains about being hurt by my lips. But to you I have not grown up. My steward trembles before you, my butler, indeed my whole household staff, shiver with fear. You won't allow me to amuse myself or make love. You want no freedom for me, but every freedom for yourself. You reproach me, you watch me like a hawk, you complain, you sigh, and you can scarcely keep your angry hand off the rod.[48] If I put on Tyrian clothes[49] or grease down my hair, you exclaim: "Your father never did

---

[46] *Paedagogues:* from the Greek *pais, paid-,* ("child") and *agogos* ("leading," "guiding").
[47] See also selections 15 and 131.
[48] Charidemus evidently believed the adage, "Spare the rod, spoil the child."
[49] *Tyrian clothes:* The traditional garment for a Roman gentleman was a drab toga made of wool. Tyrian clothes were, in contrast, a rich purple color and were perhaps made of silk. Such garments suggested an extravagant, prodigal lifestyle, unbecoming to a serious Roman. The purple dye was produced in the city of Tyre, hence "Tyrian."

that." You wrinkle your forehead and count every glass of wine I drink, as if the bottle came from your own cellar. Stop it! I cannot stand a freedman who acts like Cato.[50] My girlfriend will explain to you that I am now a man.

GUARDIANS

Appointing Guardians

When a man died, guardians (who were usually relatives) were appointed for his sons, if they had not yet come of age, and for his daughters, regardless of their age or marital status. (For example, a forty-year-old married woman would be assigned a guardian when her father died.) The main function of the guardian was to oversee and protect the financial and legal affairs of his ward.[51]

44   Ulpian, *Rules* 11: 1, 21, 27, 28

Guardians are appointed both for males and females; for males only when they have not yet reached puberty and are therefore of tender age; for females both before and after puberty because they are the weaker sex and are ignorant in business and legal matters. . . .

The Senate decreed that if a woman is about to marry and her guardian is a deaf-mute or is insane, she shall be assigned another guardian who will arrange her dowry. . . .

A woman needs the authority of her guardian in the following matters: if she is engaging in a lawsuit, if she is undertaking a legal or financial obligation, if she is transacting civil business. . . .

Males are released from their guardians at the time of puberty. . . . Women are released from their guardians . . .[52]

ORPHANS

An Appeal for Help

We have noted above that many women died while quite young, leaving motherless children.[53] When a child's father died as well, the orphan had to seek assistance

---

[50] *Cato:* Cato the Elder, who lived 234–149 B.C. He was a conservative who abhorred foreign influences because he thought they were corrupting the moral fiber of the Roman people. Although the real Cato had some human failings (see selections 160 and 184), he was represented by later generations as a paragon of moral virtue.

[51] For examples of child-guardian relationships, see selection 49.

[52] The passage is incomplete in the manuscript, but we know from other sources that, according to the Papia-Poppaean Law passed during the time of Augustus (see selections 33, 34, and 35), freeborn women with at least three children or freedwomen with four children might apply for and receive release from their guardians.

[53] See also selection 287.

from his or her relatives since the state did not operate orphanages. Upper-class families were well able to handle the financial burden of an extra child.[54] Lower-class orphans may have had a much more difficult time finding relatives who would support them. In this letter, written in the fourth century A.D., an orphaned girl named Tare living in Apamea, Syria, appeals to her aunt in Egypt for help.

45　　　　　　　*Les Papyrus Bouriant (P. Bour.)* 25 (*Select Papyri* 165)

Before all, I pray God that my letter finds you healthy and happy; this is my prayer. Please be informed, dear aunt, that my mother, your sister, has been dead since Easter.[55] While my mother was with me, she was my whole family; since her death, I have remained here alone in a strange land with no one to help. Please remember me, dear aunt, as if my mother were still alive, and if you find someone to help, please send him to me. Please give my greetings to all our relatives. May the Lord protect you and keep you in good health for many peaceful years.

WELFARE ASSISTANCE

Most of the information about Roman family life was written by members of the upper class, and we therefore know unfortunately little about lower-class families; but the life of the poor was undoubtedly harsh. We have already seen that some families, unable to support all their children, were forced to put some up for adoption, to sell them into slavery, or even to kill them through exposure. These were acts not of cruelty but of necessity. And certainly the plight of many orphans must have been dismal. Fortunately, steps were sometimes taken both by the state and by private individuals to alleviate the misery of the poor. The assistance was, however, sporadic, and we should not conclude that it reached every family in need.

Public Assistance

In the imperial period, the emperors occasionally made funds available to communities to encourage people to keep their children (rather than exposing or selling them) and to assist people in raising them. The following regulation[56] was published in A.D. 315.

---

[54] Turia (selection 288) took care of quite a few young female relatives; Pliny's wife, Calpurnia, had been raised by an aunt (see selection 54); Ummidia Quadratilla (see selection 295) had raised her grandson; Pliny's friend Mauricus (see selection 49) became guardian of his niece.

[55] The girl and her aunt appear to be Christians.

[56] *The Law Code of Theodosius;* see Appendix I.

46   *The Law Code of Theodosius* 11.27.1

A law shall be written on bronze tablets or waxed tablets or on linen cloths and clearly posted throughout the towns and municipalities of Italy to prevent parents from killing their infants and to turn them to better alternatives. It should be the concern of your office that, if any parent should report to you a child which he is unable, because of poverty, to raise, there be no delay in issuing food and clothing, since the raising of a newborn infant cannot withstand delays. We offer funds for this program from our treasury and our private account.

Private Charity

Sometimes wealthy people established and endowed charity foundations to help support children in their community.[57] The following passage is a translation of an inscription on a monument set up in Sicca, North Africa, between A.D. 169 and 180.

47   *CIL* 8.1641 (*ILS* 6818)

To my fellow townsmen of Cirta[58] and to my beloved Siccenses,[59] I, Publius Licinius Papirianus, wish to give 1,300,000 sesterces. I trust to your good faith, beloved townsmen, that from the 5 percent interest on this sum there may be fed and maintained each year 300 boys and 300 girls, the boys from the ages three to fifteen, each boy receiving two and a half denarii a month, the girls from the ages three to thirteen at two denarii a month. Residents as well as townsmen should be chosen, as long as the residents reside in buildings within the boundaries of our colony-town. If these arrangements seem acceptable to you, it will be best for the duovirs[60] of each year to choose the children; but you must take care that a replacement at once be found for each child who reaches adult age[61] or dies, so that the full number may always be fed and maintained.

[57] See selection 129.
[58] *Cirta:* town in Numidia (North Africa); see map 5.
[59] *Siccenses:* citizens of Sicca, a town in Numidia.
[60] *duovirs:* literally "two men" (Latin *duo* = "two," *vir* = "man"). The *duovirs* were two men elected annually to be the highest public officials in a town.
[61] *adult age:* apparently thirteen for girls and fifteen for boys.

III

Marriage

THE AGE OF MARRIAGE PARTNERS

Child Brides

The Romans entered upon marriage at a very young age; both partners might be in their teens at the time of marriage. It was not, however, unusual for a girl in her early teens to be married to a man considerably older than herself who had already been married once or twice before.[1] Some girls were even married before they reached puberty. The following inscription, a first-century B.C. epitaph found at Rome, tells us about Aurelia Philematium, who was married at age seven.

48   *CIL* 1.2.1221 (*ILS* 7472)

I was called,[2] while alive, Aurelia Philematium, a woman chaste and modest, unsoiled by the common crowd, faithful to her husband.

My husband, whom, alas, I now have left, was a fellow freedman.[3] He was truly like a father to me.

When I was seven years old he embraced me. Now I am forty and in the power of death.

Through my constant care, my husband flourished.

---

[1] Consider selection 54. Pliny, for example, was about forty when he married Calpurnia and had been married twice before.

[2] *I was called:* Roman tombstone inscriptions often contain messages from the dead person to the living. And Roman tombs were frequently placed alongside major roads such as the Via Appia. Here Aurelia Philematium is addressing, from her tombstone, those who pass by and read the inscription.

[3] For more on her husband, see selection 57. Although Aurelia Philematium was a freedwoman at the time of her death, she and her husband may have been slaves at the time of their marriage.

ARRANGED MARRIAGES

Matchmakers

Marriages were generally arranged by family members, and the bride and groom had little to say about the choice of their marriage partner.[4] This letter from Pliny to Junius Mauricus, who is trying to arrange a marriage for his niece (her own father is dead),[5] informs us of the criteria important to upper-class families who were making a match.[6]

49   Pliny the Younger, *Letters* 1.14

You have asked me to look for a husband for your niece; and quite rightly have you entrusted this task to me rather than anyone else. For you know how deeply I admired and loved that outstanding man,[7] and with what encouraging words he inspired me in my youth, and also how he praised me in a way that made me seem worthy of his praises. You could not entrust to me a more important or more agreeable task; and I could not undertake a more honorable task than that of choosing a young man worthy of fathering the grandchildren of Arulenus Rusticus.

Such a person would indeed take a long time to find, if Minicius Acilianus were not right at hand, provided by fate, as it were. He loves me with that very friendly familiarity which a young man frequently feels toward another young man (for he is younger than I by only a few years), but yet he respects me as he would an old man. Indeed he is as eager to be instructed and molded by me as I was by you and your brother.

His hometown is Brixia,[8] a city in that same region of Italy that I come from,[9] a region which still retains and preserves much of the modesty, frugality, and even rural simplicity of the good old days.[10]

His father, Minicius Macrinus, is a leading figure in the equestrian order,[11] but

---

[4] On the *patria potestas,* see selection 14.

[5] On guardians, see selection 44.

[6] Among upper-class families marriage arrangements frequently reflected the families' desire for a political or business alliance. Such considerations were of little importance in lower-class marriage arrangements. For an apparently happy lower-class arranged marriage, see selection 266.

[7] *that outstanding man:* the girl's father, Arulenus Rusticus. He was a courageous man who throughout his life had offered resistance to the tyranny of the emperors. He was eventually executed by Emperor Domitian in A.D. 93. His brother (the girl's uncle, Junius Mauricus, to whom Pliny addresses this letter) was also involved in the opposition to the emperors and was sent into exile by Domitian in A.D. 93. For other acquaintances of Pliny who were exiled or executed in A.D. 93, see selection 290, and genealogy chart 3.

[8] *Brixia:* modern Brescia, in northern Italy; see map 3.

[9] *same region:* northern Italy, Transpadane Italy (Latin *Transpadanus* = "beyond the Po River"—*trans* = "beyond," *Padus* = "Po River").

[10] The urbanized Romans loved to talk about their agricultural heritage and about the moral rectitude of farm life and "the good old days." Compare selections 177 and 307.

[11] Members of the equestrian order were wealthy businessmen. Politicians and statesmen

has no desire for any higher social status. Indeed, although he was chosen by the deified Vespasian[12] to hold the rank of praetor,[13] he very steadfastly preferred a dignified life out of the public eye rather than this political service—or shall I say political turmoil—of ours.[14]

His maternal grandmother is Serrana Procula, from the municipality of Patavium.[15] You know the puritanism of that area; Serrana, however, is a model of strictness even to the Patavians. And he has, for an uncle, Publius Acilius, a man of almost unique dignity, good judgment, and integrity. To sum up, there is nothing in his entire family which would not make you happy even in your own.

Acilianus himself possesses an abundance of energy and diligence, combined with the greatest modesty. He has already passed very creditably through the offices of quaestor, tribune, and praetor[16] and has thus already spared you the necessity of campaigning for him.[17] He has the countenance of a gentleman, a very healthy and ruddy complexion, an aristocratic attractiveness in his whole body, and a certain senatorial elegance. These are features which I think should not be overlooked, for this, a bridegroom's good looks, ought to be given to a girl as a reward for her chastity.

I don't know whether I should add that his father has substantial wealth. When I consider the priorities of you, for whom I am seeking an in-law, I suspect that I should leave his wealth unmentioned. When, however, I take into account current moral standards and even state laws, which arbitrate that a scrutiny of a man's financial status must be given top priority,[18] then I suspect that I should not pass over his wealth in silence. And certainly this consideration must be taken into account, when one is arranging a marriage, if we are planning for grandchildren—and for many of them at that.[19]

---

belonged to a higher order—the senatorial—but Minicius preferred to live "out of the public eye" and to remain an equestrian.

[12] Vespasian was emperor from A.D. 69 to 79. After his death he was deified, officially declared to have become a god.

[13] *praetor:* In the republican period (more than 100 years before the reign of Vespasian) the praetor had been an elected city magistrate whose main function was to oversee the administration of justice. In the imperial period men were sometimes appointed by the emperor (rather than publicly elected) to hold the honorary rank of praetor. Such distinction gave one the right to a seat in the Senate.

[14] Once appointed to the rank of praetor, Minicius Macrinus had the right to attend meetings of the Senate and to offer his "political services." In the republican period the Senate had controlled both the domestic and foreign affairs of Rome (see selection 238). Its members were therefore extremely powerful figures, and the Senate was the arena for heated debates and, frequently, political turmoil. By Pliny's time, 100 years into the imperial period, the Senate had lost much of its power, since the emperor now controlled state affairs, but Pliny still takes his position as a senator quite seriously and likes to stress both the political service and the turmoil of the Senate.

[15] *Patavium:* modern Padua, in northern Italy.

[16] *quaestor, tribune, and praetor:* elected magistrates (see Chapter X).

[17] Relatives were expected to assist in political campaigns. Acilianus, however, has already campaigned successfully and will thus expect no political favors from his in-laws. On political campaigns, see selection 236.

[18] A certain property qualification, fixed by law, was necessary for admission to both the equestrian and the senatorial orders. See the introduction to Chapter I.

[19] The production of legal heirs was the main reason for marriage. For a most unromantic view of marriage, see selection 161: "When one of his brothers died, he [Crassus] married his widow and had his children by her."

Perhaps you think that I have been overwhelmed by my affection for Acilianus and that I have therefore exaggerated his merits beyond what the case will bear. But I promise you, on my honor, that you will find everything far better than what I am telling you now. Certainly I love the young man very warmly, as indeed he deserves; but it is characteristic of a lover not to overload with praise the one he loves.

WEDDINGS

A Wedding Song

The celebration of a Roman wedding included much laughter and singing. Songs were sung, sometimes by a trained chorus, sometimes by the wedding guests, during the banquet and then during the procession through the streets when the bride was escorted from her old home to her new one. Catullus, one of Rome's finest poets, who lived in the first century B.C., wrote several poems which imitate the style of these wedding songs. The poem translated here celebrates the wedding of Manlius Torquatus and Junia Aurunculeia.

50   Catullus, *Poems* 61.1–5, 11–20, 56–75, 96–100, 106–110, 116–130,
                           151–160, 171–175, 181–185, 211–225, 230–235

Invocation to Hymen Hymenaeus, the god of weddings: the god is praised, invited to attend the wedding, and asked to bless the marriage of the newlyweds.

O you who dwell on Mount Helicon,[20]
who are the son of Urania,[21]
who give to a husband a tender virgin,
O Hymen Hymenaeus,
O Hymen Hymenaeus, . . .

inspired by this joyful day
sing wedding songs
with your shrill voice,
and shake the ground with your dancing,
and in your hand brandish the pine torch.[22]

For—as Venus
once approached Paris[23]

[20] *Mount Helicon:* mountain in Boeotia, Greece, sacred to Apollo and the Muses.

[21] *Urania:* the Muse of astronomy. She was the mother of Hymen; his father was Apollo.

[22] Torches made of pitch-pine were lit and brandished at weddings and thus became a familiar symbol of the wedding itself.

[23] Paris, prince of Troy, was required by the gods to award a golden apple to the most beautiful of the goddesses. Venus, goddess of love, promised him the most beautiful of mortal women if he would award her the apple. For another description of this incident, see selection 336. Paris gave her the apple, and she in return made Helen, wife of a Greek king, fall in love

now Junia approaches
Manlius; a good maiden
will marry with good omens.[24] . . .

It is you, Hymen, who transfer
the blossoming girl from her mother's lap[25]
into the hands of a lusty young man,
O Hymen Hymenaeus,
O Hymen Hymenaeus.

Without your blessing, Hymen,[26]
love cannot have the advantages
which a good reputation establishes;
with your blessing, peerless god,
it can.

Without your blessing, no home
can produce legitimate heirs,[27] no parent
can count on progeny;
with your blessing, peerless god,
it can.

Without your rites,
no land could protect
its boundaries;[28]
with your rites, peerless god,
it could. . . .

The timid bride is encouraged to come forward so that the procession to her new home may begin.

Come forward, new bride.
Don't be afraid. Hear our words.
See! Our torches
burn like golden hairs.
Come forward, new bride. . . .

---

with Paris and run away with him to Troy. Hence arose the Trojan War. Here the bride's beauty is compared to that of Venus (and the groom's charm to that of Paris).

[24] *omens:* The wedding ceremony began with a taking of auspices (an examination of prophetic signs) to determine if the omens were good, i.e., if the gods were favorably disposed. See selection 368.

[25] One wedding custom, perhaps a survival of primitive "bride-stealing," involved the ritualistic seizing of the bride from her mother's arms by the groom's party (although surely many brides in their early teens may have clung to their mothers because of real fear rather than custom).

[26] *Without your blessing, Hymen:* i.e., without a marriage ceremony. Hymen presides over and blesses marriage ceremonies. A marriage ceremony guarantees the good intentions and good reputation of the bride and groom.

[27] Children born out of wedlock could not be legitimate heirs.

[28] The gods are favorably disposed to and will protect the home of a lawfully married couple.

As the clinging grapevine
embraces the nearby tree,
so will you fold your new husband
in your embrace. But the day is waning.
Come forward, new bride. . . .

What joys await your new lord,
what pleasures
during the dark night,
or even at midday. But the day is waning.
Come forward, new bride.

The bride appears, ready for the procession.

Raise up your torches, boys!
I see her saffron veil.[29]
Come on, sing in harmony:
"O Hymen Hymenaeus,
O Hymen Hymenaeus."

The procession begins, and the wedding party proceeds to the bride's new home.

Shout out the dirty Fescennine jokes.[30]
And you, slave-boy, once your master's favorite
in bed, though you hear
you have lost his love,
give nuts[31] to the young boys.

And you, bride, don't deny to your husband
the things that he wants
lest he seek them elsewhere.
O Hymen Hymenaeus,
O Hymen Hymenaeus.

The wedding procession arrives at the bride's new home.

But look, your husband's home!
How large and expensive it seems!

[29] The bride's traditional wedding dress included a saffron (orange-yellow) veil.

[30] *Fescennine jokes:* obscenities in verse form shouted at the bride and groom. The custom represents a common primitive superstition. During moments of great good fortune and happiness a person may be subject to jealous attacks by the "evil eye"; his friends try to deceive and cheat the power of the evil eye by abusing the person with obscenities and making him appear less fortunate and happy than he really is. During military triumphal processions the troops also shouted abusive and obscene verses at the victorious general. Fescennine jokes are apotropaic, meant to turn away evil spirits (Greek *apo* = "away," *tropos* = "turn").

[31] *nuts:* During the procession nuts were scattered among the crowd by boys taking part in the procession. Perhaps the casting aside of nuts symbolizes the casting aside of childish toys by the bride and groom. Or perhaps the nuts (and the Fescennine jokes) have connotations of fertility.

May it serve you well!
O Hymen Hymenaeus,
O Hymen Hymenaeus. . . .

And look within—your husband
is lying on a purple couch,[32]
totally intent on you.
O Hymen Hymenaeus,
O Hymen Hymenaeus. . . .

Young boy, release the little girl's[33]
small, smooth arm. Let her
now approach her husband's bed.
O Hymen Hymenaeus,
O Hymen Hymenaeus. . . .

Bride and groom, play as you wish,
and soon have children of your own.
For so ancient a family name should not
be without heirs; it should always
produce new generations.[34]

I hope that a little Torquatus,[35]
sitting on his mother's lap,
will stretch out his tender hands
towards his father and laugh
sweetly with smiling lips.

May he be similar to his father Manlius,
and may he be easily recognized
even by strangers,
and may he confirm, by his facial features,[36]
his mother's fidelity. . . .

Close the doors, bridesmaids,
We've joked long enough.
Live well, newlyweds,
and spend your youth
in constant lovemaking.

---

[32] The groom arrives before the bride so that he may formally welcome her to share his home. The bride was accompanied in the procession to her new home by young boys (see next stanza: "Young boy").

[33] We are reminded that the bride is in fact a girl. She who was just now taken from her mother's lap (stanza 4) will soon hold a baby of her own on her lap (stanza 18).

[34] On the importance of children in a marriage, see selection 24.

[35] *little Torquatus:* a son. The groom's name is Manlius Torquatus.

[36] *facial features:* i.e., identical to those of his father. If a child looks like the bride's husband, her fidelity to her husband is established.

A Marriage Contract

The following marriage contract was drawn up in Egypt in 13 B.C. Since Egypt did not become a Roman province until 30 B.C., it is unlikely that the form of this contract was influenced by Roman procedure. Certain attitudes toward marriage, however, were shared by both the Roman and Egyptian cultures. Marriage was, for example, a practical rather than a romantic matter; the couple mentioned in this contract "have come together for the purpose of sharing their lives with one another." The basic function of a marriage was to provide a stable environment for the production and rearing of family heirs. The bride's family, moreover, was expected to provide a dowry; the dowry would help the groom's family defray the living expenses ("all necessities and clothing") of the new wife.

51   *BGU* 1052 (*Select Papyri* 3)

To Protarchus,[37] from Thermion daughter of Apion, accompanied by her guardian Apollonius son of Chaereas, and from Apollonius son of Ptolemaeus:—

Thermion and Apollonius son of Ptolemaeus agree that they have come together for the purpose of sharing their lives with one another. The above-mentioned Apollonius son of Ptolemaeus agrees that he has received from Thermion, handed over from her household as a dowry, a pair of gold earrings . . .[38] From now on he will furnish Thermion, as his wedded wife, with all necessities and clothing according to his means, and he will not mistreat her or cast her out or insult her or bring in another wife; otherwise he must at once return the dowry and in addition half again as much. . . . And Thermion will fulfill her duties toward her husband and her marriage, and will not sleep away from the house or be absent one day without the consent of Apollonius son of Ptolemaeus and will not damage or injure their common home and will not consort with another man; otherwise she, if judged guilty of these actions, will be deprived of her dowry, and in addition the transgressor will be liable to the prescribed fine. Dated the 17th year of Caesar.[39]

WIVES

The Duties of a Wife

From this epitaph, found at Rome, which dates back to the second century B.C., we learn what type of behavior was expected of a wife and matron.

[37] *Protarchus:* government official to whom contracts were submitted for legal approval.

[38] The papyrus is mutilated or illegible at this spot.

[39] *Caesar:* here the emperor Augustus. Caesar was part of the surname of Julius Caesar, the dictator, and of his adopted son, Augustus Caesar, who became the first emperor. Each succeeding emperor assumed the name Caesar, and it thus became a title for the emperor. It is also the origin of the titles *czar* and *kaiser*.

52 *CIL* 1.2.1211 (*ILS* 8403)

Stranger,[40] I have only a few words to say. Stop and read them.—This is the unlovely tomb of a lovely woman. Her parents named her Claudia. She loved her husband with all her heart. She bore two sons; one of these she leaves here on earth, the other she has already placed under the earth.[41] She was charming in speech, yet pleasant and proper in manner. She managed the household well. She spun wool.—I have spoken. Go on your way.

A Perfect Marriage

The passage translated here is taken from a letter written by Pliny to his friend Geminus and reporting the sad news of the death of a friend's wife. The couple had been married thirty-nine years and had lived, according to Pliny, in perfect harmony. Literary accounts such as these not only record the virtues of the specific people being discussed but also indicate the qualities which the Romans thought desirable in a marriage. Since almost all of the literary accounts are written by men, we may be receiving a masculine perception of the ideal marriage.

53 Pliny the Younger, *Letters* 8.5.1 and 2

Our friend Macrinus has suffered a terrible blow: he has lost his wife, a woman of rare virtue, who would have been remarkable even in the good old days.[42] He lived with her for thirty-nine years without a single quarrel or bitter word. With what respect she treated her husband! And thus, of course, she herself earned the greatest respect. She brought together and combined in her own character many admirable qualities taken from the various stages of life. Indeed Macrinus has this one great consolation: he was able to keep such a treasure for so long.

Pliny's Wife

When Pliny was about forty years old, he married a young girl named Calpurnia.[43] (He had been married twice before.) In this letter to Calpurnia's aunt, who raised Calpurnia after her mother died,[44] Pliny describes his happiness with his young wife.[45] He is delighted by the fact that she has devoted herself completely to him, his work, and his writings.[46]

[40] *Stranger:* see note 2 of this chapter.

[41] On infant mortality, see the introduction to selection 23.

[42] On "the good old days," see note 10 of this chapter.

[43] On the age of marriage partners, see selection 48.

[44] On orphans, see selection 45.

[45] We have already read another letter about Calpurnia; see selection 24, where Pliny reports her miscarriage.

[46] See the previous passage, where Pliny praises Macrinus's wife for treating her husband with respect.

54   Pliny the Younger, *Letters* 4.19.2–4

My wife is very sensible and very thrifty.[47] And she loves me, surely an indication of
her virtue. She has even, because of her affection for me, taken an interest in literature.
She has copies of my books, she reads them over and over again, and even learns them
by heart. What anxiety she feels when I am going to plead a case in court, what great
relief when I have finished! She even stations slaves to report to her on the approval
and the applause I receive, and on what verdict I obtain in the case. And whenever I
give a recitation,[48] she sits nearby, concealed behind a curtain, and listens very eagerly
to the praise I win. She even sets my poems to music and sings them, to the accompaniment of a lyre. No musician has taught her, but love itself, the best of instructors.

Calpurnia

The following passage is taken from a letter which Pliny wrote to Calpurnia when
she was in the country recovering from an illness.

55   Pliny the Younger, *Letters* 7.5

It is incredible how much I miss you, because I love you and then because we are not
used to being separated. And so I lie awake most of the night haunted by your image;
and during the day, during those hours I used to spend with you, my feet lead me,
they really do, to your room; and then I turn and leave, sick at heart and sad, like a
lover locked out on a deserted doorstep. The only time I escape these torments is when
I am in the Forum, wearing myself out pleading cases for my friends. Judge for yourself what my life is like when I find relaxation in work and relief in problems and
anxieties.

Love for a Wife

This epitaph, found in Roman France, honors the memory of a very young wife.
She and her husband, a plasterer, were of a much lower social class than people
like Pliny, but obviously valued just as much a happy and harmonious marriage.
Note that the wife was only thirteen years old when she was married.

---

[47] *thrifty:* i.e., she managed the household well, a traditional virtue of a Roman matron.
Pliny was a wealthy man, and his wife did not, therefore, need to skimp. He is praising her
here for not being a spendthrift.

[48] *recitation:* a type of entertainment popular among upper-class Romans of the early imperial period. A man would invite his friends to his home, or perhaps to a rented hall, and
entertain them with readings of his own literary works; see selection 320, where Pliny describes
a recitation at his house.

56 *CIL* 13.1983 (*ILS* 8158)

To the eternal memory of Blandinia Martiola, a most faultless girl, who lived eighteen years, nine months, five days. Pompeius Catussa, a Sequanian[49] citizen, a plasterer, dedicates to his wife, who was incomparable and very kind to him, who lived with him five years, six months, eighteen days without any shadow of a fault, this memorial which he had erected in his lifetime for himself and his wife and which he consecrated while it was still under construction. You who read this, go bathe in the baths of Apollo,[50] as I used to do with my wife. I wish I still could.

A Good Wife

This inscription is a companion to one translated earlier. Lucius Aurelius Hermia was the husband of Aurelia Philematium.[51] The behavior for which this man praises his wife is in many respects similar to the behavior promised in modern marriage vows.

57 *CIL* 1.2.1221 (*ILS* 7472)

Lucius Aurelius Hermia, freedman of Lucius, a butcher on the Viminal.[52]

She who preceded me in death was my one and only wife, chaste in body, with a loving spirit, she lived faithful to her faithful husband, always optimistic, even in bitter times, she never shirked her duties.

HUSBANDS

Battered Wives

Not all marriages, unfortunately, were happy and harmonious. The following passage, although written by an author of the first century A.D., concerns an incident from the earliest period of Roman history. The story illustrates the harshness of the early laws which the Romans themselves attributed to Romulus, their legendary first king;[53] a husband might inflict a death penalty on his wife if her family agreed with him that her behavior warranted such punishment. And overindulgence in wine was apparently considered a capital offense in a wife. Although it is un-

---

[49] *Sequanian:* living near the Seine River. Latin *Sequana* = Seine River.

[50] *baths of Apollo:* a public bath. On public baths, see the introduction to the section on baths in Chapter XIV.

[51] See selection 48.

[52] *Viminal:* one of the seven hills of Rome.

[53] Compare the *patria potestas,* the father's power of life and death over his children. The Romans believed that the powers of the husband and the father had been defined by Romulus, but we cannot ascertain the precise origin of these practices.

likely that many men killed their wives, with the consent of the wife's family, wife-beating was not a crime; nor was it limited to the early years of Roman history. Battered wives had no legal recourse and could only hope for the intervention of their families.

58   Valerius Maximus, *Memorable Deeds and Words* 6.3.9

Egnatius Mecenius beat his wife to death with a club because she had drunk some wine. And not only did no one bring him to court because of this deed, but no one even reproached him, for all the best men thought that she had deserved the punishment for her example of intemperance. For assuredly any woman who desires to drink wine immoderately closes the door to all virtues and opens it to all vices.

Love for a Husband

The following inscription was found at Rome.

59   *CIL* 6.18817 (*ILS* 8006)

Furia Spes, freedwoman of Sempronius Firmus, provided this memorial[54] for her dearly beloved husband. When we were still boy and girl, we were bound by mutual love as soon as we met. I lived with him for too brief a time. We were separated by a cruel hand when we should have continued to live in happiness. I therefore beg, most sacred Manes,[55] that you look after the loved one I have entrusted to you and that you be well disposed and very kind to him during the hours of night, so that I may see him,[56] and so that he, too, may wish to persuade fate to allow me to come to him, softly and soon.

IN-LAWS

In-Law Interference

Some things never change. In-laws, for example, were as eager in ancient Rome as they are today to give "helpful advice" about marriages. Cicero's brother Quintus[57] was married to Pomponia, the sister of Cicero's good friend Atticus. You will not be surprised to learn, when you have read this letter (written in 51 B.C.), that Quintus and Pomponia were eventually divorced.

---

[54] *this memorial:* i.e., funerary inscription.
[55] *Manes* (two syllables, Ma-nes): protecting spirits of the dead.
[56] *see him:* in a dream?
[57] For more on Quintus Tullius Cicero, see the introductions to selections 205, 236, and 278.

60 Cicero, *Letters to Atticus* 5.1.3–4

With regard to the comment scribbled sideways at the end of your last letter, the comment about your sister, these are the facts of the case. When I arrived at Arpinum[58] and my brother met me, we first had a long talk about you. Then I drew the conversation to those remarks which you and I had made about your sister when we were at my villa in Tusculum.[59] I have never seen anything as gentle or kind as my brother's conduct then toward your sister; if they had been quarreling about money and expenditures, it was not apparent. The day passed quietly.

The next day we left Arpinum. A festival required Quintus's presence in Arcae. I went to Aquinum,[60] but we met for lunch at Arcae (Quintus has a villa there, as you know). When we arrived, Quintus said very politely, "Pomponia, why don't you invite the women and I'll look after the men." Nothing, as far as I'm concerned, could have been gentler than his words and attitude and expression. But she, within everyone's hearing, said, "Oh, but I'm just a stranger here." I think she said that because Statius, and not she, had been sent ahead to make the luncheon arrangements.

Then Quintus said to me, "See! That's what I put up with every day."

You will probably say, "So, what's wrong with that?" A great deal! She really annoyed me. She answered with such rudeness and bitterness. I hid my anger. We all lay down to lunch[61] except her! Quintus sent some food to her room. She sent it back.

In short, I thought that my brother could not have been more patient, or your sister more ill-tempered. And I won't even mention many other things which Quintus seemed to overlook but which turned my stomach.

I left for Aquinum. Quintus stayed at Arcae and met me the next morning and told me that she had refused to sleep with him and that when she left the villa she was as bad-tempered as when I saw her. So much for that! You have my permission to tell her that in my opinion she showed a lack of good manners that day.

DIVORCE

A Divorce Agreement

By the late republican and early imperial periods, divorce was common among the upper-class families of Rome. Since many upper-class marriages were political and/or financial arrangements, divorces, too, often took place for political and financial reasons.[62] We have very little information about the prevalence of divorce among the lower class, for whom political advancement was not a concern, but it is

[58] *Arpinum:* the town southeast of Rome where Cicero was born.

[59] *Tusculum:* town about fifteen miles southeast of Rome. Cicero referred to his villa at Tusculum in selection 16.

[60] *Arcae, Aquinum:* small towns near Arpinum.

[61] The Romans of Cicero's time often reclined on couches to eat their meals.

[62] See the history of Augustus's family in selection 67; on Pompey's marriages, see note 87 of Chapter X.

suspected that the divorce rate of the lower class was considerably lower than that of the upper class. Another reason for divorce might be infertility.[63] The passage below is a divorce agreement made in Egypt in 13 B.C., the same year as the marriage contract above and only seventeen years into the Roman period of Egypt. Although the form of the agreement was not influenced by Roman procedure, the bride's family has demanded the return of the dowry, as would a Roman family of this same period.

61   *BGU* 1103 (*Select Papyri* 6)

To Protarchus,[64] from Zois daughter of Heraclides, accompanied by her brother and guardian Irenaeus son of Heraclides, and from Antipater son of Zeno: —
    Zois and Antipater agree that they have separated from one another and severed their arrangement to live together. . . . And Zois agrees that Antipater has returned to her, handed over from his household, the items he received as her dowry, namely clothing valued at 120 silver drachmas[65] and a pair of gold earrings.[66] Both parties agree that henceforth the marriage contract will be null and void . . . and from this day it will be lawful for Zois to marry another man and for Antipater to marry another woman, with neither party being liable to prosecution.

ADULTERY

Because marriages were family arrangements rather than love matches, the Romans had always allowed married men occasional sex with slaves or lower-class women. By the late republican and early imperial periods, however, we hear of men having affairs with married upper-class matrons. Perhaps young women, married to men much older than themselves, looked to other men for excitement and novelty. Once again, we have scant information about the lower class, but we can perhaps assume that women living in cramped apartments and raising their children without the help of nurses had little time or opportunity for adulterous affairs.

Where to Meet

In his poem *The Art of Love,* Ovid advises men on where to meet women and how to begin an affair. Since most women were married in their early teens, Ovid is in fact recommending adulterous affairs. The emperor Augustus was angered by

---

[63] Turia suggested divorce to her husband when she did not bear him children; see selection 288.
    [64] *Protarchus:* see footnote 37 of this chapter.
    [65] *drachma:* a Greek coin, approximately the value of a Roman denarius; for denarius, see Appendix II.
    [66] In the case of divorce, the husband was required to return his wife's dowry to her family.

Ovid's flouting of traditional morality, and in A.D. 8 he banished Ovid (who was now fifty years old) to a small town, Tomis, in an uncivilized area of the Black Sea coast. In this section of *The Art of Love,* Ovid recommends the racetrack as a great place to flirt.

62   Ovid, *The Art of Love* 1.135–163

Don't neglect the horse races if you're looking for a place to meet your girlfriend. A circus[67] crowded with people offers many advantages. You don't have to use a secret sign language here or be content with a slight nod to acknowledge one another's presence.[68] Sit right next to your girlfriend—no one will stop you—and squeeze up beside her as closely as possible. It's really easy to do. The narrowness of each seating space forces you to squeeze together; in fact the rules for seating compel you to touch her!

Conversation should begin with no problem; just start out with the same comments that everyone else is making. Be sure to ask with great interest which horses are running and then immediately cheer for the same one, whichever it is, that she cheers for.

Perhaps a speck of dust will settle on your girlfriend's breast (it often happens); be sure to brush it off with your hand. Even if there is no speck of dust, pretend—and keep brushing off nothing! Take advantage of every opportunity. If her skirt is trailing too far along the ground, pick up the edge of it and carefully lift the soiled part off the dust. At once you'll receive a reward for your careful concern: you'll be able to look at her legs, and she won't mind.

In addition, turn to whoever is sitting behind her and ask him not to jab her in the back with his knees. These little touches win over simple female hearts. Many men have found it useful to bring along a cushion which they can offer. It's also helpful to fan her with the racing program and to give her a stool for her dainty feet. Yes, the circus provides many opportunities for initiating a love affair.

Deceiving One's Husband

More advice from Ovid on how to conduct an adulterous affair. This passage also supplies interesting information about behavior at (some) Roman dinner parties.[69]

63   Ovid, *Love Affairs* 1.4.1–6, 9–11, 15–28, 35–54, 63–70

So your husband will be attending the same banquet as us! I hope it will be his last supper! Am I supposed to act like a mere guest toward the woman I love? Shall I only look on, while someone else has the pleasure of being caressed by you, while you snuggle up to him and warm his breast, while he casually puts his arm around you? . . . I'm not a wild animal, but I can scarcely keep my hands off you. Well then, pay attention and learn what you must do. . . . When your husband takes his place on the din-

---

[67] *circus:* the Roman word for "racetrack." Circus Maximus means the "largest race track" (*maximus* = "largest").

[68] On the sign language of lovers, see the next passage (selection 63).

[69] See Augustus's behavior (selection 67).

ing couch,[70] put on an appearance of great innocence and go, as the faithful wife, to lie down beside him; but, as you pass, touch my foot without anyone's noticing. Watch me carefully, look for my nods and facial expressions. Figure out those secret unspoken messages and send me some of your own. Without speaking a word, I will tell you things by raising my eyebrows; you will read notes marked out by my fingers which are wet with wine. When memories of our lovemaking fill your mind, put your delicate finger on your rosy cheek. If you have some objection to the way I am behaving, rest your tender hand on your earlobe. When, dearest, I say or do something which pleases you, play with your ring and keep turning it with your fingers. When you are praying that some great disaster befall your husband (he deserves it), touch the table with your hand. . . .

Don't let your husband lean against you. And don't rest your pretty head on his ugly chest. Don't let him put his fingers on your soft breasts, and try not to let him kiss you. If you kiss him, I swear I will no longer be able to conceal my love for you. I'll grab you and shout, "Those kisses should be mine!"

And yet these are only the things I will be able to see. I will be much more worried and fearful about the things which may go on under the covers,[71] things I can't see. Don't press your thigh against his, don't rest your leg on his, don't put your dainty little foot next to his big clumsy foot. I am tormented by my fear; I know these things happen because I've done them all myself—many times! I am tortured by the fear of my own behavior. My girlfriend and I often pulled a cloak over us and proceeded to enjoy the full delights of a good screw. I know you won't do this with him, but, just so that I won't worry, take off your cloak before dinner and put it away. Encourage your husband (but not with kisses) to drink and, while he is drinking, keep pouring wine in his cup if you can. Once he is sprawled out in a drunken stupor, circumstance will suggest to us a course of action. . . .

Yet after the banquet, when you have returned home, your husband will take from you kisses—and more than kisses. What you give to me stealthily, you are forced by the laws of marriage to give to him. But at least do so with reluctance and act like a woman under duress. You can manage that. Don't whisper any "sweet nothings"; let your lovemaking be churlish and unwilling. I hope that he will not enjoy it, or at least that you certainly will not. But *whatever* happens when you get home, tomorrow tell me in a sincere tone of voice that *nothing* happened.

Poems to a Mistress

The poet Catullus had a very passionate affair with a woman whom he calls in his poems "Lesbia" but who in real life was named Clodia.[72] She was a member of an

---

[70] *dining couch:* see note 61 of this chapter.

[71] *covers:* flowing cloaks or capes which the guests would wear to the party (as we would wear an overcoat). Since guests reclined on couches during dinner, they might spread their cloaks over them like sheets and thus conceal their sexual activities.

[72] Clodia was the sister of Clodius who, as tribune in 58 B.C., promoted legislation for the free distribution of grain to Roman citizens; see the introduction to selection 153. *Lesbia:* literally "woman of Lesbos." Lesbos was a Greek island off the coast of Asia Minor which was the home of Sappho, a Greek female lyric poet of the seventh century B.C. The word *Lesbia* would summon up in a Roman audience evocations of the passion, sensuality, and artistry of Sappho. Catullus's poem 51, translated here, is itself a translation from Greek to Latin of one of Sappho's poems.

old and distinguished upper-class family. When their affair began she was married to Quintus Metellus Celer (who died in 59 B.C.). In many of his poems Catullus describes his emotions during this relationship with Clodia: ecstasy, happiness, disillusionment, and finally despair when the affair ended.

64   Catullus, *Poems* 5, 51

Poem 5

Let us live, my Lesbia, and let us love,
and let us value all the criticisms
of prudish old men at one penny.
The sun can rise and set,
but we, once our brief life has run its course,
must sleep through an eternal night.
So—give me a thousand kisses, and then a hundred,
and then another thousand and another hundred.

Poem 51

He seems to me to be equal to a god,
to surpass the gods, if I may say so,
who sits opposite you and, again and again,
    sees you and hears you

laughing sweetly. This thought snatches away
all my senses; for, as soon as
I look at you, Lesbia, nothing remains
    of my senses, nothing.

My tongue becomes numb, a slender flame
spreads through my limbs, my ears ring
with a sound of their own, and both my eyes
    are veiled by darkness.

Another Perspective

Clodia (the "Lesbia" of Catullus's poems) did not confine her attentions to Catullus. Another of her lovers was Marcus Caelius Rufus, a young political friend of Cicero.[73] When their affair ended, Clodia was instrumental in bringing Caelius to court on a charge of attempted murder. The prosecution attempted to show that Caelius had in the past often acted immorally and unscrupulously and that the attempted murder was quite in keeping with his character. Cicero, however, who undertook Caelius's defense (this passage is taken from his speech for the defense), tried to persuade the jury that Caelius was an honest, naive young man who had fallen under the influence of an evil woman—Clodia herself—whom Cicero implies acted not like a proper upper-class Roman matron but like a common prostitute.

[73] *Marcus Caelius Rufus:* for more about this man, see selection 343.

65   Cicero, *Speech in Defense of Caelius,* 20:48–49

If anyone here thinks that young men should be forbidden association even with prostitutes, he is certainly very stern; but he is also in disagreement not only with the permissiveness of this century, but even with the custom and indulgences of our ancestors. When was such a thing not done, when was it censured, when not allowed, when finally was that which is now permitted not permitted? I will now clarify my point, without, of course, mentioning any woman by name; I will leave this open.

If a woman without a husband[74] opens her home to every man's lust and publicly establishes herself in the lifestyle of a prostitute and makes it a practice to attend dinner parties with strange men, if she does this in the city, on her estate, and among the crowds of people at Baiae;[75] if in fact she behaves in such a way that not only her manner,[76] but her clothes and her associates, not only the lust in her eyes and the lewdness of her speech, but also her hugging and kissing on the beach, during boat cruises and at dinner parties proclaim her to be not only a prostitute, but even a shameless and brazen prostitute—then if some young man might by chance find himself in her company, would you consider him her corruptor or her customer, would you think that he wanted to defile her chastity or satisfy her lust?

Laws to Control Adultery

The emperor Augustus expressed great concern over various social problems in Rome. Adultery was widespread and divorce common; many upper-class men chose not to marry; married couples often remained childless. Augustus was disturbed by the decreasing population of native Italians, particularly among the upper class; he also claimed that he was dismayed by the relaxed moral standards of his time and that he wanted to return Rome to the standards of the "good old days." He therefore passed laws (18 B.C., the Julian Laws regulating adultery and marriage; A.D. 9, the Papia-Poppaean Law regulating marriage) meant to encourage marriage and to discourage adultery. Here are some passages from these laws.[77]

66   *ADA* pp. 113–116, 123, 126

"Henceforth no one shall commit adultery or rape knowingly or with malice aforethought." The words of this law apply both to him who abets and him who commits the crime.

The Julian Law to control adultery punishes not only those who violate the marriages of others. Under the same law, the crime of debauchery is punished, when anyone seduces and violates, even without force, either a virgin or a respectable widow.

---

[74] Caelius's trial took place in 56 B.C. Clodia's husband, Quintus Metellus Celer, had died in 59 B.C.

[75] *Baiae:* a fashionable seaside resort near Naples.

[76] Compare Claudia (selection 52) who was "proper in manner."

[77] For other passages from these laws, see selections 33, 34, and 35.

By the second section of the law, a father is permitted, if he catches his daughter's seducer, in his own home or in his son-in-law's home, . . . to kill the adulterer with impunity, even as he may immediately kill his daughter.

A husband is permitted to kill his wife's seducer. . . . He is permitted to kill a pimp, actor, gladiator, criminal, freedman, or slave who is caught in the act of adultery with his wife in his own home, but not in the home of his father-in-law. . . . And he must divorce his wife without delay.

A husband who does not divorce his wife when she has been caught in adultery, and who allows the adulterer to go unpunished, is himself punished as a pimp.

A husband who makes any profit from the adultery of his wife is flogged.

Women convicted of adultery are punished by confiscation of half of their dowry, and a third of their property, and by exile to an island. The male adulterers are punished by a similar exile to an island (provided they are sent to different islands) and by confiscation of half their property.[78]

Augustus's Own Behavior

Although Augustus, when emperor, expressed dismay over the widespread adultery, divorce, celibacy, and childlessness, he had not always been so concerned with moral standards, as we learn from this passage of Suetonius's biography of Augustus. Before he became emperor and before he received the title "Augustus,"[79] he had been married three times. He had only one child, a daughter, Julia. And even when emperor, he did not hesitate to force his kin into marriages and divorces which they did not want.

67   Suetonius, *The Lives of the Caesars: Augustus* 62, 63, 69

Octavian had, in his youth, been betrothed to the daughter of Publius Servilius Isauricus, but after he and Mark Antony had settled their initial disagreement and become reconciled,[80] their soldiers asked them to become further allied by forming some tie

---

[78] Exile and confiscation of property were penalties assigned to the upper class; see selections 5 and 6.

[79] "Augustus" was a title bestowed by the Senate in 27 B.C. on a man whose name was first Gaius Octavius and then, after his adoption by his granduncle (Julius Caesar), Gaius Julius Caesar Octavianus. On the use of the name Caesar as a title, see footnote 39 of this chapter. The name Octavianus is translated into English as Octavian.

[80] Immediately after the assassination of Julius Caesar in 44 B.C., Octavian, who was only eighteen years old, had led his troops into battle against Mark Antony's troops ("their initial disagreement") in a struggle for power. Within a few months, however, they both realized it was more politically expedient to be "friends" and allies rather than enemies. They, and another man named Lepidus, formed an alliance which was, however, always shaky. After numerous quarrels and reconciliations, Octavian crushed Mark Anthony and Cleopatra at the battle of Actium in 31 B.C.

Genealogy Chart 1.
The Julio-Claudians[a]

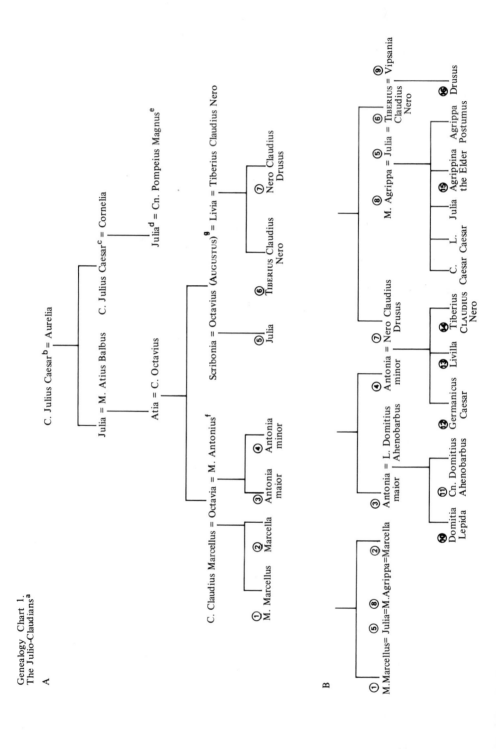

56

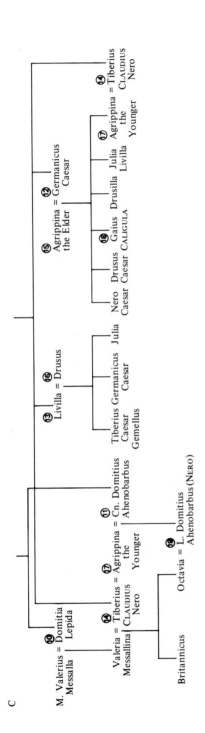

C

a. *The Julio-Claudians*: the family of emperors who were members of the Julian family (*gens Julia*; cf. the name "Julius Caesar") and of the Claudian family (*gens Claudia*; cf. the name "Claudius Nero"). *Note*: not every family member has been recorded in these charts.

b. C. = an abbreviation for the Roman *praenomen* Gaius. Cf. M. = Marcus. Cn. = Gnaeus, L. = Lucius

c. Member of the First Triumvirate (see note 104 of Ch. VII); dictator: assassinated on the Ides of March, 44 B.C.

d. Died in childbirth in 54 B.C. (see note 87 of Ch. X). Note that her name, Julia, is the feminine form of her father's *nomen*, Julius. Cf. Octavius, Octavia; Antonius, Antonia; Marcellus, Marcella.

e. Member of the First Triumvirate.

f. Member of the Second Triumvirate (see note 80 of Ch. III).

g. *Octavius*: after his adoption by his great-uncle, C. Julius Caesar, his name became C. Julius Caesar Octavianus (Octavian); see note 79 of Ch. III. The title "Augustus" was bestowed on him by the Senate in 27 B.C.

①,②, etc.: these numbers identify people in the charts and allow for cross-referencing.

⑤ *Julia*: banished from Rome in 2 B.C. by her father, Augustus (see note 83 of Ch. III). Married first to ① Marcellus, then to ⑧Agrippa, then to ⑥Tiberius.

⑧ *M. (Vipsanius) Agrippa*: 63–12 B.C.: a successful military commander and a good friend of the emperor Augustus. Married first to Pomponia Attica, then to ②Marcella, and then to ⑤Julia.

⑥ *Tiberius*: emperor A.D. 14–37. Married first to ⑨Vipsania, then to ⑤Julia.

⑨ *Vipsania*: daughter of ⑧M. (Vipsanius) Agrippa by his first wife.

⑭ *Claudius*: emperor A.D. 41–54. Married to Valeria Messallina, the daughter of his cousin, then to ⑰Agrippina the Younger, his niece.

⑱ *Caligula*: emperor A.D. 37–41.

⑲ *Nero*: emperor A.D. 54–68.

of kinship. He therefore married Claudia, Antony's stepdaughter and Fulvia's[81] daughter by Publius Clodius, a girl barely of marriageable age. However, when hostility arose between him and Fulvia, now his mother-in-law, he divorced Claudia, still chaste and a virgin. Soon afterward he married Scribonia, who had been married twice before, both times to men of consular rank; she had children from one of these previous marriages. He divorced her also because, as he himself wrote, "I was sick of her perverse nature." He immediately stole Livia Drusilla away from her husband, although she was pregnant at the time, and married her and loved her and was from then on satisfied with her alone.

By Livia he had no children, although he deeply desired them. One child was conceived but born prematurely. By Scribonia he had a daughter, Julia. He first married Julia off to Marcellus, son of his sister Octavia, when he was still a boy. Then, after Marcellus died, he married Julia to Marcus Agrippa, but he had to obtain permission from his sister to cause a divorce in her family; for at that time Agrippa was married to Marcella (daughter of Octavia who was Augustus's sister) and the couple had children. When Agrippa also died, Augustus spent a long time considering many possibilities for marriage alliances. Finally he chose Tiberius, his stepson,[82] and he forced him to divorce his wife, who was pregnant at the time and by whom he already had children, and to marry Julia.[83] . . .

Not even his friends deny that Augustus committed adulteries, although they excuse them, it is true, as committed not because of lust, but because of shrewd planning: he could more easily discover his opponents' schemes through their women. Mark Antony protested not only that he had married Livia so hastily but also that he had, at a dinner party, taken the wife of an ex-consul from her husband's dining room, right before his eyes, and led her into a bedroom; he brought her back to the dinner party with her ears glowing and her hair disheveled.

---

[81] *Fulvia:* the wife of Mark Antony in 43 B.C. She had been married twice before. Antony later married Octavia (sister of Octavian), then divorced her (she had been married once before) and went to live with Cleopatra.

[82] *Tiberius:* the son of Livia by her first husband, Tiberius Claudius Nero. Tiberius became Augustus's heir and succeeded him as emperor.

[83] The marriage of Tiberius and Julia was bitterly unhappy. Julia, who was obviously a pawn in her father's political games, was later accused by him of immorality and in 2 B.C. banished to a tiny island where she died. Julia's mother, Scribonia, whom Augustus had divorced because he "was sick of her perverse nature," chose to live with her daughter in exile; they had probably been separated since the divorce.

IV

Housing and City Life

SINGLE-FAMILY HOUSES IN THE CITY

Designs for City Houses

A family's housing depended very much on its financial situation, as is, of course, still true today. In a large city such as Rome the price of a single-family house[1] was beyond the means of most people, and such houses were therefore owned by the wealthy (who might own several). In smaller cities and towns, houses were undoubtedly cheaper than in Rome.[2] Excavations at Pompeii and Herculaneum[3] have uncovered many houses and have given us an excellent idea of Roman floor plans. All houses had in common certain rooms, such as the atrium, as every modern house has a living room, a kitchen, bedrooms, and so on.

Archeological excavations thus provide one source of information about Roman housing. Another source is an ancient "textbook for architects," from which the following passage is taken. The author, Vitruvius, reports that house designs should vary according to the owner's professional needs. A politician, for example, needed a large reception area, a lawyer needed office space, and a salesman needed areas to store and display his wares. A man's profession might therefore be ascertainable from the design of his house.

68   Vitruvius, *On Architecture* 6.3.3–8, 6.4.1–2, 6.5.1–2

The atrium. The length and breadth of the atrium[4] is determined according to three plans:

---

[1] *house:* Latin *domus* (cf. "domicile," "domestic"). The term *single-family* is somewhat misleading; a domus would provide living accommodation for a married couple, their children, perhaps some relatives, and all their slaves. Indeed the Latin term *familia* denotes the people living under one roof, both owners and slaves.

[2] See selection 72.

[3] *Pompeii and Herculaneum:* two towns buried by the volcanic eruption of Mount Vesuvius in A.D. 79; see map 2.

[4] *atrium* (plural *atria*): the main reception area or salon of a Roman house.

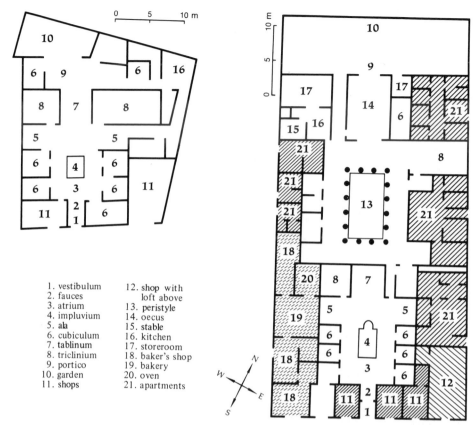

1. vestibulum
2. fauces
3. atrium
4. impluvium
5. ala
6. cubiculum
7. tablinum
8. triclinium
9. portico
10. garden
11. shops

12. shop with loft above
13. peristyle
14. oecus
15. stable
16. kitchen
17. storeroom
18. baker's shop
19. bakery
20. oven
21. apartments

Figure 1. The House of the Surgeon at Pompeii (so named because of a set of surgical instruments found inside it) was built before 200 B.C. Although it was later remodeled, it was still simpler in design than the House of Pansa (Figure 2), and it lacked Hellenistic features such as the peristyle.

Figure 2. The House of Pansa, one of the largest and most elaborate houses in Pompeii, occupied an entire city block. It has a large peristyle area and at the back a portico and garden. By the first century A.D., many areas of the house had been divided off and rented as shop, bakery, and apartment space.

1. Ratio of length to width is 5 to 3.

2. Ratio of length to width is 3 to 2.

3. Draw a square, each side of which equals in measurement the width of the atrium. Draw a diagonal line across the square. The length of the diagonal gives you the length for the atrium.

The height of the atrium, up to the underside of the cross-beams, should be ¾ of the length. Let the dimension of the ceiling and roof above the beams be the remaining ¼.

The alae. The width of the alae,[5] on the right and the left sides of the atrium, should be determined as follows:

1/3 the length of the atrium when its length is 30–40 feet[6]

2/7 the length of the atrium when its length is 40–50 feet

[5] *ala* (plural = *alae*): literally "wing"; a small room off the atrium.

[6] One Roman foot was about one-third inch shorter than the modern British or American foot.

1/4 the length of the atrium when its length is 50–60 feet

2/9 the length of the atrium when its length is 60–80 feet

1/5 the length of the atrium when its length is 80–100 feet

The lintel beams of the alae should be placed at such a height that the height of each ala equals its width.

The tablinum. The width of the tablinum[7] should be determined as follows:

2/3 the width of the atrium when its width is 20 feet

1/2 the width of the atrium when its width is 30–40 feet

2/5 the width of the atrium when its width is 40–60 feet . . .

The height of the tablinum up to the cross-beams should be set at ⅛ more than its width. The paneled ceilings should rise above the cross-beams by ⅓ the width.

The fauces. The fauces[8] for smaller atria should be ⅔ the width of the tablinum; for larger atria, ½. The ancestral images[9] with their ornaments should be set at a height equal to the width of the ala. . . .

The compluvium. The opening of the compluvium[10] should be, in width, not less than ¼, and not more than ⅓, the width of the atrium. In length, let it be in proportion to the length of the atrium.

The peristyle. The peristyle,[11] lying crosswise, should be ⅓ longer than it is deep. Its columns should be as tall as the portico[12] is wide. The distances between the columns should be not less than 3, and not more than 4 times the diameter of the columns.

The triclinium. The length of the triclinium[13] ought to be twice its width. The height of all oblong rooms should be determined in the following manner: add together the length and width measurements and then take half of this sum. This figure supplies the height measurement for an oblong room. But the height of an exedra[14] or a square oecus[15] should be increased to 1½ times the width. . . .

Winter dining rooms and baths should face west, first because the sun's light is needed in the evening, and second because then the setting sun looks directly and brightly at us, gives off heat and therefore makes this area of the house warmer in the evening. Cubicula[16] and reading rooms should face the east, for their purposes require the morning light. The books[17] in the reading rooms, moreover, will not become moldy; for in rooms which face south and west, books are damaged by book-

---

[7] *tablinum* (plural = *tablina*): a room or alcove off the atrium where family records were kept; possibly used as an office by the homeowner.

[8] *fauces:* literally "jaws"; the hallway leading from the door of the house into the atrium.

[9] *ancestral images:* an image, usually made of wax, of a distinguished ancestor. These images were put on display in the hallway or in the atrium. See the introduction to selection 115.

[10] *compluvium:* a quadrangular opening in the roof over the atrium. Rainwater flowed through this opening into a small pool (called the *impluvium*) below. Latin *pluvia* = "rain."

[11] *peristyle:* Latin *peristylium* (from a Greek word), an open courtyard or garden area surrounded by a colonnade.

[12] *portico* a walkway covered by a roof which is supported by columns.

[13] *triclinium:* dining room.

[14] *exedra:* oblong room or hall used for entertaining guests.

[15] *oecus:* room used for entertaining; a small salon.

[16] *cubicula* (singular = *cubiculum*): rooms which could be used as bedrooms or sitting rooms.

[17] *books:* i.e., papyrus rolls.

worms and by the moisture which prevailing humid winds cause. These winds, by scattering moist air particles, destroy papyrus rolls through mold.

Spring and autumn dining rooms should face east. They are then exposed fully to the sunlight in the morning, and the intensity of the sun then moves westward, making them temperate at the time when they are usually used. Summer dining rooms should face north because a northern exposure, turned away from the sun's course, is always cool, healthy, and pleasant for use when other exposures, at the solstice, become sultry with the heat. Art galleries, embroiderers' weaving rooms, and painters' studios should similarly have a northern exposure so that the colors in their works may remain of uniform quality because of the consistency of the light.

Having settled the arrangement of the rooms with regard to the position of the sun, we must now turn our attention to the principles on which should be constructed those areas in private houses which are used by the family alone and those areas which are shared with visitors. Those rooms into which no one has the right to enter un-invited are considered private rooms, such as bedrooms, dining rooms, bathrooms and other rooms which have similar functions. However, the common rooms are those into which people, even uninvited, can by right enter, such as vestibula,[18] courtyards, peri-styles, and other areas which have similar functions.

Therefore men of ordinary means do not need magnificent vestibula, tablina, or atria because they fulfill their social obligations by going around and visiting others rather than by being visited by others.[19]

Those who depend for an income on farm produce must have, in their vestibula, stalls for livestock and display counters, and, within their houses, cellars, granaries, storerooms and other areas which are designed for storing produce rather than for displaying elegance.

Similarly bankers and publicans[20] should have more comfortable and more im-pressive homes, and ones safe from burglars. Lawyers and public speakers should have more elegant and more spacious homes, to accommodate their audiences. Men of high rank, who hold political offices and magistracies and must fulfill social obligations to the citizens, should have lofty, palatial vestibula, very spacious atria, and quite broad tree-lined promenades which furnish a visible sign of their authority. In addition, libraries and basilicas[21] should be constructed in a magnificent style similar to that of public buildings because quite often public meetings and private lawsuits and legal hearings are held in the homes of these men.

---

[18] *vestibula* (singular = *vestibulum*): vestibule; the area just in front of the main entrance of the house.

[19] In Roman society, a client was expected to visit his patron regularly; see selections 9–13.

[20] *publicans:* wealthy Roman businessmen who earned their wealth by bidding on public contracts for construction, military provisions, etc. See selections 162–164.

[21] *basilica:* an oblong room (as here) or building used for meetings; see note 81 of Chap-ter XI.

APARTMENTS

Complaints from an Apartment Dweller

Most people who lived in Rome could not afford to own a house and therefore lived in rooms or apartments which they might own or rent. Apartments might be located in an apartment building, in one section of a private house,[22] above a shop or factory, or in a house which had been converted into a multiple-family dwelling. In Rome and in other ancient cities, as also in modern cities, there were many poorly designed and cheaply constructed apartment buildings. In the passage translated below, the satirist Juvenal, who lived on the top floor of such a building,[23] voices many of the same complaints which modern renters have.

69   Juvenal, *Satires* 3.193–202

We live in a city which is, to a great extent, propped up by flimsy boards. The manager of your apartment building stands in front of the collapsing structure and, while he conceals a gaping crack (a crack many years old), he tells you to "Sleep well"—even though a total cave-in is imminent! It's best, of course, to live where there are no fires and no panics in the dead of night.[24] Here, one neighbor discovers a fire and shouts for water, another neighbor moves out his shabby possessions. The third floor, where you live, is already smoking—but you don't even know! Downstairs there is panic, but you, upstairs, where the gentle pigeons nest, where only thin tiles protect you from the rain, you will be the last to burn.

A Dingy Apartment

Roman apartments were often cold, dark, and cramped, as Martial here complains.

70   Martial, *Epigrams* 8.14.5–6

I live in a little cell, with one window which doesn't even fit properly. Boreas[25] himself would not want to live here.

A Landlord's Problems

Cicero describes to his friend Atticus some buildings he owns.

---

[22] See Figure 2.
[23] In today's world of elevators and running water, the top floor is often a desirable location. In ancient Rome, ground-floor apartments were probably preferred.
[24] On the frequency of fires and collapses of buildings in ancient Rome, see selection 161.
[25] *Boreas:* the North Wind.

71   Cicero, *Letters to Atticus* 14.9

Two of my buildings have fallen down, and the rest have large cracks. Not only the tenants, but even the mice have moved out!

HOUSE PRICES

The High Cost of Living in Rome

House prices and apartment rents were higher in Rome than in small towns or rural areas. Many people, however, preferred to live in Rome, even in a small, dingy apartment, because they enjoyed the excitement of life in the big city.

72   Juvenal, *Satires* 3.223–225

If you can tear yourself away from the chariot races in Rome, the finest home in Sora or Fabrateria or Frusino[26] can be bought outright for as much as you now pay in a year's rent for your dark hovel.

RENTAL ADVERTISEMENTS

The Romans apparently advertised rental property by painting "For Rent" notices on the outer walls of buildings, and a number of these advertisements have been found painted on the walls of buildings in Pompeii. The two notices translated below were found in Pompeii.

Shops and Apartments for Rent

73   *CIL* 4.138 (*ILS* 6035)

The Arrius Pollio Apartment Complex
owned by Gnaeus Allius Nigidius Maius
FOR RENT from July 1
streetfront shops with counter space,
luxurious second-story apartments,
and a townhouse.
Prospective renters, please make arrangements
with Primus, slave of Gnaeus Allius Nigidius Maius.

[26] *Sora, Fabrateria, Frusino:* small towns in the countryside around Rome.

74   *CIL* 4.1136 (*ILS* 5723)

FOR RENT
from August 13, with a 5-year lease
on the property of Julia Felix, daughter of Spurius:
the elegant Venus Baths,
streetfront shops and booths,
and second-story apartments.

HOMEOWNER'S INSURANCE

Fire Insurance

Fire was a constant threat in ancient cities because wood was a common building material and people used open fires and oil lamps. However, some people may have deliberately set fire to their property in order to collect insurance money.

75   Martial, *Epigrams* 3.52

Tongilianus, you paid 200,000 sesterces for your house. An accident, too common in this city, destroyed it. You collected 1,000,000 sesterces. Now I ask you, doesn't it seem possible that you set fire to your own house, Tongilianus?

THE BENEFITS OF CITY LIFE

People living in Roman cities had both the advantages and disadvantages of life in an urban center. They enjoyed public services and conveniences not available in rural areas, but they endured more noise and congestion.

Aqueducts

The Romans used their engineering skills to improve the quality of life and to provide an efficient system of public services. For example, people need a constant supply of fresh water, but in a city it is difficult for each person to be responsible for finding and maintaining his own water supply. The Romans solved this problem by building an amazing system of aqueducts which carried water to their cities from areas many miles away.[27] Since the lives of the residents depended on this water supply, it was essential that the aqueducts be kept in good repair and that the water flow freely. The aqueducts were so well constructed and maintained that many are still standing today. On the other hand, enemy troops sometimes forced

[27] *aqueduct:* Latin *aqua* = "water," *ductum* = "brought," "led."

a city into surrender by destroying its aqueducts and thus cutting off its water supply.

The passage translated here provides insights into the problems which government water commissioners faced and the regulations which were established to protect the city's water supply.

76   Frontinus, *The Aqueducts of Rome* 2.103, 124, 126, 127

I shall now discuss what matters the water commissioner must give his attention to, that is, the law and the senatorial decrees which delineate his spheres of authority and activity. Concerning the right to pipe in water to private homes,[28] he must watch carefully that no one does so without a written authorization from the emperor, that is, that no one draws off public water which he has not been officially authorized to, and that no one draws off more than he has been authorized to. . . . The water commissioner must exercise great vigilance against many forms of fraud. He must inspect the channels of the aqueducts outside the city carefully and repeatedly to check up on the authorized quantities. The same thing must be done for the reservoirs and public fountains so that the water may flow day and night without interruption. The commissioner has been instructed to do this by a decree of the Senate. . . .

No one, I think, would disagree that the aqueducts nearest the city (that is, those built of squared-stone masonry and within the seventh milestone[29] must be especially protected both because they are structures of a very great height and because each one carries several water channels. If it were ever necessary to interrupt these, the city would be deprived of the greater part of its water supply. There are, however, contingency plans even for this problem: a temporary structure is built up to the level of the defective channel, and a conduit made of lead troughs, filling the gap created by the broken channel, continues the flow of water. . . . A decree of the Senate ensures that landowners may not deny access to contractors hired to repair aqueducts. . . .

Often, in fact, repairs become necessary because of the illegal acts of landowners who damage the channels in numerous ways. First, they obstruct either with buildings or with trees open space around the aqueducts which, by decree of the Senate, must be kept clear. The trees do the greater damage because their roots cause the vaultings and the sides to split open. Second, they run local and rural roads right over the aqueduct structures themselves. Finally, they shut off access for maintenance and repairs. All these things have been forbidden by a decree of the Senate from which I quote.

"The consuls[30] Quintus Aelius Tubero and Paulus Fabius Maximus have reported that the routes of the aqueducts which come into the city are being

[28] Most people went to the public fountains (into which the aqueducts flowed) to obtain their water. A privileged few were authorized to tap the aqueducts and set up a system of pipes which would bring water right into their homes.

[29] *within the seventh milestone:* i.e., within seven miles of the city. On Roman highways stone pillars were used to mark off the miles. Distances were counted from a marker in the Roman Forum; hence, "all roads lead to Rome." The Roman mile was equal to about ninetenths of an American mile.

[30] *consuls:* the highest magistracy in the government of Rome; in the republican period two consuls were elected each year for a one-year term of office; see selections 229–232. On decrees of the Senate (*senatus consulta*), see selection 238.

obstructed with tombs and buildings, and planted with trees. They have asked the Senate what action it wishes to take. With respect to this matter the Senate has decreed as follows: since obstructions damage the public aqueducts and hinder their repair, by decree of the Senate a space of 15 feet on each side of the springs, the arches, and the walls must be kept clear; a space of 5 feet must be left clear on each side of the underground channels and conduits within the city and within buildings adjoining the city; from this time forth no tomb or building may be erected in these vacant spaces, nor may trees be planted; if there are now trees in these areas, they must be cut down unless they are adjacent to a villa or surrounded by buildings. If anyone acts contrary to these decrees, his fine will be 10,000 sesterces for each violation, of which amount half will be given as a reward to the accuser, through whose efforts a violator of a Senate decree has been convicted, and half will be paid into the public treasury. In these cases the water commissioners will be the judges and will conduct the investigation."

Roads, Sewers, and the Campus Martius

The Romans were a practical people who directed their amazing engineering skills to the problems of everyday life: transportation, water supply, and disposal of waste matter. In this passage from his *Geography Book,* Strabo, a Greek author who lived from about 60 B.C. to about A.D. 24, describes with admiration the projects of Roman engineers.

77　　　　　　　　　　　　　　　　　　　　　Strabo, *Geography Book* 5.3.8

To the blessings which nature has bestowed upon their city the Romans have added others which can be attributed to their foresight. For the Greeks were renowned for their successful endeavors in the area of city planning because they sought out locations which were naturally beautiful, and also easily defended, which had harbors and also rich soil. The Romans however were especially farsighted about matters to which the Greeks gave little thought, such as the construction of roads and aqueducts, and of sewers which could wash out the waste matter of the city into the Tiber. They have constructed roads throughout the countryside, cutting through hills and filling in depressions, so that now their wagons can carry loads equivalent to those of boats. The sewers, covered with a vault of tightly fitted stones, have room in some places for hay wagons to drive through them. And the quantity of water brought into the city by aqueducts is so great that rivers, as it were, flow through the city and the sewers; and almost every house has water tanks, service pipes, and plentiful streams of water. . . . In short, the ancient Romans[31] gave little thought to the beauty of Rome because they were occupied with other, greater and more necessary matters.

However, the later Romans, and in particular those of today and of my own time, have not been deficient in this respect but rather have filled the city with many beautiful structures. In fact Pompey,[32] the deified Caesar[33] and Augustus, and Au-

[31] Since Strabo lived from about 60 B.C. to about A.D. 24, when he refers to ancient Romans he means those who lived before the first century B.C.

[32] *Pompey:* Gnaeus Pompeius, general and statesman, 106–48 B.C. Although an ally of Julius Caesar for a long time, he became his opponent in the civil war; see note 81 of Chapter V and note 86 of Chapter X.

[33] *the deified Caesar:* Gaius Julius Caesar, who was assassinated on the Ides of March,

gustus's sons, friends, wife[34] and sister[35] have exceeded all others' eagerness and expense in their building projects. The Campus Martius[36] contains the majority of these projects, thus acquiring, in addition to its natural beauty, also the splendor which has resulted from their foresight.

Toilets

In many Roman cities there were public toilets, in the marketplace, for example, which were flushed out by a sewer system. In their own apartments and homes, however, the Romans generally used chamberpots. The following passage was found scratched on a wall in Pompeii.

78   *CIL* 4.4957

Dear host, I'm afraid I've wet the bed. "Why?" you ask. Because there was no chamberpot in my room.

Roads

Any large urban community must deal with the problems of transportation and communication: bringing in supplies—food, construction material, raw materials for factories—and taking out the manufactured products for export and sale. The commercial and economic stability of Rome, as well as its administrative and military supremacy, depended on an efficient network of roads throughout the city itself, throughout Italy, and throughout the Empire. These well-constructed roads (many are still in use today) allowed the Romans to communicate quickly with any part of the Empire and to transport supplies, businessmen, messengers, bureaucrats, or military troops cheaply and safely. Roman engineers encountered and solved many difficult problems of road construction.[37] Construction work was done by slaves, local workers, or soldiers.[38] One source of information about their work has been the inscriptions on the milestones which they erected on the roads.[39] Two

---

44 B.C. After his death he was deified, officially declared to have become a god (Latin *deus* = "god," *fieri* = "to become").

[34] *Augustus's wife:* Livia; see selection 67.

[35] *Augustus's sister:* Octavia, who had been married to Mark Antony (her second husband) before he became involved with Cleopatra; see note 81 of Chapter III.

[36] *Campus Martius:* the Field of Mars (Latin *campus* = "field," *Martius* = "belonging to Mars"). Mars was the god of war. This flat, open area was used to muster the army and to assemble citizens for elections. It was also used as an exercise area. See map 1.

[37] "When in 1850 the French General St. Arnaud marched his legions through the Kanga pass in the Atlas mountains he reasonably believed that he was the first man who had ever traversed so impassable a defile. Then he found carved on a rock an inscription stating: 'The Legio III Augusta built this road in A.D. 145.'" Victor W. Von Hagen, *The Roads That Led to Rome* (Cleveland and New York, 1967), p. 53.

[38] On soldiers as construction workers, see note 72 of Chapter XI.

[39] For more on miles and milestones, see note 29 of this chapter.

examples of those milestone inscriptions appear here, the first from the lower Danube area, set up in A.D. 100, and the second from North Africa, set up in A.D. 152.

79   *CIL* 3.8267 (*ILS* 5863)

The emperor Caesar Nerva Trajan Augustus Germanicus[40] . . . had this road built. Its construction involved cutting through mountains and leveling irregularities.

80   *L'Annee Epigraphique* 17 (1904) 21

The emperor Caesar Titus Aelius Hadrianus Augustus Antoninus Pius[41] . . . repaired this road through the Numidian Alps which had deteriorated through age. Construction work involved rebuilding bridges, draining swamps, and reinforcing sections which were sinking.

THE PROBLEMS OF CITY LIFE

Crowds, Traffic, and Muggers

81   Juvenal, *Satires* 3.232–248, 254–261, 268–314

Here in Rome many sick people die from lack of sleep. Noise deprives them of sleep, and they develop indigestion and burning ulcers which in turn produce illness. But what rented rooms ever allow sleep? In this city, sleep comes only to the wealthy.[42] This is the source of the disease: carts creaking through the narrow and winding streets[43] and the curses of drivers caught in traffic jams will rob even a deaf man of sleep.

If social duty calls,[44] the rich man will be carried above the heads of the crowd by his tall Ligurian litter bearers. As people give way he will be swiftly transported to his destination, and, inside the litter, he will read or write or sleep, for a litter with the windows closed induces sleep. Without any personal strain, he will arrive before us. Whereas we, although we hurry, are blocked by a wave of people in front of us. And the great crowd behind crushes us. One man hits me with his elbow, another with a hard pole; one man strikes me on the head with a wood beam, another with

[40] Trajan was emperor A.D. 98–117.

[41] Antoninus Pius was emperor A.D. 138–161.

[42] The wealthy could afford the privacy of a large home such as that described by Vitruvius in selection 68. Or, like Pliny and Cicero, they could escape to the peace and quiet of country villas (selections 16 and 87).

[43] No vehicles (except litters carried by slaves) were allowed to pass through the streets of Rome during daylight hours. This regulation was first put into effect by Julius Caesar.

[44] *social duty:* see selections 11–13 and 169.

a wine jar. My legs are covered with thick mud. Then, on all sides, big feet step on me, and a nail from a soldier's boot pierces my toe. . . .

One wagon carries fir-wood timber, another carries pine.[45] They are piled high and they sway, posing for the crowd a threat of danger. For if a wagon carrying marble should tip over and dump its load of mountain rock on top of the throng of people, what would remain of the bodies? Who would find the limbs or the bones? The crushed body would utterly disappear, like the soul. . . .

Now consider the various and diverse dangers at night: how high it is to the lofty roofs (from which roof tiles fall and hit you on the head), how often cracked and broken pots fall from windows, with what weight they mark and damage the pavement when they strike it. You could be considered thoughtless and careless about sudden accidents if you were to go out for dinner without first making a will. For indeed there are as many potential disasters as there are open windows where you are passing by at night. You should therefore pray and carry with you this pitiable wish: that people may be content to empty over you, from their windows, only an open basin.[46]

The violent drunk who has had the misfortune to mug no one feels unsatisfied; he tosses and turns, unable to sleep. For some men, a good mugging induces sleep. Yet, though young and heated with wine, he avoids the man whom a scarlet cloak, a very long line of attendants, and many torches and oil lamps warn should be avoided. Me, however, whom the moon usually escorts or, at best, the thin light of a candle whose wick I carefully nurture—me he fears not. Now imagine the preliminaries to this street fight, if indeed you can call it a fight when he does the beating and I am only beaten. He stands in front of me and orders me to halt. You have to obey. What else can you do when a maniac, and one stronger than you, coerces you? "Where are you coming from?" he shouts. "At whose house did you have your dinner of vinegar and beans?[47] What shoemaker shared with you his leeks and lips of a boiled sheep? You won't answer? Speak or I'll kick you. Tell me where you hang out. In what Jews' prayer-house can I find you?"[48] Whether you try to speak, or shrink back in silence, it's all the same. In either case they mug you, and then in a violent rage make you pay for permission to escape. This is the poor man's freedom: having been mugged and battered with fists, he begs and entreats his assailant to allow him to go away with a few teeth left. Yet these things are not all you have to fear. For there is always someone who will rob you even when your house is securely bolted and after all the shops everywhere are locked and quiet with their shutters closed. Sometimes the burglars even carry weapons! And whenever armed police are sent to the Pomptine marsh and Gallinarian forest[49] to secure the area, all the thieves and criminals run from there to Rome, as if to a game preserve. What forge, what anvil is not now producing heavy chains? So much iron is used to make chains that we may well fear

---

[45] Vehicles carrying building materials for public buildings were allowed in the city during daylight hours, an exception to the rule cited in footnote 43.

[46] *open basin:* i.e., a basin of dirty water or food slops, not a chamberpot. (See selection 78.)

[47] The foods mentioned—beans, leeks, and sheep lips, and vinegar to drink—suggest the dinner of a poor lower-class man; see the introduction to Chapter V.

[48] Juvenal despised, in general, all foreigners, but particularly those from the eastern Mediterranean areas; see selection 212.

[49] The Pomptine marsh was in the south of Latium. The Gallinarian forest was in Campania, near Cumae.

that there will not be enough for plows and that there will be a shortage of mattocks and hoes. Happy were our ancestors. Happy were those generations long ago who lived under kings and tribunes and saw Rome content with one jail.

Noise

82 Martial, *Epigrams* 12.57.1–14, 18–21, 24–28

Do you want to know why I often seek refuge in my small fields and squalid villa at arid Nomentum?[50] Because, Sparsus, there is no place in the city where a poor man may have a quiet moment for thought. In the morning schoolteachers won't let you live;[51] before dawn bakers disturb you; and the whole day the hammers of copper-smiths jar your nerves. Over here the moneychanger idly jangles Neronian coins on his filthy table; over there a man hammering Spanish gold dust pounds his well-worn stone with a shiny mallet. The frenzied band of Bellona's priests[52] never stops chanting; nor does the sailor, who survived a shipwreck but lost a limb, ever cease his begging; and the Jew, taught by his mother to panhandle, and the half-blind huckster of sulphur products continually solicit money from passers-by. . . . You, Sparsus, know nothing of these things, nor can you ever know, you who enjoy the luxury of a mansion, you whose home looks down on the hilltops, you who own a country estate right here in Rome. . . . You enjoy deep sleep and a stillness disturbed by no voices; the daylight never shines in unless you let it.[53] But I am awakened by the laughter of the passing crowd, and all of Rome, it seems, stands near my bed. So, whenever I am weary of these torments and wish to sleep, I go to my villa.

Theft

This message was painted on a wall in Pompeii.

83 *CIL* 4.64

A copper pot is missing from this shop. I offer a reward of 65 sesterces for its return, and a reward of 20 sesterces for information leading to its return.

[50] *Nomentum:* a town in Latium, northeast of Rome. Martial was, of course, fortunate to have a country villa, however small, to which he could retreat. The poor had no such opportunities to escape the noise of Rome.

[51] Classes began at dawn and were frequently held outdoors. The voices of the school-teachers might therefore disturb people living near the school. See selection 125.

[52] Bellona: the Roman goddess of war; her priests were called "frenzied" because they gashed their arms with knives during sacrifices to her.

[53] Compare the comments of Juvenal in the previous passage: "In this city, sleep comes only to the wealthy."

Burglary

This document, written in the town of Tebtunis, Egypt in the second century A.D., records an official complaint about a burglary.[54]

84   *Tebtunis Papyri* 330

To Bolanus[55] from Ptolemaeus, son of Patron, of the town of Tebtunis:—

Upon my return from a trip out of town, I found that my house had been burglarized and the entire contents had been stolen. Therefore, since I cannot remain silent about such behavior, I am filing with you this document of complaint, and I am requesting that it be deposited in the registry so that, if anyone is shown to be guilty, I may deal with his case.

Urban Alienation

From this passage we learn that apartment buildings were constructed very close to one another (thus increasing the fire danger). However, neighbors sometimes did not know or speak to one another.

85   Martial, *Epigrams* 1.86

Novius is my neighbor; we can reach out our windows and touch hands. Who would not envy me and think I am happy every single hour since I can enjoy so close a companion?

Yet he is as far away from me as Terentianus who now is governor of Syene[56] on the Nile. I cannot dine with him, nor even see him or talk with him; in the whole city there is no one who is so near and yet so far from me.

I must move farther away, or he must. You have to be Novius's neighbor, or live in the same apartment building if you don't want to see Novius.

HOUSING IN RURAL AREAS

Farm Houses

Farm families who owned or rented small plots of land lived in little huts.[57] Much of the agricultural land in Italy, however, was divided into large tracts owned by

---

[54] For more information about papyrus documents, see selection 19 and Appendix I.

[55] *Bolanus:* strategos or magistrate appointed to oversee the district which included Tebtunis.

[56] *Syene:* a town in southern Egypt; i.e., "Novius might as well be as far away as Egypt for all I get to see him."

[57] See *selection 88:* "a tiny cottage thatched with straw and marsh reeds." See also selection 174.

wealthy families.[58] Frequently these wealthy landowners lived in the city and visited their estates only occasionally; the land was worked by farmworkers, who might be free men or slaves, and a manager or overseer managed the farming operations, which brought considerable profit to the owner. There would be on the estate a large building complex called a villa which contained within its exterior walls sleeping and living quarters for the landowner and his family, the overseer, the farmworkers, and often even the livestock, as well as work rooms and storage rooms.

Much of modern land use is specialized; one farmer plants only corn, another only wheat. The following passage, taken from a Roman "Manual for Rural Life," gives a good idea of the self-sufficiency of Roman farms which could produce a wide variety of agricultural products. Farm work today is highly mechanized; the work on a Roman farm was done by slaves and by hired help. This passage offers information about the different tasks required on the farm, the different treatment accorded the various classes of workers, and the different types of housing provided in the villa.

86   Columella, *On Agriculture* 1.6.1–11, 18–24

The size of a villa or housing structure should be determined by the total area of the farm; and the villa should be divided into three sections: one section resembling a city home [for the landowner], one section like a real farmhouse [for the workers and livestock], and the third section for storing farm products.

The landowner's section of the villa should be further divided into a winter apartment and a summer apartment. The winter bedrooms should face southeast and the winter dining rooms due west. The summer bedrooms, on the other hand, should face due south, but the dining rooms for this same season should face southeast. The baths should be turned toward the northwest so that they may be lighted from midday until evening. The promenades should have a southern exposure so that they may receive both the maximum of sun in the winter and the minimum in the summer.

Now in the farmhouse part of the villa there should be a large kitchen with a high ceiling, and for two reasons: so that the wood beams may be secure against the danger of fire, and so that household slaves may conveniently stop by here during every season of the year. The best plan will be to construct the cells for unchained slaves facing south. For those in chains let there be an underground prison, as healthful as possible, and let it be lighted by many narrow windows which are built so far from the ground that they cannot be reached with a hand.

For livestock there should be, within the villa, stalls which are not subject to either cold or heat. For draft and pack animals there should be two sets of stalls, winter ones and summer ones. For the other livestock which it is appropriate to keep within the villa there should be places, partially roofed, partially open, and surrounded by high walls, so that the animals may rest (in the former during winter, in the latter during summer) without being attacked by wild beasts. The stables should be spacious and arranged so that (1) no liquid may flow in, and (2) any liquid produced

---

[58] For more on the division of agricultural land, see the section on agriculture in Chapter VII. Agricultural land and its products were a major source of wealth for Roman society's upper class.

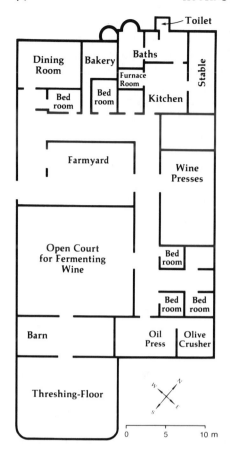

Figure 3. Plan of a farm villa (*villa rustica*) at Bosco-reale, about two miles north of Pompeii. The living quarters, stables, and wine and oil production areas were enclosed within the same set of walls. There may have been larger bedrooms on the second floor for the landowner's family.

in the stable may drain out as quickly as possible. In this way neither the bases of the walls nor the hoofs of the animals will rot. It will be suitable for the stalls to be 10, or at least 9, feet wide,[59] a width which allows the animal to lie down and also allows the herdsman to move around freely while tending it. It is a good idea for the mangers to be built no higher than an ox or pack animal can conveniently reach in order to eat while standing.

Cells for oxherds and shepherds should be placed next to their animals so that running out to care for them may be convenient. All herdsmen, however, ought to live as close as possible to one another in order to minimize the surveillance duties of the foreman, who might otherwise make rounds in several directions, and in order that the herdsmen themselves might be observers of one another's diligence and negligence.

The third part of the villa, that designated for storing produce, is divided into rooms for oil, for oil and wine presses, for aged wine, and for wine not yet fermented; into lofts for hay and straw; and into areas for warehouses and granaries. The rooms which are on the ground floor serve to store liquid products, such as wine and olive oil, which are destined for the market; however, dry products, such as grain, hay, leaves, straw, and other fodders, should be stored in lofts. The granaries should be reached by ladders and should receive ventilation through tiny little openings on the

[59] On Roman feet, see note 6 of this chapter.

north wall. For that direction is the most cold and the least humid, two factors which contribute to a long preservation for stored grain. For the same reason, the wine room is placed on the ground floor; but it should be far removed from the bathrooms, the oven, the manure pile, and other filthy areas giving off a foul stench, and just as far from cisterns and running water that release a liquid which spoils the wine. . . .

The rooms for wine and oil presses especially, and the storerooms for olive oil, should be warm because every liquid is more readily thinned by heat, but thickened by great cold; and if the oil freezes (which seldom happens), it becomes rancid. But, as it is natural heat which is needed—heat which depends on the position of the sun and the angle of its rays—fire and flames are unnecessary, since the flavor of the oil is spoiled by smoke and soot. Therefore the press room should receive sun from the south so that we do not find it necessary to use fires and lamps when the olives are being pressed.

The cauldron room, where new wine is boiled down, should be neither narrow nor dark so that the servant who is boiling down the must can move around without inconvenience. The smoke room, too, in which recently cut timber may be rapidly seasoned, can be placed in the farmhouse part of the villa, adjoining the servants' baths. For it is also important that there be baths in which the household slaves may bathe, but only on holidays; for frequent use of baths is not consistent with physical toughness. Storerooms may be advantageously located in those places from which smoke often arises since those wines age more quickly which reach an early maturity through a certain kind of smoke. For this reason, there should also be another loft to which the wines may be moved so that they do not, on the other hand, become tainted by too much smoking.

Enough has been said about the villa and the arrangement of its various sections. Now the following things ought to be near the villa: an oven and flour mill, as large as the anticipated number of tenant-farmers may require; at least two ponds, one for the use of geese and cattle, the other for soaking lupines, elms, twigs, branches, and other things which have been adapted to our needs. There should also be two manure pits, one to receive fresh dung and to keep it for a year, the other to provide old dung, ready to be carted off. But both should be placed on a slope with a gentle incline, in the manner of fishponds, and be built up and covered with a hard floor of earth so that they do not lose moisture. For it is very important that the moisture not evaporate and that the manure retain its potency, and that it therefore be soaked constantly with liquids so that any seeds of thornbushes or grasses which are mixed in with the straw or chaff may rot, and not be carried out to the field and thus make the grain fields full of weeds. And therefore, when experienced farmers carry out any waste matter from the sheep folds or cattle stalls, they cover it by throwing branches on top; nor do they allow it to dry out or to be burned by the sun's beating down.

The threshing floor should be situated, if possible, so that it can be watched from above by the owner or at least by the manager. And this floor is best paved with hard stone because then (1) the grain is quickly threshed out since the ground does not give way under the pounding of hoofs and threshing sledges, and (2) after winnowing, the grain is cleaner and free from the small stones and clods of earth which a dirt floor usually tosses up during the threshing. A shed should be connected to the threshing floor (especially considering the variability of weather in Italy) in which half-threshed grain may be stored and covered if a sudden shower comes along. For in certain regions across the sea, where there is no rain in summer, this is unnecessary.

It is also a good idea to enclose fruit trees and gardens with a fence and to plant them close to the villa, in a place to which all the manure seepage from the barnyard and the bathrooms can flow, as well as the watery dregs squeezed from the olives. For both vegetables and trees also thrive on fertilizers of this sort.

Vacation Villas

In some of the passages above, the authors refer to the luxury of a villa in the country, far from the noise and the traffic of the city.[60] Though only a small number of people could afford such a luxury, these same people frequently owned several vacation retreats—one in the mountains, another by the sea or a lake, for example—to which they escaped for rest and relaxation from the hectic life of a city like Rome. These villas might be located on a working farm, such as the one described above, but very often the main requirements for a country retreat, such as that described by Pliny to his friend Gallus in the passage translated here, seem to have been proximity to Rome and breathtaking views of the surrounding countryside and seashore. Pliny's villa is designed for leisure; he has libraries, flower gardens, exercise areas, and baths. (In the previous passage Columella had suggested that the farmworkers bathe only on holidays; frequent baths might sap the physical strength needed for farm labor.) The Romans—at least the very privileged few—enjoyed their visits to their peaceful country retreats but did not want to be too far from civilization. Pliny describes with delight the clusters of nearby villas, and he mentions the proximity of the town of Ostia as an advantage.

87   Pliny the Younger, *Letters* 2.17

You are surprised that I am so fond of my villa at Laurentum—but you will cease to be surprised once you know about its charm, the convenience of its location, and the extent of its ocean frontage. It is only seventeen miles from Rome, and therefore you can carry out a full day of business in the city, and still be here before sunset. And it is accessible by more than one road because both the Laurentine and Ostian highways come this way, although you must turn off the Laurentine highway at milestone 14, and off the Ostian highway at milestone 11.[61] From either direction, each access road has a sandy stretch part of the way, and is therefore a little difficult and slow for a team pulling a carriage, but fast and easy on horseback. The scenery varies from one spot to the next; sometimes the road narrows, with forests on both sides, sometimes it opens up and widens through very broad meadows where many flocks of sheep and many herds of horses and cattle, which have been driven down from their mountain pastures by the winter, grow fat on the grass and the warmth of spring.

The villa is roomy enough for my needs, and its maintenance is not expensive. At the front of the villa is an atrium[62] which is modest but not shabby. Then there are two porticoes, both of which curve round to produce a shape similar to the letter D and which together enclose a small but pleasant courtyard. These porticoes create a

---

60 For examples of villa ownership, see selections 60 and 82.
61 On Roman miles and milestones, see note 29 of this chapter.
62 *atrium:* see selection 68.

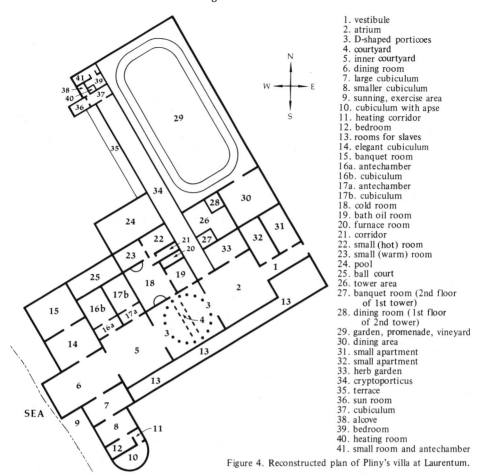

1. vestibule
2. atrium
3. D-shaped porticoes
4. courtyard
5. inner courtyard
6. dining room
7. large cubiculum
8. smaller cubiculum
9. sunning, exercise area
10. cubiculum with apse
11. heating corridor
12. bedroom
13. rooms for slaves
14. elegant cubiculum
15. banquet room
16a. antechamber
16b. cubiculum
17a. antechamber
17b. cubiculum
18. cold room
19. bath oil room
20. furnace room
21. corridor
22. small (hot) room
23. small (warm) room
24. pool
25. ball court
26. tower area
27. banquet room (2nd floor of 1st tower)
28. dining room (1st floor of 2nd tower)
29. garden, promenade, vineyard
30. dining area
31. small apartment
32. small apartment
33. herb garden
34. cryptoporticus
35. terrace
36. sun room
37. cubiculum
38. alcove
39. bedroom
40. heating room
41. small room and antechamber

Figure 4. Reconstructed plan of Pliny's villa at Laurentum.

splendid retreat from stormy weather, because their walkways are protected by windows[63] and, even better, by the overhang of the roof.

Facing the middle of this area is an inner courtyard and then a rather pretty dining room which fronts on the sea and is gently washed by a few weak waves, remnants of a storm far from shore where the southeast wind has ruffled the sea. This room has folding doors or windows as large as doors on every side, and therefore provides, from the sides and from the front, three views of the sea. From the front of the room, you can turn and look back at the inner courtyard, the portico, the little courtyard, the other portico, then the atrium, the forests beyond, and even the distant mountains.

To the left of the dining room, but set back somewhat from the sea, is a large cubiculum, and then, beside it, another smaller one with two windows, one to catch the rays of the rising sun, the other the rays of the setting sun. This second window looks over the sea, but from a distance, and therefore offers a nice, but not dramatic view. The angular area formed by the projection of the dining room beyond the cubicu-

[63] There may have been sheets of mica or glass between the columns. Very few people could afford glass. In apartment buildings windows were simply open areas in the walls, which could be closed on rainy days by means of wooden shutters.

lum traps and intensifies the brightest sunlight. This area serves as a winter sunning place and also as an exercise enclosure for my household.[64] No winds blow here except those which bring with them overcast skies; these winds carry off first the clear weather, and then, consequently, the special feature of this little corner.[65]

Connected to this area of the villa is a cubiculum whose wall is curved like an apse; because of all its windows, it is able to trace the daily movement of the sun. Built into the wall of this room is a cupboard, or bookcase, which contains books which should be not just read but studied. A heating corridor connects this room with a bedroom. The heating corridor has a hollow floor and hollow walls; from the floor and the walls it receives air warmed to a healthy temperature, and then distributes and supplies this air in all directions.[66]

The remaining rooms on this side of the villa are reserved for the use of slaves and freedmen although most of them are elegant enough to accommodate guests.

On the other side of the villa is a very elegant cubiculum; then there is a room—either a large cubiculum or an unpretentious banquet room—which is brightened by a great deal of sunlight and a very extensive sea view. Behind this room is a cubiculum, with an antechamber, which is suitable both for summer use, because of its high ceiling, and for winter use, because it is protected and sheltered from all the winds. Another antechamber and cubiculum are connected to this one by a common wall.

Next comes the broad and spacious cold room of the baths. It contains two bathing tubs which project outward, from opposite walls, with curved rims; they are quite large, especially considering how close the sea is. Nearby are the room for applying bath oil, the furnace room, a corridor, and then two small rooms which are more tasteful than sumptuous. Adjacent to these is a marvelous warm pool from which swimmers look out over the sea. Not far away is the ball court which receives the very warm afternoon sun.

At this point there rises up a tower. On its ground floor are two rooms, and, in the tower itself, there are another two rooms as well as a banquet room which looks out over the very broad expanse of the sea, the very long stretch of coastline, and the very delightful villas of my neighbors. There is, moreover, a second tower with a cubiculum which is lit by both the rising and the setting sun. Behind this are situated a wine cellar[67] and a grain storage room. Beneath this room is a dining room in which you can hear only a faint and subdued echo of the crash and roar of a stormy sea.

This dining room looks out over a garden and promenade. The promenade, which encircles the garden, has a border of evergreen shrubs, or rosemary where there are no evergreen shrubs, since the shrubs flourish in places sheltered by buildings, but wither under an open sky, an open wind, and the spray of the sea, however far away. Adjacent

---

[64] *household:* includes family, slaves, and free servants; see the definition of *familia* in note 1 of this chapter.

[65] *special feature:* i.e., it is no longer sunny.

[66] The floor of the heating corridor was raised from the ground on short pillars of masonry. A hollow or space was thus created between the ground and the floor. Into this space heated air from a furnace was conducted. The walls of the room might also be hollow, and the hot air would then fill the cavity in the walls. The heating corridor itself was quite warm, and hot air passed from it into adjoining rooms through flues.

[67] Not really a wine "cellar" since the wine is not stored underground; rather, a wine storeroom, perhaps on the second floor of the tower. In the previous passage Columella recommended storing wine near rooms with furnaces, such as the baths. The Romans thought that smoke from the bath furnace helped to age the wines.

to the promenade, and within the garden area it encloses, is a small, shady vineyard, whose soil is spongy and soft even to bare feet. Mulberry and fig trees grow luxuriantly in the garden because the soil is especially suitable for these two, although rather unsuitable for other types of trees. There is a dining area here which is, of course, some distance from the sea, but which enjoys a view of the garden that is not at all inferior to a view of the sea. Bordering the rear of the dining area are two small apartments whose windows overlook the vestibulum of the villa and another garden, a lush herb garden.

From this point there extends a cryptoporticus[68] which is almost as long as a cryptoporticus of a public building. It has windows on both sides, although more of them on the side facing the sea; on the garden side there is only one window for every two in the opposite wall. When the sky is clear and the air still, all these windows are left open; but when a breeze is blowing from either direction, only those windows on the side where the wind is not blowing can be kept open without danger.

In front of the cryptoporticus is a terrace fragrant with violets; the warmth of this terrace area is increased by the reflection of the sun pouring down on the cryptoporticus, which checks and wards off the north wind at the same time as it absorbs the sun's warmth; it is therefore as warm in front of the cryptoporticus as it is cool in the back. It offers a similar barrier to the southwest wind, and breaks the force of or brings to a standstill winds from any direction. This is the special attraction of this part of the villa in winter, an attraction even greater in the summer: before noon the shade from the cryptoporticus keeps the terrace cool; after noon, it keeps cool the nearest part of the promenade and garden. As the days grow longer or shorter, the cryptoporticus casts a shorter or longer shadow in one place or the other. But the cryptoporticus itself is least sunny when the sun burns brightest and stands directly over its roof. In addition, when the windows are open, westerly winds enter and circulate through, and the air of the cryptoporticus never seems heavy, stale, or stagnant.

At the end of the terrace and the cryptoporticus is a garden apartment, my real favorite; I had it constructed myself. It contains a sun room, one side of which looks over the terrace; another side looks over the sea, and both sides receive sunlight. In this apartment is a cubiculum which has a view of the cryptoporticus from its folding doors, and a view of the sea from its window. Across from the center wall is a very elegant recessed alcove which can be connected or separated from the cubiculum by opening or closing the curtains and glass doors. It contains a couch and two chairs. Below is the sea, behind are villas, in front is the forest. From its three windows you can see these three views either separately or in one sweeping panorama.

Adjacent to this alcove is a bedroom for sleeping or taking naps. Neither the voices of young slaves, nor the murmur of the sea, nor the gusty winds of storms, nor the flash of lightning, nor even the daylight penetrate this room unless the windows are open. The explanation for this deep and very secluded peacefulness is as follows: a corridor lies between and separates the wall of the bedroom and the wall of the garden, and this intervening empty space absorbs every sound. Attached to the bedroom is a heating or furnace room which, by means of a small glass window, gives off or retains, as the situation demands, the heat radiating from its hollow floor. Next a small room with an antechamber stretches out toward the sun; it holds until the afternoon the warm rays of the rising sun which it catches at an angle. When I retire

[68] *cryptoporticus:* a galleria or covered walkway.

to this apartment, I feel far away even from my own villa; and I take particular pleasure in it during the Saturnalia[69] when the other parts of the house resound with the merrymaking and holiday cheer of this season; for here I don't disturb the festivities of my household, and they don't disturb my studies.

Running water[70] is the one thing missing amid all these amenities and charm, but there are wells—or rather springs, for the water flows up to the surface. And this part of the coastline is quite remarkable in nature; wherever you dig you hit water, ready to gush up. And the water is pure and not even a little brackish despite its proximity to the sea. The neighboring forests offer an abundant supply of wood. And the town of Ostia[71] stocks all other necessities. Indeed even in the nearby village, which is separated from my villa by just one villa, has resources adequate for the moderate man. It has three public baths,[72] which are very handy if by chance a sudden arrival or a rather brief stay make it inconvenient to heat up the baths at the villa.

The roofs of other villas, some clustered together, some rather isolated, decorate the shoreline with a very pleasing diversity and create an impression of a series of cities, whether you view them from the sea or from the shore. Sometimes a long period of fair weather makes the beach dry and soft, but, more often, frequent and pounding waves make it wet and hard. The sea does not, it is true, abound in expensive types of fish, yet it does supply sole and excellent lobsters or prawns. And agricultural products are also abundant along this coast, milk in particular, because cattle gather here from their pastures whenever they want water or shade.

Don't you agree, then, that I have good reason to visit, live in, and love my country retreat? You are too much a "city slicker" if you do not yearn for it. I wish you did! I could then add the very great pleasure of your company to the many fine attractions of my little villa.

[69] *Saturnalia:* a festival in honor of the god Saturn. Its official date was December 17, and it was a time for revelry and good cheer. See selections 376 and 377.

[70] In the city of Rome, some homeowners were allowed to run pipes from the aqueducts into their homes and thus to have running water; see note 28 of this chapter.

[71] *Ostia:* the harbor or port of ancient Rome. Even today it is a popular seaside resort. It is only a few miles from Rome and accessible by public transportation; on Sundays its beaches are crowded with modern Romans.

[72] Consider the popularity of bathing among the Romans; a small country village could support three public baths.

V

Domestic and Personal Concerns

MEALS

Most Romans apparently took three meals a day, although we know very little about their breakfasts or lunches. In the passage below which describes a schoolboy's day, the boy has a light lunch of bread, olives, cheese, dried figs, and nuts.[1] The main meal of the day was taken in the early evening; Martial says dinnertime was the ninth hour, which would, in fact, be the late afternoon.[2] Dining customs and menus varied considerably, of course, depending on whether you were poor or rich, and whether you were dining alone or with guests. The upper class reclined on couches during dinner.[3] It is unlikely, however, that the poor had enough space in their cramped apartments for dining couches. They probably sat on chairs or stools. And while the wealthy preferred to dine outdoors in their private garden areas[4] when the weather was fine, the poor were restricted to their stuffy rented quarters. There was also a wide variation in the type of food eaten by people of different classes. Wheat was the main item in the diet of a poor Roman. Gaius Gracchus's legislation of 122 B.C. made the price of grain artificially low; Publius Clodius's legislation of 58 B.C. made free grain available to those who were eligible for the "grain dole."[5] The poorest Romans ate little other than wheat, either crushed and boiled with water to make porridge or *puls*,[6] or ground into flour and baked as bread—if they were lucky enough to have an oven available. Boiling was probably more common than baking because few poor people would have their own oven.[7] Boiled wheat or bread was not a side dish, as it is today; for many Romans it was frequently their only dish. We have already read about some of

[1] See selection 131.
[2] See selection 146.
[3] See note 61 of Chapter III.
[4] *garden area:* peristyle; see selection 68.
[5] On the legislation of Gaius Gracchus and Clodius, see the introduction to selection 153. On Clodius's sister, Clodia, see selections 64 and 65.
[6] *puls:* This boiled wheat dish would be similar to cream of wheat cereal, grits, or couscous. Scholarly opinion is divided on the question of whether the ancient Romans made pasta noodles.
[7] On breadmaking, see selection 174. Bread could be purchased at bakeries if you did not have an oven to bake your own. Perhaps some neighborhoods had communal ovens.

the other food items eaten by the poor: beans, leeks, and sheep lips.[8] The wealthy, of course, could afford a wide variety of meats, vegetables, cheeses, and fruits, and the slaves to cook and serve them.[9] Wine was the most common drink; poor people drank cheap wine or vinegar. Both the wine and the vinegar were mixed with water before drinking it; only at the most intemperate of parties was wine drunk straight.

A Peasant's Dinner

The following passage is taken from Ovid's long poem, *Metamorphoses,* in which he describes various mythological metamorphoses or transformations. For example, one day Jupiter and Mercury decided to find out how hospitable the people of Phrygia, a country of Asia Minor, were. They disguised themselves as needy travelers and wandered through Phrygia, knocking on doors and asking people to give them food and shelter. Again and again they were refused help. Finally they came to a tiny hovel in which lived a very poor old couple, Philemon and Baucis. But these two, though they had barely enough food for themselves, welcomed warmly the needy travelers at their door and prepared for them a dinner that was lavish by their own modest standards but would seem humble to Ovid's readers. Jupiter and Mercury were so pleased that they cast aside their disguises and revealed themselves as gods. They promised to grant the generous old couple any wish. And the couple's wish was that they die together, so that neither one would have to live alone. The gods agreed, and when their time of death was near, Philemon and Baucis were, at the same moment, transformed into trees, in which form they lived on together forever.

88   Ovid, *Metamorphoses* 8.630–634, 646–650, 664–668, 674–678

In a tiny cottage thatched with straw and marsh reeds lived Baucis, a god-fearing old woman, and Philemon, her husband, her equal in age and piety. They had been married in that very cottage when they were young, and they grew old together in that cottage, making their poverty easier to bear by accepting it without complaint or bitterness. . . .

Baucis stripped off the outer leaves of a cabbage which her husband had picked from their well-watered garden. Philemon reached up with a forked stick and retrieved a side of smoky pork hanging from a sooty beam.[10] He cut off a small piece of the meat, which they had been preserving for so long,[11] and put it in boiling water. . . . Baucis put on the table both green and black olives, and cornel-berries picked in autumn and preserved in dregs of wine, and endive and radishes, and cheese, and eggs cooked gently over a low flame. Everything was served in earthenware bowls. . . . For dessert there were nuts, figs, and wrinkled dates, and plums, and sweet-smelling ap-

---

[8] See selection 81. In selection 184, Cato suggests that slaves be given the following food items: wheat or bread, figs, discarded olives and the dregs of fish-sauce.

[9] On food prices in the fourth century A.D., see selection 152.

[10] The pork was hung from a beam (1) for storage in the cramped hovel, and (2) to be smoked.

[11] *preserving:* saving for special occasions. Philemon and Baucis were poor and could seldom afford to eat meat.

ples in a wide basket, and fresh-picked purple grapes. In the center of the table was a shiny honeycomb. And beside the table beamed the kindly faces of the old couple who were wealthy and generous with their good will.

A Modest Dinner

Invitations to dinner were evidently a minor literary genre. Martial wrote a number of poems which include not only the invitation but also the menu and a description of the after-dinner entertainment. These poems therefore provide valuable information about the foods which the Romans ate. Usually both the menu and the entertainment mentioned by Martial are quite modest, although far better than what the poorest Roman could afford.[12]

89   Martial, *Epigrams* 5.78

If you are worried about a lonely dinner at home, Toranius, you can come share your hunger with me. If you are accustomed to an appetizer, you won't be disappointed; there will be cheap Cappadocian lettuce and strong leeks and tuna fish garnished with sliced eggs.[13] Then a fresh, green cabbage which has just left the cool garden will be served in a black dish (you must pick it up with scorched fingers).[14] We will also have a small sausage served on a bed of white grits,[15] and pale beans with red bacon.[16] If you want the delights of dessert,[17] you will be offered shriveled grapes and Syrian pears and Neapolitan chestnuts roasted in a slow heat. The wine you will make good by drinking. After dinner, if further drinking should perhaps stir your appetite, as it frequently does, you will be nourished by tasty olives which Picene[18] branches recently produced and hot chickpeas and warm lupines. This is a humble little dinner—who can deny it?—but you will neither say nor hear a dishonest word and you will recline relaxed and at ease.[19] Your host won't read to you from a thick and dull book,[20] nor will lasciv-

[12] Although Martial complains frequently about his "poverty," he was fortunate enough to own a country villa; see selection 82.

[13] The appetizer course of a Roman dinner (the *gustatio* or *promulsis*) consisted of raw vegetables and often fish and egg dishes. Eggs were so commonly served at the *gustatio* that the Latin expression which describes a many-course dinner and corresponds to our phrase "from soup to nuts" is *ab ovo usque ad mala*, "from the egg to the apples."

[14] The second course (called *prima mensa* or "first table") consisted usually of cooked vegetables and meats. Thus the cabbage is hot and scorches the fingers when picked up.

[15] grits: *puls;* see note 6 of this chapter.

[16] Martial apparently believed that attractive color combinations made food more appealing.

[17] *dessert: secunda mensa* = "second table."

[18] *Picene:* a district of central Italy on the Adriatic coast. On the price of Picene wine, see selection 152.

[19] Except with the very best of friends, one could not be too cautious in social conversations during the imperial period. The emperors did not like criticism, and their spies were everywhere; see selections 91 and 247. In addition, one would not want to risk offending people who might be of use to you in the future. Behavior at many Roman parties must have been no less artificial than behavior at the modern cocktail party. See Pliny (selection 169), who enjoyed his country villa because it removed him from social posturing and political obligations.

[20] *book:* Latin *volumen* = "roll of papyrus." Some hosts entertained guests by reading aloud from their own writings; see selection 320.

ious girls from lewd Gades wiggle their hips with skillfully obscene swaying.[21] I will provide entertainment which is neither serious nor frivolous: you will hear the music of a small flute. Such will be my little dinner party.

A Dinner Invitation

90   Martial, *Epigrams* 11.52

You will dine well, Julius Cerialis, at my house. If you have no better invitation, come on over. You will be able to spend the eighth hour as usual.[22] Indeed we will bathe together; you know how close to my house the baths of Stephanus are. The first course[23] will be lettuce (a useful digestive aid[24]), and tender shoots cut from leek plants, and then a pickled young tuna which is larger than a small lizard fish[25] and will be garnished with eggs and rue leaves. And there will be more eggs, these cooked over a low flame, and cheese from Velabrum Street,[26] and olives which have felt the Picene cold.[27] That's enough for the appetizers. You want to know what else we are having? I'll lie, so that you will be sure to come. Fish, oysters, sow's udder, stuffed wild fowl and barnyard hens which even Stella[28] does not usually serve except at rare and special dinners. And I promise you more: I will not recite to you,[29] even if you read aloud to me your whole *Giants,* or your *Pastorals* which rank next to those of immortal Vergil.[30]

A Rejected Host

In the letter below, Pliny pretends to be very angry at Septicius, who accepted an invitation to dinner but did not come. Pliny playfully threatens to charge Septicius for the cost of the dinner, and thus itemizes each dish. He accuses his friend of having been lured away from his company by the prospect of more expensive and exquisite food and more exotic entertainment.

91   Pliny the Younger, *Letters* 1.15

So! You promise to come to dinner, and then you don't come! You will be tried and fined the full cost of the dinner, and not a penny less. My kitchen staff had prepared

---

[21] The dancers from Gades (modern Cadiz in Spain) are meant to represent a type of entertainment which is the total opposite of learned readings.

[22] *As usual:* i.e., at the baths; see selections 146 and 308.

[23] *first course: gustatio;* see note 13 of this chapter.

[24] The Romans considered lettuce a mild laxative.

[25] *lizard fish:* Latin *lacertus,* some type of saltwater fish.

[26] *Velabrum Street:* a street in Rome on the Aventine Hill.

[27] *Picene:* see note 18 of this chapter.

[28] The identity of Stella is unknown.

[29] On recitations, see selection 89.

[30] Cerialis is apparently the author of two books of poetry: *Giants,* perhaps an epic poem, and *Pastorals,* a collection of poems with pastoral themes; on pastoral themes, see the introduction to selection 175. Vergil wrote both epic and pastoral poetry (see Appendix I).

one head of lettuce for each of us, three snails and two eggs each, barley soup along with mead[31] and snow[32] (you'll pay for the snow first, although it melted right in the dish), olives, beets, cucumbers, onions, and a thousand other items no less sumptuous.[33] You would have heard comic actors or a reader or a lute player or, such is my generosity, all of them.[34] But you preferred the oysters, sow's wombs,[35] sea urchins, and dancers from Gades[36] at someone else's house. You will pay for this, though I haven't decided how. You behaved badly and spitefully to me and even to yourself. How much we could have joked and laughed and learned![37] You can dine more splendidly at the homes of many other men, but not with more cheerfulness, more frankness, and less caution[38] than at my home. So, in conclusion, at least try a dinner at my house. Then, in the future, if you prefer to dine with others, well, keep making your excuses to me.

Recipe for Fish Sauce

Cookbooks were available for Roman cooks who wanted to try new recipes or learn old ones. One of the most popular ingredients in Roman cooking was a fish sauce called *garum* or somtimes *liquamen*. It was so popular, in fact, that large amounts were shipped to Roman governors, staff members, businessmen, and soldiers in the provinces and thus introduced to the provincials. Its popularity apparently even spread beyond the borders of the empire. Rumor has it that Worcestershire sauce is a descendant of garum which was exported to India in the Roman period, and that British governors and staff members in India in the nineteenth century enjoyed it so much that they introduced it to Britain, or rather reintroduced it, since the Romans had probably carried it to Britain 1800 years earlier. Today Lea and Perrins, manufacturers of Worcestershire sauce, list anchovies as an ingredient. At any rate, garum was a favorite Roman sauce, and garum manufacture became a major industry in towns near the sea. Garum factories have been discovered, for example, at Pompeii. You could buy a jar of readymade garum, but if you wished to make your own, recipes were certainly available.[39]

92   *Geoponica* 20.46.1–5

Garum, also called liquamen, is made in this way. The entrails of fish are placed in a vat and salted. Also used are whole small fish, especially smelts, or tiny mullets, or

---

[31] *mead: mulsum,* wine mixed with honey.

[32] Wealthy Romans used snow, brought down from the mountains, to cool their wine.

[33] *sumptuous:* ironic, since the food which Pliny mentions is quite modest.

[34] After-dinner entertainment consisted of slaves reciting a scene from a comedy or reading poetry aloud.

[35] Sow's wombs were considered a delicacy. See Martial's list of delicacies in selection 90. The Romans wasted very few parts of any animal they slaughtered.

[36] *dancers from Gades:* see selection 89.

[37] *learned:* Pliny had a puritanical, but traditionally Roman, streak in him. He thought he and his guests should be edified by the entertainment and by their dinner conversation. See his remarks on recitations (selection 319) and on chariot racing (selection 348).

[38] On the need for caution at dinner parties, see note 19 of this chapter.

[39] For the fourth century A.D. prices of fish sauce, see selection 152.

small sprats, or anchovies, or whatever small fish are available. Salt the whole mixture and place it in the sun. After it has aged in the heat, the garum is extracted in the following manner. A long, thickly woven basket is placed into the vat full of the above-mentioned fish. The garum enters the basket, and the so-called liquamen is thus strained through the basket and retrieved. The remaining sediment is allec.[40]

The Bithynians make garum in the following manner. They use sprats, large or small, which are the best to use if available. If sprats are not available, they use anchovies, or lizard fish or mackerel, or even old allec, or a mixture of all of these. They put this in a trough which is usually used for kneading dough. They add two Italian sextarii of salt to each modius of fish[41] and stir well so that the fish and salt are thoroughly mixed. They let the mixture sit for one night and then transfer it to a clay vat which is placed uncovered in the sun for two or three months, stirring it occasionally with sticks. Then they bottle, seal, and store it. Some people also pour two sextarii of old wine into each sextarius of fish.

If, however, you wish to use the garum at once, do not leave it in the sun, but rather cook it in the following manner. Take some brine which has been strained and refined, and test it by putting an egg into it to see if it floats; if the egg sinks, the brine does not contain enough salt. Put the fish into the brine in a new pot, add wild marjoram, and put it over a moderate flame until it boils, that is, until it begins to thicken a bit. Some people also add sapa.[42] After it has cooled, strain it again and again and again until it runs clear. Store in a sealed jar.

Numidian Chicken

Ancient Roman cooking differed from the cooking of modern Italy. Many of the ancient recipes include fruit, honey, and vinegar, and the cooked dishes must therefore have had a sweet-and-sour flavor. Liquamen is also an ingredient in most of the recipes; it is not certain, however, whether liquamen was the pungent fish sauce of the last passage used full-strength, a watered-down version of the fish sauce, or a general term for stock, broth, or other cooking liquid. The author or authors of the cookbook from which the following recipes are taken did not, unfortunately, give measurements. If you are willing to experiment, however, it is possible to use these recipes to produce some delicious dishes.

93   Apicius, *Cookbook* 6.9.4

Clean the chicken, poach it, and then remove it from the water. Sprinkle with assafoetida[43] and pepper, and broil it. Grind together pepper, cumin, coriander seed, assafoetida root, rue, dates, and nuts. Pour over these vinegar, honey, liquamen, and olive oil. Stir. When it boils, add starch as a binder. Pour this mixture over the chicken. Sprinkle with pepper and serve.

[40] *allec:* also spelled *alec* or *halec.*
[41] *sextarii, modius:* see selection 152.
[42] *sapa:* must (new wine) or grape juice boiled until thick.
[43] *assafoetida:* a spice used today in North African and Middle Eastern cooking.

Rabbit with Fruit Sauce

94

Apicius, *Cookbook* 8.8.13

Cook the rabbit in wine, liquamen, and water, with a little bit of mustard, anise, and a whole leek. When the rabbit is done, prepare this sauce: pepper, savory, onion ring, dates, two damson plums, wine, liquamen, caroenum,[44] and a small amount of olive oil. Thicken with starch and allow the mixture to boil for a short time. Pour this fruit sauce over the rabbit in a serving dish.

Liver Sausage

95

Apicius, *Cookbook* 2.1.4

Grind together pepper, rue, and liquamen. Grill pork liver, and cut into bits. Combine the liver and spices, grind together, and mix well. Stuff the mixture into casings. Place one bay leaf in the center of each sausage. Hang the sausages to smoke for as long as you wish.[45] When you want to eat them, remove them from the smoke and grill them again.

Anchovy Delight without the Anchovies

96

Apicius, *Cookbook* 4.2.12

Take as many fillets of grilled or poached fish as you need to fill a dish of whatever size you want. Grind together pepper and a little bit of rue. Pour over these a sufficient amount of liquamen and a little bit of olive oil. Add this mixture to the dish of fish fillets, and stir. Fold in raw eggs to bind the mixture together. Gently place on the top of the mixture sea nettles,[46] taking care that they do not combine with the eggs. Set the dish over steam in such a way that the sea nettles do not mix with the eggs. When they are dry, sprinkle with ground pepper and serve. No one at the table will know what he is eating.

Sweet and Sour Pork

97

Apicius, *Cookbook* 4.3.6

Put in a pot olive oil, liquamen, and wine. Chop a dried shallot. Dice cooked pork shoulder. Add these ingredients to the pot. When this mixture has been well heated, grind together pepper, cumin, dried mint, and anise. Pour over them honey, liquamen, passum,[47] a little vinegar, and juice from the meat mixture. Combine the spices with

---

[44] *caroenum:* like sapa, a reduced wine, but less reduced than sapa.
[45] On smoking meat, see selection 88.
[46] *sea nettles:* Latin *urticae marinae;* perhaps jellyfish.
[47] *passum:* a sweet cooking wine or raisin wine.

the meat. Add fruit from which the pits and seeds have been removed, bring the mixture to a boil, and heat thoroughly. Crumble pastry over the mixture to bind it. Sprinkle with pepper and serve.

ILLNESS

The Romans were subject to most of the same illnesses and ailments which afflict us today. Their medical care, however, was far inferior, and diseases or conditions which are minor problems today were often life-threatening to the Romans. We cannot list here every sickness or disorder known to the Romans; the two passages which follow, however, inform us of personal reactions to illnesses, one temporary and one chronic.

Dysentery

98   Cicero, *Correspondence with Family and Friends* 7.26

For ten days now[48] I have been suffering from severe intestinal pains. I could not, however, convince those who wanted to avail themselves of my services that I was really ill, because I didn't have a fever, and so I have retreated from Rome to my Tusculan villa.[49] For two days I have fasted so completely that I have not even drunk water. I am worn out by my weakness and hunger. . . . It was at the Augural Banquet at Lentulus's house[50] that such a severe attack of diarrhea seized me that only today has the illness seemed to begin its remission. Ironically, I, who easily abstained from oysters and lampreys, was deceived by a beet and a mallow.[51] And so, from now on, I'll be more careful.

Since you had heard about my illness from Anicius (for he actually saw me vomiting), you had good reason not only to send a message but even to come and visit.[52] I think I will remain here at my villa until I've recovered, because I've lost strength and weight. But if I can shake this disease, I'll easily, I hope, get back my strength and weight.

[48] This letter was written in December, 57 B.C., to Marcus Fadius Gallus.

[49] Cicero had a villa near the town of Tusculum; see selection 16. In Rome, he was continually disturbed by clients.

[50] In 57 B.C. the son of Cicero's friend Publius Cornelius Lentulus Spinther had just been made augur. His father was celebrating the occasion with a banquet. Augurs were officials of the state religion; on their functions, see selection 368.

[51] Cicero had been careful to avoid the rich seafood, thinking that simple foods like beets and mallows would be harmless.

[52] Gallus had evidently tried to visit Cicero at his house in Rome but discovered that Cicero had gone to Tusculum.

Asthma

99   Seneca the Younger, *Letters* 54.1–4, 6, 7

Ill health had not disturbed me for a long time, but suddenly it has attacked me again.
"What kind of illness?" you ask. And well you may ask! There is really no illness unknown to me. However, I have been marked out, as it were, for one illness in particular. I see no reason to call it by its Greek name;[53] it can be adequately described as
"labored breathing." The attack is very brief, like a squall. Within an hour it has usually
passed. For who could keep drawing his last breath for long?[54] Every physical pain or
life-threatening ailment has visited my body, but none seems to me more distressing
than this. For with other ailments you are sick, but with this one you are losing your
soul's breath. And for this reason doctors call asthma a "rehearsal for death," because
sooner or later that breath does just what it has often tried to do.[55] Do you think that
I am elated to be writing this to you, since this time I have escaped death? I would be
foolish to rejoice and equate the end of an asthma attack with perfect good health, as
foolish as a man who thought he had won a legal case when he had only postponed the
day of trial. . . . Little by little this labored breathing, which had now become pant-
ing, came on at longer intervals, and slowed down, and finally abated. But, although it
has abated, my breathing does not flow naturally. I feel a certain hesitation and obstruction. Let it do as it wishes, as long as I don't really gasp for breath. But take my word
for it: I will not be afraid when the final moment comes; I am prepared now,[56] and do
not plan anything a full day ahead. Learn to praise and emulate the man[57] who enjoys
life but is not reluctant to die. For where is the virtue in leaving[58] when you are being
kicked out anyway? And yet there is some virtue in my situation: I am indeed being
kicked out, but I am leaving willingly. Of course, the truly wise man is never in the
position of being kicked out, because that would imply that he is being expelled from
a place which he leaves unwillingly. But the truly wise man does nothing unwillingly.
He escapes necessity because he chooses to do, of his free will, whatever necessity would
later force him to do.[59]

[53] The Greek word is *asthma*.

[54] It is so difficult for the asthmatic person to draw a breath that he feels each breath
may be his last.

[55] *What it has often tried to do:* i.e., leaves the body for good.

[56] Seneca believed that his asthma attacks, which brought him to the brink of death, had
prepared him to meet death without fear. He had rehearsed death. On Stoic preparation, see
selections 424 and 425.

[57] *the man:* not Seneca himself, but the perfect wise man, the model for Stoics.

[58] *leaving:* i.e., life.

[59] The Stoic concept of free will sees the truly wise man as so in harmony with the fate
of the universe that he chooses freely and willingly to do what fate (*i.e.,* necessity) had
planned for him to do; see selection 420. He cannot be kicked out of life because he leaves
life willingly. The Stoics explained the relationship between man's fate and free will in the
following way. A dog on a leash will be moved from point A to point B. This is fate. He may
choose to walk happily and comfortably from A to B, not even noticing the leash; this is free
will. Or the dog may resist and struggle, but he will then be dragged from A to B. By resisting
fate, dog—or man—causes his own suffering and pain.

MEDICAL TREATMENTS

We have already learned a little about Roman medical theory and practice in the sections dealing with fertility, contraception, and abortion.[60] The following recommended medical treatments are taken from a book which was written by a man interested in natural science rather than by a medical practitioner.

Jaundice

100   Pliny the Elder, *Natural History* 28.64 (227)

A cure for jaundice: use the ashes of a deer's antlers, the blood of an ass diluted with wine, or the first manure excreted by an ass foal after its birth, in a quantity the size of a bean, mixed with wine. This potion cures the disease within three days. (The manure of a horse foal is similarly effective.)

Broken Bones

101   Pliny the Elder, *Natural History* 29.65 (227)

A quick remedy for broken bones: the ashes of the jawbone of a boar or pig. Or lard boiled and then packed around the broken bone mends it with amazing rapidity. For fractures of the ribs, goat's manure mixed in wine is particularly recommended.[61]

Strains and Bruises

102   Pliny the Elder, *Natural History* 28.72 (237, 238)

Strains and injuries received from a blow are treated with wild boar's manure which has been collected in the springtime and dried. This same treatment works for chariot drivers who have been dragged or run over or badly bruised in any way,[62] even if the manure is smeared on while still fresh. Some people think that it is more useful to boil the manure in vinegar. They claim also that this manure can heal ruptures and sprains, if it is ground to a powder and mixed in a drink, or dislocations if it is mixed with vinegar. Quite respectable people drink the powder mixed with water, and they say that the emperor Nero used to refresh himself with this drink because he wanted to prove to the professional horsemen that he was a real chariot driver.[63]

---

[60] Selections 23 and 27–30. See also selections 296 and 297 for medical theory on the causes, symptoms, and cures of hysteria.

[61] See selection 408 on another remedy for fractures.

[62] On the hazards of chariot racing, see selections 346 and 350.

[63] On Nero's success as a chariot driver, see note 190 of Chapter XIV.

DOCTORS

Our knowledge about illnesses and injuries has increased dramatically in the last hundred years, and so, correspondingly, has our ability to treat successfully the various scourges of mankind. Through most of his history, however, man has been much less successful in his medical treatments. Because cure rates were low, many people in Roman society were skeptical or even scornful of doctors. And their skepticism is easily understood. There were no licensing boards and no formal requirements for entrance to the profession. Anyone could call himself a doctor. If his methods were successful, he attracted more patients; if unsuccessful—well, his patients died and he found himself another occupation! Many doctors were freedmen,[64] and the social standing of doctors was quite low.[65] Certainly there existed skillful, sympathetic, and conscientious doctors who worked very hard to diagnose and cure illnesses, but there surely also existed numerous quacks.

Medical Training

Some men "trained" as doctors by following around another doctor, such as Symmachus.

103   Martial, *Epigrams* 5.9

I felt a little ill and called Dr. Symmachus. Well, you came, Symmachus, but you brought 100 medical students with you. One hundred ice-cold hands poked and jabbed me. I didn't have a fever, Symmachus, when I called you—but now I do.

Change of Profession

104   Martial, *Epigrams* 1.47

Until recently, Diaulus was a doctor; now he is an undertaker. He is still doing, as an undertaker, what he used to do as a doctor.

105   Martial, *Epigrams* 8.74

You are now a gladiator, although until recently you were an ophthalmologist. You did the same thing as a doctor that you now do as a gladiator.

---

[64] See selection 224 on the freedman who became a physician, surgeon, and oculist.
[65] See selection 147.

Distrust of Doctors

In this passage Pliny the Elder, who reported the cures for jaundice and bone fractures which were translated above, expresses his distrust of the Greek attitude toward medicine, an attitude which he feared the Romans were adopting.

106   Pliny the Elder, *Natural History* 29.8.16–18

Our ancestors did not condemn the act of healing, but rather the pursuit of medicine as a profession; in particular they refused to believe that a profit should be made from saving lives.[66] . . . Of all the Greek sciences, only medicine has not yet gained wide interest among us sober and serious-minded Romans.[67] Very few of our citizens are attracted even by its considerable monetary rewards, and those who are immediately begin to act like Greeks.[68] In fact, medical writers, unless they write in Greek, are not accepted as authorities even by the ignorant or by those who do not know Greek. Indeed, people tend to trust advice about their own health less if they understand the language in which it is spoken.[69] Medicine is the only profession, by Jove, where any man off the street gains our immediate trust if he professes to be a doctor; and yet surely no lie would be more dangerous. But we don't worry about that; each one of us is lulled by the sweet hope of being healed. And we don't even have laws against the ignorance which endangers our lives. Doctors risk our lives while they are learning; their experiments lead to deaths; and yet for doctors, and only doctors, there is no penalty for killing a man. In fact, they pass on the blame, reproach the deceased for his lack of moderation and his self-indulgence!

Midwives

The passage translated here, on the qualities of a good midwife, offers us quite a different, certainly more favorable view of the type of medical treatment available to the Romans.

[66] Compare this with the Roman attitude toward law and politics, that those who had the advantages of an education were obligated to help those less fortunate but to receive no monetary payment; see the introduction to selection 147.

[67] *sober and serious-minded Romans:* i.e., Romans who emulated the respected and traditional patterns of behavior. On the Roman character, see selection 1, the introduction to selection 334 and the introduction to the section on agriculture in Chapter VII.

[68] Although the Romans respected the Greeks of fifth-century Athens, they despised the Greeks of their own period, whom they considered degenerate. Much of the Roman prejudice against freedmen arose from the fear that these "foreigners" would destroy the moral fiber of the Roman people, that they would, for example, convince the Roman people that it was not wrong to charge money for saving a life. See selections 81, 209–212, and 228.

[69] And today, ironically, doctors impress people by using Latin words and phrases. And prescriptions, of course, are written in Latin. What would Pliny think of this use of his native language?

107 Soranus, *Gynecology* 1.2.4

It is necessary to discuss the qualities found in the best midwives, not only so that the best may recognize themselves, but also so that students of midwifery may look at them as models and so that the public may know whom to call when there is need. . . . We label someone "the best midwife" if she is knowledgeable about theory in addition to handling actual cases, and particularly if she is trained in all branches of therapy (for some cases require special diet, some require surgery, some must be treated with drugs) and is able to prescribe hygienic rules, to observe both general and individual symptoms, and to discover from them what needs to be done. . . . She will be calm and unruffled in crises, and able to give a clear account of the procedures she is using. She will provide reassurance to her patients and will be sympathetic. . . . She will be prudent and always sober, since she is never sure when she will be summoned to a woman in danger. She will be discreet since she will share in many secrets of life. . . . She will not be superstitious and will not overlook a possible remedy because of a dream or an omen or a ritual or a vulgar superstition.

LIFE EXPECTANCY

It is not difficult to find examples from Roman history of people who lived to an advanced old age. Cato the Elder was eighty-five years old when he died. Augustus, Rome's first emperor, lived for seventy-six years, his wife Livia for eighty-six years. Tiberius, Livia's son and Rome's second emperor, died in his seventy-ninth year. Yet such statistics can be misleading because the longevity of these people was unusual. Most people in Roman society could not expect to live this long. Not only was the rate of mortality in infants and children high,[70] but many people died while in their twenties and thirties, a period which we now consider the prime of life.[71] It is important to consider what effect this brevity of life had on Roman society. For example, a Roman could expect to die at an age when we today expect to begin our adult lives. Yet adult life began much earlier for a Roman, who might have a job, a spouse, and even children when still a teenager.[72] A person in his or her early thirties might well be a grandparent. On the other hand, the high incidence of death among young adults also meant that few children would know their grandparents, many children would be orphans,[73] and some people would outlive two or three spouses.[74] Most of our information about mortality rates in ancient

[70] See selection 25 for the record of the infant who died at age one year, six months, and twenty-five days.

[71] Consider, for example, Tullia who died at thirty (selection 16), Tertius who died at 31 (selection 21), and Malius Firminus who died at twenty-four years of age (selection 22). See also selections 284, 300, and 301 for records of women who died when thirteen, nineteen, and twenty.

[72] Consider the example of a woman who was married at eleven, bore six children (only one survived), and died at age twenty-seven (selection 286).

[73] On the fate of orphans, see selection 45.

[74] Many children therefore had stepparents and stepbrothers and sisters.

Roman society comes from epitaphs. The following inscriptions were found at Rome.

Lutatia Secundina

108   *CIL* 6.21738

Lutatia Secundina, a very sweet child, lived four years, six months, and nine days.

Magnilla

109   *CIL* 6.21846

O serene peace of the inhabitants of the underworld and you renowned spirits of the pious who dwell in the sacred areas of Erebus,[75] conduct innocent Magnilla through the groves and the Elysian fields directly to your resting places. She was snatched away in her eighth year by the importunate fates while she was enjoying the time of tender youth. She was beautiful and sensitive, and clever, elegant, sweet, and charming far beyond her years. This unfortunate child who was deprived of her life so quickly must be mourned with perpetual lament and tears.

Mercurius

110   *CIL* 6.22417

Mercurius lived twenty-five years, six months, twenty days, and four hours. His very loving brother and his mistress Julia provided this memorial for him because he was well deserving.

DEATH

Cicero's Grief

Grief is a universal emotion; the ancient Romans felt the same wrenching pain of bereavement that we do. We earlier read a letter which Cicero wrote to Atticus about the desolation and despair he experienced as a result of the death of his daughter Tullia.[76] Another of his letters to Atticus, written about one month after her death in 45 B.C., is translated here.

[75] *Erebus:* a name for the underworld. Erebus was a god of darkness, the son of Chaos and the brother of Night. See note 91 of this chapter.
[76] See selection 16.

111   Cicero, *Letters to Atticus* 12.15

I have isolated myself, in this lonely region, from all human conversation. In the morning I hide myself in the dense, impenetrable forest and don't emerge until nightfall. Next to you, solitude is my best friend. My only form of communication now is through books, but even my reading is interrupted by fits of weeping. I resist as best I can these urges to cry, but I am not yet strong enough. I will, however, write to Brutus as you urge. You will have this letter tomorrow.

Condolences

The letter translated here is one of many letters of condolence which Cicero received from his friends after the death of Tullia. The writer of this letter was Servius Sulpicius Rufus, a man of senatorial rank who achieved prominence as a jurist and orator. Letters of condolence formed a minor literary genre,[77] and Sulpicius's letter displays a studied elegance of composition and thought. This careful attention to style does not, however, detract from the sincerity of the letter. Sulpicius was truly grieved by Tullia's death and by the sorrow which it brought to Cicero, and he tried to alleviate some of his friend's suffering.

112   Cicero, *Correspondence with Family and Friends* 4.5.1, 4–6

After I received the message about the death of your daughter Tullia, I was, as surely I ought to have been, deeply and painfully overwhelmed by grief, and I felt that this misfortune had struck me as well as you. If I had been in Rome,[78] I would have come to you and made my grief known to you in person. This type of condolence is, of course, painful and bitter because those very people who must offer it are relatives and friends, who are themselves suffering the same distress and cannot attempt any condolence without many tears. The result is, in fact, that they themselves seem to need the condolences of others more than they seem able to offer their services to others. Nevertheless, I have decided to write to you a brief account of the thoughts which have come to my mind at this time, not because I think that such thoughts are unknown to you, but because you may perhaps be less conscious of them now that you are struggling with your grief. . . .

I want to tell you something which brought me no small comfort; perhaps this same thought can lessen your grief. When I was returning from Asia,[79] sailing from Aegina toward Megara, I began to look at the regions all around me. Behind me was Aegina, in front was Megara, on the right Piraeus, on the left Corinth.[80] These were once flourishing towns, but now they lay lifeless and ruined before my eyes. I began to think to myself: "Ah! Are we little men, whose lives are necessarily too brief, indig-

---

[77] *condolence:* Latin *consolatio;* the Latin verb *consolari* means "to comfort," "to soothe."
[78] Sulpicius wrote this letter in Athens in March, 45 B.C. He was the governor of Greece, which had become a Roman province.
[79] *Asia:* the Roman province of Asia.
[80] *Aegina, Megara, Piraeus, Corinth:* see map 4.

nant if one of us dies or is killed, when in one place so many corpses of towns lie abandoned? Please pull yourself together, Servius, and remember that you were born a mortal man." Believe me, I was strengthened considerably by this thought. If it seems to you wise, please put this same image before your eyes. Just a short time ago, so many illustrious men perished, so serious a weakening of the power of the Roman state took place, all our provinces were shaken to their very foundations;[81] are you moved by such deep sorrow if we lose the frail little soul of one frail little woman? Even if she had not died at this time, she must nevertheless have died a few years from now because she was born a mortal. Take your mind and your thoughts away from these things and reflect instead on things which are worthy of the person that you are. Consider, for example, that she lived as long as it was necessary, that is, she lived while the republic lived.[82] She saw you, her father, a praetor, then a consul, and an augur;[83] she was married to men from noble families;[84] she enjoyed almost all of life's blessings. And she departed from life when the republic died. How, then, can you or she complain about fate on this account?

Do not, in short, forget that you are Cicero, a man who was accustomed to counsel others and to give advice. Don't act like a bad doctor who professes to have medical knowledge about other people's ailments but is unable to cure himself. Instead, bring to your own attention and place before your mind that advice which you are accustomed to offer to others. There is no grief which the passage of time does not lessen or soften; but it is unworthy of you to wait for the time to pass rather than anticipating this result with your own good sense. And if any consciousness remains in those who have gone below,[85] her love for you and her devotion[86] to all her family were such that she certainly does not wish you to behave like this. Yield to her, though she is dead, yield to others, your friends and family, who sorrow because of your grief, yield to your fatherland so that, if need arises, it can use your service and counsel. . . .

I am embarrassed to write more to you about this matter lest I seem to lack confidence in your good sense. I will therefore end my letter by making this one proposal. We have, on a number of occasions, seen you sustain good fortune very decorously and thereby gain great glory. Now act in such a way that we may know that you can also sustain bad fortune just as decorously and that it does not seem to you a greater burden than it should be, lest you, who are endowed with all fine qualities, appear to lack this one.

As for me, I will inform you about what is going on here and about the condition of the province[87] whenever I learn that you have achieved more peace of mind.

[81] Sulpicius is referring to the civil war. In 49 B.C. Julius Caesar led his army against his former ally, Pompey, and many of the aristocrats of the Roman state. Pompey and his supporters (Cicero was one of them) claimed to be fighting for the very existence of the republic, although in truth they were fighting to maintain the power of the Roman aristocracy (see note 24 of Chapter I). After Caesar defeated the army of Pompey, he tried to establish an autocratic system of government, but was assassinated in 44 B.C. by aristocrats who, understandably, did not wish to lose their power.

[82] the republic: on the meaning of this word, see note 23 of Chapter I. When Cicero and Sulpicius lament the death of the republic, they are really lamenting the death of the aristocracy and the reappearance of a monarchy (or imperial government).

[83] Cicero was praetor in 66 B.C. and consul in 63 B.C.

[84] Tullia was married three times; see selection 16.

[85] gone below: i.e., to the underworld; see note 91 of this chapter.

[86] devotion: Latin pietas; see the introduction to selection 1.

[87] province: i.e., Greece; see note 78 of this chapter.

FUNERARY LAWS AND FUNERALS

Funerary Laws

113 *FIRA* 2, pp. 334, 335 (Paulus *Opinions* 1.21.2–5, 8–14)

One is not allowed to bring a corpse into the city lest the sacred places in the city be polluted. Whoever acts contrary to these restrictions is punished with unusual severity.

One is not allowed to bury or cremate a body within the walls of the city.

Whoever strips or exposes to the rays of the sun a body entrusted to permanent burial or left for a short period of time in some place, commits sacrilege. And therefore if he is *honestior* he is usually sent to an island; if he is *humilior* he is usually sent to the mines.[88]

Whoever vandalizes a sepulcher or takes something from a sepulcher is, according to his social rank, either sent to the mines or exiled to an island. . . .

Whoever erases a tombstone inscription or knocks down a statue or removes anything from that place, such as a stone or a column, is viewed as having vandalized the sepulcher.

In a sarcophagus or grave where a body has already been deposited, one is not allowed to put another body. Whoever does so can be prosecuted for violation of a sepulcher.

Whoever buries someone and incurs some expense for this burial can demand reimbursement from the heir or the father or the master.

A husband can retain from his wife's dowry the amount which he spent on her funeral.[89]

It is forbidden to place a dwelling right next to a sepulcher or above it, for such close human contact is considered a sacrilege. Whoever acts contrary to these restrictions is punished, according to his social rank, either by public labor or by exile.

Parents and children over six years of age can be mourned for a year, children under six for a month.[90] A husband can be mourned for ten months, close blood relations for eight months. Whoever acts contrary to these restrictions is placed in public disgrace.

Whoever is in mourning ought to refrain from dinner parties, jewelry, and other adornments, and purple and white clothing.

[88] On *honestior* and *humilior,* and on the determination of punishment according to class, see Chapter I.

[89] The bride's family usually stipulated in the marriage arrangement that the dowry had to be returned in the case of divorce or death.

[90] A mother's grief for her child would undoubtedly extend well beyond a month. One month is, however, the official mourning period. The social demand that they suppress their grief may well have caused hysterical symptoms in many women; see selection 297.

Curses on Graverobbers

Although public laws prohibited the violation of sepulchers, some people in addition threatened would-be violators with a personal curse. The following inscription was found on the road leading from Rome to Ostia.

114   *CIL* 6.36467 (*ILS* 8184)

Gaius Tullius Hesper had this tomb built for himself, as a place where his bones might be laid. If anyone damages them or removes them from here, I wish for him that he may live in physical pain for a long time and that the gods of the underworld may not admit him when he dies.[91]

Funerals

Most Romans had fairly simple funerals. Upper-class families, however, arranged very elaborate funerals, particularly for members who had achieved fame and glory as statesmen or military leaders. Whereas the body of a lower-class person was removed from the city soon after death, and by the shortest route possible,[92] the body of an illustrious man might lie in state. And the funeral procession out of the city was allowed to travel a lengthy route along major streets, even stopping in the Forum for a eulogy. Many people unrelated to the deceased gathered in the Forum to hear the eulogy and to mourn the death as a loss to the state.

All Romans expressed great reverence toward their ancestors. We have already seen examples of the Romans' respect for "the good old days" and the customs of their ancestors. Families who numbered consuls, praetors, or curule aediles among their ancestors were allowed to display, in public, representations of these illustrious men. A representation, called in Latin *imago,* in Greek *eikon* or *icon,* was a wax mask portrait of the deceased.[93] Public display of these images was a privilege granted only to the upper class, but it was thought to stimulate pride in all Roman citizens and to inspire them to noble deeds.

The author of this passage, Polybius, lived in the second century B.C.

115   Polybius, *History of the World* 6.53–6.54.3

Whenever someone from the ranks of the illustrious dies, as a part of his funeral procession out of the city he is carried into the Forum and to the Rostra.[94] Usually his body is displayed in an upright pose; sometimes, but rarely, he is lying down. When all

---

[91] According to Roman eschatology, souls went to the underworld after death rather than to heaven or hell. Those souls whom the gods of the underworld would not admit were destined to wander in a horrible limbo for eternity.

[92] Interment was not allowed within the city walls; see selection 113.

[93] See note 9 of Chapter IV.

[94] *Rostra:* speaker's platform in the Roman Forum.

the people are standing round, a grown-up son, if the deceased has left one and if he happens to be present, or, if not, some other relative gets up on the Rostra and speaks about the virtues and lifetime achievements of the deceased. And thus it happens that, when these achievements are recalled and brought before their eyes, most people, not only those who shared in these achievements, but even those who had no part, feel such sympathy that the loss appears to be not a personal one, limited to the family, but a common one, felt by all the people.

After the interment and the performance of the customary rites, a wax image of the deceased is placed in a very conspicuous spot in the house, in a little wooden shrine. This image is a mask made strikingly similar to the facial features and expression of the deceased. The family puts these images on display during public sacrifices, arranging them with great care. When any illustrious family member dies, the family takes the images or masks to the funeral, putting them on men who seem to be most similar in height and size to the men represented by the masks. These "actors" put on a purple-bordered toga, if their "character" was a consul or praetor,[95] an entirely purple toga if he was a censor, and a gold-embroidered toga if he had celebrated a triumph[96] or done some other such thing. They all ride in chariots, and, according to the respective rank of political office held by each "character" during his lifetime, the "actors" are preceded by the fasces, axes, and other such things which usually accompany the magistrates.[97] When they reach the Rostra, they all sit down on curule seats.[98] It would not be easy to find a more splendid sight for a young man who loves honor and virtue to behold. For who would not be moved by the sight of the images of men renowned for their excellence, all together in one place, portrayed as if still alive and breathing? What finer spectacle could there be than this? And, in addition, when the speaker who delivers the funeral oration for the man to be buried has finished this speech, he then mentions the achievements and accomplishments of each of those other men whose masks are present, beginning with the most ancient. And therefore, since the renown of these noble men and their reputation for excellence is constantly being recalled to mind, the fame of men who have done great deeds is made immortal, and the glory of those who have faithfully served the fatherland becomes well known to the people and is handed down as a model to future generations. The most important thing, however, is that young men are inspired to endure or suffer anything on behalf of the common good in order to achieve the glory that surrounds men who are brave.

A Funeral Club

In order to defray the expenses of a respectable funeral, many people in the lower class joined funeral clubs.[99] Members of these clubs paid an initiation fee and monthly dues. When they died the club paid their funeral expenses, and club mem-

---

[95] *purple-bordered toga:* men of the senatorial order wore a white toga with a broad purple border.

[96] On triumphs, see selection 267.

[97] On *fasces*, see note 80 of Chapter X.

[98] *curule seats:* special ivory chairs, a privilege which, like the display of images in public, was granted only to consuls, praetors, and curule aediles.

[99] *funeral clubs:* Latin *funeraticium collegium* = "funeral college." The Latin word *collegium* means "an association of people sharing a similar interest."

bers attended their funerals. Club members met once a month, at a dinner meeting, to pay their dues. Funeral clubs thus also served the function of bringing lower-class people together for social activity. For many people, the social events of the club were as important a reason for joining as the defrayment of funeral expenses. The constitution of one of these clubs has been preserved on a marble tablet.

116   *CIL* 14.2112 (*ILS* 7212)

On January 1, in the consulship of Marcus Antonius Hiberus and Publius Mummius Sisenna,[100] the funeral club of Diana and Antinous[101] was founded. . . .

Here follows a section from the decree of the Senate of the Roman people: Let the members join together and have a collegium. Let those who wish to contribute monthly dues to be applied toward funeral expenses join this club. But let them not meet in the form of a club except once a month and except for the purpose of contributing money with which deceased members will be buried.[102] . . .

The Constitution of the Collegium

It was decided unanimously that anyone who wished to join this club should pay an initiation fee of 100 sesterces and an amphora of good wine. Then each month he should pay five asses.

It was also decided that if any member has not paid his fair share for six months in a row, and then meets death, arrangements will not be made for his funeral, even if he has made a will.[103]

It was also decided that if any member of this club has paid his dues regularly and then dies, 300 sesterces will be allotted from the club treasury for his funeral. From this amount 50 sesterces will be used to reimburse participants in the funeral procession. The 50 sesterces will be divided up at the site of the funeral pyre. However, participants must walk.[104]

It was also decided that if any member should die beyond the twentieth milestone from this municipality,[105] and word has been received of his death, three men chosen

---

[100] A.D. 133; it was customary in dating to give only the names of the consuls for that year.

[101] *Diana:* goddess of the moon, sister of the sun god Apollo. *Antinous:* a beautiful young man who was a favorite of the emperor Hadrian (who ruled A.D. 117–138). After Antinous drowned in A.D. 130, Hadrian kept alive the memory of him by erecting statues and building temples in his honor as if he were a god. He was frequently depicted in divine form, as Apollo, for example, the brother of Diana. The members of this funeral club held Diana and Antinous in special honor and hoped that their reverence would be rewarded by the good will of these two divine figures.

[102] The Senate had set strict limitations on the functions of *collegia* and the size of their treasuries in order to prevent people from establishing clubs whose real purpose might be political subversion or labor unrest. Some collegia were clubs established by men of the same occupation, and they were somewhat similar to guilds.

[103] . . . and left in the will provisions for payment of the monthly dues he owes.

[104] Participants would not be reimbursed for the expense of hiring a vehicle to carry them in the procession out of the city. Club members were expected to participate in the funeral processions of fellow members.

[105] The municipality in which this funeral club was established was Lanuvium, a town about twenty miles south of Rome.

from our club should go to that place and make arrangements for his funeral; they should then render an account to our members without willful deceit. If anything in their accounts is found to be a case of fraud, let their fine be fourfold. To these men will be paid the cost of the deceased's funeral, and to each in addition will be given 20 sesterces for travel expenses there and back. But if the man has died beyond the twentieth milestone and word of his death could not be announced, then whoever it was who buried him should bear witness to this fact, presenting letters sealed by the seals of seven Roman citizens. When his statement has been approved, he ought to be reimbursed according to the constitution of the club for the funeral expenses of the deceased. . . .

It was also decided that if any member of this club who was a slave should die, and if his body should not be handed over to us for interment because of the unfairness of his master or mistress, or if he has not left a will, a funeral will be held for an effigy of him. . . .

It was also decided that if any member of this club who was a slave should be manumitted, he ought to donate an amphora of good wine.

It was also decided that if any member, when it is his turn according to the membership list and his year as chairman to arrange for the dinner, does not fulfill his obligations or make the arrangements, he will pay into the club treasury 30 sesterces, and the next man in order ought to arrange for the dinner and take his place.

The order of the dinners: March 8, the birthday of Caesennius[106] . . . ; November 27, the birthday of Antinous; August 13, the birthday of Diana; August 20, the birthday of Caesennius Silvanus; . . . 4, the birthday of Cornelia Procula . . . ; December 14, the birthday of Caesennius Rufus, patron of the municipality.

Chairmen for the dinners, four at a time, selected in turn according to the membership list, ought to provide one amphora each of good wine, and bread worth two asses, proportionate to the number of club members, and four sardines,[107] and a room for the dinner, and hot water, and a waiter. . . .

It was also decided that if any member moves about from one seat to another simply to cause a commotion, let his fine be 4 sesterces. If any member speaks abusively to another or becomes obstreperous, let his fine be 12 sesterces. If any member speaks abusively or insolently to the club president during dinner, let his fine be 20 sesterces.

It was also decided that the club president, on religious holidays during his term of office, should clothe himself in white, and make offerings of incense and wine, and perform other such duties. And on the birthdays of Diana and Antinous he should provide, in the public bath building, oil for club members before they dine.

Final Words: an Epitaph

The following inscription was found at Padua.

---

[106] The Caesennii were members of Lanuvium's most important family. There are some gaps in the text (chips in the marble) at this point.

[107] It is not clear whether members contributed or paid for additional food. In any case, the dinners were undoubtedly quite modest because funeral club members were not wealthy.

117   *CIL* 5.2893 (*ILS* 8164)

I was not, I was, I am not, I care not.

PERSONAL MESSAGES

The Walls of Pompeii

We have already read some messages which were painted or scratched on the walls of buildings in Pompeii by its inhabitants.[108] Translated below is a miscellany of graffiti which appeared on the walls of this city which was frozen in time by the eruption of Mount Vesuvius.

118   *CIL* 4.6702, 1842, 5305, 1321, 3794, 8417, 6701,
                                                             813, 4993, 4917

>Aufidius was here.
>Gaius Pumidius Dipilus was here on October 3.
>Successus was here.
>Publius Comicius Restitutus stood here with his brother.
>Aemilius Celer lives here.[109]
>A benevolent god dwells here in this house.
>Burglar, watch out!
>This is no place for idlers. On your way, loafer.
>Ampliatus Pedania is a thief.
>Albanus is a bugger.

119   *CIL* 4.2409a, 3061, 1650, 1937, 116, 8972,
                                                       8162, 1926, 5112, 5279

Stronnius is a know-nothing.
I don't want to sell my husband.
Gaius Julius Primigenius was here. Why are you late?
Let anyone who invites me to dinner prosper.
I have a head cold.
On April 19 I baked bread.
We were here, two dear friends, comrades forever. If you want to know our
    names, they are Gaius and Aulus.
Epaphra is not a ball-player.

---

[108] See selections 26, 78, and 83.
[109] Aemilius Celer was a sign painter; see selections 237 and 338.

Learn this well: While I am alive, you are my enemy, Death.
When you are dead, you are nothing.

120 *CIL* 4.7086, 3117, 4498, 1951, 5251, 2175, 2246, 4091, 1649, 8408, 1904

Marcus loves Spendusa.
Serena hates Isidore.
Thyas, don't love Fortunatus.
Sarra, you're not acting very nicely, leaving me all alone.
Restitutus has deceived many girls many times.
I have screwed many girls here.
When I came here, I screwed. Then I returned home.
Let him who loves, prosper. Let him who loves not, perish. And let him who forbids others to love, perish twice over.
Let him who chastises lovers try to fetter the winds and block the endless flow of water from a spring.
Lovers, like bees, lead a honey-sweet life.
I am amazed, o wall, that you have not collapsed and fallen, since you must bear the tedious stupidities of so many scrawlers.

VI

Education

THE ROMAN IDEAL

A Traditional Education

In the early period of Roman history education was informal. Children learned in their own homes, usually from their fathers, just enough "reading, writing, and 'rithmetic" to enable them to understand simple business transactions and to count, weigh, and measure. Equally important to their education was the inculcation of respect for tradition and a solid comprehension of *pietas*.[1] It was a father's responsibility to make of his children good citizens and to train them to be hardworking, obedient, steadfast, and ready to sacrifice themselves for family and country. Job training was also a family matter, and was gained by imitating family members or through apprenticeship.[2] As the centuries passed, however, and Rome grew to be a world power, some parents preferred a more formal education for their children, one which went beyond a rudimentary knowledge of the three R's; they therefore began to hire teachers to do this academic training (although a child's moral education was still, of course, the responsibility of his parents[3]). However, even when it became common to send children to school to learn academic skills, the Romans continued to cherish an ideal of the father as his son's teacher.

Cato the Elder (Marcus Porcius Cato) lived from 234 B.C. to 149 B.C., a period during which Rome first began to establish itself as a world power. His family was wealthy, and he became prominent in politics as spokesman for the ultra-conservatives. A reactionary and an isolationist, he strongly opposed Roman expansion in the East because he feared that contact with the Greeks would change the traditional Roman way of life (as indeed it did). He was undoubtedly a stubborn and difficult man, but to later generations of Romans he represented a paragon of Roman virtues: austerity, frugality, sobriety, gravity, and, above all, respect for traditions.[4] In this passage from his biography of Cato the Elder, Plutarch, a

---

[1] *pietas:* see the introduction to selection 1.

[2] For an apprenticeship contract, see selection 135.

[3] Consider, for example, Horace's father (selection 15) and Agricola's mother (selection 17).

[4] For more information about Cato, see footnote 50 of Chapter II.

Greek author of the first century A.D., recounts with great admiration Cato's adherence to the Roman tradition of the father as his son's teacher.

121   Plutarch, *The Life of Marcus Cato* 20.4–7

After the birth of his son, Cato considered no business (except government business) so urgent as to prevent him from being present while his wife bathed the infant and wrapped it in swaddling clothes. And she herself nursed it with her own milk.[5] . . .

And when the child was old enough to learn, Cato himself took charge and taught him to read and write, even though he owned an accomplished slave, named Chilon, who was a teacher and who instructed many boys.[6] But Cato did not think it proper, as he himself said, for his son to be criticized by a slave, or to have his ears tweaked by a slave when he was a slow learner, or to owe to a slave so precious a gift as his education. Therefore Cato himself was his reading teacher, his law professor, his athletic coach. He taught his son not only to hurl a javelin, to fight in armor, and to ride a horse, but also to box, to endure both heat and cold, and to swim strongly through the eddies and undercurrents of a river. He also says that he wrote his book (the one titled *History*) in large letters and in his own handwriting[7] so that his son might have the opportunity at home to become familiar with his society's ancient customs and traditions. And he was careful to avoid indecent language no less in his son's presence than if he were in the presence of the Vestal Virgins.[8]

A CHILD'S EARLY YEARS

The Role of the Parents

The Romans realized that a child's earliest years are also the most formative, and parents were therefore advised to take an active interest in their child's upbringing. The following passage from Quintilian is a continuation of the passage above where he recommends that parents select nurses whose grammar is correct.

122   Quintilian, *The Elements of Oratory* 1.1.6–8, 15–17, 20

With regard to the parents, I would prefer that they be as well educated as possible. And I am not speaking only about the fathers; for we know that Cornelia, the mother of the Gracchi, contributed a great deal to her sons' eloquence.[9] Indeed her letters

---

[5] For the practice of hiring or buying nurses, see selection 41.

[6] *many boys:* perhaps slave boys; on educated slaves, see note 12 of this chapter.

[7] Most authors dictated their work to scribes or secretaries (who were usually slaves).

[8] For the Vestal Virgins, see selections 379 and 380.

[9] Cornelia's sons, Tiberius and Gaius Gracchus, were both excellent public speakers; see selection 170. Cornelia lived about two hundred years before Quintilian, but her personal letters had been preserved.

have preserved for us today examples of her very elegant style. . . . And even those women who were not themselves fortunate enough to receive a good education should not therefore show a less active interest in their children's education; on the contrary, they should simply be more diligent in other matters.

I would give the same advice about the slaves who will help raise the boy as I gave about nurses.[10] About the choice of paedagogue I will speak at greater length. A paedagogue should either be truly well educated (I recommend that this type be your first choice) or know that he is not well educated. For there is nothing worse than a man who assumes in his own mind the false opinion that he is learned when in fact he has progressed only slightly beyond the rudiments of an education. This type of man refuses to accept criticism or advice, and, with that particular air of authority with which all men of his type seem to be swollen, he imperiously, sometimes even cruelly, instructs others in his own stupidity. . . .

Some people think that children under the age of seven should not be given lessons in reading and writing because not until seven can they really comprehend their lessons or endure the mental strain. . . . A wiser attitude, however, is that which recommends that a child's mind at no time be left unoccupied. . . . For why should the age which is suitable for learning moral principles not be suitable for learning to speak correctly? . . .

I am not so foolishly unaware of a child's stages of development as to think that young children should be harshly forced to begin the three R's or should have real work pressed upon them. Above all else we must take care that a child who is not yet old enough to love learning should not come to hate it and to dread, even when he is older, an experience which was once bitter. Let his lessons be fun, let him volunteer answers, let him be praised, and let him learn the pleasure of doing well. If, on occasion, he refuses instruction, bring in someone to serve as a rival, someone with whom he can compete;[11] but let him think that he is doing well more often than not. Encourage him with the rewards or prizes in which his age group delights.

TEACHERS AND SCHOOLS

Private Tutors

Some families had private tutors in their own homes. These tutors might be slaves purchased by the family,[12] or free men or freedmen hired by the family. Cicero engaged a Greek named Tyrannio as a tutor for his son and his nephew, Quintus the Younger, who was living with Cicero in 56 B.C. while his father was in Sardinia

---

[10] *advice:* i.e., that they speak correctly; see selection 41.

[11] For other comments on encouraging competition among children, see selection 39.

[12] Many slaves were well educated. In their homelands they may have been wealthy men who had received a good education and held positions of dignity and power. They had been taken captive during a war or abducted by pirates, transported to Rome, and sold as slaves. Or a slave-dealer or slave-owner might provide his slaves with a basic education in order to increase their market value. Or perhaps paedagogues, who accompanied children to school, picked up enough of an education to become teachers when they were freed.

on government business. The passage below is taken from a letter by Cicero to his brother.[13]

123   Cicero, *Letters to his Brother Quintus* 2.4.2

Your son Quintus is an exceptional boy and an outstanding student. I have recently begun to notice this more because I now have Tyrannio here in my home as tutor.

Orbilius, the Schoolteacher

Most families could not afford the expense of a private tutor and therefore sent their children to schools. There were three levels of education. At the lowest level, the teacher was called a *magister* or *litterator;* he taught the basic three R's and also required his students to memorize large quantities of material (legends, laws, aphorisms, poetry). At age ten or eleven, some boys went on to study with a *grammaticus.* (Boys of poor families would by now be working or serving as apprentices; girls would of course be preparing for marriage and childrearing.) The grammaticus refined the student's style of writing and speaking, taught him to analyze poetry, and taught him Greek if he did not yet know it. Only a very few boys went on, at age fourteen or fifteen, to study with a *rhetor,* who trained the student for a career in public speaking, law, and politics. Schools were privately financed and varied widely in quality. As we have seen, Horace and his father were quite scornful of Flavius's school in Venusia.[14] Anybody could set himself up as a teacher, but the financial rewards of teaching were so slim that many teachers were freedmen who could find no other work or free men whom adverse circumstances had left impoverished.[15] Suetonius's brief biography of Orbilius gives us some idea about the life of a schoolteacher. Orbilius was a grammaticus.

124   Suetonius, *A Book about Schoolteachers* 9

Lucius Orbilius Pupillus was born in Beneventum.[16] He was left an orphan when both his parents were killed on the same day by a treacherous plot of their enemies. First he obtained a job as a menial servant for the town magistrates. Then he joined the army, was decorated, and eventually was promoted to the cavalry. When he had completed his years of service, he returned to his studies and thus fulfilled an ambition he had had since boyhood.

For a long time he lived as a teacher in his hometown, but then in his fiftieth year (the year of Cicero's consulship[17]), he moved to Rome and taught there. However, he earned more fame than money. In one of his books, written when he was an old man,

---

[13] See selection 60 on the marriage of Cicero's brother; see selection 236 for Quintus's advice on political campaigns.

[14] See selection 15.

[15] On the social status of teachers, see selection 147.

[16] *Beneventum:* town in the southern part of Italy, east of Naples.

[17] *Cicero's consulship:* 63 B.C. For consuls and their functions, see selections 229–232.

he complains that he is "a pauper, living in an attic." He also published a book called *My Trials and Tribulations* in which he complains about the insults and injuries done to him by negligent or ambitious parents.

He had a fiery temper which he unleashed not only on his rival teachers, whom he castigated on every occasion, but also on his students. Horace[18] called him "the teacher who loved the whip," and Domitius Marsus[19] wrote that many of his students suffered floggings and whippings. Even men of rank and position did not escape his scathing sarcasm. . . .

He lived to be almost 100 years old. . . . In the Capitol at Beneventum, in the area to the left, there is a marble statue of him on display. He is seated, and holds in his hands two books.[20] He left a son who was also named Orbilius and who was also a schoolteacher.[21]

A Schoolteacher's Hours

When we speak of a Roman school we are seldom referring to a detached building whose only function was to provide classroom space. As we have seen, Roman schools were privately operated and dependent on tuition fees which were usually very low. Teachers rented classroom space wherever it was available; some schools might occupy a small room in an apartment building or a little street-level shop.[22] However, many teachers met their students outdoors and held classes on the sidewalks or in piazzas. There were, of course, many disadvantages to outdoor schools. Traffic noise and street crowds must have been very distracting for the students, and inclement weather was surely a problem. However, sidewalk schools avoided rent and lighting costs.[23] Teachers started classes at daybreak, to make maximal use of the sunlight and to allow a few hours of relative quiet before the bustle of morning traffic.[24] Classes continued until noon. Sometimes more classes were held after the lunch break. A teacher's day was long and demanding, but he would receive little sympathy from Martial, who in the passage below complains that a teacher in the street outside his apartment building begins classes even before daybreak and thus awakens all the sleeping tenants.[25]

---

[18] Horace, *Epistles* 2.1.70: ". . . poems which I remember Orbilius, the teacher who loved the whip, used to dictate to me when I was a little boy."

[19] *Domitius Marsus:* poet who lived in the period of Augustus.

[20] Literally "two bookcases," i.e., two containers of papyrus rolls.

[21] Literally "also a grammaticus."

[22] On the location of shops, see selections 73 and 74 and also Figures 2 and 5.

[23] Roman schoolchildren had chairs but no desks; the teachers had no blackboards; books were rare and writing materials expensive. Many teachers recited passages to their students and expected them to memorize these passages for future reference.

[24] One function of the paedagogue was to protect schoolboys walking to school before dawn. On paedagogues, see selection 42. On traffic dangers, see Juvenal's comments in selection 81.

[25] See selection 82.

125   Martial, *Epigrams* 9.68

What do you have against us, spiteful schoolteacher? We know you are hated by all the boys and girls[26] you teach. Before the crested rooster has even crowed, you shatter the silence with your harsh voice and with lashes of your whip. The noises you make ring out as loudly as bronze beaten on an anvil when a metal sculptor is fashioning a lawyer mounted on a horse. Shouts in the Colosseum, when the crowd is cheering on its favorite gladiator,[27] are not so deafening as your thunderous voice. Now we neighbors are not demanding that we be allowed to sleep without disturbance for the whole night; to be awakened briefly is a minor irritation. But to be kept awake is a serious vexation. So send your students home. Would you be willing, you old windbag, to accept the same pay for being silent as you now receive for shouting out lessons?

A Schoolteacher's Salary

126   Juvenal, *Satires* 7.215–243

What grammaticus, even the most learned, ever receives the salary which his hard work deserves? And then this amount, however small (certainly less than a rhetor earns), is further diminished by bribes to greedy paedagogues[28] and fees to accountants. But give in, Palaemon,[29] and resign yourself to losing a little money in this way, just as a salesman of winter clothing loses a little money during a summer discount sale. As long as you get *some* money for sitting in a classroom in the middle of the night when no laborer or woolworker would be on the job! As long as you get some money for enduring the stink of oil lamps[30]—one per student—whose black soot totally discolors the copy of Horace and whose sticky grime soils the copy of Vergil![31] And yet rarely do you get your money without a court case. But still the parents set impossible standards for you. You must know the rules of grammar perfectly, memorize history books, and

[26] Fewer girls than boys went to school, and even girls who attended school seldom advanced beyond the primary level, because they were married in their early teens. Roman men did not appreciate well-educated women. Pliny (selection 54) praises his wife for having enough education to appreciate *his* intelligence, talent, and wit. Juvenal (selection 293) bitterly criticizes a woman who tries to carry on an intelligent conversation at dinner. Sallust (selection 291) implies that Sempronia had too much education for her own good. Roman women were expected to be charming, that is, to make their men feel superior. Gary Miles, in an unpublished paper, compares the education, training, and expectations of an upper-class Roman matron with those of the upper-class women of the antebellum southern United States.

[27] *gladiator:* see the introduction to the section on amphitheater events in Chapter XIV.

[28] *bribes to greedy paedagogues:* it is quite possible that teachers bribed paedagogues to put in a good word with students' parents.

[29] *Palaemon:* Quintus Remmius Palaemon, a well-known grammaticus of the first century A.D. See also Juvenal's comments in selection 293 on women who read Palaemon's treatises on grammar.

[30] Since some schools began before daybreak, students carried with them lamps fueled by animal fat, which is smoky and smelly. In a small room these lamps undoubtedly irritated both the eyes and the nose. (Outdoor schools could avoid this problem, of course.) In addition, soot from the lamps covered all the books and school materials.

[31] Horace and Vergil were two of Rome's greatest poets; see Appendix I. Very soon after their deaths, their works began to be used as schooltexts.

have at your fingertips the contents of every textbook so that if by chance someone should question you while you are on your way to the baths, you can tell him who Anchises' nurse was,[32] the name and homeland of Anchemolus's stepmother, how many years Acestes lived, and how many jars of Sicilian wine he gave to the Trojans. Parents insist that you mold the tender minds of their sons as a sculptor molds a face from wax.[33] You are supposed to act like the father of this mob of boys and make sure they don't get into trouble or develop bad habits. It's not an easy task. Then the parents say, "Do your job well, and, when the end of the year comes, we'll pay you for the twelve-month period the same amount that a chariot driver earns in one race."[34]

Incentives for Learning

Considering the hardships of a teacher's life, such as long hours, low pay, and an unsympathetic public, it is not surprising that many, like Orbilius, were bitter men who took out their frustrations on their students. However, we also hear of kind and patient teachers. The author of the next passage is Horace, who had once been a pupil of Orbilius and therefore knew about cruel as well as kind teachers.[35]

127　　　　　　　　　　　　　　　　　　　Horace, *Satires* 1.1.25–26

Coaxing teachers sometimes give cookies to their students to encourage them to learn the alphabet.

Book Awards

As boys grew older and their schoolwork became more demanding, they needed rewards and incentives more sophisticated than cookies.

128　　　　　　　　　　　　　Suetonius, *A Book about Schoolteachers* 17

Marcus Verrius Flaccus, a freedman, was renowned for his methods of teaching.[36] He used to make his students compete against one another in contests in order to stimulate their minds and encourage them to study. He gave them a topic on which to write an essay and then awarded a prize to the author of the best essay. The prize was always an old book, valuable for its beauty or its rareness.

[32] This, and the following facts, are examples of useless and trivial information.
[33] On wax images, see the introduction to selection 115.
[34] *Chariot driver:* see selections 346–353. For examples of teachers' salaries, see selection 152. The chariot driver, usually a slave, would not be allowed to keep the purse won in the race.
[35] As a young student Horace had evidently disliked memorizing poems dictated to him by Orbilius; as an adult he became one of Rome's greatest poets, and after his death his poems were ironically used as texts for young students to memorize.
[36] Indeed he was so famous that he was chosen by the emperor Augustus to teach the children of the imperial family.

An Endowment for a School

We have previously read letters in which Pliny discussed his wife's virtues, his seaside villa, and the affairs of his friends. Here he informs his friend Tacitus[37] of his plan to endow a school in his hometown of Comum.[38]

129   Pliny the Younger, *Letters* 4.13.3–10

. . . When I was in my hometown recently, the young[39] son of one of my fellow townsmen came around to pay his respects.[40] I asked him, "Do you go to school?"[41] "Yes," he replied. "Where?" I then asked. "In Milan,"[42] he said. "Why not here?" I asked. "Because," answered his father (who had in fact brought the boy to my house and was now standing beside him), "we have no teachers here." "No teachers," I said with astonishment. "But surely it would be in the best interests of you who are fathers" (and quite opportunely there were some fathers present and listening) "to have your children attend school here if at all possible.[43] For where else could they live more happily than in their hometown, and where else could they be chaperoned more closely than under the eyes of their parents, and where else could they be maintained at less expense than at home? Once the money for salaries has been raised, it is no great task to hire teachers. And, as far as raising money, isn't it easy to apply to a salary fund the amount which you now spend on your sons' board and room, travel, and other items which must be purchased when one is away from home? In fact I, who do not yet have children,[44] am prepared to act for the benefit of our town, as I would for the benefit of a daughter or a parent, and to donate one-third of whatever sum it will please you to collect. I would even promise the whole amount if I were not afraid that my endowment might someday provide an opportunity for political corruption, as I see happening in many towns where teachers are hired by public officials.[45] This ugly problem can be avoided by only one course of action: the authority to hire must be given

[37] Gaius Cornelius Tacitus, the famous orator and historian, lived about A.D. 55–118. For his views on education, see selection 137 and 141.

[38] *Comum:* town in northern Italy, modern Como.

[39] *young:* literally "still wearing a *toga praetexta,*" the garment worn before a boy reached manhood. It was a white toga with a purple border.

[40] *pay his respects:* i.e., at the *salutatio;* see note 44 of Chapter I. Pliny was a wealthy man who had gained prominence in the political and legal circles of Rome. Many residents of his hometown would therefore consider his patronage valuable and would seek to attach themselves to him as clients.

[41] His question implies that not all young boys did go to school.

[42] *Milan:* the modern name; the Latin name was Mediolanum. Milan is about sixty miles south of Como.

[43] For an opposing view on schools in small towns, see selection 15.

[44] On Pliny's hope for children, see selection 24.

[45] The first recorded employment of teachers (in this case rhetors) by the state occurred under Vespasian, emperor A.D. 69–79. In this program rhetors were hired to teach in Rome and were paid out of the state treasury. Quintilian (see Appendix I) was one of the first rhetors so hired. It should be noted, however, that Pliny is talking here not about a publicly financed, publicly administered school but about a privately endowed school administered by parents.

to the parents alone, and then their conscientious performance of this task of careful selection can be ensured by forcing them to contribute money. For men who will perhaps be negligent about another's money will certainly be diligent and careful about their own, and I can rest assured that a teacher who will receive money from them will be quite worthy of receiving money from me. So then, come to some agreement, act in unison, and, from my enthusiasm, gain some greater enthusiasm of your own. For I want the amount which I will have to contribute to be as large as possible. You can offer to your children no gift more worthwhile, to your hometown no gift more welcome. Let them be educated where they are born and from infancy grow accustomed to love and honor their native land. And I hope that you will attract here teachers so famous that, just as your children now seek an education in distant regions and flock from here to other towns, in the near future children of other regions will flock to our town."

I thought it wise to tell you about this matter in detail and from the beginning so that you might better understand how grateful I would be if you would undertake the favor I am about to ask. I ask and, in line with the importance of the matter, I beg that you keep an eye open, in that crowd of students who cluster around you because they admire your skill and intelligence, for teachers whom we can interview, under this condition, however, that I cannot give a promise of employment to anyone. I support complete freedom of selection for the parents; let them judge, let them choose. I claim for myself only the trouble and the expense.[46]

A Letter Home

Like the boy mentioned in the previous passage, the boy who wrote the letter translated here attended school away from his hometown. The letter was written on papyrus in Roman Egypt in the early third century A.D. The boy, away at school, makes a plea for a visit from his father.

130   *Sammelbuch* 6262 (*Select Papyri* 133)

First of all, Father, I pay you my respects, as I do every day. And I pray to the household gods[47] of my present living quarters that I may find you and our whole family in good health. Now, look, this is my fifth letter to you! And you have not written to me, except once! You haven't written about your health, and you haven't come to see me, even though you said, "I am coming." But you haven't come, not even to find out if the teacher is helping me or not. In fact the teacher himself asks about you almost every day and whether you are coming. And I just say, "Yes."

---

[46] Several inscriptions have been found which record that the very generous Pliny donated to his hometown money not only for a school but also for a library, baths, and support of poor children. See also selection 47 for the record of a private benefactor in North Africa.

[47] *household gods:* deities whose particular function was to watch over a specific household. See note 34 of Chapter VIII.

THE LITTERATOR

A Day in the Life of a Schoolboy

The following passage is taken from a glossary which itself dates back to the medieval rather than the classical period, but which contains elements which are as early as the third century A.D. The glossary was used by language teachers; there is Greek on one side of the page, Latin on the other. The story is easy to read and therefore suitable for beginning language students. (One might compare the stories in an elementary French or Spanish textbook.) It provides us, however, with very useful information about a schoolboy's day and about classroom routine. Note the great emphasis on memorization.

131 *Corpus Glossariorum Latinorum* III, pp. 645–647
(Colloquia Monacensia)

I awoke before dawn; I arose from my bed; I sat down and put on my socks and shoes. I requested water for my face; I washed my hands first and then my face; I wiped them dry. I took off my sleeping clothes and put on my tunic; I did up the belt. I greased down my hair and combed it. I put a scarf around my shoulders; on top of that I put a white cloak, and over that a rain mantle.[48] I left my bedroom with my paedagogue and nurse and went to greet my father and mother; I greeted them both and kissed them. Then I left home.

I went to school. I entered and said, "Hello, teacher," and he kissed me and greeted me in return. My slave[49] who carries my books handed me my waxed tablets, my writing box, and my writing instruments. Sitting in my place, I smoothed over the tablets.[50] I printed the assigned sentence.[51] When I had finished it, I showed it to the teacher. He corrected it, wrote over my errors, and bid me to read it aloud. Having been bidden, I recited it to another student. Immediately afterward a fellow student dictated to me.[52] "And you," he said, "dictate to me." I said, "First recite." And he said to me, "Didn't you see? I recited before you did." And I said, "You're lying; you didn't recite." "I'm not lying!" "Well, if you're telling the truth, I will dictate." In the midst of this quarrel, the little boys, who were so bidden by the teacher, lined up in two groups for their elementary exercises; one of the older boys gave one group of them

[48] Did young boys always wear so much clothing? It is more likely that the author of this textbook wishes to introduce as much new vocabulary as possible.

[49] *My slave:* my paedagogue.

[50] For waxed tablets, see note 54 of this chapter. Schoolboys wrote on waxed tablets. Papyrus was too expensive for school exercises.

[51] *assigned sentence:* perhaps an aphorism or epigram. Compare the next selection.

[52] Because books were expensive and scarce, students shared them and were required to commit to memory large passages for future reference. The teacher or a fellow student would dictate or read aloud a passage; the student would copy it down and read back his copy. Later he might be required to memorize the passage and recite it from memory.

syllables to spell.[53] The other group recited word lists, in order, to the assistant teacher; they print the words and then print lines of verse. I, who am in the advanced class, was given a dictation exercise. When we sat down, I went through my word lists and notes on grammar and style. Called up to the head teacher to read aloud, I listened to his comments on narration, speech construction, and characterization. I was questioned about grammatical theory, and I gave my answers. "Do you say 'to whom'?" "What are the parts of a speech?" I declined nouns and parsed sentences. When we had finished this, the teacher dismissed us for lunch. After being dismissed, I came home. I changed clothes and ate some white bread, olives, cheese, dried figs, and nuts. I drank cold water. After lunch I returned to school.

Morals and Memorization

The litterator was responsible for teaching young children the basics of reading, writing, and arithmetic. Often the reading material had a moralizing tone. For example, rather than learning to read "Dick and Jane see Spot," a young Roman might be required to learn and memorize "Forune helps the brave" or "Only the virtuous are truly happy." The passage translated here was found on a waxed tablet discovered in Egypt.[54] It provides information about writing lessons for elementary students. At the top of the waxed tablet a Greek teacher of the second century A.D. carefully wrote out two maxims (the first by Menander, a famous Greek poet); the pupil practiced his writing skills by copying these maxims on ruled lines in the waxed tablet. The pupil was not yet skilled in forming letters, and his printing looks much more awkward than the teacher's. The writing exercise is on one leaf of a diptych (two waxed tablets connected by a hinge); on the other leaf is a multiplication table and a list of words.

132   *Catalogue of the Literary Papyri in the British Museum* 253
                                         (Inv. No. Add. MS 34186, part 1)

Teacher's writing

From a wise man seek advice.
Do not blindly trust all your friends.

Student's writing

From a wise man seek advice.
Do not blindly trust all your friends.

---

[53] While the teacher was busy with one group of students, older students helped younger students in another part of the room. The practice is reminiscent of the one-room country schoolhouse in the United States.

[54] *waxed tablet:* a wooden tablet coated with wax. The writer used a sharp-pointed instrument (*stilus* or *stylus*) and scratched the letters into the wax. The other end of the *stilus* was blunt and could be used to smooth over the wax (erasing previous writing). In the previous passage the young schoolboy smoothed over his tablet when he first arrived at school. Waxed tablets were cheaper than papyrus and therefore used for school exercises and for notes to friends. The dimensions of this particular tablet are 17.8 cm by 26 cm; the waxed portion alone is 12.8 cm by 21.1 cm.

An Arithmetic Lesson

133

Horace, *Epistles* 2.3.325–330

Roman boys[55] learn to divide a penny into 100 parts by long, elaborate calculations. This is a typical lesson at school.

Teacher: Tell me, Albanson,[56] if you subtract 1/12 from 5/12, what is left? (Pause) You should have had the answer by now.

Student: 4/12 or 1/3.

Teacher: Good! You will certainly be able to look after your money. Now, if you add 1/12 to 5/12, what do you get?

Student: 6/12 or 1/2.

Enough Education for the Average Man

Most Roman boys did not advance in their formal education beyond the level of the litterator. Their parents had sent them to school only to learn skills of practical value, and when this had been accomplished the boys left school and found jobs. In this passage from Petronius's *Satyricon,* written in the first century A.D., one of the guests at Trimalchio's banquet describes the extent of his education (and implies that no man need know more).[57]

134

Petronius, *Satyricon* 58.7

I didn't learn geometry and literary criticism and useless nonsense like that. I learned how to read the letters on public inscriptions. I learned how to divide things into hundreds and work out percentages,[58] and I know weights, measures, and currency.

VOCATIONAL TRAINING

Apprenticeship to a Weaver

Children of wealthy families might expect to spend their childhood being trained and educated for positions in upper-class society: girls would be trained to assume

---

[55] *Roman boys:* as opposed to Greek boys, who Horace, earlier in the poem, says are taught to appreciate eloquence. He laments the Roman emphasis on practicality which leads Roman teachers to stress business arithmetic.

[56] *Albanson:* literally "son of Albanus" (Latin *filius Albani*).

[57] For more opinions on education from the guests at Trimalchio's banquet, see selection 210.

[58] Compare the previous selection. The value of learning to divide into hundreds and work out percentages was to enable a person to figure out interest rates for loans and other financial activities.

the role of upper-class matrons, and boys would receive a formal education which would equip them for careers in law and politics. For children of poor families (and most people were poor), formal education was a luxury. Some families could not afford the schoolteacher's fee, however low it might be, and their children remained illiterate. Other lower-class families might send their sons for a few years of schooling, but they wanted them out working and earning money as early as possible. After a brief period with a litterator, a child might take up the same job as his father or might be sent to be an apprentice to a craftsman. Here he would learn the skills necessary to ensure employment in a specific trade. The following passage, found at Oxyrhynchus, Egypt, records an agreement between a weaver and a man who wishes his son, who has not yet reached puberty, to learn the weaver's trade. The document was written on papyrus in A.D. 53. Since the weaver receives no fee for teaching the boy, we can probably assume that he expects the boy to work very hard around his shop and to earn his lessons.

135   *Wisconsin Papyri* 16.4

Pausiris, son of Ammonius, and Apollonius, a weaver, son of Apollonius, have reached the following agreement:

Pausiris has given as an apprentice to Apollonius his son Dioskus, who is still under age, so that he may learn the weaver's trade, all of it, as he himself knows it, for a period of one year from the present day. And Dioskus shall work for Apollonius and do everything he is told to. Apollonius has received for the boy, who will be clothed and fed by the weaver for the whole period of the agreement, 14 drachmas to cover the costs of clothing, and Pausiris will give him 5 silver drachmas a month to cover the costs of food.[59] And Pausiris, the father, is not allowed to take the boy away from his master within that period of time. If the boy does not do all his work, he must pay his master one silver drachma for each day on which he is negligent and lazy, or he may offer to remain an equal number of days longer. The penalty for taking the boy away before the end of the period agreed upon is 100 drachmas and an equal sum payable to the Treasury office. If the master weaver should fail to instruct the boy, he must pay the same penalty.

THE GRAMMATICUS

Curriculum

Some boys, usually those from wealthier families, went on to study with a grammaticus. Although the grammaticus was, in the most narrow sense, a teacher of language and literature, he required that his students also learn music, astronomy, philosophy, natural science, and other disciplines. It is interesting, however, to note that the study of astronomy and philosophy, for example, are justified only in their application to the study of literature; that is, one does not study astronomy solely for the sake of astronomy, but rather to understand better a poet's words.

59 *Drachma:* see note 65 of Chapter III.

136 Quintilian, *The Elements of Oratory* 1.4.1–5

As soon as a boy has learned to read and write, it is time for him to study with a grammaticus. I won't distinguish between Greek and Latin teachers, although I would prefer that priority be given to a Greek teacher. But both offer the same curriculum. And this curriculum can be divided very briefly into two main subjects: the art of speaking correctly and the interpretation of poetry. However, the curriculum offers much more in the details of the program than is at first apparent on the surface. For example, the art of speaking and the art of writing are connected. And flawless reading precedes interpretation. And critical judgment is required in all these cases. . . .

It is not sufficient to have read only poetry. Every kind of writer must be thoroughly investigated, and not simply for his topic or theme, but for his vocabulary, because words often acquire authority according to the writer using them.

And your studies with the grammaticus cannot be complete without the study of music because this education should include a discussion of meter and rhythm.

You cannot understand the poets if you know nothing about astronomy since the poets so often use the rising and setting of the constellations (to give one example) in indicating time.

Nor should this level of education overlook the study of philosophy, not only because many passages in almost every poem require our understanding of an intricate or minute detail of natural science[60] but also because some poets, such as Empedocles among the Greeks, and Varro and Lucretius among the Romans,[61] actually wrote down doctrines of philosophy in verse.

No small powers of eloquence are needed by someone wishing to speak appropriately and fluently on each one of those topics which we have just mentioned. . . . Unless the foundations for the future orator have been carefully laid by the grammaticus,[62] the whole superstructure will collapse.

THE RHETOR

A small number of boys, whose parents wanted them to become statesmen, politicians, lawyers, and public speakers, went on to study with a rhetor. A rhetor was, strictly speaking, a professor of rhetoric, but the study of rhetoric encompassed a

[60] The study of philosophy was connected in the ancient mind with the study of natural science. On the three branches of ancient philosophy, see note 351 of Chapter XV.

[61] *Empedocles:* c. 493–433 B.C. He wrote a poem in Greek hexameter verse titled *About Nature. Varro:* 116–27 B.C. Only two of his prose works are fully extant today. *Lucretius:* c. 99–55 B.C. One of Rome's great poets, he wrote a poem, in six books of Latin hexameter verse, titled *About the Nature of the Universe.* See selections 412–417 for passages from this poem.

[62] Quintilian's purpose in writing *The Elements of Oratory* was to explain what sort of training was needed to produce a first-rate orator or public speaker. It was the function of the rhetor to teach rhetoric or oratory, but Quintilian believed that the proper foundations for this training must be laid much earlier, by the grammaticus, by the litterator, even by the child's parents, nurses, and paedagogues; see selections 41 and 122.

number of scholarly disciplines, and therefore studying with a rhetor was in some senses similar to enrolling in the liberal arts program of a modern university.

The Good Old Days

We noted earlier that the Romans cherished an ideal of a child learning through experience and being taught the three R's by his father.[63] The ideal clashed with the reality, of course, since most children in the late republican period and in the imperial period were taught the three R's by professional educators. Similarly, training in public speaking was, by the late republican period, acquired in formal lessons from a rhetor; however, writers of the early imperial period, such as Tacitus, liked to talk about the good old days when young men learned rhetorical skills not through formal lessons from a rhetor but through careful observation of their elders. The young man's family made arrangements with a statesman and public speaker who would allow the young man to accompany him to the law courts and assembly meetings and to listen to him speak. In the time of Cato the Elder (300 years before Tacitus) this type of informal apprenticeship may have been the only way to train as a lawyer and politician. By the time of Cicero (150 years before Tacitus) young men received formal training from a rhetor but, in addition, attached themselves to a prominent public speaker for informal lessons.

137   Tacitus, *A Dialogue on Orators* 34.1–6

Among our ancestors, a young man was trained for public speaking in the following manner. Once he had been prepared by instruction at home and had been crammed full of worthwhile learning, he was taken by his father or a close relative to an orator who held a prominent position in the state. The young man would then accompany him and follow him about and be present during all his speeches whether in the law courts or the assembly meetings, so that he listened to debates and heard legal disputes and learned to fight battles by being, I think I may say, right in the battle. Under this system, young men acquired, right from the start, a great deal of experience, self-possession, and good judgment because they were studying in broad daylight and in the very middle of the battle, where no one can safely say anything stupid or inconsistent without its being rejected by the judge or denounced by an opponent or even, at worst, scorned by one's own legal assistants. Therefore young men were immediately imbued with true and perfect eloquence; and although they were "attached" to one man, nevertheless they became acquainted with all the lawyers of their period by attending a very great number of legal hearings and trials. They also had abundant experience with very diverse kinds of public audiences; from this experience, they could easily ascertain what the people liked or disliked about any given speaker. And thus they never lacked a teacher, and the best and most excellent teacher at that, who would teach the practice of eloquence, not the theory.[64] . . . Under teachers of this kind, the young man who was a disciple of the orators, a listener in the Forum, and an observer in the law courts be-

---

[63] See selection 121 on the education of Cato's son.

[64] Tacitus is comparing the practicing orator with the rhetor who teaches the theory of speaking well but does not himself give speeches in the Forum or courts. See selection 141.

came educated and trained by watching the experiences of others. Every day he learned the laws by hearing them discussed; he became familiar with the judges' faces; the procedures at the public assemblies were continually before his eyes; through frequent observation he learned to recognize the moods of public audiences. In short, whether he undertook an assignment as prosecuting lawyer or defense attorney, he was immediately, and without assistance, equal to any case.[65]

Classroom Exercises

Young men who studied with a rhetor learned history, law, astronomy, geography, philosophy, music, literature, mythology, and geometry. However, their studies in these areas were always subordinate to their study of rhetoric. It was the task of the rhetor to make of his students skillful orators who could speak persuasively in the law courts and in public assemblies. Exercises to promote this fluency included phrase composition, sentence composition, and paragraph composition. Students learned how to choose the right word, how to use rhetorical figures, how to arrange words in the most effective form and with the best prose rhythm. When they could compose sentences and paragraphs with ease and with brilliance, they were given topics and asked to compose speeches of varying lengths. Speech topics were divided into two broad categories: *suasoriae* (singular: *suasoria*) and *controversiae* (singular: *controversia*). A suasoria was a speech intended to persuade someone to adopt a certain course of action. Practice at composing suasoriae was thought to prepare one to make speeches of exhortation at public assemblies. A controversia was a speech in which one argued for one side of a point of law. Practice at composing controversiae equipped one for a career as a lawyer. Listed below are topics assigned by rhetors as composition exercises.

138   Seneca the Elder, *Suasoriae* 3, 6, 7

Suasoriae

Agamemnon at Aulis has been warned by the prophet Calchas that it is against the will of the gods for him to set sail until he has slaughtered his daughter Iphigenia.[66] Agamemnon deliberates: should he slaughter Iphigenia?

Each student would be expected to compose a speech exhorting Agamemnon either to slaughter or not to slaughter Iphigenia.

Antony has issued an order for Cicero's execution.[67] Cicero deliberates: should he beg Antony for mercy?

[65] This was, of course, the goal of rhetorical training, whether acquired by observing public speakers or by attending a rhetor's school: to be able to speak fluently and persuasively on any topic, for any length of time.

[66] For this story, see *Mythology* by Edith Hamilton or *Myths of the Greeks and Romans* by Michael Grant.

[67] On Antony, see notes 80 and 81 of Chapter III. Cicero was executed by Antony in 43 B.C.

Each student would be expected to compose a speech exhorting Cicero either to beg for mercy or not to beg.

Cicero deliberates: should he burn his writings,[68] since Antony has promised that he will be left unharmed if he does?

139   Seneca the Elder, *Controversiae* 1.1, 1.2, 1.6, 4.5, 5.5, 10.3 (32)

Controversiae

The law states: children should support their parents, or be cast into prison.

Two brothers quarrel among themselves. One has a son. The uncle falls on hard times. Although his father forbids him to do so, the young man supports his uncle; for this reason, his father disowns him. His uncle adopts him. His uncle receives an inheritance and becomes wealthy. His father falls on hard times. Although his uncle forbids him to do so, the young man supports him. His uncle disowns him.

Each student would be expected to argue either for or against the justice of the father's and uncle's actions. Remember, fathers expected absolute obedience from their children and could punish recalcitrant children even with death.[69]

The law states: a priestess must be chaste and pure.

A young woman was captured by pirates and offered for sale. She was bought by a pimp and set up as a prostitute. She persuaded men who came to her to give her the money as a gift [i.e., without any sex act]. However, she could not persuade a soldier who came to her. When he seized her and tried to force her, she killed him. She was brought to trial, acquitted, and returned to her family and homeland. She files a petition to become a priestess. Her petition is opposed.

Each student would present an argument explaining either why the woman should be admitted to the priesthood or why she should not.

A man who was captured by pirates wrote to his father for ransom money. His father did not ransom him. The daughter of the pirate captain made him swear that he would marry her if he escaped. He so promised. The girl left her father and went off with the young man. He returned to his father and married her. A wealthy widow comes along, and the father orders the son to divorce the daughter of the pirate captain and to marry the widow.[70] When the son refuses, the father disowns him.

A man disowned his son. The disowned son became a medical student. When the father became ill and his doctors said they could not cure him, his son cured him. He reestablished his son as his heir. Later his stepmother became ill and the doctors held

---

[68] Antony had been angered by speeches published by Cicero in which he bitterly attacked Antony.

[69] On *patria potestas*, see selection 14.

[70] Fathers had the power to arrange marriages and divorces for their children. The absolute power of the Roman father (*patria potestas*) is the topic of many of these controversiae.

out no hope. The father asked the son to cure his stepmother. When the son refused, he disowned him. The son appealed his action.

The law states: he who knowingly and with malice aforethought causes damage should make restitution at four times the value of the damaged object; he who unwittingly and without malice aforethought causes damage should make a simple one-for-one restitution.

A rich man asked his neighbor, a poor man, if he would sell him a tree which he said blocked his view. The poor man refused. The rich man set fire to the tree, but the poor man's house burned up along with it. The rich man promised to compensate his neighbor at four times the value of the tree, but only at equal value for the house.

An accusation of insanity: During a civil war, a woman found her father and her husband on different sides. She followed her husband. His faction was defeated and her husband was killed. She returned home to her father. When he would not let her into the house, she asked: What must I do to appease you? He replied: You must die.[71] She hanged herself in front of his door. Her brother accused their father of insanity.[72]

Pity the Teacher

Pity the teacher who spent all day listening to the schoolboys' controversiae.

140   Juvenal, *Satires* 7.150–154

The man who teaches declamation[73] must be made of iron, to listen to each boy in a large class denounce the cruel tyrants.[74] Each boy stands up and recites at great length what he has just finished writing. Each boy says the same thing in the same sing-song fashion. These stale rehashings[75] could kill a poor teacher!

Criticism of the Rhetor's Exercises

Tacitus complained, with some justice, that in his day classroom exercises had become very far removed from real situations. Boys were not being prepared to speak effectively in the law courts or assemblies;[76] they were, rather, encouraged to develop a florid style and to embroider their speeches with melodramatic but ir-

[71] A father (or guardian) retained his power over his daughter even when she was married; see selection 44.

[72] A son whose father had been legally declared insane might win release from the *patria potestas*.

[73] *declamation:* see note 78 of this chapter.

[74] *cruel tyrants:* a frequent topic in school exercises.

[75] *stale rehashings:* the Latin is literally "reheated cabbage."

[76] One might argue, of course, that opportunities for public speaking became more limited in the politically repressive atmosphere of the imperial period and that the rhetors of the imperial period therefore effectively trained their students to make empty but politically safe speeches.

relevant details. The topics of their speeches were much more akin to prose fiction than to legal actions or court cases. We can see even in the controversiae listed by Seneca the Elder (who lived 100 years before Tacitus) that the topics contained elements suitable for novels or melodrama: pirates, poisonings, rapes, disinherited sons, family feuds, murders, white slave trade, tyrants, torture, and insanity. By Tacitus's time, some students evidently concentrated on the melodramatic elements and lost sight of the legal disputes.

141   Tacitus, *A Dialogue on Orators* 35.1, 3–5

Nowadays[77] our young men are taken to the schools of the rhetors. . . . The classroom exercises to a large extent defeat their purpose. There are two kinds of material handled by the rhetors: suasoriae and controversiae. Since the suasoriae are clearly easier and require less maturity of judgment, they are assigned to the boys. To the young men, who are more prepared, are assigned the controversiae. But, my word, what poor quality! And how incredible they are in content! The subject matter is far removed from reality and, in addition, the style of delivery used is sheer declamation.[78] And thus it happens that problems which are rarely or never at all debated in the Forum[79]—such as "The Reward for the Tyrant-Killer" or "The Alternatives of the Raped Woman" or "The Remedy for the Plague" or "A Mother's Incest" or other problems debated every day in the rhetor's school—are discussed and described by students in grandiose language.

Criticism of the "New Style"

In the previous passage Tacitus had complained about the artificiality of the themes used in the rhetorical exercises of the imperial period. In the passage translated here Quintilian complains about the artificiality of the style of composition which was fashionable in the same period. He deplored the fact that speakers and writers were placing more emphasis on brilliance of style than on content.

142   Quintilian, *The Elements of Oratory* 8.
                                                  Preface. 22–26; 12.10.73

The result of this emphasis on brilliance is usually a deterioration of our oratorical skills, primarily because the best expressions are those which are least contrived and

[77] *Nowadays:* as compared to the good old days when boys learned how to speak well by listening to public orators in the law courts and assemblies. Tacitus lived in the second half of the first century A.D. See selection 137.

[78] *sheer declamation:* i.e., a style more suited to stage performance than to public oratory. (On the similarities between actors and orators, see selection 143.) Declamation was originally a minor subject in the curriculum of a student of rhetoric. In declamation classes, rhetors taught their students how to project and modulate their voices. However, by Tacitus's day, declamation occupied a large part of the curriculum, and many rhetors, he complains, concentrated more on the delivery of a speech than on the content.

[79] *Forum:* site of the law courts.

which have an air of simplicity, as if deriving from truth itself. For those expressions which betray their artfulness and strive to appear polished and carefully designed fail to produce a pleasing effect and do not win credibility. In addition, they cloud over the senses and choke out the crop, as it were, with their luxuriant growth. For, in our passion for words, we express periphrastically what could be said simply, we repeat what has already been said sufficiently, we envelop with many words what could be clearly expressed with one word, and we think it better to speak allusively than to speak in plain language. Nowadays ordinary language no longer delights us; can any expression be elegant if someone else has already used it? We borrow figures of speech and tropes from the most decadent poets; and then we consider ourselves obviously ingenious if our audience must be geniuses to understand us. And yet Cicero clearly informed us that the greatest fault in public speaking is to depart from the patterns of everyday speech and the rules of common sense.[80] But Cicero, of course, was inelegant and unlearned.[81] And we, of course, are superior; we find intolerable any mode of expression prompted by Nature. We search not for poetic embellishments but for meretricious ornaments—as if words have any value when they are not connected to solid fact! . . .

Those who think that the "new style" of oratory is appealing to the public and persuasive are very much deceived. It is flawed and rotten. It exults in an unbridled kind of diction and delights in childish little epigrams. Or it swells with unrestrained embellishments or runs wild with meaningless banal sayings. It glitters with flowery little phrases which will fall off if lightly touched. It thinks that a pointed style[82] can equal a sublime style; and it substitutes insane raving for freedom of speech.

The Ideal Orator

It is unquestionably true that the Roman system of education underwent many changes from the time of Cato to that of Cicero, and then of Seneca the Elder, and then of Tacitus and Quintilian. Yet it is also true that Romans of all periods would have agreed with Cato's succinct definition of the ideal orator: "a good man skilled in speaking." Although classroom exercises and classroom emphases varied from generation to generation, the purpose of an education in rhetoric was to produce a well-trained orator.[83] In the passage here, from his book *About the Orator,* Cicero describes the virtues, talents, and qualifications of the ideal orator. His words provide us with valuable information about the goals and the breadth of an education in rhetoric.

[80] Cicero lived at the end of the republican period. He is considered by many critics, both ancient and modern, to have been Rome's greatest orator.

[81] Quintilian is, of course, being facetious. He is suggesting that some rhetoricians of his period (about 150 years after Cicero) have called Cicero "inelegant and unlearned" because his style is clear and comprehensible.

[82] *pointed style:* replete with clever, witty, and abbreviated constructions.

[83] Compare Quintilian's definition in *The Elements of Oratory* 1. Preface. 10: "The man who is truly a citizen and fit for the administration of public and private business, who can guide cities by his advice, regulate them by his laws, reform them by his judgments—this man is none other than the orator."

143　　　　　　　　　　　　　　　Cicero, *About the Orator* 1.16–20

The study of oratory is more demanding, and involves a combination of more disciplines and sciences than men realize. And, if you consider the very large number of students, the very great abundance of teachers, the outstanding talents of men, the infinite variety of cases, and the most ample rewards for eloquence, what other reason is there, do you think, for the small number of good orators except the incredible magnitude and difficulty of the study of oratory? The student of oratory must acquire knowledge of a great many things, without which knowledge fluency of speech is empty and ridiculous. The student must develop his style by careful attention not only to word choice but also to sentence construction. He must be thoroughly acquainted with all the emotions which nature has bestowed on the human race because he must use all his power and ability at speaking to calm or, alternatively, to stir up those who listen to him.[84] He should also include in his style of speaking a certain charm and wit, erudition worthy of a well-bred man, quickness and brevity both in replying and in rebutting, as well as refined elegance and urbanity. He must, moreover, memorize all of history and a wealth of precedents, and not neglect knowledge of the laws and civil code. Need I speak further about delivery itself? Delivery of a speech must be reinforced by bodily movement, gesture, facial expression, and by modulation and variation of the voice.[85] The power of these skills, alone and in themselves, to move an audience is proved by the frivolous art of actors on the stage.[86] All the would-be actors work hard at controlling their facial expressions, voices, and gestures, but everyone knows how few actors there are or ever have been whom we can watch with patience. And what can I say about memory, the treasure chest of all experience? Unless memory is made the guardian of carefully formulated and clearly considered words and ideas, we know that all the skills of the orator, however excellent they be, will be of no avail.[87] And therefore we should cease to wonder what the reason is for the scarcity of eloquent orators; eloquence encompasses all sorts of skills, of which the mastery of even one by itself would be a notable achievement for the ordinary man. Therefore let us encourage our children, and others whose glory and honor is dear to us, to comprehend fully the magnitude of the study of oratory. . . . In my opinion, no one can be an orator possessed of every praiseworthy skill unless he has acquired knowledge of every important matter and art, for his style of speaking should be adorned and enriched by his learning. Unless the orator thoroughly grasps and understands his subject matter, his style of speaking will be empty and puerile declamation.

[84] Psychology was an important element in the curriculum at a rhetor's school.

[85] On declamation, see note 78 of this chapter.

[86] Students of oratory learned the same histrionic techniques as actors. Indeed Cicero seriously, though not permanently, injured his voice through his rigorous exercises for voice modulation. Later writers, such as Tacitus and Quintilian, complained that contemporary teachers of rhetoric spent too much time teaching declamation or techniques of delivery. In this passage, Cicero is willing to admit the close correspondence between declamatory and acting techniques, although he labels the actor's art as "frivolous" (for prejudice against actors, see the introduction to selection 335). Actors, according to Cicero, learn only techniques of delivery; the student of oratory must learn these, as well as composition, history, laws, psychology, and so on.

[87] Memory training began very early in the Roman system of education; see selections 131 and 132.

A YEAR ABROAD

Studying in Athens

After studying with a rhetor in Rome, some young men went abroad, to Greece or Asia Minor, to study rhetoric, oratory, declamation, and philosophy with the Greek "masters." Cicero's son went to Athens to complete his education, and his father provided him with a very handsome allowance which would enable him to pay tuition fees, to rent a spacious and comfortable apartment, and to maintain slaves. However, Cicero Jr. found the allurements of wine and women stronger than the allurements of rhetoric and philosophy; he squandered a good part of his allowance on parties. Rumors of his dissolute lifestyle began to drift back to Rome, and his father threatened to cut off funds if Cicero Jr. did not take his studies more seriously. In 44 B.C. Cicero Jr. therefore wrote to his father's secretary, Tiro, a letter, translated here, in which he claims that he has reformed and in which he describes his keen interest in his classes and his long hours of hard work at his studies. He evidently hoped that Tiro would believe him and speak on his behalf to his father. Can we believe Cicero Jr.'s account of his daily activities? We might compare a common modern situation. A college undergraduate, away from home for the first time, spends more time at parties than in classes or the library. His father writes and complains about his report card. The son writes back, professing to have reformed and to be working hard in his classes. To lend veracity to his letter, he gives specifics: he is really enjoying Professor Smith's anthropology class and Professor Brown's economics lectures.

144   Cicero, *Correspondence with Family and Friends* 16.21

Although I eagerly expected your letter-carriers every day, they finally arrived—forty-six days after they had left you.[88] Their arrival delighted me a great deal. And although I received the greatest pleasure from the letter from my very kind and dearly beloved father, yet certainly your most delightful letter set the seal on my joy.[89] . . .

I have no doubt that you find pleasing and welcome the rumors about me which reach you, dearest Tiro. I will undertake to work hard so that this new but growing good opinion of me doubles and increases every day. . . . For the errors of my youth have brought me such pain and such torment that not only does my mind shrink from contemplating these deeds, but my ears as well shrink from hearing them mentioned. . . . And because I then caused you grief, I will now undertake to double your joy on my account.

I should tell you that I have formed a very close attachment to Cratippus,[90] indeed not that of a pupil, but rather that of a son. For not only do I listen with pleasure to

---

[88] Mail delivery in the first century B.C. was about as efficient as our modern postal service. The ancient Romans had no public postal system. Letters were carried by private couriers.

[89] A little flattery will go a long way!

[90] *Cratippus:* head of the Peripatetic or Aristotelian school of philosophy.

his lectures, but I cherish greatly his personal charm. I am with him whole days at a time, and sometimes part of the night, because I beg him to dine with me as often as possible. Now that we have established this familiarity, he often drops in on us when we are having dinner and don't expect him;[91] throwing off his cloak of philosophic severity, he jokes with us in a very amiable manner. Therefore try to meet, as soon as possible, this special man, so affable and so distinguished.

What can I say about Bruttius?[92] I never allow him out of my sight. He leads a frugal and austere life, but he is nonetheless a very pleasant companion. A jovial mood pervades our discussions of "les belles-lettres"[93] and our daily joint "recherches." I have rented a room for him near mine, and, as far as I can, I alleviate his poverty out of my own meager allowance.[94]

In addition to all this, I have begun declamation lessons in Greek with Cassius;[95] however, I also want to practice declamation in Latin with Bruttius. I am a friend and daily companion of those men whom Cratippus brought with him from Mytilene; they are scholars for whom he has the highest esteem. I spend a lot of time, for example, with Epicrates, an important man in Athenian society,[96] and Leonides,[97] and others similar to these two. Well, "c'est tout" about me.

As for what you write about Gorgias,[98] yes, he was useful for daily practice in declamation. However, I considered everything else less important than obedience to my father's orders.[99] And he had written to me in explicit terms to get rid of Gorgias "tout de suite." I didn't want to hesitate or play for time lest my "ardeur" arouse some suspicion in him. And anyway, it struck me as a serious matter indeed for me to pass judgment on my father's judgment. However, your interest and advice are always welcome and gratefully received. . . .

I am indebted to you for carefully carrying out my instructions. But, please, send me a secretary as quickly as possible, most preferably a Greek.[100] I would be relieved of a lot of the labor of copying out lecture notes. Take care of yourself so that we can "discuter" literary matters together. I commend Anterus[101] to you.

---

[91] In other words, please send more money—for groceries.

[92] *Bruttius:* nothing else is known of him; his name suggests he is Italian.

[93] Cicero Jr. wrote, of course, in Latin but liked to toss in a few Greek phrases (here translated into French) to indicate that he was educated and cultured!

[94] *meager allowance:* In reality, Cicero Jr. had a very generous allowance which enabled him to support himself in a very lavish style. Of course, now that he is supplying dinners for one teacher and renting apartments for another teacher, he needs a larger allowance!

[95] *Cassius:* another professor with a Latin name.

[96] *Epicrates:* nothing else is known of him.

[97] *Leonides:* an Athenian who had, ironically, reported to Cicero Sr. the scandalous behavior of his son.

[98] *Gorgias:* a well-known rhetorician, but with a reputation for indecorous behavior. Cicero had forbidden his son to have further dealings with him.

[99] Would his father believe this expression of *pietas?*

[100] A modest request! On the use of secretaries, see note 7 of this chapter.

[101] *Anterus:* the courier who delivered the letter.

VII

Occupations

For the men of Roman society,[1] a good part of each day was occupied by one's "public life," that is, by work, business affairs, activities in the law courts, and so on.[2]

THE DAY'S ACTIVITIES

Dividing Up the Day

For much of their early history, the Romans had no device with which to divide the day into small segments such as hours. In order to measure the passage of time during the day, they depended on direct observation of the sun's position and could therefore mark with precision only three points during the day—sunrise, midday, and sunset—although they undoubtedly used the length of shadows to estimate other points—midmorning or midafternoon, for example.[3] In 263 B.C., a sundial was brought to Rome from Sicily and set up in the Forum.[4] This device enabled the Romans to divide the day (sunrise to sunset) into twelve equal segments, or hours, and they began to regulate their activities according to the "first hour" (the hour after sunrise), the "second hour," the "sixth hour" (the hour of midday), the "twelfth hour" (the hour before sunset), and so on. However, since the period from sunrise to sunset is shorter in the winter than in the summer, the twelve equal segments, or hours, were correspondingly shorter in the winter than in the summer. Some people had their own sundials, but most would still depend on personal observation of the sun's movement and of shadows.[5] Arrangement

---

[1] The position of women in Roman society is dealt with in Chapter XIII.

[2] Some men chose the military as an occupation. Chapter XI contains information about the activities of soldiers.

[3] *midday:* Latin *meridies;* therefore *ante meridiem* (a.m.) = "before midday," "morning," and *post meridiem* (p.m.) = "after midday," "afternoon."

[4] The sundial evidently became a favorite meeting place, and some idlers went there simply to pass the time, to see and to be seen.

[5] Sundials or water clocks might be set up in public buildings or squares. The public bath described in selection 309 had both a sundial and a water clock. Trimalchio, in selection 210, was wealthy enough to have a clock in his dining room.

for meetings must have been quite flexible. A "third hour" appointment probably meant more or less three hours after sunrise, and each party would expect to wait quite a while for the arrival of the other.[6]

The following passage is taken from the dialogue of a second-century B.C. Roman comedy. One of the characters in the play is complaining about these new-fangled devices which now regulate his life and eating habits.

145   Aquilius (O. Ribbeck, *Scaenicorum Romanorum Fragmenta* 1.33)

May the gods destroy that man who first discovered hours, the very man who first set up a sundial here, who smashed my day, alas, into fragments. When I was a boy, my stomach was my sundial, and the best and most accurate by far of all your time-telling devices. It always told you when you needed to eat (except when there was nothing to eat). But now, even when there is something to eat, you can't eat unless the sun agrees. And so now the town is filled to overflowing with sundials, but most people here crawl around all dried up with hunger.

City Life

Romans of all social classes began their day's activities at sunrise, or the first hour; and they retired early, usually not long after sunset. Artificial lighting was of such poor quality[7] that the Romans planned all their activities for daytime, when the sun's light could be utilized.[8] Even theater events, which we now think of as evening activities, were held by the Romans during the daytime in open-air structures.[9]

146   Martial, *Epigrams* 4.8.1–6

The first and second hours wear out the morning greeters.[10] The third hour taxes the talents of strident lawyers.[11] Rome continues her various labors well into the fifth hour. The sixth promises rest for the weary, and the seventh will bring an end to their work.[12]

[6] Compare selection 119: "Gaius Julius Primigenius was here. Why are you late?"

[7] See note 30 of Chapter VI on lighting at schools and the problems with lamps.

[8] And most activities were held either outdoors, in the Forum or Campus Martius, for example, or in open-air (roofless) structures, such as a *basilica* (law court), *macellum* (market), or peristyle.

[9] Few Romans ventured out after dark. On the dangers of being out at night, see selection 81.

[10] On "morning greeters," see selections 9–12. Most Romans would not be occupied, at least not every single day, with the *salutatio*. Most went directly to work at dawn. For mention of early-rising workers, teachers, and students, see selections 82 and 125.

[11] Since most lawyers were patrons, legal activity in the Forum probably did not begin until the morning greeting period was over.

[12] Most people quit work around noon (they had been working since dawn) for a light lunch and siesta period. Many probably returned to work for a few more hours later in the day. In modern Rome many people still work until 1:00 p.m. and then return to work from about 4:00 to 7:00 p.m. Schoolboys often attended two daily sessions; see selection 131.

The eighth hour provides time for the sleek gymnasia,[13] and the ninth bids us to sink down on cushions which have been piled high.[14]

WORKING FOR A LIVING

Scorn for the Working Class

The majority of men spent the day working to earn money to support their families. A small number of men, however, who lived off the income of their ancestral estates or their own investments, did not work for money; they could therefore occupy their time with unpaid "public service" positions such as magistracies,[15] priesthoods, legal counseling, jury duty, and Senate membership. They believed, moreover, that they were superior to the working class because they did not labor for wages. We have seen earlier how this attitude of superiority pervaded many aspects of Roman society. Because lower-class citizens could not afford to assume unpaid positions in the government (or to pay for many years of formal education), the upper class treated them as people who were incompetent to assume government positions.

In the passage translated here, Cicero discusses the occupations suitable for a gentleman. He and his friends believed that agriculture was the most honorable source of wealth. They did not, of course, work the land themselves, but rather lived off the profits accrued by the work of people in the lower class. In general, any paid labor was considered vulgar, but manual labor was particularly so.[16] The following passage indicates the stratification of Roman society according to occupations.

147   Cicero, *An Essay about Duties* 1.42, 2.25

We generally accept as true the following statements about trades and occupations, with regard to which are suitable for gentlemen and which are vulgar. First of all, those occupations are condemned which bring upon you people's hatred, such as tax collecting and usury.[17] Also vulgar and unsuitable for gentlemen are the occupations of all hired workmen whom we pay for their labor, not for their artistic skills; for with these men,

---

[13] The most popular time for attending the public baths, which included gymnasia, was after a light lunch. The gymnasia are called sleek because people were massaged with oil before exercising.

[14] The cushions have been piled up on dining couches which will be used during the evening meal. Dinner was apparently eaten rather early.

[15] Unless public officials are paid a salary, these positions will always remain the monopoly of the wealthy. Someone who works to support a family cannot afford to take time off to volunteer for public service.

[16] *vulgar:* Latin *vulgus* = "crowd," "mass of people," "rabble"; *manual:* Latin *manus* = "hand."

[17] Cicero condemns the individual who actually collects the money, not the businessman who profits from it; on tax collection and moneylending, see selections 157, 158, and 165.

their pay is itself a recompense for slavery. Also to be considered vulgar are retail merchants, who buy from wholesale merchants and immediately turn around and resell; for they would not make a profit unless they lied a lot. And nothing is more shameless than lying.[18] All craftsmen, too, are engaged in vulgar occupations, for a workshop or factory can have nothing genteel about it. And the most shameful occupations are those which cater to our sensual pleasures, "fish sellers, butchers, cooks, poultry raisers, and fishermen," as Terence says.[19] Add to these, if you like, perfume makers, dancers, and all of vaudeville.

However, occupations which involve a greater degree of intelligence or which provide no small service to society—such as medicine or architecture or teaching of liberal arts—these are proper for men whose social position they suit.[20] Trade, however, if it is small scale, must be considered vulgar; but if it is large scale, and involves importing many different items from throughout the world, and bringing many things to many people without lying or misrepresentation, it should not be greatly censured.[21] Indeed it appears that large-scale trade could even be praised under the most stringent law of respectability if a man engaging in it, once he was tired of it, or rather once he felt satisfied that he had achieved his goals, then moved himself from the harbor to a country estate, as he had often moved from the deep sea into a harbor.[22] For, of all the occupations from which profit is accrued, none is better than agriculture, none more profitable, none more delightful, none more suitable to a free man.[23] . . .

When Cato was asked what was the most profitable aspect of property ownership, he replied, "Raising livestock with great success." And then? "Raising livestock with some success." And after that? "Raising livestock with little success." And fourth? "Raising crops." And when the person asking questions said, "What about moneylending?" Cato replied, "What about murder?"[24]

Tradesmen and Craftsmen

However scornful they might be of the working class, the wealthy continued to employ their services and to purchase their products. The following passage from a Roman comedy written in the second century B.C. indicates the variety of specialized tradesmen and craftsmen in a large ancient city who catered to the whims of wealthy men and women.

[18] Cicero himself was a politician!

[19] Terence was a writer of Roman comedy who lived in the second century B.C.; see Appendix I. These words are taken from his play, *The Eunuch* (line 257).

[20] They would not be suitable for anyone like Cicero, in the upper class, but for lower-class men they are quite honorable.

[21] Cicero is being very careful not to offend the powerful large-scale traders, the equestrian class, to which many members of his family belonged. Compare his comments about the tax collector, and see selection 240.

[22] As a harbor literally provides security and relief from the stormy sea, so too rural life and land ownership figuratively provide security and relief from the stormy life of business and harbor trade.

[23] On the Roman idealization of rural life, see selections 177–180. Here Cicero at least mentions that the main goal of land ownership is profit. Only the wealthy could afford to own property as a business (as opposed to subsistence farming).

[24] Selection 160 provides quite different information about Cato's financial ventures.

148 Plautus, *The Pot of Gold* 505–522

Wherever you go nowadays, you see more wagons in front of city homes[25] than you would see in the country if you went to visit a farm. But even this is a welcome sight compared to when the tradesmen and craftsmen come around to collect payment. On your doorstep stand the clothes cleaner, the clothes dyer, the goldsmith, the wool weaver, the man who sells lace and the man who sells underwear, makers of veils, sellers of purple dye, sellers of yellow dye, makers of muffs and shoemakers who add balsam scent to their shoes, linen retailers, bootmakers, squatting cobblers, slipper makers, sandalmakers, and fabric stainers. They all demand payment—the cleaners, the dyers, the tailors, the belt makers, and the girdle makers. And just when you think you've paid them all, they leave, but others appear, three hundred more, demanding payment—purse makers, weavers, fringe makers, manufacturers of jewelry cases—all cluttering up your atrium. You owe them money and they want it. "Now," you think, "I've paid them all." But into your atrium come more dyers (these use saffron color!) and any other wretched gallows-bird[26] who wants some money.

Workers

Most of our information about workers in Roman society comes from pictorial sources—mosaics, wall-paintings, reliefs—rather than literary sources. The people who toiled every day to earn a living did not write down (if they could write) their feelings about their jobs. We therefore have very little written evidence about working conditions, job requirements, and so on. Literary sources sometimes make brief mention of jobs; we have already, for example, read of plasterers and butchers,[27] cart drivers, shoemakers and construction workers,[28] bakers, teachers and metalsmiths,[29] clothing peddlers and wool workers,[30] civil servants,[31] public criers and money collectors,[32] cooks, factory workers, merchants and fish sellers,[33] cleaners, dyers, and tailors.[34] Often we cannot ascertain whether the job mentioned was filled by a free man or a freedman, or even a slave. A bakery or textile worker, for example, might be free, freed, or slave. In addition, employers for factories and construction firms sometimes used slave labor for permanent jobs but hired free workers for temporary or part-time positions because free workers were cheaper; they did not need to be fed or clothed when they weren't working. However, although we do not know whether a bakery worker, for example, mentioned

---

[25] The wagons are making deliveries. The transportation industry employed many people; see selection 151. This passage was written before the implementation of the law forbidding vehicle traffic in Rome during the day; see notes 43 and 45 of Chapter IV.

[26] *gallows-bird:* the Latin is *crux,* "cross," "one who is destined for crucifixion."

[27] See selections 56 and 57.

[28] See selection 81.

[29] See selection 82.

[30] See selection 126.

[31] See selection 124.

[32] See selection 15.

[33] See selection 147.

[34] See selection 148.

in a poem or depicted in a wall-painting was free, freed, or slave, the workers themselves were well aware of the distinctions, and a lower-class free man undoubtedly considered himself socially superior to a slave or even a freedman doing the same job.[35] Moreover, although Cicero and his upper-class friends might be scornful of wage earners and shopkeepers, their arrogant attitude did not infect the way the wage earners and shopkeepers felt about themselves and their jobs. For the average Roman worker the aristocrats were about as far removed from his life as British royalty is from the British worker.

Political endorsements, painted on walls of buildings in Pompeii, provide evidence of a variety of occupations. They also indicate that people involved in the same occupation formed associations and were proud to be identified with that particular occupation.

149   *CIL* 4.206, 113, 710, 960, 826, 864, 336, 677, 743, 497, 7164,
                    7273, 373, 7473, 490, 6672 (*ILS* 6411c, 6412a, 6419c,
                    6419d, 6423, 6425, 6426, 6428a, 6428b, 6429)

The fruit sellers ask you to elect Marcus Holconius Priscus as aedile.[36]
The mule drivers ask you to elect Gaius Julius Polybius as duovir.[37]
All the goldsmiths ask you to elect Gaius Cuspius Pansa as aedile.
All the carpenters ask you to elect Cuspius Pansa as aedile.
All the fishermen say: "Elect Popidius Rufus as aedile."
The cloth dyers ask you to elect Postumius Proculus as aedile.
The innkeepers urge you: "Make Sallustius Capito aedile."
The bakers urge you: "Make Trebius aedile."
The barbers want Trebius as aedile.
The porters[38] and movers ask you to elect Aulus Vettius as aedile.
The fullers[39] ask you to elect Holconius Priscus as duovir.
The millers and their neighbors want Gnaeus Helvius Sabinus as aedile.
The chicken sellers ask you to elect Epidius and Suettius as duovirs.
The mat makers ask you to elect Lollius as aedile.
The farmers ask you to elect Marcus Casellius Marcellus as aedile.
The grape pickers ask you to elect Casellius as aedile.

Pride of Workmanship

Artisans frequently put their names on articles they made. The first "signature" below was found on a bronze *strigil*,[40] the second on a shallow bowl, and the third on a mold for a bowl. The articles were made about 220 B.C.

[35] On the prejudice against freedmen, see selections 210–212.
[36] *aedile:* city magistrate who had the superintendence of public buildings, works, and markets; see selections 229–231.
[37] *duovir:* see note 60 of Chapter II.
[38] *porters:* see selection 151.
[39] *fullers:* people who make and clean cloth.
[40] *strigil:* a scraper used by bathers. After a massage with oil, bathers would use a *strigil* to remove the excess oil from their skin. They would then enter the hot air, hot water room of the bath; see selection 309.

150   *CIL* 1.2.2437 (*ILS* 9444), 406, 2489

Lucilius made me.
Made by Lucius Canuleius, son of Lucius, from Cales.[41]
I am from the factory of Lucius Canuleius.

Temporary Employment

The traveling companions in Petronius's *Satyricon*[42] could not afford to buy and
keep a slave, and so they hired a free man when they needed a porter to carry
their baggage during the trip.[43] The porter is an example of the large class of poor
free workers who had no steady income and probably lived a marginal existence.[44]

151   Petronius, *Satyricon* 117.11, 12

We hired a man named Corax, who complained constantly about the job and kept putting down our luggage and cursing us for walking too fast and swearing that he would
either throw our luggage away or run off with all of it. "What do you think I am?" he
said. "A pack animal or a cargo ship? I hired myself out to do the work of a man, not
a horse! I'm no less a free man than you people, even if my father did leave me a pauper." And not content with swearing at us, he immediately lifted up his leg and filled
the street with the noise and odor of a fart.

Wage and Price Control

By the third century A.D., inflation was wildly out of control. In an attempt to
stabilize the economy, the emperor Diocletian fixed a ceiling on wages and prices
throughout the whole Roman Empire. At the very beginning of the fourth century, in A.D. 301, he published an edict on maximum prices. Anyone, anywhere
in the Empire, who tried to charge or to pay more than the maximum price could
be punished by death or exile. However, it proved impossible to enforce the edict
and it was finally revoked.

The passages here show but a small sample of the very extensive list of
items and services whose prices were controlled by the edict. They allow us, however, some understanding of the standard of living of the lower class. For example, a mule driver or a farmworker had to work one day and a carpenter or a
baker had to work half a day in order to earn the money to purchase two pounds
of pork.[45] And a mule driver's boots would cost him five days' wages.[46] Nowadays

---

[41] *Cales:* a town in southern Italy.
[42] *traveling companions:* see also selections 194 and 210.
[43] Carrying baggage and market goods was considered a very undesirable type of employment; see note 42 of Chapter IX.
[44] Compare the use of temporary free workers on farms; see note 176 of this chapter.
[45] The Italian pound weighed about twelve British or American ounces.
[46] Fine-quality leather boots are still expensive today, although they can be purchased

even minimum-wage earners can purchase the same amount of pork after just one or two hours of work. The average family of Roman society was far less affluent than the average family of modern American society.

152   *CIL* 3, pp. 805, 806, 808, 809

Food Prices

ITEM	AMOUNT	PRICE
wheat	1 army measure[47]	100 denarii
barley	1 army measure	60 denarii
rye	1 army measure	60 denarii
millet, ground	1 army measure	100 denarii
millet, whole	1 army measure	50 denarii
beans, ground	1 army measure	100 denarii
beans, not ground	1 army measure	60 denarii
lentils	1 army measure	100 denarii
peas, split	1 army measure	100 denarii
peas, not split	1 army measure	60 denarii
chick-peas	1 army measure	100 denarii
vetch	1 army measure	100 denarii
oats	1 army measure	30 denarii
fenugreek	1 army measure	100 denarii
lupines, raw	1 army measure	60 denarii
lupines, cooked	1 army measure	40 denarii
beans, dried	1 army measure	100 denarii

Wine Prices

Picene[48]	1 Italian sextarius[49]	30 denarii
Tiburtine[48]	1 Italian sextarius	30 denarii
Sabine[48]	1 Italian sextarius	30 denarii
Falernian[48]	1 Italian sextarius	30 denarii
aged wine, first quality	1 Italian sextarius	24 denarii
aged wine, second quality	1 Italian sextarius	16 denarii
vin ordinaire	1 Italian sextarius	8 denarii

Oil Prices

olive oil, fresh	1 Italian sextarius	40 denarii
olive oil, second quality	1 Italian sextarius	24 denarii
vinegar	1 Italian sextarius	6 denarii

---

with less than five days' wages. Today, however, we have the advantage of being able to purchase cheaper boots made of synthetic materials. Thus, more people today can afford to have boots.

[47] *measure:* Latin *modius* = one peck. (There are four pecks in a bushel.)

[48] *Picene, Tiburtine, Sabine, Falernian:* regions of Italy from which the wine came.

[49] *sextarius:* a Roman liquid measure equivalent to about one pint.

liquamen,[50] first quality	1 Italian sextarius	16 denarii
liquamen, second quality	1 Italian sextarius	12 denarii
salt	1 army measure	100 denarii
honey, best quality	1 Italian sextarius	40 denarii
honey, second quality	1 Italian sextarius	24 denarii

Meat Prices

pork	1 Italian pound	12 denarii
beef	1 Italian pound	8 denarii
goose, fattened	1 Italian pound	200 denarii
goose, not fattened	1 Italian pound	100 denarii
chicken	1 Italian pound	60 denarii
lamb	1 Italian pound	12 denarii
goat	1 Italian pound	12 denarii

Fish Prices

fish, second quality	1 Italian pound	16 denarii
freshwater fish, first quality	1 Italian pound	12 denarii
freshwater fish, second quality	1 Italian pound	8 denarii

Wages

farm laborer, with meals, daily	25 denarii
painter, walls, with meals, daily	75 denarii
painter, pictures, with meals, daily	150 denarii
carpenter, with meals, daily	50 denarii
baker, with meals, daily	50 denarii
camel driver or donkey driver, with meals, daily	25 denarii
shepherd, with meals, daily	20 denarii
mule driver, with meals, daily	25 denarii
veterinary, for trimming hoofs, per animal	6 denarii
veterinary, for bleeding and cleaning the head, per animal	20 denarii
barber, per man	2 denarii
sewer cleaner, full day's work, with meals, daily	25 denarii
tailor, for cutting and sewing a hooded cloak of first quality	60 denarii
tailor, for cutting and sewing a hooded cloak of second quality	40 denarii
tailor, for breeches	20 denarii
tailor, for heavy stockings	4 denarii
elementary teacher, per boy, monthly	50 denarii[51]
arithmetic teacher, per boy, monthly	75 denarii

[50] *liquamen:* fish sauce; see selection 92.

[51] An elementary teacher thus needed at least 15 students in order to earn as much as a mule-driver.

grammaticus (Greek or Latin language and literature, geometry), per student, monthly	200 denarii
teacher of rhetoric or public speaking, per student, monthly	250 denarii
teacher of architecture, per boy, monthly	100 denarii
clothing guarder at baths,[52] per bather	2 denarii
bath attendant, per bather	2 denarii

Prices for

boots, mule drivers' or farmworkers' first quality, without hobnails	120 denarii
boots, soldiers', without hobnails	100 denarii
shoes, patrician	150 denarii
shoes, senatorial	100 denarii
shoes, equestrian	70 denarii
boots, women's	60 denarii

The Grain Dole

The population of the city of Rome in the early imperial period was about one million. Some people had been forced to move to the city to seek employment when slave laborers had replaced them on the farms.[53] Others were attracted to the city because it was the political, financial, and entertainment capital of the Western world. And some people were brought to Rome as slaves but remained there as freedmen. Jobs were increasingly more difficult to find, and slaves and freedmen occupied many positions which, in another society, would be filled by free citizens of the lower class. In general, the life of the lower-class urban worker was harsh. Wages were low, prices were high, and jobs were sometimes only temporary. Free workers had no job security, no retirement benefits, no medical plans, and no unemployment insurance. Indeed, some free workers led harsher lives than some slaves, who were fed, clothed, and given medical care by their masters. Some people, both free and freed, therefore attached themselves to patrons who might help them along with gifts or money. Unfortunately, some patrons expected their clients to grovel in return for a handout.[54] The state provided welfare assistance in the form of a grain dole. In 122 B.C., Gaius Gracchus, a tribune,[55] brought forward a law to insure a low and unvarying grain price for Roman citizens. The government was to maintain a supply of grain[56] in public warehouses in Ostia[57] and to sell it in fixed monthly rations at a low price to

[52] A bather might bring his own slave to guard his clothes while he was bathing, or he might hire someone at the baths. On public baths, see selection 309.

[53] See selection 170.

[54] See selections 10–13.

[55] *tribune:* an elected public official; see selections 229 to 231. On Gaius Gracchus and his brother Tiberius, see selection 170.

[56] The grain came to Italy from the provinces, especially from Sicily, Egypt, and Africa. Some of it was grain paid by these provinces as "tribute"; see note 74 of this chapter. Grain was a staple of the Roman diet.

[57] *Ostia:* the harbor of Rome; see note 71 of Chapter IV.

Roman citizens. In 58 B.C., Publius Clodius Pulcher,[58] a tribune for that year, ingratiated himself with the urban proletariat by bringing forward a law which allowed Roman citizens to receive public grain free rather than at a reduced price. The Roman lower class became very dependent on these monthly grain handouts, prompting more than one critic to say that the Romans were interested only in "bread and circuses."[59]

153   Tacitus, *Annals,* 6.13, 12.43

[In A.D. 32] a revolution almost occurred because of a serious problem with the grain supply. For several days, protests in the theater,[60] protests directed toward the emperor,[61] were more frequent and more outspoken than usual. The emperor was infuriated and blamed the magistrates and the Senate because they had not kept the common people in check with the authority vested in them as public servants. He also made clear from what provinces he was bringing in grain and how much greater an amount of grain he was bringing in than his predecessor Augustus had. . . .

Many prodigies occurred [in A.D. 51]. . . . A shortage of grain and the resulting famine were regarded as prodigies. And the complaints of the people were not kept low or private. Instead they surrounded Claudius[62] with angry clamoring when he was in court hearing cases; then they pushed and shoved him roughly to the very edge of the Forum until he escaped the hostile mob with the help of a band of soldiers. It was learned that the city had only fifteen days of grain left. Only the benevolence of the gods and the mildness of the winter relieved this desperate situation.

BUSINESS AND INVESTMENTS

Most people in Roman society could make only enough money to cover their family living expenses. A lucky few, however, had capital to invest in something which would produce more capital which could, in turn, be invested. For these people, income was derived from business operations and investments rather than from wages for hired work. Of course, not all businessmen were wealthy. A man might have only enough capital, for example, to purchase one store or one factory[63] which he then ran as a family business. A cobbler's shop might therefore

[58] *Publius Clodius Pulcher:* see note 72 of Chapter III and also selection 206.

[59] *bread:* the free grain was ground into flour and made into bread.

circuses: chariot races; see selections 346–353.

There were flaws in the grain dole system, as there are flaws today in the welfare system. Some unscrupulous Romans obtained grain dole privileges and then turned around and sold the free grain. However, the grain dole did keep many unemployed families from starvation.

[60] It was very common for people to use the theater as the public place in which they would voice their complaints.

[61] *the emperor:* in A.D. 32, Tiberius, stepson of Augustus.

[62] *Claudius: emperor* in A.D. 51. He was Augustus's grandson and Tiberius's nephew.

[63] *factory:* Latin *facere* = "to make"; compare *manufacture,* from the Latin *manus* = "hand," *factum* = "made."

be a factory and the cobbler a self-employed businessman living very modestly. A husband and wife might produce and bottle fish sauce and therefore own a fish sauce factory. The word *factory* need not automatically imply a high-volume business employing many workers. Similarly, a man who owned one store, or one restaurant, or one mule which he used to transport other people's goods, was "in business" although his basic standard of living might not have been higher than that of a hired worker. However, ownership of a business did give him a property value above that of a man who had no money to invest,[64] and the small businessman might therefore be viewed in a separate category of the lower class.[65] There were also, of course, big businessmen, men who had vast amounts of money to invest. These people possessed the property value necessary for admission to the equestrian or senatorial orders and therefore belonged to the upper classes of Roman society.[66]

The most common and the safest investment was real estate, and the wealth of the senatorial families was tied up largely in agricultural lands and urban rental property. For adventurous investors, however, many other investment opportunities existed.

The Roman Attitude toward Profit

The Roman attitude toward profit is best revealed not by Cicero's lofty pronouncements on the shamefulness of trade[67] but rather by popular expressions. The following phrases were set into the mosaic pavement of houses in Pompeii, and they leave no doubt about the interest in moneymaking in Pompeii.

154   *CIL* 10.874, 10.875

Hello Profit!

Profit Is Happiness!

[64] Every five years a census was taken to determine the property value of Roman citizens; Latin *censere* = "to assess."

[65] There were undoubtedly middle businessmen as well, people who owned two or three shops or factories, for example. Some historians believe that these people formed a middle class of Roman society. We should remember, however, that such people lived comfortably, rather than affluently.

[66] We have seen that the plural *lower classes* probably better describes the divisions of Roman society than the singular *lower class* because there was a range in both the incomes and the social status of Rome's humble masses. There were free men and freedmen, men who worked for a very low wage, men who were hired for temporary jobs, men who owned some property, men who owned none, and so on. Similarly, there was not one upper class. The old aristocratic families treated the *nouveau riche* with disdain, and senators and equestrians were often suspicious of one another's interests. On the hostility toward wealthy freedmen, see selection 210.

[67] See selection 147.

Traders

From the earliest period of Roman history, traders were busy, buying goods in one location and selling them in another. As Rome's dominance expanded, first in Italy then throughout Europe and the Mediterranean world, the opportunities for trade also increased. Wealthy men began to invest in cargo loads of merchandise and also in the ships needed to move the merchandise.[68] Roman traders traveled to every province and shipped goods from Rome to Britain and Syria, from Britain to Greece and Egypt, and from Spain and North Africa to Rome. But enterprising traders went far beyond the frontiers of the Roman Empire. Items manufactured in Italy have been found, for example, in Scandinavia, and trade connections were established even with India and China. Some traders were self-employed; others were agents of large trading companies which were owned by wealthy investors. Wherever the Roman legions went, Roman businessmen followed closely in their wake. And the superb Roman roads built by these legions were used as much for the rapid transport of trade items and business records as for the movement of troops and military supplies. One duty of Roman garrisons in the provinces was to protect the interests, and lives, of Roman businessmen.[69] And these businessmen seemed to control the economy of many provinces.

155   Cicero, *Speech in Defense of Fonteius* 11

I say this with confidence, gentlemen; I do not make this assertion rashly. Gaul[70] is crowded with traders and packed with Roman citizens. No one in Gaul ever does business without the involvement of a Roman citizen. There is not a penny jingling in Gaul which has not been recorded in the account books of Roman citizens.

Rome, The World Trade Center

Aelius Aristides was a Greek rhetorician who lived in the second century A.D. He wrote a eulogy on the city of Rome, from which this passage is taken.

156   Aelius Aristides, *In Praise of Rome* 200, 201 (349–351)

Large continents lie all around the Mediterranean, and from them, to you,[71] flow constant supplies of goods. Everything is shipped to you, from every land and from every sea—the products of each season, of each country, of each river and lake, the crafts of

---

[68] On the rise of this new upper class, see the introduction to Chapter I.

[69] See the introduction to Chapter XII. Also compare the "opening up" of the New World. Trading companies—Spanish, Dutch, French, Portuguese, and British—had a vested interest in "pacification." Military expansion was a political issue supported by businessmen, and these same businessmen demanded military protection. In the history of the world, many wars have been undertaken for financial profit.

[70] *Gaul:* the Roman provinces of Gallia; see map 5.

[71] *to you:* that is, to the people of Rome.

Greeks and other foreigners. As a result, if anyone wants to see all these items, he must either travel through the whole world to behold them, or live in this city. Everything that is grown or manufactured by each people is not only always present here, but is present in abundance. So many ships land here bringing cargo from all over, during every season, after every harvest. And thus the city seems like a common market for the world. You can see so many cargoes from India or, if you wish, from Arabia Felix,[72] that you might think the trees in those countries had been left permanently bare and that the inhabitants would have to come to Rome if they needed anything, to beg for their own goods. Clothing from Babylonia and ornaments from foreign lands beyond arrive here in greater quantity and more easily than goods shipped from Naxos or Cythnos to Athens.[73] Egypt, Sicily, and the cultivated part of Libya are your farms.[74] The arrival and departure of ships never cease. And consequently it is quite amazing that there is enough room in the sea, much less the harbor,[75] for the ships. . . . Everything comes together here: trade and commerce, the transportation industry, agriculture, metallurgy, every skill which exists now and has existed, all that is produced and grows.

Moneylending

Moneylending was as common in ancient Rome as it is today. Today, however, most people borrow large sums of money from a bank or savings and loan institution; in ancient Rome, "bankers" were private individuals with enough capital to make loans. And, despite Cicero's denigration of moneylending, some of the "best" people made their fortunes by lending money, although they may have concealed the fact by using agents.[76]

This passage records the activities of a moneylender in a Dacian goldmining village.[77] The document was written on waxed tablets[78] in A.D. 162.

157   *FIRA* 3, p. 393 (*CIL* 3, pp. 934, 935)

Julius Alexander, the lender, required a promise in good faith that the loan of 60 denarii of genuine and sound coin would be duly settled on the day he requested it. Alexander, son of Cariccius, the borrower, promised in good faith that it would be so settled, and declared that he had received the sixty denarii mentioned above, in cash, as

---

[72] *Arabia Felix: felix* = "lucky," "prosperous." The epithet *felix* is not particularly appropriate because only the land on the west coast of Arabia was fertile. However, it was the west coast which was visited by traders.

[73] *Naxos, Cythnos:* Greek islands in the Aegean. Aristides, who is writing in Greek, makes a comparison which will be easily understood by his Greek audience.

[74] Egypt, Sicily, and Libya (North Africa) shipped grain to Rome in large quantities. Much of this grain was given to the government of Rome as tribute payment. The influx into Rome of this free grain had a negative effect on the domestic grain farmer but helped to provide cheap food for the urban masses; see selection 153.

[75] Rome's harbor was at Ostia.

[76] See note 103 of this chapter; also see selection 280.

[77] *Dacia:* a Roman province; see map 5.

[78] *waxed tablets:* see note 54 of Chapter VI.

a loan, and that he owed them. Julius Alexander required a promise in good faith that the interest on this principal from this day would be one percent per thirty days[79] and would be paid to Julius Alexander or to whomever it might in the future concern. Alexander, son of Cariccius, promised in good faith that it would be so paid. Titius Primitius stood surety[80] for the due and proper payment of the principal mentioned above and of the interest.

Transacted at Alburnus Maior, October 20, in the consulship of Rusticus (his second consulship) and Aquilinus.[81]

Loan Companies

Sometimes two or more individual moneylenders would combine resources and form a loan company.[82] The following passage is a translation of a document written on a waxed tablet in Dacia in A.D. 167. One of the partners is the same Julius Alexander whom we met in the previous passage.

158   *FIRA* 3, p. 481 (*CIL* 3, pp. 950, 951, 2215)

A partnership for moneylending has been formed between Cassius Frontinus and Julius Alexander, to continue from December 23 of last year, when Pudens and Polio were consuls,[83] until next April 12. They agreed that they would be obligated to assume in equal proportions whatever happened to the capital invested in this partnership, whether profit or loss occurred.

Julius Alexander contributed to this partnership 500 denarii . . . and Secundus, slave and agent of Cassius Palumbus, contributed 267 denarii for Frontinus. . . .[84]

In this partnership, if either member is discovered to have perpetrated a fraud with malice aforethought, he will be obligated to pay the other one denarius for each *as*, and 20 denarii for each denarius. And when the term of the agreement has expired, they will be obligated to recover the sums mentioned above, allowing for loans still outstanding, and to divide up any profit. . . .

This agreement was made at Deusara on March 28[85] in the consulship of Verus (his third consulship) and Quadratus.[86]

[79] *one percent per thirty days:* twelve percent per year.

[80] He promised to be responsible for the payment of the loan. If Alexander, the borrower, did not pay, Titius Primitius would have to.

[81] A.D. 162. It was customary in dating to give only the names of the consuls for that year.

[82] Though moneylenders have throughout history been the objects of scorn and hatred, most were only occupying the role now played by banking institutions. And the twelve percent interest charged by Julius Alexander in the previous passage seems reasonable by modern standards.

[83] A.D. 166. It is interesting that this contract, like the previous one, was written quite some time after the oral agreement was made. In other words, the contract was really the oral agreement made in the presence of witnesses; the written document, written later, is only evidence that a contract had been entered into.

[84] The text, on waxed tablets, has been mutilated in some spots.

[85] The agreement extends only until April 12. The document was written only a few days before the expiration of the contract (the oral agreement).

[86] A.D. 167.

War Bonds

In the early years of the Second Punic War, Hannibal and his army ravaged much of Italy.[87] The Romans were in a desperate position; there were severe shortages both of supplies for the army and of money to purchase the supplies. The government appealed to private individuals to make loans to the state (compare the modern system of war bonds). In 210 B.C., some individuals did lend to the state money which was to be repaid in three installments. By 200 B.C., the third installment had not yet been paid.[88]

159   Livy, *A History of Rome* 31.13

[In 200 B.C.] when the consuls were ready to set off to their provinces,[89] a group of private businessmen appealed to the Senate. The state owed them that year the third installment of payment for loans which they had made in the consulship of Marcus Valerius and Marcus Claudius.[90] However, the consuls had said that, because the state treasury had scarcely enough funds for the new war, which required a large fleet and large armies,[91] there were no funds at present to pay them the third installment. The Senate could not ignore them or their complaints. If the state planned to use for the Macedonian War the money which they had lent it for the Punic War, and if one war after another arose, what would happen? In return for their generosity, their money would be confiscated, as if for some crime on their part![92]

Since the creditors, on the one hand, were making a just request, but the state, on the other hand, was not able to pay off the debt, the Senate decreed a middle course between what was just and what was expedient; it decreed that, because many of the creditors had spoken of land in various areas which was for sale, land which they urgently wished to buy,[93] they should have the opportunity to obtain public land within

[87] The Second Punic War was fought from 218 to 201 B.C. between the Romans and the Carthaginians (who were also known as Punici). Hannibal, a Carthaginian general, moved his army from Spain, across the Alps, into Italy during the first year of the war, and stayed in Italy until 203 B.C. The Romans eventually won the war after moving troops into North Africa (Carthage was in North Africa); see Appendix III.

[88] It was not, in fact, paid until 195 B.C.

[89] The consuls were not only urban magistrates, but also commanders-in-chief of the Roman army. Each was therefore assigned a province or sphere for military activity during his one-year term of office.

[90] 210 B.C.

[91] In 200 B.C., the Second Punic War was over, but Rome had now declared war against Philip of Macedon. The Macedonian War ended in 196 B.C. Philip was forced to pay a huge war indemnity, part of which was used in 195 B.C. to make the third and final installment of the loan discussed in this passage.

[92] That is, if the loan were not fully paid, the lenders would lose their money; they would feel that the state had confiscated their money, just as it confiscated, through fines, the money of convicted criminals.

[93] This passage provides another viewpoint of a topic discussed in selection 170. Real estate investors were busy purchasing, at a low price, farmland which families were forced to sell because their menfolk were away at war, or because they had been devastated by the occupation of Hannibal's troops. The state's creditors wanted payment on their loans so that they would have cash available to purchase land.

the fiftieth milestone from the city.[94] The consuls were to place a cash value on the land and then impose a rent of one as for each acre[95] to indicate that the land was still public.[96] Then, when the state was able to discharge its debt, if any of the creditors preferred to have his money, rather than the land, he could give the land back to the state.[97] The private businessmen happily accepted this arrangement.

Cato's Financial Activities

In an earlier passage, Cicero quoted Cato as comparing moneylending to murder.[98] However, as we learn from this biography of Cato by a Greek author, Cato apparently found moneylending more profitable than agriculture.

160   Plutarch, *The Life of Marcus Cato* 21.1, 3, 5–7

Cato owned many slaves; he usually bought prisoners of war who were young and could be raised and trained like puppies or colts. . . . Since he believed that the main reason slaves misbehaved was their sexual frustration, he arranged for his male slaves to have intercourse with his female slaves, but for a fixed price.[99] . . .

Once he applied himself more seriously to the business of making money, he viewed agriculture more as an amusement than as a profitable venture, and he invested his capital in safe and sure things: he bought ponds, hot springs, land rich in fuller's earth,[100] areas which produced pitch, land with natural pastures and woods—all of which produced for him a great deal of money and could not, as he himself used to say, "be ruined by Jupiter."[101]

He also engaged in the most frequently criticized type of moneylending, namely on ships.[102] This was his method. He required the borrowers to gather many partners. When there were fifty partners and as many ships, he acquired one share in this company through an agent, his freedman Quintio,[103] who sailed with the borrowers and worked with them. Thus, he did not carry the entire risk himself, but only a small part of it, and his profits were great.

[94] *public land:* when the Romans conquered territory in Italy, they confiscated a portion of land and said that it now belonged to Rome. It became state-owned land or "public land"; see selection 170.

[95] *one as:* a very nominal fee indeed; see Appendix II.

[96] The land would remain public and the creditors would rent it until such time as the state could pay the third installment in cash.

[97] Otherwise he would keep the land in lieu of the third payment. He would then receive clear title to the land. We have no idea how many creditors chose the land in lieu of money when the state offered in 195 B.C. to make the third payment.

[98] See selection 147. For more information about Cato, see selections 121, 184, and 292.

[99] Payable to Cato, of course.

[100] *fuller's earth:* hydrous silicate of alumina, used by the Romans in the cleaning of woolen garments such as togas.

[101] The gods might be responsible for weather which destroyed crops, but they could not harm Cato's moneymaking ventures: the sale of water, fuller's earth, pitch, wood, and pasturing leases.

[102] Also known as bottomry loans. The lender provides money to a shipowner to cover the expenses of a voyage. The ship is the security. If the ship sinks, the lender loses his money.

[103] Notice that Cato, a member of the senatorial order, worked through a freedman agent.

A Real Estate Speculator

Marcus Licinius Crassus was born into an aristocratic family and served with distinction in a number of military campaigns. He was a very shrewd businessman and became extremely wealthy. Since he preferred business interests to the senatorial interests of his ancestors, he is usually labeled by historians as an equestrian. His family was, however, senatorial, and he himself was elected consul for 70 B.C. and 55 B.C. But, as consul, he promoted the interests of the equestrian order and weakened the senatorial order. After his first term as consul, he controlled Roman politics and protected equestrian interests from behind the scenes. With his enormous wealth he "bought" many politicans. In 60 B.C., he became a member of the First Triumvirate[104] which used vast sums of money and threats of violence and civil war to dominate the Roman state.

161   Plutarch, *The Life of Crassus* 1, and 2.1–6

Marcus Crassus was the son of a man who had been censor[105] and had celebrated a triumph.[106] He was raised in a small house with two brothers. While their parents were still alive, his brothers married, but everyone continued to live under the same roof, which may well explain why Crassus was temperate and moderate throughout his life. When one of his brothers died, he married his widow and had his children by her. In his family life, he was as well disciplined as any Roman.[107] However, some years later he was accused of consorting with Licinia, one of the Vestal Virgins,[108] when Licinia was prosecuted by a certain Plotius. But she owned some nice suburban property which Crassus was hoping to get for a low price, and that's why he was always hanging around her and flattering her (at least until he fell under suspicion). And, in a way, he was cleared of the charge of corrupting a Vestal Virgin and was acquitted by the jurors because of his avarice.[109] But he did not leave Licinia alone until he had acquired her property.

The Romans say that Crassus's many virtues were overshadowed by this one vice, avarice. It seems that one vice became stronger in him than all his other faults and actually weakened the others. The main proofs of his avarice are considered to be his

---

104 *triumvirate:* Latin *tris* (or *tres*) = "three," *viri* = "men." A triumvirate was a political alliance of three men. The First Triumvirate was an alliance formed by Caesar, Pompey, and Crassus. The Second Triumvirate was formed by Octavian (Augustus), Antony, and Lepidus; for this alliance, see selection 80 of Chapter III.

105 Every five years, two men were elected censors. They had an eighteen-month term of office during which they supervised the census (the register of people and property); see note 64 of this chapter. Usually these elected officials were men of very high rank in the Senate, for the censorship was considered a very distinguished appointment. For more on the duties of the censors, see selections 229 and 230.

106 *triumph:* see selection 267.

107 The ancient Romans were noted for their discipline and pragmatism, not their romanticism. The author of this passage is a Greek. (For a Roman view of the Greek character, see selection 212).

108 *Vestal Virgins:* see selections 379 and 380.

109 His avarice was so well known that everyone agreed that it, and not passion, had kindled his interest in Licinia.

method of obtaining wealth and the amount of his wealth. For in the beginning he possessed no more than 300 talents,[110] but during his consulship[111] he not only dedicated one-tenth of his property to Hercules and provided a feast for all the people, but even gave from his own pocket to every Roman enough to live on for three months.[112] And yet, when he made an inventory of his property before his Parthian expedition,[113] he discovered he was worth 7100 talents.

Most of this money, if one must tell the truth, however scandalous, he acquired through fire and war, making public disasters his greatest source of income. For example, when Sulla took control of Rome and sold off the property of those men proscribed by him,[114] considering it and calling it "spoils of war,"[115] he wanted to implicate in his crime as many of the most influential men as he could. And Crassus was not at all hesitant to accept or to buy this property from Sulla. In addition, since he realized how familiar and how common at Rome were calamitous fires and collapses of buildings because the structures were too heavy and too close together,[116] he bought slaves who were architects and builders.[117] When he had over 500 such slaves, he used to buy houses that were on fire, and houses next to those on fire, since the owners would sell at a very low price because of their fear and uncertainty. Thus, the greater part of Rome came into his possession. . . . And although he owned many, many silver mines and very valuable agricultural land with workers on it, yet one might consider all this a mere pittance in comparison with the values of his slaves, so many and so talented were the slaves he owned.

[110] This was no mean amount. Compare selection 280; the people of Salamis, the whole town, owed Brutus 106 talents and were unable to pay him.

[111] 70 B.C. His colleague in the consulship that year was Pompey. He was consul again in 55 B.C. (again with Pompey). See Appendix III.

[112] It was not uncommon for an elected official to curry favor with the general populace by bestowing lavish gifts paid for from the official's pocket. When, however, the official received an appointment as governor of an overseas province, he tried to recoup his financial losses by extorting money from the provincials. Consider Verres's behavior in selection 281.

[113] After his year as consul of 55 B.C., Crassus was sent as proconsul (governor) to govern Syria. With his army he invaded Syria's neighbor, Parthia. The expedition was a disaster. The Parthians were superb horsemen and archers who defeated the Roman infantry in every encounter. Crassus himself was killed in 53 B.C. at the battle of Carrhae. Over two-thirds of his soldiers were also killed in this battle.

[114] Sulla was a Roman general who imposed himself as dictator of Rome from 81 to 79 B.C. (On the office of dictator, see selection 231). He eliminated his enemies by proscribing them, that is, marking them for execution. Their names would be published on a proscription list; then anyone could kill them with impunity. Sulla confiscated the property of proscribed men and sold it to enrich his treasury. For more on Sulla and his proscriptions, see selection 215.

In 43 B.C., Cicero was proscribed by Antony and executed; see notes 67 and 68 of Chapter VI. Turia's husband was also persecuted by Antony, although he escaped execution; see selection 288.

[115] It was in fact Roman land, taken from Roman citizens, in a civil war.

[116] On the dangers of fires and building collapses in ancient Rome, see selections 69 and 71.

[117] Compare Cicero's comments on the social standing of architects in selection 147.

A Government Construction Contract

Once the Senate or town council had approved a construction project, it accepted bids from private contractors. The contract translated below is for work to be done in the town of Puteoli (modern Pozzuoli, near Naples). The work was approved by the town council of Puteoli, and the contract was awarded in 105 B.C. to Gaius Blossius. The inscription was found on a marble tablet.

162   *ROL* 4, pp. 274–278 (*CIL* 1.2.698)

Contract for building a wall[118] in the vacant lot in front of the temple of Serapis[119] across the road:

The contractor shall provide bondsmen[120] and shall register their properties as securities at the discretion of the duovirs. In the middle of this wall, which is in the vacant lot across the road and which is near the road, he shall make an opening for a doorway. He shall make it six feet wide and seven feet high. From the wall he shall extend out toward the sea two columns two feet long and one foot three inches thick. Above the doorway he shall place a lintel of oak wood eight feet long, one foot three inches wide, and nine inches thick.

The contract continues with detailed specifications for construction of the wall, the porch, and the doors, including the type of materials used.

He shall complete the whole project at the discretion of the duovirs and the council of ex-duovirs who govern Puteoli, provided that not less than twenty members are present when the matter is discussed. Whatever is approved by twenty of them on oath shall be legally binding; whatever is not approved by them shall not be legally binding.

Day for the work to begin: next November 1.

Day of payment: one-half the total payment shall be made when the properties of the bondsmen have been registered. The other half shall be paid when the work has been completed and approved.

A Government Contract for Military Provisions

As Rome became involved in wars fought on many fronts and with many soldiers, supplying military provisions became a lucrative business. Usually the contractors

---

[118] In fact, the wall already exists, and the contract is actually for remodeling and reconstruction.

[119] *Serapis:* an Egyptian divinity. His cult was closely associated with that of the Egyptian goddess Isis; see selection 391. The temple of Isis at Pompeii is surrounded by a wall, to create a sacred precinct. Perhaps the wall in this contract is similarly a precinct wall, separating the temple of Serapis from nearby buildings.

[120] The bondsmen will stand surety; see note 80 of this chapter.

were paid as soon as their work was completed. In a military emergency, however, they might be asked to accept a promise of deferred payment (probably with interest). In this passage, we learn of such a special appeal which the Roman Senate made, during the Second Punic War, to businessmen (1) to make loans to the state and (2) to enter into contracts for the supply of provisions to the army on the Spanish front.

163   Livy, *A History of Rome* 23.48.4–6, 10–12; 23.49.1–3

[In 215 B.C.] at the end of the summer, a letter arrived for the Senate in Rome from Publius and Gnaeus Scipio, announcing the extent and success of their campaign in Spain. They added, however, that the army needed pay, clothing, and grain, and the navy needed everything. With regard to the pay, they would, they said, initiate some plan by which they might obtain the money from the Spaniards if the state treasury was empty. The other supplies, however, had to be sent out from Rome or else the army could not be kept in Spain, and Spain could not be kept as a province.[121] When the letter was read aloud to the Senate, everyone agreed that the statements were true and the requests just. . . . They decided that the praetor,[122] Fulvius, should appear before the popular assembly, should inform the people of this public crisis, and should urge those men who had increased their family fortunes with state contracts for revenue collection[123] to make loans to the state from which they acquired their wealth and to contract to supply what was needed by the army in Spain, with the condition that the debts to them be the first settled when there was money in the state treasury.[124]

The praetor therefore presented these proposals before the popular assembly and set a date on which he would issue the contract for supplying the army in Spain with clothing and grain, and the navy with the other things it needed. When that day arrived, three companies of nineteen men came forward to enter into the contract, but they had two stipulations: (1) they should be exempt from military service while they were engaged in this public business, and (2) the cargo on their ships should be insured by the state against the threats of enemies or storms.[125] When both these stipulations were agreed to by the Senate, they entered into the contract, and public affairs were conducted with private funds.[126]

---

[121] *province:* Latin *provincia.* The word has two meanings: (1) a sphere of military activity or (2) a territorial possession. At the beginning of the Second Punic War, Spain was ruled by Carthage, and was thus, to the Romans, a *provincia* in the first meaning. At the end of the war, the victorious Romans gained Spain as a territorial possession, and it became a *provincia* in the second meaning.

[122] *praetor:* see selections 229, 230, and 231.

[123] That is, state contracts for the collection of taxes, tolls, tariffs, and tribute.

[124] They were not going to be paid as soon as they had supplied the provisions. This delayed payment clause might explain the reluctance of businessmen to enter into contracts at this time.

[125] Shipping was a very risky business; these men wanted the state to assume financial responsibility for any losses they incurred.

[126] "Private funds" because the businessmen used their capital to gather and ship provisions, and they would not be reimbursed for some time.

Contract Fraud

The incident described here occurred in 212 B.C.

164   Livy, *A History of Rome* 25.3.9–13

Marcus Postumius was a publican[127] who for many years had no equal in the Roman world for fraud and avarice except Titus Pomponius Veientanus. . . . Because the state had agreed to insure against damage from storms the cargo which was being carried to the army, not only had these two men invented false reports of shipwrecks, but in fact those shipwrecks which had been truthfully reported had occurred not by accident but by their foul play. They used to put a few things of little value into battered old ships, and when they sank out at sea (the sailors were picked up in little boats prepared for this purpose), they falsely reported that the cargo had been much larger in quantity and value than it actually was. The year before [213 B.C.], Marcus Aemilius, a praetor, had exposed this fraud and brought it to the attention of the Senate, but the senators had not censured it in any decree because they did not wish to offend the publicans at such a critical time.[128] The popular assembly, however, was a more severe avenger of fraud. Spurius and Lucius Carvilius, two tribunes of the plebs,[129] were finally so angered when they contemplated this hateful and disgraceful behavior that they proposed a fine of 200,000 asses.

Government Contracts for Tax Collection

The expansion of the Empire benefited many Roman businessmen; military conquests opened up new areas for real estate speculation, trade, banking, and government contracts. Among the most lucrative of government contracts were those dealing with the collection of public revenues. These public revenues included not only harbor taxes and customs tariffs but, more importantly, indemnities and poll taxes. An indemnity was a large sum of money paid by a conquered nation to Rome in order to compensate Rome for the expenses it incurred in fighting the war. A poll tax was an annual tax paid to Rome to reimburse it for the costs of maintaining a governor and a military force in a province (the Romans claimed that the governor and soldiers were there to protect the provincials).[130] The amount of the indemnity or poll tax was fixed by the Senate, but the collection of these public revenues was delegated, through bids and contracts, to private individuals or, more commonly, to private corporations.[131] These corporations made

---

[127] *publican:* one who deals with public revenue.

[128] The state depended on the support of the publicans during military emergencies when, for example, they might ask them to make loans or supply provisions with a promise of deferred payment; see selection 163.

[129] *tribunes of the plebs:* see selections 229 and 231.

[130] See selections 282 and 283.

[131] The tax collector, mentioned with such scorn by Cicero in selection 147, would be an employee of the contractor(s).

a profit, and a substantial one. The provincials were often squeezed unmercifully by the publicans, who might expect military assistance from the governor since one of his duties was to protect Roman citizens in the provinces.

Poll taxes were based on census returns, and heads of households were expected to return to their places of origin to declare their census information. The proclamation translated here was issued in Egypt in A.D. 104.

165 *P. Lond.* 904, ll. 18–38 (*Select Papyri* 220)

Proclamation of Gaius Vibius Maximus, prefect of Egypt: Since plans for the house-to-house census are now underway, it is necessary that all persons who are for whatever reason away from their place of origin be summoned to return to their own hearths, so that they may take care of the customary business of registration.

166 *New Testament*, Luke 2.1–5

And it came to pass in those days, that there went out a decree from Caesar Augustus, that all the world should be taxed.

And this taxing was first made when Cyrenius was governor of Syria.

And all went to be taxed, every one into his own city.

And Joseph also went up from Galilee, out of the city of Nazareth, into Judaea, unto the city of David, which is called Bethlehem (because he was of the house and lineage of David):

To be taxed with Mary his espoused wife, being great with child.

Moneylending in the Provinces

Frequently communities or countries could not pay the required war indemnity, or they might not be able to pay the poll tax. They were then forced to borrow the money from Roman businessmen who often charged exorbitant interest rates—forty-eight percent per annum was not unusual! And the provincials, sometimes unable to pay even the interest on these loans, got deeper and deeper into debt, while the Roman publicans and moneylenders grew wealthier and wealthier. The publicans and the moneylenders were the main reason for the provincials' hatred of Roman rule. Festering resentment and frustration sometimes led to rebellions. In 88 B.C., the people of the province of Asia rose up and massacred thousands of Roman citizens living there. Unfortunately, their attempt to free themselves of Roman oppression brought them even greater distress. A Roman army under Sulla[132] crushed the rebellion, and Sulla then imposed an enormous indemnity of 20,000 talents. In order to pay the Roman treasury, the cities of Asia (the province) had to borrow the money from private Roman moneylenders at a very high rate of compound interest. Within a few years, their debt had grown to a staggering 120,000 talents.

132 *Sulla:* see note 114 of this chapter.

In 51–50 B.C., Cicero was governor of the province of Cilicia, which included not only the southern coastal area of what is modern Turkey but also the island of Cyprus. Upon his arrival in the province, he found its inhabitants in very great distress, as he reported in a letter to his friend Atticus.

167   Cicero, *Letters to Atticus* 5.16.2

On July 31 I arrived in this desperate and in fact totally and permanently ruined province. My arrival had been eagerly awaited. . . . I have heard nothing except complaints: people cannot pay the mandatory poll tax; communities have become bankrupt. I have listened to groans and laments from these communities. I have heard about monstrous deeds, deeds of some savage beast, not of a man.[133] In short, these people are very weary of life.

Kingmakers

The following passage gives a good idea of the scope of some equestrian business ventures. In 58 B.C., Ptolemy Auletes, king of Egypt, was expelled by his people. Gabinius, governor of Syria at the time, accepted a 10,000-talent bribe from the king to invade Egypt with his Roman soldiers and restore Ptolemy to the throne. When Gabinius returned to Rome in 54 B.C., he was prosecuted for having left his province to wage war on Egypt and for having accepted a bribe. He was convicted. In the wake of this investigation, Rabirius Postumus was brought to trial, since he had loaned so much money to the king and might have been implicated in the bribing of Gabinius. Cicero was his defense attorney; he was acquitted.

168   Cicero, *Speech in Defense of Rabirius Postumus* 2.4–3.5

Gaius Rabirius Postumus was involved in many business deals, invested his money in many ventures, and made successful bids on many public contracts. He loaned money to whole nations.[134] He had business and banking enterprises in many provinces. He offered his financial services even to kings. He had previously lent large sums of money to the king of Alexandria himself.[135] And yet, while making a fortune for himself, he never ceased to enrich his friends, employing them in his overseas business, giving them shares in his investments, promoting them with his wealth, and supporting them with his credit. . . .

Meanwhile Ptolemy had been driven out of his own kingdom and had come to Rome with deceit in mind, as Postumus later learned. . . . Postumus unfortunately lent money to Ptolemy, who was in need and begged him. And this wasn't the first time. Postumus had lent him money when he was still on the throne, even though

---

[133] Cicero is referring to Appius Claudius Pulcher, his predecessor as governor of Cilicia. Appius had supported the interests of the Roman businessmen over the interests of the provincials.

[134] Compare the loans made by Brutus and Pompey (selection 280).

[135] *king of Alexandria:* Ptolemy Auletes. Alexandria was the capital of Egypt.

Postumus had never met him. And he didn't think this latest loan was a risk because no one doubted that Ptolemy would be restored to his throne by the Senate and the Roman people. However, in giving gifts and giving credit, he went too far, lending not only his own money but even that of his friends. A foolish move. Who denies it? Or who will now dare to think well planned a deed which turned out disastrously? But it is difficult not to follow to the bitter end a venture which you began with great hope. The man asking for credit was a king; he asked again and again; he promised him the world. Finally Postumus began to fear that he might lose what he had already lent if he now imposed a limit on Ptolemy's credit.

ACTIVITIES OF THE SENATORIAL CLASS

Pliny's Activities

Men of the senatorial class, whose income was derived from real estate and other investments, occupied their time with public services for which they received no direct monetary reward.[136] If they had been elected to one of the annual magistracies, their days were filled with official duties. But even if they were not serving a term as magistrate, their days were occupied by various activities such as Senate meetings and jury duty.[137] They were expected, moreover, to make themselves available for legal consultation and to assist their clients wth court cases. In addition senators spent a good part of their time at social events which they might well consider a duty more than a pleasure.[138] It was important to the political careers of these men that they be seen and heard frequently in public, that they make contacts, maintain political alliances, and know the right people.[139] They therefore appeared at such social functions as morning receptions,[140] parties, and recitations.[141] The letter translated here provides a glimpse of the hectic schedule of a senator of Rome.[142] Although the senators of the imperial period, when Pliny lived, had much less real power than their counterparts in the republican period,[143] their daily round

[136] Their rewards were less tangible but probably more satisfying than money: public respect, privilege, power, control over the lives of others. And many senators received indirect rewards such as gifts or, in the case of corrupt senators, bribes.

[137] Jury panels were composed of men of the senatorial order and sometimes of the equestrian order (see note 43 of Chapter XII). A lower-class man would never, therefore, have an opportunity to be judged by his peers. In fact, most cases involving lower-class defendants never went to a jury trial but were decided by a magistrate or his staff. On the differentiation between upper-class and lower-class defendants, see the introduction to selection 5. (Women were never chosen for jury duty.)

[138] Compare modern business lunches, campaign dinners, and cocktail parties.

[139] Compare the advice of Quintus Cicero to his brother Marcus (selection 236).

[140] *morning receptions:* Martial (selection 146) suggests that the first two hours of the day were occupied by these receptions (and that patrons then went to the law courts to plead cases).

[141] *recitations:* see selections 318–320.

[142] Other letters by Pliny provide additional information about his activities, such as matchmaking (selection 49), hiring teachers for a school he is funding (selection 129), and attending recitations (selection 319).

[143] The emperors reduced the power of the senatorial order; see selection 248.

of activities was similar. Pliny made frequent trips to his many vacation villas, where he could relax and escape the pressures of senatorial life in Rome.[144]

169 Pliny the Younger, *Letters* 1.9

It's remarkable, isn't it, how you can offer a satisfactory account, or apparently satisfactory account, of your time in the city on any single day, but fail to make a satisfactory account of your time when you put all the days together. For if you ask someone, "What did you do today?" he will answer, "I went to a coming-of-age-party;[145] I attended an engagement party and then a wedding; one man asked me to be a witness at the signing of his will, another asked me for legal advice, a third asked me to sit in court." On the day you did these things they seemed essential and important, but if you consider that you did them day after day after day, they seem trivial and useless. And how much more trivial they seem when you are away from the city! For then the thought comes to you: "I've wasted so many days on such dreary and fruitless activities."

I think about this whenever I'm at my Laurentine villa reading or writing or just getting my body in shape (a sound mind needs a sound body!). I hear and say nothing which I might later regret. No one comes to me with malicious slander about someone else. I criticize no one (except myself—when I'm not writing well). I'm not agitated by any hopes or fears, or irritated by any gossip. I speak only to myself and my books. What a decent and healthy life! A leisure, so pure and sweet, and more rewarding than almost any activity.[146] O sea, o coastline, the true and private home of the Muses. How many things you have inspired me to compose!

Leave behind, Fundanus, as soon as you can, the noise and the meaningless running about and the really silly occupations of the city, and exchange them for leisure and for time to read. As our friend Atilius very cleverly and wittily said, "It is better to be idle than to do idle things."

AGRICULTURE

The citizens of Rome believed that they were the descendants of sturdy, self-reliant farmers who owned the small plots which they worked and who were will-

---

[144] For a description of his villa at Laurentum, see selection 87.

[145] When a boy was about fifteen or sixteen years old, he came of age. He dedicated to the household gods his boyhood toga, with its purple border (*toga praetexta:* see note 39 of Chapter VI) and his *bulla* (his childhood good-luck charm; a girl made a similar dedication before her wedding). He then put on the plain white toga of manhood (*toga virilis*) and was escorted by family and friends to the Forum where he was formally introduced as a citizen and where his name was inscribed on the register of his family's tribe (on tribe, see notes 12 and 48 of Chapter X). A sacrifice was then offered to Jupiter at the temple on the Capitoline Hill, and the rest of the day was devoted to parties and banquets. Many families chose March 17, the Liberalia, as the day for this ceremony, but other dates are also mentioned.

[146] Pliny did not completely ignore his social obligations when away from Rome. See selection 129 where he describes a *salutatio* at his country home at Comum.

ing to fight bravely to defend the land which they owned. They believed, in addition, that their ancestors had succeeded both in farming and in war because they had possessed qualities such as diligence, determination, and constancy, and these qualities became enshrined by generation after generation as traditionally Roman virtues.[147] Small Roman farms, according to legend, had produced great military heroes who embodied these virtues and, with them, conquered all of Italy. The legends of these men were passed on from generation to generation, and there became firmly entrenched in the Roman national consciousness the notion that "Rome owed her greatness to a sturdy breed of smallholders, content with little above bare subsistence, and working their plots with their own hands."[148] This traditional belief contains two important theses: (1) the early Roman farmer owned the land he worked, and (2) rural virtues were the source of imperial greatness.

It is perhaps true that, in Rome's earliest history, virtually all of its citizens owned a plot of land which they farmed and that they thus knew well the harsh realities of agricultural life. However, by the middle republican period, ownership of much of the agricultural land in Italy had become concentrated in the hands of a wealthy few. The wealthy landowners did not, of course, work the land themselves. They preferred life in the towns and cities to the exhausting toil of farm work, however virtuous it might be. Most farmers therefore were either tenants working rented land, or hired help on large estates. Yet the myth of the landowning farmer and his rural virtues persisted. Indeed, wealthy property owners continued to foster this myth, even at a time when few families actually owned land, because it served as proof that they were the true conservators of ancestral custom and were thus properly the people who governed the state. The urban population, moreover, cherished a romantic notion that farm life bred purity and simplicity and that the countryside offered a retreat from the vices, complexities, and stress of urban life.[149] The longing to escape to the country is particularly prominent among authors of the late republican and early Augustan periods which were filled with turmoil and anxiety.[150] A striking ambivalence developed in the Roman attitude toward agriculture, particularly in the attitude of the upper class. For example, Roman senators extolled in their writings the simple virtues of rural life and praised the lot of the peasant farmer as austere but happy; however, as landowners,[151] politicians, and statesmen, these same senators did little to help the peasant farmer who was, in fact, by the end of the republican period, in a very desperate plight. Thus, Roman literature reflects the traditional, romantic picture of Roman

[147] See selection 1.

[148] K. D. White, *Country Life in Classical Times* (Ithaca, 1977), p. 5: "This powerful, almost obsessive, morality myth is peculiar to the Romans." One might argue that a similar myth persists in modern America.

[149] One might compare American romantic notions about rural life and pioneer spirit.

[150] The first century B.C. was a period of great political unrest. See note 81 of Chapter V on Caesar's rise to power. After his assassination, Antony and Octavian (Augustus) contended for power. Turia and her husband (selection 288) suffered in the proscriptions of the Second Triumvirate.

[151] It is important to remember that most large landowners were involved in the politics and government of their local community and were often members of the Senate of Rome as well. They thus controlled legislation affecting land ownership, sale of agricultural products, and so on. Their own interests might well conflict with those of the actual farmers, yet because they had the political power, their will prevailed.

agriculture; but Roman history, which documents the lack of political support, or even sympathy, for the small landowner and the farmworker, reflects the reality of the situation.

Early in Rome's history, only property owners[152] were eligible for military service.[153] It was assumed that property owners would be better soldiers than non-property owners because they would be fighting to protect their own investments. However, Rome was for centuries almost continually at war, and these prolonged military campaigns produced many changes in the structure of the community. Farmers might be away from their land for several years, or even die in service. Often their families could not maintain the farm without them, and therefore they sold the land. Or enemy forces in Italy ravaged the farmlands and rendered them unproductive.[154] Subsistence farmers were forced to sell out. Eventually most of the farmland belonged to only a few families. These families were not subsistence farmers; they bought the land as real estate investments and then sold the produce of the land to provide themselves with an income. Large farms and ranches thus replaced the earlier small farms, and displaced farmers went to the city to seek employment. The gap between the landed wealthy and the landless poor widened.

The wealthy absentee landlords did not hire displaced farmers to work their land. Instead they imported slaves captured in Rome's many foreign wars.[155] It is indeed one of the great ironies of history that Roman farmers who went to war to defend their property against a foreign enemy ultimately lost their property to fellow Romans and also lost farming jobs to slaves whom they themselves had helped capture. And, to add further to the irony, some countries defeated in war by these peasant farmers were forced to send to Rome an annual tribute of free grain which was then distributed among the urban population;[156] the few peasant farmers left could scarcely compete with the large farms, slave labor, and the artificially low grain prices. Their lives were wretched, and they were never far from starvation.

An Attempt at Land Reform

Although the plight of the peasant farmer was desperate, and although the influx to the city of displaced farmers created unemployment problems, very little was ever done to ease the situation because most of the land was in the hands of wealthy, politically powerful families. In other words, the politicians who might have instituted changes were themselves the wealthy landowners who benefited most from the inequitable distribution of land. The following passages describe one of the very few attempts ever made to remedy the problems caused by this inequitable distribution.

[152] The property might be real or personal. Most people, however, put their money into real property (real estate) and were thus landowners.

[153] This regulation is taken as proof that in the early republican period most men did own some land. Otherwise Rome would not have had an army large enough to make the conquests it did; see the introduction to Chapter XI.

[154] Hannibal's troops, for example, during the Second Punic War.

[155] In the American South, slaves were imported because there were no workers available to farm the land. The American colonists were creating farms where none had existed before; Roman landowners were simply taking over land which had been cultivated for centuries.

[156] On the distribution of this grain, see selection 153.

The first paragraph describes Rome's acquisition of "public land." Public land was land which had been confiscated by the Romans from peoples whom they had conquered in war. This land now belonged to the state of Rome and could be (1) given to Roman colonists, (2) sold, or (3) rented.[157] If sold or rented, the income went into the state treasury.

170   Appian, *The Civil Wars* 1.1.7, 9, 10, 11

Little by little, the Romans conquered in war the peoples of the Italian peninsula.[158] Then they would confiscate part of their (the Italians') land and build towns there,[159] or they would select Roman colonists to send to already existing towns, intending these colonists to serve as garrisons.[160] That portion of the land acquired in war which was still under cultivation was distributed immediately to Roman colonists, or was sold or leased. The majority of the confiscated land, however, was, because of the war, no longer under cultivation, and since the Roman magistrates did not have the time to distribute it, they announced by public proclamation that in the meantime[161] the land could be used by anyone who wished to, upon payment of a tax, namely one-tenth of the grain harvest and one-fifth of the fruit harvest, or, for people pasturing animals, a percentage of both the large and the small animals. They adopted these policies to encourage proliferation of the Italian peoples, whom they considered very solid and sturdy, so that they might have many allies close to home.

However, something quite different happened. Wealthy men took over the majority of the undistributed public land and were encouraged by the passage of time to think that they would never be evicted. Moreover, they gained possession of adjacent plots and whatever other little parcels were farmed by poor families, sometimes persuading the person to sell, sometimes taking it by force. Thus, they were farming vast acreages instead of small plots and using slaves as farmworkers and herdsmen because free workers could be taken away from agriculture for military service. At the same time, their ownership of slaves brought them considerable profit because the slaves had many children[162] with no threat of their being called for military service. And therefore certain powerful men became extremely wealthy, and the class of slaves increased throughout the country, but the Italian people decreased in numbers and strength since they were hard pressed by poverty, taxes, and military service.

In 133 B.C., Tiberius Sempronius Gracchus, a Roman of impeccable upper-class breeding, was elected tribune.[163] He brought forward a bill, discussed in the

[157] Compare selection 159.

[158] This was early in Rome's history, in the fifth, fourth, and third centuries B.C.

[159] The new towns would be settled by colonists from Rome, not by people native to the region. Sending people to colonies was one early attempt to provide land for landless Romans.

[160] Very often the colonists were retired soldiers; see Horace's remarks in selection 15 about centurions' sons in his hometown. Soldiers were given a plot of land upon retirement as a reward for good service. See selection 274 for complaints which some soldiers had about the land given to them.

[161] That is, until they had time to formulate a distribution policy.

[162] The children would, of course, become the property of the landowner. See note 30 of Chapter VIII.

[163] *tribune:* see selections 229–231. (On the mother of Gracchus, see note 32 of Chapter II and note 9 of Chapter VI; also genealogy chart 2.)

passage translated below, to create farms for the landless. He hoped to accomplish at least two things: (1) to strengthen the Roman army (property ownership was still, in 133 B.C., a requirement for military service[164], and (2) to lessen the threat of slave rebellions by decreasing the number of slaves in Italy. He encountered considerable opposition from the Senate, which was composed of wealthy landowners. Although the bill was passed by the popular assembly, Tiberius had made many enemies in the Senate and he was assassinated. A commission was set up to organize the distribution of public land (Tiberius's brother Gaius was one of the three commissioners[165]), but the reform measure was not a real success. It was impossible for the small farm family to compete with owners of vast estates who used slave labor, particularly (1) when small farmers were called away for military service, and (2) when grain coming to Rome from the provinces as tribute kept grain prices artificially low.

Tiberius Gracchus, a famous and illustrious man, eager for glory, a very powerful speaker, and for all these reasons well known to all, while he was tribune delivered a solemn speech about the Italian people, pointing out that these people, who were so brave in war[166] and were related in blood to the Romans, were little by little declining into poverty and being reduced in numbers, and had no hope of correcting the situation. He complained about the large population of slaves who were useless for military service and never faithful to their masters, citing as proof the recent suffering which slaves in Sicily had caused their masters.[167] . . . After recounting these things, he again proposed the law providing that no one should use more than 500 Roman acres[168] of public land. However, he added a provision that two sons of the present occupant might each hold an additional 250 Roman acres. The rest of the land,[169] however, was to be divided among the poor by three elected commissioners who would change each year.

This proposal was extremely distressing to the wealthy because they could no longer disregard the law, as they had before, since now there were commissioners; nor could they buy land from those poor to whom it was allotted because Tiberius Gracchus had foreseen this problem and forbidden them to sell.[170] The wealthy gathered

---

[164] He did not, unfortunately, realize that military service was in fact the reason why so many families had originally lost their land. See the introduction to Chapter XI.

[165] Gaius was also the author of the legislation to sell grain at a fixed low price (see the introduction to selection 153), a measure which helped the urban populace but ruined farmers.

[166] They had been attached to the Roman state as "allies" and had served in Roman military campaigns for many years. Some were Roman citizens whose ancestors had been colonists. All free Italians became Roman citizens in 89 B.C.; see the introduction to Chapter I.

[167] There was a slave revolt in Sicily in 135 B.C. See selection 196.

[168] 500 Roman acres (iugera) = about 300 British acres. In ancient times, 500 acres was a very large farm. Many subsistence farmers had fewer than 10 acres; see selection 266. A similar law, limiting use of public land, had been passed as early as 367 B.C. but virtually ignored by the upper class.

[169] If a wealthy family with two sons had been squatting on, for example, 2000 Roman acres of public land, they now received clear legal title to 1000 Roman acres and the remaining 1000 acres of the 2000 was distributed to the landless in small plots.

[170] It was very difficult for many of these new farmers to survive on their little plots, for reasons stated above. Tiberius was assassinated in 133 B.C. His brother Gaius continued his work. In 121 B.C., when Gaius was serving as tribune, he too was assassinated. Not long after his death, the Senate overturned Tiberius's law which forbade recipients of the land allotments

Genealogy Chart 2. The Families of Scipio Africanus and Tiberius Gracchus

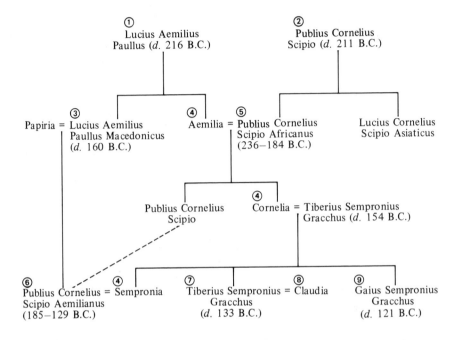

① As one of the two consuls for 216 B.C., Paullus died leading the Roman forces against Hannibal in the disastrous battle at Cannae.

② Consul in 218 B.C.; defeated by Hannibal in the battle at Trebia River; died in Spain in 211 fighting the Carthaginians.

③ Consul in 182 and 168 B.C.; received the title Macedonicus because he defeated Perseus, king of Macedonia, in 168.

④ Note that a woman received as a name the feminine form of her father's family name; Aemilia is the daughter of (Lucius) Aemilius (Paullus).

⑤ Received the title Africanus because he defeated the Carthaginians in Africa in 202 B.C. at the battle of Zama and thus put an end to the Second Punic War (see note 87 of Chapter VII); for more on Scipio Africanus see selection 307.

⑥ Although Lucius Aemilius Paullus was his natural father, he was adopted by Publius Cornelius Scipio and given the name of his adoptive father. He also had, however, the cognomen Aemilianus (="of the family Aemilius") which indicated the identity of his natural family. Cf. the name of the emperor Augustus – Gaius Julius Caesar Octavianus – whose natural father was Octavius but who was adopted by Gaius Julius Caesar. (His sister's name was Octavia, the feminine form of Octavius.)

⑦ Tribune in 133 B.C.; he proposed land-reform measures; see selection 170; assassinated by his political opponents in 133.

⑧ A descendant of the famous Appius Claudius, censor in 312 B.C., who was responsible for the construction of the Via Appia and Aqua Appia (see note 106 of Chapter XIV).

⑨ Tribune in 123 and 122 B.C.; killed by his political opponents in 121; see note 170 of Chapter VII.

together in groups and wailed, alleging that cultivated fields and vineyards and farm buildings which had been theirs for years and years were now being given to the poor. . . . There was wailing and cursing throughout the whole upper class.[171]

However, the lower class was moaning, too, complaining that they were being reduced from an adequate standard of living to poverty, and then even to childlessness because they were unable to raise their children.[172] They pointed out the military service which they had rendered and by which this public land had been acquired, and expressed anger that they should be deprived of this public land. They rebuked those who used slaves instead of hiring free men, citizens, and soldiers, pointing out that slaves were always untrustworthy and hostile. . . .

Gracchus had in mind, when he proposed this measure, not an abundance of money but an abundance of men. Believing greatly in the usefulness of work, that Italy could never possess anything better or more admirable than her hard-working men, he didn't worry about the difficulties of his proposal. When the proposal came to a vote, he put forward at great length many arguments, and in particular he raised the questions of whether it was not just to divide public land among the public, whether a citizen did not deserve more consideration than a slave, whether a veteran was not more useful than a man who had never done military service, and whether a man who had a share in his country's land was not more concerned about public affairs. . . . He bid the wealthy to consider these things carefully and to hand over this land, as a gift if necessary, to men who would raise children. Only thus could hopes for the future be realized. He warned them not to overlook larger issues while quarreling about smaller ones. They would receive adequate compensation for improvements made to the land by obtaining, free of charge, absolute title, guaranteed forever, to 500 Roman acres and, for those who had sons, 250 Roman acres per son, up to two sons. After saying many more things of this nature, and stirring up the poor and even some wealthy men who were moved by reason rather than by desire for profit, he ordered the clerk to read out the proposed law.

Tillers of the Fields

Tiberius Gracchus's proposed law was passed in 133 B.C. Within twenty years, however, the plan had proved to be unsuccessful, and both the urban and the rural poor were as badly off as they had ever been. The following passage, written by an author of the late republican period,[173] describes the categories of farmworkers.

---

to sell their land. "Immediately the wealthy began to buy the allotments of the poor, or found some pretext to seize the land by force. And thus the plight of the poor became even harsher than before" (Appian 1.4.27).

[171] And the Senate, which should have been concerned about the plight of the landless, was upper class.

[172] They were forced to expose the children at birth or sell them into slavery. Compare selections 31, 32, 37, and 218.

[173] *author:* Varro, who also wrote the passage on managing farm slaves (selection 185).

All fields are tilled by men—either slaves, or free men, or both. Free men are either (1) those who till their own fields, as many poor people do with the help of their families,[174] or (2) those who are hired when the major farming operations, such as vintage and haying, are performed with the assistance of hired free men, or (3) those who are working off debts.[175] There are still many in this final class in Asia, Egypt, and Illyricum. With regard to all these classes of free men, I have this to say: it is more profitable to work unhealthy areas with hired workers than with slaves.[176]

Tenant Farmers

In the republican period, it was common to work the large farms and ranches with slave labor. Although buying slaves involved a considerable initial outlay of capital, and then feeding and clothing them required money, nevertheless landowners at first thought that slave labor was more economical than the labor of free men. A free man, who owned any small amount of property, was eligible for military service and might be called up just when the landowner most needed him. Also, in theory at least, it seemed that slaves could be forced to work harder than free men. However, free men were hired to work in unhealthy or dangerous areas where an owner did not want to risk losing a slave to disease or accident.

By the late republican and imperial periods the expense of buying and maintaining slaves outweighed the advantages of slave labor. Free workers did not need to be fed and clothed or nursed when sick. They could be laid off when ill or when bad weather interrupted the farm work. And free men worked harder than slaves because they needed the employment to feed and clothe their families. Also, changes in the system of army enlistment meant that free men in Italy were seldom called away for military service.[177]

In addition to running a large estate as one operation managed by an overseer and worked by slaves and hired help, landowners often divided their property into rental units which were worked by tenant farmers. These tenant farmers paid a cash rental fee; often they were also required to work a few days a year for the landowner. Some landowners found that renting the land was unprofitable, and therefore they leased the land to sharecroppers, families who paid the owner a

---

[174] These families may rent rather than own the land they farm. Varro calls them "poor people." Wealthy people did not till their own fields.

[175] That is, indentured servants. They are not actually slaves, but they are bound to their master until they have worked off their debt. The Latin for indentured servant is *obaerarius* (*ob* = "on account of"; *aera* = "copper coins," "money").

[176] *unhealthy areas:* very hot (or very cold) areas, or areas infested by malaria mosquitoes. It was more profitable to use hired workers here because when they became ill they could be laid off; a slave, who was property, had to be fed during his illness (although Cato, in selection 184, recommends reducing the rations of sick slaves). The death of a slave, moreover, represented a financial loss (a loss of property) to the owner, while the death of a hired worker did not. In many ways, the life of a hired worker might be harsher than that of a slave. Who would feed or clothe him when he was ill?

[177] *enlistment:* see the introduction to Chapter XI.

certain percentage of their harvest (and also worked a few days a year for him). The roots of the medieval feudal system, of lords and serfs, can be traced back to the Roman system of large estates worked by tenant farmers and sharecroppers.

172   Columella, *On Agriculture,* 1.7.6–7

On far-off estates, to which visits by the owner are not easy, it is in the long run preferable to keep the land under free tenant farmers rather than under slave overseers. This is true of all types of land, but particularly of grain-producing land, which a tenant farmer can injure only minimally (as he might injure vineyards or orchards). Slaves, however, damage grain land very seriously. They rent out the oxen; they do not feed them or the other animals well; they don't plow the land with the necessary energy; they record the sowing of far more seed than they have actually sown;[178] as for the seed which they have sown, they don't look after it in the way necessary for it to grow correctly; and when they bring the harvest to the threshing floor, day after day while they are threshing, they lessen the total amount by outright dishonesty or by carelessness. They themselves even steal it, and they certainly don't guard against theft by others. And they don't even record the amount of stored grain honestly in their account books. The result is that both overseer and slaves commit crimes, and the land quite often gets a bad reputation.[179] Therefore, as I have said before, if the owner cannot be present, I think that a farm of this type should be leased out.

Sharecroppers

The life of both tenant farmers and sharecroppers was very harsh. Despite endless toil, they lived at subsistence level; if illness or injury occurred, or if the crops were damaged by bad weather, the family faced starvation. Often the landowner was unaware of or unconcerned about their plight. Pliny's problems with tenants who did not pay their rent led him to try a sharecropping system.

173   Pliny the Younger *Letters* 9.37

It is certainly not in your nature to demand from your close friends public expressions of support if it is inconvenient for them; and I have been your faithful friend too long to fear that you might interpret things other than I would wish if I don't come to town on the Kalends[180] to see your inauguration as consul. The reason for my absence is this: I am detained by the necessity of leasing my estates and settling these lease arrangements for several years to come. I must adopt a new system. During the past five-

---

[178] It would be interesting to know what the slaves do with the seed they don't sow. Do they sell it and pocket the money? Do they eat it because they are hungry? Do they secretly plant it somewhere else and raise their own crop?

[179] *bad reputation:* that is, as being unproductive.

[180] *Kalends:* the name given to the first day of each month; compare Ides, note 8 of Chapter II.

year period,[181] despite considerable decreases in rents, the arrears increased.[182] As a result, many of my tenants are no longer concerned about reducing their debts to me since they feel they have no hope of being able to pay them off. They even seize and eat the produce of the land,[183] like people who think they no longer have to be frugal since the property is not theirs anyway. I must face these mounting problems head-on and remedy them. One plan for remedying them would be to lease the land not for cash but for a share of the produce, and to place some of my own men as overseers to supervise the work and guard the produce. Certainly there is no return on an investment fairer than that offered by the land, the weather, and the seasons. This experiment demands great honesty, keen watchfulness, and many working hands. Nevertheless, I must try it and, just as with a chronic disease, experiment with every possible remedy. So, you can understand that it is not a whimsical reason which prevents me from being present on the day of your consular inauguration. But I will celebrate it with as much joy, rejoicing, and prayers for good fortune as if I were present.

A Farmer's Life

The passages translated here deal primarily with attitudes toward agriculture and with problems of land ownership, rather than with descriptions of farming operations. K. D. White has collected many descriptions of such operations in his book, *Country Life in Classical Times*.[184]

The life of the peasant farmer (and of his wife and children) was filled with endless, back-breaking toil: clearing, plowing, planting, hoeing, pruning, weeding, irrigating, and harvesting grain, grapes, olives, vegetables, fruit, and fodder; feeding, cleaning, breeding, raising, shearing, milking, slaughtering goats, cattle, sheep, pigs, poultry, and draft animals; building barns, fences, and sheepfolds; cutting firewood; making and repairing tools and equipment; squeezing grapes, pressing oil, grinding grain; making baskets, jars and boxes for storage. The list of chores is endless.[185]

Exhausting toil and grinding poverty were the lot of the farmer. The title of this anonymous poem, *Moretum,* is the name given to a food item common among the poor. It consisted of a medley of vegetables and herbs, ground together and mixed with vinegar, oil (if available), and sometimes cheese (if available). The poor, who often could not afford oil and cheese, mixed whatever plants, domestic or wild, were available to them.[186] Although some scholars translate *moretum* as

[181] Five years was a regular period for leases in the ancient Roman world; see selection 74.

[182] Pliny does not explain why his tenant farmers have not been able to pay their rent. Was there a drought? Did bad weather destroy the crops? Although Pliny reduced the rent, he shows no further compassion for his tenants.

[183] They are eating the produce rather than selling it to raise rent money or saving the seed to plant for next year's crops. Pliny does not explain whether they were hungry and needed to eat the produce.

[184] See note 148 of this chapter. Another of his books well worth looking at is *Roman Farming* (Ithaca, 1970).

[185] Compare the list of chores which Cato assigned to his farmworkers on rainy days and holidays (selection 184) and the operations described by Columella in selection 86.

[186] Wild plants may have kept alive the families of subsistence farmers during years of crop failure.

"salad," it was probably much more similar to modern pesto sauce, which is also a combination of ground herbs, oil, and cheese.

174   *Moretum* (anonymous) 1–24, 27, 29–37, 52–54, 117–122

And now night had completed twice five winter hours, and the winged sentry announced the new day with his crowing.[187] Simulus, the peasant farmer of a meager little plot, worried about gnawing hunger on this coming day. He slowly raised his weary limbs from his ugly little cot. With anxious hand he groped through the stagnant darkness and felt his way to the fireplace, burning his hand when he touched it. One tiny spark remained from a burned log, but the ashes concealed the glow of live flames underneath. Stooping over, he moved his lamp forward, close to these embers, and drew out with a needle the dry wick. With frequent huffs and puffs, he stirred up the sluggish fire. Finally, when the fire had caught and the lamp was lit, he turned away, using his hand to shield the wick light from a draft.

He unlocked the cupboard door with a key. Spread out on the cupboard floor was a paltry pile of grain. From this he took for himself as much as his measuring bucket held. He moved over to the mill and put his trusty lamp on a small shelf built onto the wall for the purpose. Then he slipped off his outer garment and, clad only in a shaggy goatskin, he swept the stones and inner portion of the mill. He put both his hands to work. [The left poured the grain into the mill, the right turned the millstone.] The grain which was ground by the rapid blows of the millstone poured out as flour. . . . At times he sang country songs and eased his labor with a rural tune. Or he shouted for Scybale. She was his only companion, an African woman, whose whole body betrayed her country of origin. Her hair was frizzy, her lips swollen, her skin dark, her shoulders broad, her breasts sagging, her waist narrow, her legs thin and her feet very large. He called her and told her to put firewood on the fireplace and to heat up some cold water.

After he had ground the grain, he mixed the flour with salt and water, formed the mixture into a round loaf, cut the impression of a cross on the top,[188] and set the loaf to cook in the fireplace.

While it baked, Simulus was not idle. He worked at another task, lest bread alone would not satisfy his hunger, and he prepared another dish to eat with the bread.

Since he had no meat, he made a *moretum* of cheese, garlic, parsley, rue, coriander, salt, olive oil, and vinegar. All these ingredients were ground in a mortar with a pestle and carefully blended together. A large portion of the poem is devoted to a description of the preparation of the *moretum*.

Meanwhile, hard-working Scybale plucked the bread out of the fireplace. Simulus

---

[187] Mock heroic style: after ten hours of cold winter darkness, the day dawned and the cock crowed. For another parody of heroic or epic style, see note 214 of this chapter.

[188] Loaves of bread of this design (round, with a cross marking off the four sections) were found in the excavations at Pompeii. Pictorial representations of these loaves also appear in wall-paintings at Pompeii.

happily took a piece in his hand.[189] Now that he had put aside the fear of hunger and was free of anxiety, at least for this day, he tied leggings on his legs, covered his head with a leather cap, yoked his obedient oxen, drove them into the field, and sank his plow into the earth.

Shepherds

Ancient writers developed a romantic image of the shepherd's life as a carefree lazy existence amid grassy meadows. The Latin word for shepherd is *pastor;*[190] a *pastoral* is defined by Webster's as "a literary work dealing with the life of shepherds, generally in an artificial manner, typically drawing a conventional contrast between the innocence and serenity of the simple life and the misery and corruption of city life." In reality a shepherd's life was at best dull, at worst almost intolerably harsh.[191] Shepherds spent months in isolation, leading their flocks from pasture to pasture. Rain or shine, sleet or hail, they were outside with their sheep, often in rugged mountain terrain. During lambing season, they might go weeks without sleep. The shepherds in pastoral poems are friendly garrulous fellows, but real-life shepherds spent most of their days without any human companionship. So difficult and lonely was the life of a shepherd that it was considered one of the least desirable of all jobs. Many shepherds were slaves.

175   Varro, *On Agriculture* 2.10.1–3

For herds of larger animals,[192] use older men; for flocks of smaller animals,[193] use boys. But in either case, the herdsmen who stay in the mountain pastures should be sturdier than those who return every day to the sheepfolds in the villa.[194] Thus, in the woodland areas you may see young men, usually armed, but close to the villa boys and even girls tend the flocks. The herdsmen must be forced to stay in the pasture all day, to let the herds pasture together during the day, but to spend the night alone, each with his own herd. . . . Neither old men nor young boys can easily tolerate the difficult terrain and the steep and rugged mountains, although herdsmen must endure these hardships, especially herdsmen who follow cattle and goats which love to pasture on sheer cliffs or in thick forests. In choosing herdsmen, examine their physique. They should be sturdy, swift-footed, quick, with good reflexes, men who not only can follow a herd, but also can protect it from predatory animals and from thieves; men who can lift loads onto pack animals; men who can run fast and hurl a javelin.[195]

---

[189] Bread or porridge with *moretum,* olives, or fish brine would be a common lower-class meal. Few people could afford meat.

[190] And the Latin word *pastor* means literally "he who feeds the sheep, takes them to pasture." Some modern churches call their ministers *pastors.* (*Minister* is a Latin word which means "servant.")

[191] This was true also of the ancient cowherd's life. One might compare the romantic American image of the cowboy with the reality of the cowboy's life: long, monotonous, and lonely hours following the herds of cattle, day and night, summer and winter.

[192] *larger animals:* cattle.

[193] *smaller animals:* sheep or goats.

[194] *sheepfolds in the villa:* see selection 86.

[195] Note in selection 152 the low pay which a free-man shepherd received.

Harassment of Shepherds

Shepherds often found themselves easy targets for thieves who lived in mountainous areas. However, in the following passage we learn of an upper-class prankster who found it amusing to terrorize poor shepherds. And this childish bully was none other than the Stoic philosopher and future emperor Marcus Aurelius.[196]

176   Marcus Aurelius, *Fronto's Letters* 2.12

When my father had returned home from the vineyards, I, as is my custom, got on my horse and set off down the road. I had gone only a short distance when I came across a large flock of sheep, standing in the road, huddled together as they do when space is tight, and four dogs and two shepherds, but nothing else. One shepherd spotted our little group of horsemen and said to the other shepherd, "Keep your eyes on those horsemen, for they often steal and cause very great damage."

When I heard this, I jabbed my spurs into my horse and galloped him into the middle of the flock. The terrified sheep quickly scattered. They ran off in all directions, bleating loudly. The shepherd hurled his staff at me, but it hit the rider who was following me. We galloped away. And, as it turned out, the shepherd, who feared to lose his sheep, lost his staff.

Do you think I made up this story? No, it's true. And there is more I could write about the incident, but a messenger is even now summoning me to my bath.

Farmers and Heroes

We have noted that the reality of the Roman agricultural world was that the landowners didn't farm and the farmers didn't own the land. Yet the aristocratic landowners perversely continued to cherish the "morality myth" that Rome owed its greatness to military heroes who were also sturdy farmers, living frugally and working their own land. Cato the Elder is the speaker in the following passage from Cicero's *Essay on Old Age*. Both Cato and Cicero, who was born almost fifty years after Cato died, were wealthy landowning aristocrats. Cato lauds the behavior of the ancient farmer-soldiers of legend and remarks on the happiness and prosperity of a farmer's life. Not surprisingly, the world he describes bears little resemblance to the real world of the tenant farmer or hired farmworker.

177   Cicero, *An Essay on Old Age* 16.55–56

I could discuss at very great length the pleasures of farming. . . . Manius Curius Dentatus[197] lived a farmer's life after his victories over the Samnites, the Sabines, and

---

[196] See selection 18. This letter was written about A.D. 143 to Marcus Aurelius's friend and teacher, Fronto (see Appendix I).

[197] *Manius Curius Dentatus:* in his first consulship (290 B.C.), he fought and defeated the Samnites; in his second consulship (276 B.C.), he defeated Pyrrhus. At the end of his military career, he retired to a small farm which he cultivated with his own hands.

Pyrrhus.[198] Whenever I look at his farm (it is not far from mine), I cannot admire enough the self-control of that man and the strict discipline of his generation. . . .

In the good old days, senators lived on farms. . . . The messenger sent to announce to Lucius Quinctius Cincinnatus that he had been appointed dictator found him plowing his fields.[199] . . . And Manius Curius Dentatus and other elders of the community were summoned from their farms to serve in the Senate. And that is why the messengers who were sent to summon them were called "travelers."[200] Surely, then, the old age of men such as these, who took such pleasure in being farmers, was not unhappy. Indeed, in my opinion, I know that nothing could be happier than a farmer's life,[201] not only because of the public service he performs, since agriculture is advantageous to the whole human race, but also because of the pleasure, which I have mentioned earlier, and the plenitude and abundance[202] of all things which are necessary for the sustenance of men and the worship of gods.[203]

Retreat from Reality

In this poem Horace presents us with a very common theme: farm life provides an escape from the evils of the city. However, his tongue is in his cheek; the speaker of the poem is a banker, who professes to be weary of the city and to long for the country, but who, at the end of the poem (not translated here), returns to his busy life of loans and investments. Horace is mocking people who love the bustle of the large city but pretend to desire the peace and quiet of the countryside. Of course, Horace's picture of farm life is quite unreal. His farmers don't sweat, get backaches, or become totally exhausted from their endless chores. They don't worry about crop failures, bad weather, or plagues of locusts. They spend a good part of the day lying in the grass, listening to a babbling brook.

178   Horace, *Epodes* 2.1–16, 23–26

Happy is the man who remains far from the world of business, as did our puritan ancestors, and who cultivates the family farm with his own oxen;[204] who refrains from

---

[198] *Samnites, Sabines:* inhabitants of central Italy; see map 3.

Pyrrhus: a Greek prince who invaded Italy in 280 B.C. and campaigned there and in Sicily until his defeat by Dentatus in 275 B.C.

[199] *Lucius Quinctius Cincinnatus:* In 458 B.C., Cincinnatus was called away from his plow and made dictator in a military emergency. In just sixteen days he defeated the enemy, saved Rome, and returned to his plowing. Would messengers ever have found Cato or Cicero plowing *their* own fields?

[200] *travelers:* Latin *viatores,* because they had to travel out to the farms to find these distinguished statesmen (Latin *via* = "road").

[201] Compare his views on moneylending, as reported by Cicero in selection 147. Plutarch, however, provides a different portrait of Cato in selection 160.

[202] Cato was wealthy and could therefore absorb a crop failure on one of his farms. However, the small farmer, with one plot of land, was never far from starvation.

[203] *the worship of gods:* animals, such as sheep, goats, pigs, and cattle, were used in sacrifices to the gods.

[204] *family farm with his own oxen:* Horace stresses that the happy man is not a tenant farmer but a landowner.

moneylending, who is not a soldier roused from sleep by the harsh trumpet or quaking in terror on a stormy sea; who avoids the Forum[205] and the haughty thresholds of our more important citizens.[206] Instead, he trains the mature tendrils of his grapevines to the tall poplar trees; or he stands in a secluded valley and surveys his herds of lowing cattle as they graze; or he prunes fruitless branches with his pruning knife and grafts on more fruitful ones; or he stores every last drop of honey in clean jars; or he shears the helpless sheep.[207] . . . How pleasant it is to lie down, sometimes under an ancient oak, sometimes on the matted grass; meanwhile the stream glides by between its high banks, and the birds warble in the trees.

The Romantic Vision

Tibullus's poem, like Horace's, presents a picture of farm life which is divorced from reality. There is, however, an important difference between the two: Horace uses his poem to mock the romantic vision; Tibullus is quite serious in his belief in this dreamworld.

179   Tibullus, *Elegies* 1.1.1, 5–8, 25–32, 43–46

Let another man heap up for himself the wealth of shining gold. . . . Let my humble means lead me through a quiet life.[208] May my fireplace continually blaze. . . . May I be content to live on a little, . . . to avoid the summer's heat under the shade of a tree upon the bank of a flowing stream.[209] And let me not think it shameful to hold a hoe once in a while[210] or to urge the slow oxen with a whip. Let me not be reluctant to lift up in my arms and carry homeward a lamb or a kid rejected by its mother. . . . When the time is right, let me tend the young vines and the large fruit trees with a farmer's deft touch. . . . A small harvest is enough for me; it's enough to lie on my own little bed and stretch out my limbs. And how pleasant it is to lie in bed and hold my loved one safe in my arms and listen to the winds raging outside.[211]

205 *Forum:* the center of legal and political activity.

206 He does not, as a client, pay his respects at the homes of patrons.

207 *helpless sheep:* helpless probably because they are "hog-tied" for shearing.

208 **Money** creates anxiety and inquietude. The impoverished farmer therefore has no worries!

209 There is always a nice stream in these pastoral fantasies. Compare the end of the previous selection. Of course, much of Italy is very dry.

210 *once in a while:* at least he won't get many blisters on his hands! Of course, he won't get much work done either. He will probably just borrow a hoe from one of his slaves.

211 A real farmer would lie awake and worry about whether the storm would destroy his crops, whether he and his family would starve in the coming year. One crop failure could spell disaster for the subsistence farmer, the tenant farmer, or the sharecropper. And on sleeping quarters for farmworkers, see selection 86. Moreover, many farmworkers were outside working even in foul weather. See selection 184.

The Country Mouse and the City Mouse

This pleasant fable is meant to teach us that city life, however luxurious, produces anxiety. Country life is simple and austere, but free of care.

180   Horace, *Satires* 2.6.79–117

Once upon a time, the Country Mouse, as the story goes, entertained the City Mouse in his poverty-stricken hole. The two mice were old friends. The Country Mouse was frugal and kept close watch on his supplies, but yet was able to relax his tight-fisted nature for the sake of hospitality.[212] In other words, he didn't begrudge his friend carefully stored chick-peas or long-grained oats, and he carried to him a raisin and a half-eaten piece of bacon fat, since he wanted to tickle the jaded appetite of his guest with this varied dinner. But the City Mouse barely touched each morsel with disdainful tooth, while the master of the house[213] lay stretched out on fresh straw and ate spelt and darnel, leaving the choicer parts of the dinner for his guest. Finally the City Mouse said to the Country Mouse, "My dear friend, why do you want to live and suffer here on the ridge of a steep forest? Wouldn't you prefer the city and human dwellings to these rugged woods? Come on, take my advice and return to the city. Earthborn creatures have mortal souls; there is no escaping death, whether you are a large or small creature. So, my good fellow, live it up, while you may; enjoy life's pleasures. Live well, but always mindful that life is short."

These words won over the Country Mouse and he lightheartedly skipped away from his home. The two mice traveled along the planned route, eager to creep under the city walls at night. And now night occupied the middle portion of the sky[214] when both mice set foot in a luxurious mansion, where coverlets dyed scarlet gleamed on ivory couches, and many courses were left over from a large banquet on the previous evening, and the leftovers were ready at hand in heaping baskets. So the City Mouse settled the Country Mouse on a scarlet coverlet, told him to stretch out, and then himself, as host, bustled about like a waiter, serving course after course, performing his waiter's duties perfectly, tasting everything which he served.[215] The Country Mouse lay back and enjoyed his changed fortune, and played the role of the happy guest surrounded by luxuries. But suddenly a loud slamming of doors tumbled both mice from their couches. In panic they raced down a long hall, and were even more terror-stricken and confused when the lofty house resounded with the barking of vicious dogs. Then the Country Mouse said, "I don't need this kind of life! Bye-bye! My forest and my little hole which is free from these dangers will console me as I eat my wild peas."

[212] Thrift was a traditional Roman virtue; see note 47 of Chapter III.

[213] *master of the house:* the Country Mouse, who is master of his little hole. Note that he follows the human custom (in the Roman world) of lying down at dinner.

[214] A parody of epic style; "it was the middle of the night when . . ." Compare note 187 of this chapter.

[215] It was customary at banquets to have an official "taster" (a slave) who tasted each dish before it was served to guarantee (1) that it was well prepared and (2) that it was not poisonous (accidentally or intentionally).

VIII

Slaves

Slavery was a common institution in all ancient Mediterranean lands. Until the third century B.C., there were relatively few slaves in Rome, and these were mainly of Roman or Italian nationality. However, the many foreign wars from the third century onward rapidly increased the number of slaves, and the number of foreign slaves, in Rome.[1]

The sources of the slave supply were inhabitants of towns or countries captured in war,[2] rebellious provincials, people seized by pirates or kidnappers,[3] people enslaved for debt,[4] people convicted of capital crimes, children exposed by their families,[5] children sold by families who were no longer able to feed them, and the offspring of slaves.[6]

BUYING A SLAVE

A Contract for the Sale of a Slave

A slave might be purchased from a private individual or from a slave-dealer. A reputable seller would be willing to certify that the slave was in good health, was not a runaway slave (someone else's property), and was not guilty of any crime. The following papyrus document, written in Egypt in A.D. 129, records the sale of a slave by Agathos Daemon to Gaius Julius Germanus.

[1] Julius Caesar reportedly created more than one million slaves during his campaigns in Gaul from 58 to 51 B.C.

[2] See selection 221.

[3] *pirates or kidnappers:* see note 29 of this chapter.

[4] The Poetelia-Papirian Law of 326 B.C. officially abolished enslavement for debt. However, indentureship was common. See note 175 of Chapter VII.

[5] *exposed:* see selection 31.

[6] *offspring of slaves:* see note 30 of this chapter.

181

Agathos Daemon, the son of Dionysius and Hermione, who resides in the city of Oxyrhynchus, by this document acknowledges to Gaius Julius Germanus, son of Gaius Julius Domitianus, that he accepts as valid the handwritten sales contract which they made concerning the female slave Dioscorous, about twenty-five years old and without distinguishing marks.[7] Julius Germanus took possession of her from Agathos Daemon just as she was. She is nonreturnable, except for epilepsy or external claim.[8] The price was 1200 drachmas of silver[9] which Agathos Daemon received in full from Julius Germanus when the handwritten sales contract was made out. For this amount Julius Germanus paid the sales tax on the aforementioned slave. A warranty on this slave has been given by Agathos Daemon according to all claims made in the sales contract.

RENTING A SLAVE

A Contract for the Rental of a Slave

Some slave-dealers rented out as well as sold slaves. Their rental customers would include people who needed a slave for only a limited period of time and who therefore did not want to invest their capital in purchasing a slave. The following papyrus document, found at Oxyrhynchus, was written in A.D. 186. It records an agreement made between Glaukios, the slave-owner, and Achillas, the rental customer. The plight of a rental slave was undoubtedly dismal. The woman in this document must work seven days a week and be on call at night. A man who bought a slave would at least care for the slave well enough to protect the money he had invested; a rental customer would be much less concerned about the welfare of his rented property.

182

Glaukios, son of Pekysis and Dieus, originally from Oxyrhynchus and now living in Sento, has rented out to Achillas, son of Harpaesis and Tesposiris, from the same town, for a period of one year his female slave Tapontos to work at the weaver's trade. Glaukios, who has rented her out, will make sure that she is absent from him neither day nor night, and that she will be fed and will receive other necessities, except clothing, from Achillas; she will be clothed by her owner. The rental fee for the whole year is 420 silver drachmas which I, Achillas, will pay to Glaukios, once the rental

---

[7] *distinguishing marks:* scars.

[8] The terminology is not clear. Perhaps if another person can rightfully claim her (make an "external claim") as his property, who had run away or been stolen, Germanus will have to return her and Agathos Daemon will have to give back his money.

[9] Compare the annual rental fee of 420 drachmas in selection 182. Also note that in selection 135 the monthly food allowance for the young apprentice is five drachmas.

contract has been ratified, in monthly installments, as due, at the end of the month
without delay. The slave Tapontos will have four days off in the month of Tybi and
similarly four days off in the month of Pachon for holidays, a total of eight days,[10]
for which nothing will be deducted from the rental fee. If, however, she will take
more time off, for festivals or illness or some pressing necessity on the part of her
master, the rental fee for those days will be deducted. If her master needs her during
the night to bake bread, he will send for her without anything being deducted from
the rental fee.[11] The rental contract is valid.

SLAVES IN THE CITY AND ON THE FARM

Slaves in the city were employed in many different ways. Some were owned by
the city and worked on city construction projects, such as roads and aqueducts, or
on the cleaning crews which maintained public buildings, such as the baths and
temples, or on the clerical staff. Other slaves were purchased by factory owners
or shop owners, and set to work in the factories[12] and shops. Transportation firms
would buy slaves to haul both raw and manufactured materials from one part of
the city to another. Among the most unfortunate of slaves were those purchased
to serve as gladiators or prostitutes.[13]

Wealthy private homes also employed large numbers of slaves as nurses,[14]
tutors, paedagogues,[15] litter-bearers,[16] secretaries,[17] cooks,[18] gardeners, dishwashers,
housecleaners, hairdressers,[19] barbers, butlers, laundrywomen, seamstresses, and
so on. It was not unusual for a wealthy man or woman to own several slaves. The
situation of slaves in a large Roman household might be compared to the situation
of servants in a large eighteenth- or nineteenth-century British household. The
treatment of slaves varied according to the disposition of their masters. However,
work in a household was usually preferable to work on a farm, in a mine or factory, or as a public (city-owned) slave because a household slave might hope to
establish some personal contact with his or her owner and thus be treated more
humanely, and to receive a *peculium*.[20] And household labor was sometimes,
though certainly not always, less physically taxing than other forms of labor.

[10] Eight days a year; compare the weekend, long weekend, and vacation time of the
average modern worker.

[11] This poor woman will sometimes work close to twenty-four hours a day!

[12] *factory:* from the Latin *factum* = "made," "produced"; see note 63 of Chapter VII.
Factory slaves might be rented as well as purchased.

[13] See selections 200 and 341.

[14] See selection 41.

[15] See selections 42 and 43.

[16] See selection 81.

[17] See selection 73. Prospective renters are asked to apply to the owner's slave. Some
slaves were obviously given considerable responsibility in the management of their masters'
affairs.

[18] See selection 188.

[19] See selection 190.

[20] *peculium:* an occasional small gift of money. See selection 197. Some slaves managed
to save enough money to purchase their freedom; see selections 210 and 224.

Since slave ownership involved an outlay of capital, one might expect slave-owners to protect their investments by keeping their slaves in good health. However, the treatment of slaves varied considerably, depending on the disposition and personality of the master or mistress. Some masters were more cruel or thoughtless than others. In general, however, slaves working in private homes were better treated than slaves working on farms and ranches or in factories and mines. Also, slaves born in the master's home were probably better treated than slaves brought to Rome from foreign countries. And slaves from "civilized" areas, Greece or Egypt, for example, were less likely to be bought for farm, factory, or mine work than were slaves from "uncivilized" areas, such as Gaul or Germany.[21] Slaves on farms were forced to do very hard physical labor, and the punishments for disobedience were severe. The slave's owner often lived in a city and visited his land only occasionally. The slave was supervised by an overseer who was also a slave, and who would probably be very demanding since he would fear demotion or punishment if the farm were not productive. The master would think of his farm slaves in much the same terms as he thought of his farm animals[22] and have less sympathy with them than with his city household slaves whom he saw daily. Seldom, for example, would a farm slave be given a *peculium*. City slaves, then, were generally better off than farm slaves. Indeed, in Roman comedy a frequent threat made to city slaves who have misbehaved is: "I'll send you to work on the farm!"

Choosing Slaves for the Farm

In a passage from Columella's book which was translated earlier, Columella discussed the location and construction of a villa. He also discussed housing for farm slaves.[23] In this passage from the same book, he gives advice on the choice and treatment of slaves. His words indicate the different nature of slave work in the city and in the country.

183   Columella, *On Agriculture* 1.8.1, 2, 5, 6, 9, 10, 11, 16, 18, 19

A landowner must be concerned about what responsibility it is best to give each slave and what sort of work to assign to each. I advise that you not appoint a foreman from that type of slave who is physically attractive, and certainly not from the type who has been employed in the city, where all skills are directed toward increasing pleasure. This lazy and sleepy type of slave is accustomed to having a lot of time on his hands, to lounging around the Campus Martius,[24] the Circus Maximus,[25] the theaters, the gambling dens, the snack bars, and the brothels,[26] and he is always dreaming

[21] On well-educated slaves, see note 12 of Chapter VI.

[22] See the references to articulate and inarticulate instruments in selection 185.

[23] See selection 86 and contrast Pliny's remarks about housing for slaves at his villa (selection 87).

[24] *Campus Martius:* see note 36 of Chapter IV. The slave would wait around while his master exercised.

[25] *Circus Maximus:* see note 67 of Chapter III. The slave would wait outside while his master watched the races.

[26] The slave is waiting for his master.

of these same foolish pleasures. If a city slave continues to daydream when he has been transferred to a farm, the landowner suffers the loss not just of the slave but actually of his whole estate. You should therefore choose someone who has been hardened to farm work from infancy, and who has been tested by experience. . . .

The foreman should be given a female companion both to keep him in bounds and also to assist him in certain matters. . . . He should not be acquainted with the city or the weekly market, except in regard to matters of buying and selling produce, which is his duty.[27] . . .

The foreman should choose the slaves' clothing with an eye to utility rather than fashion, and he should take care to protect them from the wind, cold, and rain with long-sleeved leather tunics, patchwork cloaks, or hooded capes. All of these garments ward off the elements and thus no day is so unbearable that no out-of-doors work can be done. The foreman should not only be skilled in agricultural operations, but also be endowed with such strength and virtue of mind (at least as far as his slave's personality permits) that he may oversee men neither with laxity nor with cruelty. . . . There is no better method of maintaining control over even the most worthless of men than demanding hard labor. . . . After their exhausting toil, they will turn their attention to rest and sleep rather than to fun and games. . . .

It should be an established custom for the landowner to inspect the slaves chained in the prison,[28] to examine whether they are securely chained, whether their quarters are safe and well guarded, whether the foreman has put anyone in chains or released anyone from chains without his master's knowledge.[29] . . .

A diligent master investigates the quality of his slaves' food and drink by tasting it himself. He examines their clothing, hand-coverings, and foot-coverings. He should even grant them the opportunity of registering complaints against those who have harmed them either through cruelty or dishonesty. . . . I have given exemption from work and sometimes even freedom to very fertile female slaves when they have borne many children, since bearing a certain number of offspring ought to be rewarded.[30] For a woman who has three sons, exemption from work is the reward; for a woman who has more, freedom.[31]

Farm Slaves and a Frugal Owner

Marcus Porcius Cato was endowed with virtues highly prized by traditional Romans: austerity, frugality, and thrift.[32] He wrote a book, *On Agriculture,* in which he gave advice to wealthy landowners on how to obtain the most profit from their

---

[27] The foreman obviously had some freedom of movement and could travel back and forth to the market, but was not to linger there to enjoy the attractions of the city.

[28] *prison:* housing for unruly or recalcitrant slaves. See selection 86. These slaves worked during the day in chain gangs out in the fields; see note 41 of this chapter. At night they were kept in prisons.

[29] Evidently travelers were sometimes kidnapped, put in the slave prison, and forced to work in the chain gangs. Their families would never discover their whereabouts.

[30] A female slave's fertility could be very profitable for her owner. A slave's children became the property of her owner, who could sell them at a slave auction, just as he might sell calves or piglets at an auction.

[31] Although the mother might be set free, her children remained as slaves.

[32] See selection 160.

land. In the passages below, it is apparent that he had little compassion for his slaves.

184   Cato the Elder, *On Agriculture* 2, 56, 57, 58, 59

When the master has arrived at his villa[33] and has paid his respects to the household *lar*,[34] he should walk around the whole farm, on the same day if possible; if not, on the next day. When he has learned how the farm is being looked after, what work has been done, and what has not been done, he should summon his foreman[35] the next day and ask how much of the work has been completed, how much remains, whether the completed work was done pretty much on time, whether the remaining work can be finished, and how much wine, grain, and other products were produced. When he has received this information, he should calculate what was done in how many days, by how many workers. When the figures are not encouraging, the foreman usually claims that he has worked diligently but "the slaves have been ill," "the weather has been bad," "the slaves have run away," etc., etc. When he has given these and many other excuses, call his attention again to your calculation of the work done and the workers used. If the weather has been rainy, remind him of the chores that could have been done on rainy days: washing out wine vats, sealing them with pitch, cleaning the villa, moving grain, hauling out manure, making a manure pit, cleaning seed, mending ropes, and making new ones.[36] The slaves might also have repaired their cloaks and hats. On festival days,[37] old ditches might have been cleaned out, the road repaired, brambles cut down, gardens dug, the meadow cleared, twigs bundled, thorn bushes uprooted, spelt[38] ground, and general cleaning done. When the slaves were sick, he should not have given them so much food.[39] When these things have been calmly pointed out, give orders for the remaining work to be completed. Look over his account books for ready cash, grain, fodder supplies, wine, oil—what has been sold, what payments have been collected, how much is left, and what remains to be sold. Order him to collect outstanding debts and to sell what remains. Order him to provide whatever is needed for the current year, and to sell off whatever is superfluous. . . . Tell him to scrutinize the herd and hold an auction. Sell your oil, if the price is right, and the surplus wine and grain. Sell off the old oxen, the blemished cattle and sheep, wool, hides, old wagons, old tools, old slaves, sick slaves, and whatever else is superfluous. . . .

Food rations for the slaves: For those who do hard labor, four measures[40] of wheat in winter, four and one-half in the summer. For the foreman, the foreman's

[33] For a definition of *villa*, see the introduction to selection 86.

[34] *lar:* the *lar familiaris* (household lar) was the spirit or deity which guarded and protected the household and its members. There was a shrine to this deity in the home, and sacrifices were made to it regularly. See selections 327 and 354.

[35] The foreman is a slave.

[36] Farm animals would have a day off when it rained; slaves, however, were to keep working, seven days a week.

[37] On religious holidays, when everyone else had a day off, Cato made only one concession to his slaves: they were free of regular farm work for the day and were bidden to do chores around the villa.

[38] *spelt:* a type of grain.

[39] Cato did not want to waste food on nonproductive slaves. For more on Cato's keen eye for profit, see selection 160.

[40] *measure:* Latin *modius*, perhaps equivalent to one peck.

wife, the taskmaster, and the shepherd, three measures. For slaves working in chains,[41] four pounds of bread[42] in the winter, five pounds when they begin to dig the vineyard, and back to four again when the figs appear.[43]

Wine rations for the slaves: When the vintage is over, let them drink *lora*[44] for three months. In the fourth month, allow one-half *sextarius*[45] of wine a day, or two and one-half *congii*[46] a month. In the fifth, sixth, seventh, and eighth months, allow a sextarius a day, or five congii a month. In the ninth, tenth, eleventh, and twelfth months, allow one and one-half sextarii a day, or one amphora a month. In addition, during the Saturnalia and Compitalia,[47] give each man three and one-half congii. The total amount of wine per person per year is seven amphorae. For slaves working in chains, add more in proportion to the work they are doing. It is not excessive if they drink ten amphorae of wine per person per year.

Relishes[48] *for the slaves:* Preserve as many as possible of the olives which have fallen to the ground. Later, when the olives are ripe, preserve those from which very little oil can be pressed. Distribute the olives sparingly so that they may last as long as possible. When the olives have been eaten, give the slaves fish sauce[49] and vinegar. Give each one a sextarius of olive oil per month. A measure of salt per person per year is enough.

Clothing for the slaves: Provide a tunic weighing three and one-half pounds and a cloak every other year. Whenever you give a tunic or cloak to any of the slaves, first get the old one back; from it, patchwork coverings can be made. You ought to give the slaves sturdy wooden shoes every other year.

Managing Your Slaves

The following passage comes from another book *On Agriculture,* this one written by Varro.

[41] Some slaves obviously worked in chain gangs. For more on the treatment of chained slaves, see selections 86 and 183.

[42] Unchained slaves are given wheat, chained slaves bread. Were the unchained slaves expected to grind their wheat and make their own porridge or bread?

[43] In the summer.

[44] *lora:* a weak wine made from water mixed with grape skins which remained after pressing.

[45] *sextarius:* a Roman liquid measure equivalent to about one pint.

[46] *congii:* singular *congius,* equal to six sextarii, or one-eighth amphora.

[47] *Compitalia:* a festival held in December, soon after the Saturnalia, honoring the *Lares Compitales.* These *lares* (see note 34 of this chapter) guarded and protected the boundaries of one's property. Latin *compitum* = "crossroads," "intersection of property boundaries." For Saturnalia, see selections 376 and 377.

[48] *Relishes:* the Latin is *pulmentarium,* which means "anything eaten with porridge or bread." Porridge or bread was the main item on the diet of almost all Romans, not just slaves. It was certainly the main staple for Roman soldiers; see selection 265, where wheat and barley are mentioned as military rations.

[49] *fish sauce:* Latin *halec* or *alec* or *allec,* the sediment left after the preparation of *garum* and *liquamen.* For these latter, see selection 92.

185   Varro, *On Agriculture* 1.17.1, 3–5, 7

The instruments by which the soil is cultivated: Some men divide these into three categories: (1) articulate instruments, i.e., slaves; (2) inarticulate instruments, i.e., oxen; and (3) mute instruments, i.e., carts. . . .

Slaves should be neither timid nor brazen. They ought to have as overseers men who have knowledge of basic reading and writing skills and of some learning. . . . It is very important that the overseer be experienced in farming operations, for he must not only give orders but also perform the work, so that the other slaves may imitate him and understand that he has been made their overseer for good reason—he is superior to them in knowledge. However, overseers should not be allowed to force obedience with whips rather than words, if words can achieve the same result. Don't buy too many slaves of the same nationality, for this is very often accustomed to cause domestic quarrels. You should make your foremen more eager to work by giving them rewards and by seeing that they have a *peculium*,[50] and female companions from among their fellow slaves, who will bear them children.[51] . . . Slaves become more eager to work when treated generously with respect to food or more clothing or time off or permission to graze some animal of their own on the farm, and other things of this kind. The result is that, when some rather difficult task is asked of them or some rather harsh punishment is meted out, their loyalty and good will toward their master is restored by the consolation of these former generosities.

SLAVES IN THE MINES

Spanish Silver Mines

Conditions for slaves who were purchased to work in mines were even more wretched than conditions for farm slaves, as we can see from the following passage which describes the silver mines in Spain.[52]

186   Diodorus Siculus, *The History of the World* 5.38.1

The slaves engaged in the operation of the mines secure for their masters profits in amounts which are almost beyond belief. They themselves, however, are physically destroyed, their bodies worn down from working in the mine shafts both day and night. Many die because of the excessive maltreatment they suffer. They are given no rest or break from their toil, but rather are forced by the whiplashes of their overseers to endure the most dreadful of hardships; thus do they wear out their lives in misery . . . although they often pray more for death than for life because of the magnitude of their suffering.

[50] *peculium:* see note 20 of this chapter. Note that it is the foremen, not the ordinary slaves, who will receive a peculium.

[51] The children became the property of the master.

[52] Spain became a Roman province after the Second Punic War; see Appendix III.

SLAVES IN A MILL

A Flour Mill

The following passage is taken from a book entitled *The Golden Ass* or *The Transformation of Lucius Apuleius of Madaura,* written in the second century A.D. The hero of this book, Lucius, was turned into an ass when he used a magic ointment. However, though a donkey in appearance, he retained his human intelligence and throughout the book records his perceptions of the people he encounters as he moves from owner to owner. In this passage from Book 9, he describes the slaves working in a grain mill.[53]

187   Apuleius, *The Golden Ass* 9.12

When the day was nearly over and I was completely exhausted, they undid the ropes attaching me to the millstone,[54] removed my harness, and tied me up at a manger. Yet, although I was extremely tired and almost dying of hunger and badly in need of some refreshment, my old curiosity, and anxiety too, kept me from eating, even though there was hay in front of me, and instead I observed, with some fascination, the routine of the detestable mill. Good gods, what scrawny little slaves there were! Their skin was everywhere embroidered with purple welts from their many beatings. Their backs, scarred from floggings, were shaded, as it were, rather than actually covered by their torn patchwork garments.[55] Some wore only flimsy loincloths. All of them, decked out in these rags, carried brands on their foreheads,[56] had their heads half-shaved, and wore chains around their ankles. Their complexions were an ugly yellow; their eyes were so inflamed by the thick dark smoke and the steamy vapor that they could barely see.

CRUELTY TO SLAVES

Flogging

Slaves were subject to various forms of cruelty from their owners. Whipping was a very common punishment; branding and various kinds of mutilation were also

---

53 For more on the adventures of Lucius, see selections 234 and 391. For more on the author, Apuleius, see Appendix I.

54 Donkeys and horses were attached to the millstone. They were blindfolded and forced to walk all day in a small circle, turning the millstone. Apuleius says they were skinny, mangy, and covered with open sores, both from chafing harnesses and from the frequent beatings they received to keep them moving.

55 On patchwork garments for slaves, see selections 183 and 184.

56 On the branding of slaves, see the first paragraph of selection 196.

used as punishments. In this passage from Martial, we learn of a cook who was flogged for a minor mistake.

188　　　　　　　　　　　　　　　　　　　Martial, *Epigrams* 3.94

You say, Rufus, that your rabbit has not been cooked well, and you call for a whip. You prefer to cut up your cook, rather than your rabbit.

Sadism

189　　　　　　　　　　　　　　Pliny the Elder, *Natural History* 9.39.77

Vedius Pollio, a Roman equestrian,[57] a friend of the emperor Augustus, found that lamprey eels offered him an opportunity to display his cruelty. He used to toss slaves sentenced to death into ponds of lampreys, not because wild animals on land were not capable of killing a slave, but because with any other type of animal he was not able to enjoy the sight of a man being torn to pieces, completely, in one moment.[58]

Brutality

Many slave-owners vented their own frustrations by treating their slaves cruelly. All slaves, but particularly female slaves, routinely serviced the sexual needs of their owners.[59] Although the slave was usually forced to perform this service against his or her will, a man's wife might nonetheless be jealous of a slave who had attracted her husband's attention. In this passage, a suspicious wife, whose husband ignores her in bed, immediately assumes that he is sleeping with the household secretary (a slave) and has her punished.

190　　　　　　　　　　　Juvenal, *Satires* 6.475–476, 480–484, 490–493

If her husband turns his back on her in bed at night, his secretary suffers! . . . Some women hire a torturer on a yearly salary. He whips, while she puts on her makeup, talks to her friends, and examines the gold thread of an embroidered dress. He lashes, while she looks over the columns of the account book. He lashes, and is exhausted by lashing—until she bellows out, "Go away." . . . Poor Psecas, whose own hair has been torn out by her mistress, and whose clothing has been ripped from her shoulders and breasts by her mistress, combs and styles her mistress's hair. "Why is this curl so high?"

---

[57] *equestrian:* see Chapter I.

[58] Once, when Augustus was dining at his home, Vedius Pollio ordered a slave who had broken a glass to be thrown to the eels. Augustus protested that this punishment was far too severe. To "persuade" Pollio to change his mind, Augustus had all the glasses in his home broken. Pollio, who obviously could not punish the emperor, could not now punish the slave for committing the same crime as the emperor.

[59] See selections 191, 198, and 210.

the mistress screams, and at once a whipping punishes Psecas for this crime of the curling iron and sin of a hairstyle.[60]

Cruel Laws

Certain Roman laws dealing with slaves seem particularly cruel. For example, if a slave were required to give evidence in a court case, he was first tortured, on the assumption that a slave would not tell the truth unless first tortured. If a free man were murdered, and the murder suspect was one of his slaves, *all* of his slaves could be executed (often by crucifixion). Many Romans felt that fear of such mass execution would (1) prevent murder plots by slaves, or (2) encourage a slave to report a plot to his master. The following passage from Tacitus's *Annals* describes a situation in A.D. 61 when a slave-owner, Pedanius Secundus, a city official, had been murdered by one of his 400 slaves. Some of his friends demanded that all 400 slaves be executed, as a warning to other slaves contemplating murder. The Senate discussed the issue[61] and voted to execute all 400 slaves. Cassius's speech to the Senate illustrates the fear which haunted Roman slave-owners who dreaded a slave uprising such as those described in selections 195 and 196. Cassius's speech also indicates the quite conservative attitude of most Romans: "the majority were of the opinion that nothing should be changed."

191   Tacitus, *Annals* 14.42–45

One of his own slaves killed Pedanius Secundus, the city prefect.[62] The slave committed the murder either (1) because Pedanius Secundus refused him his freedom after agreeing to the "purchase price,"[63] or (2) because the slave was in love with some young man and could not tolerate his master as his rival.[64] Now, according to ancient custom, every single slave living under the same roof was supposed to be executed.[65] However, a crowd of protesters, trying to protect so many innocent lives, gathered and even began to riot. They besieged the Senate house. Within the Senate house, some senators were anxious to eliminate excessive cruelty, but the majority were of the opinion that nothing should be changed. Among the latter was Gaius Cassius who, when asked his opinion, spoke as follows:

"I have often, senators, been present in this chamber when we discussed senatorial

---

[60] For more on the cruelty of women toward their hairdressers, see selection 299.

[61] Fifty-one years earlier, however, in A.D. 10, the Senate had passed a law stating that all slaves in a household where the master had been murdered need not *necessarily* be executed.

[62] *city prefect:* an official responsible for maintaining public order in the city; see selection 242.

[63] If a slave had managed to save up some money (from his *peculium* or from gifts and tips from his master's friends), he might be able to purchase his own freedom, if he and his master could agree on a selling price. Obviously, some masters might promise freedom for a certain purchase price and then later refuse it, or agree on a certain price and then later raise the price. (On the amounts which some former slaves paid for their freedom, see selections 210 and 224.)

[64] The young man in this homosexual triangle may be a fellow slave.

[65] However, see note 61.

decrees which were innovative and contrary to the laws and customs of our ancestors. Nor did I oppose them, although I had no doubts that the ancient provisions were in every case superior and more correct and that the innovations were changes for the worse. . . . But now a man who was once a consul has been murdered in his own home by a treacherous slave whom no fellow slave thwarted or betrayed, even though the senatorial decree which threatens every household slave with execution has never been repealed. By Hercules, go ahead and vote for impunity then. But if reverence for rank could not protect the city prefect from murder, whom will it protect? How many slaves will we need to protect us if 400 slaves could not protect Pedanius Secundus? What owner will household slaves ever help, if not even fear motivates them to an interest in plots against us? . . . Do you really think that a slave who had taken the notion to murder his master did not let slip to his fellow slaves one hint of a threat? Did not utter one rash word? But supposing he did conceal the plot and did obtain a murder weapon without anyone's noticing. Could he have passed the guards, opened the bedroom door, carried in a lamp, and killed his master—with every other slave blissfully ignorant? There are many clues which presage a crime. If our slaves tell us when they notice these clues, we can live, though one among many, safely and securely because *they* are afraid. Or, if we must die, we will not be unavenged nor will the guilty survive.

Our ancestors were suspicious of their slaves, even though the slaves were born right on their own farms and in their own homes, and from birth received the affection of their masters. But nowadays our household slaves represent many different nations, with a variety of customs, with strange religions—or no religion at all.[66] You cannot control these dregs of society except through fear. Yes, it's true that innocent people will suffer. But remember that when every tenth man in a defeated army is beaten to death, even the bravest soldier must draw a lot.[67] Every punishment that is used to provide a negative example contains some element of injustice, but the individual injustices are outweighed by the advantages to the community as a whole.''

No one dared to oppose Cassius's statements, although some people voiced their disagreement by reminding him of the large number of the female slaves or of the young slaves or of the majority who had protested their undoubted innocence. However, the senators who favored execution prevailed.

A large angry mob, with rocks and torches, at first prevented the carrying out of the execution order. Then Nero chastised the people in an official edict and lined with troops the whole route along which those condemned to death were taken for execution.

---

[66] Actually, there were more "home-bred" slaves in the imperial period than in the late republican period because there were fewer wars in the imperial period and therefore fewer war prisoners to be enslaved. However, in the early republican period, which may be the period Tacitus is thinking of, most slaves were Roman or at least Italian; see the introduction to this chapter.

[67] If a group of soldiers was charged with cowardice or neglect of duty or disobedience, the punishment was the execution, by beating or stoning, of one-tenth of the men in the group. This process was called decimation (from the Latin *decem* = "ten"). The men to be executed were chosen by lot. See selection 265.

RUNNING AWAY

Slave Collars

It is not surprising that some slaves tried to run away from their masters, although, if caught, they were severely punished. They might, for example, be sold to a man who arranged gladiator shows and thence be "fed to the lions."[68] To help identify fugitives, some masters branded their slaves.[69] Others had identification collars, or collars with identification tags fastened around the slaves' necks. The following passages record the inscriptions on two of these collars.

192   *CIL* 15.7194 (*ILS* 8731)

I have run away. Capture me. When you have returned me to my master, Zoninus, you will receive a reward.

193   *CIL* 15.7172 (*ILS* 8727)

I am Asellus, slave of Praeiectus, who is an administrative officer in the Department of the Grain Supply. I have escaped from my post. Capture me, for I have run away. Return me to the barbers' shop near the temple of Flora.[70]

A Search for a Fugitive Slave

A fugitive slave would be hunted down by professional slave-hunters who knew there was a reward for his return; he was considered a criminal because he had stolen himself (i.e., the property of his master). His master would use heralds to announce his escape and the reward.

194   Petronius, *Satyricon* 97.1–8, 98.1

While Eumolpus was talking privately with Bargates, a herald[71] came into the hotel,[72] followed by a policeman and a small crowd of people. Brandishing a torch which gave out more smoke than light, the herald made this announcement:

"Attention, please. A short time ago, a slave boy wandered away from the baths.[73]

---

[68] See selections 200 and 201.

[69] See the first paragraph of selection 196.

[70] *Flora:* the goddess of flowers.

[71] *herald:* Latin *praeco;* see note 11 of Chapter II.

[72] *hotel:* Latin *stabulum* (from which we derive the English word *stable*) frequently implies a brothel as well as a hotel; see selection 326. On public lodging, see also selection 323.

[73] *baths:* see selections 308 and 309.

He is about sixteen years old, has curly hair and a delicate complexion, is good-looking, and is named Giton. Anyone who is willing to return him or give information concerning his whereabouts will receive 1000 sesterces."[74]

Ascyltus, who was standing not far from the herald, wore a garment of many colors and held up for display the "lost slave" announcement and the promised reward on a silver plate. I[75] ordered Giton to get under the bed at once and to grab on to the framework with his hands and feet, and thus escape the hands of the search party. Giton did not hesitate at all and, in a moment, he had stuck his hands into the webbing of the bed and outdone Ulysses at his own crafty game.[76] In order not to leave any opportunity for suspicion, I fitted the bed with clothing and made the shape of a man about my own size.

In the meantime, Ascyltus, who had gone through all the hotel rooms with the policeman, reached my room and became more hopeful because he found the doors[77] very carefully bolted. The policeman swung with his ax at the bolts which joined the doors and broke them. . . . Then he snatched a long rod from the innkeeper, moved it back and forth under the bed, and even poked it into the cracks in the wall. To avoid the rod, Giton flattened his body against the bedframe, very anxiously held his breath, and even touched the bedbugs with his mouth.

SLAVE REVOLTS

Most Roman slave-owners, and especially those who owned hundreds of slaves, lived with the fear that their slaves might revolt. The decision by the Senate to execute all 400 slaves of Pedanius Secundus, for example, was certainly motivated by fear. The senators hoped that the executions would cause terror among slaves and discourage any further plots against masters. Punishments for slaves who revolted were particularly brutal. The Romans tried to deal with their own fear of slave rebellions by instilling great fear of punishment among the slaves. However, sometimes hatred of a cruel master or despair about working conditions overrode the slaves' fear of punishment, and they were willing to risk torture and death for the chance to escape.

Revolt within the Household

195   Pliny the Younger, *Letters* 3.14

What a shocking story I have to tell you, and one worthy of more than just a simple letter! Larcius Macedo, a man of praetorian rank,[78] suffered a terrible fate at the hands

---

[74] *1000 sesterces:* compare the reward for the lost pot in selection 83.

[75] *I:* the name of the narrator is Encolpius; see selections 151 and 210.

[76] In *Odyssey* 9.425 ff., when Ulysses was trying to escape from the Cyclops's cave, he hung on to the belly of a large ram which the Cyclops allowed out to graze.

[77] *doors:* instead of one door, many Roman buildings had double doors. When closed, they were joined together by bolts.

[78] *praetorian rank:* he had once been a praetor. For praetor, see selection 229.

of his slaves. (Admittedly he *was* an arrogant and cruel master who remembered too little, or perhaps too well, that his own father had once been a slave.[79]) He was bathing in his villa at Formiae.[80] Suddenly his slaves surrounded him. One began to strangle him, another punched him in the face, yet another beat him on the chest, stomach, and even (it makes me sick to report) the genital area. When they thought he was dead, they threw him onto the red-hot floor to see if he was still alive.[81] He, whether unconscious or pretending to be, lay stretched out and still, confirming their opinion that death had come. Finally they carried him out of the bath as if he had been overcome by the heat.[82] His more faithful slaves took his body, and his concubines[83] ran up, wailing and shouting. But then, awakened by their voices and refreshed by the cool air, he raised his eyelids and moved his body to indicate that he was still alive (since it was now safe to do so). The treacherous slaves fled in all directions, but many were caught, although a few are still being sought. He himself, although barely kept alive for a few days, nonetheless did not die without the satisfaction of revenge since the slaves were punished while he was still alive in the same way that murderers are punished.[84] Do you realize how many dangers, how many injuries, how many abuses we may be exposed to? And no one can feel safe, even if he is a lenient and kind master. Slaves are ruined by their own evil natures, not by a master's cruelty.[85]

A Widespread Revolt

In selection 186, the Greek historian Diodorus described the appalling conditions for slaves working in mines. In this passage he describes a slave revolt.

In 135 B.C., a group of slaves on a large farm in Sicily began a revolt which lasted almost four years and eventually involved over 70,000 slaves before the Roman army quelled it in 132 B.C. This revolt is described in the following passage.[86] Two other widespread uprisings have been recorded in Roman history, one in Sicily again, in 104–101 B.C., and one on the Italian peninsula which began in gladiators' barracks near Naples,[87] lasted from 73 to 71 B.C., and was led by

[79] For another slave's son who did well in life, see selection 15. One might have expected the son of a slave to treat his slaves humanely, but in this case the opposite seems to have been true. It is interesting that Pliny, who seems to have been a reasonably kind master (selection 197) and who admits that Larcius Macedo was cruel, does not pardon these slaves at all for trying to revolt. Rebellion was the one crime for which no Roman could forgive a slave.

[80] *Formiae:* a seaside town between Rome and Naples.

[81] *red-hot floor:* hot air was piped from the furnace room to the bathing rooms by a system of pipes set under the floor; see note 66 of Chapter IV. The floor near the furnace room would be very hot to touch.

[82] These slaves pretended that he had died a natural death so that they would escape punishment.

[83] *concubines:* Latin *concubinae; concubare* or *concumbere* = "to lie together, have sexual intercourse." The women were probably slaves or freedwomen.

[84] Probably by crucifixion.

[85] A curious philosophy, but one which explains Pliny's lack of sympathy toward Macedo's slaves. Compare the comments of Columella, in selection 183, on a "slave's personality"; contrast the comments of Seneca in selection 198.

[86] For another comment on this slave revolt, see note 167 of Chapter VII.

[87] Most gladiators were slaves; see the introduction to the section on amphitheater events in Chapter XIV.

Spartacus. At the end of this latter uprising, 6000 slaves who had been recaptured were crucified on crosses set up along the Appian Way, a major road leading from Rome to Capua.

196 Diodorus Siculus, *The History of the World,* fragments of Book 34:2

The slave war in Sicily began for the following reasons. The Sicilians who had done well and accumulated large reserves of wealth bought huge numbers of slaves. They brought herds of them to Sicily from the places where they had been raised and immediately branded them and put identifying marks on their bodies. They used the very young boys as shepherds; the others they used as needs arose. They treated them harshly, worked them too hard, and were little concerned about their food and clothing. . . . Crushed by their physical hardships and mistreated, almost beyond reason, with frequent beatings, the slaves could no longer patiently endure. When they had the opportunity to do so, they met together and talked about a revolt, until finally they put their plan into action. . . .

The revolt actually began in this way. There was a man in Enna[88] named Damophilus, very wealthy but also very arrogant. He was excessively cruel to his slaves, and his wife, Megallis, was every bit his rival in torture and other inhumane treatment of the slaves. Having been so savagely abused, the slaves turned into wild animals and plotted an uprising and the murder of their master and mistress. . . . They quickly collected 400 of their fellow slaves and, when the opportunity arose, they armed themselves and attacked the city of Enna. . . . They entered the houses and wrought great slaughter. They did not even spare suckling babies, but tore them from the breast and hurled them to the ground. It is not possible to express in words how they brutalized and degraded the women, and right before the eyes of their husbands. They added to their numbers a multitude of city slaves who first murdered their own masters and then turned to the slaughter of others. . . .

They chose, as their king, Eunus, a slave from Syria, not because he was so strong or because he was a military genius, but only because he could foretell the future and because his name seemed to be a good omen predicting a benevolent ruler.[89] When he had been established by the rebels as king over all of them, he summoned an assembly and executed all the people of Enna who had been taken prisoner, except those who were skilled in making weapons. . . . In three days he armed over 6000 men as best he could, and mustered others who were using axes with single and double blades, slings, sickles, stakes, and even kitchen skewers. He led them on a pillaging spree through the whole countryside. When he had collected countless more slaves, he dared to do battle even with Roman generals, and he defeated them in battle many times by the sheer force of numbers since he had over 10,000 "soldiers." . . .

When news of this success spread, there sprang up slave revolts in Rome, involving 150 slaves who conspired together; in Athens, involving over 1000 slaves; in Delos;[90] and in many other places. However, in each of these places the local magis-

---

[88] *Enna:* a city in central Sicily; see map 3.
[89] *Eunus,* a Greek word, means "benevolent," "kindly."
[90] *Delos:* a Greek island in the Aegean, one of the centers of the Mediterranean slave trade.

trates quickly suppressed the revolts by speedy action and by severe torture as punishment, thus quelling those who were on the verge of joining the revolt. But in Sicily the evil only increased, and cities were captured, their inhabitants were enslaved, and many armies were cut down by the rebels, until the Roman general Rupilius recaptured Tauromenium[91] after besieging it so that it was completely sealed off, and bringing the rebels to such an indescribable state of suffering and hunger that they ate human flesh, first eating the children, then the women, and finally eating one another. . . . Eventually a Syrian slave named Sarapion betrayed the citadel, and Rupilius overpowered all the fugitive slaves in the city. He first tortured them and then killed them. From there he marched to Enna and besieged that city in a similar manner, reducing the rebels to the most extreme suffering and dashing their hopes. . . . And this city, too, fell because of betrayal, for it could not otherwise be captured since it was very secure against any human attack. Eunus summoned his 1000 bodyguards and fled like a coward to a steep precipice. His bodyguards, who realized they could not escape death since the general Rupilius was marching toward them, cut off one another's heads. Eunus, on the other hand, the quack prophet and the king, cravenly fled to a hiding place among the rocks, but was dragged from there . . . and put in prison, where his body was ravaged and eaten away by lice, a fitting fate considering his penchant for fraud. Thus he died.

HUMANE TREATMENT

Not all slave-owners were cruel; in every period of Roman history there were undoubtedly kind masters. However, the treatment of slaves seems generally to have improved during the imperial period. The increased compassion toward slaves is reflected both in literary works of the period and in new legislation.

Sympathy

We should be wary of attributing too much compassion to the slave-owners. Although Pliny says in this letter to his friend Paternus that he was upset by the death of some household slaves, we must remember the attitude he expressed in the letter translated above: "Slaves are ruined by their own evil natures."[92] Moreover, Pliny was a very wealthy man; the slaves working on the farms he owned may have received less sympathy from him than did his household slaves.

197   Pliny the Younger, *Letters* 8.16

The illnesses of my slaves, and now the deaths of some of the young men, have upset me. Two thoughts console me; though not equal to the weight of my grief, they are

[91] *Tauromenium:* city on the east coast of Sicily.
[92] See selection 195.

still consolations. First, my willingness to manumit slaves:[93] for I don't feel that I have lost them to a totally untimely death if they die as free men.[94] Second, I permit my slaves to draw up documents which resemble wills, and I treat them as if legal wills. They give instructions and make requests about what they wish done, and I carry out their instructions as I have been ordered. They divide up their property, make bequests, and leave gifts, only within the household, of course; for to a slave, the household is the political unit, his city or state as it were.[95]

However, although I am comforted by these thoughts, I am crushed and shattered by that same compassion which led me in the first place to grant these kindnesses. Not that I would wish to be less compassionate! Of course I know that some people call tragedies of this kind nothing more than a loss of money,[96] and even imagine themselves therefore to be great and wise human beings. Well, I don't know whether they are great or wise, but I do know that they are not very human. For surely it is a human characteristic to be affected by grief and to admit emotions, though one may first resist them, and to welcome consolation, indeed to need consolation. I have probably said more about this matter than I should have, but less than I wished to. There is admittedly a certain pleasure even in grief, especially if you can cry on the shoulder of a friend, a friend who has ready a word of assurance or a word of sympathy for your tears.

A Stoic View of Slavery

Seneca the Younger was a disciple of Stoic philosophy.[97] He and his fellow Stoics believed that all men are equal inasmuch as all men are citizens of the universe. They also believed that an angry and cruel slave-owner does himself much damage since he allows himself to be dominated by his most destructive emotions. The Stoics of the imperial period therefore preached compassion and humane treatment toward slaves[98] and were perhaps instrumental in changing the general attitude toward slaves. They did not, however, preach abolition of slavery, but rather accepted slavery as a natural occurrence in the human world. Seneca, for example, who was a very wealthy man and owned many slaves, may have treated them kindly (knowing that their fate could as easily have been his[99]), but did not

[93] *manumit:* to free, to send out of one's hands (Latin *manus* = "hand," *mittere* = "send").

[94] Pliny apparently manumitted slaves who were on the verge of death. For the financial considerations of manumission, see the introduction to Chapter IX.

[95] Although Pliny's permission to his slaves to make wills may seem to us a small favor, it was in fact a large favor. According to Roman law, the slave's *peculium* remained technically the property of the master; when the slave died, the *peculium* ordinarily reverted to the master, not to the slave's family or friends. Pliny, however, allowed his slaves to bequeath the *peculium* to whomever they wished, provided the beneficiary was a member of his household (Pliny thus retained legal control over the money). Pliny's slaves apparently saved up money and property received as tips or gifts.

[96] They view the death of a slave only as a loss of the capital they invested in him.

[97] *Stoic philosophy:* see selections 418–425. Seneca the Younger was also the author of selection 99 about dealing with asthma.

[98] The Stoics shared this teaching with certain religions which became popular during the imperial period, for example, the worship of Isis, of Mithra, and of Christ.

[99] The Stoics expected each man to accept his fate without complaint or resistance. A slave should not, then, be unhappy simply because he was a slave. Wealth or lack of it, free-

manumit them all. In this letter to his friend Lucilius, he discusses his attitudes toward slavery.

198 Seneca the Younger, *Letters* 47

I was happy to learn from people who had just visited you that you live on friendly terms with your slaves. This attitude is quite in keeping with your good sense and your liberal education. Some people say, "They're just slaves." But they are fellow human beings! "They're just slaves." But they live with us! "They're just slaves." In fact, they are our fellow slaves, if you stop to consider that fate has as much control over us as it has over them.

And therefore I have to laugh at those silly people who think it is degrading for someone to eat dinner with his slave. Why do they think this way? Only because we have this very arrogant custom of surrounding a master who is dining with a crowd of slaves standing at attention. The master eats more than he can hold and with monstrous greed loads down his swollen stomach which finally gives up trying to perform the function of a stomach, so that he vomits up everything with more effort than he swallowed it. But the poor slaves are not allowed, while all this is going on, to move their lips to speak. A whip punishes any murmur and not even accidents—a cough, a sneeze, a hiccup—are let pass without a beating. Any sound which interrupts the silence is paid for with a heavy penalty. . . . We have a common saying about this very arrogance: "You have as many enemies as you have slaves." More correctly, we *make* them enemies.[100] I will not dwell on our cruel and inhuman treatment of them, the fact, for example, that we abuse them as if they were pack animals rather than human beings.[101] Or when we are lying down at dinner, one slave wipes up our spittle, another stands ready to clean the mess made by drunk diners. Yet another slave, the one who pours the wine, is decked out in feminine clothing and fights a losing battle against age. He is a boy approaching manhood, but he must present a boyish appearance. Thus, although he has the bodily build of a soldier, he remains beardless because his hairs are rubbed away or pulled out by the roots. He is awake all night, dividing his time between his master's drunkenness and sexual desires. In the bedroom, he is a man; at the dinner table, he is a boy. . . . I don't want to engage in a lengthy discussion about the treatment of slaves, toward whom we are very arrogant, very cruel, and very abusive. However, this is the essence of my advice: "Treat those of lower social rank as you would wish to be treated by those of higher social rank."[102] . . . "What!" (I can hear you saying) "Am I to bring all my slaves to my dinner table?" No; no more than you would invite every free man. You are wrong, however, if you think that I would reject someone because his job was menial or "dirty," because he was a mule driver, for example,

---

dom or lack of it, did not in Stoic theory affect one's ability to be happy or to lead a good life. The Stoics, moreover, elevated moral freedom or freedom of the soul far above physical freedom or freedom of the body.

[100] Contrast the comments of Pliny in selection 195.

[101] Compare Varro's comment in selection 185 about "articulate instruments" and Cato's comment in selection 184: "Sell off the old oxen, the blemished cattle and sheep, . . . old slaves, sick slaves, and whatever else is superfluous."

[102] The Golden Rule; compare "Do unto others as you would have them do unto you."

or a cowherd. I wish to judge men not by their jobs but by their character.[103] Fate assigns to us our jobs; but each man decides his own character. Let some slaves dine with you because they deserve to, let others so that they may become thus deserving. If there is any "slavish" quality in their behavior which results from their humble associations, the company of better-educated men will dispel it. There is no reason, my dear Lucilius, why you should look for friends only in the Forum or in the Senate house. If you pay attention, you will find friends even in your own home. Often good material lies unused, waiting for an artist. Try it. He is foolish, isn't he, who goes to buy a horse and inspects the saddle and bridle but not the horse? Well, just as foolish is the man who judges a human being by his clothes or his social position (which we "put on" like an article of clothing).

"He's just a slave." But perhaps in spirit he's a free man. "He's just a slave." Shall that damn him? Show me someone who isn't a slave. One man is a slave to lust, another to greed, another to ambition. And all of us are slaves to hope and fear. Let me present to you a man of consular rank[104] who is a slave to his girlfriend, or a man of immense wealth who is a slave to a little serving maid. I could show you young men of the finest aristocratic families who are slaves to pantomime actresses.[105] And there is no slavery more degrading than voluntary slavery. So there is no reason why these snobbish people should deter you from behaving with good humor toward your slave rather than appearing arrogantly superior. Let your slaves respect you rather than fear you.[106]

Of course, now someone will say that I am encouraging slaves to don the freedman's cap[107] and hurl their masters off the roofs of their houses, just because I said "respect rather than fear." . . . Anyone who says this has forgotten that what is good enough for God[108] cannot be too little for a master. He who is respected is also loved. And love cannot be mixed with fear. And therefore I think you are very right in not wishing to be feared by your slaves and in using words, not whips, for chastisement. Let whips chastise only dumb animals. . . . For otherwise minor annoyances drive us into a fit of anger, and soon anything which fails to cater to our slightest whim causes anger.[109] We even begin to assume the attitude and temperament of a tyrant.[110] . . .

But I won't keep you any longer. You certainly don't need my advice. Good character has, among other things, this quality: it is content with itself and it is abiding.[111] Bad character, on the other hand, is fickle and constantly changing—not for the better, but into other forms of evil behavior.

[103] Contrast Cicero's comments in selection 147.

[104] *consular rank:* a man who has once been consul.

[105] *pantomime actresses:* pantomime was considered a low form of entertainment. See selections 295 and 336.

[106] Contrast the opinions expressed by Cassius in selection 191.

[107] *freedman's cap:* a felt cap, made to fit close to the head and shaped like half of an egg. It was given to a slave at his enfranchisement as a sign of freedom.

[108] That is, God asks for respect and love, not fear. Therefore, a man should be content with the respect of his slaves, not their fear.

[109] According to the Stoics, anger was the most dangerous and devastating of the emotions; see selection 421.

[110] An angry man is an irrational man; the angrier he becomes, the more irrational are his actions, until eventually he degenerates and begins to act like a tyrant. The Stoics opposed tyrants because tyrants restricted or prevented the rational actions of others; for more on the Stoic opposition to the emperors, see selection 290.

[111] On the self-sufficiency and constancy of the Stoic wise man, see selection 425.

Laws to Curb Cruelty

The following passage, from Suetonius's biography of the emperor Claudius (emperor A.D. 41–54), indicates both the cruelty of some slave-owners and official action taken to curb such cruelty.

199   Suetonius, *The Lives of the Caesars: Claudius* 25

Certain slave-owners abandoned their sick and worn-out slaves on the island of Aesculapius[112] since they were loathe to provide them with medical care. Claudius ordered all slaves so abandoned to be granted their freedom. And if they recovered, they were not to be returned to the control of their master. He also decreed that anyone who chose to kill a slave rather than abandon him should be arrested on a charge of murder.

Hadrian's Legislation

200   *Scriptores Historiae Augustae*
(Aelius Spartianus, *The Life of Hadrian*) 18.7–11

Hadrian forbade masters to kill their slaves; capital charges against slaves were to be handled through official courts and execution, if necessary, carried out by these courts. He forbade a master to sell a male or female slave to a pimp or to a gladiator trainer without first showing good cause.[113] . . . He forbade private prisons.[114] . . . If a slave-owner was murdered in his own home, not all his slaves were to be tortured for evidence but only those who were close enough to have had some knowledge of the case.

Reiteration

201   *The Digest of Laws* 48.8.11 (Modestinus)

A slave cannot be assigned to fight wild animals in an arena[115] unless he has been so condemned by an official court. Otherwise both the buyer and the seller of the slave will be charged with an illegal action. . . . A master no longer has the authority on his own to assign slaves to fight wild animals. However, if he has a just complaint regard-

---

[112] *Aesculapius:* the Greek and Roman god of medicine and healing. There was a famous sanctuary of Aesculapius on an island in the Tiber River; see selection 360.

[113] For centuries, people had bought slaves and forced them to be prostitutes or gladiators. According to this law of Hadrian such sales could no longer take place unless the slave had proved refractory and incorrigible; sale to a pimp or gladiator trainer thus became a punishment.

[114] See note 28 of this chapter.

[115] One form of entertainment which took place in an amphitheater such as the Colosseum was the wild animal fight. Lightly armed men were sent into an arena to fight hungry lions or bears or angry bulls. Very rarely did the men leave the arena alive.

ing a slave's behavior,[116] and the complaint has been recognized by an official court, fighting wild animals may be the punishment handed down to the slave.

Humane Interpretation of the Laws

A few centuries after Cato had advised his readers to sell off old and sick slaves and after Varro had described slaves as "articulate instruments,"[117] Roman jurists recognized the need for a humane interpretation of the laws.[118]

202 *The Digest of Laws* 50.17.32 (Ulpian)

According to our code of law, slaves are considered nonentities. However, this belief is not valid under natural law because, according to the law of nature, all men are equal.

Slave Families

203 *The Law Code of Theodosius* 2.25.1

Who can tolerate that children should be separated from parents, sisters from brothers, wives from husbands? Therefore anyone who has separated slaves and dragged them off to different owners must recover these slaves and place them with one single owner. And if anyone should lose slaves because of this policy of reuniting families, substitute slaves should be given to him by the man who has received the above-mentioned slaves. Take care that from now on no complaint persist about the separation of slave families.

[116] Compare "showing good cause" in selection 200.

[117] See selections 184 and 185.

[118] The very period portrayed by novelists and by Hollywood filmmakers as "the decline of the Roman Empire," the age of depravity and immorality, was, in actual fact, the period which saw the passage of much humane legislation and an increasing compassion among Romans of all classes; compare selections 46 and 47 on welfare assistance for children.

IX

Freedmen

A freedman was a slave who had been manumitted, that is, freed. Manumission was widely practiced in ancient Rome, and it is an aspect of Roman society which sets it apart from other slave-owning societies. For example, very few slaves in the American ante-bellum South were ever manumitted by their owners. In Rome, however, slaves were not only freed but were also given Roman citizenship and thus assimilated into Roman society and culture. Yet, although manumission was a common practice, not every slave could hope to be manumitted. Wealthy slave-owners could much better absorb the cost of manumission (loss of property) than could moderate-income slave-owners. And slaves working in a private household, whose job had been to attend to a master's personal comfort and who were therefore known well by the master, were the most likely to receive freedom. Slaves whose work brought profit to an owner—that is, slaves working on a farm or ranch, in a mine or factory, as a prostitute or gladiator—were least likely to be manumitted. Such slaves had been chosen for their physical stamina rather than their intellect, and it was thus easy for Roman owners to adopt the same protective attitude used by slave-owners of the American South: "He's not bright enough to do anything else; if I freed him, he would never make it on his own." Slaves owned by a city or corporation, rather than by a private individual, were also poor candidates for manumission.

Although there were a number of ways by which a slave might be legally manumitted, two were most common: (1) the slave and master would appear before a magistrate (either praetor or consul) who would touch the slave with a rod or wand and thus signify that he was now free; or (2) the master would state in his will that he wished some or all of his slaves manumitted upon his death. The advantage of the latter procedure was that the owner enjoyed the use of his slaves right up to his death, but still appeared to be a generous man.[1] Some owners would free slaves only if the slaves could buy their freedom, that is, pay back the original purchase price or whatever price the owner deemed reasonable.[2] Most slaves would save up the money from occasional gifts and tips; slaves employed in

---

[1] His heirs were left to deal with the problems which the loss of so much property (slaves) might cause.

[2] One slave paid 50,000 sesterces for his freedom; see selection 224. In selection 191 Tacitus reports that an owner and his slave had apparently agreed on a purchase price, but then the owner reneged.

the civil service had the advantage of receiving bribes. Sometimes freedmen who were friends or family members would buy the slave from the owner and then manumit him.[3]

The new freedman, with his new freedman's cap,[4] was not now independent of his former owner; he became his client and owed him not only loyalty but also a certain number of days' work each year.[5] In fact, many freedmen continued to work full-time for their former owners at the same jobs they had held as slaves. Of course, now they were paid employees, but they had to provide for their own food, clothing, and lodging. Some freedmen found new employers but in the same line of work. Some freedmen had learned skills when slaves which helped them find jobs, and surely some returned to occupations they had held before being enslaved. A few went into business for themselves, often with the help of their ex-master or patron who loaned them some capital or left them a bequest.[6]

REASONS FOR MANUMISSION

Although there were certainly in the Roman world kind slave-owners whose compassionate natures led them to manumit slaves, it would be a mistake to think that kindness was the only reason for freeing slaves. An owner might feel compassion toward a slave who had once, before his capture and sale as a slave, been a wealthy businessman, a powerful politician, or a distinguished professional man in his own country—or he might feel nervous and inferior in his presence. He might prefer to manumit such a slave but continue to utilize his talents. A manumitted slave, a freedman, became the client of his former master, who now became his patron. A freedman client could travel without restriction throughout the city, or throughout the Empire, mingle with all classes of society, and perhaps establish important connections for his patron.

Some men manumitted slaves in order to impress their friends with their generosity and their wealth;[7] since the loss of a slave involved the loss of a capital investment, a man who freed many slaves would appear quite wealthy.

A very common reason for manumission was to offer incentive to other slaves to work hard. Roman slave-owners kept their slaves in check with a combination punishment-reward system: fear of beating and hope of manumission. If a man's slaves knew that freedom was the reward for good service, they would work much harder.

Some men fell in love with slave women and freed them so that they could

---

[3] A freedman or freedwoman might buy his or her own children who had been born into slavery, were property of the owner, and therefore not freed when the parent was. Or a freedman might buy the slave woman he had loved when he was a slave, and then marry her; see selection 210.

[4] *freedman's cap:* see note 107 of Chapter VIII.

[5] On freedmen as clients, see the introduction to selection 9.

[6] See selection 210.

[7] "The behaviour dictated by fashion or the canons of taste sometimes did duty for that dictated by morals—one of the saving graces of a class-conscious society," Susan Treggiari, *Roman Freedmen during the Late Republic* (Oxford, 1969), p. 14.

then legally marry them. Some men became very attached to slave children born in the household and freed them so that they could adopt them as legal heirs.

There were baser reasons, too, for manumission. Some men, who were defendants in criminal cases, freed their slaves before they were asked to provide evidence for the court. Because slaves were routinely tortured when providing evidence,[8] a man might free his slaves rather than risk their disclosure of incriminating information under torture. And some men freed old or sick slaves because they no longer wanted to feed and clothe them. Since such slaves had no resale value, it was cheaper to free them and let them fend for themselves (though it is unlikely that an old or sick slave could support himself; most probably starved to death).[9]

Recognition of Talent and Intelligence

204   Suetonius, *A Book about Schoolteachers* 27

Lucius Voltacilius Pilutus is said to have been a slave and even to have been chained to the doorpost as a doorman[10] until he was manumitted because of his intelligence and interest in education. . . . Then he became a teacher of rhetoric.[11]

In 53 B.C., Marcus Tullius Cicero manumitted his slave Tiro. The passage translated below is a letter to Marcus from his brother Quintus, who was obviously very pleased by the news of Tiro's manumission.[12] Tiro was apparently a well-educated and talented man whom both Marcus and Quintus Cicero felt deserved a better fate than slavery. After his manumission, he worked as Cicero's personal secretary and trusted confidant. Tiro won not only the admiration but also the warm affection of Cicero and his family.[13]

205   Cicero, *Correspondence with Family and Friends* 16.16

My dear Marcus, with regard to Tiro, I swear by my hope to see you, and my son Cicero, and little Tullia, and your son,[14] that you gave me the very greatest pleasure when you decided that he, who did not deserve his bad fortune, should be our friend rather than our slave. Believe me, when I finished reading your letter and his, I jumped for joy. And now I both thank you and congratulate you. For if Statius's faithful service brings such great pleasure to me,[15] of what great value should these same fine qualities be in Tiro, especially when we take into account his literary skills, his conver-

---

[8] This practice was forbidden in the imperial period. See selection 200.

[9] The thrifty Cato sold rather than freed his old and sick slaves; see selection 184.

[10] It was evidently common to chain the doorman to his post so that he could not run away.

[11] See selections 124 to 126 on the social status of teachers.

[12] On relations between Marcus and Quintus Cicero, see selections 60, 123, and 236.

[13] For a letter from Cicero's son to Tiro, see selection 144.

[14] On Tullia (Marcus Cicero's daughter) and the sons of Marcus and Quintus, see selections 16, 111, 123, and 144.

[15] Statius was a slave who had been manumitted by Quintus.

sational abilities, and his breadth of knowledge, qualities which are more significant than his ability to perform personal services for us.

Freeing Possible Witnesses

In 52 B.C., Titus Annius Milo was on trial for the murder of Publius Clodius Pulcher.[16] His defense attorney was Marcus Tullius Cicero. Before the trial began, Milo manumitted all his slaves. The prosecution suggested he had done so in order that they might not be tortured into supplying incriminating evidence against him. In the following passage, Cicero tries to explain away the sudden manumissions.

206   Cicero, *Speech in Defense of Milo* 57, 58

Why, then, did Milo manumit them? You suggest, of course, that he feared that they might incriminate him, that they might not be able to endure the pain, that they might be forced under torture to confess that Publius Clodius was murdered on the Appian Way[17] by Milo's slaves. Why would you need torture? What information are you looking for? Do you want to know whether or not Milo killed Clodius? Yes, of course he killed him![18] Was the homicide justifiable or unjustifiable? There is no reason to use a torturer to decide that. The rack is used to ascertain factual information; the court is used to ascertain justification under law. We are here today to investigate questions appropriate to the court; we have already admitted what you wish to discover by torture. . . .

What reward can be great enough for slaves so devoted, so brave, and so loyal, for slaves who saved their master's life? . . . Amidst all his troubles and misfortunes, there is nothing which Milo finds more comforting than the fact that, whatever calamity may strike him, these slaves have already been given a well-deserved reward.

Adoption

The boy commemorated in this sepulchral inscription, found in Macedonia, had been born a slave but later was freed and adopted by his owner.

207   *CIL* 3. 14206.21 (*ILS* 7479)

Here lies Vitalis, first the slave, then the son of Gaius Lavius Faustus. I was born in his home as a slave.[19] I lived sixteen years and I was a salesman in a shop. I was pleasant

---

[16] Clodius was the proposer of legislation in 58 B.C. to provide free grain to Roman citizens; see the introduction to selection 153. He was also the brother of the notorious Clodia, on whom see selections 64 and 65.

[17] *Appian Way:* Via Appia; see selection 323.

[18] Milo did not deny killing Clodius. However Cicero was trying to prove that Clodius' death was self-defence, not murder. (The jury convicted Milo of murder; his punishment was exile; on exile as a punishment, see selections 5 and 6.)

[19] His mother was a slave, and he therefore became the property of her owner.

and well liked, but I was snatched away by the gods. I beg you, travelers and passers-by, if ever I shortchanged you to bring more profit to my father, please forgive me. And I beg you, by the gods above and below, that you treat my father and mother with kindness and respect. Farewell.

Marriage

These two laws were apparently passed to prevent a patron from imposing himself on a freedwoman, and to prevent a slavewoman from promising to marry her master if freed, but then "dumping" him once she gained her freedom.

208   *The Digest of Laws* 23.2.28 (Marcianus), 29 (Ulpian)

1. A patron cannot force a freedwoman to marry him against her will.
2. However, if the patron manumitted her for this reason (marriage), she must marry him.

Criticism of the Manumission Process

Dionysius was a Greek rhetorician and writer of history who had been born in Halicarnassus, a Greek city in Asia Minor, but who lived in Rome for many years before he died around 8 B.C. He wrote a history of the Roman people. Dionysius was not the only resident of Rome to notice the abuses of the manumission process. In 2 B.C., under the emperor Augustus, a law was passed prohibiting a master from freeing more than a hundred slaves in his will, although apparently no limit was placed on the number of slaves he could free during his lifetime.

209   Dionysius of Halicarnassus, *Roman Antiquities* 4.24.4–8

In ancient Rome, most of the slaves who were manumitted received their freedom as a gift because of their hard work and fine service. This type of manumission from an owner was considered the most desirable. A few slaves, however, paid a ransom fee which they had saved up from just and honest labor.

This is not, however, the case today. Matters have reached such a state of confusion and the fine traditions of the Roman people have become so corrupt and so debased that men who have become wealthy through theft, housebreaking, prostitution, and every other sordid means, buy their freedom with this wealth and immediately become Roman citizens. Others who are witnesses or even accomplices to their masters in poisonings, in murders, in crimes against the gods or the republic, receive from their masters freedom as a favor or reward.[20] . . . Others are manumitted because of their master's passing whim or his vain thirst for popularity.[21] I know that some men have granted freedom upon their deaths to all their slaves so that they might, when dead, be

[20] See selection 206.
[21] See selection 210.

called good men and so that many people wearing freedmen's caps might follow their bier in the funeral procession.[22] . . . Most people, however, when they look upon these stains which are difficult to wash away from the city, bitterly dislike and condemn the custom, since it is not at all suitable for an imperial city, a city which aspires to rule the world, to create citizens of such men. . . . I don't think this law[23] ought to be abolished lest some greater evil break out and damage the state. But I do think that it should be amended as far as possible . . . and that the magistrates should scrutinize each and every person who is manumitted each year and find out who they are and for what reason and in what manner they have been freed. . . . Those whom they find worthy of citizenship . . . they should allow to remain in the city, but they should expel from the city the foul and polluted herd.

ROMAN ATTITUDES TOWARD FREEDMEN

There were many freedmen in a large city such as Rome.[24] Though freedmen could vote, they could not run for public office, nor could they be officially enrolled in the equestrian or senatorial orders even if they became wealthy enough to meet the property qualifications for these orders. However, only one generation of a family was "freed." The sons of a freedman were "free" citizens;[25] they did not owe their father's patron a certain number of working days a year (though they might choose to be his clients), and they were eligible for public office and equestrian and senatorial rank (should they be lucky enough to meet the property qualifications).

Many free men were prejudiced against freedmen because they disliked the fact that foreigners were becoming voting citizens of their city.[26] They also resented the fact that freedmen occupied many jobs which would otherwise be available to them. They feared, moreover, that foreigners, with their foreign customs and religions, who were ignorant of the traditional Roman values, would corrupt and debase their society.[27] Certainly the presence in Rome of these numerous freedmen changed the character of the city, but it is impossible now to say whether for better or worse.

[22] A man's clients would march in his funeral procession. The more clients in the procession, the more important would the dead man appear to have been.

[23] *this law:* the law allowing manumission.

[24] See M. I. Finley, *The Ancient Economy* (Berkeley and Los Angeles, 1973), p. 72. He notes that for the early imperial period there are more sepulchral inscriptions for freedmen than for free men and conjectures that there were therefore more freedmen than free in the population of Rome. Unfortunately, we do not have enough information to reach a firm conclusion on this issue.

[25] The poet Horace, for example, was the son of a freedman; see selection 15.

[26] Of course, these foreigners had not asked to come to Rome; they had been captured, taken away from their own countries, and brought to Rome as slaves; see selection 221. Moreover, in the imperial period, most slaves were home-bred, born in Rome and therefore not really foreign. Also, there were few free families that did not have a freedman ancestor somewhere in the family tree.

[27] Consider the attitude of Dionysius in selection 209: "They should expel from the city the foul and polluted herd." Ironically, Dionysius was himself a foreigner.

The Stereotype of the Wealthy Freedman

In the section of the *Satyricon* where he describes a banquet at the home of a wealthy freedman named Trimalchio, Petronius presents a Roman stereotype of the wealthy freedman: vulgar, boorish, ostentatious, and completely lacking in the cultural refinement expected of a Roman gentleman. We should remember two things when reading this passage: (1) that very few freedmen ever became even moderately well-off; most lived in poverty; and (2) that Petronius was a satirist and therefore exaggerates elements of the characters and the story. Yet his portrayal of Trimalchio and Trimalchio's freedman friends would have delighted those Roman citizens who detested, feared, and envied the few freedmen who actually had gained wealth and power. Clever and ambitious freedmen, since they were barred from political careers and excluded from "polite" society, often turned their talents to banking and business investments. Though forced into this situation, they were then criticized by others as venal and rapacious. And yet Petronius's portrayal of these freedmen is quite ambivalent. Although they seem, on the one hand, vulgar and unrefined,[28] yet they are hard-working and self-reliant, and therefore worthy of our sympathy. We have already met one of these freedmen in an earlier passage.[29]

210   Petronius, *Satyricon* 26.9; 32.1–3; 37.1–6, 8, 9; 38.6–7;
                                  46.3, 5–8; 57; 71.1–4; 75.8–11; 76.1–9; 77.4, 6

Your host today is Trimalchio. He's terribly elegant, has a clock[30] in his dining room. . . .

We[31] were about halfway through some very elegant hors d'oeuvres when Trimalchio himself was carried in to the sound of orchestra music and placed on a pile of pillows. This spectacle surprised us and made us laugh. His shaved head peered out from under a scarlet cloak.[32] He had wrapped around his neck a napkin with a broad purple stripe[33] and a dangling fringe. On the little finger of his left hand he wore an enormous gold-plated ring, and a smaller one on the tip of the next finger. . . .

When I couldn't eat another bite, I turned to the man next to me and began to ask him who the woman was who was running back and forth. "Trimalchio's wife," he said. "Her name is Fortunata[34] and she counts her money by the bushel-load. And what was she before? Before? Please pardon my saying so, but you wouldn't have wanted to take

---

[28] I have not been able to translate the odd and sometimes incorrect Latin grammar used by these men who were probably foreign-born and learned their Latin as slaves. When reading the passage, one might perhaps think of the accented, grammatically peculiar speech of an immigrant who has moved from rags to riches.

[29] See selection 134.

[30] *clock:* either a sun dial or a water clock. Clocks were expensive; see the introduction to selection 145.

[31] *We:* Encolpius and Ascyltus, who appeared in selection 194.

[32] *scarlet cloak:* a sign of wealth; see selection 81.

[33] Perhaps mocking the toga with a broad purple stripe of the senatorial order, for which Trimalchio, a freedman, was not eligible; see note 95 of Chapter V.

[34] *Fortunata:* a Latin name meaning "Fortunate" or "Lucky Lady."

a piece of bread from her hand. But now, without rhyme or reason, she has reached Cloud Nine, and she means the whole world to Trimalchio. In fact, if she tells him at high noon that it's dark, he will believe her. He doesn't even know how much he has, he's so wealthy. But this bitch[35] looks after everything, even where you wouldn't think to look. . . . Trimalchio himself has estates as far as the falcon flies, and million upon million in dollars.[36] There is more silver lying in his doorman's cubicle[37] than anyone else has as his entire fortune. As for slaves, wow! I don't think that even a tenth of them know who their master is, by Hercules. . . .

"And don't turn up your nose at the rest of the freedmen here. They are dripping with money. See that guy lying on the farthest couch? Today he's worth 800,000. And he built up his fortune from nothing. Not long ago, he used to haul wood on his back for a living." . . .

"And now my kid will soon be your pupil.[38] He can already divide by four. . . . He has a good foothold in Greek and he is beginning to be quite interested in Latin, even though his teacher has too high an opinion of himself . . . and is not willing to work very hard. He has another teacher who is not quite as learned but is hard-working and actually teaches the boy more than he himself knows. In fact, it's his habit to come to our house even on holidays, and he's happy with whatever amount you pay him.[39] So I bought my son a few law books because I want him to get a taste of the law, at least enough for home use. You can even earn your bread at this sort of thing. He's dabbled enough in literature.[40] . . . I'm resolved that he should learn a trade—barber or auctioneer[41] or at least court bailiff—something that can't be taken from him, except by death, of course. I tell him this every day: 'Believe me, son, whatever you learn, you learn for yourself. Look at Phileron, the bailiff. If he hadn't studied, he couldn't fend off starvation today. Not long ago, not long ago at all, he was carrying loads of market goods on his back for a living;[42] now he can walk proud even in front of Norbanus.' "[43] . . .

Ascyltus, always a man of unrestrained impulsiveness, was making fun of everything, and throwing up his hands and laughing until he cried. Finally one of Trimalchio's fellow freedmen flared up (the one lying next to me, in fact) and shouted, "What are you laughing at, you smelly sheep-face? Does our host's elegance not meet with your approval? I suppose you are wealthier and used to finer dinners! I swear by the guardian spirits of this place that if I were lying next to him I would knock that bleating out of him. What a rotten apple he is—laughing at other people. . . . I hope that I now conduct my life so that no one can laugh at me. I'm a man among men; I hold up my

---

35 *bitch:* Latin *lupatria.* The exact meaning of the word is unknown, but the word *lupa* means both a female wolf and a prostitute. Perhaps the speaker is implying something about Fortunata's past.

36 *dollars:* the Latin actually says "silver coins."

37 The doorman may have been chained in his cubicle or guardhouse at the front of Trimalchio's home; see note 10 of this chapter.

38 A wealthy freedman is here talking to Agamemnon, a professor. There is a great contrast between the refined Latin of Agamemnon and the vulgar Latin of the freedman.

39 Most teachers were poorly paid and overworked; see selection 126.

40 We have already read the opinion about education of another freedman at Trimalchio's banquet; see selection 134.

41 *auctioneer:* Latin *praeco;* see note 11 of Chapter II.

42 *carrying loads of market goods on his back:* for another reference to the occupation of porter, see selection 151.

43 *Norbanus:* a prominent townsman.

head when I walk; I don't owe anyone a cent. . . . I bought myself a bit of land and saved up some cash. I feed twenty bellies and a dog. I bought freedom for the slave woman who had shared my bed, so that no one could wipe his filthy hands on her breast. For my own freedom I paid 1000 silver coins. . . . You are such a busybody that you can't see your own faults. You see the louse on someone else, but not the flea on yourself. Only to you do we seem ridiculous. . . . I was a slave for forty years. . . . I arrived in this town when I was a young boy—the courthouse hadn't even been built yet. I worked hard, and pleased my master. . . . I made my way successfully—and that's real success! Being born a free man is as easy as saying 'Boo.' So what are you staring at now, you stupid, smelly goat?" . . .

Then Trimalchio said, "My friends, slaves are human beings, too, and drink the same milk as the rest of us, even if bad luck has overtaken them. But as long as my luck doesn't change, my slaves will soon have a taste of freedom. You see, I have manumitted them all in my will. And I've even left a farm to Philargyrus, plus I'm leaving him his girlfriend, a fellow slave. And to Cario I'm leaving an apartment building, his five percent manumission tax,[44] and bedroom furniture. I'm making Fortunata my heir and I am entrusting her to the care of all my friends. I'm announcing all this publicly so that my household slaves will love me as much now as if I were dead."[45]

All the slaves began to thank their master for his kindness. He dropped his playful attitude and ordered a copy of his will to be brought in. He read out the whole thing, from beginning to end, while his household slaves stood around wailing and sobbing.[46] . . .

"Please, enjoy yourselves, my friends. I was once what you are now, but I got where I am now because of my intelligence. It's the brain that makes the man; the rest is all rubbish. I buy at the right time; I sell at the right time. Someone else will tell you something different. But I'm bursting with good fortune. —Hey, you over there, the snorer, are you still crying? I'll make sure that you have something to cry about!— But as I was saying, it was my thriftiness that brought me to my present good fortune. When I first came from Asia,[47] I wasn't any taller than this candlestick. In fact, every day I used to measure myself against it. And in order to grow a beard more quickly, I used to smear my cheeks with lamp oil. When I was fourteen, I became my master's 'favorite.' I mean, what's wrong with doing what your master wants? Of course, I was doing it for my mistress, too. You catch my meaning? I don't publicize it because I don't like to boast.

"Well, as the gods willed it, I took control in the house, and, to be blunt, I took my master's fancy. And, in the end, he made me co-heir with the emperor,[48] and I received a senator's fortune.[49] But nobody ever has enough. I wanted to go into business. To be brief, I built five ships and loaded them with wine—it was as good as gold at the

---

[44] A five percent tax on a slave's value paid at manumission.

[45] Compare selection 209.

[46] This is all happening, of course, during the dinner party. The reading of the will is but one of many grotesque events at Trimalchio's banquet.

[47] As a slave.

[48] Wealthy men often left part of their estate to the emperor in order to avoid outright confiscation. Some emperors executed wealthy men and seized their property.

[49] *a senator's fortune:* enough money to qualify for the senatorial order although, as a freedman, Trimalchio was not eligible to be a senator. Obviously, a slave freed by a wealthy owner might be better off financially than a slave freed by a poor or moderate-income owner.

time—and sent them to Rome. You would have thought I had ordered this accident,[50] it was so total—all the ships were wrecked. That's fact, not fiction! In one single day Neptune swallowed thirty million! Do you think that I gave up? Listen, this loss wasn't even a drop in the bucket; it was as if nothing had happened. I built other ships—larger, better, luckier—so that no one could say I wasn't a brave man. You know, a great ship has great courage. I loaded them again with wine, bacon, beans, perfumes, and slaves.[51] . . . What the gods want, quickly happens. In one trip, I made ten million. I bought back all the estates which had belonged to my former owner. I built a house. I bought slaves and draft animals. Whatever I touched grew like a honeycomb. Once I began to own more than the whole country put together, I quit. I retired from business and began to lend money to freedmen.[52]

". . . I built this house, as you know. It was a shack; now it's a temple. It has four dining rooms, twenty bedrooms, two marble colonnades, an upstairs dining room, a bedroom in which I sleep, a suite of rooms for this viper here,[53] a really nice cubicle for the doorman,[54] and many guest rooms. . . .

"Believe me: have a penny and you're worth a penny. If you have something, you'll be considered 'someone.' ""

Resentment

Although native-born Romans may have been galled by the success of some freedmen, we should keep things in perspective and remember that during the period of Martial and Juvenal a large percentage of the population of Rome was either freedmen or descended from freedmen and that therefore the prejudice against this class cannot have been as pervasive as it may seem when we read the Roman satirists.

211 Martial, *Epigrams* 10.76

Fortune, do you really think this situation is fair? Maevius, who was not born in Syria or Parthia or bought at a Cappadocian slave auction, but who was native-born, a descendant of Romulus and Numa,[55] a citizen who is pleasant, honest, a blameless friend, who knows both Latin and Greek, Maevius whose only flaw (though admittedly a great one) is the fact that he is a poet, Maevius shivers in a cheap gray garment, while Incitatus, a freedman, a former mule driver, shines forth in scarlet.

---

[50] Evidently some shipowners rigged accidents at sea in order to collect the insurance money; see selection 164. For fire insurance fraud, see selection 75.

[51] Trimalchio, himself an ex-slave, has no qualms about making his fortune in the slave trade. Note that he puts slaves in the same category as bacon and beans.

[52] At a high rate of interest, of course. On charging interest, see selection 134.

[53] *this viper:* his wife, Fortunata.

[54] On doormen, see notes 10 and 37 of this chapter.

[55] *Romulus:* the founder and first king of Rome.
Numa: the second king of Rome.

Prejudice against Foreigners

Juvenal disliked foreigners in Rome, whether they were slaves, freedmen, or free men. His views are probably typical of those native-born Romans who saw foreigners getting ahead of them and who resented their success. Like many Romans of his period, Juvenal particularly distrusted and disliked the Greeks.[56]

212   Juvenal, *Satires* 3.58–65, 69–78, 81–87, 100–106

There is one race of men which the very wealthiest among us find highly acceptable socially, but which I find particularly repulsive. About this race I am eager to speak, and no artificial sense of decorum will silence me. Citizens, I cannot bear a Rome that has become a Greek city. And yet, what portion of the dregs in our city is Greek? For a long time Syrian Orontes[57] has poured its sewage into our Tiber—its language, its customs, its flutes, its string instruments, its foreign tambourines,[58] and the prostitutes who are sent to hang out at the race track.[59] . . . On our Roman streets you see men from Sicyon, Amydon, Andros, Samos, Tralles, and Alabanda.[60] They are heading for the Esquiline and the Viminal,[61] aiming to become the owners and future lords of these magnificent mansions. Quick wit, incurable brashness, a ready tongue (more glib than any rhetorician)—that's a Greek for you! Look, tell me what you think that man over there does for a living. He has brought with him to Rome any number of personalities: teacher, rhetorician, geometer, painter, trainer of wrestlers, prophet, tightrope walker, doctor, or magician. These hungry little Greeks know everything! He will fly above the clouds if you ask him. . . . Should men such as these sign documents before I do[62] or receive a better seat at a dinner party,[63] men who were brought to Rome as cargo along with the Damson plums and Syrian figs?[64] Does it not count at all that we breathed our first infant breath right here on the Aventine[65] and were nourished by Sabine olives?[66] And besides, these people are extremely clever at flattery; they praise the conversational skills of the biggest dimwit and the physical beauty of an ugly friend. . . . Greece is a

[56] See note 68 of Chapter V.

[57] *Orontes:* a river in Syria.

[58] Roman writers often express distaste for oriental music which, to the Roman ear, seemed harsh and unmelodic. See note 241 of Chapter XV.

[59] The circus, or race track, was evidently a popular place for prostitutes to meet prospective customers.

[60] All are Greek areas; see map 4.

[61] *the Esquiline and the Viminal:* two hills in Rome on which were situated some of the most expensive and luxurious houses in the city. Juvenal is jealous of foreigners and freedmen who can afford homes in those areas. On Juvenal's apartment, see selection 69.

[62] When a document needed the signature of witnesses, the witnesses signed in order of their social importance, the most prominent man signing first and the least prominent signing last. Juvenal resents being asked to sign after a Greek.

[63] *better seat:* more literally, a better position on the dining couches.

[64] On ship cargoes, see selection 210.

[65] *Aventine:* another of Rome's Seven Hills.

[66] *Sabine:* the Sabines were one of the most ancient and powerful of the peoples of central Italy.

nation of actors. Laugh, and they laugh with you. Cry, and they cry too, although they feel no grief. If you ask for a little heat during the winter, a Greek will put on his endromis.[67] If you say, "I'm hot," he sweats. But we are never equal. He has the advantage of being always, night and day, able to assume a mask, a personality, which matches another's expression.

FREEDMEN AND THE JOB MARKET

Freedmen in the lower class worked at the same jobs as did free men.

Construction Work

This inscription was found at Beneventum.

213 *CIL* 9.1721 (*ILS* 7668)

Publius Marcius Philodamus, construction worker, freedman of Publius, built this tomb for himself and his family. Here was buried his beloved Jucunda.

Herald

This inscription, found on a marble tablet at Rome, was done about 100 B.C.

214 *CIL* 1.2.1210 (*ILS* 1932)

This silent stone asks you, who pass by,[68] to stop while it reveals what he, whose body it covers, entrusted it to reveal. Here lie the bones of Aulus Granius, an auctioneer and herald,[69] a man of honor, integrity, and great trustworthiness. He wanted you to know this. Aulus Granius, auctioneer and herald, freedman of Marcus.

Teacher

Mention has already been made of freedmen who became teachers. Some had been well educated before their enslavement; some received their education while in slavery.

[67] *endromis:* a Greek word (Juvenal sarcastically uses many in this Satire) which means "heavy woolen cloak."
[68] *who pass by:* see note 2 of Chapter III; also selection 207.
[69] *auctioneer and herald:* see note 11 of Chapter II.

215   Suetonius, *A Book about Schoolteachers* 13

Staberius Eros was a Thracian[70] who was captured and sold at a slave auction. He was manumitted because of his interest in education.[71] He became a teacher and taught, among others, Brutus and Cassius.[72] Some people say that he was endowed with such great generosity that during the time of Sulla[73] he taught the sons of proscribed men[74] for free and enrolled them in his school at no charge.

Slaughterer

This inscription was found at Capua.

216   *CIL* 1.2.1604 (*ILS* 7642)

Here lie the bones of Quintus Tiburtius Menolavus, freedman of Quintus, who made a living slaughtering animals for sacrifices.[75]

Maid

This inscription was found at New Carthage in Spain.

217   *CIL* 1.2.2273 (*ILS* 8417)

Here lies Plotia (also known as Phryne), a maid,[76] freedwoman of Lucius and Fufia. This memorial indicates her behavior toward her patron, her patroness, her father, and her husband.[77] Farewell. Be well.

FREEDMEN AND THEIR PATRONS

Most freedmen maintained a close relationship with their patrons or ex-masters. Sometimes they continued to work for their ex-masters.

[70] *Thracian:* a native of Thrace, a country in the Balkan peninsula.

[71] Compare selection 204.

[72] *Brutus and Cassius:* two of the assassins of Julius Caesar. Although they did not achieve their alleged goal—restoration of the republican government—later generations looked on them with fond nostalgia as "liberators." See note 24 of Chapter I and note 81 of Chapter V.

[73] *Sulla:* a brutal Roman general, dictator of Rome from 81 to 79 B.C.; see note 114 of Chapter VII.

[74] *proscribed men:* on proscriptions, see selection 161.

[75] On the sacrifice of animals in religious ceremonies, see selection 372.

[76] Plotia may have continued to do the same work for her patron (ex-master) as she had done when a slave.

[77] That is, she behaved well and therefore they have honored her with this memorial.

Marcus Aurelius Zosimus

This freedman praises highly his patron, Marcus Aurelius Cotta Maximus,[78] who has been very supportive. It is interesting to note that the patron ordered his freedman to raise his (the freedman's) children. This statement suggests that some, if not many, freedmen gave away or exposed their infants because they were too poor to support them. The inscription was found on the Appian Way near Rome.

218 *CIL* 14.2298 (*ILS* 1949)

Marcus Aurelius Zosimus, freedman of Marcus Aurelius Cotta Maximus and business agent for his patron. I was a freedman, I confess; but in death I have been honored by my patron Cotta. He generously gave to me the equivalent of an equestrian's fortune.[79] He ordered me to raise my children, he helped support them, and he was always generous to me with his money. He provided dowries for my daughters[80] as if he were their father. He obtained for my son Cottanus the rank of military tribune which he proudly held in the imperial army.[81] What did Cotta not do for us? And now he has with sadness paid for this message which can be read on my tombstone.[82]

Another Kind Patron

It was not uncommon for a patron to allow his freedmen to be buried in his family tomb. This inscription was found at Ostia.

219 *CIL* 14.4827

Gaius Calpenius Hermes built this tomb for himself and his children and his freedmen and freedwomen and their children and for his wife, Antistia Coetonis.

Selective Kindness

This inscription was found near Rome. Apparently not every patron-freedman relationship was happy.

[78] Upon manumission, ex-slaves assumed the *praenomen* (i.e., Marcus) and the *nomen* (i.e., Aurelius) of their former owner. The name by which they had been known as slaves (i.e., Zosimus) was appended as a third name or *cognomen*. Thus, Marcus Aurelius Zosimus was the freedman of Marcus Aurelius Cotta. Compare the names in selections 221 and 222.

[79] *an equestrian's fortune:* enough money to qualify for the equestrian order (see the introduction to Chapter I), although as a freedman Zosimus was not eligible to be enrolled in the equestrian order. However, his son, Cottanus, undoubtedly became a member of the equestrian order.

[80] Daughters were less desirable than sons (and therefore girl infants were more frequently exposed or sold into slavery than boy infants) because of the difficulty of providing them with dowries; see selections 31 and 32.

[81] There was considerable social prestige attached to the rank of military tribune; see selection 272 and also the introduction to selection 265.

[82] Cotta, the patron, has paid for this tombstone inscription which praises his own generosity.

220   *CIL* 6.11027 (*ILS* 8285)

Marcus Aemilius Artema built this tomb for his well-deserving brother Marcus Licinius
Successus and for Caecilia Modesta, his wife, and for himself, and for his children and
his freedmen and freedwomen and their descendants, with the exception of his freedman Hermes whom he forbids, because of his ungrateful and offensive behavior, to approach, walk around, or draw near to this tomb.

PRIVATE AND SOCIAL LIFE

There would have been, in ancient Rome, no market for books written by freedmen about a freedman's life; yet many freedmen wanted to leave some permanent
record of their achievements. Therefore, the little we know about the family and
social life of freedmen must be implied from their sepulchral inscriptions, some
of which we have already read.[83]

A Life Story

221   *CIL* 11.137 (*ILS* 1980)

Gaius Julius Mygdonius, born in Parthia, born to a free man, was captured in his youth
and sent as a slave into Roman territory.
     Once I became a freedman and a Roman citizen, thanks to a benevolent fate, I
saved up a nest egg for the time when I reached fifty. Ever since my youth I have been
traveling toward old age.
     Now, o grave stone, receive me willingly. With you I shall be released from my
cares.

Friendship between Freedmen

Slaves who formed friendships when they worked in the same household or factory
often remained close friends after manumission. Since slaves were frequently
separated from their families by sale and resale, these friendships must have been
especially important to them (as also undoubtedly were their marriages to fellow
freedwomen). This inscription was found on the Appian Way near Rome.

222   *CIL* 6.22355a (*ILS* 8432)

Aulus Memmius Urbanus erected this memorial for his very dear friend and fellow
freedman, Aulus Memmius Clarus.[84]

---

[83] On the comparatively large number of sepulchral inscriptions for freedmen, see note
24 of this chapter.
[84] The name of their patron was Aulus Memmius.

I was never aware of any quarrel between me and you, my highly esteemed fellow freedman. With this memorial I call to witness the gods of heaven and of the underworld that you and I were sold as slaves at the same time and that we became freedmen at the same time in the same household, and that nothing has ever separated us except your day of death.

Mother and Daughter

This epitaph, found at Reate, was written by a freedwoman, Quarta Senenia, for her daughter, Posilla Senenia. Although many people considered daughters undesirable, this mother's love for her daughter is indeed touching. We do not know whether the daughter was born after her mother was manumitted, and was therefore free born, or whether she was born while her mother was still a slave; in the latter case, she would have been born a slave. Her mother, once manumitted, may have purchased the freedom of her daughter. Perhaps Quarta Senenia had other children, born as slaves and sold off, and therefore lost forever to their mother. Many freedmen cherished ties of friendship and family since as slaves they had been torn away from their parents and children.[85]

223

CIL 1.2.1837

Stop, traveler,[86] and read what is written here. A mother was not allowed to enjoy her only daughter. Some god, I don't know which, begrudged her to me. Since I, her mother, was not allowed to dress her while she was alive, I performed this task as was fitting after she died, when her time on earth was over.[87] A mother has honored with this memorial the daughter whom she loved.

Buying Respectability

Wealthy freedmen frequently tried to buy respectability for themselves and their families by financing the building of temples and other publicly used structures. This inscription was found at Assisi.

224

CIL 11.5400 (*ILS* 7812)

Publius Decimius Eros Merula, freedman of Publius, physician, surgeon, and oculist, member of the Board of Six.[88]

For his freedom he paid 50,000 sesterces. For his membership on the Board of Six he contributed 2000 sesterces to the public treasury. He donated 30,000 sesterces for the erection of statues in the temple of Hercules. For building roads he contributed 37,000 sesterces to the public treasury. On the day before he died, he left an estate of . . . sesterces.[89]

---

[85] Imperial legislation forbade the separation of slave families; see selection 203.
[86] *traveler:* see note 2 of Chapter III.
[87] She dressed the corpse for burial or cremation.
[88] *Board of Six:* a community group involved in public building projects.
[89] The final figures of the inscription are illegible.

X

Government and Politics

THE ASSEMBLIES

The history of ancient Rome can be divided into three periods: the monarchy, the republican period, and the imperial period.[1] During the republican period, every male citizen enjoyed the privilege of voting (1) on legislation and (2) in the election of government officials.[2] Casting of votes was done in meetings or assemblies of the eligible voters.[3] Thus, each voter was a member of the popular[4] assemblies, assemblies which met outdoors in order to accommodate the large number of voters. Once a year, for example, all voters would assemble in one location to elect the coming year's consuls. Today American voters cast their votes for president at polling stations near their homes, rather than all assembling in one location, such as Washington, D.C. In the ancient Roman world, eligible voters had to be in Rome to cast their votes. This system was equitable while Rome was a small town and citizenship was confined to residents; by the late republican period, however, many Roman citizens did not live in or near Rome.[5] Thus, although all male citizens enjoyed the privilege of voting, many were not in a position to exercise this privilege. We have no way of ascertaining how many of the eligible out-of-town voters traveled to Rome to vote, or what influence they had on the outcome of the voting; it is likely that only a few of these citizens had the wealth or leisure to make the journey.

Popular assemblies were convoked to legislate as well as to elect. Since each eligible voter could, theoretically, attend the assembly and cast a vote, the Romans had a direct democracy, rather than a representative democracy such as Americans have, who elect people to represent them at legislative assemblies rather than attending the assemblies themselves. Once again, however, it is not clear to us how many eligible voters did in fact attend each convocation of the assemblies.

1 On the dates for these periods, see Appendix III.
2 Prior to the mid-second century B.C., male citizens had also on occasion been convoked to hear and to decide by voting criminal cases involving capital offenses.
3 *eligible voters:* male Roman citizens.
4 *popular:* Latin *populus* = "the people." Popular assemblies are "assemblies of the people."
5 On the extension of Roman citizenship to Italians in 89 B.C., see the introduction to Chapter I.

In the republican period, there were three assemblies: the Comitia Centuriata, the Comitia Tributa, and the Concilium Plebis.[6] Every eligible voter, whether patrician or plebeian,[7] belonged to both of the first two assemblies (the *comitia*).[8] At the Comitia Centuriata, which met in the Campus Martius, voters were divided into voting units called centuries;[9] division was made according to property value and age, so that all the wealthiest people over forty-six years, for example, were put in the same century.[10] There were 373 centuries in all.[11] In the Comitia Tributa, which met in the Forum, the very same voters were now divided into voting units called tribes;[12] there were 35 tribes in all.[13] Each citizen voted within his own century and his own tribe, and the votes were tabulated there. Then the majority vote of each century (or tribe) was announced as the vote of the century (or tribe), and each century (or tribe) had but one vote.[14] Thus, in the Comitia Centuriata, there were 373 votes in all; in the Comitia Tributa, 35. The Concilium Plebis[15] was restricted to plebeians, but the voters were divided into the same 35 tribes as in the Comitia Tributa, and they also met in the Forum. Plebeians thus voted in three assemblies, patricians in only two. In the elective functions of the assemblies, the Comitia Centuriata elected consuls, praetors, and censors;[16] the Comitia Tributa elected quaestors and curule aediles, and the Concilium Plebis elected tribunes and plebeian aediles. In their legislative functions, it is important to realize that the assemblies met only to vote, not to discuss or to initiate action. The legislation was initiated by a magistrate and discussed by the Senate, and only then taken to one of the assemblies for a vote. In other words, the senators, who were members of Rome's upper class,[17] controlled the nature of the legislation which reached the assemblies; and therefore the government of Rome during the republican period was more truly an aristocracy than a democracy.[18]

[6] A fourth and ancient assembly, the Comitia Curiata, was rarely convoked.

[7] On the distinctions between patricians and plebeians, see Chapter I.

[8] Do not confuse the Latin word *comitia* with the English word *committee*. The word *comitia* means a general assembly of all eligible voters.

[9] *century:* Latin *centuria* = "a group of 100" (Latin *centum* = 100). In actual fact, the number of men in each century varied greatly.

[10] When a voter reached the Campus Martius, he then located the enclosure marked out for his particular century and voted there. On the location of the Campus Martius, see note 20 of this chapter and note 36 of Chapter IV.

Men forty-six and under were called *iuniores* ("juniors," "younger men"); men forty-seven and over were called *seniores* ("seniors," "older men"). *Iuniores* were eligible for military service.

[11] This was the number during the time of Cicero.

[12] *tribes:* division into tribes was probably based on geographic considerations, one's place of origin or one's ancestors' place of origin.

[13] This was the number during the time of Cicero.

[14] For example, in a century of 100 men, if 71 voted yes on a piece of legislation and 29 voted no, the single vote of the century was recorded as a yes. It was then tallied with the single votes of the other centuries. If the majority of centuries had a yes vote, the legislation passed.

[15] *Concilium Plebis:* "meeting of the plebeians." Do not confuse the Latin word *concilium* with the English word *council*. The Latin word implies a much larger gathering of people.

[16] The duties of these elected officials are discussed in selections 229–235.

[17] Lack of money—to obtain a good education, to finance a political campaign, and to serve in an unpaid public position—prevented all but the wealthiest citizens from running for political office and gaining a seat in the Senate; see the introduction to selection 147.

[18] For Cicero's views on aristocracy, democracy, and monarchy, see selection 2.

The Comitia

225   Aulus Gellius, *Attic Nights* 15.27.5

When voting is done according to property value and age, the assembly is called the
Comitia Centuriata; when according to districts and localities, it is called the Comitia
Tributa. It is unlawful for the Comitia Centuriata to assemble within the city limits because it is unlawful for the army to be mustered within the city limits; the army should
be mustered outside the city limits.[19] Therefore, it was a custom for the Comitia Centuriata to be assembled and the army to be mustered in the Campus Martius.[20]

Comitia and Concilium: Some Differences

226   Aulus Gellius, *Attic Nights* 15.27.4

He who summons a meeting not of all the people[21] but of only the plebeians should announce the meeting not as the comitia, but rather as the concilium.[22] Tribunes do not
summon patricians to meetings nor can they present to them any motions requiring a
vote.[23] Therefore, motions which have been presented by the tribunes of the plebs and
have been approved by a vote are properly called plebiscita, not leges.[24] Until 287 B.C.,

[19] The division of the male citizens into centuries began early in Rome's history as a way
of organizing military forces. The wealthiest men, who could afford the best equipment, were
grouped into the same centuries; men of lower property value were put in centuries with men
of similar property value. Thus, men with similar equipment fought together as a unit; see
selection 265. Men forty-six and under, the "juniors," were still eligible for military service
and were therefore placed in different centuries from men forty-seven and over. The Comitia
Centuriata began, then, as a mustering of the militia, an assembly to vote on war declarations
and to organize for military campaigns; and it was presided over by the consuls, the commanders-in-chief of the army. However, the consuls began to convoke the Comitia Centuriata
during peacetime, for various legislative, judicial, and electoral functions.

It was unlawful for the army to assemble within the city limits; this ancient restriction
was probably established to lessen the possibility of civil wars or army coups.

[20] *Campus Martius:* the Field of Mars, god of war. This large, open area was outside
the ancient city limits.

[21] *all the people:* that is, Latin *populus,* both patricians and plebeians. Since women did
not have the right to vote, *populus* or "people" in this context means male patricians and
plebeians.

[22] The Concilium Plebis.

[23] Soon after the expulsion of Rome's last king, Tarquinius Superbus, in 509 B.C., the
plebeians, who were distressed because the patricians had assumed total control in the state,
formed their own legislative assembly (Concilium Plebis) and elected their own magistrates
(tribunes) to protect them from the patrician magistrates. Thus, historically patricians were
barred from attending the Concilium Plebis.

The tribunes of the plebs were elected in the Concilium Plebis and presided over it, that
is, convoked it and introduced legislation to it.

[24] *plebiscita:* English *plebiscites,* from the Latin *plebs + scitum = "ordinance," "decree,"*
that is, "decrees of the plebeians."

leges (singular is *lex*): statutes or laws passed by the comitia (that is, all voting citizens,
both patrician and plebeian). The English word legislation is derived from the Latin *leges +
latum = "proposed."*

the patricians were not subject to such legislation, but in that year Quintus Hortensius, the dictator, enacted a law that all citizens[25] should be subject to whatever legislation the Concilium Plebis should enact.

Lex and Plebiscitum

227   Gaius, *Institutes* 1.3

A lex is what the populus[26] orders and establishes. A plebiscitum is what the plebs orders and establishes. The plebs differs from the populus in this respect: all the citizens, including the patricians, are indicated by the term *populus;* however, the term *plebs* denotes all the citizens except the patricians.

Contio

As noted above, the function of the three assemblies was simply to vote on electoral or legislative matters, and no opportunity for discussion was provided. However, an informal public meeting in which discussion was allowed was often held a few days before a convocation of the assemblies. Such a meeting was called a *contio.* There was no division of those present into voting groups and, of course, no voting. Moreover, not only male citizens, but also women, slaves, and foreigners could attend a contio. The purpose of a contio was to acquaint people with the issues which would be voted on in the comitia, or with the candidates who were up for election. Sometimes, however, a consul might summon a contio simply to inform people about matters of general interest and to let them know how he was handling each specific matter.[27] The people who attended the contiones were frequently quite vocal in their expressions of approval or disapproval. In the passage translated here, Cicero complains that the people are too vocal and too rowdy; he seems to fear that issues were being decided, albeit unofficially, in the contiones, and that, as a result, the traditional structure of voting according to voting groups in the comitia was being undermined. Senators and conservatives such as Cicero felt threatened by these changes because, whereas they had manipulated the voting groups for many years, they had little control over the moods or whims of the often volatile contiones.[28] It is curious that Cicero blames these changes on Greek influences and particularly singles out the Greek practice of sitting at meetings; the Romans had, in the past, always stood in their assemblies.[29] For some reason, Cicero attributes disorderly conduct to sitting down.

[25] *all citizens:* whether patrician or plebeian. Patricians were thus now subject to legislation on which they had no vote.

[26] *populus:* all the male citizens, patrician and plebeian, meeting in either the Comitia Centuriata or the Comitia Tributa.

[27] See, for example, selection 387.

[28] Cicero and other members of the senatorial class believed that the lower classes were incapable of making sound judgments and that they therefore needed careful guidance by the senatorial class; see selections 2 and 147.

[29] Roman assemblies were held in open areas such as the Forum and the Campus Martius. Greek assemblies were held in theaters which had seats.

228   Cicero, *Speech in Defense of Flaccus* 15, 16

Oh, if only we would preserve the outstanding traditional system of citizens' assemblies which we inherited from our ancestors. But now it is somehow slipping out of our hands. Our very wise and venerable ancestors did not want any power to reside in the contiones. They instituted these regulations about what the plebs decreed or the populus ordered. Only after the contio had been adjourned; after the voting citizens had been distributed into their proper tribes or centuries according to rank, class, and age; after the men who proposed the legislation had spoken;[30] after the proposal had been published and understood well in advance; only then did our ancestors wish the people to vote and thereby approve or reject a proposal. Among the Greeks, however, all public business is conducted quite irresponsibly by a contio where people sit down. . . . And ancient Greece, which once flourished with wealth, power, and glory, was ruined by this one evil: the excessive liberty and license at its contiones.[31] When men who were inexperienced, incompetent, and ignorant[32] sat down in the theater, they would decide to embark on futile wars, they would choose lawless men as magistrates, and they would expel from the city the very citizens whom they should have thanked for good service.

MAGISTRATES

Men were not elected to the Senate; rather, in the middle and late republican period, a man was automatically admitted to the Senate once he had been elected by the comitia or concilium to his first magistracy. However, once admitted he became a member for life.[33] Since the Senate held the real power in Rome and the Empire, men of the "right" families hoped to win election to their first magistracy in their early thirties, and therefore to be Senate members from then until their deaths. The magistrates were the public officials of Rome and of the Empire—the mayor, the chief justice, the chief engineer, the public treasurer, the army chief of staff, and so on. They had executive, judicial, legislative, diplomatic, military, and even religious functions. The term of office for the magistrates was just one year, but a senator would expect to be elected to at least two or three magistracies during his lifetime.

Magistracies were usually sought in a particular order. One's first political office, for example, was the quaestorship; the consulship was the top rung of the political ladder.[34]

---

[30] The proposers of legislation would always be magistrates and therefore senators; see the introduction to selection 238.

[31] For more on Roman opinions about Greeks, see selection 212, the comments of Juvenal, who lived about 100 years after Cicero.

[32] Is this Cicero's opinion of the common people of Rome? Compare selection 2.

[33] He could be removed by the censors if he were guilty of shameful or criminal behavior; the historian Sallust (author of selection 291) was expelled from the Senate for alleged immorality; see Appendix I.

[34] Today also one would not run for president without first having held some lower offices. We speak of "running for office." The Latin phrase for political career is *cursus honorum*, "the race or course of honors." On the meaning of *honors*, see note 28 of Chapter I.

The Functions of the Magistrates

The passage translated here is taken from a work in which Cicero describes what he considered an ideal political system. However, the functions of the magistrates in this ideal system resemble very closely the actual functions of Roman magistrates, and the passage therefore provides helpful information.

229   Cicero, *A Book about Constitutions* 3.3.6–9

In the army there will be military tribunes who will command those over whom they are placed. In the city, there will be officers [quaestors] who will administer the public finances. . . .

There will be aediles who will oversee the city's markets, merchandise, and food supplies, and also the regularly held games.[35] . . .

The censors will record the ages, children, slaves, and property value of all citizens. They will undertake construction of temples, roads, and aqueducts in the city,[36] and will audit the records of the public treasury. They will divide the citizen body into tribes; they will also make other divisions, according to wealth, age, and class.[37] They will enroll young men in the cavalry and the infantry. They will regulate the morals of the people and will allow no one guilty of shameless behavior to remain in the Senate. . . .

There will be a praetor, an arbitrator of legal disputes, who will himself judge or will arrange to have judged civil suits.[38] He will be the administrator of civil law. And there will be as many praetors,[39] all with the same power, as the Senate shall decree or the "people" order.[40]

There will be two magistrates with royal power[41] . . . who will be called consuls. They will have supreme authority in military matters, and everyone will obey them. Their most important charge will be the safety of the people. . . .

There will be tribunes, ten officers whom the plebeians have elected to help protect them from violence. And whatever they veto[42] and whatever legislation has been

[35] *regularly held games:* games or public entertainments which were sponsored every year by the state. See the section on spectacles in Chapter XIV.

[36] The censors decided on new construction and were responsible for letting the contracts. The aediles were responsible for the maintenance and repair of public works.

[37] New citizens were enrolled into tribes and centuries. It is not clear to us today on what criteria the assignment to a particular tribe was based; see note 12 of this chapter. However, the assignment to a particular century was based on wealth and age.

[38] The praetor could judge the case himself, assign the case to his assistants, or send the case to a comitia to be judged (see note 2 of this chapter).

[39] In 366 B.C., there was one praetor; by 241 B.C., there was a second praetor. As the Romans acquired overseas provinces, the number of praetors was increased. By 197 B.C., there were six praetors, and by 80 B.C., there were eight.

[40] *the "people":* either the comitia tributa or comitia centuriata in their legislative functions; see notes 21 and 26 of this chapter. In the translations which follow, the "people" refers specifically to these two voting assemblies, and not to the general populace (= the people).

[41] *royal power:* the consuls assumed many of the duties of the king after the monarch was expelled in 509 B.C.

[42] *veto:* a Latin word meaning "I forbid." The plebeian tribunes had the unique power to veto or forbid any action or plan of action occurring within the city of Rome, provided

passed by the Concilium Plebis, over which they preside, will be binding. And they will be sacrosanct.[43]

The Titles of the Magistrates

The titles of the Roman magistrates were at least as old as the beginning of the republican period, and therefore the Romans of later periods were as uncertain as we are today of the derivation of these titles. In the passage translated below, Varro, a scholar of the first century B.C., provides an etymological study of the origins of these titles.

230   Varro, *A Book about the Latin Language* 5.14.80–82

The *consul* was so named as the one who should *consulere* ["consult," "ask the advice of"] the people and the Senate; Accius, however, gives a different etymology in his tragedy *Brutus*,[44] where he writes: "Let him who gives correct *consilium* ["advice"] become the *consul*."

The *praetor* was so called as the one who should *praeire* [*-ire* "go"; *prae-* "before"; "take the lead before"] the law and the army.[45] And therefore Lucilius[46] said: "It is thus the duty of the *praetors* to go in front and before."

The *censor* was the one according to whose *censio*, that is "judgment" or "rating," the people should be *censeri* ["assessed," "rated"].[47]

The *aedile* was the one who should look after sacred and private *aedes* ["buildings"].

The title *quaestor* was derived from *quaerere* ["to inquire"] since they are the ones who should inquire into the public finances. . . . The *tribuni militum* ["military tribunes"] were so called because long ago there were sent to the army three *tribunes* from each of the three *tribus* ["tribes"].[48]

The *tribuni plebei* ["tribunes of the plebeians"] were so called because it was from the military tribunes that the tribunes of the plebeians were first created, for the purpose of defending the plebeians. . . .

---

they did so in person. A tribune might thus obstruct the plans of the Senate or of a magistrate. The tribunate had been established to protect the plebeians from the patricians early in Rome's history, when the patricians held all the public offices; see note 23 of this chapter.

[43] *sacrosanct:* inviolable; protected by religious sanction against harm. See note 167 of this chapter.

[44] *Accius:* Roman tragedian of the second century B.C. *Brutus* was the title of one of his tragedies.

[45] In the early republican period, praetors both made and enforced laws and served as generals in military campaigns. By the middle republican period, however, their powers were restricted to law and justice, and the consuls assumed the military role.

[46] *Lucilius:* Roman satirist of the second century B.C.

[47] See notes 64 and 105 of Chapter VII.

[48] In very early Rome there were only three tribes. (The word *tribus,* "tribe," is itself derived from the Latin word for "three," *tris* or *tres*.) However, by the end of the republican period, the number of tribes had increased from three to thirty-five. On military tribunes, see the introduction to selection 265.

The *dictator* was so named because he was appointed by the consul as the one to whose *dictum* ["command"] all should listen.[49] The *magister equitum* ["master of the cavalry"] was so named because he has supreme power over the *equites* ["cavalry-men"], just as the *dictator* has supreme power over the people and is therefore sometimes also called *magister populi* ["master of the people"].

The Development of the Magistracies

In the passage translated here, a writer of the imperial period tries to trace the historical development of the magistracies.

231   *The Digest of Laws* 1.2.16–28 (Pomponius)

After the kings had been driven out, the consulship was established, and two consuls took office.[50] A law was passed that the supreme authority in the state should rest with them. They were called consuls because they, above all else, consulted about, or looked after, the state. In order, however, that they not appropriate to themselves in all matters the power formerly wielded by the kings, a law was passed which stipulated that there be a right of appeal from their decisions and that they not be able to inflict capital punishment on a Roman citizen without an order from the "people."[51] One power, however, was left to them: the power to arrest men and to order them to be imprisoned.

Later, when the taking of the census began to occupy more time, and the consuls could not handle this duty in addition to their others, the office of the censors was established.

As the population increased and wars became frequent (some rather bitter ones were started by neighboring peoples), occasionally, when the situation required, it was decided to establish a magistrate with power greater than any other magistrate. And thus dictators were appointed, from whom there was no right of appeal and to whom had been granted the power to inflict capital punishment. Since this magistrate had absolute power, it was unconstitutional for him to be kept in office for more than six months.[52] And a master of the horse was assigned to the dictator as his second-in-command or chief of staff.

About this same time, the plebeians . . . created for themselves tribunes, who were to be plebeian magistrates. They were called tribunes because . . . they were elected by a vote of the tribes.[53] And similarly, in order that there might be magistrates

---

[49] *dictum*: "command," from the Latin *dico*, "I say."

[50] The consuls, who were always patrician until 367 B.C. when plebeians were allowed to run for the consulship, took over the functions of the monarch but did not themselves become monarchs because (1) the two consuls had to share power, and (2) their terms expired after one year.

[51] *the "people"*: the Comitia Centuriata or the Comitia Tributa.

[52] It was therefore unconstitutional for Sulla to hold the office of dictator for three years (see note 114 of Chapter VII) or for Julius Caesar to declare himself dictator for life. On the repercussions of Caesar's declaration, see note 24 of Chapter I.

[53] That is, by the tribes meeting as the Concilium Plebis.

to look after the temples in which the plebeians deposited all their plebiscites,[54] two men were elected from the plebeians and called aediles.[55]

And when the state finances began to increase in size and complexity, in order that there might be magistrates to administer them, quaestors were elected to manage state funds. And they were called quaestors because they inquired into and supervised the state funds. . . .

Several years after the Twelve Tables had been passed,[56] strife arose between the plebeians and the patricians because the plebeians wanted consuls to be elected from their group, as well as from the patricians; the patricians at first refused to allow this. . . . Later, however, it was agreed to elect consuls also from among the plebeians, and thus they began to be elected from both groups.[57] Then, in order that the patricians might retain some distinction of rank, it was agreed to elect from among the patricians two magistrates who became curule aediles.[58]

Since the consuls were called away by wars with neighboring peoples, and there was no one in the city who could administer justice, it came about that a praetor was elected who was called the *praetor urbanus* because he administered justice in the city.[59] Some years later, when this praetor could no longer manage all his duties because large numbers of foreigners had crowded into the city, another praetor was introduced, who was called the *praetor peregrinus* because primarily he administered justice to foreigners.[60]

The Duties of the Consuls

232   Polybius, *History of the World* 6.12.1–9

The consuls, until they leave the city as commanders of the legions, serve in Rome as the chief administrators of all public affairs. All the other magistrates, except the tribunes,[61] serve under them and obey them. They introduce foreign ambassadors to the Senate. In addition, they present to it for discussion matters of urgency, and they

[54] *plebiscites:* see note 24 of this chapter. Legal documents were deposited in temples for safekeeping.

[55] *aediles:* for the etymology, see selection 230. There were actually two groups of aediles: the plebeian aediles (who were always plebeian) and the curule aediles (who might be patrician or plebeian).

[56] *Twelve Tables:* the first written code of Roman law, passed about 450 B.C. Previously laws had been handed down orally from generation to generation. The establishment of a written code was a landmark in Roman legal history. See the introduction to the section on legislation in this chapter.

[57] In 367 B.C.

[58] In 367 B.C.; later, however, plebeians were also admitted to the curule aedileship. The plebeian and curule aediles had similar functions: superintendence of public buildings and works (temples, roads, aqueducts, etc.), of markets, and of public entertainments.

[59] Although the praetorship may have existed from the beginning of the republican period, in 366 B.C. the office of the *praetor urbanus* was established (*urbanus* = "of the city," from *urbs* = "city"). Henceforth the praetorship became less concerned with military leadership and almost exclusively concerned with the administration of justice in the city.

[60] *praetor peregrinus: peregrinus* = "concerning foreigners." This office was established during the First Punic War (264–241 B.C.) to deal with legal cases in which one or both parties were foreigners.

[61] The tribunes were responsible directly to the Concilium Plebis.

carry out in entirety the execution of the Senate's decrees.[62] And then, in connection with all the matters pertaining to public affairs which must be managed by the "people,"[63] it is the duty of the consuls to consider these matters their concern, and to summon assemblies, to introduce resolutions, and to execute the decrees of the "people."[64]

In preparations for war and in the military operations in the field, the consuls have almost absolute authority. It is in their power to give any order they wish to the allies, to appoint military tribunes, to levy soldiers, and to select those who are suitable. In addition, they have the authority while in the field to punish whomever they might wish of those men under their command. And they have the power to spend from the public treasury any amount that they may decide upon, and they are accompanied by a quaestor who readily does everything they bid him. Therefore, if anyone were to look at this branch of the government, he might with justification say that the constitution is simply a monarchy or kingship.[65]

The Responsibilities of a Magistrate

Cicero spent most of his adult life in the political arena of Rome. He was quaestor at age thirty-one, aedile at thirty-seven, praetor at forty, and consul at forty-three.[66] Because his family was equestrian and because no one in his family had ever before achieved the rank of consul, Cicero was looked down on by many of the old, established Roman senatorial families as a "new man."[67] Yet Cicero held the same traditional upper-class opinions as these families. He believed, for example, that property rights were sacred, and that it was the responsibility of government officials to protect property owners from any attempt to damage or decrease their property or to impede their acquisition of wealth.[68] Since only a few men in Roman society could afford to own significant amounts of property, and since these same few men often held the public offices, they were in effect responsible to themselves and to their own class, rather than to the Roman people in general, and they frequently worked to protect their own interests, even when this might mean ignoring the interests of the common people.[69]

The passage translated here is taken from Cicero's three-volume work, *An*

---

[62] *Senate's decrees:* the *senatus consulta;* see note 125 of this chapter.

[63] *the "people":* the Comitia Centuriata and the Comitia Tributa.

[64] The consuls could not summon meetings of the Concilium Plebis; this was the prerogative of the tribunes.

[65] However, the consuls served for only one year, and there were two consuls each year so that no one man would possess supreme authority.

[66] For more on Cicero's political career, see selection 236.

[67] *"new man":* Latin *novus homo;* on the political difficulties of a "new man," see selection 236.

[68] In the middle and late republican periods, when most people in Roman society could not afford to own land, the educated upper class continued to cherish the legends of the heroic landowner-soldiers of early Roman history who fought bravely to protect their property; see the introduction to selection 177. The upper class was, in effect, trying to preserve the historic validity of an ideal which fostered its own current interests.

[69] Compare the reaction of the senatorial class to the land reform proposal of Tiberius Gracchus (selection 170).

Essay about Duties,[70] which he dedicated to his son[71] and completed in November, 44 B.C.[72] Cicero's upper-class biases show through very clearly in his denunciation of agrarian and debt laws and in his interpretation of a magistrate's responsibilities. It is important to realize, however, that his interpretation is not unique and that most magistrates would agree with him.

233   Cicero, *An Essay about Duties* 1.34.124; 2.21.73; 2.22.78, 79; 2.23.84; 2.24.85

It is the specific duty of a magistrate to understand that he is the representative of the whole citizen body and that he must therefore uphold the dignity and honor of the state, defend its laws, render justice, and remember that all these powers have been entrusted to him as a sacred trust. . . .

And he who holds public office must especially see to it that each man keeps what belongs to him and that private citizens suffer no loss of property through public legislation. . . . It was particularly for this reason that governments and states were established: so that each man might keep what belonged to him. Although men originally banded together because their nature so urged them, yet it was in the hope of protecting their possessions that they sought the defensive safety of cities. . . . And men who wish to be *populares*[73] and who therefore either try to pass some agrarian law, in order that the occupants may be driven away from their residences,[74] or think that money loaned should be remitted to the debtors,[75] are undermining the foundations of our society; they are, in the first place, disrupting public harmony, which cannot exist when money is taken away from one group and given to another, and, secondly, they are abolishing equity, which is completely swept away if each man is not allowed to keep what belongs to him. . . . How, for example, is it fair or equitable if a man who has never before held property should now hold land which someone else has occupied for many years or even generations,[76] but a man who previously held prop-

---

[70] For another passage from this work, see selection 147.

[71] On Cicero's son, see selection 144.

[72] Caesar had been assassinated eight months earlier, March 15, 44 B.C. Cicero hoped that the republic would be restored and that his son would have the same political opportunities he had had. This was not, however, to be. Caesar's death was followed by many years of civil war until Octavian assumed absolute control over the state. Octavian, as Augustus, greatly curtailed the political power of the senatorial class. See note 81 of Chapter V, and the introduction to selection 242.

[73] *populares*: politicians who sought the support of the common people (i.e., "popular" support; Latin *populus*) by catering to their demands; see selections 236 and 239.

[74] Cicero is careful not to say "from the land they own." He is referring to the public lands on which the wealthy were "squatting." Almost 100 years earlier, Tiberius Gracchus had passed an agrarian law which forced these wealthy squatters to stop using the public land and to allow its distribution among the poor (see selection 170). Cicero expresses here the opinions both of the many wealthy senators who bitterly opposed Gracchus in 133 B.C., and of the many in his own lifetime who feared such "popular" legislation because it threatened them financially.

[75] Many people were burdened with debts because they had borrowed money at high interest rates. Every few years some politician would suggest a complete cancellation of debts, but no such legislation was ever passed. However, in 49 B.C., Caesar had passed a law which allowed debtors to settle their debts by deducting from the principal the interest already paid.

[76] Occupied, but not really owned, because it was public land.

erty should now lose it? . . . What else is that but to rob one group of its property, and to give another group property which belongs to someone else? And what favorable arguments can be made for the remission of debts, except that you may now buy a farm with my money and then you have the farm but I don't have my money?[77] . . . And therefore men who hold public office must steer clear of that kind of generosity which takes property from one group and gives it to another. And they will especially take care that each man keeps what belongs to him through the just application of laws and legal decisions.

Friends in Power

Lucius was the unfortunate man who was accidentally changed into an ass.[78] The passage translated below is taken from an early part of his story, prior to his metamorphosis. This incident occurred in Thessaly, where Lucius was visiting.[79] It illustrates well the type of petty official—all too familiar to us today—whose ego is inflated by his sense of his own importance.

234   Apuleius, *The Golden Ass*, 1.24, 25

I went to the marketplace to buy something for dinner. The fish store there was well stocked with fish for sale. I asked the price; the clerk said twenty-five denarii; we haggled, and I bought them for twenty denarii. Just as I was leaving, Pythias, who had been a fellow student with me in Athens, bumped into me. After some hesitation, he recognized me and affectionately threw his arms around me. He embraced me and kissed me in a friendly manner and said, "Dear, dear Lucius, it's been a long time since I last saw you, in fact not, by Hercules, since we finished our schooling with Vestius. What's the reason for this trip of yours?"

"I'll tell you about it tomorrow," I said. "But what about you? I'm glad you have achieved success. I see, for example, that you have attendants and fasces[80] and clothing which befits a magistrate."

"Yes," he said, "I'm in charge of the market here; I hold the position of aedile,[81] and if you want to buy something for dinner, I'll be happy to help you."

I declined his help since I had already bought enough fish for dinner. However, when Pythias saw my shopping basket, he shook it a bit so that he could have a closer look at the fish. "And how much," he asked, "did you pay for this garbage?"

---

[77] That is, if a man borrowed money and bought a farm, he would owe the lender the principal plus interest. If, however, all debts were remitted by law, the lender would lose both principal and interest, but the borrower would keep his farm. Cicero is, however, grossly exaggerating the threat of such legislation. Even under Caesar's debt law, the lenders lost only some interest.

[78] See selection 187.

[79] *Thessaly:* a district in northeastern Greece.

[80] *fasces:* a bundle of rods carried by the men who attended a magistrate. The rods were used to punish men by beating them. The fasces were thus a symbol of the magistrate's authority. From the Latin *fasces* is derived the English word *fascist*.

[81] This book was written in the second century A.D., when Greece was a province of Rome. The superintendent of markets, a position which had long existed in the Greek world, is here designated by the Roman term *aedilis*, "aedile."

"With some difficulty, I convinced the fish seller to sell them for only twenty denarii," I said.

When he heard this, he quickly grabbed my hand and led me back into the Forum. "From which person," he asked, "did you buy this trash?"

I pointed out the old man who was sitting in a corner. Pythias immediately went into action as aedile and lashed out at him in a very gruff voice. "All right! All right!" he said. "You won't even deal fairly with my friends and with guests in our fair town. You have to charge such exorbitant prices, do you, for such worthless fish. With your extortionate prices for food you are going to reduce this town, which is the flower of Thessaly, to a barren piece of rock! But I won't let you get away with this. You are going to learn how you riff-raff will be punished as long as I am aedile." Then he dumped the fish out of my basket and ordered one of his flunkeys to jump up and down on them until he crushed them all. Satisfied that he had exhibited the proper severity, my good friend Pythias suggested that I leave. "I've shamed the old man quite enough," he said, "with this harsh treatment." I was astonished and dumbfounded by what had happened, but I went off to the baths, having lost both my money and my dinner because of the stern punishment exacted by my quick-witted fellow student.

Abuse of Power

235   Aulus Gellius, *Attic Nights* 4.14

Aulus Hostilius Mancinus was a curule aedile. He brought before the "people" an accusation against the prostitute Manilia because (he claimed) he had been hit by a stone thrown from her apartment at night. He even showed the wound made by the stone. Manilia appealed to the tribunes of the plebs.[82] She told them that Mancinus had come to her home wearing his party clothes.[83] It was not, however, convenient for her to let him in. When he tried to force his way in, she drove him off with stones. The tribunes decided that the aedile had been rightfully refused admittance to a place which it was unseemly for him to enter with a garland on his head.[84] And so the tribunes forbade[85] the aedile to bring this accusation before the "people."

POLITICAL CAMPAIGNS

During the republican period, the most important activity in life for the small group of families who constituted the senatorial class was the pursuit of political power—for one's self, one's family, and one's friends. A man of senatorial rank

[82] There were ten plebeian tribunes. Ordinarily it was sufficient to appeal to just one tribune.

[83] That is, he was dressed for a night on the town rather than in his magistrate's robes. As an aedile, he might make an official inspection visit to a brothel, and Manilia would have to admit him. On this night, however, his visit had nothing to do with official business.

[84] Partygoers frequently wore garlands. The garland on Mancinus's head proved that his visit was not official and that he had no right to demand entry.

[85] *forbade:* exercised their power of veto; see note 42 of this chapter.

would spend his whole adult life planning, scheming, manipulating, negotiating, creating a public image, ingratiating himself, attracting supporters, dispensing favors. A boy's rhetorical education and a young man's activities in the law courts were preparations for a political career. Friendships and marriages were often a matter of political convenience,[86] and more than one divorce was prompted by a desire to form new political alliances.[87] The percentage of the population which was so deeply involved in politics was small—in the republican period there were only about 300 Senate members—but the stakes were high: control over Rome, Italy, and a far-flung empire. And it is the men of the senatorial class—men like Sulla, Caesar, Cato, and Cicero—and their activities that are for us the best-known elements of Roman history.

Since each senatorial family felt that its members and friends had a god-given right to rule Rome, rivalry was intense and political campaigns were bitter. And because elections were held every year,[88] the process of campaigning was virtually unending.[89] Campaigns were not only bitter, but also expensive since candidates, as a matter of course, spent huge sums of money "buying" votes; bribery was more common than it is even today.[90]

Planning a Campaign

The following passages are selections from a letter of advice on running for public office. Many scholars believe that the letter was written by Quintus Tullius Cicero to his more famous brother, Marcus Tullius Cicero in 64 B.C. when Marcus was running for the consulship of 63 B.C. Other scholars argue that the letter was written at least 100 years later, as a literary exercise. If, however, it is a literary exercise rather than a genuine letter, it is very cleverly composed, because the author has described so well the political realities of the final years of the republican period. (One would not expect a writer of the imperial period, when the emperor controlled all public offices and when popular elections had been suspended, to be so well informed about republican politics.)

Whoever the author may be, his letter provides very valuable information

[86] For example, Julius Caesar married off his daughter, Julia, to his sometime political ally, Pompey, a man older than himself. The marriage, which took place in 59 B.C., was intended to strengthen the ties between the two men. Julia died in childbirth in 54 B.C., and soon afterward the uneasy political alliance between the two men was violently ruptured; see note 81 of Chapter V.

[87] Julia was Pompey's fourth wife (he married a fifth wife after her death). He had divorced his first wife to marry Aemilia, the stepdaughter of Sulla, presumably because he wanted to strengthen his ties to Sulla (see note 114 of Chapter VII). At the time that Pompey and Sulla arranged this marriage, Aemilia was pregnant and living with her husband. She was forced to divorce him and marry Pompey. She died in childbirth soon afterward. The younger Cato (great-grandson of the elder Cato; see selection 121) had actually divorced his own wife, Marcia, and married her off to Hortensius to strengthen their friendship. When Hortensius died, he remarried Marcia.

[88] The term of office for quaestor, aedile, tribune, praetor, and consul was only one year.

[89] Even if you were not yourself running for office, you were expected to campaign for family members and family friends; see note 17 of Chapter III. You were also expected to lobby for the legislation of your political allies and against that of your opponents, and to maintain a high profile by speaking out in the courts, Senate, and assemblies.

[90] See note 59 of Chapter XII.

about running for office in the late republican period. The advice—make connections, establish a broad base of support, keep a high profile, and promise everyone everything—was applicable to all political aspirants (and still is), but was particularly appropriate for a *novus homo*. A "new man" was someone whose family had never before had a consul in its rank. Cicero was a "new man." He was born in Arpinum, a town southeast of Rome, in 106 B.C.; his family was wealthy ("new men" were never poor) and equestrian; he received an excellent rhetorical education. Cicero was apparently driven by his ambition to achieve political success in Rome and, while still a young man, acquired a reputation as a brilliant lawyer and public speaker.[91] His political career followed a "normal" course, that is, he was elected quaestor, the lowest rung of the political ladder, in 76 B.C., when he was thirty years old, and served as quaestor in 75 B.C., at age thirty-one, the youngest age by law at which he could hold the quaestorship. He was elected aedile in 70 B.C. (served in 69) and praetor in 67 B.C. (served in 66), also at the youngest ages allowed by law. Thus, by 64 B.C., when he ran for the consulship, Cicero had already served in the Senate for twelve years[92] and held three magistracies. One might well think that he had proved himself a capable and conscientious politician. He had certainly tried very hard to become part of the establishment. But the old senatorial families, however bitter the rivalries among themselves, would always jealously close ranks against a "new man," an upstart, as they thought, invading the political arena, *their* arena. Cicero was forced to work very diligently to acquire a solid and broad base of support. No doubt he used the tactics described in this letter; in 63 B.C. he became the first "new man" in over thirty years to hold the consulship.[93]

236   Quintus Tullius Cicero, *Some Thoughts about Political Campaigns*
                 1.1–5; 8.29–31, 33; 9.34–38; 11.41–45; 12.48; 13.53; 14.54, 55

Although you are well equipped with every advantage which men can acquire through intelligence, experience, and hard work, yet I don't think it is inappropriate for me, who loves you, to write to you the suggestions which have come into my mind whenever I have thought about your campaign for the consulship. I don't think that you will learn anything new from these, but at least the various strategies which now seem random and unconnected will be set into one framework and will have a unifying

[91] Another native of Arpinum and another "new man" who became consul was Gaius Marius, who was elected consul in 107 B.C. (see the introduction to Chapter XI). Both Marius and Cicero were individuals of exceptional talent, Marius in military matters and Cicero in oratory. The latter used public speaking to gain the reputation necessary to political success in Rome; the former gained fame as a military man. Neither "new man" would have achieved the rank of consul had each not been an individual of exceptional talent. "New men" had to work much harder for each political success than the sons of old, established senatorial families who could count on family support. Do not, however, think that "new men" were poor or politically naive. Cicero and Marius both came from wealthy families, prominent in their hometowns. They simply did not have the network of support available to families long active in Roman politics.

[92] He was admitted to the Senate upon being elected quaestor; see the introduction to selection 238.

[93] Even after holding the consulship Cicero still met with hostility, petty jealousy, and suspicion from some senatorial families who continued to view him as a "new man."

plan and arrangement. Although natural ability is a strong advantage, yet in a campaign of only a few months, duplicity can defeat natural ability. Therefore, consider carefully what city this is, what office you are running for and who you are. Every day, as you walk down to the Forum,[94] you must remind yourself: I am a "new man," I am running for consul, and this is Rome.

You will be able to compensate for the "newness" of your name to a large extent by your fame as a speaker.[95] . . . Then make sure that both the large number of your friends and also their high ranks are quite apparent. For you have friendships[96] which few "new men" have had: with all the publicans, almost all the equestrian order,[97] many municipalities with special attachments to you, many men of every class who have been defended by you,[98] some private clubs, a large number of young men devoted to you because of their enthusiasm for eloquence, and the daily assistance and attendance of your personal friends. Take care that you retain these supporters by reminding them of your campaign, by asking for their votes, and by using every method to make sure that the people who owe you favors understand that there will never be another opportunity for them to return the favor, and that the people who desire your help understand that there will never be another opportunity for them to put you under obligation to them.[99]

This also, it seems to me, can assist greatly a "new man": the good will of men of noble, and especially of consular rank. It is advantageous to be thought worthy of a particular rank by those very men into whose ranks you wish to enter. All these men must be diligently courted by you; you must entreat them and persuade them that we have always supported the *optimates* in affairs of state, and have not been *populares*.[100] . . .

Make sure that you have firm support in all the centuries[101] by means of your many and varied friendships. First of all, win over to your side the Roman senators and equestrians and the active and influential men of all the other social classes. There

[94] Cicero owned a home on the Palatine, one of Rome's Seven Hills. He would thus walk down the hill to the Forum. Houses on the Palatine were among the most expensive in Rome; the English word *palace* is derived from the Latin *palatium* (Palatine). In the imperial period, the emperors' residence was on the Palatine. Like other wealthy Romans, Cicero had several country homes as well as his city home; see selections 16 and 98.

[95] Selections 65, 168, 206, 239, and 281 are taken from Cicero's speeches.

[96] The Latin word *amicitia* (English "amicable," French "ami") means both personal friendship and political alliance. For many people in the upper class, no distinction was made between personal and political friendships.

[97] Cicero's family was equestrian.

[98] Legal services were paid for not with money but with political help (see selections 7 and 8). It was therefore important for aspiring politicians to provide legal assistance to as many people as possible. Cicero was a very successful lawyer.

[99] In ancient Rome, favors were always reciprocal. People who had in the past received favors from Cicero (he had helped them with a lawsuit, loaned them money, written a letter of recommendation, etc.) now owed him the favor of assisting in his campaign. People who wanted his help in the future promised him their votes now (i.e., a favor) and expected him to return the favor later.

[100] *populares:* see note 73 of this chapter. The *optimates* were the larger and conservative part of the Senate; see selection 239. It was important that Cicero convince these men that, although he was a "new man," he would not resort to "popular" tactics to win support. (Since Cicero had already been a Senate member for twelve years before running for consul, the *optimates* should have known well his political inclinations.)

[101] *centuries:* see notes 9 and 10 of this chapter.

are many hard-working men in the city and many influential and active freedmen in the Forum. Both in person and through mutual friends exert every possible effort to make them your supporters; pursue them, entreat them, show them that they are bestowing upon you the very greatest favor. Then develop a plan for the whole city, for all private clubs, for the country districts and the neighboring regions.[102] If you can win over to your side the leading men in these groups, you will with their help easily gain the votes of the other members of the groups. Next, make sure that you have in your mind and memory a plan of all of Italy divided and arranged by tribes[103] so that you do not allow to go unnoticed any municipality, colony, or prefecture, indeed any place at all in Italy in which you do not have sufficient support. Search for and track down men from every region. Become acquainted with them, entreat them, encourage them. See to it that they campaign for you in their own neighborhoods and that they are candidates, so to speak, for your cause. . . .

I think that the centuries of equestrians[104] can very easily be kept on your side with a little hard work. First, become acquainted with the equestrians (there are not many of them in the top centuries); then, court them (for youth[105] is much more easily attracted to friendship). In the end, you will have on your side all the finest young men and those most devoted to honorable behavior. . . . And the eagerness of these young men in voting for you, in working for you, in giving you publicity, and in attending upon you is both wonderfully important and wonderfully respectable.

And, since I have brought up the topic of attendants, make sure that you are attended every day by men from each class, order, and age group. . . . Your attendants can also be divided into three groups: (1) those who come to your home for the morning salutation, (2) those who escort you from your home,[106] and (3) those who follow you through the city.[107] The morning greeters are more common than the other two groups and more numerous, because this is now the fashion. You must be sure to make the slightest little service they do seem especially gratifying to you. Indicate to those who come to your house that you are aware of their attention. Make it known to their friends (who will, of course, report your words to them). And tell them often, in person. When several candidates are campaigning and men see that there is one who really appreciates the services of his attendants, they frequently desert the other candidates and pledge themselves to him. . . . As for the group who escort you from your home, whose service is greater than that of the morning greeters, clearly indicate to them that it is also more gratifying to you. Come down to the Forum at the same time every day; for a large crowd of escorts every day brings you great renown and great respect. Now the third group in this classification are those who attend you assiduously. Some do so voluntarily; make sure that they know that you will be under

---

[102] By 64 B.C., when Cicero was running for consul, all citizens of Italy were Roman citizens, and the men of Italy were therefore eligible to vote in elections for Roman magistrates.

[103] *tribes:* see notes 12 and 13 of this chapter.

[104] *centuries of equestrians:* in Cicero's time, there were 373 centuries. Of these, only eighteen centuries were equestrian. The equestrian centuries were composed of men under forty-seven years of age (*iuniores:* see note 10 of this chapter) with the highest property qualification in the state. Not everyone in the equestrian order was placed in an equestrian century; assignment to a century was the job of the censors; see selection 229.)

[105] *youth:* because men in the equestrian centuries were under forty-seven.

[106] That is, down the Palatine to the Forum.

[107] These men stay with Cicero all day long.

obligation to them for this enormous favor. Some, however, owe you this service; simply demand that they repay you; those whose age and occupation will allow it should attend you constantly, but those who cannot personally attend you should assign their relatives to this duty.[108] I strongly urge, and I think it important, that you always appear with a group of attendants. And you will particularly gain great respect and renown if your attendants are men who have been defended by you in court and who have been acquitted. Simply demand from them that they repay you with this service since they, through your efforts and at no cost to themselves,[109] won a court case, or preserved their reputations, or kept their lives and their property, and never again in the future will there be a time when they can show their gratitude to you.[110] . . .

Enough has been said about establishing friendships. We must now discuss the other aspect of a political campaign: what is done to win over the common people. Here you need flattery, constant attention, courtesy, good reputation, prominence in public life, and the knowledge of each man's name. In fact, make it very clear that you do know men's names, and add to the list so that every day you become even better at this.[111] Nothing, as far as I am concerned, is so popular or so pleasing. And then, although you are not by nature a flatterer, persuade yourself that you must give the appearance of complimenting people in a very natural fashion. Certainly you possess that affability which befits a good and pleasant man, but you really need the gift of flattery which, although it is wicked and reprehensible in all other aspects of life, yet is essential in a political campaign. Actually, when flattery makes a man worse it is bad, but when it makes him more supportive of you it shouldn't be censured. It is certainly essential for a candidate, whose expression and appearance and speech must be changed and adapted to the opinions and wishes of everyone he meets.

Constant attention implies . . . that you campaign continually, that you appeal to the same people again and again. . . . Courtesy belongs in the services which you should offer to the common people. Take care that they have easy access to you day and night, not only through the doors of your home[112] but even through your open and sincere appearance, which is the door to your mind. . . . Men want to hear promises when they make requests of a candidate, and they want to hear lavish and creditable promises. And so make it clear that you will do whatever you do with enthusiasm and generosity. It is rather difficult, and more appropriate to the demands of your campaign than to your own nature, to promise what you cannot accomplish. . . . But it is the strategy of a good campaigner. . . . If you make a promise, its fulfillment is never a definite matter; it is a question of the right opportunity, and it concerns only a few people. If, however, you refuse to make a promise, you alienate definitely and immediately many people. In any case, far more people ask for the promise of a favor than ever demand its fulfillment. . . .

In this campaign you must especially see to it that the public thinks that you are honest and trusts that you will serve well in office. Politics is not simply a matter of

---

[108] The favor must be repaid.

[109] Lawyers did not receive fees; see note 98 of this chapter.

[110] *gratitude:* from the Latin *gratia* = "favor"; compare *ingratiating.*

[111] A politician was (and still is) expected to greet everyone warmly and by name. Ancient politicians were assisted by a slave called a *nomenclator* whose duty it was to memorize names and identify people (Latin *nomen* = "name," *clamo* = "call out"; compare English *nomenclature*).

[112] A man with political aspirations needed a large reception area in his home; see selection 68.

success in the campaign, or in the Senate, or in the popular assembly, but rather these things must be kept in mind: the Senate should think that you will be a defender of its authority from the fact that you have in the past been its defender; the Roman equestrians and other honorable and wealthy men[113] should think from your past life that you will be eager for peace and tranquility;[114] and the masses should think, from the fact that in your speeches in the assemblies and in court you supported the rights of the people, that you will not be opposed to its interests. . . .

Rome is a city-state formed by the coming together of many nations; in Rome you must endure much treachery, deceit, vices of every kind, arrogance of many men, scorn, malevolence, pride, hatred, and harassment. I see that anyone who lives in the midst of so many vices of every sort and of such scale and of so many men must have great prudence and skill to avoid giving offense, to avoid gossip and treachery. Only one man can adapt to such a variety of characters and forms of expression—you! Therefore, continue always to maintain the course which you set for yourself: excel in public speaking! By this are men in Rome controlled, and attracted, and discouraged from hindering or harming you.[115]

Campaign Literature

Political messages were painted on the walls of buildings in Pompeii (and presumably of cities like Rome as well). We have already read some of these messages;[116] here are some others.

237   *CIL* 4.7463, 579, 275, 6628, 7213, 635, 787, 7866, 7221, 3409, 6625, 920, 3775, 429, 1147, 235, 581, 576, 575, 2887

Elect Pansa aedile. He deserves the position.

Magonius supports Cuspius Pansa for aedile.

Saturninus and his pupils urge you to elect Gaius Cuspius Pansa aedile. He is a worthy candidate for our government.

Make Gnaeus Helvius Sabinus and Marcus Samellius Modestus aediles; they are worthy candidates for our government.

Amandio and his friends urge you to elect Gnaeus Helvius Sabinus aedile. He is a worthy candidate for our government.

Proculus, make Sabinus aedile and he will make you aedile.

[113] Notice the differentiation in rank. Members of the equestrian order needed a property qualification of 400,000 sesterces. Other businessmen, well-off but with less than 400,000 sesterces, would share the same interests as the equestrian order.

[114] Businessmen were interested in peace and tranquility because the volume of trade increased when conditions were stable; see the introduction to selection 155.

[115] Cicero won fame as a public speaker in the law courts, the assemblies, and the Senate. His skill as a speaker made him a man to be admired, but also to be feared. He had demolished more than one political opponent with his brilliant oratory. Consider his attacks on Clodia in selection 65 and on Verres in selection 281.

[116] See selection 149.

All the worshipers of Isis[117] urge you to elect Gnaeus Helvius Sabinus aedile.

Maria[118] urges you to elect Gnaeus Helvius Sabinus aedile.

Ismurna urges you to elect Lucius Popidius aedile.

Rufinus, support Popidius Secundus for aedile, and he will do the same for you.

His neighbors urge you to elect Marcus Lucretius Fronto aedile.

Proculus, give up your office to Fronto.

His neighbors urge you to elect Lucius Statius Receptus duovir with judicial power.[119] He deserves the position. Aemilius Celer, his neighbor, wrote this.[120] If you spitefully deface this sign, may you become very ill.

Elect Gaius Julius Polybius aedile. He supplies good bread.

Ballplayers, I urge you, make Aulus Vettius Firmus aedile: he is a worthy candidate for our government.

Faventinus and his friends urge you to elect Marcus Cerrinius Vatia aedile.

All the late drinkers[121] urge you to elect Marcus Cerrinius Vatia aedile. Florus and Fructus wrote this.

The petty thieves urge you to elect Vatia aedile.

All the late sleepers urge you to elect Vatia aedile.

Let anyone who opposes the election of Quintius go sit by an ass!

THE SENATE

The Senate in the Republican Period

In the republican period, the Senate was composed of men who had been elected by the assemblies to one of the magistracies. A man did not, therefore, "run" for the position of senator, but once elected quaestor, for example, for a one-year term of office, he was admitted into the Senate for life. All the magistrates were thus also senators, and all senators were men who had once been magistrates and who hoped for further magistracies for themselves or their family members. All magistrates and senators, moreover, were wealthy. Therefore, although the func-

---

[117] *Isis:* an Egyptian goddess; see selections 391 and 392.

[118] *Maria, Ismurna:* barmaids.

[119] *duovir:* see note 60 of Chapter II.

[120] *Aemilius Celer:* for more on this sign painter, see selections 118 and 338.

[121] It is not clear whether the "late drinkers," the "petty thieves," and the "late sleepers" were respectable clubs or associations which had given themselves humorous names (compare the Oddfellows); in this case, their political endorsements were probably useful. Or "late drinkers" may, in fact, mean exactly that: people who drink late into the night. In this case, the "endorsements" may have been written by Vatia's political enemies.

tions of the magistrates differed from those of the senators, every magistrate would have interests similar to those of his fellow senators, and he would work in close consultation with them. Indeed, historically the function of the Senate was to provide advice to the chief executives of Rome. In the monarchy, senators were the elders of the state,[122] chosen by the king to be his advisors. After the expulsion of the monarchy, the Senate remained during the republican period as an advisory body for the new chief executives, the two consuls elected each year (who were, of course, also senators). The consuls introduced to the Senate proposals for legislation. The senators discussed the proposals and, if they approved them, advised the consuls to present the legislation to one of the popular assemblies for a vote. Thus, although Rome was in name a democracy since the "people" elected magistrates and voted on legislation, the Senate had tight control over what legislation actually reached the assemblies.[123] The Senate could not technically pass laws,[124] but its "advice," called a *senatus consultum*,[125] came to have the force of a law.[126] The Senate controlled both domestic and foreign affairs. It decided how much money to collect in taxes, tributes, public rents, etc., and how much and where to spend it.[127] The Senate administered the provinces and sent its own members out to be governors. All aspects of public life, and many aspects of private life, too, both in Rome and throughout the Empire, were controlled during the republican period by the Senate. As Rome's power, territory, and wealth increased, so too did the power of the Senate. The common people were, for the most part, content with this system. The administration of the Empire had become a very complex matter, and the people therefore depended more and more on the senators, who were well educated, had considerable experience (since each senator had held at least one magistracy, may have been a Senate member for years, and may have traveled to the provinces), and had the wealth and leisure to devote to government service. The almost absolute authority of the Senate was acquired gradually and imperceptibly; as territorial expansion brought new problems of administration, the common people, out of necessity, left these matters to the Senate. By the end of the republican period, by the time of Caesar, the power of the Senate was supreme. (The author of this passage, Polybius, lived in the second century B.C.)

238   Polybius, *History of the World* 6:13; 14.1, 2; 15.2–9; 17.1–9

The Senate, first of all, has control of the public treasury; for it controls almost every income and expenditure. With the exception of payments made to the consuls, the

---

[122] The Latin word *senator* is related to the words *senex* ("old man") and *senere* ("to be old"). The senators were sometimes called *patres*, "fathers."

[123] Tiberius Gracchus, when tribune, had angered his fellow-senators, and was assassinated by certain elements of the Senate, because he took his agrarian law proposal directly to the *Concilium Plebis* for a vote even though the Senate had advised against it; see selection 170.

[124] *laws:* that is, *leges;* see note 24 of this chapter.

[125] *senatus consultum* (often written as one word: *senatusconsultum*): "advice (*consultum*) of the Senate." For examples, see selections 76 and 388.

[126] See selection 252.

[127] See selections 159, 163, and 164, which mention the Senate's role in financing military campaigns.

quaestors are not allowed to make any payments for any necessary items or services without a decree of the Senate. And the expenditure which is by far heavier and of greater importance than any other, I mean the amount which the censors use every five years for the repair and construction of public works, this expenditure is regulated by the Senate, and a disbursement of funds is made to the censors by the Senate. Any crimes which have been committed in Italy and which require a public investigation, such as treason, conspiracy, poisoning, and murder, are the concern of the Senate.[128] In addition, if any private individual or any town in Italy needs arbitration or censure or help or protection, all these matters are the concern of the Senate. And if it is necessary to send an embassy to any country outside of Italy, in order to resolve a dispute, or to make a demand, or to give an order, or to receive submission, or to declare war, the Senate makes this task its concern. Similarly, when embassies arrive in Rome, everything—how it is necessary to treat them and what answer they should be given—is in the hands of the Senate. All in all, none of the matters mentioned above is controlled by the "people." And therefore, again, if someone resided in Rome at a time when the consuls were absent, to him the constitution appears entirely aristocratic. And many Greeks and many kings are convinced of this, because the Senate handles almost all matters having to do with them.

Someone might therefore ask, and not unreasonably, what part and how much of a part is left for the "people" in this constitution, considering that the Senate has control over each of the items which I mentioned above and, most importantly, that the Senate handles every income and expenditure; and again considering that the consuls have absolute authority as generals over the preparations for war, and absolute power in the field. . . .

When the consul sets off with his army, endowed with the powers I mentioned above, he seems to have absolute authority to carry out the task set for him. However, he is dependent on the "people" and the Senate,[129] and he is not able to bring his projects to a conclusion without them. It is clear that the army must continually receive supplies, but, without the good will of the Senate, neither grain, nor clothing, nor pay can be supplied to the army.[130] And so the plans of the generals are never carried out if the Senate decides to be negligent and obstructive. The fulfillment or nonfulfillment of the general's long-range goals and objectives also lie with the Senate, for it has the power to supersede him, when his year of office has come to an end, or of making him proconsul and retaining him in command.[131] And the Senate also has the power to heighten and amplify the successes of the generals, or on the other hand to obscure and minimize them. The public salutes, which the Romans call triumphs, in which the generals bring before the eyes of the citizens clear evidence of their achievements, cannot be properly organized, and sometimes cannot be held at all, unless the Senate agrees and allots the necessary funds.[132] . . .

Similarly, the "people" are dependent upon the Senate, and must aim to please

---

[128] See selections 387 and 388 on the Senate's role in suppressing Bacchanalia.

[129] The consuls were, of course, themselves senators and therefore not quite as rigidly separate from the Senate as Polybius would seem to imply.

[130] On military provisions, see selection 163.

[131] If a consul's year of service had ended but the Senate allowed him to retain his military authority in the provinces, he was called a *proconsul*. He no longer, of course, retained any civilian authority in Rome. Latin *pro* = "in place of"; thus *proconsul* = "in place of a consul." There were also *propraetors*. Governors of provinces were proconsuls or propraetors.

[132] On military triumphs, see selection 267.

it both in public and in private. The censors assign numerous contracts for the construction and repair of public works throughout all of Italy, so many, in fact, that one could not easily count them. There are in addition many contracts relating to the use of rivers, harbors, orchards, mines, and farmlands, in short everything that falls under Roman sovereignty. Now it happens, of course, that all the work which the above-mentioned contracts entail is carried out by the masses, and almost everyone is involved in these contracts and the work they entail. Some men do the buying of the contract from the censors; other men are their partners; still others stand surety for the buyers; and some offer their own money to the state for these purposes.[133] But it is the Senate which has control over all the matters just mentioned. The Senate can grant extensions of time; if an accident occurs, it can ease the requirements of the contract; and if the project turns out to be totally impossible, it can cancel the contract. And there are many different ways in which the Senate can greatly harm or greatly help those who deal with public revenues.[134] To it, for example, are referred all the matters mentioned above. And, most importantly, from it are selected jurymen for most legal suits, of both public and private nature, especially where the charges are very serious.[135] Therefore, because everyone is put at the mercy of the Senate and is fearful and uncertain about how it may act, they are cautious about obstructing and resisting its decisions.

The Senate and the People

There was no opportunity for a lower-class man to run for political office. Even the "new men" came from wealthy families who had at least a few connections with the well-known Roman political families. It is not surprising, then, that the Senate showed little sympathy for the lower classes and little interest in their needs. The senators were generally occupied by their personal struggles for power against other aristocrats. Some senators did, however, sponsor legislation which would benefit the masses. A few were genuinely compassionate and eager to alleviate the problems of the less fortunate. More commonly, however, senators who sponsored such legislation were actually scheming to win the support of the masses, who could in the popular assemblies elect, or not elect, candidates for office, and who could pass, or not pass, legislation presented to them. In other words, some senators appeared to be champions of the people so that they could strengthen their own positions.[136] Once they had the support of the popular assemblies, they could pass any legislation they wished and win election to any office they wished (or

---

[133] Polybius is here not really talking about the masses but rather about the equestrians. The ordinary man-on-the-street was not terribly concerned about contracts, although construction projects did, of course, provide employment opportunities.

[134] Compare selections 164 and 240 on Senate-equestrian relations.

[135] The jurymen in the standing courts of Polybius's day (mid-2nd century B.C.) were members of the senatorial order. In 122 B.C. Gaius Gracchus replaced the senatorial jurors with jurors from the equestrian order. In 80 B.C. Sulla restored the courts to the senatorial order. For the composition of the courts at the time of Cicero, see notes 43 and 46 of Chapter XII.

[136] The tribunes of the plebs, who had originally been established as champions of the common man, had become by the middle and late republican period part of the political establishment. Most tribunes had no desire to alienate their fellow senators by taking the side of the people against the Senate.

prevent their opponents from doing so). In this passage, Cicero suggests that the members of the Senate could be divided into two groups: the *optimates,* the "best" men,[137] whose political tactics were honorable and respectable; and the *populares,*[138] who were dishonorable, who courted the masses, and who supported extremist legislation dangerous to the stability of Rome, in order to win personal power. Cicero's views are blatantly biased. He himself desperately longed for the approval of the optimates and curried favor with them by his laudatory comments here.[139]

The passage translated here indicates clearly that the interests of the lower classes and the senatorial class often differed substantially.

239   Cicero, *Speech in Defense of Sestius,* 45.96, 97; 48.103

There have always been in this state two groups of men who were eager to participate in the government and, by doing so, to make themselves more prominent. One of these groups wished to be considered, and in fact to be, populares, "popular"; the other, optimates, "best." And those who wanted everything they did and said to be pleasing to the masses were considered populares; but those who conducted themselves so as to win for their policies the approval of all the best citizens were considered optimates. . . .

All are optimates who are neither malevolent, nor shameless in behavior, nor insane, nor embarrassed by family problems.[140] It therefore follows that these men . . . are honest, of sound mind, and comfortably settled in their domestic arrangements. . . .

Tiberius Gracchus proposed an agrarian law.[141] The people were pleased with it because it seemed to relieve the situation of the poorer classes. The optimates, however, opposed it because they saw that it roused dissension;[142] they also thought that the state would be stripped of its prime defenders if the wealthy were evicted from land they had long occupied. Gaius Gracchus proposed a grain law.[143] The people

---

[137] *optimates:* Latin *optimi* = "the best." It was the optimates themselves, obviously, who gave themselves the title of "best men." Latin *optimi* corresponds to the Greek word *aristoi;* on the meaning of *aristocracy,* and for Cicero's views on aristocracy, see selection 2.

[138] *populares:* for a definition, see note 73 of this chapter; Caesar and Pompey were considered populares.

[139] For Cicero's difficulty in gaining acceptance with the old nobility, and for his brother's advice, see selection 236.

There were not rigid boundaries between the optimates and the populares. A man might enter a political alliance with optimates one year, with populares a few years later. Cicero himself, early in his career, had supported populares candidates and legislation.

[140] Cicero is, of course, hinting that the populares are malevolent, shameless, insane, and so on.

[141] For Tiberius Sempronius Gracchus, his agrarian law, and the Senate's reaction to it, see selection 170. Tiberius Gracchus is Cicero's prime example of a *popularis* (singular of *populares*) and a dangerous demagogue. Most modern historians view him as a well-intentioned reformer, genuinely concerned about a difficult situation.

[142] The optimates were conservatives who traditionally, sometimes fanatically, opposed any legislation which would disturb the status quo. In the case of Gracchus's agrarian law, they were especially afraid that they would suffer personal financial losses.

[143] On Gaius Gracchus's legislation to sell a fixed monthly ration of grain at a low and unvarying price to any Roman citizen, see the introduction to selection 153.

were delighted with it because it provided an abundance of food without work.[144] The good men, however, fought against it because they thought the masses would be attracted away from hard work and toward idleness, and they saw that the state treasury would be exhausted.[145]

The Senate and the Equestrians

The equestrians exerted considerable influence on the politics of the Roman state. As early as the third century B.C., senators were afraid to offend wealthy contractors.[146] As the Empire expanded and as business opportunities increased, the conflicts became more frequent. To complicate matters, senators, who were not supposed to bid on public contracts, sometimes became silent partners or loaned to the provincials money with which they paid their taxes.[147] A governor was caught in the middle. The provincials, whom he was, after all, sent to protect, asked for his help against greedy and violent publicans and moneylenders; but the publicans and moneylenders demanded his assistance in collecting their money. It was difficult to deny assistance to the latter group because they were politically powerful and might even be friends or allies of the governor. In Rome, too, the Senate all too frequently found itself giving in to shameless requests from the equestrians rather than risk offending the equestrians (and their silent partners). In the letter translated here, we find Cicero in an awkward situation. He felt compelled to support an equestrian demand which he himself considered dishonorable because he feared that the alienation of the senatorial and equestrian orders might cause a civil war.[148]

240   Cicero, *Letters to Atticus* 1.17.8, 9

We live in a commonwealth which is weak, despondent, and unstable.[149] I suppose that you have already heard that our friends the equestrians have broken off almost completely any relationship with the Senate. . . . They made a proposal which was

[144] Cicero has grossly distorted the real situation. Gaius's grain law was an attempt, like his brother's agrarian law, to deal with the plight of large numbers of unemployed citizens in Rome. The sale of grain at a low price prevented such people from starving.

[145] Cicero's discussion of the optimates and their conservative opposition to reform measures probably has on the modern reader an effect quite contrary to what Cicero intended. The optimates appear stubborn and insensitive; populares like the Gracchi seem sympathetic. In Cicero's day, however, many populares were agitators, like Catiline (see selection 291) or Clodius (see selections 153 and 206), who threatened the security of the state. Cicero cannot separate positive reform from dangerous demagogy because he is so frightened by the possible collapse of order in the state.

[146] See selection 164 on contract fraud.

[147] See selection 280.

[148] Compare selection 147 where Cicero declares that small business is shameful but big business is honorable. He was afraid to offend the big businessmen, the equestrians.

[149] The date of this letter is 61 B.C. The formation of the First Triumvirate and the election of Julius Caesar to the consulship of 59 B.C. were in part the result of the rift between equestrian and senatorial orders mentioned by Cicero in this letter. And the formation of the First Triumvirate led ultimately to the civil war which Cicero had so feared.

outrageous, almost intolerable—yet I not only tolerated it, but even spoke eloquently on its behalf! The publicans who had bid successfully on the tax contract for Asia were now complaining in the Senate that they had been distracted by their desire for profit and had bid too high, and were requesting that the contract be canceled.[150] I was their principal supporter, or rather their second strongest supporter; for Crassus had encouraged them to dare to make this request in the first place.[151] An irritating matter, a disgraceful request, and an admission of reckless behavior on their part. Yet there was a very great and real danger that they would have alienated themselves completely from the Senate had their request been denied.[152]

GOVERNMENT IN THE EARLY
IMPERIAL PERIOD

The assassination of Caesar in 44 B.C. effectively marked the end of a type of government which historians have labeled the Roman Republic but have defined as an aristocracy. The republic, however, had been ailing for decades before Caesar's death, partly because the aristocrats all too frequently put pursuit of personal power above the common good and partly because the constitution which the Romans had developed to serve a small, homogeneous city was ill suited to the powerful, imperialistic, and cosmopolitan city Rome had become. It was not until about 30 B.C., however, that Octavian finally conquered all rivals, gained supreme power in Rome, became, in fact, Rome's first emperor, and thus changed its political system forever.[153] The people who were most affected by Octavian's rapid rise to absolute power were his fellow aristocrats, the senators. Many greatly resented his position, particularly since, as he consolidated his own power, he curtailed theirs. And the power of the Senate declined further under each successive emperor. In the republican period, the Senate had governed Rome and its provinces; in the imperial period, when government was controlled by the emperor, the Senate was but a shadow of its former self, an honor society or exclusive club for wealthy aristocrats, with all the trappings but little of the power it had once held.

The Powers of Augustus

In September of 31 B.C., Octavian and his troops defeated the combined forces of Antony and Cleopatra in a sea battle off the coast of Greece. Octavian was now

[150] They had promised to collect more money than they could actually squeeze out of the province. They would therefore make no profit, and so they wanted out of the contract.

[151] *Crassus:* see selection 161; Crassus may have been a silent partner in the tax contract.

[152] Their request was denied, and Crassus angrily formed a political alliance with Pompey and Caesar—the First Triumvirate—which used money and violence to force the Senate to listen to equestrian demands.

[153] *Octavian (Augustus):* see notes 79 and 80 of Chapter III. Octavian was only eighteen years old when his granduncle Julius Caesar was killed; but he was shrewd, ruthless, and ambitious, and set out immediately to obtain for himself the absolute power his granduncle had desired.

the undisputed master of the Roman Empire. He had learned, however, from the fate of his granduncle, Julius Caesar, that military supremacy alone could not ensure that his position would be unchallenged. In February of 44 B.C., Caesar had himself appointed dictator for life; a month later he was dead, murdered by senators who resented his attempt to gather all political power into his own hands.[154] Octavian, therefore, was very careful not to give the impression that he was creating a monarchy, although that was exactly what he was doing. Instead, he held only the regular magistracies—but he held several at once, and he continued to hold them year after year. He thus maintained a facade of constitutionality—he could say, "I'm not a dictator; I'm just a consul, as my ancestors and yours were"[155]—but, in fact, he had unlimited and absolute control over Rome and its empire. The following passage, from the historical writings of Greek author Dio Cassius, explains the nature of the powers Octavian assumed, as well as indicating how he weakened the power of the senatorial class. It is difficult for us now to determine just how many people were deceived by this facade of constitutionality. Most Romans were so weary of civil war that they welcomed a strong leader who promised peace, and they perhaps chose not to notice his "stretching" of the republican constitution.

241   Dio Cassius, *Roman History* 53:12.1–3, 16.1, 6–8;
                    17.1–11; 18.1–3; 19.1; 21.3, 6, 7

Augustus wanted to be considered democratic. Therefore, although he accepted responsibility for all the care and management of government business, on the ground that it required considerable attention, he said that he would not himself assume the administration of all the provinces, and that, in the cases of those provinces which he did personally govern, he would not do so forever. In fact, he did return to the Senate the weaker provinces, on the ground that they were peaceful and not at war, but he retained control over the stronger provinces, on the ground that they were unstable and explosive, and either had hostile neighbors or were themselves able to foment a serious revolt. He claimed to have done this in order that the Senate might without anxiety enjoy the best portions of the Empire, but in actual fact he did this in order that, having carried out his plan, the senators might be unarmed and unprepared for battle, while he alone had arms and maintained soldiers. . . .

Caesar[156] would obviously have absolute power in all matters for all time because he controlled the state finances (ostensibly he had separated public monies from his own, but in reality he spent the former also as he chose) and also because he commanded the soldiers. . . .

The name Augustus was bestowed upon him by the Senate and the people. They wanted to address him by some special name, and while they were proposing one name or another, and deciding on it, Caesar was extremely eager to be called Romulus.[157]

---

[154] See note 24 of Chapter I.

[155] And consuls continued to be elected, year after year, to serve along with Augustus (Octavian); theoretically they held the same powers as the consuls of the republican period, but in fact they would scarcely dare to oppose or anger Augustus.

[156] *Caesar:* here Octavian (Augustus); see note 39 of Chapter III.

[157] *Romulus:* Rome's first king.

When he perceived, however, that people therefore suspected him of yearning for a position as king, he no longer sought this title, but instead accepted the title Augustus, as if he were somewhat more than human; for everything that is most valuable and most sacred is called *augustus*.[158]

And so the power both of the people and of the Senate passed entirely into the possession of Augustus, and from this time on there existed a true monarchy; for monarchy would be the most accurate term.[159] . . . Now the Romans hated this term *monarchy* so much that they did not call their sole rulers dictators[160] or kings or any such thing. Since, however, the final and highest level of political power rests with these rulers, it is not possible to see them as anything but kings. Of course, the original constitutional magistracies[161] still exist even now (except the office of censor),[162] but everything is planned and carried out strictly in accordance with what the one man who holds permanent power wishes. However, in order that the emperors may at least seem to hold this power through constitutional measures rather than through their own personal dominance, they have taken for themselves all the offices and titles, except the dictatorship, which were politically strong positions during the republic, when the people voted.[163] For example, they frequently became consuls, and they always hold the title *proconsul* whenever they are outside the city limits. And they hold the title *imperator*[164] for life. . . . Because they hold these titles, they receive the power to make levies, to collect money, to declare war, to make peace, to rule foreigners and citizens alike, anytime, anywhere—so that they can even execute equestrians and senators within the city limits—and to do everything else that was once allowed to the consuls and other magistrates. Because they hold the censorship, they inquire into our lives and our morals, compile property lists, enroll some men in the equestrian and senatorial classes, and remove others, however they please.[165] Because they control all the priesthoods,[166] . . . they have control over all things, sacred and profane. The so-called tribunician power, which was once held by the most promising young men, allows emperors to block the proposals or actions of anyone else if they do not approve, and prevents them from being assaulted. And if they appear to be mistreated, even slightly, not just physically but even verbally, they are allowed to execute the offender, as someone polluted or accursed, without a trial.[167] Of course, the emperors do not think it right actually to be tribunes, inasmuch as they are con-

---

[158] In Latin, the adjective *augustus* means "majestic," "magnificent," "venerable," "worthy of honor."

[159] *monarchy:* "rule by one man"; see note 25 of Chapter I.

[160] *dictators:* the Romans considered the dictatorship a temporary position; see selection 231.

[161] That is, the consulship, the praetorship, and so on.

[162] Dio Cassius was writing around A.D. 200.

[163] On the end of popular elections, see selection 245.

[164] *imperator:* originally the title of a military commander-in-chief (Latin *imperium* = "supreme command"). In the *imper*ial period, however, it came to mean "sole authority," "*emper*or."

[165] On the duties of the consuls and censors in the republican period, see selections 229–232.

[166] The emperor was the *pontifex maximus,* "high priest" of the state religion. For more on the Roman priesthoods, see selection 378.

[167] A tribune was sacrosanct, that is, inviolable or secured by religious sanction against assault. If a tribune or a man with tribunician power was assaulted, his assaulter could be executed without trial.

sidered patricians; however, they take on the full power of the tribunes as it was in the period of the tribunate's greatest power.[168] . . . They have thus taken over these positions just as they existed during the republic, and continued to use the long-established titles so that they might appear to have no power except what has been legally given to them.[169] In addition, however, they have acquired something which was given to no Roman of the past without some restriction, and with this alone they could do everything just mentioned, and other things as well: they have been made exempt from the laws; that is, they are free from all compulsion of the law and are bound by no written statutes. And so, by assuming these republican offices and titles, they have embraced every power which exists in this state with the result that they possess all the powers of kings, but without the vulgar name. The names Caesar or Augustus, of course, bestow on them no particular power, but merely indicate, in the one case, the succession or heirship from Julius Caesar and, in the other, the magnificence of their rank. And the title "Father" gives them perhaps a certain added authority over us, such as fathers once used to have over their children.[170] Originally, however, the title "Father" was used both as a title of honor and as a warning to the emperors to love their subjects as they would their own children, and to the subjects to respect the emperors as they would their own fathers. . . . And so the system of government was changed, both for the better and to make the state healthier and more stable; for it was no doubt completely impossible for the people of the republic to have a stable and secure government.[171] . . .

Augustus did not enact all laws on his own;[172] there were some which he presented in advance to the popular assembly in order that he might learn about and correct any part which displeased them. And he encouraged everyone to offer him advice, anyone who might think of something to improve the law, and he allowed them considerable freedom of speech, and even rewrote some parts.[173] . . . The Senate judged legal cases, as it had during the republican period, and dealt with some of the ambassadors and delegations from both foreign governments and kings; and the "people" and the plebeians still assembled as they had in the past.[174] Nothing, however, was

[168] The office of tribune, or the tribunate, had existed from the earliest days of the republic. It had been established to provide plebeians with protection from the patricians, and thus only plebeians could be tribunes. The emperors did not hold the office of tribune, but rather assumed for themselves the powers of the tribunes, such as the veto.

[169] Augustus did not create any new positions or titles for himself or his successors. He simply assumed positions which had existed for hundreds of years: the consulship, the censorship, tribunician power, the priesthood, the title *imperator*. He could thus say, "I haven't done anything new or revolutionary; I'm just a legally appointed magistrate." However, he held all these positions at the same time, which was revolutionary. During the republican period, one man could never have been consul, censor, tribune, and *pontifex maximus* all in the same year, and certainly not for life. Thus, Augustus, and his successors as emperor, held virtually all the powers of all the magistrates all the time.

[170] The emperor held the title *Pater Patriae*, "Father of the Fatherland." On paternalism in Roman society, see the introduction to selections 7–13.

[171] For the instability of the late republican period, see selections 112, 240, and 288.

[172] On sources of law in republican Rome, see selection 252. The last known legislation to be voted and passed in the popular assembly was passed in A.D. 97. Henceforth, legislation consisted of edicts and imperial constitutions.

[173] Augustus's successors were much less generous or amenable. Later emperors, in fact, were quite despotic.

[174] Tiberius, Augustus's stepson and immediate successor, put an end to popular elections; see selection 245.

done which did not please Augustus. And it was Augustus who selected and nominated men to hold the magistracies.[175]

The Prefect of the City

Augustus knew that his survival as an absolute ruler depended to a great extent on his ability to weaken the power of his opponents in the Senate. One method of doing this was to concentrate the powers of the magistracies in his own hands. Augustus did not, of course, abolish the traditional magistracies, and these continued to be held by men of senatorial families, although these men now "shared" their power with Augustus. However, he created new positions and filled them with men of his own choosing. One of the most important of the imperial appointments was the office of city prefect.[176] For this office, Augustus and succeeding emperors chose men of senatorial rank, but certainly men loyal to them. The passage translated here lists some of the duties and powers of this prefecture. Many of these duties seem to duplicate those of the magistrates; in fact, the prefect's powers often superseded those of the magistrates. The consulship, praetorship, aedileship and quaestorship continued to exist but became positions with more prestige than real power.

242   *The Digest of Laws* 1.12.1, 11–13 (Ulpian)

The prefect of the city has the authority to punish all crimes, not only those which are committed in the city but also those which are committed outside the city but within Italy. . . .

It is also his job to see that meat is offered for sale at a fair price, and for this reason the swine market is also in his jurisdiction. Similarly, other livestock which are used to provide meat are within his jurisdiction.[177]

It is also the responsibility of the prefect of the city to maintain public order and discipline at the games.[178] He should certainly keep soldiers stationed at various locations to maintain public order and to report to him anything which happens anywhere.

The prefect of the city can forbid entrance into Rome or into any of the districts of Rome. And he can deny permission to engage in business or professional or legal activity, either temporarily or permanently. He can also deny entrance to the games.

---

[175] Magistrates continued to hold office, although their power was greatly reduced because Augustus's power was so immense. The consulship, for example, was reduced to a term of six months and became a position of honor rather than of real power.

[176] *prefect:* Latin *pr(a)eficere, pr(a)efectum* = "to put in charge," "having been put in charge." Pedanius Secundus, who was murdered by one of his slaves, was city prefect; see selection 191.

[177] Compare the duties of the prefect of the city with those of the praetors and aediles of the republican period; see selections 229–231.

[178] *games:* see the introduction to the section on spectacles in Chapter XIV.

Careers in the Government

At the same time that Augustus knew that he could not allow any ambitious man of the senatorial class to become a rival for power, he also realized that he needed to create a stable civil service which would be free of the political rivalries that had destroyed the republic and which would be accountable ultimately to him. He wanted to secure the assistance of talented, experienced, but also loyal men, and he therefore courted men of the equestrian order and offered them positions in his administration. The equestrians, for their part, supported Augustus because he brought to the Roman Empire peace and prosperity after decades of turbulence.[179]

There were many advantages to this system of imperial appointment. It allowed Augustus to create a strong, loyal, experienced imperial bureaucracy or civil service. One fault of the republican constitution had been the lack of continuity in the magistracies; republican magistrates had served only one year and were frequently inexperienced. Imperial civil servants spent many years in one job and learned it well; moreover, they had time to develop good working relationships with people in other civil offices.

During the imperial period, therefore, opportunities existed for talented and ambitious men to plan careers in the government.[180] Good service at one level was rewarded by promotion to a higher level. At the top of the career ladder were the governorship of Egypt and the prefecture of the Praetorian Guard.[181] During the first century A.D., many of the men in the middle- and upper-level positions were equestrians who had begun their careers as military officers and then moved into positions of civil administration. By the time of the emperor Hadrian,[182] however, one might pursue a totally military or a totally civil career. The passages translated here indicate the types of careers in the imperial government which an ambitious man might pursue.

This inscription was found in Sardinia.

243   *CIL* 10.7584 (*ILS* 1359)

To Marcus Cosconius Fronto, son of Marcus, of the Pollian tribe; chosen chief army engineer by the consul, prefect of the First Cohort; . . . military tribune of Legion I Italica; imperial procurator[183] for the 5 percent inheritance tax revenue from Pontus, Bithynia, Inner Pontus, and Paphlagonia; imperial procurator again for the 5 percent inheritance tax revenue from Asia, Lycia, Phrygia, Galatia, and the Cyclades islands;

---

[179] For comments on the equestrians' interest in pacification, see the introduction to selection 155.

[180] During the republican period, men of the senatorial class had careers in politics rather than government administration. A republican magistrate held his office for only one year.

[181] The Praetorian Guard was an elite corp of about 5000 soldiers stationed in and near Rome whose duty it was to protect the emperor. The senatorial families resented these appointments because they felt military commissions and provincial governorships belonged to them.

[182] *Hadrian:* emperor A.D. 117–138.

[183] *procurator:* Latin *procurare* = "to take care of," "to manage."

subprefect for the grain supply of the city;[184] imperial procurator for the revenue of the iron mines in Gaul; imperial procurator and prefect of the province of Sardinia; Lucretius, imperial recordkeeper of the province of Sardinia [dedicates this memorial] to his excellent and very conscientious director.

This inscription was found at Praeneste.

244   *CIL* 14.2922 (*ILS* 1420)

To Titus Flavius Germanus, son of Titus, curator of the very successful second German triumph[185] of . . . [186] honored . . . [187] with the most illustrious priesthood, the Pontifex Minor; procurator of the 5 percent inheritance tax; procurator of inherited estates; procurator of the Great Games;[188] procurator of the Morning Games;[189] procurator of city districts with the additional duty of paving streets in two parts of the city; procurator of the 5 percent inheritance tax from Umbria, Etruria, Picenum, . . . and Campania; procurator for child welfare assistance in Lucania, Bruttium, Calabria, and Apulia;[190] curator for the repair of public works and sacred buildings; aedile; duovir; priest of the deified Augustus;[191] duovir quinquennalis;[192] patron of the colony;[193] Cerdo, his freedman [dedicated this memorial] to his incomparable patron, with his sons, Flavius Maximinus, Germanus, and Rufinus, who have been honored with equestrian rank.[194]

The End of Popular Elections

In the republican period, all male citizens had been eligible to vote in the popular assemblies for the election of magistrates. These elections were energetically, often bitterly, contested by candidates from the senatorial class. Soon after Tiberius

184 *the city:* Rome. On the city grain supply, see selection 153.

185 On triumphs, see selection 267. In the imperial period, only members of the imperial family were allowed to celebrate triumphs.

186 Commodus was emperor A.D. 180–192. He was hated by many and was assassinated in A.D. 192. After his death, his name was chiseled out of inscriptions. Hence there is a gap in this inscription where the name Commodus originally stood: "the very successful second German triumph of *Emperor Caesar Lucius Aurelius Commodus Augustus.*"

187 "honored *by Commodus.*"

188 *Great Games:* an annual celebration held in honor of Jupiter, September 4–19.

189 *Morning Games:* nothing is known about these.

190 On child welfare assistance, see selection 46.

191 After his death, Augustus was declared to have become a god, to have been deified, and a cult of the deified Augustus was established; see selections 381 and 382.

192 *duovir quinquennalis:* duovir = duo ("two"), vir ("man"); quinquennalis = "occurring every five years." A commission of two men was selected every five years for a specific purpose such as taking a census.

193 *colony:* Praeneste, a town about 20 miles southeast of Rome. On the Roman colonization of Italian towns, see footnotes 159 and 160 of Chapter VII.

194 It was an honor, not just a privilege, to be enrolled in the equestrian order. Equestrians were easily distinguished from the common folk because they wore special gold rings and white togas with a narrow purple border. Senators wore white togas with a broad purple border.

became emperor in A.D. 14, he abolished popular elections in Rome.[195] Henceforth the emperor nominated at least some of the candidates for the magistracies, and voting took place only in the Senate, by senators.[196] Tiberius's action robbed the common people of any voice in the selection of magistrates and substantially reduced the political activities of the senatorial class. In the republican period, a man of the senatorial class spent a good part of his life involved in public election campaigns for himself, his family, and his friends, and, for his efforts, he gained wide public recognition. In the imperial period, a Senator's prominence and influence would be fairly limited. (This diminishing of senatorial authority was, of course, the purpose of Tiberius's action.)

245   Tacitus, *Annals* 1.15

Then, for the first time, elections were transferred from the Campus Martius[197] to the Senate. Up until that day, certain things were still done according to the will of the voting tribes,[198] although the most important matters had been decided by the *princeps*.[199] However, the people did not complain (except for a few idle grumblings) that a right and privilege had been taken away from them. And the senators supported this move eagerly, since it would relieve them of the expenses of bribery and degrading campaigns.[200] And Tiberius, for his part, acted with moderation, nominating no more than four candidates (their candidacies, however, had to be accepted, and they did not have to campaign).

Freedom of Speech

The last decades of the republican period were years of turmoil and violence. Seldom, however, has the world seen a period which enjoyed such unlimited freedom of speech.[201] We need only look at Cicero's speech about Verres[202] to recognize both the bluntness and the ferocity with which politicians assailed their opponents. Cicero risked incurring the wrath of Verres's political allies, of course, but was in no danger of any official restriction on his freedom of speech. The imperial period, however, presents a stark contrast. Augustus had ended the turmoil

---

[195] Towns like Pompeii continued to elect local officials. Most of the political advertisements found printed on building walls in Pompeii date to the imperial period.

[196] The popular assemblies met for the last time to pass legislation about A.D. 100.

[197] *Campus Martius:* the Comitia Centuriata met here for elections; see note 20 of this chapter.

[198] *voting tribes:* see note 12 of this chapter.

[199] *princeps:* the Roman emperors held the title *princeps,* which meant "first" or "foremost." The English word *prince* is derived from *princeps.* Both the "people" and the senators had already lost many of their powers during Augustus's principate.

[200] A cynical view of political campaigns during the republican period.

[201] "Freedom of speech was an essential part of the Republican virtue of *libertas,* to be regretted more than political freedom when both were abolished." Sir Ronald Syme, *The Roman Revolution* (Oxford, 1939), p. 152.

[202] See selection 281.

and violence, but the price was liberty. Peace could be maintained only if the emperor's power remained absolute and unquestioned. The emperors could not allow any criticism of themselves, and detractors were punished harshly.

The following passages, the first from the republican period and the second from the imperial period, reveal the enormous difference between the freedom of the republican period and the repression of the imperial period.

The poet Catullus[203] lived from about 84 B.C. to about 54 B.C., a period which witnessed the rise to power of Sulla, Caesar, Pompey, Cicero, and many other prominent republican politicians. Catullus apparently loathed Caesar and consequently reviled him in poems which would today be considered libelous. Yet he feared no lawsuit and no public prosecution, despite the fact that Caesar was a member of the triumvirate which virtually ruled Rome at this time.[204]

246   Catullus, *Poems* 93, 57

I have no very great desire, Caesar, to make an effort to please you, or even to know whether you are white or black.[205]

They suit one another well, these two lewd lechers, Mamurra[206] and Caesar with his unnatural lusts. And no wonder! They have both been stained with an equal number of blotches which cannot be washed away,[207] one picking them up in the city, the other at Formiae,[208] equally diseased, equally debauched, like twins, both learned scholars in affairs of the bed, both renowned for their adulterous appetites, friendly rivals also of young girls.[209] Yes, they suit one another well, those two lewd lechers.

Epictetus was a Stoic philosopher who lived in Rome during the first century A.D. He was expelled from Rome in A.D. 89 by the emperor Domitian.[210]

247   Epictetus, *Lectures Collected by Arrian* 4.13.5

In Rome, reckless men are trapped by soldiers in the following manner. A soldier in civilian clothing sits down beside you and begins to vilify the emperor. Then, as if you had received from him a pledge of good faith just because he began the abuse, you, too, say what's on your mind—and the next moment you are handcuffed and led away.

---

203 Some of his poems are translated above, in selections 50 and 64.

204 On the First Triumvirate, see note 104 of Chapter VII and note 149 of this chapter.

205 *whether you are white or black:* a proverbial expression in Latin, comparable to the English expression "whether you're dead or alive."

206 *Mamurra:* a Roman equestrian who served in Gaul under Caesar.

207 A reference to a venereal disease.

208 *Formiae:* town south of Rome; Mamurra's hometown. See note 80 of Chapter VIII.

209 That is, they were attracted also to boys and therefore competed with young girls for the favors of handsome boys. One of Caesar's contemporaries is said to have remarked that Caesar was "a man for all women and a woman for all men."

210 On Epictetus, see Appendix I.

The Emperor and the Senate

During Augustus's reign as emperor, many members of the Senate were men who had entered the Senate during the republican period and who therefore remembered well the power and prestige they had held in that period. It was these men who were most resentful of the new form of government.[211] By the time Tiberius abolished popular elections, however, few of these senators were still alive. And by the time Claudius became princeps in A.D. 41, not only had the Senate and the magistrates lost many of their powers, but the very composition of the Senate had changed. Many of the senators were "new men" rather than the sons and grandsons of the republican senators. Since, from the time of Tiberius on, most candidates for the magistracies were nominated by the emperor, he would obviously choose men on whose loyalty he could depend. And, although magistrates were now elected in the Senate, as the Senate became filled with "emperor's men," they would in turn elect candidates favored by the emperor.[212] In this passage, from a speech preserved on papyrus in Egypt, the emperor Claudius chides the Senate for its servile behavior. He is apparently encouraging the senators to speak their own opinions freely, but other sources indicate to us the dangers of frankness during the imperial period.[213]

Claudius was but one of a long line of emperors, and relationships between emperor and Senate varied considerably from reign to reign. The Senate never regained, however, the supremacy in the state which it had held in the republican period.

248   *FIRA* 1, p. 287 ff. (*B.G.U.* 611)

And so, senators, if my proposals seem good to you, express your approval at once, candidly and openly. If they do not seem good to you, find some other solutions, but do it here. If perhaps you want more time to think about this, take it, as long as you remember that you must express your own opinion regardless of the order in which your names are called. It is not at all befitting the dignity of this group for one man alone, the consul-elect, to express an opinion which he has copied word for word from the motion of the consuls, and for the rest of you to speak just one word, "I agree,"[214] and then to leave saying, "We gave our opinions."

[211] The opposition to the principate came mainly from the senatorial class in Italy, and it was effectively silenced by Augustus. We have virtually no information about how the lower classes in Italy and in the provinces felt about the changes made by Augustus, but it is unlikely that many people felt anger or expressed opposition. The lower classes, particularly outside of Rome, probably felt far removed from what must have seemed to them a power struggle between the aristocratic senators and the aristocratic Augustus. Moreover, Augustus's rise to power had brought peace and stability to Roman society.

[212] There continued to be opponents of the principate among the senatorial class; see note 7 of Chapter III and note 28 of Chapter XIII. However, the opposition was usually not widespread and apparently did not make appeals for popular support.

[213] See selections 89 and 91.

[214] In Latin, *adsentior,* one word, means "I agree."

The Benefits of Imperial Rule

The people most bitter about imperial rule were the aristocrats, who had lost the political power which had always belonged to their ancestors. The average Roman had never held more than a token share of this power and could not, therefore, grieve too deeply when the monarchy of the emperor replaced the aristocracy of the Senate. In fact, many Romans welcomed this new system of government because it brought peace, stability, and therefore prosperity. In the republican period, the fate of the common man was frequently dependent on magistrates who changed every year and who were willing to sacrifice the welfare of other people to achieve their own political and financial ambitions. In the imperial period, affairs of state were conducted by bureaucrats, not politicians; by men who had served in one office for a long time and who had no illusions of securing for themselves supreme control over the Roman world. In the first two centuries of the imperial period, the common people of Rome, Italy, and the provinces enjoyed remarkable prosperity and security.[215]

Strabo was a historian and geographer who was born in Pontus[216] but spent some years in Rome. He lived from about 60 B.C. to about A.D. 24 and therefore lived through the last, turbulent decades of the republican period, the struggle for power between Octavian (Augustus) and Antony, the establishment by Octavian of the principate, the death of Augustus, and the accession by Tiberius which ensured the continuity of the principate.

249   Strabo, *Geography Book* 6.4.2 (end)

It is difficult to control and administer an empire as large as Rome's other than by entrusting it to one man, as to a father.[217] And indeed the Romans and their allies have never enjoyed such an abundance of peace and prosperity as that which Augustus Caesar provided from the time when he first assumed absolute power, and which his son and successor, Tiberius, is now providing. Tiberius has made Augustus the model of his administration and ordinances, as have his children, Germanicus and Drusus, who are helping their father.

Velleius Paterculus was a historian who lived during the reigns of Augustus and Tiberius.

---

[215] For more on the progress in social reforms during the imperial period, see selections 46 (on child assistance) and 198 to 203 (on the treatment of slaves).

[216] *Pontus:* a Roman province in Asia Minor; see map 5.

[217] On the emperor's title, *Pater Patriae,* see note 170 of this chapter. On the failure of the republican constitution to provide for the proper administration of a far-flung empire, see selections 278 to 281.

250 Velleius Paterculus, *A History of Rome* 2.126.2–5

Trust has returned to the Forum; dissension has been removed from the Forum, campaigning from the Campus Martius,[218] discord from the Senate house. Justice, equity, and diligence, long buried and forgotten, have been restored to the state. Magistrates once more have authority; the Senate, honor; the courts, dignity. Riots in the theater have been suppressed.[219] Everyone has either been inspired with desire, or forced by necessity, to behave honestly. Right is honored, wrong is punished. The humble man respects the man of power, but does not fear him. The man of power has precedence over the humble man, but does not despise him. When were grain prices more reasonable? When was peace more auspicious? The peace of Augustus has spread into the regions of the rising sun and of the setting sun, to the boundaries of the southernmost and northernmost lands. The peace of Augustus protects every corner of the world from fear of banditry. . . . The provinces have been liberated from the outrageous misconduct of magistrates.[220] Honor[221] lies waiting for those who deserve it; and the wicked do not escape punishment. Fairness has replaced influence and favoritism; real merit has replaced clever campaigning.[222] And the best emperor[223] teaches his citizens to do right by himself doing right. Although he is very great in his authority, he is even greater by his example.

LEGISLATION

Law was Rome's most original and most enduring achievement. Even today the law codes of most Western European countries are based on the code of ancient Rome. The Roman mind—pragmatic, prudent, methodical, orderly, yet adaptable and able to compromise, which had made outstanding developments in military science and engineering—seemed particularly well suited to the study of law as a science.

The written history of Rome's legal code begins in the fifth century B.C., not long after the expulsion of the monarchy and the establishment of the republic. As a result of agitation by the plebeians, who felt that knowledge and proper interpretation of the unwritten laws were denied to them, the laws were collected, written down, and published, and this, Rome's first written code, was known as

---

[218] On the location and function of the Campus Martius, and on the abolition of popular elections, see selection 245.

[219] On the use of theaters for the expression of political dissent, see note 60 of Chapter VII.

[220] Verres, for example; see selection 281.

[221] On the meanings of the Latin word *honor,* see note 28 of Chapter I.

[222] On campaign practices during the republican period, see selections 236 and 281. Once popular elections were abolished, political campaigns no longer took place. Velleius suggests that the selection of magistrates by an emperor who recognizes real merit is preferable to their selection by popular elections since voters can be swayed by clever and dishonest campaign practices.

[223] Velleius is here referring specifically to Tiberius.

the Twelve Tables.[224] The Twelve Tables were never formally repealed, although many sections fell out of use in later centuries. About six hundred years after the publication of the Twelve Tables, about A.D. 160, a Roman jurist[225] named Gaius wrote a textbook on Roman law, entitled the *Institutes,*[226] which was a collection of and commentary on Roman laws. About four hundred years after Gaius, about A.D. 540, the emperor Justinian[227] appointed a commission of jurists to publish a complete body of law. These jurists published (1) the *Digesta* (or *Pandectae*),[228] which was a collection of legislation and valuable commentaries by earlier jurists; (2) the *Justinian Code,* which was a collection of the imperial constitutions; (3) the *Institutes,* a textbook; and (4) the *Novellae Constitutiones,* or new imperial constitutions. These four legal works commissioned by Justinian are known by the collective title *Corpus Iuris Civilis*[229] and form the code of Roman law which was inherited by modern Europe.

These four works, and the writings of earlier jurists such as Gaius,[230] provide us with a detailed knowledge of Roman law. Other sources of information are contracts and documents,[231] speeches and correspondence,[232] and even references in literature.[233] It is not the function of this brief section to list even a portion of the actual laws.[234] Instead, we will see where the laws were made and then look at some of the general principles and basic concepts of Roman law.

Although we have an apparent wealth of information about Roman law, our knowledge about its application is quite limited. The people who studied and

[224] The traditional date for the publication of the Twelve Tables is 451–450 B.C. On plebeian agitation subsequent to the publication of the Twelve Tables, see selection 231.

[225] *jurist:* a jurist was a man learned in the law who gave advice, either oral or written, to judges and lawyers. The opinions and decisions of the jurists frequently influenced legal procedure. The Latin word for jurist is *jurisconsultus:* "skilled" (*consultus*) "in the law" (*iuris*); or *jurisprudens:* "experienced" (*prudens*) "in the law" (*iuris*).

"When a rule of law is expressed in a permanent written form it is fixed and immutable: the dispute which may arise about it will be as to its meaning and the only way in which it can be adapted to meet new needs is by agreeing that its words have a different meaning from that which was originally attributed to them. What the meaning of legal words is must be decided by one who is considered to have an authority, derived from special learning or experience, to give a decision on such matters, and the possessor of this authority is *iuris prudens* (or *iuris consultus*), a person skilled in the law." J. W. C. Turner, *Introduction to the Study of Roman Private Law* (Cambridge, 1953), p. 86.

[226] *Institutes:* Latin *institutiones* = "principles," "elements of instruction."

[227] Justinian lived in Constantinople in the Byzantine period. In the fourth century A.D., the Roman Empire had been divided into a western realm (whose capital was Rome) and an eastern realm (whose capital was Constantinople). During the fifth century A.D., Rome was sacked a number of times by Goths, Huns, and Vandals. In A.D. 476, the last western emperor of the Roman Empire was deposed, and henceforth the eastern emperor in Constantinople became the sole ruler of what was left of the Roman Empire. See Appendix III.

[228] *Digesta:* the Latin word *digesta* means a collection of writings arranged or distributed under certain headings. The alternative title, *Pandectae,* is a Greek word meaning "universal encyclopedia."

[229] *Corpus Iuris Civilis:* literally "body of civil law."

[230] Brief biographies of the jurists Gaius, Paulus, and Ulpian appear in Appendix I.

[231] See, for example, the moneylending contracts in selections 157 and 158.

[232] See, for example, Cicero's comments on interest rate regulations in selection 280.

[233] Legal terms are common in Latin poetry. Roman poets received a rhetorical training which strongly emphasized legal terminology and forensic debate.

[234] Examples of Roman laws are found in selections 5, 6, 33, 46, 66, 76, 113, 152, 199–203, 388, and 405.

wrote about law, who initiated legislation, who served as judges, jurors, and lawyers, were male and upper-class, concerned in their writings largely with their own social group. We know much less about the application of Roman law to women and the lower classes. In addition, the writers may tell us about the application of legal rules but almost never discuss the social, political, or economic reasons for these legal rules. And we have little information about the extent to which legal rules might be subverted by bribery, corruption, or the threat of force.[235] We speak, moreover, of Roman law, but we do not have a clear understanding of how it was applied to the peoples of the Empire, to the Greeks, the Spaniards, the Egyptians, for example, who certainly had retained many of their own laws.

The Roman Science

The Romans were quite aware of, indeed proud of, their passion for order, organization, and obedience. In the passage translated here, the poet Vergil expresses the Romans' pride in what they considered their most remarkable achievement: the establishment of world peace and the dissemination of Roman law.

251   Vergil, *Aeneid* 6.847–853

Other men will shape molten bronze with greater artistry; other men will fashion living faces from marble; others will plead cases with more skill,[236] and will draw with a stick the wandering movements of the heavenly bodies, and will predict the rising constellations. You, Roman, do not fail to govern all people with your supreme authority. *These* will be your skills: to establish law and order within a framework of peace,[237] to be merciful to those who submit, to crush in war those who are arrogant.

Sources of Legislation

Some of the sources of law mentioned here have already been mentioned above.

[235] Consider Verres's conduct in selection 281.

[236] Vergil has deliberately minimized Roman achievements in art and oratory so that he can emphasize the particularly Roman skills: the establishment of peace and order and the development of law. However, we should not forget that Rome produced some of the greatest orators in history. And, although Greek sculptors are justly famous for the beauty and grace of their marble statues, Roman artists are equally renowned for their attention to realistic detail.

[237] For a different view of the *pax Romana* ("Roman peace"), see Tacitus's comments in selection 282. Keep in mind, however, that Tacitus lived well over one hundred years after Vergil.

252 Gaius, *Institutes* 1.2–7

The laws of the Roman people consist of *leges*, plebiscites, decrees of the Senate, imperial regulations, edicts of those who have the right to issue them, and responses of jurists.[238]

A *lex* is what the *populus* orders and establishes. A *plebiscitum* is what the *plebs* orders and establishes.[239] . . .

A decree of the Senate is what the Senate orders and establishes. It has the force of a *lex* although its nature has been disputed.[240]

An imperial regulation[241] is what the emperor establishes by decree or edict or letter.[242] It has never been disputed whether this has the force of a *lex* since the emperor himself receives his power through a *lex*.[243]

The right of issuing edicts[244] is possessed by the magistrates of the Roman people. The use of this right is seen most often in the edicts of the two types of praetor, the *praetor urbanus* and the *praetor peregrinus*.[245] And in the provinces, the jurisdiction of the *praetor peregrinus* is possessed by the governors.[246] . . .

The responses of jurists are the decisions and opinions of those to whom authority has been given to make rulings. If all these learned men agree in an opinion, their opinion has the force of a *lex*. If, however, they disagree, the judge may adopt whichever of their opinions he pleases.

Categories

The Romans recognized a division into public law (legal rules and concepts which dealt with the functioning of the state) and private law (which dealt with relations between individuals). By far the majority of juristic literature, however, concerns private law, which was itself divided into three categories, discussed below.

253 *The Digest of Laws* 1.1.2–4 (Ulpian)

Law is divided into two categories: public law and private law. Public law is that which pertains to the affairs of the Roman state. Private law is that which pertains to the

---

[238] *responses:* Latin *responsa* (singular: *responsum*). *jurist:* see note 225 of this chapter.

[239] This paragraph has been translated in selection 227.

[240] *decree of the Senate: senatus consultum;* see the introduction to selection 238.

[241] *imperial regulation:* Latin *constitutio principis,* "regulation of the prince (emperor)." On the word *princeps (principis),* see note 199 of this chapter.

[242] For an example of an emperor's letter (called a *rescriptum*), see Trajan's letter to Pliny (selection 399), which is an official imperial response to a query.

[243] On the emperor's legal position, see selection 241.

[244] *edicts:* Latin *edictum; edico =* "I proclaim," "I pronounce."

[245] At the beginning of his year's term of office, a praetor would issue an edict which would state what actions at law he would allow or in what circumstances he would grant a legal action (see Cicero's edict on interest rates in selection 280). Praetors' edicts allowed the continual addition of more flexible institutions to the rigid system of established statute, and thus enabled the Roman legal system to keep pace with social and economic developments and increasing contact with foreign peoples.

[246] Governors were propraetors or proconsuls; see note 131 of this chapter.

interest of individuals; for some things are in the interest of the state, and some in the interest of private individuals. Public law is concerned with sacred matters, priests, and magistrates.[247] Private law is tripartite since it has been collected from three different sources: from the rules of natural law, of "international" law, and of civil law. Natural law is that which nature has taught all animals; it is not peculiar to the human race, but is common to all animals that are born on land and in the sea, and to birds as well. From natural law comes the union of male and female, which we call matrimony. From it comes the procreation and raising of children. And we observe that other animals, too, even the wild ones, are judged by their familiarity with this law. "International" law is the law which the nations of men employ.[248] We can easily understand how it differs from natural law: natural law is common to all animals, including man; "international" law is common only to all men.

254   Gaius, *Institutes* 1.1

Every group of people that is governed by legal rules and by customs employs, in part, laws which are peculiar to itself and, in part, laws which are common to all mankind. The body of laws which each group establishes for itself is called civil law, since it is peculiar to that particular group of citizens.[249] The body of laws which natural reason establishes among all men is observed by all groups of people equally and is called "international" law, since it is employed by all nations. Therefore, the Roman people employ partly their own peculiar law and partly the common law of all mankind.

255   *The Digest of Laws* 1.1.6 (Ulpian)

Civil law is that which neither differs totally from natural law or "international" law, nor follows it in every regard. When we add to or subtract from natural or "international" law, we create our own peculiar law, that is, civil law. And this law of ours exists either in writing or without writing.

[247] On Roman state or public religion, see Chapter XV. The chief priest of this religion was elected, and many of the priesthoods were political appointments.

[248] I have used the phrase "international law" to translate the Latin phrase *ius gentium* (more literally "law of nations"), although *ius gentium* does not correspond precisely to our concept of international law. *Ius gentium* (*gentes* = "nations," cf. "gentile") suggests rather laws which are common to all men, the prohibition against murder, for example, which all societies establish independently. Compare the definition given in the next passage.

An example of "international" law which is cited by another jurist deals with protecting oneself from violence and injury. "Whatever a man does to protect himself, he is considered to have done lawfully; and since nature has established a certain kinship among all human beings, it follows that it is unlawful for one man to attack another man." *The Digest of Laws* 1.1.3 (Florentinus).

[249] The Latin word *civilis* means "pertaining to citizens"; *civis* = "citizen," and *civitas* = "state" or "community."

Definitions

Roman jurists were preoccupied with a definition of law which would be, in theory at least, precise, objective, and fair to all peoples through all generations.[250]

256   *The Digest of Laws* 1.1.1 (Ulpian)

A man who plans to devote himself to law should first know the origin of the word *law*. The word *ius* ["law"] is derived from the word *iustitia* ["justice"]. . . . And law is the art of "the good" and "the fair."[251] We jurists, who may deservedly be called priests of the law, cherish justice and profess knowledge of the good and the fair, separating the fair from the unfair, discriminating between what is permitted and what is not permitted, striving to make men honest not only through the fear of punishments but also through the encouragement of rewards.

Equity

Roman jurists realized that the law, the legal rule, was not in itself an absolute. It required interpretation,[252] and if "the good" and "the fair" were to be pursued, interpretation must consider the spirit or intent, as well as the letter of the law.[253]

257   *The Digest of Laws* 50.17.90 (Paulus)

In all matters certainly, but especially in legal matters, equity[254] must be observed.

258   *The Digest of Laws* 50.16.6 (Ulpian)

The expression "according to the laws" must be interpreted as "according to the spirit of the laws" as well as "according to the letter of the laws."

259   *The Digest of Laws* 50.16.219 (Papinianus)

In contracts, it is best to consider the intent of the parties involved rather than the words.

[250] Other Roman definitions of law have appeared in selections 3 and 4. Though the application of the laws was supposed to be unbiased, the assignment of penalties for breaking the laws varied widely according to class; on *honestiores* and *humiliores,* see selection 5.

[251] Or of "goodness" and "fairness."

[252] The *controversiae* (selection 139) indicate Roman awareness of the claims of equity.

[253] The largest amount of interpretive material comes from the commentaries of jurists of the imperial period. Many of these commentaries were incorporated into Justinian's *Digest of Laws.*

[254] *equity:* the Latin word is *aequitas:* "justice," "fairness."

260   *The Digest of Laws* 1.3.17, 18 (Celsus)

To know the laws does not mean simply to understand their wording, but rather to understand their force and potential. Laws must be interpreted rather liberally so that we preserve their intent.

261   *The Digest of Laws* 50.17.56 (Gaius)

When in doubt, the more liberal interpretations should always be preferred.

262   *The Digest of Laws* 48.19.5 (Ulpian)

The deified Trajan[255] wrote that no one should be found guilty on the basis of suspicion alone. It was, he wrote, better for the crime of a guilty man to remain unpunished than for an innocent man to be condemned.

263   *The Digest of Laws* 22.3.2 (Paulus)

The burden of proof lies with he who accuses, not with him who is accused.

The Force of Custom

As the Romans expanded their Empire, they encountered not only people whose laws differed from their own but also situations for which no laws had been formulated. In their search for a fair and valid definition of law, Roman jurists recognized that custom must sometimes have the force of statute, because both were ultimately determined by the will of the people.

264   *The Digest of Laws* 1.3.32 (Julian)

When we encounter situations about which no written statutes have been established, we should uphold that precept which has been established by custom and usage. If such a precept is lacking, we should uphold a precept which is nearest to it in intent. If even this is not available, we should then maintain the law which is observed in the city of Rome. Longstanding usage is quite deservedly upheld as a substitute for statute, and we call this the law established by custom. Indeed, since the statutes themselves are binding on us for no other reason than because they have been approved by the will of the people, surely we should all deservedly be bound by those precepts which the people approve, although without written confirmation. For why does it matter whether the people declare their will by vote or by actual deed and fact?

[255] *deified Trajan:* Trajan was emperor A.D. 98–117.

XI

The Roman Army

THE ARMY DURING THE REPUBLICAN PERIOD

The army played a major role in the development of Roman society. Rome was a militaristic community, and warfare dominated the lives of its citizens as the community grew from a small isolated village to a large cosmopolitan city controlling a vast empire. The Empire was, of course, the fruit of the army's constant campaigning. Wars of expansion continued through the republican period to the early imperial period; in the imperial period, however, the army was occupied primarily with defending the borders of the far-flung Empire. Roman citizens owed to their army both the material prosperity and the cultural advancements which territorial expansion brought. And to the conquered areas the army brought the *pax Romana,* the "Roman peace," which could be viewed cynically as repression and loss of freedom, or more generously as an opportunity to share in the security, order, and prosperity of the Roman Empire.

The Roman army was for centuries composed of citizen property owners,[1] and supplemented by allies.[2] It was not a standing army; men were called into service only for a specific campaign.[3] However, since Rome was frequently at war, men eligible for service were called up year after year. We have already seen the problems which the system of a property-owner army caused. Families lost their land when the owner was often away on campaign; when the number of property owners decreased, fewer men were eligible for military service; meanwhile landless families fled to the cities, seeking employment, but were often unemployed or underemployed.[4] The Gracchan land reform measures were an honest but quite unsuccessful attempt to solve these problems. However, at the end of the second century B.C., a general named Gaius Marius made a far-reaching change in the

[1] *property owners:* the property might be real or personal. However, people usually invested in real estate and were thus landowners.

[2] People who were conquered by the Romans in war were thereafter required to provide troops for the Roman army. These troops were called "allies" or "auxiliaries."

[3] Men were eligible for service for sixteen to twenty years (i.e., on a draft registration list for twenty years) but were only called up for service when needed for a specific campaign.

[4] See the introduction to selection 170, which describes the Gracchan land reform measures.

composition of the Roman army. Marius had served as a soldier in many campaigns. Although his family had not in the past been politically active,[5] Marius ran for the consulship of 107 B.C. and was elected, largely on the basis of his distinguished military record. As consul,[6] he received command of the Roman army in a war in Africa. In order to build up the size of the army, he began to enroll men who did not meet the old property qualification.[7] In the past, soldiers who owned land were often eager to return home; for them, army service was a duty, not a career. Marius's new recruits, however, many of them landless and unemployed, were eager to make the military a career. Marius's reform, therefore, not only eased the problem of urban unemployment and a shrinking citizen army but also began the development of a professional army. Marius's soldiers stayed in the army for twenty years.[8] When not engaged in actual battles, they continued to train and occupied their time building roads, bridges, and aqueducts. At the end of their twenty-year term (twenty-five for allies), they were often given land in the province where they had served.[9] The army became increasingly more professional as Rome changed from a republic to a principate, and it offered men throughout the Empire a career with steady employment, good pay, and opportunities for advancement. And soldiers from the provinces, the "allies" or "auxiliaries," received Roman citizenship upon retirement.[10]

The Army before Marius's Reforms

Polybius was born in Greece about 204 B.C. In 168 B.C., after the Romans captured Macedonia, Polybius was one of 1000 Greeks taken to Rome as hostages. He lived in Rome for seventeen years, returning to Greece in 150 B.C. During his stay in Rome, he became a close friend of Publius Cornelius Scipio Aemilianus Africanus, an excellent military officer from a very distinguished patrician family.[11] Polybius came to admire the Romans; the passage translated here is taken from his *History of the World*.[12] The army he describes is that of his own period, before Marius's reforms. At that time, there were four legions, with 4000 to 5000 infantrymen in

[5] Marius was born in Arpinum, a town east of Rome. The people of Arpinum had received Roman citizenship in 188 B.C. Another native of Arpinum, and another *novus homo*, was Marcus Cicero. On the meaning of *novus homo*, see the introduction to selection 236, Quintus Cicero's advice on political campaigns.

[6] A consul was a commander-in-chief of the Roman legions as well as a civic official; see selection 232.

[7] It is quite possible that some non-property owners were enrolled before Marius became consul, but he regularized such enrollments and vastly increased their number.

[8] They served for twenty years, as opposed simply to being eligible for twenty years.

[9] Roman soldiers were forbidden to form legal marriages during their terms of service. Many, however, had common-law wives, raised families, and, upon retirement, settled in the provinces where they had served. In A.D. 197, the emperor Septimius Severus lifted the prohibition of marriage for soldiers.

[10] Before A.D. 212, when the emperor Caracalla granted Roman citizenship to all free people within the borders of the Roman Empire, service in the Roman army was one way for provincials to acquire Roman citizenship.

[11] See genealogy chart 2.

[12] In passages from this book translated above, Polybius described the duties of the Roman Senate and consuls; see selections 232 and 238.

each legion and 300 cavalry.[13] The allies also supplied four legions, with the same number of infantrymen in each, but with about 900 cavalry. Each legion was divided into 60 centuries, and each century contained about 100 men. The division of the citizen body into centuries for military purposes was the same as the division made for the Comitia Centuriata. In other words, a man was placed by the censors in a particular century according to his age and the amount of property he possessed, and he remained with that century whether he was summoned to vote or to fight. Thus, the Comitia Centuriata met in the Campus Martius for elections and legislation, as well as for muster, because it was in origin a method of organizing the militia.

The two consuls were the commanders-in-chief; under them were 24 officers called military tribunes[14] (or, in the allied legions, prefects); under the tribunes were officers called centurions. The military tribunes were generally young aristocrats whose appointments as officers were "political."[15] The centurions, however, were officers who had begun their military service as common soldiers and who had been promoted because of their ability.[16] Each centurion commanded a century.

In Polybius's time, there was a fighting unit called a *maniple* which consisted of two centuries. Thus, there were 30 maniples in each legion. Marius introduced a unit called a *cohort,* which contained about 600 men; there were henceforth 10 cohorts in each legion.

265   Polybius, *History of the World* 6.22–24, 26 (5, 7, 10),
              31 (10–14), 33 (6, 7, 12), 34 (5–11), 37–39

The youngest soldiers, the *velites,*[17] are ordered to carry a sword, javelins, and a small shield. The shield is of durable construction and of sufficient size to offer protection, being round and measuring three feet in diameter. They are also equipped with a plain helmet, sometimes covering it with a wolf's skin or something of this sort, both to protect it and at the same time to make it distinct so that those men who are stoutly bearing the brunt of the battle, and those who are not, will be clearly visible to their officers. The wooden shaft of the javelins is about two cubits[18] in length and the width of a finger in breadth. The tip is a span[19] long and sharpened to such a fine point that it is necessarily bent by the first impact[20] and the enemy cannot then hurl it back. Otherwise the javelin could be used by both sides.

[13] In 31 B.C., when Antony and Augustus were battling for power (see note 80 Chapter III), there were seventy legions; when Augustus became *princeps,* he reduced the number of legions to twenty-eight.

[14] *military tribunes:* not to be confused with the tribune of the plebs.

[15] See selections 218 and 272.

[16] *centurions:* see Horace's comments in selection 15 about the centurions in his hometown.

[17] *velites:* "light-armed" (*velox* = "quick," "swift").

[18] One cubit equals the distance from the elbow to the end of the middle finger, about 18 inches.

[19] One span equals the distance between the tips of the thumb and the little finger, about 9 inches.

[20] The metal tip would enter the flesh and then bend so that it could not be pulled out without tearing a large section of flesh.

The men next in age, the *hastati*,[21] are ordered to wear a panoply.[22] The Roman panoply consists of: (1) An oblong shield, which is 2½ feet in width and 4 feet in length. The thickness at the rim is one palm's breadth.[23] It is constructed of two sheets of wood fastened with glue. The outer surface is covered first with linen cloth and then with calfskin. A strip of iron is placed on the upper and lower rims to protect it from downward thrusts of swords and [from damage] when it is propped up on the ground. It also has an iron boss attached to it which deflects direct hits by stones, pikes, and heavy missiles in general. (2) A sword, which is carried on the left thigh and called a Spanish sword. It has a blade which is sharp on both edges, and thus suitable for upward and downward thrusts, and which is strong and stable. (3) Two javelins. (4) One brass helmet. (5) Greaves. There are two types of javelins: thick ones and thin ones. . . . Each is fitted with a barbed iron head which is the same length as the wooden shaft. . . . In addition to all this, they adorn their helmets with a crown of feathers—three purple or black feathers standing straight up, about a cubit in height—which, since it is placed on the top of the head, above all the other arms, makes the soldier appear twice his real size and gives him a fine appearance, guaranteed to strike terror in the enemy.

Most of the soldiers also wear a bronze breastplate, one span square, which is placed in front of the heart and therefore called a heart protector. This completes their equipment. Soldiers who have a property value of more than 10,000 drachmas[24] wear, instead of a heart protector, a protective covering of chain mail. The *principes* and the *triarii* are armed in the same fashion, except that the *triarii* carry spears instead of javelins.

Twenty centurions are selected according to merit from each of the classes mentioned above except the youngest, the *velites*.[25] . . . These officers then choose from the ranks two of the most vigorous and most noble of soldiers to be the standard-bearers[26] in each maniple.[27] . . . When both centurions are present in battle, the first

[21] *hastati:* literally "armed with a spear" (*hasta*), although by Polybius's day these men wore a panoply.

[22] *panoply:* a complete set of armor and weapons; from the Greek *pan* = "all" and (*h*)*opla* = "arms."

[23] One palm equals about 4 inches.

[24] The drachma is a Greek coin approximately equivalent to a Roman denarius. Polybius, a Greek historian, has converted a Roman denomination to a Greek denomination. Ten thousand drachmas or ten thousand denarii was a large amount of money. All soldiers had to pay for their own panoply. Men who were wealthy, who had a large property value, could afford the more expensive chain mail; poorer soldiers wore the breastplates.

[25] The *hastati,* the *principes,* and the *triarii* each supplied from their ranks 20 centurions, for a total of 60 centurions per legion. The *velites* would not supply centurions from their ranks because they were young and therefore inexperienced.

[26] Selection as standard-bearer was an honor. Since the standard-bearer was expected to remain with the standard, however dangerous his position, and to inspire courage in the other soldiers, only men who could remain cool under heavy attack were selected. Frequently, standard-bearers were later promoted to the rank of centurion.

[27] *maniple:* a fighting unit consisting of two centuries. There were 30 maniples in a legion: 10 maniples of *hastati,* 10 of *principes,* 10 of *triarii.* The *velites* were distributed equally among all 30 maniples. During the time of Marius, the light-armed troops, the *velites,* were discarded and the army became entirely heavy-armed infantry. Marius also introduced the cohort, a fighting unit of six centuries.

centurion[28] commands the right half of the maniple and the second centurion the left, but if one centurion is absent,[29] the remaining centurion commands the whole maniple. The Romans wish the centurions to be not so much daring and adventurous in spirit but rather steadfast and persevering and with good leadership ability.[30] They do not want men who will rush thoughtlessly into battle or who will initiate the fighting, but rather men who will hold their ground when outnumbered and hard pressed and who will die at their posts. . . .

The organization and command of the allies is assumed by officers who are appointed by the Roman consuls and are called prefects. . . . Regarding the total number of allied forces, the number of infantrymen is usually equal to that of the Roman infantry, but the number of cavalrymen is three times as many.[31] . . .

When assignments to the four classes and to maniples have been made, the military tribunes take command of both the Romans and the allies and make a camp. The Romans have one simple plan for a camp which can be utilized at all times and in all places. . . . The whole plan of the camp forms a square, but in details, such as the division of the camp into streets and the arrangement of housing, it has the appearance of a town.[32] The palisade stands 200 feet from the tents on all sides. The open space [between the tents and the palisade] is of great use for several reasons. First, it is useful and necessary for assembling and dispersing troops; for all the men enter this open space, each from his own street, rather than assembling in one of the streets and tripping over and jostling one another. Also the livestock are gathered here, as is the booty from the enemy, and guarded during the night. Most importantly, during night assaults, neither fire[33] nor missiles can reach the soldiers, except for a very few missiles, and these are almost harmless because of the great distance they must travel and because of the open space surrounding the tents. . . .

The maniples take turns providing the following services to the tribunes.[34] When they encamp, they pitch his tent and level the ground around his tent. And if any of his baggage needs to be fenced around for protection, they take care of it. They also supply him with two units of guards—each unit consisting of four men—one of which is stationed in front of his tent and the other behind it, next to the horses. . . . Each maniple in turn, on a daily rotation, provides a unit of guards for the consul, both to protect him from plots and at the same time to enhance the dignity of his office. . . .

Every day at dawn, all the cavalry officers and centurions go to the tents of the military tribunes and wait while the tribunes go to the consul's quarters. The consul announces to the tribunes things which must be done that day, the tribunes pass on his

---

[28] Each maniple contained two centuries and therefore two centurions. First centurion was a higher rank than second centurion.

[29] He may be wounded, or he may be at a strategy session.

[30] Steadfastness and perseverance were qualities highly prized by the Romans. Compare the description of Horatius at the bridge in selection 1, and also the Stoic emphasis on steadfastness in selection 425.

[31] The Romans never developed a highly efficient fighting cavalry; they depended on the auxiliary forces to provide cavalry.

[32] Compare Vegetius's description of a Roman camp in selection 270: "Wherever the legion builds its camp, it builds an armed city."

[33] *fire:* from flame throwers.

[34] There were six tribunes in each legion.

orders to the cavalry officers and centurions, and they, in turn, give these orders to the soldiers when it is time.

They take the following provisions for informing the camp of the password for the night. From the tenth maniple of each class of infantry[35] and cavalry [the maniple at the bottom of the street at the farthest end of the camp], one man is chosen who is relieved of guard duty. Instead he goes every day at sunset to the tent of the tribune, receives from him the password [the password is written on a wooden tablet], and heads back to his maniple. When he has returned to his maniple, he gives the wooden tablet and the password, before witnesses, to the officer of the next maniple, who likewise gives it to the officer of the next. Everyone repeats the process until the password reaches the first maniples [those camped nearest the tents of the tribunes]. The first maniples must return the tablet to the tribunes before dark. When all the tablets distributed are returned, the tribunes know that the password has been given to all the maniples and, having passed through all, returned to them. . . .

A panel composed of all the military tribunes tries the offender.[36] If he is found guilty, he is bludgeoned in the following manner. A tribune takes a wooden club and just touches the condemned man with it. Once this has happened, everyone in the camp beats him with a club or stones him. Usually they kill these condemned men right in the camp, but even those men who are able to escape do not find safety. How could they? They are not allowed to return to their homes, nor would any of his relatives dare to receive such a man in their homes. And therefore those who once fall into such misfortune are completely ruined. . . .

The rank-and-file soldiers must obey the military tribunes; the military tribunes must obey the consuls. The tribune (or, for the allied forces, the prefect) has the right to inflict fines, to seize property for nonpayment of debt, and to punish by flogging. Bludgeoning to death is the punishment for anyone who steals anything from the camp, for anyone who gives false evidence, for any young man who is discovered abusing his body, and also for anyone who has already been fined three times for the same offense. These actions, then, are punished as crimes. The following culpable actions [also punished by bludgeoning] are considered unmanly and disgraceful in a soldire: reporting falsely to the tribune about one's valor in order to gain military honor; similarly, abandoning an assigned position because of fear after one has been ordered to remain at that station; similarly, throwing away any of one's arms in actual battle because of fear. Therefore, men ordered to remain at a station await certain death, unwilling to leave their positions although the enemy vastly outnumber them, because they fear punishment from their own side. Some men who have dropped a shield or a sword or some other arm in the heat of battle throw themselves recklessly into the midst of the enemy, hoping to regain possession of the weapon they have lost or resigning themselves to escape, by this death, certain disgrace and the taunts of their friends and relatives.

If ever these same things happen to occur among a large group of men, if, for example, entire maniples abandon their positions when exceedingly hard pressed, the officers reject the idea of bludgeoning or slaughtering all the men involved. Instead they

---

[35] That is, from the tenth maniple of *hastati*, the tenth of *principes*, and the tenth of *triarii*. The tenth maniples were the lowest-ranking maniples, and their first centurion was of a lower rank than the first centurion of the first maniple.

[36] Roman military discipline was very severe. The offense being discussed here is falling asleep while on night guard duty, an offense punished by death.

find a solution for the situation which is at one and the same time useful and terrifying. The tribune assembles the legion, leads those who abandoned their positions into the center of the assembly, and chastises them bitterly. Finally, he chooses by a lottery system sometimes five, sometimes eight, sometimes twenty of these men, always calculating the number in this group with reference to the whole unit of offenders so that this group forms one-tenth of all those guilty of cowardice. And these men who are chosen by lot are bludgeoned mercilessly in the manner described above.[37] The tribune gives the others in the guilty unit rations of barley instead of wheat and orders them to camp outside the palisade and safety of the regular camp. Therefore, the danger and the fear of the lottery hang over everyone equally since it is never certain to whom the lot will fall. And because everyone in the guilty unit is equally made an object lesson by receiving barley instead of wheat, this practice is considered the most effective of their customs both for inspiring terror and for correcting such incidents.

However, the Romans also encourage young soldiers with praise to face danger. Whenever an encounter has taken place and some of them have acted in a courageous manner, the consul summons an assembly of the troops, presents to them the men who, it seems to him, have done something outstanding, then first of all delivers a speech of praise about the courage of each one and about anything else in their lives which is worthy of mention as a noble deed, and then afterwards presents the following military honors: to the man who has wounded an enemy, a javelin; to the man who has killed and stripped an enemy of armor, a drinking bowl (for infantry) or a bridle (for cavalry). These honors are not given to men who have wounded or stripped enemy in regular battle or during an assault on a city, but only to those who have voluntarily and deliberately engaged in skirmishes or other such situations where there is no necessity to fight in single combat. The first man to scale the wall when a city is being stormed receives a gold crown. . . . By such incentives they stir to rivalry and emulation in battle not only the men who are present and listening, but also those who remain at home. For the men who receive such gifts, apart from their renown among the troops and their immediate fame at home, hold distinguished positions in religious processions after their return home since no one is allowed to wear decorations except those men alone who have been honored for bravery by the consuls. And in their houses they display in the most conspicuous places the spoils they have won because they consider them the symbols and evidences of their valor. Since such great attention and importance are given to both the rewards and the punishments in the army, it is inevitable that the outcome of every war the Romans fight is successful and brilliant.[38]

Foot soldiers receive a salary of two obols a day; centurions receive twice as much, and cavalry soldiers receive a drachma.[39] . . . However, the paymaster deducts from

---

[37] This procedure is called decimation. Compare note 67 of Chapter VIII.

[38] Polybius, a Greek, is giving an implied warning to the Greek world that Rome's military might is irresistible; compare the attitude of Josephus in selection 268.

[39] *obols, drachma:* again, Polybius has used Greek denominations because his readers were Greek (his book was written in Greek). One drachma equaled roughly one denarius. One obol was one-sixth of a drachma. In Polybius's time, a private in the infantry received about 120 denarii a year. Cavalrymen received more money because, from their salary, they had to pay not only their own expenses but also the expenses of their horses. Inflation made pay raises necessary. By the time of Caesar, a private in the infantry made 225 denarii a year. Domitian (emperor A.D. 81–96) raised the pay to 300 denarii; Septimius Severus (emperor A.D. 193–211) raised it to 450 denarii; and Caracalla (emperor A.D. 211–217) raised it to 675 denarii.

the pay of the Roman soldiers a fixed price for the grain, clothing, and any arms they need.

A Good Republican Soldier

Before Marius's reform, which allowed men without property to make the army a twenty-year career, the army was composed of men with property who remained on the draft registration list for about twenty years but who were called up only for specific campaigns. A man who held the rank of first centurion in one campaign did not automatically obtain that ranking in his next campaign. He might, in fact, be drafted as a rank-and-file soldier. In 171 B.C., when the consuls were drafting men for a campaign in Macedonia,[40] men who had earlier served as high-ranking centurions protested when their ranks were not renewed for this campaign. The passage translated here is a speech given by a veteran soldier, Spurius Ligustinus, who tried to appease both the angry former centurions and the military tribunes who were drafting for the new campaign. Spurius Ligustinus's speech reveals him as an ideal Roman soldier: a man of peasant stock who fights bravely for his country.

266   Livy, *A History of Rome* 42.34

Fellow citizens: I, Spurius Ligustinus, am descended from the Sabines.[41] My father left me an acre of farmland[42] and a small cottage, in which I was born and raised. And I live there even today. As soon as I reached manhood, my father married me to his brother's daughter,[43] who brought with her nothing except her free birth and chastity[44] and, with these, her fertility which would have filled even a wealthy home. We have six sons and two daughters, both of whom are now married. Four of our sons wear the *toga virilis*, two still wear the *toga praetexta*.[45]

  I became a soldier in the consulship of Publius Sulpicius and Gaius Aurelius.[46] In the army which was taken to Macedonia to fight King Philip, I spent two years as a private. In the third year, because of my valor, Titus Quinctius Flamininus put me in charge of the tenth maniple of *hastati*.[47] After Philip and the Macedonians had been

---

[40] In 168 B.C., at the conclusion of this war, the Romans brought to Rome 1000 Greek hostages, including Polybius; see the introduction to selection 265.

[41] *Sabines:* see footnote 66 of Chapter IX.

[42] *an acre of farmland:* a very small farm indeed, but perhaps typical for the peasant farmer. Ligustinus volunteered for many campaigns rather than waiting to be drafted. Perhaps he needed his military pay to supplement the family income. (The senatorial opponents of the Gracchan reforms, described in selection 170, were angry that they were being given clear title to only 500 acres.)

[43] Neither bride nor groom had any choice in this arrangement, but their marriage was apparently a happy one.

[44] Her family did not have enough money for a dowry.

[45] *toga virilis, toga praetexta:* see note 145 of Chapter VII.

[46] 200 B.C. The date of Ligustinus' speech is 171 B.C. He has therefore been campaigning over a period of thirty years.

[47] He became first centurion of the lowest-ranking maniple. (The tenth maniples of *principes* and *triarii* were higher ranking than the tenth maniple of *hastati*.)

defeated, when we were brought back to Italy and discharged, I immediately set out for Spain as a volunteer soldier with the consul Marcus Porcius Cato.[48] Those of you who served under him and under other generals, too, in a long army career, know that no one of all the generals now alive was a more perceptive observer and judge of valor. This general judged me worthy of commanding the first maniple of *hastati*.[49] I became a volunteer soldier again for the third time in the army which was sent against King Antiochus and the Aetolians.[50] Manius Acilius made me first centurion of the first century. When King Antiochus had been driven back and the Aetolians beaten, we were brought back to Italy. Two more times after that I served in campaigns where the legions were on duty for a year. Then I campaigned twice in Spain, once when Quintus Fulvius Flaccus was praetor[51] and again when Tiberius Sempronius Gracchus was praetor.[52] I was brought back from the province of Spain by Flaccus to appear with him in his triumph,[53] along with others whom he brought back because of their valor. Asked by Tiberius Gracchus to return to the province, I returned. Four times within a few years I was chief centurion of the *triarii*.[54] Thirty-four times I was rewarded by my generals for valor. I have received six Civic Crowns.[55] I have served twenty-two years in the army, and I am over fifty years old.[56] . . . But as long as anyone who is enrolling armies considers me a suitable soldier, I will never try to be excused from service.[57] It is the prerogative of the military tribunes to judge me worthy of a rank, whatever that may be. I, for my part, will take care that no one in the army surpasses me in valor. That I have always done so, both my generals and those soldiers who served with me are my witnesses.

A Triumph

The following passage describes a triumph during the republican period. Roman generals considered the triumph the greatest honor their country could bestow on them for a military victory. However, Augustus and subsequent emperors forbade these celebrations since they attracted too much attention to one individual military man; the emperors could not afford rivals for power. In the imperial period, the honor of a triumph was reserved for the emperor and his family.

[48] *Marcus Porcius Cato:* see selections 121, 160, 184, and 292. The campaign in Spain began in 195 B.C.

[49] That is, made him centurion of the highest-ranking maniple of *hastati*.

[50] In 191 B.C.

[51] In 181 B.C.

[52] In 180 B.C. Tiberius Sempronius Gracchus was the father of Tiberius and of Gaius Gracchus who proposed reforms in the distribution of public lands. See genealogy chart 2.

[53] *triumph:* see selection 267.

[54] The highest centurion rank.

[55] *Civic Crown:* a decoration awarded for saving the life of a Roman citizen.

[56] Only eight of the last thirty years has he not been on campaign. Generally men over forty-six ("seniors"; see note 10 of Chapter X) were not drafted. Ligustinus is enlisting voluntarily for this campaign.

[57] An expression of Ligustinus's *pietas*. Military service is a duty to the state.

A parade celebrating a military victory is called a triumph and takes the following form. Whenever a great and noteworthy victory was achieved, the general was immediately hailed by his soldiers as *imperator*.[58] He would bind sprigs of laurel around the *fasces*[59] and give them to runners to carry to the city and announce the victory. When he returned home, he would assemble the Senate and ask it to have a triumph voted for him. And if he obtained a favorable vote from the Senate and from the popular assembly, the title of *imperator* was also ratified for him. If he was still in the office which he held when he won the victory,[60] he remained in that office for the celebration of the triumph. If, however, his term of office had expired, he assumed some other title appropriate to the office, because it was forbidden to allow a triumph for a private citizen.

Dressed in triumphal garb and wearing bracelets on his arms and a crown of laurel on his head, and holding a branch in his right hand, he summoned the people together. Then he praised the soldiers who had served under him, both collectively and, in some cases, individually, and made them gifts of money and honored them also with military decorations, presenting arm bracelets to some and spears (but without iron tips) to others, crowns—some gold, some silver—each crown bearing the name of the honored individual and a representation of his particular brave deed. If he was the first over the wall, for example, his crown bore the likeness of a wall. A man who won a sea battle received a crown adorned with ships. A man who was outstanding in a cavalry charge received a crown with an equine motif. But a soldier who had saved the life of a fellow citizen in battle or in some other danger or in a siege won the greatest praise and received a crown of oak leaves, which was considered a much greater honor than all the crowns of silver and gold.[61] And these decorations were given not only to individuals distinguished for their valor, but also to units and even whole legions.

A large amount of the booty was also distributed to the soldiers who had served in the campaign.[62] However, some triumphant generals also gave it to the entire populace and defrayed the expenses of the triumph and made the booty public property. If any was left over, they spent it on temples, porticoes, and other public works.

When these ceremonies had been completed, the triumphant general mounted his chariot. This chariot, however, did not resemble a racing chariot or a war chariot; it was constructed to look like a round tower. And the general did not stand alone in the chariot, but, if he had children or relatives, he took the girls and the male infants in the chariot with him and put the older male relatives on the chariot horses. If there were

---

[58] In the imperial period, this title was assumed only by the emperor. In fact, the English word *emperor* is derived from the Latin *imperator;* see note 164 of Chapter X.

[59] *fasces:* a bundle of rods carried by the men who attended the general; see note 80 of Chapter X.

[60] Many generals were consuls or praetors, and these offices had only one-year terms. A general might be out of office before the date of his triumph.

[61] Ligustinus (selection 266) had been awarded six crowns.

[62] The emperors dispensed with this practice because it encouraged soldiers to fight for the sake of booty and to attack without provocation. Also, it made successful generals (those who could provide much booty) far too powerful and popular among the soldiers. As compensation, the emperors would periodically make cash awards, called *donatives,* which came from the imperial treasury and were thus dissociated from a particular general or a particular campaign.

many relatives, they rode in the procession on horses, as out-riders for the general. None of the other people in the triumph was mounted; all marched along wearing laurel wreaths. However, a public slave[63] rode in the chariot with the general, holding above his head a crown with precious gems set in gold. And the slave kept saying to him, "Look behind!" warning him to consider the future and events yet to come,[64] and not to become haughty and arrogant because of present events.[65]

. . . Thus arranged, they entered the city. At the head of the procession were the spoils and trophies, placards bearing representations of captured forts, cities, mountains, rivers, lakes, and seas, indeed all the things they had captured. And if one day was sufficient for the exhibition of these things, fine. If not, the exhibition continued for a second or even third day. When all the men[66] ahead of him had reached the concluding point of the procession, the general [who was at the end of the procession] finally was escorted into the Roman Forum.

He ordered some of the captives to be led to prison and executed,[67] and then he drove up to the Capitol. There he performed certain religious rites and made offerings. And he dined in the porticoes there. Toward evening he was escorted to his home to the accompaniment of flutes and Pan's pipes. And such were the triumphs of old.[68]

THE ARMY DURING THE IMPERIAL PERIOD

Reasons for the Army's Success

Flavuis Josephus was born in Jerusalem in A.D. 37. In A.D. 63, he traveled to Rome, where he became a friend of Poppaea, the second wife of the emperor Nero. He returned to Jerusalem and at first tried to restrain its citizens from a rebellion against the Romans but finally joined the rebellion himself. He was taken prisoner by the Romans, but was freed after two years, and he became a friend of the emperor Vespasian and his son Titus. After the siege and destruction of Jerusalem by Titus in A.D. 70, he went to live in Rome, where he died about the turn of the century. Like Polybius, who had lived almost 250 years before him, Josephus was a foreigner who was awed by Roman military might. Polybius had been a hostage, Josephus a prisoner of war, yet both admired Rome's energy and achievements.[69]

---

[63] *public slave:* one who belonged to the city rather than to a private individual.

[64] The Romans thought that the future came up on you from behind, catching you unaware if you had not looked behind you. Today we think that the future is ahead of us; we speak of looking ahead.

[65] The slave warns the general that he is mortal. No mortal knows his fate. One day he may be healthy, the next day ill or dead; one day he may be wealthy and famous, the next day poor and reviled by all.

[66] *the men:* his soldiers who had fought in the victorious battle. Ligustinus (selection 266) marched in the triumph of Fulvius Flaccus.

[67] Important prisoners of war were dragged in chains during the triumphal procession, mocked and spit at by the crowds, and then executed. Cleopatra committed suicide rather than suffer the disgrace of appearing in Octavian's (Augustus's) triumph.

[68] *of old:* of the republican period.

[69] *Polybius:* see selection 265.

268   Josephus, *A History of the Jewish War*
                                                              3.71–97, 104, 105, 107, 108

If you study carefully the organization of the Roman army, you will realize that they possess their great empire as a reward for valor, not as a gift of fortune. For the Romans, the wielding of arms does not begin with the outbreak of war, nor do they sit idly in peacetime and move their hands only during times of need. Quite the opposite! As if born for the sole purpose of wielding arms, they never take a break from training, never wait for a situation requiring arms. Their practice sessions are no less strenuous than real battles. Each soldier trains every day with all his energy as if in war. And therefore they bear the stress of battle with the greatest ease. No confusion causes them to break from their accustomed formation, no fear causes them to shrink back, no exertion tires them. Certain victory always attends them since their opponents are never equal to them. And so it would not be wrong to call their practice sessions bloodless battles and their battles bloody practice sessions.

The Romans are never caught unexpectedly by an attack of the enemy. Whatever hostile territory they invade, they do not engage in battle until they have built a camp. And they do not build this camp randomly or inconsistently, with everyone working on his own or without a master plan. Rather, if the ground happens to be uneven, it is first leveled. Then a square campsite is measured out. And a multitude of carpenters and tools needed for building accompany the army.

The interior of the camp is divided into areas for tents. The outer circuit has the appearance of a wall and is equipped with towers at regular intervals. On the spaces between the towers they set up catapults and stone throwers and every type of ballistic engine, all ready for firing. Four gates are then built, one on each side of the encircling wall, wide enough for the easy entrance of draft animals and for the rapid exit of troops if necessity arises.

The camp is divided symmetrically into streets. In the middle are the tents of the officers and, in the very center, the headquarters of the general, which resembles a small temple. And so a city suddenly appears, with a marketplace, workmen's quarter, and assembly area where officers pass judgment if any differences arise. The surrounding wall and everything within it are built quicker than thought, thanks to the number and the skill of the workmen. If there is need, a ditch is dug around the camp, on the outside of the wall, four cubits both in depth and in width.

Once they have completed the fortifications, the soldiers take up lodging, unit by unit, in a quiet and orderly fashion. All their duties are performed with the same discipline, the same safety precautions: gathering wood, securing food if supplies are low, hauling water—all these are done in turn by each unit. Nor does each man eat breakfast or dinner whenever he feels like it; they all eat together. Trumpets signal the hours for sleep, guard duty, and waking. Nothing is done except by command. At dawn, the rank-and-file soldiers report to their respective centurions, the centurions go to salute the tribunes, and all the tribunes go with their officers to the general. He gives them, according to custom, the password, as well as orders to deliver to the men under their command. Even in battle they act in the same orderly fashion: they quickly get into formation whenever they are required, and, both during an advance and during a retreat, they move as one unit.

When it is necessary to break camp, the trumpet sounds. No one remains idle. Immediately at this signal, they take down the tents and get everything ready for departure. Again the trumpets sound, this time the signal to prepare for the march. The soldiers immediately load the baggage on the mules and other pack animals and stand alert, as if ready to sprint forward at the start of a race. They set fire to the camp, first because it is easy for them to construct another one at their next stop, and second so that this camp may never be used by the enemy. The trumpets sound a third time, another signal for departure, to hurry along those who are slow, whatever their excuse, so that no one is left behind by his unit. Then the herald, standing on the right of the commanding officer, asks three times in the native tongue of the soldiers whether they are ready for war.[70] Three times the soldiers shout their reply loudly and enthusiastically: "We are ready!" Sometimes they even anticipate the question, and, filled with the spirit of war, they raise their right arms in the air as they shout.

Then they march forward, everyone silent and in correct order, each man maintaining his particular position in the ranks, just as he would in battle. The infantry are equipped with breastplates and helmets, and carry a sword on both sides.[71] The sword on the left side is the longer by far of the two. That on the right side is no more than a span in length. The infantry chosen to guard the general carry a spear and a small round shield. The rest of the soldiers carry a javelin and an oblong shield. However, they also carry a saw, a basket, a shovel, and an ax, as well as a leather strap, a scythe, a chain, and three days' food rations. As a result, an infantryman differs little from a loaded pack mule.[72]

Cavalrymen are equipped with a large sword on their right side, a long pike for their hand, an oblong shield placed sideways on the horse's flank, and, in a quiver hanging by their side, three or more shafts with broad points, equal in length to spears. The helmet and breastplate are similar to those worn by all the infantrymen. The cavalry chosen to guard the general does not differ in equipment from the horsemen in the regular ranks. The division which is to lead the marching army is always chosen by lot. . . .

Absolute obedience to the officers creates an army which is well behaved in peacetime and which moves as a single body when in battle—so cohesive are the ranks, so correct are the turns, so quick are the soldiers' ears for orders, eyes for signals, and hands for action. . . .

One might rightfully say that the people who created the Roman Empire are greater than the Empire itself. I have discussed the army at some length not so much wishing to praise the Romans as wanting to console those they have conquered and to deter those thinking about revolt.[73]

[70] By the time of Josephus, most of the auxiliary forces came from non-Latin-speaking areas and served their time in non-Latin-speaking areas. For example, Syrian garrisons were stationed in Egypt; see selections 269 and 271.

[71] Compare and contrast the equipment of Roman soldiers in the time of Polybius (selection 265) who lived in the second century B.C.

[72] The tools were used not only for constructing camps but also for road and bridge construction when the army was not actually fighting. When Marius introduced the concept of the professional career soldier, he was obligated to find some method of occupying his soldiers when there was no fighting (previously the soldiers had simply been dismissed and sent home). Marius set them to work at construction projects. His soldiers, with their packs of construction equipment, were sarcastically called "Marius's mules."

[73] Josephus, who was living in Rome when he wrote this *History,* which goes on to describe the destruction of Jerusalem, may be warning the peoples of the eastern part of the

Enlistment

The following passage is a translation of a letter written in Latin and addressed by the prefect of Egypt, Gaius Minicius Italus, to Celsianus, prefect of the Third Ituraean Cohort.[74] The letter announces the enrollment in the cohort of six recruits, who are identified by name and distinguishing marks (if any). The letter was written on papyrus in A.D. 103; upon receipt, it was entered in the archives of the cohort.

269   *P. Oxy.* 1022 (*Select Papyri* 421)

Order the six recruits who have been approved by me to be entered on the rolls of the cohort which you command, effective February 19. I have appended to this letter their names and distinguishing marks.

Gaius Veturius Gemellus, aged twenty-one, no distinguishing mark;

Gaius Longius Priscus, aged twenty-two, distinguishing mark on his left eyebrow;

Gaius Julius Maximus, aged twenty-five, no distinguishing mark;

[?] Lucius Secundus, aged twenty, no distinguishing mark;

Gaius Julius Saturninus, aged twenty-three, distinguishing mark on his left hand;

Marcus Antonius Valens, aged twenty-two, distinguishing mark on the right side of his forehead.

Received[75] on February 24, in the sixth year of our emperor Trajan,[76] through Priscus, orderly.

I, Avidius Arrianus, adjutant of the Third Cohort of the Ituraeans, declare that the original letter is in the archives of this cohort.

Training

In the passage translated here, Vegetius is describing the Roman army of the fourth century A.D. Like Polybius and Josephus before him, he stressses the Roman emphasis on discipline and obedience.

Empire not to consider rebellion against the Romans. (The *History* is written in Greek and therefore intended for an eastern rather than western audience.)

[74] *Cohort:* see the introduction to selection 265.

Ituraea: district in southern Syria, on the northeast border of Palestine. Augustus gave Ituraea, which had been hitherto ruled by native princes, to the family of Herod. This cohort was stationed in Egypt but named after the region in which its original soldiers had been first recruited (Ituraea). The six new recruits mentioned in this letter, however, were probably Egyptian.

[75] This last section of the document, acknowledging receipt of Minicius Italus's letter, is in another handwriting.

[76] A.D. 103, counting inclusively from A.D. 98, the first year of Trajan's reign.

270   Vegetius, *A Book about Military Affairs* 1.1, 9–11,
14, 18, 19, 21; 2.23, 25

We see that the Roman people have subjugated the whole world by no means other than thorough training in the use of weapons, strict discipline in the military camps, and practice in warfare. . . . We owe our success against all other people to our skillful selection of recruits; to our teaching, as I mentioned earlier, of the use of weapons; to our hardening the soldiers with daily exercise; to our acquainting them in field maneuvers with everything that can happen on the march and in battles; and to our severe punishment of idleness. Knowledge of military affairs nurtures boldness in battle; no one fears to do what he is confident that he has learned well. . . .

At the very beginning of their training, recruits must be taught the military pace. For nothing else must be checked more carefully, on the march or in battle, than that all the soldiers maintain their ranks while moving. This cannot be done unless they learn by continuous practice to march quickly and in time. For an army which is separated and lacks orderly ranks always finds itself in the most serious danger at the hands of the enemy. Therefore, 20 Roman miles[77] at the military pace should be completed, during the summer months, in five hours. At the full pace, which is quicker, 24 Roman miles should be completed in the same number of hours. . . . A soldier must also be trained in jumping in order that ditches may be leapt or an obstacle of some height may be negotiated, so that when difficulties of this type present themselves, they can be crossed without effort. . . . In the summer months, every recruit should learn how to swim, for rivers cannot always be crossed by bridges, and a retreating or pursuing army is frequently forced to swim. During sudden rains or snowfalls, streams become torrents, and danger arises from ignorance not only of the enemy but of water itself. . . .

Our ancestors, as we learn from their books, trained recruits in this way. They made round wickerwork shields that had twice the weight that a regular shield usually has. And, instead of swords, they gave the recruits wooden blades, which were also of double weight. And they trained at the stakes[78] not only in the morning but also in the afternoon. . . .

The recruit who has trained at the stake with a wooden blade should also be made to hurl wooden shafts, which are heavier in weight than real javelins, at the stake as if at a man. . . . In this exercise, they increase the strength of their upper arms and acquire skill and experience in hurling missiles. . . .

Vaulting onto horses should be practiced strictly and constantly not only by recruits but also by trained soldiers. It is clear that this custom has been passed down to our own time, although we neglect it. Wooden horses were set up in a covered hall in the winter, or out in the field in the summer. Young soldiers were ordered to vault over these, first without weapons until practice made them perfect, and then in full armor. So much time was devoted to this exercise that they learned to leap up on the horse and to leap down, from both the right side and the left, holding unsheathed swords or pikes. . . .

---

[77] Twenty Roman miles are equal to approximately 18½ British or American miles.

[78] *stakes:* each recruit set firmly in the ground a wooden stake about 6 feet high. He practiced against this stake as if he were fighting a real enemy, aiming sometimes at the "head" or "face," sometimes at the "knees" or "legs."

Young soldiers must very frequently be required to carry loads up to 60 pounds[79] and to march at the military pace, for on arduous expeditions there will be pressing need for them to carry food supplies as well as arms.[80] . . .

Every recruit must learn how to construct a camp. Nothing else is found to be so advantageous and so necessary in war. If a camp is built correctly, the soldiers spend their days and nights securely inside the rampart, even if the enemy besieges them. It is like carrying around a walled city with you everywhere. . . .

In the winter, porticoes for the cavalry were covered over with tiles or shingles or, if these were lacking, with reeds, rushes, or straw. For the infantry there were halls resembling basilicas[81] in which the army was trained in the use of arms under cover if the weather was stormy or windy. But on some winter days, once the snow or rain stopped, the soldiers were required to exercise in the field so that no interruption of their training would weaken their spirits or bodies. They should very frequently cut down trees, carry heavy loads, jump ditches, swim in the sea or in rivers, march at full pace, or even run with their armor and baggage so that tasks which are daily labor in peace will not seem difficult in war. . . .

The legion ought to carry everywhere with it all the things which are considered necessary for every kind of warfare,[82] so that wherever it builds its camp, it builds an armed city.[83]

A Letter Home

The following passage is a letter written to his family in the second century A.D. by a soldier from Egypt who has been shipped to Italy.

271　　　　　　　　　　　　　　　　　*B.G.U.* 423 (*Select Papyri* 112)

Apion sends warmest greetings to Epimachus, his father and lord:

Before all else, I pray that you are in good health, and that you always remain healthy and flourishing, and that my sister and her daughter and my brother are also well. I thank Lord Serapis[84] because he immediately kept me safe when I was in

[79] One Roman pound equals .721 British or American pounds. Therefore, 60 Roman pounds equals about 43 British pounds.

[80] Compare Josephus's description in selection 268 of the many construction implements carried by a Roman soldier.

[81] *basilicas:* in the Roman period, the word *basilica* designated the design, not the function, of a building (basilica did not mean "church" or "building with religious function"). A basilica was a rectangular hall divided inside into a nave and two side aisles.

[82] The army carried with it all kinds of construction equipment; small boats for making pontoon bridges; siege equipment, such as battering rams, movable towers, flame throwers, and rock-throwers. The Roman soldiers excelled at taking towns by siege. They would cut off food supplies to the town and might poison the water supply. In addition, they had very elaborate techniques for undermining the town's walls, sometimes even diverting a stream to cause flooding. Roman military engineers were extremely skillful and well trained.

[83] Roman army camps (*castra*) in the provinces sometimes did become cities, whose existence continued after the Roman Empire fell. The city of Chester in western England is one example. Its name is a corruption of the Latin word *castra,* "army camp." Chester began as a Roman army camp when Britain was part of the Roman Empire.

[84] *Serapis:* an Egyptian god; see note 119 of Chapter VII.

danger during the sea voyage. When I arrived at Misenum,[85] I received from the emperor three gold pieces to compensate me for traveling expenses. And so I am well.

I ask you now, lord and father, to write me a letter, first telling me about your own health, secondly about the health of my brother and sister, thirdly allowing me to do reverence to your handwriting because you educated me well, and I therefore hope to advance quickly, may the gods be willing. Give my love to Capiton, and to my brother and sister, and to Serenilla, and to my friends. I have sent you, with the messenger Euctemon, a portrait of myself. My name is Antonius Maximus.[86] I pray that you are well. The name of my century is Athenonica.

Address: To Philadelphia,[87] to Epimachus from his son Apion.

Deliver this letter from Apion to his father Epimachus to the First Cohort of the Apameni,[88] to Julianus the under-secretary.[89]

A Letter of Recommendation

Enough money and the right friends would earn one a rapid promotion. Pliny wrote this letter to his friend Pompeius Falco, a praetorian legate.

272   Pliny the Younger, *Letters* 7.22

You will be less surprised by my earlier pressing request that you confer the military tribuneship[90] on a friend of mine when you learn who he is and what sort of man he is. However, now that you have promised to promote him, I can tell you his name and describe him to you. His name is Cornelius Minicianus, and he is the shining light of our region, both in nobility and in character. He comes from a splendid family and is loaded with money, but loves hard work as much as poor people usually do. He is a very honest judge, a very bold lawyer, and a very faithful friend. You will realize that I have done you a favor when you examine him closer and see that he is a man equal to any job and to any distinction. But I won't say anything more to glorify such a very modest man.[91]

How to Advance Quickly

It was apparently not uncommon for soldiers to buy their advancements. For other comments on the prevalence of bribery in the Roman army, see selection 274. This letter, found at Karanis, Egypt, dates to the second century A.D.

[85] *Misenum:* promontory in Campania, near Naples.

[86] His Egyptian name is, of course, Apion, but he has been given a Roman name because he is in the Roman army. Compare the names of the recruits in selection 269.

[87] *Philadelphia:* town in the Fayum area of Egypt.

[88] *Apameni:* Apamea was a town in Asia Minor (see map 4). The original soldiers in this cohort were Apameni, men from Apamea. See notes 70 and 74 of this chapter.

[89] The letter is sent from Italy first to the cohort headquarters in Alexandria, where it will be forwarded by the under-secretary to Apion's family in Philadelphia.

[90] On the rank of military tribune, see the introduction to selection 265. This rank was generally the preserve of young aristocrats. Men who were promoted through the ranks might hope to be a centurion or even a prefect, but not a military tribune.

[91] For another recommendation letter from Pliny, see selection 49.

273   *P. Mich.* 8.468 (35 ff.)

I hope to live frugally, God willing, and to be transferred to a cohort. But around here, nothing happens without money. And letters of recommendation are of no use unless you can help yourself.

A Mutiny

In A.D. 14, when news of Augustus's death reached the legions in Pannonia and on the Rhine,[92] some soldiers stirred up a mutiny, perhaps thinking that Rome's new emperor, Tiberius, would be so preoccupied with other matters that he would quickly yield to their demands. The grievances of the soldiers are made quite clear in the following passages.

The speaker in this first passage is Percennius, leader of the mutineers in Pannonia.

274   Tacitus, *Annals* 1.17, 20, 23, 32, 35

"Enough mistakes have been made, over so many years, because of our inaction. For example, old men, and many men whose bodies have been maimed by war wounds, endure thirty or forty campaigns. But even discharge does not bring an end to their military service; stationed near the legion's standard, they endure the same hardships under a different name.[93] And if a soldier survives the many hazards of military life? He is still dragged into far-flung regions where he receives, under the name of "farmland," a marshy swamp or a barren mountainside.[94] Yes indeed, military service itself is harsh and unprofitable. Your body and soul are valued at a few cents a day.[95] And from that pittance, clothing, weapons, and tents have to be paid for—as well as bribes to mollify the cruel centurion and to escape onerous tasks. By Hercules, lashings and injuries, severe winters and withering summers, terrible war or barren peace—there is no end. Nor will there be any relief unless military life can be entered under fixed regulations: pay of one *denarius* a day[96] and an end to active service after sixteen

---

[92] *Pannonia:* see map 5. Roman control in this area extended to the Danube River, but not beyond.

The Romans also controlled the territory west of the Rhine River.

[93] After a soldier was discharged, he was still required to live near the camp for five more years and serve in the "reserves." Many veterans wanted, of course, to settle near the camp with their "wives" and families (see note 9 of this chapter), and many were given land near the camp after discharge, but they resented the reserve duty.

[94] For centuries it had been a military custom to give a parcel of farmland to retiring soldiers. Usually the soldiers received land in the areas where they had been stationed and had raised families with local women. However, as the best land in these areas became occupied, soldiers began to receive parcels far from their army camp and sometimes in infertile areas.

The settling of Roman soldiers with local wives in the provinces was a successful way of Romanizing the area. Also, the sons of these soldiers frequently enlisted in the army.

[95] The Latin says 10 *asses*, the salary per day. On the *as*, see Appendix II.

[96] Infantrymen were currently receiving 225 *denarii* a year. They wanted 365 *denarii* a year. Compare the military pay in Polybius's day (note 39 of this chapter).

years,[97] no detention for further service as reserves, and our veteran's bonus to be paid in cash,[98] right here in the camp." . . .

Some maniples had left the camp before the mutiny began, having been sent out to build roads and bridges and other construction projects.[99] When they heard of the turmoil back in the camp, they tore up the standards, plundered neighboring villages— and attacked the centurions, who tried to restrain them, with jeering and insults, and finally with blows. Their anger was directed chiefly against Aufidienus Rufus, camp prefect, whom they dragged out of a wagon, loaded down with baggage, and led to the front of the line, asking him in mocking voices whether he enjoyed such huge loads and such long marches. . . .

They killed one centurion whose name was Lucilius, but to whom they had, as a camp joke, added the nickname "Old Give-me-another," because whenever he broke a cane[100] on a soldier's back, he would demand in a loud voice: "Give me another, and another." . . .

[About the same time and for the same reasons, the legions on the German front rose in mutiny.]

In a mad frenzy, they suddenly attacked the centurions with swords drawn. Centurions are a longstanding object of soldiers' resentment and the main cause of their anger. They threw them on the ground and beat them, sixty to one (in order to correspond to the number of centurions). Then they threw them outside the camp or into the Rhine River—broken, mangled, some even dead. . . .

[Germanicus[101] rushed to the German front to quell the mutiny.]

When Germanicus mentioned the mutiny and asked what had happened to their soldierly dignity and the glory of their ancient discipline, and where they had driven their military tribunes and centurions, they all bared their bodies and reproached him by exposing the scars of their wounds and the marks of the whippings. And then, with all shouting at one time, they complained about the expense of bribes for work exemptions, the small amount of their pay, and the severity of their duties, naming specifically the defensive wall and ditches,[102] the gathering of fodder, construction material, and firewood, and whatever else they were ordered to do, either for reasons of necessity or to prevent idleness in the camp. The fiercest clamor arose from the veteran soldiers who, listing their thirty or more campaigns, begged him to provide relief for weary men and to assure them not of death under these same hard conditions, but of an end to their severe military service, not of a poverty-stricken retirement, but of quiet rest from duty.

[97] instead of after twenty years.

[98] Retiring soldiers received a bonus, but its payment was frequently delayed and sometimes payment was made in kind, not in cash.

[99] The work of the army during peacetime; see note 72 of this chapter.

[100] *cane:* the staff carried by the centurion as a mark of his rank. He used it to punish soldiers with a beating.

[101] Germanicus was the nephew of the emperor Tiberius (the son of Tiberius's brother Drusus). He spent many years with the legions in the northern provinces. Germanicus's son was Caligula, who became emperor in A.D. 37. Caligula was a nickname; it meant "little army boot" and was given to the child by soldiers who were fond of his father.

[102] That is, the construction work they were obliged to do.

The Height of Recruits

The population decline in the late imperial period had an adverse effect on the Roman army, and thus on all of Roman society, because, without enough soldiers to keep the borders of the Empire secure against invaders, people within the Empire lived under constant threat of attack. To keep the number of soldiers up to the necessary level, the height requirements for new soldiers were lowered.

Flavius Vegetius Renatus lived at the end of the fourth century A.D., 300 years after Josephus and 550 years after Polybius. The Roman army had undergone many changes during these years.

275   Vegetius, *A Book about Military Affairs* 1.5

I know that the height of recruits has always been required to conform to a standard measurement, so that only men who stand 6 feet or at least 5 feet 10 inches[103] have been accepted for service in the cavalry or in the first cohorts of the legions.[104] But in those days, the population was larger, and more men entered the armed forces, because the civil service was not then drawing away our most eligible young men. And therefore, if the need is pressing, it is fine to take account not so much of a man's stature as of his physical strength.

The following regulation was put into effect in A.D. 367.

276   *The Law Code of Theodosius* 7.13.3

Let there be held a levy of men 5 feet 7 inches tall.[105]

Avoiding the Draft

Marius's reform at the end of the second century B.C. had made the draft unnecessary, because so many men throughout the Empire wanted to enlist and to make the army a career. However, 500 years later, enlistments were down, the size of the army was shrinking, and the draft again became necessary. Some men tried to avoid the draft by mutilating themselves. The regulation translated here went into effect in A.D. 381.

[103] The Roman foot was a third of an inch shorter than the modern British or American foot; hence the height requirement was 5 feet 10 inches or 5 feet 8 inches in modern measures.
[104] The cavalry and the first cohorts were the highest-ranking, elite units, and may have demanded that recruits for their units be taller than recruits for lower-ranking cohorts. Perhaps the height requirement for the sixth cohort was more like 5 feet 6 inches.
[105] Or, in modern measure, 5 feet 5 inches. These may be recruits for lower-ranking cohorts.

277 *The Law Code of Theodosius* 7.13.10

Whoever tries to evade the bearing of arms by the shameful amputation of a finger shall not escape the service which he flees; but he shall be branded, and he who has declined military service as an honor shall endure it as a forced labor.

XII

The Provinces

PROVINCIAL ADMINISTRATION

During its first 250 years as a republic, the city of Rome gradually extended its influence throughout Italy, sometimes by military force, sometimes by diplomacy, until the whole Italian peninsula was under Roman domination. The peoples of the various towns and regions of Italy were allowed a moderate degree of autonomy, but they were enrolled as "allies" of Rome and forced to supply auxiliary contingents for the Roman army.[1] In addition, they sometimes lost land in confiscations and had colonies of Roman citizens imposed upon them.[2] They were, moreover, ultimately subject to decisions made by the magistrates, Senate, and popular assemblies in Rome. However, the Romans did not change the internal structure of a town's laws and government or send in Roman overlords. Instead they solicited the support of the ruling class which already existed in the town. And although the Italian allies eventually rebelled in 90 B.C. and demanded the rights and privileges of Roman citizenship,[3] all in all the Roman system for the pacification of Italy worked well.

Until 241 B.C., Rome had no overseas territory under its domination. At the conclusion of the First Punic War,[4] however, the defeated Carthage yielded to Rome its control over Sicily, and Sicily became Rome's first province. The Romans did not make Sicily an ally, but chose instead to treat the island as a subject territory which had to pay a tribute to Rome in return for enjoying its "protection." This protection was provided by a Roman governor and Roman troops stationed

[1] See the introduction to Chapter XI.

[2] On colonies and land confiscations, see notes 159 and 160 of Chapter VII.

[3] On the Social War, see note 2 of Chapter I.

Part of the reason for Rome's success in pacifying Italy was the fact that it made separate treaties of alliance with each town or region rather than forcing each newly dominated area to accommodate itself to some master plan. Each town thus thought of itself as directly allied to Rome. Moreover, loyal towns were often rewarded with special privileges or even citizenship. For example, the citizens of Arpinum, the hometown of Marius and Cicero, received the right to vote in the *comitia* of Rome in 188 B.C., 100 years before the Social War. The leading citizens of the town, such as Marius and Cicero, were thus eligible to run for political office in Rome. On the other hand, disloyal towns were punished brutally.

[4] First Punic War: 264–241 B.C.

on the island. The Romans did not establish a new government agency to deal with Sicily, such as an "Office of Provincial Affairs," but instead gave responsibility for the administration of Sicily and subsequent provinces to the Senate. Two centuries later, Rome controlled most of the Mediterranean world, and what had at first appeared a fairly simple task—maintaining order in Sicily—became a very complex operation as the number of provinces increased.[5] Rome's first province had been close to it, both geographically and culturally. Spain, however, and Gaul, Syria, Bithynia, and Africa, were all far from Rome and had their own special customs and presented their own special problems.

The Senate decided to choose men from its own rank to serve as governors of the provinces. Since the governor was the commander of the troops stationed in the province, he was usually a man who had already been consul or praetor, and he was thus called a proconsul or propraetor.[6] The assignment of provinces to governors was done by lot, although provinces requiring serious military action were reserved for proconsuls.[7] The main duty of the governor was to maintain peace and order in the province, and this meant (1) protecting it against foreign enemies and domestic agitators, and (2) serving as a judge in legal disputes.[8] The Romans demanded, however, that the provincials pay for these services, through indemnities and poll taxes. An indemnity was a large sum of money paid by a conquered nation to Rome in order to compensate Rome for the expenses incurred in fighting the war. A poll tax was an annual tax paid to Rome to reimburse it for the costs of maintaining a governor and a military force in the province. The Senate fixed the amount of the indemnity or poll tax but delegated the collection of these public revenues to private corporations. The employees of these corporations were often unmerciful in their collection of taxes, but the governor was expected to back them, with military force if necessary, since the revenues they were collecting belonged to the Roman people and he was a servant of the Roman people. If the province could not pay the indemnity or the poll tax, it frequently borrowed money from Roman businessmen (often the same men who had the contracts for tax collection) and was charged an exorbitant interest rate. Sometimes the provincials could then not pay even the interest on these loans and they sank deeper and deeper into debt. The behavior of the Roman publicans and money-lenders was one of the main reasons for the provincials' hatred of Roman rule.[9]

[5] As the Senate became more involved in foreign affairs and provincial administration, it accumulated more power in the state until its supremacy was unchallenged; see the introduction to selection 238. In the imperial period, Augustus weakened the Senate by removing provincial administration from its control; see selection 241.

[6] On the meaning of these terms, see note 131 of Chapter X.

[7] Consuls generally had more military experience than praetors. The Latin word *provincia* has two meanings: territorial possession or sphere of military activity. Governors were sent to territorial possessions, where there might, or might not, be military activity. Any new sphere of military activity in an area outside of Roman territory was usually the concern of that year's consuls, although a proconsular governor might invade neighboring territory on the pretext of maintaining peace in his own; consider Gabinius's invasion of Egypt, discussed in the introduction to selection 168.

These remarks about the selection of governors are true for the republican period; in the imperial period, the selection of governors rested ultimately with the emperor.

[8] Usually the governor's court moved about from district to district within the province; the governor had a fixed number of circuits.

[9] On equestrian activities in the provinces, see selections 167 and 168.

And the senatorial governors did little to redress the injuries caused by the publicans and moneylenders.[10] In addition, the opportunities for exploitation of the provincials by the governor and his staff were considerable, and few governors could resist the temptations. Indeed, exploitation in the provinces is one of the most scandalous aspects of Roman history. Roman politicians callously assumed that their positions gave them a license to plunder and that they would use their term in the provinces to enrich themselves at the expense of the provincials. They would blithely run up huge campaign debts, knowing that election to the consulship or praetorship meant a provincial governorship and a chance to amass a fortune. The most common form of exploitation was the demanding and accepting of bribes, not only from the provincials but also from Roman businessmen in the provinces. However, there were many other ways of extorting money—and the Roman governors knew them all.

The Publican Problem

Cicero's brother, Quintus Tullius Cicero,[11] was governor or propraetor of the province of Asia from 61 to 59 B.C.[12] Cicero wrote him a lengthy letter, only part of which is translated below, in which he discussed the duties and problems of a governor. The greatest problem, which Cicero himself encountered later in Cilicia, was reconciling the demands of the publicans with the welfare of the provincials. Some governors shamelessly ignored the welfare of the provincials and chose to assist the publicans—for a tidy profit, of course.

278   Cicero, *Letters to His Brother Quintus* 1.1.11 (32–34); 12 (35)

The publicans pose a serious problem to your efforts to be benevolent and diligent in your provincial administration. If we oppose them, we will alienate from both ourselves and the government a class[13] which has deserved the best from us and has, through our efforts, begun to reconcile itself with the government. Yet, if we defer to them in every situation, we will allow to be ruined utterly those people whose safety and welfare must be our concern. To tell the truth, this is the only problem in your whole administration. The other requirements—to be temperate, to control your emotions, to keep your staff in check,[14] to uphold a fair system of justice, to show yourself to be gracious in investigating legal cases and in listening to and giving audiences to men—these are not problems but rather grand opportunities because they demand no real exertion but simply strong determination and inclination. The depth, however, of the bitterness which this question of the publicans causes among our allies has been impressed upon us recently by our own citizens. When the harbor taxes in Italy were lifted, they complained not so much of the taxes as of certain offenses by the tax col-

---

[10] On relationships between the senatorial and equestrian classes, see selection 240.
[11] For more on Cicero's brother, see selections 60, 123, 205, and 236.
[12] *province of Asia:* see map 5.
[13] *a class:* the equestrian class.
[14] The governor's staff was often as venal as the governor.

lectors.[15] I therefore know what happens to our allies in far-off lands when I hear such complaints from citizens in Italy. And to act in such a way that you satisfy the publicans, especially when their contract for tax collection has proved unprofitable, yet do not allow our allies to be ruined—this apparently requires a certain divine excellence which you, of course, possess. . . .

Asia should bear in mind that the calamity both of foreign war and of internal strife would befall her if she were not part of our Empire. This Empire, however, cannot in any way be maintained without taxes, and she should therefore happily pay for this continual peace and tranquility, which benefits her, with some portion of what she produces.[16] If the allies will patiently put up with the idea and the name of "publican," then all other aspects of our rule can be mitigated for them by your wisdom and prudence.

Cicero as Governor

When Cicero was appointed governor of Cilicia for 51–50 B.C., he was an unwilling appointee. A new regulation, requiring a five-year interval between the consulship and proconsulship meant that the consuls of 51 B.C. could not become proconsuls in 50 B.C.[17] Therefore, ex-consuls, such as Cicero, who had been consul in 63 B.C., were pressed into service as governors. Although Cicero did not want to leave Rome at this critical period,[18] he accepted the appointment as a duty. He tried to be a fair and considerate governor, and to alleviate the suffering caused by Appius Claudius Pulcher, his predecessor as governor.[19]

279   Cicero, *Letters to Atticus* 5.16.2, 3; 5.21.7

In short, these people are very weary of life. However, these wretched and impoverished towns are gaining some relief because they are burdened by no expenses for me or my staff officers or the quaestor[20] or anyone else in my retinue. I'll have you know that not only do we not accept fodder, or any other contribution which can be made under the Julian law,[21] but none of us will accept firewood or anything else except four

---

[15] Collection of harbor taxes, customs taxes, and revenue from public lands was let out in contracts by the Senate; see the introduction to selections 165 and 166.

[16] For similar justifications of the Roman position, see selection 283.

[17] Previously a consul had gone to a province as proconsul as soon as his one-year term of office in Rome expired.

[18] The alliance between Caesar and Pompey had ruptured. Pompey was in Rome; Caesar was in Gaul, as governor, with command of a huge army. His political enemies were attempting to have him recalled. He was threatening to use the Roman legions under his command to protect himself. (In January of 49 B.C., Caesar did lead his troops into Italy and seize power in Rome.)

[19] For more on the suffering caused by Appius Claudius, see selection 167. (This selection is a continuation of the letter translated in that selection.)

[20] It was customary for one quaestor to be appointed financial secretary to the staff of each governor. In 75 B.C., for example, Cicero had been quaestor in Sicily; see the introduction to selection 281.

[21] The governor traveled about his province regularly to hear legal cases. He was allowed to demand supplies from the inhabitants of each town he visited. The townspeople would

beds and a roof, and, in many places, not even a roof since we usually camp in a tent. . . .

During the first six months of my administration, the people of my province received from me no requisitions for supplies and endured no billeting. Before my term as governor, this period each year had been used for making a profit. The wealthy districts used to pay great sums of money to the governor to avoid having Roman soldiers billeted there over the winter. Indeed the people of Cyprus used to pay 200 Attic talents.[22] While I am governor, however, not a single penny will be demanded.

The Noble Brutus

It was not only the equestrians who exploited the provincials and made fantastic profits from money lending and tax collection in the provinces; many a senator was a silent, or not so silent, partner in these ventures. Cicero was, however, shocked to find, while he was governor of Cilicia, that the noble Brutus[23] was involved in a particularly shameless moneymaking venture. The following passage is a translation of several selections from two letters from Cicero to Atticus. We learn from it much about the role of both the senatorial and the equestrian orders in exploiting the provincials.

280   Cicero, *Letters to Atticus* 5.21.10–12; 6.1.3–6, 16

Let me tell you about Brutus. Your friend Brutus is a close associate of certain creditors of the city of Salamis in Cyprus, namely Marcus Scaptius and Publius Matinius.[24] In fact, he warmly recommended them to me. I have not yet met Matinius, but Scaptius came to visit me in camp. I promised him that I would make sure, for Brutus's sake, that the people of Salamis paid him his money.[25] He thanked me and asked me for a position as prefect. I told him, as I have told you, that I have always refused to appoint businessmen to my staff.[26] . . . Our friend Appius had given him command of cavalry

therefore be required to feed and stable his horses, and to feed and house him and his staff. Many governors abused this privilege and made excessive or unreasonable demands on the townspeople. The Julian law of 59 B.C., which was named after its initiator, Gaius Julius Caesar, tried to regulate what supplies could be demanded by a governor. Cicero could legitimately have required fodder, firewood, and comfortable housing for himself and his staff, but he chose not to.

[22] *talents:* Billeting must have been a ruinous expense on a community if the provincials were willing to pay the governor such a huge bribe to escape it. A talent was a Greek weight equivalent in monetary value to 6000 drachmas. One Greek drachma was approximately equivalent to one Roman denarius.

[23] *Brutus:* Marcus Junius Brutus. He was later one of the assassins of Julius Caesar; see note 72 of Chapter IX.

[24] At this point, Cicero has not yet learned that these men are in fact business agents for Brutus.

[25] *his money:* the money loaned to the people of Salamis; the amount was 106 talents. They had borrowed it to pay off an already existing loan. Cicero thinks the money belonged to Scaptius.

[26] It was a wise decision on Cicero's part to try to keep separate the business and military personnel in the province.

squadrons with which he could force the Salaminians to make their loan payments; he also gave him the prefecture.[27] He was harassing the Salaminians. I ordered the cavalrymen to leave Cyprus. Scaptius was very angry. However, in order to keep my promise to him,[28] I ordered the Salaminians, when they and Scaptius came to see me at Tarsus,[29] to pay off the debt. They complained at length about the loan and about their mistreatment by Scaptius. I refused to listen. I urged and begged them to settle this matter in respect for my good services to their community. Finally I said that I would force them. These men then did not refuse to pay, but even declared that they would be paying at my expense, since I had not accepted the money which they usually gave to the governor.[30] . . . "Good," said Scaptius, "let us calculate the total amount owed." Now I had, in my praetor's edict,[31] stated that I would observe an interest rate of 1 percent per month compounded annually. But Scaptius demanded 4 percent according to the terms of his loan.[32] "That's ridiculous," I said. "I can't act in contradiction to my own edict!" But he produced a decree of the Senate, passed in the consulship of Lentulus and Philippus,[33] which ordered the governor of Cilicia to make his judgments according to the terms of this loan contract! . . . These friends of Brutus, relying on his political influence, had been willing to lend money to the Salaminians at 48 percent interest if the Senate would protect them with a decree.[34]

Cicero's second letter to Atticus was written a few days after the first. He has now learned that it was Brutus's money that was loaned to the Salaminians at 48 percent interest and Brutus's money that was protected by a senatorial decree. First, however, he tells Atticus about another community driven to bankruptcy by the greed of Roman moneylenders.

Pompey's agents have begun to put pressure on King Ariobarzanes.[35] . . . The money owed to Pompey is now being paid off at the rate of 33 Attic talents per thirty days, and this sum comes from taxes, but still it is not enough to cover even the

[27] Appius (see selection 167) was less wise and more greedy than Cicero. Scaptius probably paid him quite handsomely for the appointment as prefect and then used his position as a military officer to order the Roman soldiers to threaten and harass the provincials who were delinquent in their loan payments. Appius, by the way, was the father-in-law of Brutus, to whom the loan money actually belonged.

[28] *promise:* that he, Cicero, would urge the Salaminians to pay their loan.

[29] *Tarsus:* the chief city of Cilicia.

[30] A provincial community expected to pay each governor large sums of bribe money or to make him gifts in return, it hoped, for his support and consideration. Cicero had made it clear upon his arrival that he did not expect these gifts.

[31] *praetor's edict:* when a praetor entered office, he issued an edict in which he explained the legal procedures he would follow and the rules he would impose during his term of office; see note 245 of Chapter X. He could always, of course, issue further legislation during his term of office.

[32] 12 percent annually versus an astounding 48 percent annually.

[33] 56 B.C.

[34] And their friends in the Senate made sure they were so protected.

[35] *Ariobarzanes:* King of Cappadocia, a district of Asia Minor bordering on Cilicia. Although Cappadocia did not become a Roman province until the reign of Tiberius, it was in Cicero's time an area "protected" by the Romans. The king had obviously become deeply in debt to Roman moneylenders. His people were taxed heavily to raise money to pay off the debts, but they were unable to raise even enough to pay the interest on the loans.

monthly interest. However, our friend Gnaeus[36] is taking this tolerantly; he receives no payment on the principal, and he is content with even less than the full interest due. The king does not pay off his debts to anyone else. He can't! He has no treasury and no revenue. He has imposed a tax system modeled on that of Appius,[37] but it produces scarcely enough to pay the interest to Pompey. . . . I am constantly writing letters to the king to beseech, persuade, and reproach him. Deiotarus also told me that he had sent to him a delegation in connection with the debt to Brutus,[38] but it had brought back to him the reply that the king did not have any money. By Hercules, I myself am convinced that no kingdom has been more thoroughly stripped of its wealth, no king has been more impoverished. . . .

Now let me tell you about the Salaminians. I see that the incident there surprised you as much as it surprised me. I never heard Brutus say that the money involved was his. In fact, I even have a document of his in which it is stated: "The Salaminians owe money to Marcus Scaptius and Publius Matinius, my friends." He recommends them to me; he even adds, as an extra incentive to me, that he had insured a large sum of money for them against his own property. I had arranged that the Salaminians pay off their debt at 12 percent compounded annually. But Scaptius demanded 48 percent. . . . And at this very moment he thrust in my face a letter from Brutus stating that he, Brutus, had made the loan from his own funds, a fact which Brutus had never disclosed to me or to you, and requesting that I award to Scaptius a prefecture. But I had already told him, through you, that I would not award a prefecture to a businessman. And even if I did, it would surely not be to Scaptius. He had been prefect under Appius and had command of cavalry squadrons with which he locked the Senate of Salamis in their senate house and besieged them. Five senators died from starvation! On the very day on which I reached my province . . . I sent a letter ordering the cavalrymen to leave the island immediately. For this reason, I suppose Scaptius has written to Brutus some rather prejudiced remarks about me. However, my mind is made up. If Brutus thinks that I ought to have imposed 48 percent interest, even though I had agreed to 12 percent throughout the whole province and had announced this publicly, and even the most hard-nosed moneylenders had approved; if he is complaining because I denied a prefecture to a businessman; . . . if he is annoyed because I ordered the cavalry out, I shall be sorry, of course, to have angered him, but much sorrier that he is not the man I thought he was.[39] . . .

You seem to be curious about how I manage the publicans.[40] With great delicacy! I humor them, I flatter them, I treat them with deference—and I make sure that they harm no one! Most amazing is this: even Servilius[41] observed the interest rates speci-

---

[36] *Gnaeus* Pompeius Magnus or, more simply, Pompey: the great Roman general and one member of the First Triumvirate. Here is another case of a Roman senator being involved in money-lending in the provinces.

[37] *Appius:* Appius Claudius Pulcher.

[38] Brutus had also loaned money to Ariobarzanes.

[39] Cicero has found himself in a very awkward position. He wants to treat the people of Salamis fairly, but he does not want to risk alienating Brutus, who was a very powerful political figure. In the end, Cicero did nothing and left the problem to his successor in office.

[40] *the publicans:* the tax collectors, who are private businessmen, not government employees. They did, however, expect the assistance of the governor.

[41] *Servilius:* an earlier governor of Cicilia who, like Cicero, had tried to treat the provincials fairly. However, he did allow the publicans to fix whatever interest rate they wished on tax contracts.

fied by the publicans in the tax contracts; but I do something else. I fix a day, well in advance, and announce that if they[42] make their payments before that date, I shall apply an interest rate of 1 percent per month. If they don't make the payment by then, they will be charged interest according to the original contract. So the provincials pay a tolerable interest, and the publicans are pleased with the arrangement.

A Most Unscrupulous Governor

In 76 B.C., when Cicero was thirty years old, he was elected quaestor for 75 B.C. During his year in office, he was sent to Sicily to work on the governor's staff. He favorably impressed the Sicilians because of his diligence and honesty. In 73 B.C., a senator named Gaius Verres became governor of Sicily and held that position for three years. He was thoroughly shameless and unscrupulous in using his position to enrich himself, and by the time he left Sicily many of its inhabitants were destitute. The Sicilians sent a delegation to Rome and brought Verres to trial on charges of extortion.[43] They asked Cicero to speak for the prosecution. He accepted the position, although it was both difficult and dangerous; Verres's defense lawyer was Quintus Hortensius, the most brilliant speaker of the period, and Verres had, as political allies, many members of the old nobility. If Cicero failed to secure a conviction, he would destroy his political future; but if he won the case, he would gain immediate fame and certainly promote his career. He chose to gamble because, as a "new man," he desperately needed the renown which a court victory would bring. Cicero traveled to Sicily and collected a mass of evidence. On the first day of the trial, he presented such damning evidence against Verres, and presented it so brilliantly, that Verres knew he would be convicted and so retired from Rome in voluntary exile.[44] Yet Cicero had presented only a small part of the information about Verres's innumerable atrocities. He therefore published five more speeches which set forth in great detail the misconduct of Verres. Cicero's success in this trial ensured strong political support for the future. In addition, he superseded Hortensius as the most distinguished orator of the period.

The passages translated below reveal all too clearly the unscrupulous exploitation to which provincials were subject. One might wish that Verres was a unique example of predatory behavior, but such governors were probably all too common. These passages from Cicero's speeches also provide an interesting insight into trial procedures in a Roman court.

[42] *they:* the provincials.

[43] In 149 B.C., the Senate had established a permanent court or standing tribunal to try cases of provincial administrators charged with extortion. All the jurymen were senators, and it was therefore very difficult for provincials to receive a fair hearing from men who would obviously protect one another's "right" to plunder the provinces. In 122 B.C. Gaius Gracchus changed the composition of the court to equestrians, but by the time of Verres's trial, the jurymen were again all senators.

[44] He went to Massilia (modern Marseilles). It was quite legal for a defendant to withdraw before the end of the trial. Since Roman citizens could not be executed, exile from Italy was the most severe punishment which the court could assign a man of senatorial rank (men of the lower-classes could be scourged or sent to work in the mines; see selections 5 and 6). Realizing that he would be convicted, Verres simply chose his own place of exile. After his departure, the court passed an official sentence of exile and a fine to compensate the losses the Sicilians had suffered. Verres died in exile in 43 B.C.

281   Cicero, *The Prosecution of Verres* 1:1–3, 10–15, 18–20, 22, 23;
2(1):32, 33, 63–67, 69, 72, 74–76; 2(2):68–71, 74, 75, 120, 121, 169,
170, 186–188, 190, 191; 2(3):56–58, 100, 101, 103, 188, 189;
2(4):1, 4, 7, 49; 2(5):139, 147, 160–162, 169, 170

Gentlemen of the jury:[45] . . . An opinion harmful both to you and to our republic
has taken root and has spread not only throughout Rome but even throughout foreign
lands and is discussed by everyone, everywhere: the opinion that no one who has
money can be convicted by the courts as they are now constituted.[46] And now, at this
critical point for the senatorial class and for your position as jurors,[47] . . . Gaius
Verres has been brought before you to stand trial, a man already condemned, in the
opinion of everyone, everywhere, by his life and his deeds, yet expecting, even predicting, acquittal because of his vast wealth.[48] . . . If you judge this man strictly and
scrupulously, you will retain the influence and authority which you ought always to
have. . . .

I can easily see what his hopes and intentions are. However, I do not understand,
when I consider the praetor[49] and members of this court, how he can be so confident
that he will fulfill his intentions. . . . Who is so shrewd, or so eloquent, or so fluent
that he could defend, even in part, the life of this man,[50] a life convicted of so many
vices and crimes, a life condemned long ago by the will and judgment of the whole
world. . . . He piled up the greatest—both in number and in consequence—demon-
strations of all his vices when he was governor of Sicily. In just three years he so
thoroughly despoiled and ruined that province that it can in no way be restored to its
former state; indeed, it scarcely seems possible that even a lapse of many years and a
succession of conscientious governors could rehabilitate it even partially. While Verres
was governor of Sicily, its inhabitants had access to neither their own laws, nor our
senatorial decrees, nor the rights universally allowed to men.[51] Each Sicilian now possesses only as much as either escaped the notice of this very greedy, very lecherous

[45] *Gentlemen of the jury:* in fact, the members of the court served both as jurors and
judges.

[46] At the time of Verres's trial, the members of the standing courts were selected from
the senatorial class; however, legislation was being proposed to include members of the equestrian class (equestrians had served as court members from the time of Gaius Gracchus to
Sulla, who switched control of the courts back to the senatorial class). This proposed legislation was prompted by people's disgust with the corruption of the senatorial courts where
bribery was rampant ("no one who has money can be convicted"). For comments on bribery
in the army, see selections 273 and 274.

[47] The senatorial class may lose their control over the courts.

[48] Cicero was a very clever speaker; at the very beginning of the trial, he has put the jury
on the spot: "The whole world thinks you are corrupt and open to bribes. The Roman people
want to remove you from the courts. Verres says openly he will bribe you and gain acquittal.
Show the world you are honest—by convicting Verres."
Notice also that a Roman lawyer could say virtually anything about his opponents. Here
Cicero insinuates that the whole world knows about Verres and has already condemned him.

[49] A praetor was the presiding officer of a standing court.

[50] We should imagine Cicero pointing his finger at Verres in court and emphasizing with
his voice, "this man," "he," and so on.

[51] The Romans accepted the concept of universal or common law; see selections 253
and 254.

swine, or remained after he glutted his lusts. For three years, not one legal case was decided without some interference by him; no one had such absolute right to his father's or his grandfather's property that the courts would not take it away from him if Verres so demanded. Countless sums of money were extorted from the pockets of the farmers under a new and immoral regulation. Our most loyal allies were treated like enemies. Roman citizens were tortured and executed like slaves.[52] The most guilty of men were acquitted in court because of their bribes, while very honest and scrupulous men were prosecuted and tried in their absence, convicted, and exiled. Heavily fortified harbors and very large, well-defended cities were left exposed to pirates and bandits.[53] Sicilian sailors and soldiers, however, our allies and friends, were starved to death. Our finest and best-equipped fleets were lost or destroyed. What an appalling disgrace for us, the Roman people! . . .

Now, about his adulteries and debaucheries—a sense of decency makes me shrink from describing his outrageous lewdness. And I also do not wish, by describing them, to add to the anguish of those who were not able to save their children and wives from his lust. . . . I don't think there is one human being alive today who has heard the name of this man and cannot also describe his loathsome deeds. And so I am more afraid that you might think I have overlooked many of his atrocities than that you might think I have invented some. Indeed, the large crowd which has assembled here today to listen to the proceedings does not, I think, want to learn from me the facts of the case, but rather to review with me the facts it already knows.[54] . . .

When Hortensius had been elected consul and was being escorted home from the Campus Martius by a large crowd of supporters, they happened to meet up with Gaius Curio.[55] . . . Curio called out to Verres by name and congratulated him in a loud voice. He didn't say a word to Hortensius himself, who, after all, had just been elected consul,[56] or to his relatives and friends who were with him. Instead, he went over to Verres, embraced him, and told him not to worry. "I hereby proclaim," he said, "that today's election results have ensured your acquittal." His remark was immediately reported to me by the many very honest men who heard it.[57] . . . How is it that a

[52] Roman courts did not normally sentence Roman citizens to execution.

[53] Piracy was a continual and serious problem in the Mediterranean world. Julius Caesar was once kidnapped by pirates and held for ransom. His family had the money to pay the ransom. Poor victims were usually murdered by the pirates or sold into slavery. It was, of course, the duty of the governor to provide military protection in his province.

[54] It was quite acceptable in Roman court procedure for a lawyer to use exaggeration or insinuation to prejudice a jury; hence the very great importance of having a skillful lawyer argue your case.

[55] On the identity of Hortensius, see the introduction to this selection. Elections for consul were held in the summer, although the consul-designate did not take office until the beginning of the next year. Thus, Hortensius was elected in the summer of 70 B.C., Verres's trial took place in the autumn of 70 B.C., and Hortensius assumed office as consul in January of 69 B.C. (The other consul-designate was Quintus Metellus, also a friend of Verres.) It is certainly to Cicero's credit that he was willing to plead the case for the prosecution when the defense lawyer was Hortensius, the famous orator and consul-designate.

Elections for consul (and praetor and censor) were held in the Comitia Centuriata which met in the Campus Martius.

Gaius Curio had been consul in 76 B.C.

[56] And therefore apparently deserved the congratulations which Curio instead gave Verres.

[57] Such unsubstantiated rumors would not be permitted in today's courts or would be excluded as hearsay.

defendant one day thinks that he is sure to be convicted, but the next day, when his lawyer has been elected consul, is acquitted?[58] . . .

I received an interesting piece of information from certain men who keep me posted about all such matters: quite a few baskets filled with Sicilian money had been handed over by a certain senator to a Roman equestrian; about ten of these baskets had been left at that senator's house, earmarked for my defeat in the elections; the bribe distributors for all the tribes had been summoned to Verres's house one night.[59] One of these distributors, who felt obligated to offer me all the assistance he could, came to my house that very same night and told me what Verres had said to them. He reminded them how generous he had been to them in the past, both when he himself had campaigned for the praetorship[60] and at the recent elections of the consuls and praetors.[61] Then he had immediately promised them as much money as they wished if they would prevent me from gaining the aedileship. . . .

I must keep close track of the time which I have been allotted for my speech to you because I intend to present every detail of this case. However, I shall pass over the extremely indecent and scandalous "first act," as it were, of Verres's life.[62] He won't hear from me one word about the scandals of his boyhood years, not one word about his debauched adolescent years (you remember what they were like). . . . Please make allowances for my sense of decency and permit me to be silent about some aspects of the lewdness of this man. As far as I am concerned, let the whole time prior to when he embarked upon a political career remain unchallenged. Let there be silence about his all-night drinking parties and orgies. Let no mention be made of the pimps, and the gamblers, and the panders. Let us pass over his squandering of his father's money and his vile behavior as a youth. . . .

Cicero describes in detail the misconduct and criminal actions of Verres when he was quaestor and when he served as legate on the staff of the governor of Cilicia.

---

[58] Cicero is cautioning the members of the court not to be intimidated and vote for Verres's acquittal simply because his lawyer is the consul-designate.

[59] Cicero's remarks indicate how prevalent election bribery was. In the summer of 70 B.C., Cicero was campaigning for the aedileship of 69 B.C. Verres and his friends tried to arrange his defeat, hoping thereby to discourage him from prosecuting Verres. They spent huge sums of money, which Cicero suggests had been illegally extorted from the Sicilians, to bribe the voters. Large bribes were given to men of equestrian rank. Money was also distributed to the lower classes through agents. Verres may have been excessive in his bribery, but he was not alone. It was evidently quite common for candidates to hire bribe distributors from each of the tribes to pass on bribes to members of the tribes. (Despite Verres's generous bribes, Cicero won the election. Thus, he was aedile-designate at the time of this trial.)

[60] Verres had been praetor in 74 B.C. and had then gone to Sicily as propraetor or governor in 73 B.C.

[61] The elections for consuls and praetors, which were held in the Comitia Centuriata, took place a short time before the elections for aediles and quaestors, which were held in the Comitia Tributa.

[62] A delightful example of the rhetorical figure praeteritio. Praeteritio is a Latin word meaning "pass over." Cicero claims he will ignore or "pass over" Verres's earlier misdeeds, but, even in claiming to ignore them, he of course brings them to the attention of the audience. The rhetorical education which boys of wealthy families received made them clever and manipulative speakers.

On the shores of the Hellespont is a town called Lampsacus, one of the most famous and well-known towns in Asia.[63] The people of Lampsacus are extremely helpful to all Roman citizens traveling there, and are moreover peaceful and quiet. . . . Verres was lodged as a guest in the home of a certain Ianitor.[64] . . . As was his custom, that is, as his shameless lusts urged him to do, he at once set his staff to work— all of them especially wicked and disreputable men—at looking around and making inquiries about whether there was any girl or woman so desirable that he should extend his stay in Lampsacus. . . . Rubrius, one of the men on his staff, reported to him that there was a certain Philodamus, who was easily the leading citizen of Lampsacus by virtue of his family background, his official position, his wealth, and his good reputation; and that Philodamus had a daughter, who lived at home since she had not yet married and who was a woman of exceptional beauty, but also, it was reputed, of impeccable chastity and modesty. When Verres heard this, he seethed with passion. [He arranged to have Rubrius lodged in the house of Philodamus.] Philodamus had always been considered very hospitable and friendly toward the Romans, and he did not want it thought that he had received even a man like Rubrius into his house unwillingly. In keeping with his position as one of the wealthiest men in town, he planned an elegant and lavish dinner party and asked Rubrius to invite anyone he pleased, reserving only one place for Philodamus himself, since even his son, an exceptional young man, would be sent out to have dinner with a relative.[65] Rubrius invited the men on Verres's staff, and Verres told them what they should do.

The guests arrived and took their places on the couches. They chatted and drank. Their host urged them to drink more, and they asked for larger goblets. The conversations and laughter grew louder and louder as everyone talked at once. When Rubrius decided that the party had warmed up enough, he said to Philodamus, "I wonder, Philodamus, why you don't have your daughter called in to see us." The eminently strait-laced and elderly father was astonished by the suggestion of this fiendish man. Rubrius pressed him. Finally, in order to say something, Philodamus said that it was not customary among the Greeks for women to attend a men's dinner party. Then someone in another part of the room cried out, "This is really quite intolerable. Let someone call the woman!" At this very moment, Rubrius ordered his slaves to shut the front door and to stand guard in the entranceway. When Philodamus realized that Verres had planned and arranged all this in order to rape his daughter, he called his slaves and told them not to worry about him, but to save his daughter. One was to run to tell his son about this great calamity at home. Within moments, the whole house was in turmoil. The town's leading citizen, a very honorable gentleman, was being pushed around in his own home while his slaves fought those of Rubrius. Everyone was fighting. And then Rubrius poured boiling water over Philodamus.

---

[63] That is, in the province of Asia.

[64] Verres was at this time legate on the staff of the governor of Cilicia. Although Lampsacus was in the province of Asia, not Cilicia, Verres had traveled there on official business. Townsmen like Ianitor were expected to entertain Roman officials free of charge; see selection 279.

[65] Although Roman women frequently attended dinner parties, Greek women (Lampsacus was a Greek town) did not. Therefore, Philodamus's daughter remained in the house, in the women's quarters, during the party. The son, however, would be expected to attend the party if he were at home. Philodamus sent him out of the house, because he did not wish his son to mix with men like Rubrius and Verres.

When the son received the message, he was terrified and immediately rushed home to save his father's life and his sister's honor. When the people of Lampsacus heard what was happening, they all became angry as they thought of the respectability of Philodamus and the magnitude of the outrage perpetrated against him. They gathered that night in front of his house. And during that night, Cornelius, one of Verres's bodyguards, who had been stationed by Rubrius along with his slaves to clear the way for the kidnapping of the woman, was killed. Several slaves were wounded, and Rubrius himself was hurt in the fray. When Verres saw what a great commotion his lust had caused, he was eager to find a method of escape. . . .

The next day, all the townspeople headed toward the house in which Verres was staying. They threw rocks at the door and beat on it with iron weapons. Then they piled wood and brush around it and set a fire. However, some Roman citizens, who were in Lampsacus on business, rushed up and pleaded with the townspeople to consider Verres's rank as legate a more serious concern than the outrage he had committed as legate. They said that they knew he was an indecent and wicked man, but, because he had not accomplished what he had attempted, and because he would not be in Lampsacus again, they, the townspeople, would be less at fault if they spared an evil man than if they murdered a legate. . . .

Verres persuaded the Roman governor of Asia to prosecute Philodamus and his son on charges of murder in connection with the death of Cornelius, Verres's bodyguard. And Verres was chosen as a member of the jury. Also on the jury were Roman administrators, military officers, and businessmen, all of whom had an interest in seeing that Roman authority in the provinces not be subject to challenge.

Gentlemen of the jury, please listen to what happened, and then have pity on our allies. Let them see that they are not mistaken in looking to you for some support. . . . Although the prosecution used all its force and all its might, although poor Philodamus had many prosecutors and not one defender, . . . although Verres himself was not only a witness but also a member of court, and had even prepared the case for the prosecution, . . . nevertheless the jury felt that Verres's behavior the night of Cornelius's death had been so outrageous, and that Verres was so unscrupulous, that they deferred their decision until a second hearing was held. . . . At the second hearing, Philodamus and his son were found guilty, but by a very small majority. In the forum of Laodicea, a cruel and barbarous spectacle occurred, a spectacle which caused pain and bitterness throughout the whole province of Asia, the spectacle of an aged father and of his son being led out for execution, the former because he tried to defend the purity of his children, the latter because he tried to save his father's life and his sister's honor. Each wept, but not for his own fate. The father wept for his son, the son for his father. . . . How deep do you think was the grief, how loud the lamentations of the people of Lampsacus? Two innocent men, two excellent men, friends and allies of the Roman people, were executed, beheaded, because of the unparalleled wickedness and cruel lustfulness of this incredibly shameless man. . . .

Sopater of Halicyae[66] was one of the wealthiest and most respected citizens of that

[66] *Halicyae:* a town in Sicily. Cicero is now describing Verres's crimes as governor of Sicily.

town. During the governorship of Gaius Sacerdos, his enemies had charged him with a criminal offense, but he had easily gained acquittal. Verres succeeded Sacerdos as governor. The same enemies prosecuted Sopater again, on the same charge. Sopater thought the trial would be no problem, both because he was innocent and because he assumed that Verres would not dare to overturn Sacerdos's judgment. He was summoned to court in Syracuse. . . . While preparations were being made for the trial, Timarchides, a freedman and agent[67] of Verres, . . . told Sopater that his prosecutors and enemies intended to offer Verres a bribe, but that Verres would prefer to receive a bribe from Sopater for his acquittal (since he would rather not overturn his predecessor's judgment). . . . Sopater gave Timarchides 80,000 sesterces. When the trial began, all of Sopater's supporters were free of fear and anxiety. After all, the charge had no basis, the case had already been judged, and Verres had received the bribe money. Who could doubt the outcome? After the first day of proceedings, however, Timarchides again approached Sopater and said that his accusers had offered Verres a much larger bribe than he, Sopater, had given him. . . . "Do whatever you like," replied Sopater, "I won't give you a penny more."

The next day, the court reconvened. Sopater's sole hope for acquittal rested entirely on this one fact: the presence and good reputation of the men on the jury. They were the same men who had before acquitted him on the same charge.

However, Verres, by a clever ruse, managed to have all the members of the jury dismissed from court. Sopater's lawyer angrily left the courtroom, refusing to plead a case when the jury had been dismissed. Verres was faced with the decision of adjourning the trial until the jury could be reassembled (in which case Sopater would be acquitted), or of convicting him, without a jury present, without a defense lawyer present, and of reversing his predecessor's judgment (in which case Verres would be hated and reviled).

His mind seethed with indecision. He leaned first this way, and then that way, not only in his mind but with his whole body.[68] Everyone in the courtroom could see that fear and greed were pulling his mind in opposite directions. There was a very large crowd of spectators present, but they were absolutely silent, waiting anxiously to see how his greed would overpower him. Timarchides, his agent, kept whispering in his ear. Finally Verres said, "Come on, then, speak your case." Sopater begged and pleaded to have the case tried before a jury, to no avail. Verres at once ordered the witnesses to be called. One or two spoke briefly. There was no cross-examination. The court clerk announced that the case had been heard. . . . Verres quickly leapt up from his seat and pronounced Sopater, an innocent man who had been acquitted by Sacerdos, "Guilty."

Cicero described many other instances where Verres encouraged the parties in legal cases to pay him bribes. He then discussed instances where Verres made appointments to public offices dependent on bribery.

---

[67] On freedmen agents, see the introduction to the section on reasons for manumission in Chapter IX.

[68] Verres is fidgeting nervously. Students of rhetoric, such as Cicero, learned both how to convey and how to describe emotional states; see selection 143.

From the testimony you have heard, you can now see that throughout Sicily, for three years, no one, in any city at all, became a senator free of charge; that no one became senator except by Verres's spoken or written order; that the appointment of every senator was, in the first place, done without an election and, in the second place, done without regard to the social rank according to which it is usually considered appropriate to select senators. Neither property value, nor age, nor any other qualification which the Sicilians normally require was given consideration. Anyone who wanted to become a senator, however young, however unqualified, however low in social rank, always became a senator if the amount of money he offered Verres was large enough.

Cicero next exposed the collusion between Verres and the businessmen in the province of Sicily.

Lucius Carpinatius was the director for the company which collected rents on public pastures in Sicily.[69] . . . He also lent money to those who wanted to buy something from Verres. His loan operation, however, was run in such a way, gentlemen of the jury, that the profit even from it came to Verres here. Carpinatius used to enter under the heading "Paid Out" the sums of money which he lent to those who negotiated loans with him. However, he entered the exact same sums under the heading "Received," either received from Timarchides or received from Verres himself.[70] . . . When I was in Syracuse looking through the company's accounts which Carpinatius kept,[71] some entries showed that the same men who had given money to Verres had taken out loans from Carpinatius. . . . And the dates at which they ransomed themselves from some desperate situation by the payment of a bribe corresponds not only year for year but actually month for month with the accounts of the company. While I was checking these figures carefully, and had the account books in my hands, I suddenly noticed some erasures, as if the tablets had been recently tampered with.[72] Filled with suspicion, I fixed my eyes and attention on certain entries. There were sums of money entered under the heading "Received from Gaius Verrucius." However, although the letters up to the second R were clear, the remaining letters had been written over an erasure.[73] There were two, three, four—a large number of entries of this kind. Since these erasures in the tablets obviously indicated some foul play and dirty dealing, I asked Carpinatius who this Verrucius was with whom he had business amounting to such large sums. Carpinatius hesitated, squirmed a bit, and blushed. . . . I had discovered, when I compared the months and the years of entries in the books, that this Verrucius had had no account with Carpinatius either before the arrival of Gaius Verres or after his departure. I demanded that he tell me who this Verrucius was. A merchant? A banker? A farmer? A rancher? Was he still in Sicily, or had he left? The Sicilians said that there had never been anyone in Sicily named Verrucius. I insisted that he tell me who this man was, where he was, where he had come from, and why the company slave who

[69] The collection of rents on public pastures was done by publicans who had a contract with the Roman state. The main directors of the company probably lived in Rome. Carpinatius was head of the "branch office."

[70] That is, Verres, through the agency of Carpinatius, was actually lending money to the same people from whom he demanded bribes.

[71] Cicero had gone to Sicily before the trial to collect evidence.

[72] The records were kept on waxed tablets. On erasing a waxed tablet, see selection 132.

[73] Cicero is suggesting that the name was originally "Verres," that the final "es" had been erased from the wax and that "ucius" had been written in the erased area.

kept the books always made a mistake when writing the name of Verrucius in a particular place. . . .

Since Carpinatius would not answer me then, you, Verres, please tell me now who you think this Verrucius is, whose family name is so similar to yours. It is impossible that you were not acquainted with a man who was, as I observed, in Sicily during your governorship and who was, as I noticed from the account books, wealthy. But, rather than prolong this issue and risk causing confusion, step forward, gentlemen of the jury, and unroll[74] this transcript and copy of the tablets so that everyone, everywhere, can see not just the tracks but the actual den of Avarice. Do you see the word *Verrucius?* Do you see how the first letters have not been touched? Do you see the last part of the name, how the tail is sitting in the erasure as if in mud?[75] So, gentlemen of the jury, these are the accounts, just as you see them. What are you waiting for? What further information do you need? And you, Verres, why do you just sit there, doing nothing? You must either produce Verrucius for us, or confess that you are Verrucius. . . .

Polemarchus was an honest, respectable citizen of Murgentia. He was ordered to hand over 800 bushels of grain from his 50-acre farm.[76] Because he refused, he was dragged off to Verres for judgment, but in Verres's own house. Verres, in fact, was still in bed! Polemarchus was brought into the bedroom, a favor usually permitted to no one except women and tax collectors. There he was beaten, punched, and kicked until finally, although he had earlier refused to hand over 800 bushels, he promised 1000. . . .

In the region near Centuripa, there were three brothers—Sostratus, Numenius, and Nymphodorus—who fled from their land because they had been ordered to hand over more than they had even harvested. Verres's henchman Apronius then went to their farm with his thugs, seized all their equipment, carried off the slaves, and led away their livestock. Later Nymphodorus went to see Apronius at Aetna and begged him to give him back his property. Apronius, however, ordered him to be seized and suspended from a wild olive tree in the forum. And so this friend and ally of the Roman people, this farmer who supplies our grain, hung from that tree in the forum of a town which is friendly to us, for as long as Apronius wanted him to.

I have introduced to you, gentlemen of the jury, the various types of Verres's innumerable injustices by providing you with but a single example of each type, and leaving unmentioned an infinite number of others. But imagine how all of Sicily suffered outrageous demands by tax collectors, seizure of their farms, the insolence of Verres here, and the tyranny of Apronius. . . .

Verres carried off the whole grain harvest of the people of Imachara, robbed them of every last kernel by his unjust behavior, and then forced these desperate and impoverished people to pay him an additional tribute by giving Apronius 20,000 sesterces. [The decree demanding these tributes is read out in court as evidence.] . . . The tax collector in the area around Mutyca harassed the farmers so terribly that, after paying to him the additional tribute, they were forced to buy wheat from farmers outside their area because they had none of their own left. And I can show that this very same thing happened in other areas as well. . . . In short, for three years, the taxes from all the

[74] On his fact-finding mission in Sicily, Cicero had copied the information from the waxed tablets onto a papyrus roll.

[75] The final "es" of "Verres" had been erased by rubbing the wax with a sharp-pointed instrument. The erasure left a slight depression in the wax into which the "tail" of the name *Verres* sank. In Latin, the word *verres* means "boar" or "pig."

[76] On the size of a Roman acre, see note 168 of Chapter VII.

farmlands that were subject to taxation were distributed thus: one-tenth of the harvest was sent to Rome,[77] and the rest was sent to Verres.[78] Many, many farmers, in fact, were left with nothing at all for themselves. And if anything was left for them, it was only the small amount which happened to remain after Verres's greed had been glutted. . . .

Verres was permitted, both by a senatorial decree and by law, to requisition grain for his household.[79] . . . It was no crime . . . that he demanded money in place of the grain; many honest, upright, and conscientious governors have done this. . . . However, although a *modius*[80] of wheat sold for 2 sesterces in Sicily, as Verres himself states in a report sent to you, or 3 sesterces at most, as the testimony of witnesses and the farmers' records have made very clear, yet Verres demanded from the farmers 12 sesterces as a substitution for each *modius* of wheat. . . .

Now I come to that particular behavior which he himself calls a hobby, which his friends call a disease or an obsession, but which the Sicilians call grand theft. I myself really don't know what label to give it. I will therefore set before you the details of this behavior, and you may judge it by its real nature, not a label. . . . In all of Sicily, a province so rich and so ancient, in so many of its towns, in so many of its wealthy families, there was not one silver bowl, not one goblet made of Corinthian or Delian metal,[81] not one jewel or pearl, not one object made of gold or ivory, not one bronze or marble or ivory statue, not one painting or tapestry that he did not seek out, examine, and, if he liked it, carry off. . . . For example, in the house of Gaius Heius in Messana, there was a very splendid and ancient chapel which had been built by his ancestors. In this chapel were four magnificent statues, of superb workmanship and artistic value, statues which could delight not only a sensitive and knowledgeable man such as Verres, but even any of us, whom Verres calls "uncouth." . . . Well, gentlemen of the jury, Verres carried off all these statues from Heius's chapel. . . .

One night Verres was at a dinner party at the house of Eupolemus. Eupolemus had set the table with unadorned silver[82] because he did not want his tableware stolen. He had, however, set out two drinking cups, neither one large but both embossed with relief work. Verres here, like a party clown determined not to leave the party without a gift, had the relief work torn off the silver right in front of the rest of the guests. . . .

Madness, the companion of Malice and Insolence, infected his unbridled and deranged mind with such great insanity that he did not hesitate for a moment to inflict on Roman citizens punishments which have always been reserved for slaves guilty of wrongdoing, and to inflict them quite openly. . . . Moreover, he had Roman citizens strangled in prison cells—a most shameful death. While he was governor, that cry, that appeal, "I am a Roman citizen," an appeal which has often brought help and rescue to many men, even in far-off lands and among barbarians, brought Roman citizens in

---

[77] Sicily supplied Rome with a large amount of grain; it was Rome's "bread-basket." The grain, which the Sicilians paid as tribute or tax was distributed to the inhabitants of Rome; see selection 153.

[78] Verres would, of course, sell the grain—at a very nice profit since he had paid nothing for it.

[79] Compare the Julian law mentioned in note 21 of this chapter.

[80] *modius:* see note 47 of Chapter VII.

[81] *Corinthian or Delian metal:* an alloy consisting of gold, silver, and copper.

[82] *unadorned silver:* objects made of pure silver but not decorated with relief work. Sometimes the relief work was done in gold. Verres evidently considered "ordinary" silver not worth the bother of stealing.

Sicily a more summary punishment and a more painful death. . . . Gavius of Consa was one of those innocent Roman citizens whom Verres put in chains and sent to the stone quarries.[83] Somehow or other, he escaped and went to Messana. He saw Italy so close by, just across the straits, and the walls of Rhegium, a town of Roman citizens. Released from the fear of death and doom, he was revived and refreshed by the light of liberty and the sweet smell of justice. He began to speak to the people of Messana and to complain to them that he, a Roman citizen, had been put in chains. He said he was going directly to Rome and would be there, ready to prosecute Verres when he arrived back from his term as governor. . . . However, Gavius was immediately arrested by spies of Verres and taken to a local officer; and, by chance, on the very same day, Verres arrived in Messana. . . . He stormed into the forum, enraged with anger. His eyes were blazing, and his whole face was streaked with cruelty. Everyone waited and watched how he would proceed or what he would do. Suddenly, he ordered Gavius to be dragged into the middle of the forum, stripped, tied, and whipped. The poor man shouted out that he was a Roman citizen, a resident of Consa, that he had served in the army under Lucius Raecius, a very distinguished Roman equestrian who was in Sicily on business and could confirm this story. Verres, however, said that he had learned that Gavius had been sent to Sicily as a spy by the leaders of a gang of deserters. (There was no evidence or personal testimony for this charge, nor any reason to suspect this.) He then ordered him to be whipped many, many times all over his body. And so, gentlemen of the jury, in the middle of the forum in Messana, a Roman citizen was flogged. And the whole time, while he suffered, while the whip cracked, no groan, no cry of any kind was heard from the tortured man except "I am a Roman citizen." In reminding Verres of his citizenship, he thought that he would escape the beating and free his body from the torture. However, not only did he not escape the flogging, but when he kept crying out and demanding the rights of citizenship, Verres ordered his staff to make for this poor tormented man a cross. That's right, a cross![84] . . . Gentlemen of the jury, this was the only cross ever set up in the part of Messana that overlooks the straits. Verres chose this spot, with its view of Italy, deliberately so that Gavius, as he died in pain and agony, might recognize that the narrow straits marked the boundary between slavery and freedom, and so that Italy might see her own son hanging there, suffering the most horrible punishment ever inflicted on slaves. To put a Roman citizen in chains is a wrong. To flog him is a crime. To execute him is almost parricide. And what shall I call crucifixion? So abominable a deed can find no word adequate enough to describe it. Yet even a crucifixion did not satisfy Verres. "Let him gaze upon his native land. Let him die within sight of justice and liberty." Oh Verres, it was not Gavius, not some unknown man, whom you tortured and crucified in that place, but the universally acknowledged correlation between liberty and Roman citizenship.

Hatred of Roman Rule

The Romans boasted that they had imposed *pax Romana* on all areas within their Empire.[85] *Pax,* a word which is usually translated into English as "peace," means

[83] On life in a mine, see selection 186.

[84] Crucifixion was usually reserved for criminals of the very lowest social class; see note 36 of Chapter I.

[85] *pax Romana:* see Vergil's comments on "Roman peace" in selection 251.

"a state of order, regularity, and harmony." The orderliness established by the Romans produced a greater freedom of travel and communication from one part of the Empire to any other part, and thus increased security, trade, and prosperity in western Europe and the Mediterranean world. Yet many people in the provinces resented Roman rule which they were forced to pay for with taxes and tribute. The Roman tax collector was a hated figure, as were the ever-present Roman soldiers[86] and government officials. The following passage is from a speech by Calgacus, a British chief who attempted to stop the advance northward of the army commanded by Agricola, governor of the Roman province of Britain from A.D. 78 to A.D. 85.[87] The speech is fictitious; Tacitus had no way of knowing what Calgacus really said to his men, so he invented a speech which he thought Calgacus might have spoken in that particular situation. Tacitus evidently knew what a provincial was likely to complain of: conscription, taxes, tribute, forced labor, and Roman arrogance.

282   Tacitus, *A Biography of Agricola* 29–31

Among the many British war chiefs was one named Calgacus, who was preeminent in valor and in birth. He is reported to have addressed in the following manner the assembled crowd of Britons who were clamoring for battle.

"Every time I consider the causes of this war and our own dire straits, I have great confidence that this day and your new unity[88] will be the beginning of freedom for all Britain. Now you have joined forces, you who have never been slaves. There is no land beyond ours, no place to flee;[89] even the sea is no longer a safe refuge because a Roman fleet threatens us there. And so war and weapons, which offer honor to the brave, will offer safety even to the cowardly. . . . Up until this day, we who live in this last strip of land and last home of liberty have been protected by our very remoteness. . . . But now the farthest limits of Britain have been opened up. . . . Beyond us, there are no tribes, nothing except waves and rocks and, more dangerous than these, the Romans, whose oppression you have in vain tried to escape by obedience and submission. Plunderers of the world they are, and now that there is no more territory left to occupy their hands which have already laid the world waste, they are scouring the seas. If the enemy is rich, they are greedy; if the enemy is poor, they are power-hungry. Neither east nor west has been able to sate them. Alone of all men they covet rich nations and poor nations with equal passion. They rob, they slaughter, they plunder—and they call it 'empire.' Where they make a waste-land, they call it 'peace.'

"Nature has planned that each man love his children and family very dearly. Yet these are torn from us by conscription to be slaves elsewhere.[90] And our wives and sisters, even if they escape rape by an enemy, are yet defiled by Romans pretending to be friends. Our possessions and our money are consumed in providing tribute; our farmland and our yearly produce are consumed in providing them with grain; our very

---

[86] Many of the soldiers, however, were themselves provincials, although not serving in their home province; see note 70 of Chapter XI.

[87] For more on Agricola, see selection 17.

[88] The Britons had not previously presented a unified military resistance to the Romans.

[89] The scene of the speech is the northeastern highlands of Scotland.

[90] For example, conscripted Britons were shipped to Germany to serve as soldiers.

bodies and hands are worn down while clearing forests and swamps for them, who beat and insult us."

The Benefits of Roman Rule

In answer to the grievances of provincials, the Roman government maintained its position that conquered nations had exchanged freedom for things more valuable: peace, prosperity, and protection. This passage is part of a speech by Petilius Cerialis, a Roman general who suppressed a revolt by the people of Gaul in A.D. 70. Like the previous speech, this one, too, is fictitious.

283   Tacitus, *Histories* 4.74

Tyranny and war always existed in Gaul until you yielded to our authority. And we, although we have been provoked many times, have imposed upon you by right of conquest only this one demand: that you pay the costs of keeping peace here. For peace among different peoples cannot be maintained without troops, and troops cannot be maintained without pay, and pay cannot be found without taxation. In other respects we are equals. You yourselves often command our legions and govern this and other provinces. You are in no respect excluded or shut out. Although you live far from Rome, you enjoy as much as we do the benefits of praiseworthy emperors; on the other hand, the cruel emperors threaten most those closest to them. You must resign yourselves to the extravagance and greed of your masters just as you resign yourselves to barren years or excessive rains or any other natural disaster. As long as there are men, there will be vices. But they are not everlasting, and they are balanced by intervals of better government. Perhaps you expect a milder type of government if Tutor and Classicus[91] assume power? Perhaps you think that they can equip armies to repel the Germans and the Britons for less tribute than you now pay us? But if the Romans are driven out—may the gods forbid!—what situation could exist except wars among all these races? The structure of our Empire has been consolidated by 800 years of good fortune and strict organization, and it cannot be torn apart without destroying those who tear it apart. And you especially will run the greatest risk, for you have gold and natural resources, which are the chief causes of war. Therefore love and cherish peace and the city of Rome which you and I, conquered and conqueror, hold with equal rights. Let these examples of good fortune and bad fortune warn you not to prefer rebellion and ruin to submission and safety.

[91] *Tutor and Classicus:* leaders of the revolt against the Romans.

XIII

Women in Roman Society

Roman women of all social classes were expected to assume, and at an early age, the traditional role of child bearer and child rearer.[1] While the male members of the society regularly spent their days outside the home working, seeing friends, arguing politics, conducting business, and so on, women generally remained close to home, first their father's home, then their husband's.[2] Men in Roman society thus had both a public and a private identity; a man was a baker or a banker or a carpenter, as well as a husband and a father. A woman had only a private life: she was somebody's daughter, somebody's wife, or somebody's mother. Women were praised only for their performances in these roles, and conspicuous behavior in any other role brought notoriety rather than praise. In every aspect of their lives, moreover, women were expected to defer to men.[3] They were treated like wards or dependents who needed constant supervision. If a woman's father died, she was entrusted to the care of a guardian.[4] Even in her role as child bearer and child rearer, a woman's life was controlled by men. An infant could be exposed without the consent of the woman who had just given it birth.[5] And a mother would lose her children if she were divorced. Men were the doers and achievers of the Roman world; women were the nourishers and sustainers, providing the men in their lives—their fathers, husbands, and sons—with encouragement and support.

CHILDHOOD

Little Women

Roman girls grew up very quickly; they received little, if any, formal education and were considered ready to assume the duties of a Roman *matrona* (matron)

[1] On the age of girls at marriage, see selection 48.

[2] Their husbands were chosen for them by their *paterfamilias* (or guardian; see selection 49).

[3] Consider the complaints which Cicero had about his sister-in-law in selection 60.

[4] On guardians, see selection 44. The function of the guardian was to protect any money or property the woman might have inherited. Few women in ancient Rome were financially independent; the vast majority were bound to the men in their lives because they had no money of their own, or no control over their money.

[5] On exposure, see selections 31 and 32.

and to become a wife and even a mother at the age of twelve or thirteen. Even before marriage they were expected to act like little adults rather than like children. In this letter to his friend Marcellinus, Pliny expresses his grief at the untimely death of a girl, named Minicia, who he thought had possessed all the qualities desirable in a thirteen-year-old Roman girl: maturity of judgment, matronly dignity, and modesty; she was serious and industrious, obedient and cheerful; she had little interest in toys or in play; and right to her death she bore her suffering courageously.

284   Pliny the Younger, *Letters* 5.16.1–7

I write this to you with a very heavy heart: the younger daughter of our friend Fundanus is dead. No young girl has ever been more charming than she, or more lovable, or, as I think, more worthy not just of a longer life, but even of immortality. She had not yet completed her thirteenth year, and yet she had the judgment of a mature woman and the dignity of a matron, but the sweetness of a little girl and the modesty of a young maiden. How lovingly she put her arms around her father's neck! How affectionately and respectfully she embraced us who were her father's friends! How she adored her nurses, her paedagogues, and her teachers, each for the special guidance that he or she had offered her! How diligently and how perceptively she used to read! How rarely and how demurely she played! With what composure, with what patience, indeed with what courage did she endure her final illness! She obeyed her doctors, she comforted her sister and father, and, even after the strength of her body failed her, she hung on by the strength of her mind. And this strength remained with her right to the very end; neither the length of her illness nor fear of death could weaken it. She has, therefore, because of her courageous attitude, left us even greater and graver reasons to feel loss and grief. O sad and quite untimely death! Indeed, I find the untimeliness of her death more cruel than the death itself. She had already been engaged to a fine young man, the day had now been set for the wedding, and we had just received our invitations. Now our joy has turned to sadness. I cannot express in words what great anguish I felt when I heard Fundanus himself making arrangements for the money he had intended to spend on his daughter's wedding clothes, pearls, and jewelry to be spent instead on funeral incense, ointments, and perfumes.

Single Women

As we have seen, young girls did not choose their own husbands, and they certainly had no choice about whether to marry or to remain single. An unmarried daughter was considered by her family an undesirable burden; it was her duty to marry the man chosen for her and to raise a family. In this passage from a poem by Catullus, we see that parents might even hate an unmarried daughter.

285   Catullus, *Poems* 62.57–65

If, when she is ripe for marriage, she enters into wedlock, she is ever dearer to her husband and less hateful to her parents. . . . So do not reject such a husband, little girl.

It is not right to reject the man to whom your father and mother gave you. You must obey them. Your virginity is not entirely yours. One-third of it belongs to your father, one-third to your mother, and only one-third to you yourself. Don't fight against your parents who have surrendered to your husband a dowry and their rights over you.

LIFE EXPECTANCY

A Brief Life

Some females died of exposure immediately after birth; some lived to be eighty. Many women, however, were married at a young age, raised families, and died before reaching "middle age." A woman's life passed rapidly; she might well be a grandmother at thirty. The woman mentioned in this epitaph from the Roman province of Pannonia was married at eleven, gave birth to six children, lost five of them,[6] and died at twenty-seven.

286   *CIL* 3.3572

Here I lie, a matron named Veturia. My father was Veturius.[7] My husband was Fortunatus. I lived for twenty-seven years, and I was married for sixteen years to the same man. After I gave birth to six children, only one of whom is still alive, I died.

Titus Julius Fortunatus, a soldier of Auxiliary Legion II, provided this memorial[8] for his wife, who was incomparable and showed outstanding devotion[9] to him.

Death in Childbirth

We have seen in many of the passages above that the duty of the Roman *matrona* was to bear legitimate heirs for her husband. Girls married in their early teens soon became pregnant; childbirth was frequently difficult and painful, and many women died. In this letter to his friend Velius Cerialis, Pliny comments on two such deaths.

287   Pliny the Younger, *Letters* 4.21.1, 2

What a sad and bitter tragedy befell the two Helvidiae sisters! Both of them died in labor, both of them died while giving birth to daughters. I am overwhelmed with grief.

---

[6] Cornelia, mother of Tiberius and Gaius Gracchus, bore twelve children, but only three lived to adulthood.

[7] On the naming of girls, see note 4 of genealogy chart 2.

[8] *this memorial:* funerary inscription.

[9] *devotion:* Latin *pietas;* see the introduction to selection 1 and the introduction to the section on ritual in Chapter XV.

And not unduly, for it seems to me so tragic that two very virtuous young women, in the prime of their youth, were snatched away from us even as they were giving life to a new generation. And I grieve over the unhappy lot of the infants, who immediately, even while being born, were deprived of their mothers.[10] And I weep for the sad fate of the husbands, who are both very fine men.[11]

PRAISEWORTHY BEHAVIOR

Women earned praise when they directed all their actions toward the welfare and preservation of their families. A man was expected to devote himself to his own career or political advancement; a woman was expected to devote herself to the advancement of others. Therefore, courage, intelligence, and strength in a woman were commendable qualities, but only when coupled with selflessness and self-sacrifice.

An Outstanding Example of *Pietas*

This inscription, which dates to the end of the first century B.C. and was discovered in Rome, honors a Roman woman whose name was perhaps Turia. She exemplified the character and behavior expected of a Roman matron. She was strong, brave, modest, prudent, faithful, and self-sacrificing. In sum, she was an outstanding example of *pietas:* an unswerving sense of duty, devotion, and loyalty to one's family, friends, country, and gods. This eulogy was written by her husband.

288   *CIL* 6.1527, 31670 (*ILS* 8393)

The day before our wedding you were suddenly left an orphan when both your parents were murdered. Although I had gone to Macedonia and your sister's husband, Gaius Cluvius, had gone to the province of Africa, the murder of your parents did not remain unavenged. You carried out this act of piety[12] with such great diligence—asking questions, making inquiries, demanding punishment—that if we had been there, we could not have done better. You and that very pious woman, your sister, share the credit for success. . . .

Rare indeed are marriages of such long duration, which are ended by death, not divorce. We had the good fortune to spend forty-one years together with no unhappi-

---

[10] Many children did not know their natural mothers; see the introduction to the section on mothers in Chapter II. In selection 284, there is no mention of Minicia's mother, who is perhaps dead or separated from her children by divorce.

[11] For more information about this family, see selections 289 and 290, and genealogy chart 3.

[12] *piety:* Latin *pietas.* It was Turia's duty to her parents to avenge their murders. In the absence of their husbands, she and her sister took a very active role in the murder investigations, but their concern was family, not personal, honor, and their behavior was therefore laudable.

ness.[13] I wish that our long marriage had come finally to an end by *my* death, since it would have been more just for me, who was older, to yield to fate.

Why should I mention your personal virtues—your modesty, obedience, affability, and good nature, your tireless attention to wool making,[14] your performance of religious duties without superstitious fear, your artless elegance and simplicity of dress? Why speak about your affection toward your relatives, your sense of duty[15] toward your family (for you cared for my mother as well as you cared for your parents)? Why recall the countless other virtues which you have in common with all Roman matrons worthy of that name? The virtues I claim for you are your own special virtues; few people have possessed similar ones or been known to possess them. The history of the human race tells us how rare they are.

Together we diligently saved the whole inheritance which you received from your parents' estate. You handed it all over to me and did not worry yourself about increasing it.[16] We shared the responsibilities so that I acted as the guardian of your fortune and you undertook to serve as protector of mine. . . .

You demonstrated your generosity not only toward your very many relatives but especially in your performance of family duties. . . . For you brought up in our home young female relatives.[17] . . . And you provided dowries for them so that they could attain a position in life worthy of your family. These arrangements which were planned by you and your sister were supported by Gaius Cluvius and me with mutual agreement; moreover, since we admired your generosity, in order that you might not reduce the size of your inheritance, we put on the market family property and provided dowries by selling our estates. I have mentioned this not to congratulate myself but in order to make known that we were compelled by a sense of honor to carry out with our own money those arrangements made by you because of your dutifulness and generosity. . . .

When my political enemies were hunting me down,[18] you aided my escape by selling your jewelry; you gave me all the gold and pearls which you were wearing and added a small income from household funds. We deceived the guards of my enemies, and you made my time in hiding an "enriching" experience. . . .

Why should I now disclose memories locked deep in my heart, memories of secret and concealed plans? Yes, memories—how I was warned by swift messages to avoid present and imminent dangers and was therefore saved by your quick thinking; how you did not permit me to be swept away by my foolhardy boldness; how, by calm consideration, you arranged a safe place of refuge for me and enlisted as allies in your

[13] Statements such as these help to correct the impression that all Romans of the late republican period had loveless marriages and were frequently divorced. For a marriage of long duration in the imperial period, see selection 53.

[14] Compare selection 52: "she spun wool." Wool making was one of the traditional duties of a Roman matron. Even upper-class matrons were praised for wool making, just as they were praised for thrift; see Pliny's description of his wife in selection 54.

[15] *sense of duty:* Latin *pietas.*

[16] It was the husband's duty and right to manage his wife's estate. It is clear, however, in the next paragraph that separate books were kept for the wife's money and the husband's money.

[17] On orphans, see selection 45. Turia considered it her duty to look after relatives who had been orphaned.

[18] When Octavian and Mark Antony formed an alliance in 43 B.C. (see note 80 of Chapter III), they began to hunt down systematically and to kill their political opponents. Turia's husband, Quintus Lucretius Vespillo, was one such opponent, but he managed to escape execution. Cicero, however, was executed by Antony (see selection 138).

plans to save me your sister and her husband, Gaius Cluvius, even though the plans were dangerous to all of you. If I tried to touch on all your actions on my behalf, I could go on forever. For us let it suffice to say that you hid me safely.

Yet the most bitter experience of my life came later. . . . I was granted a pardon by Augustus,[19] but his colleague Lepidus[20] opposed the pardon. When you threw yourself on the ground at his feet, not only did he not raise you up, but in fact he grabbed you and dragged you along as if you were a slave. You were covered with bruises, but with unflinching determination you reminded him of Augustus Caesar's edict of pardon. . . . Although you suffered insults and cruel injuries, you revealed them publicly in order to expose him as the author of my calamities.[21] . . .

When the world was finally at peace again and order had been restored in the government,[22] we enjoyed quiet and happy days. We longed for children, but spiteful fate begrudged them. If Fortune had allowed herself to care for us in this matter as she does others, we two would have enjoyed complete happiness. But advancing old age put an end to our hopes for children. . . . You were depressed about your infertility and grieved because I was without children. . . . You spoke of divorce and offered to give up your household to another woman, to a fertile woman. You said that you yourself would arrange for me a new wife, one worthy of our well-known love, and you assured me that you would treat the children of my new marriage as if they were your own. You would not demand the return of your inheritance;[23] it would remain, if I wished, in my control. You would not detach or isolate yourself from me; you would simply carry out henceforth the duties and responsibilities of my sister or my mother-in-law.

I must confess that I was so angered by your suggestion that I lost my mind. I was so horrified that I could scarcely regain control of myself. How could you talk of a dissolution of our marriage before it was demanded by fate![24] How could you even conceive in your mind of any reason why you should, while still alive, cease to be my wife, you who remained very faithfully with me when I was in exile, indeed almost in exile from life! How could the desire or need for having children be so great that I would break faith with you! . . .

I wish that our old age had allowed our marriage to last until I, who was the elder, had passed away; it would have been fairer for you to arrange a funeral for me. . . . But by fate's decree, you finished the race of life before I did, and you left me all alone, without children, grieving and longing for you. . . . But inspired by your example I will stand up to cruel fortune, which has not stolen everything

---

[19] *Augustus:* Octavian.

[20] *Lepidus:* member of the political alliance with Octavian and Antony (the Second Triumvirate); see note 104 of Chapter VII.

[21] Although Turia here appeared conspicuously in public and even dared to contradict a man, Lepidus, she did so on behalf of her husband and is therefore praised, not censured.

[22] That is, when Augustus (Octavian) established the principate; see selection 241.

[23] Roman husbands by law assumed control of their wives' money. Turia's husband managed for her the money she had inherited from her parents. In the case of divorce or death, the husband was required to return the wife's dowry to her father or, if he were dead, to her guardian; see selection 61. However, Roman funerary laws provided that "a husband can retain from his wife's dowry the amount which he spent on her funeral"; see selection 113. The vast majority of Romans were lower-class and not fortunate enough to have inheritances and large dowries to worry about. Consider selection 266; Ligustinus's wife brought to the marriage "nothing except her free birth and chastity."

[24] *fate:* death.

from me since it allows the memory of you to grow brighter and stronger through praise. . . .

I conclude my oration with this: you have deserved all, and I can never repay you completely. I have always considered your wishes my commands. I will continue to do for you whatever I still can.

May the Manes[25] grant to you and protect your eternal peace, I pray.

Emotional Control

In this letter to his friend Nepos, Pliny describes the courage of Arria, the wife of Caecina Paetus. When her husband was ordered by the emperor Claudius in A.D. 42 to end his life,[26] he hesitated to do so. Arria picked up a sword, stabbed herself, handed the bloody sword to her husband, and said, "Paetus, it does not hurt." The incident related in this passage took place, of course, before Paetus's suicide. Arria's strength of mind is viewed as praiseworthy because it was directed toward the welfare of her husband.

289   Pliny the Younger, *Letters* 3.16.3–6

Arria's husband, Caecina Paetus, was ill. So was her son, and neither was expected to recover. The son died, a boy of exceptional beauty, remarkable modesty, and dear to his parents for all sorts of reasons in addition to his being their son. Arria made arrangements for his funeral and attended the funeral without her husband's knowing. In fact, whenever she entered his room, she pretended that their son was alive and even feeling better. And whenever her husband asked how the boy was doing, she replied, "He has rested well and has his appetite back." Then, when the tears which she had held back for a long time overwhelmed her and gushed forth, she left the room and only then gave way to grief. After she had wept, she dried her eyes, regained her composure, and returned, as calm as if she had left her feeling of bereavement outside the room. Her best-known deed was, of course, heroic, when she unsheathed the sword, stabbed herself in the breast, pulled out the sword, and handed it to her husband, saying these immortal, almost divine words: "Paetus, it does not hurt." But still she had before her eyes, as she was acting and speaking thus, the hope of fame and immortality. How much more heroic was it to conceal her tears when she had little chance of gaining immortality, to hide her grief, with little chance of fame, and to continue acting like a mother after she had lost her son.

Loyalty

In this letter, Pliny tells his friend Priscus about the illness of Fannia. Fannia was the granddaughter of Caecina Paetus and Arria, who were mentioned in the pre-

---

[25] *Manes:* see note 55 of Chapter III.

[26] Upper-class Romans who had incurred the wrath of an emperor were frequently invited to end their lives or commit suicide, and thus save their families the embarrassment of a public execution.

Genealogy Chart 3. Helvidii

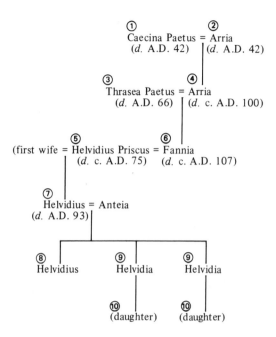

① *Caecina Paetus:* involved in a plot to overthrow the emperor Claudius; tried, found guilty, and forced to commit suicide.

② *Arria (the elder):* committed suicide with her husband ("Paetus, it does not hurt"); see selection 289.

③ *Thrasea Paetus:* involved in opposition to the emperor Nero; charged with treason, and forced to commit suicide.

④ *Arria (the younger):* wanted to follow her mother's example and share her husband's fate. He persuaded her to remain alive for sake of their daughter, Fannia.

⑤ *Helvidius Priscus:* exiled by Nero in A.D. 66; put to death in exile by the emperor Vespasian.

⑥ *Fannia:* accompanied her husband into exile; see selection 290.

⑦ *Helvidius (the elder):* accused of treason against the emperor Domitian and executed in A.D. 93.

⑧ *Helvidius (the younger):* brother of the two women who died in childbirth; see selection 287.

⑨ *Helvidia:* the two sisters who died in childbirth.

⑩ *daughters:* infant girls born to the two sisters who died.

vious passage. Her husband was Helvidius Priscus, a Stoic philosopher and writer[27] who was prominent in the opposition to the emperors and who was put to death by the emperor Vespasian around A.D. 75.[28]

[27] On Stoicism and the Stoics of this period, see selections 418–425.

[28] Fannia and her husband were related to Arria, who was mentioned in the previous passage, and the two sisters of the Helvidian family who died in childbirth (selection 287); see genealogy chart 3. Many of the men in the family were exiled and even executed for their political beliefs. For other acquaintances of Pliny who were exiled or executed by emperors, see selection 49.

290 Pliny the Younger, *Letters* 7.19.1, 3, 4, 6

Fannia's illness worries me. . . . Her fever lingers, the cough grows worse, and she is extremely thin and weak. . . . I grieve that so great a woman is being snatched away from the sight of our citizens; I don't know whether we will see another like her. What purity she had! What integrity! What dignity! What loyalty! Twice she followed her husband into exile; the third time, after his death, she herself was banished when she tried to preserve his writings. . . . For when the Senate, through fear and imperial pressure, decreed that her husband's books be burned, she kept them safe (even though all her own possessions were confiscated) and took them with her into exile.[29]

This same woman was charming and friendly and—a quality possessed by only a few—both loved and respected. Will there in the future be anyone whom we can offer to our wives as a model? Will there be anyone in whom we men can find an example of courage, whom we can all admire, even as we see and speak with her, as much as the heroines we read about in books?

UNACCEPTABLE BEHAVIOR

Scandalous Conduct

Women who exhibited independence of thought or concerned themselves with matters outside the home and family were subject to criticism. One of the most fascinating women in Roman history is Sempronia, who is described in the passage below from Sallust's account of *The Catilinarian Conspiracy*. Catiline was a young upper-class Roman of good family who in 63 B.C. planned a revolution to overthrow the state. The conspiracy was discovered by Cicero, consul in 63 B.C., and the conspirators were either killed in battle or arrested and executed.[30] Sempronia, an intelligent, well-educated, and talented upper-class Roman matron, had supported Catiline and thereby scandalized the "decent" citizens of Rome. They were scandalized because she had apparently acted independently, had assumed a public role in the political life of Rome, and had done so not in support of her family but for personal reasons. Thus, while women like Turia and Arria were seen to exhibit "strength of mind," Sempronia was viewed as "willful." Sallust's portrait of her reveals his ambivalent reactions to her character: disgust at her flouting of the traditional female role, but honest admiration for her considerable talents.

291 Sallust, *The Catilinarian Conspiracy* 25

Sempronia had often in the past acted with a masculine daring and boldness. Yet Fortune had blessed her quite adequately, first with beauty and good birth, and then with

---

[29] Fannia, like Pliny's wife, Calpurnia (selection 54) was intelligent and educated enough to appreciate the value of her husband's writings. Neither woman sought fame on her own as a writer.

[30] One father executed his son for his involvement in this conspiracy; see the introduction to selection 14.

a husband and children. She had studied Greek and Latin literature. She could play the lyre and dance, although with more skill than is necessary for an honest woman.[31] And she had many other talents which lead to moral dissipation. But there was nothing she valued less than honor and decency; it would be difficult to decide which she squandered more—her money or her reputation. She was so filled with burning lust that she more often made advances to men than they did to her. Even before meeting Catiline, she had often broken promises, dishonored credit agreements, been an accessory to murder, and plunged headlong into poverty because of her extravagance.[32] And yet her abilities were far from contemptible; she could write poetry, be droll, converse modestly or tenderly or coarsely, as the situation demanded. In fact, she was a woman of great wit and great charm.

Women and Politics

In 215 B.C., after a stunning defeat by Hannibal at Cannae,[33] the Romans passed a law (the Oppian Law) which curtailed women's purchases of luxury items, such as gold jewelry and expensive clothing. The Romans hoped this austerity measure would increase the money available for the war effort. A few years after the end of the war, in 195 B.C., two tribunes brought before the Concilium Plebis a proposal to repeal the Oppian Law. The proposal was discussed at great length and often bitterly. Since the Oppian Law had directly affected women, one would expect that women would have had strong opinions about its repeal. And they did! They poured out into the streets and into the Forum, where the assembly met, and, although they could not themselves vote, they tried to persuade their menfolk to vote for repeal. Ultimately, the proposal for repeal was passed by the assembly, but one of its reactionary opponents, Marcus Porcius Cato,[34] expressed dismay and disgust at the behavior of the Roman women who had dared to express an opinion about a political matter and had lobbied for support. This passage is taken from one of his public speeches.

292   Livy, *A History of Rome,* 34.2.1, 2, 8–11, 14

If each of us men, fellow citizens, had undertaken to keep the right and the authority of the husband out of the hands of the women of the family, we would have less trouble with groups of women. But as it is now, at home our freedom is trampled on by feminine rages, and here in the Forum it is crushed and trod underfoot. Because we were unable to control each woman as an individual, we are now frightened by women in groups. . . .

[31] The Romans enjoyed watching dance performances but thought the dancers themselves were low-class and contemptible. Most dancers were slaves or foreigners. However, Sempronia's fault is not so much that she dances, but that she dances well; a woman's talents were not to be conspicuous.

[32] Sallust's description of Sempronia's personal behavior may well have been colored by his distaste for her political involvement.

[33] *Hannibal:* Carthaginian general who ravaged much of Italy during the Second Punic War; see note 87 of Chapter VII.

Cannae: town in eastern Italy.

[34] *Marcus Porcius Cato:* see selections 121, 160, and 184.

Indeed, it was with some embarrassment that I came a few minutes ago to the Forum right through a crowd of women. If I had not held in respect the dignity and basic decency of each woman as an individual (it would mortify them to be seen receiving a scolding from a consul), I would have said: "What kind of behavior is this, running around in public and blocking streets and talking to other women's husbands? Could you not have asked your own husbands the same thing at home? Are you more persuasive in public than in private, with others' husbands than with your own? And yet it is not right, even in your own homes (if a sense of shame and decency were to keep you within your proper limits), for you to concern yourselves about which laws are passed or repealed here." That's what I would have said.

Our ancestors were not willing to let women conduct any business, not even private business, without a guardian. They wanted them to remain under the control of their fathers, brothers, and husbands. We, for heaven's sake, now allow them to take part in politics and to mingle with us in the Forum and to attend assemblies. . . . To be quite honest, they desire freedom, nay rather license in all matters. And if they win in this matter, what will they not attempt?

Women and Education

Roman women were expected to have enough education to appreciate their husbands' work, wit, writing, and opinions; they were not, however, expected to express opinions of their own. In public they were best seen—nodding in agreement or smiling appreciatively at their husband's wit—but not heard. An intelligent and talented woman had to be careful not to appear more clever than the men around her.[35]

Juvenal's Sixth Satire is a scathing attack on women. Many of his criticisms involve an exaggeration of the situation but nonetheless reveal what sort of behavior irritated Roman men. Apparently Roman men were embarrassed by, and thus disliked, women who were openly more learned than they.

293   Juvenal, *Satires* 6.434–456

Really annoying is the woman who, as soon as she takes her place on the dining couch,[36] praises Vergil,[37] excuses Dido's suicide,[38] compares and ranks in critical order the various poets, and weighs Vergil and Homer[39] on a pair of scales.[40] Gram-

[35] Sempronia, vehemently criticized by Sallust in selection 291, evidently did not conceal her talents.

[36] *dining couch:* the Romans reclined at dinner parties.

[37] *Vergil:* Rome's greatest epic poet; author of the epic poem *Aeneid* which recounts the journey from Troy to Italy of Aeneas, a Trojan prince who survived the Trojan war.

[38] An episode from the *Aeneid*. Dido, queen of Carthage, a city in North Africa, had fallen in love with Aeneas when he landed there. After a few months, however, Aeneas sailed away to continue his journey to Italy. The unhappy Dido committed suicide. Readers of the *Aeneid* have either blamed Aeneas for deserting a friend and causing her suicide or, like the woman at the dinner party, excused Aeneas for Dido's suicide because *pietas* demanded that he continue on to Italy. On Aeneas's *pietas*, see note 88 of Chapter XV.

[39] *Homer:* Greek epic poet who composed the *Iliad* and the *Odyssey*.

[40] A figurative expression; she tries to determine the "weightiness," the value, of each poet's work.

mar teachers[41] surrender, professors of rhetoric[42] are defeated, the entire group of guests is silent; neither a lawyer nor an auctioneer nor even another woman will get a word in. So loud and shrill are her words that you might think pots were being banged together and bells were being rung. . . .

Like a philosopher she defines ethics. If she wants to appear so learned and eloquent, she should shorten her tunic to midcalf![43] . . . Don't marry a woman who speaks like an orator—or knows every history book. There should be some things in books which she doesn't understand. I hate a woman who reads and rereads Palaemon's[44] treatise on grammar, who always obeys all the laws and rules of correct speech, who quotes verses I've never even heard of, moldy old stuff that a man shouldn't worry about anyway. Let her correct the grammar of her stupid girlfriend! A husband should be allowed an occasional "I ain't."

Women and Luxuries

In the same satire from which the previous passage came, Juvenal, who lived around A.D. 100, blames women's immorality on Rome's affluence. In the "good old days," life was hard and women were pure, or so Juvenal thought.

294   Juvenal, *Satires* 6.286–295, 298–300

Do you wonder where these monsters come from? In the good old days, poverty made our Latin women chaste; small huts didn't provide opportunities for immoral behavior. Hard work, lack of sleep, hands rough and callused from working wool,[45] Hannibal[46] near the city, their husbands performing militia duty—these things just don't allow vices to develop. Now, however, we are suffering the ill effects of a long peace. Luxury, more destructive than war, threatens the city and takes revenge for the lands we have conquered.[47] No crime or lustful act is missing, now that traditional Roman poverty is dead. . . . Obscene wealth brought with it foreign customs,[48] and unmanly luxuries and ugly affluence weakened each generation.

[41] *grammar teachers:* Latin *grammatici;* see selection 136.

[42] *professors of rhetoric:* Latin *rhetores;* see selection 137.

[43] The tunic (Latin *tunica*), which reached about midcalf, was a man's garment; the woman's garment was a *stola* which extended to the feet. Juvenal is saying, let her wear men's clothing if she wants to act like a man.

[44] *Palaemon:* see note 29 of Chapter VI.

[45] On wool working as a matron's duty, see note 14 of this chapter.

[46] *Hannibal:* see note 33 of this chapter.

[47] Lands conquered by Rome in war sent money to Rome for taxes and tribute. These lands also offered Roman capitalists new territory in which to expand their business ventures. However, as Rome became more affluent and prosperous, it also became, according to Juvenal, weaker and immoral, and thus conquered lands could indirectly cause the downfall of Rome.

[48] On Juvenal's prejudice against foreigners, see selection 212.

Women and Theatrical Performances

In this letter to a man named Geminus, Pliny reports the death of Ummidia Quadratilla, a woman more fond of theatrical performances than was considered proper for an upper-class Roman matron.

295   Pliny the Younger, *Letters* 7.24.1, 4, 5

Ummidia Quadratilla passed away a little before her eightieth birthday. She was in good health until the end, a woman with a figure more solid and plump than is usual even for a matron. . . . She owned a company of pantomime dancers[49] and enjoyed their performances with more enthusiasm than was proper for a woman of her social rank. However, her grandson Quadratus, who was brought up in her household, never saw their performances, either in the theater or at home, and she certainly never encouraged him to. She herself told me, when she was asking me to supervise his rhetorical training, that she, during the idle hours which women have,[50] used to relax by playing checkers or watching pantomimes; but when she was about to do either, she always told her grandson to go and study.

HYSTERIA

The word *hysteria* is derived from the Greek word *hystera,* "womb." Greco-Roman medical writers believed, as did the Egyptians before them, that hysteria was an illness caused by violent movements of the womb and that it was therefore peculiar to women. The illness had a clearly recognizable pattern of symptoms: suffocation, inability to speak, and sometimes convulsions. Men exhibiting similar symptoms were not considered hysterical, since they did not have a *hystera,* or "womb," and they were therefore assumed to have a different illness, such as epilepsy. The Greco-Roman theory of hysteria as an illness of physiological origin influenced doctors for the next 2000 years. During these millennia hysteria continued to be considered a feminine ailment attributable to disturbances of the womb. Not until the time of Freud did doctors begin to recognize that the symptoms of hysteria were caused by emotional tensions arising from unconscious sources; these tensions are converted from emotional manifestations into a physical ailment, into the symptoms of hysteria. It is interesting that the symptoms of hysteria vary from culture

[49] *owned a company:* performers were usually slaves; therefore, this woman literally owned the performers.

    pantomime: a performance in which dancers depicted the actions of characters, usually mythological, in various situations; see selection 336. The woman in this letter loved pantomime but thought it would corrupt her grandson. Most Romans enjoyed the stage but despised the actors. On Roman ambivalence toward theatrical performance, see the introduction to selection 335.

[50] Upper-class women, attended by many slaves, might have "idle hours," but lower-class women would have precious few moments of leisure. Pliny's perspective was upper-class.

to culture and are adapted to the ideas and mores current in each particular culture. . . . "Hysteria has become an apparently infrequent illness. In this century behavior that includes 'kicking about' and 'waving the arms and legs' is met with distaste and lack of sympathy. . . . It has been suggested that, unlike the psychotic patient, the patient suffering from hysteria retains a sense of reality in the course of the seizure and is thus able to control his manifestations and to keep them within the limits permissible in his ambient setting. Unacceptable today would be the fainting ladies of the Victorian period . . . because they would altogether fail to evoke any sympathetic response in their social environment. . . . Hysteria has become subjectively unrewarding."[51]

In the passages below, medical writers of the Roman world describe the origins, symptoms, and cures of hysteria. Their ideas seem curious, particularly since we now recognize that hysteria is caused, in both men and women, by anxiety and emotional tensions, and also since we seldom today see such examples of hysteria. However, we may well wonder why hysteria was so prevalent in the Roman world. What were the pressures, tensions, and anxieties which tormented so many Roman women and found a socially acceptable outlet only in the manifestation of hysterical symptoms?[52]

Symptoms

296   Aretaeus, *Medical Writings* 2.11.1–3, 6.10.1–4

In women, in the hollow of the body below the ribcage, lies the womb. It is very much like an independent animal within the body for it moves around of its own accord . . . and is quite erratic. Furthermore, it likes fragrant smells and moves toward them, but it dislikes foul odors and moves away from them. . . . When it suddenly moves upward[53] and remains there for a long time and presses on the intestines, the woman chokes, in the manner of an epileptic, but without any spasms. For the liver, diaphragm, lungs, and heart are suddenly confined in a narrow space. And therefore the woman seems unable to breathe or speak. In addition, the carotid arteries, acting in sympathy with the heart, compress, and therefore heaviness of the head, loss of sense perception, and deep sleep occur. . . . Disorders caused by the uterus are remedied by foul smells,[54] and also by pleasant fragrances applied to the vagina. . . .

The uterus follows after sweet-smelling things as if it experiences pleasure from them, and flees from stinking and foul-smelling things as if it experiences pain from them. If any bad-smelling thing irritates it from above, it flees downward, even beyond the genital organs. But if a fetid odor is applied below, it is forced upward, away from

---

[51] Ilza Veith, *Hysteria: The History of a Disease* (Chicago and London, 1965), p. 273. See also p. 209: "The symptoms, it seems, were conditioned by social expectancy, tastes, mores and religion, and were further shaped by the state of medicine in general."

[52] Consider, for example, the repressed behavior of Arria in selection 289. Or consider the strain on a woman who was forced to expose her child (selections 31 and 32).

[53] That is, toward a fragant smell.

[54] The uterus "flees from" foul smells. Therefore, a foul-smelling object near the hysterical woman's nose or throat will cause the uterus to flee downward, back to its position in the lower body. A pleasant-smelling object near the vagina will attract the uterus and draw it down to its desired position.

the odor. . . . If the uterus wanders upward, it very quickly causes the woman to suffocate and choke by cutting off her breathing. She cannot even struggle in pain or shout and call for help. In many cases, inability to breathe strikes immediately, in others inability to speak. . . . Old urine[55] rouses the senses of someone in a death-like state and drives the uterus downward. Sweet fragrances must be applied with pessaries to the area of the uterus.

Causes and Cures

297   Soranus,[56] *Gynecology* 3.26, 3.28.2, 3.29.5

The term *hysterical suffocation* derives from both the affected organ and one symptom, suffocation.[57] It denotes cessation of breathing, together with inability to speak and a loss of sense perception, caused by some condition of the uterus. In the majority of cases, the illness is preceded by repeated miscarriage, premature childbirth, long widow-hood, retention of menses, menopause, or inflation of the womb.[58] Among women suffering the disease, these symptoms occur: swooning, loss of speech, labored breath-ing, seizure of the senses, clenching or grinding of the teeth, convulsive contraction of the extremities (though sometimes only weakness and collapse), swelling of the abdo-men, retraction of the uterus, dilation of the chest area, bulging of the veins which criss-cross the face, chilling of the body, perspiration, and a failed or failing pulse. In general, the women recover quickly from the seizure, and usually they remember what happened. . . .

One should make the patient lie down in a room which is moderately warm and bright, and rouse her as gently as possible from her seizure by moving her jaw, placing warm compresses over the whole middle part of her body, slowly straightening out each cramped limb, restraining the spasm of each extremity, and warming each chilled part by the laying on of bare hands. Then one should wash the face with a sponge soaked in warm water, for sponging the face in some way revives the patient. . . .

I strongly disagree with all those men who immediately irritate the inflamed areas and cause drowsiness or torpor by effluvia of foul-smelling substances. For the uterus does not issue forth like a wild animal from its lair, attracted by pleasant fragrances, nor does it flee from fetid smells.[59] It is, rather, displaced or contracted because of constrictions caused by inflammation.

[55] That is, applied to the nose.

[56] Earlier passages from this same author discussed fertility, contraception, and abortion; see selections 23, 27, and 29.

[57] *hysterical suffocation:* Greek *hysterike pnix* from *hystera*, "womb," and *pnix*, "suffoca-tion."

[58] Although Soranus recognized that hysteria most often occurred in women who were unable to have children, he did not understand that its cause might be the psychological stress of being childless in a society which believed that a woman's main function was to bear chil-dren. In contrast with other ancient medical writers, however, Soranus did not believe that virginity was physically harmful.

[59] Soranus thus disagrees with Aretaeus, the author of the previous passage, a Greek medical writer who lived in the second century A.D.

COSMETICS

For the Skin He Loves to Touch

Ovid, the poet who advised men on where and how to meet women,[60] also advised women about cosmetics which would help to attract men.

298   Ovid, *A Book about Facial Cosmetics* 51–60, 63–68

Now we will learn how we can appear bright and radiant even in the morning when sleep first deserts our tender limbs. First strip away the husks and the chaff from some barley, preferably the variety sent from Libya by boat. Clean two pounds of this barley. Moisten an equal amount of vetch with ten eggs. When the barley has dried in blowing breezes, crush it with a rough millstone turned by a lazy donkey.[61] Grind up along with the barley the horns of a lively young stag. . . . Add twelve narcissus bulbs stripped of their outer layers and pulverized on pure marble. . . . Then add nine times as much honey. If you pamper your face with such a mixture, your skin will be smoother and more radiant than your own mirror.

The Dangers of Hair Dyes

Roman men and women used various mixtures to dye their hair. Henna, for example, was quite popular. One of Ovid's girlfriends, however, had an unfortunate experience with one dye. Besides the information about hair dyes, this passage offers insights into how Roman women treated their slaves.

299   Ovid, *Love Affairs* 1.14.1–18, 27, 28, 43–46

Didn't I tell you to stop messing around with the color of your hair? Now you have no hair left to dye! If you had left it alone, who had thicker hair than you? And when you let it down, it used to hang to your waist. It was very fine—so fine that you hesitated to curl it with curling irons—like the silk fibers the Chinese produce, or the threads which the spider spins with her slender legs when she weaves a delicate web under a deserted beam. But it was neither raven black nor golden blond; it was a mixture of the two, the color of cedar wood when the bark has been stripped away. And it was easy to manage, naturally curly, and didn't cause you any trouble. You didn't have to worry about hair pins or combs being caught in tangles and hurting you when they were pulled out. Your hairdresser was never bruised or scratched.[62] I used to watch her combing and

---

[60] See selections 62 and 347.

[61] For the situation of a donkey in a mill, see selection 187.

[62] Obviously many women would physically abuse their hairdressers (who were usually slaves) when combing out the tangles in their hair caused them pain. On the treatment of slaves, see Chapter VIII.

arranging your hair, and you never had to grab a hair pin and stab her in the arm. . . .

I used to cry out to you, "It's a crime, a real crime, to burn such naturally lovely hair with dyes. You cruel woman, have pity on your head." . . .

Now your hair has fallen out, and you alone are responsible. You yourself mixed the poison and put it on your head. Now Germany will send you her captured locks of hair,[63] and a conquered race will save you from the embarrassment of baldness.

WORKING WOMEN

Since the literary works which we use as source material for Roman civilization were written by upper-class men, we have much more information about men than about women, and more information about upper-class women than about lower-class women.[64] Yet there were obviously thousands and thousands of women in the Roman world who were working wives and mothers, women who were slaves or freedwomen or free women of the lower class. We know virtually nothing about their daily existence or how they coped with the often conflicting demands of work, children, and marriage.[65] They did not themselves write, and no one else wrote about them. Only their tombstones provide evidence that they once existed, and their epitaphs—a few from Rome are given here—tell us only the nature of their employment, not their feelings about it.[66] Note how young these women were at death.

A Dressmaker

300   *CIL* 6.9980 (*ILS* 7428)

To Italia, dressmaker of Cocceia Phyllis. She lived twenty years. Acastus, her fellow slave, paid for this tombstone because she was poor.

A Hairdresser

301   *CIL* 6.9732 (*ILS* 7420a)

Psamate, Furia's hairdresser, lived nineteen years. Mithrodates, the baker of Flaccus Thorius, put up this tombstone.

[63] She will buy a wig. Wigs made from the hair of Germans captured in battle were very popular because the hair was naturally blond.

[64] An upper-class Roman *matrona*—Arria, Fannia, Calpurnia, and Tullia are all examples— certainly did not work outside the home. And within the home, they had many slaves to cook, clean, and look after the children. Compare Pliny's description of Ummidia Quadratilla in selection 295: "during the idle hours which women have."

[65] Roman women did not have careers; they worked because they were forced to if they were slaves, or because their families would otherwise starve. Women without husbands were often destitute; see selection 37 on the woman forced to give away her daughter.

[66] On midwives, see selection 107; on prostitutes, see selection 326.

A Fishmonger

302   *CIL* 6.9801 (*ILS* 7500)

Aurelia Nais, a freedwoman of Gaius, sold fish in the warehouses of Galba. Gaius Aurelius Phileros, a freedman of Gaius, and Lucius Valerius Secundus, a freedman of Lucius, paid for this.

XIV

Leisure and Entertainment

LEISURE ACTIVITIES

The people of ancient Roman society occupied their leisure with a variety of activities. Many of these activities were available to people of all social classes. For example, most men enjoyed drinking wine in the company of their friends. Poor men could probably not afford to host these gatherings, nor did their tiny apartments allow room for parties. Rather, they met their friends in bars which served wine (at room temperature or heated until warm[1]) and snack food.[2] Excavations at Pompeii have revealed a surprisingly large number of bars.[3] Lower-class Roman men must have made regular visits to the neighborhood tavern to discuss politics, exchange gossip, and tell jokes.[4] The wealthy had the money and the facilities for private entertaining, and the upper classes enjoyed social events such as receptions, parties, and banquets.[5] Elaborate weddings offered further opportunities for expensive socializing.[6] Of course, the splendid wedding processions of the wealthy, and even their funeral and triumphal processions,[7] wending their way through the city streets, provided entertaining diversions for the lower classes as well, as do royal weddings today.

[1] Heated wine was a favorite Roman drink.

[2] The bars may also have served food "to go" like a modern deli, since few people had space in their apartments for cooking more than grits.

[3] At Pompeii archeologists have discovered 20 inns and 118 bars.

[4] Lower-class women had fewer opportunities to get out of the house, to meet friends, and to relax. It was socially unacceptable for women to frequent bars. The only women found in bars were barmaids and prostitutes (frequently one and the same).

[5] Besides ordinary dinner parties, there were parties to celebrate births, election victories, and so on. In selection 98, Cicero spoke of an augural banquet; in selection 169, Pliny spoke of a coming-of-age party.

[6] Because Roman women were allowed to attend private parties, upper-class women were less confined than lower-class women. Some even managed to carry on extramarital affairs (see selections 62 and 63). Possession of slaves, who managed the household and cared for the children, also gave upper-class women greater freedom than lower-class women. It would be interesting to know whether the mental health problems associated with "cabin fever" were less serious among upper-class women.

[7] On wedding, funeral, and triumphal processions, see selections 50, 115, and 267.

The Pleasures of Life

The following inscription was an epitaph discovered at Rome.

303   *CIL* 6.15258 (*ILS* 8157)

Baths, wine, and sex ruin our bodies. But what makes life worth living except baths, wine, and sex?

304   *CIL* 8.17938

This sentiment was found in the mosaic pavement of a town in North Africa.

> Hunting, Bathing, Playing,[8]
> Laughing—That's Living.

Gambling and Gaming

People of all social classes were fond of gambling and gaming, and vast numbers of dice and knucklebones have been discovered by archeologists in sites throughout the Roman Empire. In one type of board game, six Latin words were inscribed on a board or tabletop. Each word consisted of six letters, and the words were so arranged that there were eighteen letters on each side of the board. Perhaps each player had a gaming piece which he moved from letter to letter, but we have no idea how the game was played. Here is one example of this arrangement of six words of six letters each.[9]

305   *Poetae Latini Minores* 4.132
                                  (pp. 119f. = *Carmina xii Sapientium*)

> SPERNE   LUCRUM
> VERSAT   MENTES
> INSANA   CUPIDO

The translation of these words reveals a message not inappropriate to a gambler.

SCORN WEALTH.[10] INSANE GREED[11] DISTURBS MINDS.[12]

[8] *playing:* probably with dice, or a board game.
[9] The Latin text of selection 304 reveals a similar arrangement of words: VENARI LAVARI LUDERE RIDERE OCCEST VIVERE.
[10] Sperne lucrum.
[11] Insana cupido.
[12] Versat mentes.

Athletic Activities

Some men liked to participate in athletic activities in their free time. One popular exercise area in Rome was the Campus Martius, which was also the area used for training the republican militia and convening the Comitia Centuriata. We have already noted that the militia muster and the Comitia Centuriata were in origin the same organization.[13] The use of the Campus Martius for recreational exercise is also probably connected in origin with its use as a military drill ground. In the early republican period, physical fitness was undoubtedly closely linked to preparation for warfare because, as long as Rome's army was a militia, each male citizen was expected to keep himself fit and ready.[14] Keeping fit thus had a practical purpose, and men would go to the Campus Martius to do exercises which developed strength and stamina, and exercises which provided training with arms (such as javelin throws). Even though the Roman attitude toward athletics changed over the centuries, from functional military training to recreational activity, the Romans continued to think of athletics mainly in terms of personal fitness, and they did not develop athletic competitions, such as the Olympic Games, popular elsewhere in the Mediterranean world.[15]

The passage translated here (which continues selection 77) mentions some of the activities which took place in the Campus Martius. Near the Campus was the Tiber River which was a popular swimming area.

306   Strabo, *Geography Book* 5.3.8

The size of the Campus is truly remarkable, for it allows chariot races and other equestrian activities to take place,[16] without interference, at the same time as a great multitude of people are involved in various physical exercises such as ballgames, running, and wrestling. The beautiful works of art scattered throughout the Campus and the grassy fields, green during the whole year, and the outlines of the hilly ridges which are on the other side of the river[17] and extend right to its banks—these provide for our visual enjoyment a landscape like the background scene-painting for a play, and a view from which you can scarcely take your eyes.

---

[13] See note 19 of Chapter X.

[14] Consider the physical activities which Cato (234–149 B.C.) planned for his son (selection 121): riding, fighting in armor, throwing javelins, boxing, and swimming. By 100 B.C., the militia had developed into a standing army; see the introduction to Chapter XI.

[15] The Olympic Games originated in Greece long before Greece became a Roman province. The Greeks held many other similar athletic competitions, both in mainland Greece and in the many Greek colonies throughout the Mediterranean world (including southern Italy). No distinction was made between amateurs and professionals (*pace* Avery Brundage), but by the Roman period most of the athletes competing in Greek games were professionals by our modern standards. (The Romans thought of them as performers; see selection 334.)

[16] *equestrian activities:* probably restricted to the wealthy.

[17] *river:* the Tiber.

BATHS

Bathing was a recreational activity enjoyed by people of all ages, sexes, and social classes. The wealthy might have bathing facilities in their own homes,[18] but most people used public establishments which were operated either by the state or by a private, profit-making company.[19] So popular were these baths that by the fourth century A.D. there were almost 1000 public bath buildings in Rome alone. And throughout Italy, indeed throughout the Roman Empire, almost every town and every village had at least one public bath building.[20] Bathing as a recreational activity had an interesting development in the Roman world. In Rome's early period, bathing and physical fitness were two quite separate issues. Bathing was strictly a matter of washing off dirt, as we shall see below in a passage from Seneca. And physical fitness was closely linked to militia training. Gradually, however, the sober, cautious, and hard-working Romans, who had thought that all activities must have a practical function, learned to relax and enjoy themselves, began to do things simply because they made them feel good, and realized that pleasure does not immediately lead to decadence. The public baths developed into fitness centers similar to our YMCA, health spas, or sports clubs. There were often areas for ballgames, jogging, various exercises, swimming, and massages as well as the baths proper which consisted of a hot-air, hot-tub room; warm-air, warm-tub room; and cold-air, cold-tub room. Other amenities frequently found in these establishments were snack shops, meeting rooms, and gardens. The baths catered to the total well-being of the person, providing the opportunity to keep fit, to relax in the warm water, and, very importantly, to socialize. The baths brought people together where they could chat, gossip, meet friends, and make contacts. The afternoon was apparently the most popular time for bathing,[21] but some baths opened in the morning.[22] Entrance fees were low,[23] and for many people a visit to the baths was part of the daily routine.

The Good Old Days

Publius Cornelius Scipio Africanus lived from 236 to about 184 B.C. He was the brilliant general who defeated Hannibal and the Carthaginians in the Second Punic

[18] See Pliny's description of his villa at Laurentum in selection 87. Larcius Macedo was attacked by his slaves while in his private baths (selection 195).

[19] See the rental advertisement in selection 74: "For rent: the elegant Venus Baths."

[20] There were four public baths in the town of Pompeii, which had a population of about 20,000. In the village near Pliny's Laurentine villa there were three public baths. Remains of Roman baths have been discovered at archeological sites throughout Europe, North Africa, and western Asia Minor. Roman baths have been discovered, for example, at Bath, England.

[21] See selection 146: "The eighth hour provides time for the sleek gymnasia."

[22] Some bathing establishments had separate facilities for men and for women; see figure 5. If separate facilities were not available, the women bathed in the morning.

[23] Occasionally a wealthy member of the community or, in the imperial period, the emperor would provide funds to cover entrance fees for everyone for a day, or even a week or a month. The donors hoped, of course, to win favor with this gesture.

War and was thus one of the great heroes of Roman history.[24] In this passage, taken from a letter to a friend, Seneca, who lived about 250 years after Scipio, describes a visit to the hero's villa. Seneca was particularly struck by the small size of the bath area and thought that the contrast between Scipio's baths and the grandiose baths of his own period reflected the contrast between ancient and contemporary Roman values.

307   Seneca the Younger, *Letters* 86.1, 4–6, 8, 11, 12

I am writing this letter to you while staying at the villa which once belonged to Scipio Africanus.[25] . . . The tiny bath area was narrow and, in keeping with ancient custom, dingy; our ancestors thought a bath should not be hot unless also dark.[26] And therefore a feeling of pleasure crept through me as I compared Scipio's customs with our own. In this little nook, the "terror of Carthage," to whom Rome is indebted for being captured only once,[27] washed a body which had been exhausted by farm work. For Scipio kept himself busy with hard labor and even plowed the land himself, as, of course, was the custom of our ancestors.[28] He stood right here, beneath this shabby roof, and this wretched floor bore his weight. Who is there nowadays who could bear to bathe in such a place? Everyone thinks himself impoverished and distressed unless the walls of his bath area sparkle with large and costly stone work, unless marbles from Alexandria alternate with marbles from Numidia, unless these marbles are coated with finishes of various colors and elaborate design, like paintings, unless the vaulted roof is covered with glass, unless Thasian marble, once a rare sight even in a temple, lines the swimming pools (into which we dip bodies from which the sweat has been squeezed[29]), unless the water pours out of silver faucets. . . . In this bath of Scipio, there are no windows, but rather very narrow slits cut out of the stone wall in such a way that light could be admitted without weakening the structure. But nowadays baths are called "moth havens" unless they are designed to receive the sun all day long through very wide windows, unless people can get clean and get a tan all at the same time, unless they have a view of meadows and ocean from their hot tub.[30] . . .

[24] On Scipio's family, see genealogy chart 2. On the Second Punic War, see note 87 of Chapter VII.

[25] Scipio's villa was at Liternum, a seaside town between Rome and Naples.

[26] A question of heat conservation rather than modesty. It was more energy-efficient to have very few windows in the hot-water room.

[27] Scipio defeated the Carthaginians and therefore prevented Rome from being captured. From its founding in 753 B.C. until the Visigoth invasion in A.D. 410, the city of Rome was captured only once, in 390 B.C. by the Gauls.

[28] On the Roman ideal of the soldier-farmer, see selections 1, 177, and 266.

[29] Seneca is contrasting the sweat produced by hard work in Scipio's day with the sweat squeezed out of the bodies of his contemporaries by massages or by long idle sessions in the *caldarium* (hot-air room).

[30] The Stabian Baths, the oldest public baths in Pompeii (see figure 5), were built about 100 B.C. They, too, were dark and dingy because there were so few windows. The designers thus hoped to prevent the heat from escaping. Bathers brought their own oil lamps to provide light, but it would be very dim light at best. However, the Central Baths at Pompeii, which were under construction when Vesuvius erupted in A.D. 79, were designed to have numerous large windows and to let in as much sunlight as possible. Some scholars believe that the wood fuel requirements of the public baths caused serious deforestation in Italy.

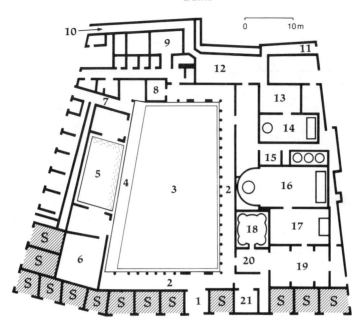

1. main entrance, men's baths
2. colonnade
3. palaestra (open-air exercise area)
4. bowling lane
5. swimming pool
6. dressing and massage room
7. side entrance, men's baths
8. office
9. toilets
10. entrance, women's baths
11. entrance, women's baths
12. apodyterium (dressing room), women's baths
13. tepidarium (warm room), women's baths
14. caldarium (hot room), with hot tub and basin, women's baths
15. furnace room, with three water tanks
16. caldarium, with hot tub and basin, men's baths
17. tepidarium, with warm tub, men's baths
18. frigidarium (cold room), men's baths
19. apodyterium, men's baths
20. vestibule
21. waiting room
S. shop

Figure 5. Plan of the Stabian Baths at Pompeii.
The Stabian Baths, the oldest of public bath buildings at Pompeii, was built in the second century B.C. but was repaired and remodeled in the subsequent two centuries. There were separate bathing areas for men and women (but no *frigidarium* for the women). Public baths with only one bathing area generally had separate hours for men and women.

Note that the two *calderia* (hot rooms for men and for women) are placed on opposite sides of the furnace and water tank room to conserve fuel. The small shops along the front and side walls of the building are not connected to the public baths, although some may have sold bath supplies, such as oil and towels, or food snacks.

Some people nowadays condemn Scipio as being extremely uncouth because he did not let the daylight into his *caldarium* through wide windows, because he did not boil[31] himself in a well-lit room, and because he didn't linger in the hot tub until he was stewed. "What an unfortunate man!" they say. "He didn't know how to live well. He bathed in water which was unfiltered, which in fact was often murky and, after a heavy rain, was almost muddy." But it didn't matter much to Scipio whether he bathed in murky water, because he came to the baths to wash off sweat, not oily perfumes![32] . . . And he didn't bathe every day. Writers who have passed on to us the

[31] Seneca is contrasting Scipio, who kept his bath water at a reasonable temperature, with people of his own time, who wanted the water to be as hot as possible and who lingered in the water rather than simply washing and leaving.

[32] *oily perfumes:* a reference to the oils that were used for massages during Seneca's time; see Martial's "sleek gymnasia" (selection 146). On the use of a *strigil,* see note 40 of Chapter VII.

ancient customs of Rome say that our ancestors washed only their arms and legs every day, since these parts of the body were covered with dirt from farm work. The rest of the body was washed only once a week. Of course, someone will at this point say, "Sure, but they were very smelly men." And what do you think they smelled of? Of the army, of farm work, and of manliness!

Living above a Public Bath Building

As was noted in the introduction to selection 69, it was common for rooms above shops or factories to be used as apartments. In the passage translated here, Seneca writes to his friend Lucilius about his apartment in Rome which was situated over a public bath building. (We might compare life in an apartment directly above a health club or the YMCA.) Seneca's letter provides valuable information not only about housing in the ancient Roman world but also about some of the activities at the public baths.

308   Seneca the Younger, *Letters* 56.1, 2

If silence is as necessary as it seems for someone who wants seclusion to read and study, then I'm really in trouble. Here I am surrounded on all sides by a variety of noises. I live right over a public bath. Just imagine the whole range of voices which can irritate my ears. When the more muscular types are exercising and swinging about lead weights in their hands, and when they are straining themselves, or at least pretending to strain, I hear groans. And when they hold their breath for a while and then let it out, I hear hissing and very hoarse gasps. But when I have to put up with an unathletic fellow, one satisfied with a low-class rub-down, I hear the slap of a hand pummeling his shoulders (the sound varies somewhat, depending on whether the hand is flat or cupped). Now, if a ballplayer comes along and begins to count his score aloud, I'm definitely finished.[33] Imagine also a quarrelsome drunk, or sometimes a thief caught in the act, or a man who loves to sing in the bath. And then imagine people diving into the pool with a great splash of water.

Besides these men, whose voices are, if nothing else, at least natural, imagine the hair plucker with his shrill and high-pitched voice, continually shrieking in order to be noticed; he's never quiet, except when he's plucking armpits and forcing his customer to shriek instead of him. I could wear myself out just listening to the variety of shouts among people selling drinks, sausages, and pastries; each restaurant or snack bar has its own huckster with his own recognizable jingle.

The Design of a Bath Building

In this passage, Lucian, a Greek author of the second century A.D., describes a bath building designed by an architect-engineer of his own period. The contrast between these baths and the baths at Scipio's villa is striking.

[33] Ballgames of various kinds were popular in the Roman world. See selections 306, 310, and 323.

The entranceway is lofty and has a wide flight of steps which are low rather than steep, for the convenience of people walking up them. You enter into a very spacious hall which provides a large waiting area for slaves and attendants. To the left of this hall are rooms designed for relaxation, and therefore particularly well suited to a bath building—elegant, well-lit, and private rooms. Next to these is a meeting room larger than one normally finds in a bath building, but necessary for reception of the wealthy. Beyond this room are two spacious locker rooms and, between them, a lofty and brightly lit hall which contains three cold-water swimming pools. It is decorated with slabs of Laconian marble and with two white marble statues. . . .

Upon leaving this hall, you enter into a large room which is long, rounded at each end, and slightly warm, rather than being confronted suddenly with intense heat. Beyond this room and to the right is a very bright room which is quite suitably arranged for rub-downs with oil. At each end it has an entryway decorated with Phrygian marble to provide access for those coming in from the exercise area. And then near this room is another large room, the most beautiful of all rooms, very well designed for standing about or sitting down, for whiling away time without fear of reproach, or for occupying your time most profitably. It, too, gleams from top to bottom with Phrygian marble.

Next you enter a passageway heated with hot air[34] and faced with Numidian marble. It leads into a very beautiful room which is filled with bright light and resplendent with purple.[35] This room contains three hot tubs.[36] Once you have bathed, you don't need to go back again through the same rooms. Instead, you can go immediately through a small, slightly warm room[37] to a cold room.[38]

Every room has a great deal of sunlight coming in. In addition, the height of each room is of good proportion, and the width corresponds well with the length. . . . The cold room lies in the north part of the building, but the rooms that need a lot of heat are situated in the south, east, and west. . . .

The building also has two privies and many entrances and exits, and provides two devices for telling time—a loud water clock and a sundial.

DINNER PARTIES

The Romans enjoyed getting together with their friends over dinner. For the poor (for whom frequent dinner guests would be a burden), funeral clubs provided

---

[34] Hot air was piped from the furnace room (see figure 5) into hollow spaces in the floors and walls of the rooms. For more information about such heating systems, see footnotes 66 of Chapter IV and 81 of Chapter VIII.

[35] Probably with porphyry, a stone or rock with purple hue.

[36] The *caldarium*, or "hot room." Hot air was piped into the floors and walls, and hot water for the hot tubs was piped from a large tank or cauldron in the furnace room.

[37] The *tepidarium*, or "warm room." Warm air was piped into the floors and walls. In some Roman baths, the *tepidarium* had a tub or a basin full of warm water piped from the furnace room.

[38] The *frigidarium*, or "cold room."

an opportunity for dinner meetings.[39] Dinner parties in private homes ranged from austere to wildly extravagant with respect to both the food and the entertainment provided.[40] The passages translated here inform us about the behavior of guests and hosts.[41]

Fishing for a Dinner Invitation

Since bathing was an afternoon activity, many bathers went from the baths directly home to dinner.[42] Some people used a visit to the baths as an opportunity to fish for a dinner invitation.

310   Martial, *Epigrams* 12.82

Whether you are in the hot room or anywhere else in the bath building, there is no way to escape from Menogenes, although you may try with all your might. He will grab the warm ball with either his left hand or his right hand so that he can add the balls he has caught to your score.[43] He will pick up from the dust and hand back to you the flabby inflatable ball, even if he has already bathed and has already put on his sandals. When you pick up your towel which is dirtier than a child's bib, he will exclaim that it is whiter than snow. While you are combing your thin hair, he will say that you are styling Achilles' locks. He will carry over to you a smoky jug of wine and wipe the sweat from your brow. He will praise everything, he will marvel at everything, until finally, having endured his thousand tedious ploys, you say, "Come and have dinner with me."

An Early Dinner Guest

311   Martial, *Epigrams* 8.67

Your slave has not yet announced the fifth hour,[44] and yet you have already arrived as my dinner guest, Caecilianus, even though the strident fourth hour[45] has only now begun to defer court appearances and the arena is still torturing wild animals at Flora's

---

[39] On funeral clubs, see selection 116.

[40] See selections 89, 90 and 91. At Trimalchio's banquet (selection 210), some of the foods served were wild boar stuffed with live thrushes, which were released when the boar was carved but then captured and cooked; dormice sprinkled with honey and poppy seed; pastry eggs with figpeckers inside; pastry thrushes stuffed with raisins and nuts.

[41] On the behavior at some parties, see selections 63, 67, and 210.

[42] Large dinner parties may also have begun early but extended into the evening hours because entertainment was provided (such as singers, dancers, and recitations). Dinner parties provided the only after-dark entertainment. Because the Romans depended on natural light (i.e., the sun), theater and amphitheater events and chariot racing were daytime entertainments. On the dangers of being out at night, see Juvenal's comments in selection 81.

[43] On the popularity of ballgames, see note 33 of this chapter.

[44] *fifth hour:* that is, after sunrise, about 11:00 a.m.

[45] See selection 146: "the third hour taxes the talents of strident lawyers." Here the hour itself is personified as strident and as engaging in legal affairs.

festival.[46] Quick, Callistus,[47] run and summon back my unwashed slaves.[48] Have the dining couches set up. Good! Now, Caecilianus, please sit down. What? You want warm water. But my cold water hasn't arrived yet.[49] My kitchen is still closed and chilly since the stove is without a fire. Better you should come at dawn. Why wait until the fifth hour? If you want breakfast, Caecilianus, you've come too late.

A Thrifty Man

312   Martial, *Epigrams* 5.47

Philo swears that he has never dined at home, and that's the truth. He just doesn't dine unless someone invites him over!

Roman Doggy Bags

The same Caecilianus who arrived for dinner so early[50] also felt no shame about taking home a few leftovers. Since Roman dinner guests brought their own napkins to parties, they could easily prepare doggy bags.

313   Martial, *Epigrams* 2.37

Whatever is placed on the table, you sweep up from all sides: teats from a sow's udder, and ribs of a pig, and a meadow bird carved for two, and half a mullet, and a whole pike, and the side of a moray, and the leg of a chicken, and a pigeon dripping with a sauce made from grits. You hide these things in your greasy napkin and give them to your slave to carry home. The rest of us recline at the table, relaxed and inattentive. If you have any shame, Caecilianus, return my food. I didn't invite you for dinner also tomorrow!

A Shameless Guest

By the imperial period, the nature of the patron-client relationship had changed a great deal; many clients were former slaves.[51] They expected regular dinner

[46] The arena, where various spectacles involving combats of men and animals took place, is here personified. *Arena* (also spelled *harena*) actually means "sand." The site of these combats was covered with sand to soak up the blood.

Flora's games: Flora was the goddess of flowers. A festival in her honor was celebrated each year from April 28 to May 3. As part of the celebration, state-financed entertainment was provided (theater performances, chariot races, and spectacles in the arena).

[47] *Callistus:* one of Martial's slaves.

[48] Martial's slaves have not yet had time for bathing, which was, of course, an afternoon activity.

[49] A slave has not yet had time to fetch water from the fountain, much less to heat it.

[50] See selection 311.

[51] See the introduction to selection 9.

invitations from their patrons or former masters, and evidently they sometimes abused their patrons' hospitality.

314   Martial, *Epigrams* 7.20

There is no one and no thing more miserly or more gluttonous than Santra. As soon as he has been invited, he rushes right off to the dinner party for which he has fished for so many days and nights. He asks for three helpings of boar's neck, four helpings of pork loin, for both hipbones of the rabbit and both shoulder blades. He doesn't even blush when he lies about the roast thrush or steals the bluish oysters from their shells. He conceals in his filthy napkin mouthfuls of cake. He also hides there grape preserves and a few apple cores and the ugly outer skin of a hollowed womb[52] and an oozing fig and a limp mushroom. But when his napkin is already bursting with his thousand petty thefts, he hides in the warm folds of his toga gnawed bones and the body of a turtle-dove (its head having been devoured). Nor does he think it disgusting to pick up with his long right arm anything the floor sweepers and dogs have left. And food is not the only object of his gluttony: he fills a jug to the brim with diluted wine.[53] When he has greedily carried all this loot home, up 200 stairs, and nervously shut himself in his locked closet apartment—then the next day he sells it!

A Napkin Thief

Catullus threatens to write (and, in doing so, actually does write) verses exposing Asinius Marrucinus as a thief who steals the napkins which other guests bring with them to dinner parties.

315   Catullus, *Poems* 12

Asinius Marrucinus, you certainly don't use your left hand[54] in a very polite way. While we are relaxed and inattentive, telling jokes and drinking, you are stealing our napkins. Do you think this is cute? Well, you're wrong, you ill-mannered fool. It's an ugly and quite vulgar type of behavior. You don't believe me? Then believe your brother Pollio,[55] who would gladly pay a talent[56] to compensate for your thefts. For he is a young man[57] full of charm and wit. And so either look out for 300 lines of scathing verse, or return my napkin to me. It's not the cost of the napkin which worries me, but it's a souvenir from my friends. Fabullus and Veranius sent me napkins

---

[52] The womb had probably been stuffed with sausage meat and served, like haggis.

[53] The Romans generally diluted their wine with water before drinking it.

[54] *left hand:* Latin *sinistra,* from which we have the English word *sinister.* The left hand was considered more capable of dishonest acts than the right hand.

[55] *Gaius Asinius Pollio:* a Roman orator and historian who lived from 76 B.C. to A.D. 5. His lifetime thus spanned the end of the republican period and the establishment of the principate.

[56] *talent:* a large sum of money; see note 22 of Chapter XII.

[57] This poem was probably written about 60 B.C. Catullus died about 54 B.C.

from Saetabis in Spain,[58] and I must cherish them as I cherish my dear Veranius and Fabullus.

A Rude Host

Some hosts were very rude to their guests, and served different foods to different guests at the same party, the quality of the food depending on the guest's social rank. Clients, in particular, often received food of a much lower quality than the host himself was eating.[59]

316   Martial, *Epigrams* 10.49

While you are drinking pints of deep purple wine, Cotta, and guzzling rich dark Opimian,[60] you set before me Sabine wine which has just been made.[61] And then you ask me, "Do you want a gold wine goblet?" Who wants a gold goblet for lead wines?

House of the Moralist

Although most dinner parties were probably quiet affairs, we have learned from Ovid and Suetonius that dinner parties were sometimes used as occasions for adulterous intrigue.[62] One homeowner in Pompeii tried to prevent such behavior, or any other disruptive behavior, by painting "rules of conduct" on the walls of his *triclinium* or dining room. His house has been labeled by modern scholars as the "House of the Moralist."

317   *CIL* 4.7698

Keep your lascivious looks and bedroom eyes away from another man's wife. Maintain a semblance of decency on your face.

Be sociable and put aside, if you can, annoying quarrels. If you can't, go back to your own home.

RECITATIONS

Wining, dining, gambling, and bathing appealed to men (and women) of all social classes. One leisure activity, however, attendance at recitations, was of interest

---

[58] Fabullus and Veranius served on the governor's staff in Spain. Saetabis (modern Javita) was in eastern Spain and was well known for its textile industry.

[59] Compare Juvenal's complaints in selection 13.

[60] *Opimian:* an excellent and rare wine which had been well aged.

[61] *Sabine:* a common wine. The wine given to Martial has not even been aged.

[62] See selections 63 and 67.

to only a very small group of people. A recitation was a reading aloud of a literary work. Boys in the upper classes of Roman society spent their school years learning how to write elegantly, to speak effectively, and to analyze literary style. Even after they had finished their formal schooling, they continued to write, to speak in public, and to read extensively. During the republican period, men found an outlet for their creative energies in public speaking; years of formal training enabled them to compose and declaim brilliant speeches for the law courts and public assemblies. In the imperial period, opportunities for public speaking were curtailed.[63] Men therefore created opportunities to present their literary work before an audience. They planned private parties to which they invited their friends and clients to hear them recite or declaim their latest literary masterpiece.[64] Poems, essays, and speeches were all proper fare for a recitation. There had been recitations in the republican period, but they became more popular as an upper-class leisure activity during the imperial period.

The Persistent Poet

Some men invited guests for dinner and then offered them, as after-dinner entertainment, a recitation of the host's literary work.[65] (One might certainly hesitate to accept a dinner invitation from a bad poet.) However, Ligurinus not only held dinner-party recitations; he recited his poems to any friend he happened to meet, anywhere.

318   Martial, *Epigrams* 3.44, 3.50

Do you want to know, Ligurinus, why it is that no one smiles when he meets you on the street, why there is a mass exodus wherever you approach, why there is a vast loneliness around you? Because you are too much a poet! This is a very dangerous character flaw. No tiger, enraged by the theft of her cubs, no serpent scorched by the tropical sun, no murderous scorpion is so feared. For who, I ask you, can endure such great ordeals? You recite to me when I'm standing up and when I'm sitting down. You recite to me when I'm jogging and when I'm taking a crap. I run to the public baths to escape—you are there, bellowing in my ear. I dive into the pool, but you won't let me swim.[66] I hurry out to dinner; you detain me at the door. I arrive at the dinner table; you drive me away even as I'm eating. Exhausted, I lie down to sleep; you wake me up even as I'm sleeping. Do you want to know just how much harm you are doing? Although you are a just, virtuous, and innocent man, people fear you!

This, and no other, is your reason for inviting me to dinner: so that you may recite to me your verses, Ligurinus. I arrive. I take off my shoes. At once you have a

---

[63] There were no opportunities, for example, to address the popular assemblies (which no longer voted; see selection 245). In the Senate and the law courts, moreover, a man had to be very careful about his choice of words and topics lest he offend the emperor; on freedom of speech in the imperial period, see selection 247.

[64] It was a client's duty to attend his patron's recitations and applaud loudly.

[65] See selections 89 and 90.

[66] On activity at public baths, see selection 308.

huge volume of verses brought in with the lettuce and fish sauce.[67] A second volume is read out, in its entirety, while the main course gets cold. A third volume is produced, and dessert has not yet been served. Then you recite a fourth and finally a fifth volume. If you keep serving me the pork dish, again and again, I'll be sick.[68] If you don't confine your awful poems to the mackerel dish,[69] Ligurinus, from now on you will dine at home, alone.

The Popularity of Recitations

Pliny seems genuinely to have enjoyed recitations. However, many people obviously considered attendance at recitations a friendly obligation, as we learn from this letter to Pliny's friend Sosius Senecio.

319   Pliny the Younger, *Letters* 1.13

This year has produced a great harvest of poets. During the whole month of April scarcely a day went by on which someone did not give a recitation. I'm pleased that literary studies are flourishing and that talented men come forward and perform, although people are reluctant to attend. The greater part sit in the vestibules and spend the recital time exchanging gossip; from time to time they ask to have it announced whether the reciter has arrived yet, whether he has read the preface, whether he has gone through most of the book.[70] Not until then, and even then slowly and reluctantly, do they enter the lecture hall. However, they don't stay; they leave before the end, some stealthily and slyly, others openly and boldly. But, by Hercules, the previous generation remembers a different kind of behavior. They say that the emperor Claudius[71] was walking one day on the Palatine[72] and heard a shout. He inquired about the source of the shout, and, when he was told that Nonianus[73] was reciting, he immediately and unexpectedly went to hear him. Nowadays, however, even people with the most time on their hands, who have been invited well in advance and reminded again and again, do not show up at recitations or, if they do show up, complain that they have wasted a day (because, in fact, they have *not* wasted it).[74] But we should praise and encourage all the more those authors who are not deterred from their love of writing and reciting by either the laziness or the haughtiness of their audiences. For my part, I scarcely

[67] *Gustatio* or appetizers; see selections 89, 90, 91.

[68] That is, he keeps serving the main dish (the pork) and does not serve dessert, because he wants to keep his guest at the dinner table as long as possible.

[69] *mackerel dish:* the *gustatio.*

[70] The Latin is literally "whether he has unrolled," since the "book" was, of course, a papyrus roll.

[71] *Claudius:* 10 B.C.–A.D. 54 (emperor A.D. 41–54). Another reference to the "good old days," although the "good old days" are relative to one's own time period. Tacitus thought Cicero had lived in the good old days (selections 137 and 141). Cicero thought Cincinnatus had lived in the good old days (selection 177). See also Seneca's comments on Scipio's baths in selection 307.

[72] *the Palatine:* one of the Seven Hills of Rome. It rises above the Forum. The Imperial Palaces were built on the Palatine; see note 94 of Chapter X.

[73] *Marcus Servilius Nonianus:* consul A.D. 35 (died A.D. 59).

[74] That is, they usually squander their day doing nothing.

ever miss a recitation. Of course, usually the people reciting are friends of mine; for there is almost no one who is fond of literary studies who is not also fond of me. For these reasons I have spent a longer time in the city than I had intended. Now I can seek seclusion[75] and write something—which I will not, however, recite lest I seem, to those whose recitations I attended, to have been not a listener but a lender.[76] In the matter of listening, as in other matters, the favor is no longer a favor if you expect a return.

A Recitation at Pliny's House

320   Pliny the Younger, *Letters* 8.21

In literary studies, as in life, it is, I think, most commendable and most civilized to interweave seriousness and joviality lest the former develop into moroseness and the latter into flippancy. Following this reasoning, I punctuate my more serious writings with witty and frivolous little pieces. I chose the most opportune time and place to publish them:[77] in order that my little writings might get used to being heard both by relaxed friends and in their own dining room, in the month of July, when the law courts are especially quiet,[78] I set up some writing desks[79] in front of the dining couches and gathered a group of friends.[80] . . . The book was a collection of little poems in different meters. This is how we, who have little confidence in our own talent, avoid the danger of being cloying. I recited for two days. The audience (which was highly approving) forced me to! Of course, I never leave anything out anyway, and I state that policy clearly. Other writers do omit some passages—and thereby implicitly brand as bad the passages they omit. But I recite everything so that I may improve everything, a possibility not open to those who read only selections. Reading only selections is the more modest and perhaps more decorous behavior, but my behavior is the more sincere and more suitable among friends. For if you treat a man as a friend, he will be your friend, and you need not fear boring him. Otherwise, what good are friends if they visit you only for their own pleasure? That man is spoiled, and no better than a stranger, who prefers to hear his friend's book in its final, polished form rather than to help him polish it.

I have no doubt that you, because of your friendship with me, wish to read my book as soon as possible, although it is not yet "ripe." You will get to read it, but after it has been corrected, since that was, of course, the point of the recitation. Yet

[75] Perhaps in his villa at Laurentum; see selection 87.

[76] *lender:* that is, that he gave them his time but expected them to give him their time when he planned a recitation.

[77] *publish:* from the Latin *publicare,* "to make public property," "to impart to the people." Thus, recitations were one method of publishing one's work.

[78] There were fewer cases heard and tried in July because (1) the courts were recessed quite a large number of days for public holidays or festivals, and (2) many lawyers took vacations in this hot month and left Rome for their cooler country or seaside homes.

[79] *writing desks:* guests were expected to write down their comments and criticisms of Pliny's work. Indeed, one purpose of recitations was to obtain the advice of friends before formally publishing one's work.

[80] In selection 54, Pliny says that his wife attended his recitations: "She sits nearby, concealed behind a curtain, and listens very eagerly to the praise I win."

you already know some of the parts. After these have been corrected (or perhaps spoiled—a danger of too long a delay!), you will find new passages and rewritten passages. And when many things have been changed, even those which were not changed seem to have been changed.

HUNTING AND LITERARY STUDIES

Pliny's Hunting Expedition

For poor men in rural areas, occasional fishing and hunting expeditions undoubtedly offered needed relaxation from hard toil on the farm and, more importantly, provided families with a supply of meat. For these families, hunting and fishing were as much a necessity as a pleasure. For the upper classes, however, who could easily afford to buy meat, hunting was a leisure activity, indulged in during a visit to one's country estate. Landowners probably invited friends to stay over for a few days to enjoy hunting parties. Some hunting involved the pursuit of the hunted animal either by horseback or on foot. In other cases, the hunters did not track down their quarry, but simply waited in one spot while beaters with dogs drove the animals into nets. Once the animals were ensnared, the "hunters" stabbed them and then claimed to have made a kill.[81] Not everyone was enthusiastic about hunting. In this letter, Pliny describes to his friend Tacitus, the famous historian, his behavior at a hunting party. It should not surprise us to learn that Pliny, who so enjoyed recitations, spent his time by the hunting nets engaged in literary composition.

321 Pliny the Younger, *Letters* 1.6

You will laugh, and well you may. I, that Pliny whom you know well, captured three wild boars, and very handsome ones at that! "You?" you will exclaim. Yes, me! Not that I interrupted my quiet and inactive studies, mind you. I just happened to be sitting by the nets. I didn't even have a spear or a lance beside me. Instead I had a stilus and some waxed tablets.[82] I was busy composing thoughts and jotting down notes so that I would bring back tablets that were full even if my hands were empty.[83] There is no reason for you to scorn this type of literary activity. In fact, it is amazing how the mind is stimulated by the movement and activity of the body. Moreover, the woods on all sides and the solitude and the very silence itself which hunting demands are also great inducements to creative thinking. And so, the next time you go hunting, take my advice and take along with you a picnic basket and a bottle of wine and your waxed

---

[81] Many Romans apparently enjoyed the kill, and watching the kill, more than the pursuit. One of the popular arena events was the wild animal "hunt." The spectators watched as animals of many different species were driven into the arena and then slaughtered by "hunters."

[82] *stilus, waxed tablets:* see selection 132.

[83] *empty:* that is, of game.

tablets certainly. You will discover that Minerva roams the mountains as much as Diana.[84]

A Day in the Country

Unlike Pliny, Marcus Aurelius was quite fond of hunting. The letter translated here was written to his friend and teacher, Fronto, between A.D. 144 and 145.[85] In fact, it was written just one day before the letter in which Marcus described his chat with his mother when he was visiting his parents' home.[86] The hunt he mentions in this letter was apparently a pursuit on horseback, but the quarry was the same as that of Pliny's hunting party: wild boar. Although Marcus Aurelius and Pliny may have had differing opinions about hunting, they shared an appreciation for literary studies. Like many men of their class, they believed that it was important to occupy a part of one's leisure with productive intellectual activities such as reading, research, and writing.[87] This emphasis on the profitable use of one's time seems to suit the practical, rather puritanical element of the Roman "self-image."[88] We must remember, however, that our sources are men who had a genuine interest in and talent for research and writing (or they would not have written these letters), and that not everyone shared this attitude that leisure should be mentally stimulating and intellectually profitable. There were undoubtedly quite a few men of leisure who would fit the modern caricature of the empty-headed, fox-hunting country squire.

322   Marcus Aurelius, *Fronto's Letters* 4.5

We are all well. Today I worked at my studies from about 3:00 a.m. to about 8:00 a.m., having arranged for some snacks in advance.[89] Between 8:00 and 9:00 a.m., wearing only slippers, I cheerfully paced up and down in front of my bedroom. Then I put on my boots and my short cape (for we had been told to come dressed in that way) and went to say good morning to my lord. We all set off on a hunt, and did daring deeds. We heard by word of mouth that boars had been caught, but we weren't able to see for ourselves. We did, however, climb quite a steep hill. In the afternoon we returned home.

[84] Minerva was the patron goddess of literary activity; Diana was the patron goddess of hunting.

[85] Marcus Aurelius was emperor A.D. 161–180.

[86] See selection 18. In selection 176, Marcus wrote to Fronto about terrorizing shepherds.

[87] In selection 87, Pliny speaks of retiring to the study of his Laurentine villa during the Saturnalia: "Here I don't disturb the festivities of my household, and they don't disturb my studies." In selection 169, he says he prefers reading at his villa to the silly occupations of the city because "it is better to be idle than to do idle things." Seneca, when complaining about his apartment over the bath building (selection 308), says he wants "seclusion to read and study." Cicero, writing from his villa about his grief at his daughter's death (selection 111), says: "Even my reading is interrupted by fits of weeping."

[88] On the Roman "self-image," see selection 1.

[89] The next day (on which the conversation with his mother occurred), Marcus spent the hours from 5:00 to 9:00 a.m. reading Cato's book *On Agriculture;* for excerpts from this book, see selections 184, 356, 366, 372, and 408.

And I returned to my books. After pulling off my boots and taking off my cape, I stayed on my couch[90] for nearly two hours. I read Cato's speech, "On the Property of Pulchra," and another in which he impeached a tribune. "Hey," you say to your slave, "go as fast as you can and bring me those speeches from the library of Apollo."[91] You will be sending him in vain, for those volumes have followed me here! You must therefore ingratiate yourself with the librarian at the library of Tiberius.[92] You might offer him a tip (which he and I will share equally when I come back to town).

Once I had read these speeches carefully, I wrote a few wretched things, which are only suitable for dedication either to water or to fire. . . .

I seem to have caught a cold; I don't know whether it was from walking in slippers in the morning or from writing badly. I do, it's true, frequently suffer nasal congestion, but today my nose seems to be running much more than usual. And so I will pour oil on my head and go to sleep.[93] I don't think I'll put one drop of the oil in my lamp today,[94] because the riding[95] and sneezing have so tired me out. Farewell, my dearest and sweetest teacher whom I miss (dare I say it!) more than Rome itself.

TRAVEL

Despite the very considerable difficulties and dangers of travel in the ancient world, some Romans were frequent travelers. For business reasons and on military service, they journeyed throughout the Roman world and beyond. Political and diplomatic missions, too, demanded trips away from home.[96] But some people traveled for pleasure as well, and made journeys on both land and sea in order to study abroad,[97] to reach their vacation villas,[98] to visit friends, and generally to see the sights. Their eagerness to travel is admirable, especially when we consider how uncomfortable the experience could be. Many people walked from place to place, carrying their own baggage. Some rode donkeys, or were carried in litters borne by slaves, or traveled in vehicles drawn by draft animals over bumpy roads.

[90] The Romans reclined on couches to read as well as to eat.

[91] This library was built by Augustus and situated in the Temple of Apollo on the Palatine. By the fourth century A.D., there were twenty-nine libraries in the city of Rome. Apparently books (i.e., papyrus rolls) could be checked out, as Marcus has done. The generous Pliny the Younger built a library in his hometown of Comum; for his other benefactions, see selection 129.

[92] This library was located in the palace of Tiberius on the Palatine.

[93] Although we read elsewhere of people pouring oil on their heads to relieve cold symptoms, the point of this procedure is not clear. The next morning, Marcus gargled with honey and water.

[94] That is, he will not need a reading lamp because he is too tired to read.

[95] *riding:* that is, on the hunt.

[96] Governors and their staffs, for example, made lengthy journeys to and within their provinces. In Italy itself, some citizens who lived outside of Rome may have traveled to that city each year for the elections. And in the provinces, some people had to travel to their "place of origin" for the census; see selections 165 and 166.

[97] The younger Cicero, for example, went to Athens; see selection 144.

[98] In selection 87, Pliny talks about traveling to his villa at Laurentum.

Dangers included highwaymen and bad roadside food. On sea voyages, travelers had very cramped quarters and were threatened by shipwreck and pirates.[99]

Along the Appian Way

The poet Horace was of humble origin; he was born in a small town in southern Italy, and his father was a freedman.[100] However, his father gave him the very best education his modest means could afford. Horace worked for a while as a clerk in the quaestor's office, but he managed to publish some poems which attracted the attention not only of other poets such as Vergil but also of a very well-known and generous literary patron named Maecenas. Maecenas was a wealthy equestrian who served as a trusted advisor to Octavian (later the emperor Augustus),[101] and it was through Maecenas that Horace was introduced to Octavian.

In the following passage, Horace describes a journey he made from Rome to Brundisium.[102] He does not explain the purpose of this journey, but he does tell us that a rendezvous was planned at Anxur with Maecenas and Cocceius, who was a close friend of Mark Antony, "both of them ambassadors, sent out on matters of great importance since they had reputations for patching up broken alliances." The alliance referred to is undoubtedly the uneasy and fragile political friendship between Mark Antony and Octavian (Augustus).[103] This journey probably took place in 38 B.C., when Maecenas and Cocceius traveled to Athens to deliver a message from Octavian to Antony. Horace and Vergil accompanied them as far as Brundisium. However, Horace has chosen not to give us any details about his historic diplomatic mission. In fact, he seems deliberately to mislead us, to describe his journey as a leisurely and carefree trip, to give emphasis to humorous but minor details, pretending, as he frequently does, that he is just a poor, simple poet, thankful for the patronage of political figures but quite unaware of the power they wield.

323　　　　　　　　　　Horace, *Satires* 1.5.1–33, 37–51, 70–97, 104

I set out on my journey and left behind me the bustling city of Rome.[104] When I reached the little town of Aricia[105] I stopped at a small inn. My traveling companion was Heliodorus, the rhetor, by far the most learned of the Greeks. From Aricia we

[99] On pirates, see note 53 of Chapter XII.

[100] For more on Horace's youth, see selection 15.

[101] On Augustus's employment of equestrians as advisors and as civil service officers, see selection 243.

[102] *Brundisium:* modern Brindisi, a town in southern Italy on the Adriatic coast. It was the regular departure point for ships to Greece. The distance from Rome to Brindisi on the Appian Way was about 370 miles.

[103] On the Second Triumvirate, see note 80 of Chapter III and note 18 of Chapter XIII.

[104] Horace headed south on the Via Appia, or Appian Way, Rome's oldest highway. It was begun in 312 B.C. to facilitate military and commercial expansion. Parts of this ancient road are still in use today.

[105] See map 2. It was about sixteen miles from Rome to Aricia. Horace probably rode or drove rather than walked. See selection 87, in which Pliny describes his journey to his Laurentine villa.

went to Forum Appii, which was crowded with boatmen and greedy innkeepers.[106] Being rather lazy, we had spread this part of the trip over two days, although more energetic travelers make it in one. But the Appian Way is less tiring if you go slowly.

Because the drinking water at Forum Appii is so incredibly foul, I endured hunger pangs and waited impatiently while my traveling companions had dinner.[107] And now night was preparing to spread her shadows over the earth and sprinkle her stars in the sky.[108] Slaves jeered at boatmen,[109] and boatmen chided slaves. "Put in here!" "You're taking on hundreds!" "Hey, that's enough!" By the time the fare was paid and the mule hitched,[110] a whole hour had gone by. The damn mosquitoes and frogs in the marsh made sleep impossible,[111] while a boatman and a passenger, both drunk from too much cheap wine, took turns serenading their absent girlfriends. Finally the passenger was exhausted and fell asleep. The lazy boatmen left the mule to graze, fastening the harness traces to a rock, and then lay on his back and snored. Day was already dawning before we noticed that the boat wasn't moving an inch. So one hothead jumped out of the boat and beat both the boatman and the mule on the head and loins with a willow club. Finally, about 10:00,[112] we had just arrived at Feronia's waters.[113]

We washed our hands and faces there and ate some breakfast. Then we crawled along for three miles, climbing steadily up to Anxur which sits atop shining, very conspicuous rocks. Maecenas, an excellent man, and Cocceius were to meet us there, both of them ambassadors, sent out on matters of great importance since they had reputations for patching up broken alliances. At Anxur[114] I smeared some black ointment on my sore eyes. Maecenas and Cocceius arrived and, with them, Fonteius Capito, a polished gentleman and Antony's best friend. . . . The following day, weary from our travels, we stopped at Formiae;[115] we had dinner at Capito's[116] and spent the night at Murena's.[117] We were eager to see the dawn of the next day because Plotius, Varius, and Vergil[118] met us that day at Sinuessa.[119] The earth has not borne souls more

[106] It was about twenty-seven miles from Aricia to Forum Appii. The town of Forum Appii ("the Forum of Appius," named after Appius Claudius, censor in 312 B.C., who initiated the building of the Via Appia, also named after him) was situated at the northern edge of a marshy plain called the Pomptine Marshes. Although the Via Appia did skirt the Pomptine Marshes, there was also a canal through the marsh, and it was thus possible to travel by canal boat. On highwaymen in the Pomptine Marshes, see Juvenal's comments in selection 81.

[107] Horace preferred to be hungry and thirsty rather than to risk dysentery.

[108] Mock-heroic style; see selections 174 and 180. The imitation of a lofty poetic style humorously jars with the subject of the following sentence: very low-class slaves and boatmen.

[109] *boatmen:* employed on the canal boats.

[110] The mule pulls the canal boat.

[111] Horace is now traveling on the canal boat.

[112] *about 10:00:* the fourth hour; on Roman divisions of time, see selection 145.

[113] Feronia was an ancient Italian goddess. There was a temple of Feronia at the southern edge of the Pomptine Marshes. It is here that Horace leaves the canal boat.

[114] It was about nineteen miles from Forum Appii to Anxur (modern Terracina).

[115] It was about twenty-six miles from Forum Appii to Formiae. Formiae was the hometown of Mamurra, who was reviled by Catullus in selection 246. Larcius Macedo (selection 195) was attacked by slaves in his villa at Formiae.

[116] Capito apparently had a vacation villa at Formiae. Travelers preferred to stay at the homes or villas of friends rather than at inns or hotels. Private homes were undoubtedly cleaner, quieter, and more comfortable.

[117] *Lucius Licinius Terentius Varro Murena:* another friend with a vacation home in the area which he made available to Horace and his traveling companions.

[118] Like Vergil, Plotius and Varius were poets.

[119] It was about eighteen miles from Formiae to Sinuessa.

splendid than these! And no one is more deeply attached to them than I. Oh, how many times we hugged one another and laughed with glee. As long as I'm in my right mind, there is nothing I could compare to a pleasant friend. A little house[120] near the Campanian bridge provided shelter for the night. . . .

The next day we traveled from there to Capua.[121] At Capua we had the mules unsaddled. Maecenas played ball,[122] but Vergil and I took a nap because playing ball is painful if you have sore eyes or indigestion. From Capua we traveled to Caudium,[123] where Cocceius entertained us at his well-stocked villa which is situated on a hill above the town and its inns. . . . We had a very enjoyable dinner there.

From Caudium we headed directly toward Beneventum,[124] where the overly eager innkeeper almost burned down his whole place while roasting some scrawny thrushes on a spit. Some sparks from the fireplace fell on the floor, and the flames spread quickly through the ancient kitchen and raced upward to lick the roof. Had you been there, you would have seen hungry guests and frightened slaves grabbing the food, and everyone trying to put out the fire.

Soon after Beneventum, Apulia began to reveal her mountains, so familiar to me.[125] They were scorched by the hot wind, and we would never have managed to crawl through them if an inn near Trivicum had not taken us in for the night.[126] But it was filled with eye-stinging smoke because there were damp branches, leaves and all, burning in the fireplace. I very stupidly waited up half the night for a deceitful girl. When I finally fell asleep, I dreamed of Venus—and wet my bedclothes.

The next day we raced along over twenty-four miles in carriages and then spent the night in a town whose name I cannot mention in verse.[127] But I can easily give you some clues: water, the cheapest of commodities everywhere else, is here sold,[128] but the bread here is by far the best anywhere, and the experienced traveler usually packs a few loaves for the journey ahead. Indeed, the bread of Canusium[129] . . . is gritty, and the town is not a jug richer in water.[130] There Varius sadly departed, leaving his friends in tears.[131]

When we finally reached Rubi, we were exhausted because we had covered a long distance[132] and the trip was made even more uncomfortable by rain. The weather improved the next day, but the road was worse, right up to the walls of the fishing town

---

[120] Possibly a posthouse maintained by the government for the reception of travelers on state business.

[121] It was about nine miles from Sinuessa to the posthouse, and about seventeen miles thence to Capua.

[122] On ballgames, see note 33 of this chapter.

[123] A journey of about twenty-one miles.

[124] About eleven miles away.

[125] Apulia, the name of the southeastern region of Italy. Horace was born in Venusia, a town in Apulia; see selection 15.

[126] It was about twenty-five miles from Beneventum to Trivicum.

[127] The name of the town does not fit into the metrical pattern of the poem and therefore cannot be mentioned.

[128] That is, water is scarce.

[129] Canusium was evidently their next stop.

[130] That is, has no more water than the town whose name could not be mentioned.

[131] Perhaps Varius went back to Rome.

[132] It was about twenty-three miles from Canusium to Rubi, twenty-three from Rubi to Barium, thirty-seven from Barium to Gnatia, and thirty-nine from Gnatia to Brundisium.

of Barium. Our next stop was Gnatia . . . and finally Brundisium, the end of a long trip, and of my papyrus.

Hotel Sign

Most travelers tried to stay with friends or with friends of friends during their trips. Horace, for example, spent most nights of his trip to Brundisium at the villas of friends. Hotels were available, but they were small in size—usually just two or three rooms above a bar, dining area, and stable—and accommodations were rather less luxurious than they are in today's Hiltons.[133] Consider Horace's descriptions of the hotels he stayed in: greedy innkeepers, fire traps, smoky rooms. The following sign was painted outside an inn or hotel in Pompeii.

324   *CIL* 4.807 (*ILS* 6036)

Guest lodging available to rent, has a triclinium with three couches, and all conveniences.

Hotel Bars

Most hotels or inns also had bars which catered to local residents as well as to travelers. Various kinds of wine would be served, and wine which had been warmed was a favorite drink. The following sign was painted on the wall of an inn at Pompeii.[134]

325   *CIL* 4.1679

> For one *as*,[135] you can get a drink here.
> For two *asses,* you will get a better drink.
> For four *asses,* you will drink Falernian wine.[136]

Hotel Prostitutes

Many hotel owners provided their guests with more than just food and lodging. The following inscription was found at Aesernia (modern Isernia), a town in central Italy.

---

[133] See Petronius's reference to bedbugs in selection 194.

[134] On the same building appeared the political endorsement from the late-drinkers which was translated in selection 237.

[135] *as:* see Appendix II.

[136] *Falernian:* on the price of Falernian wine in the fourth century A.D., see selection 152. Since this bar sign was found in Pompeii, it cannot be later in date than the eruption of Vesuvius in A.D. 79.

326 *CIL* 9.2689 (*ILS* 7478)

"Innkeeper, my bill please!"

"You had one *sextarius*[137] of wine, one *as* worth of bread, two *asses* worth of relishes."[138]

"That's right."

"You had a girl for eight *asses*."

"Yes, that's right."

"And two *asses* worth of hay for your mule."

"That damn mule will ruin me yet."

Homesickness

Many messages similar to this one have been found scrawled on the walls of Pompeii.

327 *CIL* 4.1227

Gladly we came here, but much more gladly do we depart, eager to see again, O Rome, our own Lares.[139]

Loneliness

328 *CIL* 4.2146

Vibius Restitutus slept here, alone, and longed for his Urbana.

No Trespassing

Ancient landowners, like modern ones, tried to restrict access to their property, as this ancient sign reveals.

329 *CIL* 1.2.1831 (*ILS* 6012)

The lower road is the private property of Titus Umbrenius, son of Gaius. Please request permission to use the road. No animal or vehicle traffic allowed.

[137] *sextarius:* see note 49 of Chapter VII.

[138] *relishes: pulmentarium;* see note 48 of Chapter VIII.

[139] *Lares:* household gods; see note 34 of Chapter VIII. In Latin, the word *Lares* is frequently used by metonymy to mean simply "home."

The Ancient Jet Set

Poor people could not afford to make frequent or lengthy trips for pleasure. Among the wealthy, however, such trips were common. These people, who owned not only homes in the city but also villas in the country and by the sea, could vary their leisure activities, relieve their boredom, and escape the summer heat with trips to their vacation homes, where they might hunt or fish. The Bay of Naples was a favorite vacation area, and its shoreline was studded with magnificent villas from which the "beautiful people" enjoyed swimming and boating and probably a continual round of parties.[140] For men like Cicero and Pliny, who led very active public lives in Rome yet found satisfaction in their work, a trip to a villa meant a chance to enjoy some uninterrupted peace and quiet. For other people, however, whose lives in Rome were occupied with empty leisure activities rather than public service, a trip provided no relief from boredom. In the passage translated here, Seneca describes frantic attempts to find peace of mind by traveling.

330 Seneca the Younger, *An Essay about Peace of Mind* 2.13

Some people undertake aimless journeys and wander up and down the coast. An unhealthy restlessness always afflicts them wherever they are, traveling by sea or by land. "Let's go to Campania."[141] But luxury proves to be a bore. "Let's hurry to Bruttium and the woodlands of Lucania."[142] Yet amidst these wild regions, they look for something refined so that they can relieve their delicate eyes of the unbroken desolation of these uncultivated areas. "Let's go to Tarentum;[143] it has a famous harbor and mild winters and is certainly opulent enough and charming." "No, let's go back to Rome." It's been much too long since their ears have heard thunderous applause.[144] And human blood would be an enjoyable sight.

SPECTACLES

In Rome's early history, the only occasions for holidays were religious festivals. Since Roman society was in origin agricultural, the purpose of the festivals was to win the support of gods or spirits who controlled the weather, crop growth, animal breeding, and so on.[145] These festivals were days of sacrifice and ritual,

---

140 See selection 65, where Cicero discusses the activities of Clodia at Baiae, a fashionable seaside resort near Naples.

141 *Campania:* a region south of Rome where the cities of Naples and Pompeii were situated.

142 *Bruttium, Lucania:* regions in the southernmost part of the Italian peninsula.

143 *Tarentum:* city on the southeast coast of Italy. It was founded by the Greeks.

144 *thunderous applause:* probably at the spectacles in the arena such as gladiatorial combats.

145 The Parilia, for example, on April 21, honored Pales, the goddess of shepherds and flocks.

but also of holiday merriment, as Easter or Christmas are for us today. In addition to holidays devoted to placating the divine spirits, there were holidays established to thank the gods for helping the Romans win a specific military victory. For example, before a battle, the general would pray on behalf of the Romans to certain gods and vow that if the Romans won they would honor those gods with a day (or days) of holiday entertainment.[146] Although each thanksgiving holiday originally marked the victory of a specific campaign, it became an annual event, and its original significance may have been forgotten. On these days, the state presented various types of entertainment which were financed with public funds. These entertainments were called *ludi,* which can be translated as "games" or "plays" or "sports."[147] Although the *ludi* were originally presented as part of the religious celebration which brought people together to honor the gods publicly, gradual changes began to occur in the celebration of Roman religious holidays. Holidays without *ludi*[148] became less important to most people than holidays with them, particularly as the city-dwelling Romans forgot their agricultural associations. And holidays with *ludi* were extended to occupy more days. The Ludi Cereales, for example, which honored Ceres, the goddess of grain, were extended from one to seven days, from April 12 to 19.[149] The Ludi Romani, which were dedicated to Juno, Jupiter, and Minerva, lasted fourteen days, from September 5 to 19. Of course, people did not take all those days off work, but the spectacles were usually presented in the afternoon when many people were free.[150] About 100 B.C., there were fifty-eight days of festivals without *ludi* each year and fifty-seven days of *ludi,* although the fifty-seven days represented only six separate celebrations.[151]

The association of holidays and public entertainment with religion was weakened when Sulla dedicated *ludi* to *Victoria Sullae*—"Sulla's (military) Victory."[152] It then became fairly common practice to celebrate personal military victories with *ludi,* and, in the imperial period, to celebrate thus the emperor's birthday or his death and deification. By the fourth century A.D., there were 177 days of *ludi* in the year.

The main spectacles[153] or shows enjoyed by people during the *ludi* were chariot racing, theater events, and wild animal "hunts." Gladiatorial combats also took place in republican Rome, but many scholars maintain that these events did not receive public funding until the imperial period.[154] Admission to the *ludi* was

[146] Such vows might also be made when asking the gods for relief from a plague or famine.

[147] *Ludus* (singular of *ludi*) can also mean "training," and the word *ludus* is used both for children's play and children's school, as well as for training schools for gladiators.

[148] The Parilia, for example.

[149] *Cereales, Ceres:* the origin of the English word *cereal.*

[150] Spectacles were not held at night because of the absence of good artificial lighting; see note 42 of this chapter.

[151] These six celebrations were: Ludi Megalenses (April 4–10), Ludi Cereales, Ludi Florales (April 28–May 3), Ludi Apollinares (July 6–13), Ludi Romani, and Ludi Plebeii (November 4–17). These were the celebrations held in the city of Rome. Other Italian cities had similar holidays with publicly financed *ludi.* As the Roman Empire expanded, the popularity of *ludi* spread to all the provinces. In the imperial period, *ludi* in the provinces were often dedicated to the cult (or worship) of the emperor; on this cult, see selection 381.

[152] *Sulla:* see note 114 of Chapter VII.

[153] *spectacle:* Latin *spectare* = "to look at," "to observe."

[154] A man with political aspirations might finance spectacles with his own private funds

free. At the beginning of each year, the Senate would decide how much money it wished to allocate for the *ludi* of each holiday. The production of the *ludi,* however, was entrusted to the aediles (or, in the imperial period, to the praetors).[155] It was their job to hire the performers,[156] buy wild animals, purchase necessary equipment, and so on. The senatorial allotment was intended to cover all these expenses, but most aediles added to this allotment large amounts of their own money because they hoped to win popularity with the voters by arranging "the greatest show on earth." The aediles were, of course, ambitious politicians with their eyes on the praetorship and consulship, and were therefore willing to buy voter support by subsidizing the public entertainments from their own private funds.[157] When Julius Caesar was aedile in 65 B.C., he almost ruined himself financially in order to stage lavish entertainments. But his near bankruptcy was a wise gamble; he went on to be elected consul and then to be appointed governor of Gaul.

Caesar's Games

Julius Caesar, when aedile in 65 B.C., not only produced *ludi* for state holidays, adding his personal funds to the senatorial allotment, but also arranged gladiatorial shows at his own expense (or, more correctly, with borrowed money).

331   Suetonius, *The Lives of the Caesars: Julius Caesar* 10

During his aedileship, Caesar . . . arranged wild animal "hunts" and theatrical performances, sometimes with the help of his colleague, Marcus Bibulus, sometimes on his own.[158] . . . He also arranged a gladiatorial exhibition, but with somewhat fewer pairs of gladiators than he had originally planned.[159] For since the group he had hired was so large, and their sheer number had terrified his political enemies, these enemies passed legislation restricting the number of gladiators which anyone was allowed to keep in Rome.[160]

---

and might include gladiatorial combats at his shows. He might use, as the occasion for these shows, a personal military victory or a desire to honor one of his dead relatives.

During the imperial period, gladiatorial shows received lavish state funding.

[155] In the imperial period, the *ludi* produced with senatorial allotments were often eclipsed in size and lavishness by *ludi* produced with funds from the emperor.

[156] Usually the aedile would negotiate a rental contract with a man who owned a company of actors or a team of chariot drivers. And since many actors and drivers were slaves, the team owner quite literally owned them.

[157] Politicians thought this money was well invested. If the aedile went on to be praetor or consul, he was also assured of a post as a provincial governor. And in the provinces he would try to fill up his empty purse by extorting money from the people he had been assigned to protect. Consider Verres's activities in Sicily, described by Cicero in selection 281.

[158] Caesar and Marcus Calpurnius Bibulus were the two curule aediles in 65 B.C. The two plebeian aediles were Gaius Vergilius Balbus and Quintus Tullius Cicero; on Quintus Cicero, see selections 60, 205, and 278.

[159] Caesar arranged the gladiatorial show to honor the memory of his father.

[160] In 73 B.C., gladiators in Italy, led by Spartacus, revolted and stirred up an ill-fated war in which thousands of slaves participated. Caesar's enemies feared either that the gladia-

Nero's Games

Once the emperor Tiberius had transferred the election of magistrates from the popular assemblies to the Senate, aspiring politicians no longer had a reason to court the favor of the masses by arranging lavish public spectacles. Although the aediles and praetors continued to execute their duties in this area, the task became a burdensome and thankless one. The emperors, on the other hand, did not fail to exploit the political advantages of entertaining the masses, and many instituted new spectacles. A well-loved emperor was a safe emperor.[161] Nero, who was emperor from A.D. 54 to 68 and who had a personal interest in performances and competitions, was particularly generous with the time and money he devoted to public spectacles.

332   Suetonius, *The Lives of the Caesars: Nero* 11, 12

Nero presented a large number of different types of entertainments: youth athletic meets, chariot races, theatrical performances, and gladiatorial shows. At the youth meets he allowed even old men of consular rank and elderly matrons to take part.[162] At the chariot races he assigned to the equestrian class[163] special boxes, separate from the ordinary seats. He even arranged for races of four-camel chariots. At the theatrical performances . . . when Afranius's play[164] *The Fire* was staged, the actors were allowed to keep the furniture which they had snatched from the burning house.[165] And throughout the entire period of the Greatest Games,[166] gifts were distributed among the people; every single day a thousand birds, all different kinds, were given away, as well as numerous food baskets and vouchers for grain, clothing, gold, silver, precious stones, pearls, paintings, slaves, horses, mules, even for tamed wild animals, and, finally, for ships, apartment buildings, and farms. Nero himself watched these plays from the edge of the stage.

At the gladiatorial show, which he had staged in the wooden amphitheater near the Campus Martius (the amphitheater had been built in just twelve months),[167] he

___

tors he had hired to fight in Rome might be emboldened by their numbers to revolt (see selection 196) or that Caesar might be gathering a private army to stage a coup d'état.

[161] The emperors did not allow private individuals to institute new spectacles. They wanted no rivals for the favor of the people, no threats of revolution or coup d'état. Similarly, the emperors did not allow military leaders to celebrate triumphs; see the introduction to selection 267.

[162] On Nero's encouragement of citizens to perform, see selection 334.

[163] Perhaps because the equestrian class had originally had "horsey" associations; see note 12 of Chapter I.

[164] *Lucius Afranius:* a playwright who had lived about 200 years earlier.

[165] Apparently a building had actually been set on fire during the performance. The Roman audience demanded realism.

[166] Nero had inaugurated these games and given them the name "Greatest."

[167] On the location of the Campus Martius, see map 1. In Rome's earliest period, gladiatorial events were held in the open area of the Forum, with standing room only for the spectators. An amphitheater was a circular seating structure built around an arena where the events took place. (For the definition of *arena,* see note 46 of this chapter.) Rome's most famous amphitheater is the Colosseum, which was completed in A.D. 80, twelve years after Nero's

allowed no one to be killed, not even convicted criminals.[168] . . . He staged a sea battle on an artificial saltwater lake with sea monsters swimming in it. He also staged some Greek ballets with young Greek dancers to each of whom he granted a certificate of Roman citizenship when their performance was over. Among these Greek ballets was one in which a bull actually mounted Pasiphae who was concealed in a wooden cow—or that's what many of the spectators believed.[169] In another ballet, Icarus fell when he first tried his wings, crashed near the emperor's couch, and spattered Nero with blood.[170]

Political Wisdom

Although games, or *ludi,* had originally been closely associated with the observance of a religious celebration, they gradually assumed an importance of their own. City dwellers, who did not feel the respect for Ceres, the grain goddess, which a farmer might, began to think of the Ludi Cereales not as an opportunity to honor Ceres but as a chance to see chariot races. And politicians were quick to see the political advantages in the people's love of games. Lavish entertainments won voter support and might even erase public memory of political blunders, since the voters could forgive a man's sins if he provided impressive spectacles. In the republican period, the *ludi* were often used by the upper class as a political tool to maintain the support of the lower class. In the imperial period, the emperor did not, of course, have to worry about winning votes. But he did need to keep the people happy and contented, since an unhappy populace might riot and demand a new emperor. The emperors therefore increased the number of annual holidays with *ludi,* perhaps hoping that these diversions would keep people's minds off problems like unemployment or food shortages. Some emperors arranged special one-time shows. When the Colosseum was opened, for example, in A.D. 80, Titus[171] arranged shows for the occasion which lasted 100 days. And in A.D. 108, Trajan[172] celebrated his military victories in Dacia with 117 days of spectacles. In the passage below, Fronto[173] discusses the political importance of public entertainments. His comments are, however, a bit misleading. Very few people, if any, would have

---

death. It was called by the Romans not Colosseum but Flavian Amphitheater since the emperors who built it were of the Flavius family.

[168] On the use of convicted criminals in these events, see selections 6, 201, and 344.

[169] The subject of the ballet was the myth of Pasiphae and the bull. Pasiphae, wife of King Minos of Crete, was consumed by an unnatural lust for a handsome white bull. She asked Daedalus, a master craftsman, to build for her a beautiful, but hollow, wooden cow. She hid in the cow and waited for the bull. The bull mated with what he thought was a cow. Pasiphae became pregnant and gave birth to a monster known as the Minotaur, half-bull, half-man.

[170] Icarus was the son of the master craftsman Daedalus. Daedalus built two sets of wings from feathers and wax, and he and Icarus set out on a flight from Crete to Athens, the first men in history to fly. Icarus flew too close to the sun. The wax melted, the wings collapsed, and Icarus plunged to his death. Perhaps the actor playing the role of Icarus in this ballet also died. The Romans appreciated realism! The role may have been played by a convicted criminal, sentenced to die in a ballet.

[171] *Titus:* the second of the Flavian emperors; ruled A.D. 79–81.

[172] *Trajan:* emperor A.D. 98–117.

[173] *Fronto:* see Appendix I, and also note 21 of Chapter II.

attended all 117 days of Trajan's spectacles. Today, for example, a person could attend a movie every day of the year, but no one does (although many people do watch TV every day). And in a large modern city, there are spectator sports events just about every day.[174] Will future historians say our century was interested only in hot dogs and baseball, or in sex and violence (as modern moralists claim)? In ancient Rome, most people worked hard for a living and attended spectacles only occasionally.

333   Fronto, *Elements of History* 18

Because of his shrewd understanding of political science, the emperor[175] gave his attention even to actors and other performers on stage or on the race track or in the arena, since he knew that the Roman people are held in control principally by two things—free grain and shows[176]—that political support depends as much on the entertainments as on matters of serious import, that neglect of serious problems does the greater harm, but neglect of the entertainments brings damaging unpopularity, that gifts[177] are less eagerly and ardently longed for than shows, and, finally, that gifts placate only the common people on the grain dole,[178] singly and individually, but the shows placate everyone.

The Road to Decadence

In the passage translated here, Tacitus, who lived from about A.D. 55 to 118, inveighs against a public entertainment which the emperor Nero instituted in A.D. 61. Tacitus's main complaint was that Nero encouraged the participation of Roman citizens in these shows.[179] Tacitus believed that the appearance of citizens in public spectacles was yet another symptom of the moral decline of Roman society. His comments provide insight into Roman attitudes toward public spectacles or entertainments.

Competitive athletics for citizens had a long tradition in the Greek world, the Olympic Games being but one example.[180] Although very few people could

---

[174] And we enjoy 104 weekend "holidays," as well as holidays on Christmas, Labor Day, Fourth of July, and so on.

[175] *the emperor:* Trajan.

[176] *free grain:* the grain dole; see selection 153. Juvenal remarked that the city mob was interested only in *panem et circenses,* "bread and chariot races." He exaggerated the situation, but it is nonetheless true that the people of Rome were in a unique position. Because Rome headed a vast empire, the state treasury was filled with tribute and tax money which could be used to provide inhabitants of the city with free grain and free entertainment. Residents in cities and towns in the rest of Italy and in the Empire enjoyed far fewer gifts.

[177] On gifts from the emperor, see selection 332.

[178] Evidently gifts were sometimes distributed only to people whose names were on the grain dole list.

[179] See selection 332: "At the youth meets he allowed even old men of consular rank and elderly matrons to take part."

[180] There were many athletic competitions in Greece, of both major and minor dimensions. Most offered handsome prizes or money to the winner, and athletes therefore traveled on a circuit, from competition to competition, as do pro golf or pro tennis players today. These

hope to reach the level of Olympic competition, excellence in athletics[181] was considered an ennobling pursuit, and therefore the training areas, the *palaestrae* and *gymnasia,* were crowded with citizens aspiring to achieve a reputation for athletic skill. In the Roman world, however, athletic skill in and of itself brought no glory to a citizen; only as an applied skill, within a functional or practical context such as battle, was the athletic excellence of a citizen praised. Physical training was a matter of personal fitness and preparation for war, not of public display, and the Romans therefore developed no athletic competition for citizens. The proper arenas for competition and excellence were the law courts, the Senate house, and the battlefield; nonfunctional displays of talent were considered mere performances.[182] Since the Romans viewed athletic, musical, dramatic, and sporting events as forms of entertainment, rather than as true pursuits of excellence, they thought that to devote oneself to training for such an event would be a frivolous and improper use of time. A Roman citizen who appeared on a theater stage would not only be making an undignified spectacle of himself; he would also be wasting his time. In fact, the serious-minded Romans disapproved of citizen participation in all public entertainments, including musical or theatrical shows, as inconsistent with the *dignitas* and *gravitas* of a Roman.

Yet the Romans were avid spectators! Because they frowned on a citizen making a public spectacle of himself, most performers were slaves, freedmen, or foreigners. The Romans were thus curiously ambivalent about their spectacles. They loved watching theatrical shows, for example, and they appreciated the skill of the actors, but they looked down on them as shameless, disreputable, and socially unacceptable.[183]

There is another curious feature to the Roman attitude toward public entertainments. Although the Romans enjoyed these entertainments from their earliest history,[184] nonetheless for many centuries the state assumed a puritanical posture toward them, asserting that idle activities led to sloth. In the early republican period, no spectator seating was provided at theatrical or gladiatorial events. At a later period, temporary bleachers were allowed, but they were quickly dismantled at the end of the performance. A temporary theater building suited the Roman self-image well; its very impermanence reminded the citizens of Rome that duty

---

athletes were not amateurs, since they earned substantial sums of money for successful performances; see note 15 of this chapter. The Greeks also had musical, dramatic, poetic, and rhetorical competitions for citizens.

[181] Or music, poetry, or drama.

[182] See Cicero's comments in selection 143 about the difference between an actor and an orator.

[183] Ummidia Quadratilla was criticized for owning a company of pantomime dancers; see selection 295. The Julian Laws stated "a husband . . . is permitted to kill a pimp, actor, gladiator, criminal, freedman, or slave who is caught in the act of adultery with his wife;" see selection 66. The same ambivalent attitude existed also in modern Europe and America until quite recently. Since actors traveled from place to place, they remained outside society and were looked upon as strange.

[184] According to Roman legend, the first public entertainment was a day of chariot racing planned by Romulus shortly after he founded Rome in 753 B.C. He and his men had no women for their new city, so he invited his neighbors the Sabines to come and watch the races in the valley where the Circus Maximus was later built; see map 1. While the Sabine men were intently watching the races, Romulus's men carried off the Sabine women (the famous "Rape of the Sabine Women").

and gravity, not leisure and frivolity, were the enduring values. The first permanent stone theater in Rome, the theater of Pompey, was not built until the end of the republican period, in 55 B.C.[185] Yet it was probably the upper classes which promoted the puritanical idea that frequent attendance at spectacles could produce moral decay, and which prevented, by senatorial decrees, the construction of permanent theaters. Nor were the senators necessarily concerned about the moral well-being of the lower classes. It is more likely that they resisted permanent theaters because they feared civil disturbances (and the loss of their own power) if masses of common folk assembled in one area.[186]

For their part, the lower classes, which had few other forms of entertainment, attended the spectacles in large and enthusiastic numbers and did not seem to worry too much about their moral decline. The fact that politicians could curry favor with the voters by sponsoring lavish games indicates the true feelings of the masses of people.

As late as the first century A.D., however, Tacitus is still arguing the traditional aristocratic opinion that spectacles had caused the disintegration of the true Roman character. However, Tacitus places the primary blame for Rome's decline[187] on the Greeks and on the introduction to Rome of the Greek custom of allowing citizens to appear as performers and competitors.[188]

---

[185] By contrast, towns in southern Italy, which had been settled or influenced by the Greeks, had permanent theaters much earlier. The town of Pompeii, for example, had a permanent theater by the early second century B.C.

In 44 B.C. Julius Caesar was assassinated in the theater of Pompey. (For more information about Pompey, see note 32 of Chapter IV.) Today's visitor to Rome can dine in Pompey's theater; the Ristorante da Pancrazio, at 92 Piazza del Biscione, occupies its ruins.

[186] See Cicero's comments in selection 228 where he compares the disorderly conduct at the *contiones* to the Greek practices of sitting at assembly meetings and of holding assembly meetings in theaters. In fact, although the Romans did not use theaters for official meetings, theater audiences often did voice their political favor or disfavor quite loudly; see selection 153 concerning protests about a grain shortage and selection 242 about the city prefect's responsibility to maintain order at the games.

The upper class had various methods of keeping the lower classes under control. It could, through senatorial decrees, prohibit or closely regulate gatherings of lower-class people. See, for example, the regulations imposed on funeral clubs (selection 116) or the worship of Bacchus (selections 387 and 388). A more subtle method of manipulating the lower classes was to promote a concept of the ideal Roman as someone who was dutiful (*pius*), hardworking, and serious-minded. The upper class claimed that it was preserving ancestral customs, and it concealed its resistance to political power for the masses by appealing to traditional procedures and virtues. Of course, to an aristocrat who had been brought up to assume a paternalistic attitude toward the lower classes and to think that the masses were incapable of governing themselves, public gatherings and moral decline may well have seemed the same thing. Compare the upper-class promotion of the traditional Roman as a rugged farmer, willing to fight to defend the land he owned (see selection 177); at a time when few families owned land, this image continued to be fostered by wealthy property owners as a kind of proof that they were the conservators of ancestral custom and were thus the proper authorities in the state.

[187] It was Tacitus's personal opinion that Rome had declined. In many respects, Rome had progressed substantially in the direction of social reform; see selections 46 and 199–203. Tacitus, however, is a moralizing author who laments the passing of the "good old days." See note 71 of this chapter.

[188] The Romans viewed Greece as a once great state which had collapsed irretrievably. The Greeks whom the Romans met were often the moral and intellectual inferiors of the fifth century Athenians. The Romans earnestly sought the causes of Greece's decline, since they

In his fourth consulship, with Cornelius Cossus as his colleague,[189] Nero instituted at Rome an entertainment which was to be held every five years and which was patterned after Greek competitive events.[190] Like all new things, this entertainment received mixed reviews. Some people said that even Gnaeus Pompeius[191] had been censured by the older men of his day for building a permanent theater. For before the building of Pompey's theater, theatrical performances used to be given on a temporary stage to an audience on makeshift bleachers. And, if you go back farther, the audience stood while watching plays, so that the people would not, by sitting in a theater, become accustomed to spending their time in idleness and sloth. The character of the ancient shows should have been preserved, . . . and no citizen should have felt obligated to compete. But, little by little, our traditional moral values weakened and then were completely subverted by an imported licentiousness, so that we began to see here in our city everything that could corrupt or be corrupted: our young men were ruined by their eagerness for foreign ways, their enthusiasm for gymnasia, for idleness, for perverted sex, and all with the approval of the emperor and the Senate, who not only granted permission for such offensive behavior but even applied pressure on Roman noblemen to disgrace themselves with stage performances of speeches and poetry. What else was left but for them to strip naked and put on boxing gloves and train for sports matches instead of for war![192]

THEATER EVENTS

The Problems of a Playwright

On holidays with *ludi,* a festive atmosphere prevailed, and the crowds were happy, restless, and eager to be amused. The various entertainments competed with one another for an audience, as they do today at a carnival. In the republican period, all performances were given in open areas, and people at one spectacle were easily distracted by the sounds of other spectacles and moved on with no hesitation. Actors sometimes lost their audience in the midst of a performance. This problem

---

feared that Rome, too, might decline, and tended to blame on the Greeks any potentially harmful changes in the structure of the Roman state.

On anti-Greek sentiment in Rome, see selections 212 and 228.

[189] The year was A.D. 61. The emperor would occasionally assume the office of consul; see selection 241.

[190] Nero loved Greek competitive events and was eager to participate in them himself. He performed in public as a lyre player, an actor, and a singer. He even traveled to Greece to compete. At the Olympic Games he entered a race for ten-horse chariot teams. Although he fell out of the chariot, had to be helped back in, and still failed to complete the course, he was awarded first prize!

[191] *Gnaeus Pompeius:* Pompey.

[192] *for sports matches instead of for war:* nonfunctional versus functional applications of athletic skills.

was alleviated by the construction of permanent theater buildings which separated the plays[193] from other activities, but that was comparatively late in Rome's history.[194] In the passage translated here, Terence, a playwright of the second century B.C., makes known the problems which writers, stage managers, and actors encountered when distractions were numerous.

The Romans enjoyed a variety of stage shows, despite their aversion to permanent theaters and their contempt for actors. The oldest type was evidently something like a vaudeville presentation. By the second century B.C., comedies and tragedies patterned after earlier Greek dramas became very popular. Only male actors were allowed on stage, even for women's roles. By the first century B.C., two other forms of stage shows were favored: mimes and pantomimes. Both used mythological stories for their themes, but there was little or no plot. There was, however, much music and dancing. Mime actors had speaking roles, but performers in pantomimes, which were apparently somewhat similar to ballets, did not. Although upper-class writers decried mimes and pantomimes as vulgar and tasteless,[195] since in them women were allowed on stage as actresses, and nudity, violence, and sex were common,[196] these shows became immensely popular and acquired far more fans than the Greek-style comedies and tragedies. Another type of show, though of more narrow appeal, was the musical concert which included lyre playing and singing.

Terence wrote Greek-style comedies, from one of which this passage is taken.[197]

335   Terence, *The Mother-in-law,* 28–57

Now, please, listen politely to my request. I am again introducing Terence's play *The Mother-in-law,* although I have never yet been able to find a quiet, attentive audience for it.[198] Bad luck has dogged it. A favorable response from you, however, and your support of my efforts, will put an end to this bad luck. The first time I tried to present this play, my rivals for an audience were some famous boxers and then a tightrope walker as well. People gathered in noisy groups; there were shouts, and women's shrieks, and all this commotion forced us off the stage before the play was over. So, in order to give this new play another chance, I tried an old trick: I staged it a second time. And I was successful in holding the audience—at least to the end of the first act.

---

[193] *plays:* the Latin phrase is *ludi scaenici,* "games on stage"; the Latin word *scaena* means "stage."

[194] Before the construction of permanent theaters, plays were presented in open areas such as the Forum where other entertainment was also presented. Since admission was free, people could spend a few moments at each event without worrying about the cost of tickets.

[195] Consider Pliny's comments in selection 295 about Ummidia Quadratilla's fondness for pantomime. See also note 105 of Chapter VIII.

[196] We have already noted examples of realistic violence and sex on the Roman stage (see selection 332).

[197] For other passages from comedies, see selections 145 and 148.

[198] This prologue is being spoken by a man who was an actor-manager-producer. He owned the company of actors (most were slaves) and may himself have been a freedman. He and the company probably traveled from place to place and would be hired or rented by a magistrate in charge of public entertainments. This is his third attempt to produce *The Mother-in-law* at Rome.

But then a rumor spread that some gladiators were going to perform—and my audience flew off in a huge crowd, pushing, shouting, fighting to get a good spot at the gladiator performance. Well, I really couldn't keep my show going. Today, however, there is no unruly mob. Everything is calm and quiet. I have been given a golden opportunity to stage this play, and you have been given the chance to pay honor to the dramatic arts.[199] Don't allow, by your neglect, music and drama to fade away, appreciated by only a few.[200] Let your support of the theater promote and encourage my own. As I have never greedily put a price value on my talent, as I have always maintained adamantly that my greatest concern was how best to serve your pleasure, so then now allow me this request. Terence, the playwright, has on good faith entrusted his work, indeed his very self, to my care and to your attention. Don't let wicked critics laugh wickedly at him, attacking him on all sides. Please, understand his situation and give us your undivided attention, so that other playwrights may be willing to write and so that I may be encouraged in the future to buy and produce new plays.[201]

Pantomime

The following passage describes a pantomime performance of the second century A.D.[202] The pantomime was accompanied by music and perhaps resembled a ballet. This pantomime told the story of Paris's choice. Paris, prince of Troy, was asked to decide which goddess was the most beautiful: Juno, Minerva, or Venus. Venus promised him the most beautiful mortal woman as his wife if he would choose her. And so he did. In return, Venus made the beautiful Helen fall in love with Paris, desert her Greek husband, King Menelaos, and run off to Troy with Paris. Paris's seduction of Helen was the cause of the Trojan War.

336   Apuleius, *The Golden Ass* 10.30–32

There appeared on stage a young man representing the Trojan prince, Paris, gorgeously costumed in a cloak of foreign design which flowed down from his shoulders. On his head was a gold tiara. He pretended to be a shepherd tending his flocks. Next there appeared a radiantly fair young boy, naked except for a small cloak which covered his left shoulder. His long golden hair attracted everyone's eyes. It flowed down his back but did not conceal his beautiful little golden wings. These wings and the herald's staff he held in his hand indicated that he represented Mercury, the messenger god.[203] He danced toward the actor representing Paris and offered him the golden apple which he

199 *dramatic arts:* Latin *ludi scaenici*, which attracted smaller audiences than *ludi circenses*, "games in the circus" (chariot races). The prologist is afraid that the *ludi scaenici* may be abandoned completely (a worry certainly shared by modern theatrical producers).

200 *music and drama:* Roman comedies included a good deal of singing and music.

201 The playwright sold his play to the producer. He did not receive royalties. Terence sold one of his plays for 8000 sesterces.

202 Mime and pantomime had long since replaced comedy and tragedy as the Romans' favorite stage shows.

203 *Mercury:* the messenger of the gods. He carried a staff with two serpents intertwined at the top. In selection 88, Mercury and Jupiter visited the cottage of Philemon and Baucis.

was holding in his right hand.[204] By his gestures, he informed him of Jupiter's command and then immediately danced gracefully away, out of our sight.

[Actresses representing Juno and Minerva appear on stage.]

Then Venus appeared, displaying to all her perfect beauty, naked, unclothed, except for a sheer silk scarf which covered, or rather shaded, her quite remarkable hips and which an inquisitive wind mischievously either blew aside or sometimes pressed clingingly against her. . . . Then two groups of attractive young maidens danced onto the stage. On one side were the very graceful Graces,[205] on the other the very beautiful Seasons, who honored the goddess by scattering flowers and bouquets around her. They danced with great skill an intricate ballet movement, paying tribute to the goddess of pleasure with the blossoms of spring. The flutes played sweet Lydian[206] melodies which soothed and delighted the minds of the spectators. But far more delightful was Venus, who began to move forward gracefully, rhythmically, slowly, swaying softly from side to side, gently inclining her head, answering the tender sound of the flutes with her delicate movements. . . . As soon as she came face to face with the judge, she appeared by her gestures to promise him that if he would choose her above all the other goddesses she would give to him, Paris, a bride who was the most beautiful of all mortals and similar in appearance to Venus herself. And then the young Trojan prince gladly handed to Venus the golden apple, thus pronouncing her victor in the beauty contest.

AMPHITHEATER EVENTS

In the republican period, the entertainments which the state financed were called *ludi.* However, at privately financed spectacles, particularly those honoring the dead, it was common to see gladiatorial matches.[207] These matches, which apparently had their origin in Etruscan funeral rites, were not called *ludi,* but rather *munera,* which means "duties," "obligations," since it was the duty of the family to honor its dead with the display of courage which gladiatorial matches involved. (Only wealthy families, of course, could afford to fulfill this obligation.[208]) Not until the imperial period did gladiatorial matches become a firmly established part of the state-financed entertainments.

Not all events in the amphitheaters involved gladiators. There were different types of events and different types of performers. The gladiators were trained fighters. Most were men who had been purchased as slaves and trained at a gladiatorial school. Often they were men who had been captured in war.[209] Some were slaves who had displeased their masters; being sold to a gladiatorial school was

---

[204] The golden apple was the official prize in the beauty contest of the three goddesses.

[205] *Graces:* Latin *gratia,* which means "pleasantness," "kindness," "charm," as well as "grace."

[206] *Lydia:* a country in Asia Minor. Lydian melodies were noted for being plaintive and querulous.

[207] The gladiatorial matches produced by Caesar (selection 331) were designed to honor the memory of his father.

[208] Which served their political purposes as well as their sense of piety.

[209] Spartacus, for example, was by birth a Thracian.

a punishment.[210] And occasionally a free man, who had no other source of income, might sign up with a gladiatorial school. Training was tough and thorough; the gladiators learned to use various types of equipment, but toward the end of their training they began to specialize with one particular type. The most agile men became net men, with nets to snare their opponents and tridents to stab them. They wore almost no clothing and could move very quickly. Heavily armed gladiators with swords were well protected with armor but moved slowly. They depended on brute force rather than speed.

The owner of the gladiators would rent them out at a profit for shows, just as the owner of an acting company would rent out his actors.[211] Matches were arranged between two fighters, one often a net man, one a heavily armed fighter. Although many gladiators certainly were killed in the arena or died later from their wounds, not every loser of a match was killed. An owner who had invested considerable amounts of money for the purchase, training, feeding, and equipping of gladiators would not want to rent out eighteen gladiators knowing that only nine would return alive.[212] A graffito from Pompeii tells us that in an exhibition of eighteen gladiators (nine matches), nine were victorious, six were spared, and three killed.[213] Some men fought as gladiators for many years, were manumitted, and then continued as gladiators, even though they were now freedmen, demanding high prices for their performances. Gladiatorial combats were extremely dangerous and frequently fatal, but in nature similar to modern boxing matches as contests of skill. It is for the other events in the arena that the Roman world has acquired its reputation for cruelty and sadism.[214]

Criminals, war captives, and other offenders who were sent to the arena for capital punishment were not expected to return alive. They received no training and no defensive equipment. If a man killed one opponent and survived one fight, he immediately faced another opponent, and then another, until he grew exhausted and was in turn slain. These spectacles were executions.

Some amphitheater events involved wild animals. For executions, the unfortunate men were placed without weapons, and sometimes were tied up as well, in an arena with hungry animals such as lions or panthers. In the wild animal

210 For disobedient female slaves, the corresponding punishment was sale to a brothel. Under Hadrian, legislation was passed which forbade the selling of a slave to a gladiatorial school or brothel unless he or she had been convicted of a crime; see selections 200 and 201.

211 From the time of Domitian (emperor A.D. 81–96) onward, all gladiators in the city of Rome were owned by the imperial administration, and private ownership of gladiators was forbidden. The emperors feared that privately owned gladiators might be employed in a coup d'état. Compare the fears which people in the republican period had of Julius Caesar's gladiators (selection 331).

212 In the late second century A.D., an ordinary gladiator was valued at about 2000 sesterces.

213 Nero once sponsored gladiatorial exhibitions in which no one was killed; see selection 332.

214 It should be remembered that Rome was not the only city which offered its citizens the spectacle of men dying. Pompeii's permanent amphitheater was completed in 80 B.C. The first permanent amphitheater in Rome was not built until 29 B.C. (Similarly, Pompeii's theater was built about one hundred years earlier than the theater of Pompey in Rome.) Amphitheater events were popular everywhere in both the eastern and western parts of the Empire. From Britain to Africa to Greece to Syria, men and animals were slaughtered to provide entertainment.

"hunts," men with weapons but no protective clothing were matched with animals. Seldom did the "hunters" leave the arena alive. Sometimes animal was pitted against animal—bears chained to bulls, or lions set upon elephants. Sometimes the animals were herded into the arena and shot by archers in the stands. The Roman world was quite inventive in the ways of cruelty and devised many different methods for slaughtering men and animals.

The popularity of gladiatorial matches, executions, and wild animal "hunts" increased in the imperial period, when they began to be supported lavishly with public funds. In the 100 days of spectacles which accompanied the opening of the Colosseum in A.D. 80, 9000 animals were killed. At Trajan's games of A.D. 108, 10,000 gladiators fought and 11,000 animals were killed.[215] And similar spectacles took place throughout the Roman Empire. We cannot excuse this cruelty by pointing to similar inhumane atrocities in other periods, including our own, but there are, at least, indications that such spectacles did not appeal to the majority of Romans. In Rome itself, there were more race tracks than amphitheaters. And the largest amphitheater, the Colosseum, held about 50,000 spectators, whereas the largest race track, the Circus Maximus, held 250,000 spectators. Amphitheater events, moreover, were certainly not everyday occurrences. The spectacles sponsored by Titus and Trajan were exceptional in both size and duration.

Advertising Amphitheater Events

In Pompeii, and presumably in other cities and towns as well, sponsors of amphitheater events advertised with messages painted on walls of buildings. The following are two examples from Pompeii.

337   *CIL* 4.1190

The gladiatorial troop hired by Aulus Suettius Certus will fight in Pompeii on May 31. There will also be a wild animal hunt. The awnings will be used.[216]

338   *CIL* 4.3884 (*ILS* 5145)

Twenty pairs of gladiators sponsored by Decimus Lucretius Satrius Valens, lifetime priest of Nero Caesar,[217] and ten pairs of gladiators sponsored by Decimus Lucretius Valens, his son, will fight in Pompeii on April 8, 9, 10, 11, and 12. There will also be a suitable wild animal hunt. The awnings will be used. Aemilius Celer[218] wrote this, all alone, in the moonlight.

[215] See the introduction to selection 333.

[216] The amphitheater at Pompeii was equipped with awnings which could be unfurled to protect spectators from the hot sun. Apparently they were not always used, and the promise here to use them is meant to attract a larger audience.

[217] Priesthoods were often political appointments. This man, a wealthy businessman, has been given the honor of serving the cult of the emperor. This honor would involve few actual duties. On imperial cults, see selection 382.

[218] On Aemilius Celer, Pompeii's busy sign painter, see note 120 of Chapter X.

Fight Statistics

Sometimes results of gladiatorial matches were painted on walls. The following are two examples from Pompeii. Sketches of the gladiators accompany the writing. The four gladiators who are mentioned were all freedmen. They may have begun their gladiatorial careers as slaves, been manumitted, and then continued to fight as freedmen. At least three of them had won quite a few matches.

339   *CIL* 4.8055 and 8056

> Oceanus, a freedman, winner of 13 matches, won.
> Aracintus, a freedman, winner of 9 matches, lost.
>
> Severus, a freedman, winner of 13 matches, lost.
> Albanus, a freedman of Scaurus, winner of 19 matches, won.

Fans

Some successful performers—whether actors, gladiators, or charioteers—acquired followings of very ardent fans and admirers.[219] Both men and women were often attracted to strong, good-looking, and/or courageous performers and idolized them as people today frequently idolize rock musicians or movie stars. Despite the adulation received by a few, however, performers as a group remained very much at the bottom of the social ladder. The passages translated here, again from the walls of Pompeii, tell of two gladiators who were the current heartthrobs.

340   *CIL* 4.4397 and 4356 (*ILS* 5142d)

CELADUS, THE THRACIAN,[220] MAKES ALL THE GIRLS SIGH.

CRESCENS, THE NET FIGHTER,[221] HOLDS THE HEARTS OF ALL THE GIRLS.

An Unsympathetic Point of View

Many fans of gladiatorial matches had little sympathy with the fighters. They came to be entertained, and they expected a good show. They didn't care if the gladia-

---

[219] On men who were attracted to pantomime actresses, see Seneca's comments on voluntary slavery in selection 198.

[220] *the Thracian:* probably not a Thracian by birth; rather "Thracian" described a type of gladiator, one who carried a small shield and a reversed sickle for slashing his opponent. Similarly, "Gaul" or "Samnite" designated not nationality but rather type of armor and weapons.

[221] *net fighter:* man armed with only a net and trident.

tors were sick, wounded, tired, thin, or frightened; they wanted action—and lots of it—and they demanded that fight officials encourage sluggish fighters to attack one another by flogging or even burning them. When the performance was over, the fighters who had appeared reluctant to fight were severely punished.

341   Petronius, *Satyricon* 45.11 and 12

What good has Norbanus[222] ever done us? He arranged a show with gladiators, sure! They were worth about two cents, the whole lot. So old and decrepit they would have fallen over if you blew on them. I've seen better wild animal fighters.[223] . . . There was one with a bit of spirit in him. He was a Thracian. But even he fought in a very perfunctory way. Finally, at the end of the show, they were all soundly flogged. They had heard the whole audience shouting, "Hit him! Hit him!" They were clearly cowards, pure and simple.

A More Enlightened View

In this letter, Cicero praises his friend Marcus Marius for his decision to miss the spectacles which Pompey had sponsored in 55 B.C. to celebrate the dedication of his theater.[224] Since Cicero was in Rome at the time, he felt obligated to attend, but he did not enjoy the shows.

342   Cicero, *Correspondence with Family and Friends* 7.1.1–3

If it was some physical ailment or ill health which kept you from attending the spectacles, I would attribute your absence more to your luck than to your wisdom. But if you decided to scorn what other men marvel at, and chose not to attend, although good health would have allowed you to, then I have two reasons to be delighted: first, because you were free of physical pain and, second, because your mind was strong, since you ignored things other men marvel at for no reason (assuming, of course, that you produced something worthwhile during your leisure!).[225] I have no doubt that, during the days of games at Rome, you were in your study at Pompeii[226] reading books . . . while your friends were watching, or rather sleeping through, hackneyed mimes. . . . All in all, the entertainments were (if you're interested) quite splendid, but certainly not to your taste. . . . They did not even have the charm which more modest entertainments often have, because the spectacle of such extravagant expense destroyed any spontaneous merriment. You were not, I am sure, upset to have missed such extrava-

---

[222] *Norbanus:* a politician; see note 43 of Chapter IX.

[223] Wild animal fighters were not trained. They were usually brought to the amphitheater for execution and simply thrown to the lions. Norbanus's gladiators, however, showed even less skill than wild animal fighters.

[224] *theater of Pompey:* see note 185 of this chapter. The mimes took place in the new theater, the other events probably in the Circus.

[225] A man of culture and refinement was expected to spend his leisure in literary pursuits; see the introduction to selection 322. He was certainly not supposed to be lazy and idle in his free time.

[226] Marius had a vacation home in Pompeii.

gance. What enjoyment can we find in 600 mules in *Clytemnestra*,[227] or 3000 punch-bowls in *The Trojan Horse,* or a variety of infantry and cavalry equipment in some battle scene or other? Things which won the applause of the common people would have given you no enjoyment. . . . I know that you certainly didn't worry about missing the athletes, since you have always been scornful of gladiators. In fact, Pompey himself admitted that he had wasted his time and money on this group. And then there were wild animal hunts, two a day for five days, very expensive ones—no one can deny that. But what pleasure can a civilized man find when either a helpless human being is mangled by a very strong animal, or a magnificent animal is stabbed again and again with a hunting spear?[228] Even if this was something to look at, you have seen it often enough before, and I, who was a spectator there, saw nothing new. The last day was the day for elephants.[229] The mob of spectators was greatly impressed, but showed no real enjoyment. In fact, a certain sympathy arose for the elephants, and a feeling that there was a kind of affinity between that large animal and the human race.[230]

Rounding Up the Animals

Public entertainments, as we have seen, were the responsibility of the aediles, and they in turn used this responsibility as an opportunity to ingratiate themselves with the voters. In the summer of 51 B.C., Cicero's friend Marcus Caelius Rufus[231] was elected aedile for the year 50 B.C. Cicero himself was in Cilicia in 51 and 50 B.C. as governor.[232] Caelius began to pester him to send to Rome Cilician panthers which would be used in the spectacles which Caelius would organize in his year as aedile. His request is but one small example of how provincial governors were prevailed upon by their friends to exhaust the resources of a province to satisfy the whims of people in Rome.

343   Cicero, *Correspondence with Family and Friends* 8.9.3, 2.11.2

Dear Cicero,
    In almost all my letters to you I have written about the panthers. You will be embarrassed! Patiscus has sent Curio ten panthers,[233] whereas you have not sent me

---

[227] The mime dramatized the myth of Clytemnestra, who murdered her husband, King Agamemnon, when he returned to Greece after the Trojan War. Evidently 600 mules were brought on stage during the performance of this mime.

[228] Six hundred lions were killed during this show.

[229] That is, the day on which elephants were slaughtered.

[230] The elephants, maddened by the pain of javelin wounds, stampeded and almost trampled the spectators. Their cries of agony stirred pity in these same spectators.

[231] *Marcus Caelius Rufus:* a very gifted young man, Cicero's junior by about twenty-five years. He was intelligent, charming, ambitious, and a fine orator. He was also self-indulgent and undisciplined. He is a figure who represents well the character of the last generation of the republican period. For comments about his love affair with Clodia, see selection 65.

[232] See selections 279 and 280.

[233] *Patiscus:* a Roman businessman in Cilicia who enjoyed hunting.
    Gaius Scribonius Curio: tribune in 50 B.C. Like Caelius, he was young, bright, resourceful, and totally without scruples. It is not clear why Patiscus sent him panthers. On Curio's father, see note 55 of Chapter XII.

the equivalent or more. And Curio gave those ten to me, plus another ten from Africa. . . . If you but remember, and if you send for some hunters from Cibyra[234] and also send orders to Pamphylia[235] (for they say that more panthers are caught there), then you will satisfy my request. I am greatly concerned about this now because I think I will have to make all the arrangements myself, without the help of my colleague. So please, dear friend, take on this task. You are usually quite willing to take on extra concerns (whereas I generally take on none). In this case, you will actually have no extra work, except to talk, that is, to give orders and instructions. As soon as the panthers have been caught, you have with you the men I sent over on financial business to feed them and arrange for shipping. . . .

Dear Caelius,

About the panthers! The matter is being handled with diligence and according to my orders by men who are skillful hunters. But there is a remarkable scarcity of panthers.[236] And they tell me that the few panthers left are complaining bitterly that they are the only animals in my province for whom traps are set. And therefore they have decided, or so the rumor goes, to leave my province and move to Caria.[237] But the matter is receiving careful attention, especially from Patiscus. Any animal found will be yours. But whether any will be found, we don't really know. I swear your aedileship is of great interest to me. Indeed, today even reminds me of it, for I am writing this letter on the opening day of the Ludi Megalenses.[238] . . .

The Harmful Results of Spectacles

In this passage, Seneca describes the revulsion he experienced when he stopped to watch a public spectacle. As a Stoic, Seneca found the show objectionable because it encouraged in the audience behavior of the worst kind.[239] Similarly, today many people argue that violence on TV breeds violence in the home and on the street.

344   Seneca the Younger, *Letters* 7.2–5

There is nothing more harmful to one's character than attendance at some spectacle, because vices more easily creep into your soul while you are being entertained. When I return from some spectacle, I am greedier, more aggressive, and more addicted to pleasurable sensations; I am more cruel and inhumane—all because I have been with other humans! Recently I happened to stop at a noon-hour entertainment, expecting humor, wit, and some relaxing intermission when men's eyes could rest from watching

[234] *Cibyra:* a town in southwestern Asia Minor.

[235] *Pamphylia:* a region on the south coast of Asia Minor.

[236] Had Roman hunters, and Roman demands for wild animal hunts, brought the panthers in Cilicia to near extinction? At Pompey's games in 55 B.C., 600 lions and 400 leopards were killed.

[237] *Caria:* a region in southwestern Asia Minor.

[238] *Ludi Megalenses:* April 4–10; see note 151 of this chapter. They were held in honor of the goddess Cybele (see selections 389 and 390) and were the responsibility of the aediles.

[239] On Seneca and Stoicism, see selections 99, 198, and 418–425.

men's blood.[240] But it was quite the opposite. The morning matches had been merciful in comparison. Now all niceties were put aside, and it was pure and simple murder.[241] The combatants have absolutely no protection. Their whole bodies are exposed to one another's blows, and thus each never fails to injure his opponent. Most people in the audience prefer this type of match to the regular gladiators or the request bouts. And why not! There are no helmets or shields to deflect the swords. Who needs armor anyway? Who needs skill? These are all just ways to delay death. In the morning, men are thrown to the lions and the bears; at noon, they are thrown to the spectators. The spectators demand that combatants who have killed their opponents be thrown to combatants who will in turn kill them, and they make a victor stay for another slaughter. For every combatant, therefore, the outcome is certain death. They fight with swords and with fire.[242] And this goes on while the arena is supposedly empty. "But one of these men is a robber." And so? "But he killed a man." Well, since he killed a man, he deserves capital punishment. But what did *you* do, you wretch, to deserve the punishment of watching?—"Kill him, whip him, burn him![243] Why does he approach combat so timidly? Why does he kill so reluctantly? Why does he die so unwillingly? Why must he be driven with whiplashes to face sword wounds? Let them expose their naked chests to one another's weapons. This is the intermission for the gladiators. So let's have some men murdered. Don't just stop the entertainment!"—Don't you understand that bad examples recoil upon those who set them?

Escaping the Tortures of the Arena

Men condemned to participate in amphitheater events realized that their deaths would be agonizing and painful. Some chose to commit suicide, and thus both spare themselves the torment and rob the hated spectators of the gory sight they craved. In a letter to his friend Lucilius, Seneca describes two such suicides. They were of interest to Seneca because they demonstrated the Stoic belief that suicide is ultimate freedom.[244]

345   Seneca the Younger, *Letters* 70.19–21, 23

There is no reason why you should think that only famous men have had the strength necessary to break the chains of human bondage. . . . Men of the lowliest rank have escaped to safety through their own heroic impulse. Even when they were not allowed to die at a time convenient to them, even when they were not allowed a real choice in the means of their death, they snatched whatever opportunity was at hand and by sheer force made for themselves lethal weapons from objects which are not by nature

240 Apparently the noon-hour intermission was often occupied by more refined entertainment, perhaps by comic actors, musicians, or jugglers.

241 What Seneca saw were not gladiatorial matches but executions, where men sentenced to capital punishment were placed in the arena to kill one another.

242 The men do not actually fight with fire. If they refuse to fight or try to leave the arena, they are burned by the officials. See selection 341.

243 That is, "Force him to fight!" Seneca is recording the comments of the spectators.

244 For more of Seneca's views on death, see selection 99. Seneca himself committed suicide in A.D. 65 when he was threatened with death by the emperor Nero.

harmful. Recently, for example, a German who was destined to be one of the wild animal fighters at a public entertainment was preparing for the morning show. He withdrew from the rest for a moment to relieve himself (he was given no other opportunity to withdraw without a guard). There, in the toilet area, he found a wooden stick with a sponge attached to the end (it was used for wiping away the excrement). He stuffed the whole thing down his throat and choked to death. . . . Though apparently without any resources, he devised both a method and a means of death. From his example you, too, can learn that the only thing which makes us hesitate to die is the lack of will. . . . Recently, again, when a man was being carted off under close guard to the morning show, he pretended to nod his head in sleep. Then he lowered his head until he had stuck it between the spokes of the cartwheel, and remained calmly in his seat until his neck was broken by the turning wheel. And so, he used the very vehicle which was carrying him to punishment to escape it.

CIRCUS EVENTS

Chariot racing was the oldest, most popular, and most enduring of the public entertainments.[245] It was a spectator sport, employing professionals and designed to make a profit for its organizers. As such, Roman chariot racing was more similar to modern pro football than to the chariot racing of the ancient Olympics. There were four chariot-racing companies in ancient Rome and at race tracks throughout the Empire: Red, White, Blue, and Green. Each was called a *factio* or "faction." Factions were owned by businessmen, as are football teams today. The faction owners owned the horses, the chariots, the stables, other equipment, and even the drivers, most of whom were slaves.[246] The aedile or praetor whose responsibility it was to organize the public entertainment would negotiate with the owners of each faction a contract to rent the chariots, horses, and drivers for the duration of the *ludi*.[247] The owners probably received a basic rental fee plus prize money for races won. Chariot racing was the most exciting of the public entertainments. Spectators appreciated not only the skills of the drivers but also the spills and the thrills. The chariots were small and flimsy,[248] the turns tight, and the drivers ruthless. Accidents were frequent and serious.[249]

[245] *Chariot racing: ludi circenses*. On the legendary origin of racing at Rome, see note 184 of this chapter. By the third century A.D., there were eight tracks in the vicinity of Rome, and the largest, the Circus Maximus, held 250,000 spectators. There were race tracks throughout the Empire, and, even after the fall of Rome in the fifth century A.D., chariot racing remained immensely popular in the eastern Empire during the Byzantine period.

[246] Compare the status of actors and gladiators. Many drivers continued to race even after they had been manumitted.

[247] The Ludi Romani, for example, lasted fourteen days, although chariot races did not take place on each of those days. The owners of acting and gladiatorial companies probably negotiated similar contracts.

[248] Do not be misled by Hollywood portrayals, such as the race scenes in *Ben Hur*. Racing chariots were lightweight, to minimize the burden on the horses. They were made of wood or wickerwork and were thus easily broken. The drivers stood, or rather balanced, on narrow floorboards, close to the hindquarters of the horses. On the design of chariots used in military triumphs, see selection 267.

[249] On remedies for chariot-racing accidents, see selection 102.

Like modern horse racing, Roman racing attracted members of all levels of society. Since admission to the *ludi* was free, the "sport of kings" could be enjoyed by everyone. We have already noted that racing was far more popular than the gladiatorial or theatrical entertainments.[250] Many emperors were personally interested in racing,[251] but even those who were not prudently concealed their disinterest and made appearances at the Circus Maximus, as British royalty today appears at Ascot. The common people liked to think that the emperors shared their own interests and amusements. Emperors who attended races usually received enthusiastic applause from the spectators and a warm display of public affection.

A Driver's Winning Techniques

A poet of the fifth century A.D., Sidonius Apollinaris, has left us a vivid account of a chariot race in which one of the drivers was his friend Consentius. In this race, only four teams competed, but at the Circus Maximus there was room for twelve teams in a race, three from each faction. Four-horse chariots were the most common, but there were also races for chariots with two horses, and all the way up to chariots with ten horses. Sidonius's account provides valuable information about racing techniques. Frequently two drivers worked as partners, as they do in this race. The *circus,* or race track, had a divider or low wall stretching lengthwise to separate the "up" stretch from the "down" stretch and prevent head-on collisions. At each end of the divider was a turning post. There were seven laps in each race and therefore thirteen sharp and dangerous turns. A race in the Circus Maximus covered a distance of about two and a half miles.

346   Sidonius Apollinaris, *Poems* 23.323–424

[The four chariot teams enter the starting gates.]

The four team colors are clearly visible: white and blue, green and red.[252] Grooms are holding the heads and the bridles of the horses, . . . calming them with soothing pats and reassuring them with words of encouragement. Still the horses fret in the gates, lean against the starting barrier, and snort loudly. . . . They rear up, prance, and kick impatiently against the wood of the gates. A shrill blast of the trumpet, and the chariots leap out of the gates, onto the track. . . . The wheels fly over the ground, and the air is choked with the dust stirred up on the track. The drivers urge their horses with whips. Standing in the chariots, they lean far forward so that they can whip even the shoulders of the horses. . . . The chariots fly out of sight, quickly cov-

---

250 For a comparison of the size of the Colosseum and the size of the Circus Maximus, see the introduction to the section on amphitheater events. Remember also that there were more race tracks in Rome than amphitheaters.

251 Both Caligula and Nero drove chariots, Caligula on private tracks, Nero in public. For Nero's "victory" at the Olympics, see note 190 of this chapter. Caligula owned a race horse named Incitatus ("Fast Runner") which he wanted to make consul of Rome, so much did he admire the horse's talents.

252 Drivers wore tunics dyed the color of their faction; see Pliny's comments on these faction colors in selection 348.

ering the long open stretch. . . . When they have come around the far turn, both the rival teams have passed Consentius, but his partner is in the lead. The middle teams concentrate now on taking the lead in the inside lane. If the driver in front pulls his horses too far right toward the spectator stands, he leaves an opening on his left, in the inside lane.[253] Consentius, however, redoubles his efforts to hold back his horses and skillfully reserve their energy for the seventh and last lap. The others race full out, urging their horses with whip and voice. The track is moist with the sweat of both horses and drivers. . . . And thus they race, the first lap, the second, the third, the fourth. In the fifth lap, the leader is no longer able to withstand the pressure of his pursuers. He knows his horses are exhausted, that they can no longer respond to his demand for speed, and he pulls them aside. When the sixth lap had been completed and the crowd was already demanding that the prize be awarded, Consentius's opponents thought they had a very safe lead for the seventh and last lap, and they drove with self-confidence, not a bit worried about a move by Consentius. But suddenly he loosens the reins, plants his feet firmly on the floorboard, leans far over the chariot, . . . and makes his fast horses gallop full out. One of the other drivers tries to make a very sharp turn at the far post, feeling Consentius close on his heels, but he is unable to turn his four wildly excited horses, and they plunge out of control. Consentius passes him carefully. The fourth driver is enthralled by the cheers of the spectators and turns his galloping horses too far right toward the stands. Consentius drives straight and fast, and passes the driver who has angled out and only now, too late, begun to urge his horses with the whip. The latter pursues Consentius recklessly, hoping to overtake him. He cuts in sharply across the track. His horses lose their balance and fall. Their legs become tangled in the spinning chariot wheels and are snapped and broken. The driver is hurled headlong out of the shattered chariot which then falls on top of him in a heap of twisted wreckage. His broken and bloody body is still. . . . And now the emperor presents the palm branch of victory to Consentius.[254]

A Day at the Races

In *The Art of Love,* Ovid advised men in search of an amorous adventure to visit the race track.[255] "Don't neglect the horse races if you're looking for a place to meet your girlfriend." In the poem translated below, he has taken his own advice. He is at the circus, seated next to the lady whose favor he hopes to win. The poem takes the form of a dramatic monologue.

347   Ovid, *Love Affairs* 3.2.1–14, 19–26, 33–38, 43–59, 61–84

I'm not sitting here because of my enthusiasm for race horses; but I will pray that the chariot driver you favor may win.[256] I came here, in fact, so that I might sit beside

---

[253] The chariots raced counterclockwise, and thus all the turns were to the left. The turns were very sharp, basically 180 degrees, quite unlike the gradual turns on a modern race track.

[254] Victorious drivers received palm branches. There were also substantial purses in regular races, but most of the money went to the faction owners, not the drivers, as today the purse goes to the owner, not the jockey.

[255] See selection 62.

[256] *Art of Love:* "immediately cheer for the same one, whichever it is, that she cheers for."

you and talk to you. I didn't want the love which you stir in me to be concealed from you. So, you watch the races, and I'll watch you. Let's each watch the things we love most, and let's feast our eyes on them.

Oh, how lucky is the chariot driver you favor! Does he have the good fortune to attract your attention? Let me, please, have that good fortune. Carried out of the starting gate by galloping horses, I will drive aggressively, sometimes giving the horses their heads, sometimes whipping their backs. Then I will graze the turning post with my inside wheel. But if I catch sight of you as I race along, I will stop and let the reins slacken and fall from my hands. . . .

Why are you edging away from me? It's no use. The seat marker forces us to touch. Yes, the Circus does offer some advantages in its seating rules.[257]

Hey, you, on the right, whoever you are, be more considerate of the lady! You're hurting her by pressing up against her. And you, too, behind us. Draw in your legs, if you have any sense of decency, and don't stick your bony knees in her back.[258]

Oh dear, your skirt is trailing a bit on the ground. Lift it up, or here, I will do it.[259] . . . (But what will happen when I see her ankles? Even when they were hidden I burned with passion. Now I am adding flames to a fire, water to a flood. From the sight of her ankles I can well imagine the other delights which lie carefully hidden under her clothing.) Would you like me to stir a light breeze by using my program as a fan?[260] . . .

But look, the procession has arrived.[261] Quiet, everyone! Pay attention! It's time for applause. The golden procession has arrived. Victory is riding in front, her wings outstretched. Be with me, Victory, and make me victorious in love. You who trust yourselves to the sea can clap for Neptune. I have no interest in seafaring; I'm a landlubber. And you, there, soldier, clap for Mars, your patron god. I hate warfare. It's peace I like, and it's in peace that you find love. Let Phoebus help the augurs,[262] and Phoebe the hunters. Minerva, seek applause from the craftsmen. Farmers, stand up! Here comes Ceres and delicate Bacchus. Boxers should show reverence to Pollux and horsemen to Castor. Now it's my turn to applaud, sweet Venus, for you and your archer cupids. Nod in support of my plans, oh goddess. Make my new girlfriend receptive to my advances and willing to be loved. Look, she nodded[263] and gave me a favor-

---

[257] *Art of Love:* "The narrowness of each seating space forces you to squeeze together; in fact, the rules for seating compel you to touch her!"

[258] *Art of Love:* "Turn to whoever is sitting behind her and ask him not to jab her in the back with his knees. These little touches win over simple female hearts."

[259] *Art of Love:* "If her skirt is trailing too far along the ground, pick up the edge of it and carefully lift the soiled part off the dust. At once you'll receive a reward for your careful concern: you'll be able to look at her legs, and she won't mind."

[260] *Art of Love:* "It's also helpful to fan her with the racing program."

[261] A day of racing began with a solemn procession (Latin *pompa*, English *pomp*) into the circus and around the track, of carriages holding statues of the gods. The *ludi* were, after all, dedicated to the gods. The noisy, boisterous spectators became hushed as the procession of carriages entered the track, but they applauded enthusiastically as the carriage of their favorite god passed by. The gods whose statues appear in Ovid's procession are Victory, Neptune (god of the sea), Mars (god of war), Phoebus (god of augury and oracles), Phoebe (goddess of hunting), Minerva (goddess of crafts and skills), Ceres (goddess of grain), Bacchus (god of wine), Pollux (god of boxing), Castor (god of horsemanship), and Venus (goddess of love). These deities served as patron saints for guilds, clubs, or groups of people with a common interest.

[262] *augurs:* see selection 368.

[263] Ovid imagines the statue of Venus has nodded assent to his prayer.

able reply. Well, then, I'm only asking you to agree to what the goddess has already promised. . . . I swear, in front of all these witnesses and by this procession of the gods, that I will cherish you as my girlfriend forever.

Oh, but your legs are dangling. You can, if you wish, rest your toes on the railing.[264]

Good, the track is clear and ready for the first big race. The praetor gives the signal and the four-horse chariots break from the starting gates. I can see the driver you're cheering for. I'm sure he'll win. Even his horses seem to know what you want.

Oh no, he's swinging wide around the turning post. What are you doing? The driver in second position is coming up from behind. Pull on the left rein with your strong hand![265] Oh, we're cheering for an idiot and a coward.

Come on, call them back, citizens.[266] Wave your togas and give them the message. Good, they're calling them back. Oh dear, don't let the waving togas mess your hair. Here, you may hide under the folds of my toga.

The starting gates are opening again, the horses break, and the different-colored teams[267] fly onto the track. Now, gallop ahead and take a clear lead! Fulfill my girl-friend's hopes, and my own. (Good! Her wishes have been granted, mine remain to be granted. He has won the palm,[268] I am still reaching for mine. Ah, she smiled, and promised me something with her sly eyes.) Enough for this place. Satisfy the rest of my desires elsewhere.

Fanatical Fans

Not quite everyone in Rome was a fan of chariot racing. Pliny, who thought recitations were entertaining,[269] could not understand the appeal of the circus.[270] In a letter to his friend Calvisius, he scoffs at the popular appeal of racing and the fickleness of fans who cheer for team or faction colors and not the skill of the drivers.

Roman race fans were perhaps the most fanatical sports fans in all of history. Because Roman chariot racing was a team sport, spectators behaved more like modern football fans, who favor a team, rather than modern race fans, who favor a horse. In the circus, team or faction supporters often sat together at the races and cheered wildly for their team. All too often they quarreled with the supporters of other teams, and riots broke out, Green fans trading punches with Blue fans, for example. Soldiers were stationed in the Circus Maximus to help control unruly crowds.[271]

[264] *Art of Love:* "It's also helpful . . . to give her a stool for her dainty feet."

[265] That is, pull your horses closer to the turning post and dividing wall (turns were to the left) because another chariot is moving up on the inside; see note 253 of this chapter.

[266] Apparently the spectators could demand a second start by waving their togas, although we do not know on what grounds the track officials would call back the drivers and start them again. The drivers in this race had already rounded the first (or far) turn before they were stopped.

[267] *different-colored teams:* each driver wore his faction's colors.

[268] *the palm:* palm branch of victory; see note 254 of this chapter.

[269] See selections 319 and 320.

[270] Or of pantomimes; see selection 295.

[271] See selection 242.

Pliny the Younger, *Letters* 9.6

I have spent the past few days quietly, but very pleasantly, involved with my notes and books. "In Rome?" you say. "How could you?" There were, of course, chariot races, but I am not the least bit interested in that kind of entertainment. There's never anything new or different about them, nothing which you need to see more than once. And so I am amazed that so many thousands of men time after time have such a childish desire to see horses racing and men driving chariots. Now, if they were attracted by the speed of the horses or the skill of the drivers, this would not be unreasonable. But as it is, they are interested only in the team uniforms.[272] It's the team colors they love. In fact, if, during the race itself, right in the middle of the race, the team colors were suddenly switched, the spectators would immediately transfer their interest and support, and abandon those drivers and those horses which they recognized from afar and whose names they had been shouting just a moment before.[273] One cheap little tunic has so much power, so much influence, and not just with the rabble, which is cheaper even than the tunic, but with certain men of weight and dignity. When I consider these men, and their insatiable interest in something so silly, so dull, and so common, I take some pleasure in the fact that I am not taken in by a pleasure such as that. And so, during the past few days, which other men have wasted on the most vacant pursuits, I have used my vacant time very cheerfully for literary work.

A Successful Driver

Most chariot drivers began their careers as slaves bought by one of the four factions. When a driver won a race, his owners were awarded the purse money.[274] It is quite likely that the happy owners often gave a winning driver a little gift of money as a reward. A highly successful driver might therefore save enough money to purchase his freedom.[275] Many drivers continued to race even after manumission; they remained with their factions and were probably paid a percentage of each purse they won. A good driver might therefore make a very comfortable living.[276] An inscription found at Rome records the very successful career of a driver named Gaius Appuleius Diocles.

[272] *team uniforms:* the drivers' colored tunics.

[273] Pliny did not appreciate team sports. Today a Jets fan or a Steelers fan would not switch allegiance just because the quarterbacks were switched. So, too, a Green fan cheered for the Greens, even if the drivers changed factions. The most successful drivers (and sometimes horses), however, did acquire followings of faithful fans; see selection 353.

[274] Today the stable owner is awarded the purse, from which he pays the jockey a percentage.

[275] Just as a household slave might save his *peculium*.

[276] Compare Juvenal's comments in selection 126 on a schoolteacher's salary: "We'll pay you for the twelve-month period the same that a chariot driver earns in one race."

Compare the careers of gladiators who continued to fight even after they had been freed; see selection 339.

349   *CIL* 6.10048 (*ILS* 5287)

Gaius Appuleius Diocles, driver for the Red Faction.

Born in Lusitania, Spain. 42 years, 7 months, 23 days old.

He drove first for the White faction, beginning in A.D. 122, and won his first victory, in A.D. 124, for the same faction. In A.D. 128, he drove for the first time with the Green faction. In A.D. 131, he won his first victory for the Red faction.

Statistics: He drove four-horse chariots for 24 years.[277] He had 4257 starts, with 1462 first-place finishes, 110 of them in opening races.[278] In single-entry races[279] he had 1064 first-place finishes, winning 92 major purses, 32 of them worth 30,000 sesterces (three of these finishes were with six-horse teams), 28 of them worth 40,000 sesterces (two with six-horse teams), 29 worth 50,000 sesterces (one with a seven-horse team), and 3 worth 60,000 sesterces.

In double-entry races he had 347 first-place finishes, including 4 with three-horse teams and purses of 15,000 sesterces.

In triple-entry races he had 51 wins.

All total, he was in the money 2900 times. Besides his 1462 wins, he was second 861 times, third 576 times, and fourth once, when the fourth prize was 1000 sesterces. He failed to place 1351 times. . . . He won a grand total of 35,863,120 sesterces.[280]

In races for two-horse chariots, he had 3 first-place finishes, 1 tie with the Whites, and 2 with the Greens.

In 815 races, he took the lead at the start and held it to the end.

In 67 races, he came from behind to win.

He won 36 races as the stablemate entry.[281]

He won 42 races in various different ways.

He won in the final stretch 502 times,[282] 216 times over the Greens, 205 times over the Blues, and 81 times over the Whites.

He made nine horses hundred-race winners, and one horse a two-hundred-race winner.

---

[277] He began racing when he was eighteen years old.

[278] The first or opening race of the day was the feature race.

[279] *single-entry races:* in these races there was a single entry from each faction, one Blue chariot, one Green chariot, and so on, four chariots in all. In a double-entry race, there were two Blue chariots, two Green chariots, and so on, eight chariots in all. In a triple-entry race, there were three chariots from each faction, twelve chariots in all. In a triple-entry race, the three Green drivers acted as a team. One driver might set a very fast pace at the beginning of the race and try to tire the horses of the other factions (see the tactics of Consentius and his partner in selection 346). One driver might try to force his opponents to make too sharp a turn, and thus to crash. The goal of the triple-entry team was to have one of the three chariots cross the finish line (and to prevent opponent chariots from finishing the race). Double-entry and triple-entry races must have resembled roller derbies. Single-entry races were more straightforward, although drivers would not hesitate to force their opponents into a crash. Diocles won far more single-entry than double- or triple-entry races, possibly because in the latter he was the second- or third-string driver, the man not expected to finish but rather to wreak havoc on the opponents.

[280] Which, of course, went to the faction owners.

[281] *stable-mate entry:* as the second- or third-string driver, of a double- or triple-entry, who was not expected to win.

[282] As Consentius had done in selection 346.

Cursing One's Opponent

Few drivers were as successful or as lucky as Diocles. Driving was a dangerous occupation. Men standing on narrow floorboards, in flimsy chariots that easily tipped over and readily broke, trying to control excited horses around thirteen sharp turns, were indeed lucky to finish a race without an accident. And when you consider the ruthless tactics which drivers used to gain an advantage by forcing another driver to crash, you may wonder how anyone survived even one race. An additional danger was the fact that the drivers wrapped the ends of the reins around their waists, which freed their whip hands but also made it likely that they would be dragged to death if they fell from the chariot. Many drivers did not wait until the actual race to begin endangering the lives of their opponents. Before a race, they invoked evil spirits and put curses on the drivers of the other factions.[283] The passage translated here is one such curse; it was found in North Africa, an area renowned for its race horses.

350   *ILS* 8753

I call upon you, o demon, whoever you are, and ask that from this hour, from this day, from this moment, you torture and kill the horses of the Green and the White factions, and that you kill and crush completely the drivers Clarus, Felix, Primulus, and Romanus, and that you leave not a breath in their bodies.

A Young Driver

Many of the drivers were just boys when their training began. Faction owners undoubtedly preferred lightweight drivers for the same reasons that horse owners today choose lightweight jockeys. Although a few drivers, like Diocles, had long, financially rewarding careers in which they won the adoration of the crowds, many drivers died young. The following epitaph, found at Rome, is from the grave of Crescens, who was born in Mauritania, North Africa, and was probably brought to Rome as a slave. He died at age twenty-two.

351   *CIL* 6.10050 (*ILS* 5285)

Crescens, driver for the Blue faction.
  Born in Mauritania, 22 years old.
  After 24 starts, he won his first victory with a four-horse chariot in A.D. 115, driving the horses Circius, Acceptor, Delicatus, and Cotynus.[284] He drove his last race in A.D. 124.[285]

[283] For more curses, see selection 411.
[284] The horses' names are Whirlwind (Circius), Hawk (Acceptor), Sweet Delight (Delicatus), and Dark Bay (Cotynus).
[285] In A.D. 115, when Crescens won his first race, he was thirteen years old, but he had probably been driving for at least a year. (Diocles drove two years before his first win.) Crescens may have started driving when he was only twelve years old.

Starts: 686
Wins: 47
  single-entry: 19
  double-entry: 23
  triple-entry   5
    stablemate entry: 1
    had lead from start: 8
    won in final stretch: 38
Places: 130
Shows: 111
He won 1,558,346 sesterces.

A Family of Drivers

Another epitaph found near Rome records the deaths of two brothers whose father had also been a chariot driver.

352   *CIL* 6.10049 (*ILS* 5286)

Marcus Aurelius Polynices, a slave by birth, who lived 29 years, 9 months, 5 days.

He won 739 palms[286]
  for the Reds: 655
  for the Greens: 55
  for the Blues: 12
  for the Whites: 17
    purses worth 40,000 sesterces: 3
    purses worth 30,000 sesterces: 26
    purses of gold: 11
      for eight-horse teams: 8
      for ten-horse teams:[287]   9
      for six-horse teams: 3

Marcus Aurelius Mollicius Tatianus, a slave by birth, who lived 20 years, 8 months, 7 days.

He won 125 palms
  for the Reds: 89
  for the Greens: 24
  for the Blues: 5
  for the Whites: 7
    purses worth 40,000 sesterces: 2

[286] *palms:* a palm branch was given to the winning driver as a symbol of his victory; see note 254 of this chapter.
[287] Imagine trying to steer ten horses around a sharp turn!

Polynices, the famous charioteer, bred and raised in Rome two sons, Macaris and Tatianus, the two brothers mentioned above.[288] They died young, snatched away by Fate even as they won glory on the race track.

A Famous Driver

Successful drivers, like successful gladiators, won the favor and the hearts of the crowds. They were admired by the men and adored by the women. Like movie stars today, they were recognized as they walked down the streets of Rome and greeted with swoons and squeals of delight. They were wined and dined by the wealthy and even by emperors like Caligula, although they could, of course, gain no real social acceptance among the upper class in a society which considered entertaining a degrading occupation. For a young slave who had been brought to Rome from the provinces, this public adulation must have been heady stuff. Despite the hazards of the race and the dark threat of a sudden and early death, many drivers showed reckless bravado on the track, hoping to win glory and fame, to become the current pet of the circus crowd. One of the most popular drivers in Rome was a man named Scorpus, who lived in the second half of the first century A.D. He won 2048 races and had a huge following of fans. The poet Martial mentioned him in a number of poems while he was still alive. He also wrote about his death, in two poems translated here. Scorpus died in a crash on the track when he was only twenty-six years old.

353   Martial *Epigrams* 10.53, 50(5–8)

Here I lie,[289] Scorpus, the pride of the noisy Circus, the darling of Rome, wildly cheered, but short-lived. Spiteful Lachesis[290] snatched me away in my twenty-sixth year. She counted my victories, not my years, and decided that I was an old man.

Alas, what a crime! You were cheated of your youth, Scorpus. You have fallen and died. Too soon have you harnessed the dark horses of death. Why did the finish line of the race, which you time and again hastened to cross, quickly covering the distance in your chariot, now become the finish of your life?[291]

---

[288] The names suggest that this family of slaves was Greek in origin.

[289] *Here I lie:* the poem is intended as an epitaph.

[290] *Spiteful Lachesis:* Lachesis was one of the Three Fates. Clotho spun the thread of life, Lachesis determined its length, and Atropos cut the thread. The Fates are called spiteful because they begrudge men the enjoyment of life and snatch them away in death.

[291] Roman tombstones sometimes show portrayals of a driver and chariot racing toward the finish line. The race in the circus became a metaphor for the race of life. See selection 288: "By fate's decree, you finished the race of life before I did."

XV

Religion and Philosophy

Religion is an element common to all human cultures. Indeed, it plays a significant role in even the most simple or primitive of societies. Yet religion is also a complex phenomenon which manifests itself variously in various societies. We thus speak both of religion (the phenomenon) and religions (the individual manifestations). To facilitate the comparative study of religions, Ninian Smart has devised a six-dimensional framework.[1] The six dimensions which Smart claims can be seen in every religion are (1) doctrine (in Christianity, the doctrine of the Trinity, for example), (2) narrative or myth (Christ's early life), (3) ethics ("love thy neighbor"), (4) ritual (prayer and sacrifice), (5) experience (personal communion with the god), and (6) social institution (the church as a community). Although no religion has equal proportions of these six dimensions, nor do any two religions share the same proportions, Smart's six-dimensional framework provides a useful tool for the comparative study of religions.

Throughout the Roman Empire there were many different religions, but the citizens of Rome considered one religion "ours," "the faith of our fathers," and it is this religion which modern scholars have labeled "the state religion." It is called the state religion not simply because most people in Rome accepted it, and had accepted it for hundreds of years, but more especially because it was the religion which, according to the Romans, had ensured and could continue to ensure the preservation and prosperity of their state. Since the very existence of the state depended on the conscientious performance of religious rites, state officials assumed responsibility for the performance of these rites. Priests, therefore, were state officials, and temples and religious festivals received state funding.[2] Centuries of military success and imperialist expansion had proved to the Romans both the efficacy of their religion and the wisdom of making religion a function of the state. Thus, the religion protected the state, and the state protected the religion. The two were interwoven, and religion was an intrinsic part of the very fabric of Roman society. In modern America, on the other hand, Christianity is the dominant religion, but it is not the state religion. In fact, the Constitution ensures the separation of church and state. Christianity teaches, moreover, that the afterlife and the kingdom of God are far more important concerns for the Christian than this life and the kingdom of men. Christ's teaching, to render unto

[1] Ninian Smart, *The Religious Experience of Mankind* (New York, 1969).

[2] On state funding of religious festivals, see the introduction to the section on spectacles in Chapter XIV.

Caesar the things that are Caesar's and unto God the things that are God's, would not have been easily comprehended by a Roman, who thought that state and religion were inseparable and that life on earth was the only reality.[3] A Roman saw nothing unusual about electing the same man magistrate one year and priest another year, since the function of both magistrate and priest was the same: to promote the welfare of the state. Julius Caesar, for example, was both consul and Pontifex Maximus.[4] Priests supervised the civil calendar, and consuls presided over religious sacrifices. Thus, if we look at the social institution dimension of Roman religion, we discover that the religion did not provide a separate community for its adherents but was in fact the very same community as the society as a whole.

The state religion had developed as an expansion of the rites performed by individual families in Rome's earliest agricultural society. The same deities who were asked by the family to provide good weather, bountiful harvests, or protection from marauders were later, as the community grew, asked also by the state to provide these blessings for the community as a whole. Rituals such as the purification of family property were paralleled by rituals such as the purification of the city. In other words, the state priests assumed the responsibility, on behalf of the community, for maintaining good relationships with the gods, just as the *paterfamilias* assumed it on behalf of his family.[5] This development was a natural one. Once individual families began to live in close proximity to one another, they began to share similar interests and similar fates. Everyone had to maintain a good relationship with the gods, because if one person in the community did not purify his property, or seek divine protection from marauders, everyone in the community might suffer. The Romans sought to preclude the larger danger which one man's negligence might cause by delegating to the state responsibility for performance of rites on behalf of the community. Individual families did not, of course, abandon their religious responsibilities. Retention and conservation were fundamental traits of the Romans, who preferred to add on new institutions rather than to replace old ones. Thus, the family religious rites continued to be performed along with the state rites.

THE GODS OF THE STATE RELIGION

By the late republican period, the religion developed by the early inhabitants of Rome had been substantially modified. Although the Romans had retained the

[3] The Roman state religion was worldly and materialistic and concerned with the success of the state. Christianity was "otherworldly." Some historians have suggested that the rise of Christianity hastened the fall of the Roman Empire because converts to Christianity were encouraged to forget the problems of their present lives and contemplate only the blessedness of the afterlife.

[4] *Pontifex Maximus:* head or "president" of the priests of the state religion (*pontifex* = "priest," *maximus* = "greatest"). In the imperial period, the emperor was Pontifex Maximus; see selection 241.

[5] The community or state was frequently viewed by the Romans as one large family. Upper-class elders were the state "fathers" who looked after the welfare of the younger or less fortunate. Senators were called *patres,* "fathers," and the words *patrician* and *patron* are derived from the word *patres;* see notes 6 and 40 of Chapter I.

deities and religious practices which had fostered their successes and had helped them evolve from an agricultural community into an imperial city, they had also added new deities and new practices introduced to them by the Etruscans and the Greeks. The Etruscans had ruled Rome in the last hundred or so years of the monarchy[6] and left a strong imprint on the developing Roman culture.[7] Greek influence in this early period had come primarily from the Greek colonists in southern Italy. The borrowing undoubtedly took the form of gradual assimilation rather than sudden importation. However, by the late republican period, the borrowed deities were, of course, no longer new. They were now firmly ensconced in the religious tradition of Rome. It is therefore very difficult for us today to separate away the borrowed elements and to determine, for example, which of the deities honored by the religious rites of the late republican period had been part of the state religion before the Roman encounters with the Greeks and the Etruscans.

Deities of the Environment

The Roman gods best known to most people today are the Olympians:[8] Jupiter, Juno, Mars, Venus, Apollo, Diana, Ceres, Bacchus, Mercury, Neptune, Minerva, and Vulcan. These are the Roman gods who paralleled the Greek Olympians, and they are well known because they share the vivid mythology of the Greek gods and have been portrayed in innumerable artistic works and literary accounts. And they are easy to portray because they look like human beings—bigger, stronger, and more beautiful perhaps, but of the same basic shape and with the same emotions.[9] However, long before the introduction of Greek elements, the Romans believed in many other deities or spirits who dwelled not on far-off Mount Olympus but in the immediate environment. Each of these deities had a very specific or narrow sphere of influence, since each was associated with a particular place or object or process. Every tree or stream of water, for example, had its own spirit. This attribution of a spirit to a natural phenomenon or to an inanimate object is called animism.[10] Since these spirits were so specialized or localized, they were countless in number, but they could affect men only in their immediate sphere of influence. Anyone plowing up a meadow would hope to keep on the good side of the spirits in that meadow, as well as the spirit of plowing, but would not otherwise think of them. Rarely were anthropomorphic features or emotions attributed to these spirits.[11] No Roman would worship all of these spirits; he would direct his devotion to those nearest his home or associated with his occupation,[12] and he might set up a shrine

[6] On the expulsion of the monarchy, see notes 4 and 5 of Chapter I.

[7] On the origin of gladiatorial combats, see the introduction to the section on amphitheater events in Chapter XIV.

[8] *Olympians:* gods who lived on Mount Olympus, the home of the gods in Greek mythology.

[9] The Greek gods were anthropomorphic, having human characteristics; Greek *anthropos =* "human," *morphe =* "shape," "form."

[10] *animism:* Latin *anima =* "spirit," "breath of life."

[11] The Roman spirits were forces of nature, without body. The spirit of a tree lived in the tree but did not have the body of a tree. Sometimes, however, people might attribute a shape or form to a favorite spirit.

[12] As today people choose favorite or patron saints; for more on the Roman deities as patron saints, see selection 347.

for their worship on his property.[13] Some spirits naturally became better known than others. The spirit of the Tiber River, for example, which flowed through Rome, received more attention than the spirit of a stream in an uninhabited area.

There were spirits in the home as well as in the fields and woods, spirits of the hearth fire and of the cupboard, for example.[14] Each household had its own *Lar* who would protect the household if properly propitiated.[15] It was the responsibility of the *paterfamilias* to establish within the home a shrine, called a *lararium,* and to keep the *Lar* appeased. As the early community at Rome expanded, the Romans recognized *Lares* which protected a whole neighborhood (*Lares Compitales*)[16] and then *Lares* who protected the whole city (*Lares Publici* or *Praestites*).[17]

354   Seneca the Younger, *Letters* 41.3

If you have ever come upon a thick grove of ancient trees which rise far above the usual height and block the view of the sky with their umbrella of intertwining branches, then the height of the forest and the seclusion of the spot and the wonder of so dense and uninterrupted a shade out of doors creates in you a belief in deity. . . . We venerate the sources of great rivers; we build altars where large streams of water suddenly burst forth from hidden regions; we worship hot springs; and we consecrate certain lakes because of their darkness or depth.

A River Spirit

In the letter to Romanus[18] translated below, Pliny describes a shrine established to honor the spirit of the river Clitumnus.[19] The shrine was located at the source of the river and contained a representation of the river god.[20] It was important to propitiate the spirits of rivers in your area because you would not want the river to flood or dry up or drown you.[21]

355   Pliny the Younger, *Letters* 8.8

Have you ever seen the source of the Clitumnus? If you have not yet seen it (and I suspect not; otherwise you would have told me), do see it. I saw it, just the other day,

---

[13] In Italy today people often set up in their homes or gardens shrines for their favorite saints.

[14] *Vesta* was the spirit of the hearth fire; the *Penates* were the spirits of the cupboard or pantry.

[15] On the *Lares,* see note 34 of Chapter VIII.

[16] On the *Compitalia,* the festival at which these *Lares* were propitiated, see note 47 of Chapter VIII.

[17] The city *Lares* protected the "family" of Rome. Propitiation of these *Lares* was entrusted to the state.

[18] Pliny's friend, Voconius Romanus, was a Spaniard living in Italy.

[19] *Clitumnus:* modern Clitunno, located in Umbria, between Trevi and Spoleto.

[20] We do not know how the spirit of the Clitumnus River was portrayed. In the *Aeneid* (bk. 8.31–34), Vergil describes the spirit of the Tiber River as an old man wearing a gray-green robe and a crown of reeds.

[21] Compare Horatius's prayer to the Tiber River in selection 1.

and I'm only sorry that I waited so long. From the base of a small hill, which is covered with shady groves and ancient cypress, issues the spring. It bubbles out of several cracks, all of different sizes. Forcing its way out in whirling eddies, it then releases these eddies in a wide pool which is so clear and glassy[22] that you can count the shiny pebbles and the coins which have been thrown in.[23] . . . The banks are fully clothed with ash trees and poplars whose green reflections appear in the clear stream like trees beneath the water. The coldness of the water could rival snow, as could its sparkle. Nearby is an ancient and holy shrine where Clitumnus himself stands, clothed in a *toga praetexta*. . . . All around are numerous shrines, each for a particular deity with its own name and its own rites.

Propitiating a Woodland Spirit

It was essential that a farmer maintain good relationships with the spirits who inhabited his property. In the passage translated here, Cato offers advice on how to propitiate the spirit of a grove of trees which one wanted to thin or cut down. Careful propitiation of deities was every bit as important to a farmer's success as careful choice of seed grain or correct plowing techniques. It is not surprising that Cato's handbook *On Agriculture*[24] should contain advice on religious ritual, since for Roman farmers religion was a practical aspect of farming.

356   Cato the Elder, *On Agriculture* 139, 140

When thinning a grove of trees, it is essential to observe the following Roman ritual. Sacrifice a pig as a propitiatory offering and repeat the following prayer: "Whether you are a god or goddess to whom this grove is sacred,[25] as it is proper[26] to sacrifice to you a pig as a propitiatory offering for the disturbance of this sacred place,[27] and therefore for these reasons whether I or someone I have appointed[28] performs the sacrifice, provided that it be performed correctly,[29] for this reason, in sacrificing this pig, I pray in good faith that you will be benevolent and well disposed to me, my home, my fam-

---

[22] *glassy:* glass was well known in the Roman world but was not widely used for windows.

[23] The custom of throwing coins into fountains and springs is very ancient.

[24] For another selection from this handbook, see selection 184.

[25] Roman prayers were very legalistic. Since the Romans did not know the sex of every single deity, they frequently addressed their prayers to "god or goddess." If the deity were female, and the suppliant said only "god," the deity could ignore his prayer. By using the "god or goddess" formula, the Romans left their deities no loopholes for ignoring prayers.

[26] *it is proper:* it is a religious duty, an aspect of *pietas*.

[27] Roman religion was concerned not with personal sin but rather with the violation of the rights of deities. The spirit of the grove has a right to remain undisturbed. The thinning of the grove is a disturbance and a violation, which must be expiated by prayer and sacrifice. The spirit does not examine the moral character of the suppliant before granting his prayer, but looks only to see if he has correctly performed the proper ritual of expiation.

[28] *I or someone I have appointed:* more legalistic formulas. Ordinarily the *paterfamilias* or landowner was expected to perform the sacrifice, but since many landowners lived in the city, the farm manager would be given the authority to perform the necessary rituals.

[29] It was essential that the ritual be performed correctly or the deity would not need to pay heed to it.

ily,[30] and my children. For these reasons therefore be honored by the sacrifice of this pig as a propitiatory offering."

If you wish to plow the cleared land in the grove, offer a second propitiatory sacrifice in the same manner but add these words: "for the sake of doing this work."

A Multitude of Deities

Some spirits, such as river spirits or grove spirits, were localized. Others presided over processes rather than places. In their obsession with legalistic exactness, the Romans had apparently attributed a spirit to almost every action by man or the natural world. The following passage is taken from Augustine, who was a hostile critic of the state religion.[31] He is mocking the detailed division of labor among the state deities, but he has not fabricated the information. The Romans did indeed have a multitude of very minor deities because they wanted to be sure that they had not neglected any potentially harmful force in their universe. We should remember, of course, that not every person worried about every deity. People worshipped only those spirits most closely associated wth their own interests.

357   Augustine, *City of God* 4.8

How could I possibly record in one passage of this book all the names of the gods and goddesses[32] which the earlier Romans could scarcely enumerate in the huge volumes in which they separated the particular and specific spirits in the environment into individual and distinct categories? They were not willing to entrust the care of all their land to just one deity, but instead assigned their fields to the goddess Rusina,[33] mountain ridges to the god Jugatinus,[34] hills to the goddess Collatina,[35] and valleys to Vallonia.[36] Nor could they find just one goddess, such as Segetia,[37] to whom they could entrust their grain crops once and for all. Instead, when the seed was sown but still under the ground, they chose to have the goddess Seia[38] in charge of it. But once the plants were above the ground and ripening, they put the goddess Segetia in charge. And then when the grain had been harvested and stored, they entrusted to the goddess Tutilina[39] the task of keeping it safe. Who would not have thought that this Segetia was quite sufficient to care for the grain crop all the way through, from its first sprouts to its ripened

---

[30] *family:* Latin *familia,* included not only relatives but also slaves.

[31] Augustine's book, *City of God,* was written in the fifth century A.D. In it he attempts to refute the charge, made after the sack of Rome by Alaric in A.D. 410, that Christianity was responsible for Rome's decline because it had interfered with the traditional rites of the state religion upon which Rome had relied for its success and prosperity. (Rome had been a Christian city since the conversion of the emperor Constantine about 100 years earlier.)

[32] Augustine says "gods and goddesses," but most of the deities he mentions were spirits or forces without form or personality.

[33] *Rusina: rus* = "field," "farmland"; English "rustic."

[34] *Jugatinus: juga* = "mountain ridges."

[35] *Collatina: collis* = "hills."

[36] *Vallonia: valles* = "valley."

[37] *Segetia: seges* = "grain crop."

[38] *Seia:* also derived from *seges.*

[39] *Tutilina: tutari* = "to keep safe."

ears? That was not, however, enough for men who loved a multitude of gods. . . . So the earlier Romans put Proserpina[40] in charge of germinating seeds, and the god Nodutus[41] in charge of the joints and knots of the stems, and the goddess Volutina[42] in charge of the husks folded over the ears; and when the husks open so that the ears may emerge, the goddess Patelana[43] is in charge. . . .

Everyone posts just one doorman[44] to guard the entrance to his home. And since the doorman is human, he is quite sufficient for this task. However, the earlier Romans assigned three gods to this task: Forculus[45] for the doors, Cardea[46] for the hinges, and Limentinus[47] for the threshold. Thus, Forculus was not capable of guarding both the hinge and the threshold as well as the door.

Naming the Deities

Almost every human activity was controlled by a deity. Most deities were too vague to receive a name;[48] those who were named usually had titles which designated their sphere of influence.[49]

358   Servius, *On Vergil's Georgics* 1.21

It is quite obvious that names have been given to divine spirits in accordance with the function of the spirit. For example, Occator was so named after the word *occatio,* "harrowing"; Sarritor, after *sarritio,* "hoeing"; Sterculinius, after *stercoratio,* "spreading manure"; Sator, after *satio,* "sowing." Fabius Pictor[50] lists the following as deities whom the *flamen*[51] of Ceres invokes when sacrificing to Mother Earth and Ceres:[52] Vervactor, Reparator, Imporcitor, Insitor, Obarator, Occator, Sarritor, Subruncinator, Messor, Convector, Conditor, and Promitor.[53]

[40] Proserpina became identified with the Greek goddess Persephone and thus acquired the form and personality of Persephone. On the identification of Roman spirits with Greek gods, see selection 359.

[41] *Nodutus: nodus* = "knot."

[42] *Volutina: volutare* = "to fold over."

[43] *Patelana: patere* = "to open up."

[44] On Roman doormen, see note 37 of Chapter IX.

[45] *Forculus: fores* = "doors."

[46] *Cardea: cardo* = "hinge."

[47] *Limentinus: limen* = "threshold."

[48] See selection 356: "whether you are a god or a goddess."

[49] See selection 357: Volutina = "She who folds over"; Nodutus = "knotted one"; Tutilina = "she who keeps safe."

[50] *Fabius Pictor:* a third-century B.C. writer.

[51] *flamen:* a priest in charge of the cult of a specific deity; see the introduction to selection 378.

[52] Ceres was identified with the Greek goddess Demeter, mother of Persephone. The Greek name *Demeter* means "Mother Earth." The Latin name *Ceres* is derived from the verb *cereare,* "to produce." The English word *cereal* is derived from the Latin *cerealis* which means "pertaining to Ceres." The Cerealia, the festival of Ceres, was celebrated on April 19. On the Ludi Cereales, see the introduction to the section on spectacles in Chapter XIV.

[53] *vervagere,* "to plow fallow land"; *reparare,* "to plow again"; *imporcare,* "to put in furrows"; *insitus,* "sown"; *obarare,* "to plow up"; *(sub)runcare* "to clear of weeds"; *messis,* "harvest"; *convectus,* "carried"; *conditus,* "stored"; *promere,* "to bring forth."

The Greek Influence

The world of the early Romans was filled with a multitude of vague spirits, each presiding over one place, one process, or one activity. The Greek gods, on the other hand, had broad spheres of influence, as well as established anthropomorphic shapes and personalities and well-developed mythologies. When the Romans encountered and were attracted to these gods,[54] they did not merely add them to their own list of gods. Instead, they identified the functions of the Greek gods with the functions of certain of their own deities. In Zeus, the Greek father of the gods, who caused thunder and lightning, they saw similarities to Jupiter, the Roman weather spirit. Aphrodite, the Greek goddess of love and beauty, seemed to preside over the same phenomena as Venus, the Roman spirit of fertility and procreation. Once the identification of similar functions had been established, the Romans began to attribute to their own deities the shapes, personalities, and mythologies of the Greek Olympians. Thus, Jupiter became the father and king of the gods, a position held by Zeus; Juno, originally a spirit whose special concern was the protection of women, became his wife and the queen of the gods, as Hera was wife to Zeus. The spirit Venus acquired the personality and beauty of Aphrodite, the irresistible goddess who was born from the sea and whose lover was the god of war. Minerva, the spirit of skilled workmanship, was equated with Athena and became the Roman goddess of wisdom.[55] Ceres, who may originally have been but one of the many spirits of plant growth, was identified with Demeter and thus became the main goddess of grain production and plant fertility. The Romans thus retained the spirits of their own religion but adopted for them a mythology and recognizable forms. The formerly vague spirits, Jupiter and Juno, could now be portrayed in art and literature, where they looked exactly the same as Zeus and Hera. The Roman deities who were identified with the Greek Olympians assumed very broad areas of control over man's life and overshadowed the many minor spirits, who remained vague and shapeless[56], but the minor spirits continued to be honored until the end of the Roman period.[57]

The following passage, which is a translation of a hymn to Diana, indicates the nature of the transformation which took place when a Roman spirit became identified with a Greek deity. Diana had been a woodland spirit, probably the type of spirit who would be propitiated by someone clearing a grove[58] or hunting in a forest. However, once she became identified in function with Artemis, the Greek goddess of woodland and wildlife, she also took on the personality and appearance of Artemis. She acquired, moreover, Artemis's family; the once vague spirit now became the daughter of Leto and sister of Apollo, two other Greek deities. In ad-

---

[54] The Romans may have been introduced to these gods by the Etruscans as well as the Greeks; see the introduction to this chapter.

[55] Minerva was the patron goddess of craftsmen; see Ovid's description of the circus *pompa* in selection 347.

[56] In selection 358, for example, Ceres was identified as a major deity who oversaw the various specialized farming spirits.

[57] Augustine (selection 357) was writing in the fifth century A.D. His criticism of the ancient belief in minor spirits indicates that the belief was still prevalent. The functions of many of these minor spirits were absorbed by Christian saints.

[58] See selection 356.

dition, Diana assumed new functions; for example, like Artemis, Diana became the goddess of the moon as well as of the woods.

Catullus's hymn is a literary exercise rather than a prayer used at an actual religious service, but it contains the formulaic elements of a Roman prayer: an address to the deity, a catalogue of his or her ancestry and powers, the reminder of a previous good relationship and an appeal for assistance.

359   Catullus, *Poems* 34

Diana,[59] we are in your care, we chaste girls and boys. Come, chaste boys and girls, let us sing in praise of Diana.

O daughter of Leto,[60] mighty offspring of mightiest Jupiter, you who were born beside the Delian olive tree,[61] queen of the mountains and the green forests and the trackless glens and the murmuring streams.

You are called Juno Lucina by women in the agony of childbirth.[62] You are called powerful Trivia. You are called Luna, with your borrowed light.[63]

You, goddess, measuring out the year's progress by your monthly phases, do fill the farmer's humble storerooms with fine produce.[64]

Hallowed be thy name, whatever name it is that you prefer.[65] And, as in years past you have been accustomed to do,[66] so now, too, protect and preserve the race of Romulus with your kindly favor.

Importing Gods

The early Romans had learned about the Olympian deities from their Etruscan overlords or from their neighbors in the Greek colonies of southern Italy, and the assimilation of Greek elements into the Roman religion had been a gradual process. Later in their history, however, the Romans began to import deities directly from Greece and Asia Minor and to introduce them suddenly into their state religion.

[59] This is the initial address to the goddess, summoning her attention.

[60] Catullus now begins the catalogue of Diana's ancestry and powers. Diana (Artemis) was the daughter of Jupiter (Zeus) and Leto, and the twin sister of Apollo. The catalogue was an essential element in Roman prayers. If one addressed the deity by the wrong name, he or she would not listen to the prayer. By listing the correct ancestry and powers, one could make sure that the deity had to listen.

[61] *Delian:* Diana and Apollo were born on the island of Delos.

[62] Diana has other names and other spheres of influence. The suppliant must mention these names or the deity might ignore his prayer. Diana was called Juno Lucina when she assisted women in childbirth. She was called Trivia when she was associated with witchcraft and the underworld. Diana was also Luna (the moon), sister of the sun.

[63] The Romans understood that the moon's light was only a reflection of the sun's.

[64] Diana was also a goddess of fertility (which may be her connection to Juno Lucina and childbirth).

[65] *whatever name it is that you prefer:* a formulaic expression found in most Roman prayers. This is an escape clause by which the suppliant covers himself in case he has missed one of the deity's names.

[66] The suppliant must remind the deity of their previous good relationship. A precedent has been set, and the deity should maintain it.

The importations occurred at times of crisis, when the Romans felt they needed some extra help in dealing with a grave situation. The passage below describes the importation into Rome in 293 B.C. of Aesculapius, the Greek god of medicine.

360 *A Book about Famous Men* (anonymous) 22

Because of a plague, and on the advice of the Sibylline books,[67] the Romans sent ten envoys under the command of Quintus Ogulnius to bring Aesculapius from Epidaurus.[68] When they had arrived at Epidaurus and were admiring the huge statue of the god, a snake, which inspired respect rather than terror, slithered out of the temple, and to the amazement of all headed right through the middle of the city to the Roman ship where it coiled up in Ogulnius's cabin.[69] . . . When the ship was sailing up the Tiber, carrying the snake to Rome, the snake jumped onto an island.[70] A temple was built there, and the plague subsided with remarkable speed.[71]

Welcoming the Gods of Your Enemy

The cautious Romans tried very hard not to offend any deity. When they were besieging an enemy city, they invited the protective deities of that city to leave and come to Rome where they would be worshipped. When the city was captured, the Roman soldiers were instructed to remove carefully the statues of the gods from the temples. This passage is a translation of the type of prayer made to the gods of one's enemy. Although the prayer is quoted by Macrobius, who was writing about A.D. 400, he claimed that it was a very ancient formula.

361 Macrobius, *Saturnalia Conversations* 3.9.7, 8

Whether you are a god or a goddess who hold under your protection the people and city of Carthage, and you also, almighty god, who have taken under your protection this city and this people, to you I pray, you I implore, you I respectfully ask to abandon the people and city of Carthage, to desert their structures, temples, sanctuaries, and urban area, and to leave them. I ask you to instill in that people and city fear, terror, and oblivion, and to come to me[72] and my people when you have left these. I ask that

[67] *Sibylline books:* see selection 371.

[68] *Epidaurus:* a town in Argolis, Greece, which was the center for the worship of Aesculapius. People traveled long distances to visit the temple and sanctuary of Aesculapius at Epidaurus and seek a cure for their illnesses and afflictions. And many astonishing cures have been recorded. Although people believed the god had cured them, the priests of Aesculapius were apparently skilled in medicine, surgery, and pharmacology.

[69] Snakes were sacred to Aesculapius because they were a symbol of renewal and reproduction.

[70] The island is in the middle of the Tiber. It is called the Tiber Island and is joined to the mainland by two bridges.

[71] Romans went to the temple to be healed. Sick slaves were sometimes abandoned there; see selection 199. There is still today a hospital on the island.

[72] The commanding officer of the besieging troops would make the vow.

our structures, temples, sanctuaries, and urban area may be more acceptable and more agreeable to you, and that you may take under your protection me and the people of Rome and my soldiers in such a way that we may know and perceive it. If you will do this, I vow that I will build for you temples and celebrate for you games.[73]

New Identities for Roman Deities

As the Roman Empire expanded, the Romans continued to absorb the deities of the people they conquered. The inscriptions translated below, which were found in far-off Britain, indicate that the Roman god Mars, who had already been identified with Ares, the Greek god of war, was now also identified with local British deities.

362　　　　　　　　　　　　　　　　　*CIL* 7.36 (*ILS* 4586a), 84 (*ILS* 4540), 176

Peregrinus, son of Secundus, willingly and deservedly fulfilled his vow[74] to Loucetius Mars and to Nemetona.

To Mars Toutatis,[75] Tiberius Claudius Primus, freedman of Attius, willingly and deservedly fulfilled his vow.

To the god Mars Braciaca, Quintus Sittius Caecilianus, prefect of the First Cohort of Aquitanians, fulfilled his vow.

Personal Devotion

By the late republican period, many city dwellers felt no personal interest in the minor deities of the state religion, whose spheres of influence were rural and whose worship seemed irrelevant to city life. In the countryside, however, these deities continued to be cherished, and people felt a particularly strong attachment to the deities or spirits who inhabited their property. In the passage below, the poet Martial, who has sold his farm, reveals his sorrow at leaving the deities to whom he has become devoted. He asks the new owner to treat well the deities of the farm.

363　　　　　　　　　　　　　　　　　　　　Martial, *Epigrams* 10.92

Marrus, advocate and admirer of the quiet life, you who make your hometown, ancient Atina, proud, I entrust to your care these twin pine trees, the glory of their untilled

---

[73] *games: ludi;* on vows to the gods and promises of *ludi,* see the introduction to the section on spectacles in Chapter XIV. The booty from the captured city would be sold to provide the funds for temples and games.

[74] These inscriptions were found on objects such as altars or plaques which were given to the gods as votive offerings. A suppliant would say, "If you do this for me, I vow to give you an altar." If the god answered his prayer, the suppliant would fulfill his vow and set up the altar.

[75] Here Mars has absorbed the identity of Toutatis. In other inscriptions, Toutatis appears as a separate deity. For Mars as an agricultural deity, see selection 365.

grove, and these holm oaks, haunted by fauns,[76] and the altars of Jupiter, the thunder god, and shaggy Silvanus[77] which my unlettered farm manager built with his own hands. The blood of many a lamb and many a kid has stained these altars.[78] I also entrust to your care the virgin goddess of the sacred sanctuary[79] and Mars, who ushers in my year and shares the sanctuary of his chaste sister,[80] and also the laurel grove of tender Flora[81] in which she takes refuge when pursued by Priapus.[82] Whether you propitiate all the kindly deities of my tiny little farm with a blood sacrifice or with incense,[83] please tell them this: "Wherever your Martial is, though absent, he is yet in spirit a suppliant with me, making this sacrifice to you. Consider him to be present and grant to each of us whatever we may pray for."

RITUAL

The divine forces which operated in all natural processes and human activities were not naturally sympathetic to man. They were basically neutral forces, in the sense that they did not concern themselves about man; their effects, however, might ultimately be harmful to man. Hail or crop disease, for example, are not deliberately spiteful, yet they can ruin a farmer's life. The Romans therefore sought to propitiate or at least neutralize these invisible spirits who influenced their lives so totally. It was the purpose of Roman religion to gain the good will of the divine forces and to keep them benevolent; and since the benevolence[84] of the gods could ensure the success and prosperity of both the individual and the community, it was essential that all citizens strive to establish a correct relationship with the gods and to maintain *pax deorum,* "peace with the gods." *Pax* was a state of order, regularity, harmony, and discipline. *Pax* meant that everything was in its proper place and was, moreover, cooperative. It was the opposite of disturbance and confusion. It was the environment in which man could be productive and successful because he was free of anxiety about disruption or disorder.[85]

Maintaining *pax deorum,* however, was a continual process. The Roman gods did not demand constant professions of faith, but they did require that men respect their power and acknowledge their participation in the universe. Acknowledgments of the gods formed the ritual of Roman religion. Since the earliest rituals

[76] *fauns:* spirits of woodland areas.

[77] *Silvanus:* spirit of uncultivated land, pastures, and wooded areas. He was pictured as shaggy or disheveled because he lived in the wilderness.

[78] Devotion to the gods was expressed by frequent sacrifices.

[79] *virgin goddess:* Diana.

[80] In the Greek mythology which the Romans adopted into their religion, Diana (Artemis) and Mars (Ares) were both children of Jupiter (Zeus).

[81] On Flora and the Floralia, see note 46 of Chapter XIV.

[82] *Priapus:* a guardian spirit of flocks of sheep and herds of goats. He was particularly concerned with the fertility of these animals. He was renowned for his insatiable lust and was depicted as a creature with an enormous phallus.

[83] A worshipper might offer to the gods either an animal or incense as an appropriate sacrificial offering.

[84] *benevolence:* Latin *bene* = "well," *volens* = "wishing."

[85] Compare *pax Romana,* the order which the Romans imposed on the lands that they conquered. For varying interpretations of *pax Romana,* see selections 251 and 282.

had been effective in securing the cooperation of the deities—the success and prosperity of Rome proved that divine forces were cooperative—the Romans preserved the rituals. Roman religion became static and formalized. Year after year, century after century, the same procedures were repeated, the same words were spoken in the same order, accompanied by the same actions. Since these rituals had proved their efficacy, no deviation was allowed. If one single word was mispronounced, one small action left out, the divine forces might not listen or might even be offended. The slightest error in a religious procedure meant that it must be done again, right from the beginning.

Two Latin words deserve definition and clarification here: *pietas* and *cultus.* The noun *pietas* denotes scrupulous and conscientious attention to maintaining a proper relationship with one's parents, relatives, ancestors, gods, friends, institutions, and fellow citizens. *Pietas* involves giving each man, each god, each institution his or its due,[86] and therefore *pietas* is often translated as "sense of duty" or, simply, "duty."[87] Although the English word *piety* has been derived from the Latin *pietas,* the Latin word has much broader connotations. *Piety* implies devotion to the gods, but in Latin devotion to the gods is only one aspect of *pietas.* The *pius* man feels a commitment or sense of duty toward much more than just the gods.[88] For a Roman, his attitude toward the gods was inseparable from his attitude toward the rest of his life. The noun *cultus* means "cultivation" or "care" or "tending of," but the object of care must be specified. For example, "cultivation of a field" is *agri* ("of a field") *cultus* (English *agriculture*). *Agri cultus* is the methodical performance of labors which will make the fields fruitful. The English derivation *cult* implies religious practice without any further specification, but Latin *cultus* has a more generalized meaning. *Cultus deorum* means "cultivation of the gods," a methodical performance of all the rites and practices which will make the gods favorably disposed. A *pius* man included scrupulous *cultus deorum* among his "duties" as a citizen.

Roman religion was a religion of *cultus,* of ritual, rather than of ideas and beliefs. And it was a religion concerned with material success rather than ethical behavior. Cicero said: "Jupiter is Best and Greatest not because he makes us just or sober or wise, but because he makes us healthy and right and prosperous."[89] The gods did not examine the moral character of a worshipper; if a prayer was recited with scrupulous attention to the correctness of its phrasing, it would be heard, whether the worshipper was a morally "good" or "bad" man. Roman religion did not teach ethics or demand good works.[90] This is not to say that the Romans were

---

[86] The legalistic Roman mind was obsessed with marking out boundaries and defining obligations. See the definitions of law and justice in selections 253–255.

[87] See selection 288.

[88] *pius:* the adjective which corresponds to the noun *pietas;* "dutiful," "devoted," "with a keen sense of duty."

Aeneas, the hero of Vergil's epic poem *Aeneid,* is described in the poem as *pius.* It is difficult for modern readers to appreciate Aeneas's heroism since it is defined primarily by an overwhelming sense of duty which makes him appear cold and even dull. But Aeneas does represent the traditional values of ancient Rome. For more on the Roman concept of heroism, see selection 1 and also note 30 of Chapter XI.

[89] *The Nature of the Gods* 3.87. The English words *Best* and *Greatest* are translations of the Latin *Optimus* and *Maximus,* two of Jupiter's titles.

[90] Thus the ethical dimension was not developed; see the first paragraph of this chapter.

an amoral people. However, morality and ethical behavior were a function of *pietas,* of family and civic responsibility, rather than of religion.

Formalism

The rituals by which the Romans established communication with their gods were sacrifice, prayer, vow, and divination. Prayers might be made by the individual, by the *paterfamilias* on behalf of the family, or by a magistrate on behalf of the state. We have already read two prayers, one to Diana and one to the deity of a forest grove. The former is a literary hymn written by a poet; the latter, which was included in a manual of practical advice, describes the precise words of the formula which must be used on a specific occasion (the thinning of a grove). Most prayers were accompanied by a sacrifice which would indicate to the gods the seriousness of one's desire to communicate with them. Although cattle, sheep, goats, and pigs were frequent sacrificial victims, especially at large state-financed sacrifices, poultry, flowers, fruit, crackers made of spelt, wine, milk, and incense were also offered to the gods, particularly in family or individual sacrifices.

In this passage, Pliny the Elder discusses the importance of having the words of the ritual spoken in the correct order at the correct time.

364   Pliny the Elder, *Natural History* 28.2(3).10, 11

It apparently does no good to offer a sacrifice or to consult the gods with due ceremony unless you also speak words of prayer. In addition, some words are appropriate for seeking favorable omens, others for warding off evil, and still others for securing help. We notice, for example, that our highest magistrates[91] make appeals to the gods with specific and set prayers. And in order that no word be omitted or spoken out of turn, one attendant reads the prayer from a book,[92] another is assigned to check it closely, a third is appointed to enforce silence.[93] In addition, a flutist plays to block out any extraneous sounds. There are recorded remarkable cases where either ill-omened noises have interrupted and ruined the ritual or an error has been made in the strict wording of the prayer.

Conservatism

The following passage is a translation of a prayer chanted by the Arval Brethren, a college of twelve priests.[94] The prayer, inscribed on a marble tablet, was discov-

[91] Prayers were offered not by priests but by civil officials—consuls or praetors—on behalf of all the citizens.

[92] A priest would read aloud the prayer, phrase by phrase, and the magistrate would repeat it after him.

[93] At a public sacrifice, a citizen's only duty was to maintain absolute silence. He did not speak the prayers along with the magistrate.

[94] *Arval Brethren:* this priesthood was concerned with the worship of deities who protected crops; Latin *arvum* = "arable land." The prayer translated here may have been a processional hymn. On priestly "colleges," see selection 378.

ered under the basilica of St. Peter's in Rome in A.D. 1778. Although the tablet is dated to A.D. 218, the formulaic words of the prayer are much older and may go back to the sixth century B.C. The antiquity of the prayer provides a good example of the conservatism of Roman religion; if the formula worked, it was repeated unchanged for century after century. It is unlikely that many city dwellers of A.D. 218 would have been interested in this prayer for agricultural prosperity, but the priests continued to chant it. The prayer invokes the *Lares*[95] and Mars, who is also called Marmar and Marmor.[96] Mars was originally a vaguely defined agricultural deity who protected farmland from invasions of disease, insects, and animal predators, including human. In this last aspect of his role, he appeared to the early Romans similar to the Greek god of war, Ares, and so later Romans identified Mars primarily as the god of war,[97] with the personality and mythology of Ares.[98] In this ancient prayer, however, he retains his role as an agricultural deity.

365   *CIL* 6.2104 (*ILS* 5039)

Then the priests closed the doors, girt up their robes, picked up their hymn books, divided into three choirs, and moved forward in three-step rhythm, chanting these words:

> Help us, Lares!
> Help us, Lares!
> Help us, Lares!
> Marmar, let not plague or ruin attack the multitude.
> Marmar, let not plague or ruin attack the multitude.
> Marmar, let not plague or ruin attack the multitude.
> Be filled, fierce Mars. Leap the threshold. Halt, wild one.[99]
> Be filled, fierce Mars. Leap the threshold. Halt, wild one.
> Be filled, fierce Mars. Leap the threshold. Halt, wild one.
> By turns call on all the gods of Sowing.
> By turns call on all the gods of Sowing.
> By turns call on all the gods of Sowing.
> Help us, Marmor!
> Help us, Marmor!
> Help us, Marmor!
> Triumph!
> Triumph!
> Triumph!

After the three-step procession had finished, a signal was given and public slaves[100] came in and collected the hymn books.

[95] On *Lares,* see the introduction to selection 354.

[96] *Marmar, Marmor:* these are not different names but simply reduplications of the name Mars; that is, Marsmars.

[97] On Mars as the god of war, see selection 347.

[98] For example, as Ares was the lover of Aphrodite, so Mars became the lover of Venus. On Mars's identification with Celtic deities, see selection 362.

[99] The priests perhaps leap into the air as they dance their processional hymn. The leaping would be imitative magic to make the crops leap up and grow high. On magic, see selection 410.

[100] *public slaves:* owned by the state and assigned to work for the priests.

Prayer

Another passage in Cato's manual *On Agriculture*[101] describes the proper procedure for a prayer and sacrifice to be made before harvest was begun in order to win the cooperation of the gods.

366   Cato the Elder, *On Agriculture* 134

Before you harvest your crops, you should offer a sow as a preliminary sacrifice in the following manner. Offer a sow to Ceres before you store up the following crops: spelt, wheat, barley, beans, and rape seed. Before you slaughter the sow, invoke Janus, Jupiter, and Juno,[102] offering incense and wine.

Offer sacrificial crackers[103] to Janus with the following words: "Father Janus, in offering to you these sacrificial crackers I humbly pray that you may be benevolent[104] and well disposed toward me and my children and my home and my family."[105]

Offer an oblation cracker to Jupiter and honor him with the following words: "Jupiter, in offering to you this oblation cracker I humbly pray that you may be benevolent and well disposed toward me and my children and my home and my family, being honored by this oblation cracker."

Afterward offer wine to Janus with the following words: "Father Janus, just as I humbly prayed when I offered to you the sacrificial crackers, so now for the same purpose be honored with sacrificial wine."

And afterward offer wine to Jupiter with the following words: "Jupiter, be honored by the oblation cracker, be honored by the sacrificial wine."

And then slaughter the sow as a preliminary sacrifice. When the internal organs have been cut out,[106] offer sacrificial crackers to Janus and honor him in the same terms as when you earlier offered him crackers. Offer an oblation cracker to Jupiter and honor him in the same terms as before. Likewise, offer wine to Janus and offer wine to Jupiter in the same terms as it was offered when you earlier offered the sacrificial crackers and the oblation crackers. Afterward offer the internal organs and wine to Ceres.

[101] See selections 184 and 356.

[102] Janus was the god of all beginnings (*January*) and thus appropriately invoked at the beginning of the harvest. He was also the god of doorways and was frequently represented as having two faces, each looking in the opposite direction, even as a door has two "faces." His specific areas of influence were defined by the epithets attached to his name. For example, as Janus Patulcius he opened doors, as Janus Clusivius he closed them. It was very important to use the right epithet in one's prayers. If you want to keep your horse in the barn, you must be careful to pray to Janus Clusivius, not Janus Patulcius. (For other door deities, see selection 357.

On Jupiter and Juno, see the introduction to selection 359. They, too, had many epithets. For example, Jupiter Lucetius was Jupiter, the bringer of light; Juno Lucina was Juno, deity of childbirth. On Jupiter Optimus Maximus, see note 89 of this chapter.

[103] Small wheat crackers were frequently used as offerings to the gods. These wheat crackers were usually accompanied by an offering of wine.

[104] *benevolent:* see note 84 of this chapter.

[105] *family: familia;* see note 30 of this chapter.

[106] The internal organs were first inspected carefully to ascertain the will of the gods (see selection 370) and then burned on the altar. The rest of the pig was eaten by the people who witnessed the sacrifice.

Vow

On some occasions, the support of the gods was invoked by means of a vow rather than a prayer. Both types of request for divine aid had a contractual nature. In a prayer, the suppliant said, "I am doing this for you" (usually offering a sacrifice). "Please do this for me."[107] The gods received a gift whether or not they answered the prayer, but it was hoped that they would honor the contract.[108] In a vow, the suppliant said, "I will, in the future, do this for you if you do this for me." The gods received a gift only if they fulfilled the suppliant's wish.[109] The request to the gods of Carthage to desert their city is a vow.[110] In 191 B.C., Rome was about to embark on a war against Antiochus, a king of Asia Minor. In enlisting divine support for the war, the Romans vowed to Jupiter ten days of *ludi*.[111]

367   Livy, *A History of Rome* 36.2.1–5

[The consuls of 191 B.C.[112] drew lots to determine which province[113] would be assigned to which consul.]

Acilius drew Greece, and Cornelius drew Italy. Once the assignments had been determined, the Senate passed a decree advising that, since the Roman people[114] had recently ordered that there be a war against King Antiochus[115] and those who were under his authority, the consuls should proclaim a period of prayer for this military undertaking, and the consul Manius Acilius should vow great games to Jupiter and gifts at all the banquet tables of the gods.[116] The consul made this vow in public, reciting after the Pontifex Maximus, Publius Licinius, the following words:[117] "If the war which the Roman people have ordered to be undertaken against King Antiochus shall be brought

---

[107] In the previous passage, for example: "Jupiter, in offering to you this oblation cracker, I humbly pray that you may be benevolent and well disposed."

[108] Inspection of the internal organs sometimes indicated whether the gods would honor the contract.

[109] The word *votive*, as in "votive offering," is from the Latin *votum* = "vow."

[110] See selection 361: "If you will do this, I vow that I will build for you temples and celebrate for you games." See also the votive offering inscriptions in selection 362.

[111] The Romans won the war, and the games did take place.

An individual might make a vow before embarking on a voyage (fulfillment depending on his safe return) or if he were ill (fulfillment depending on his recovery).

[112] Manius Acilius Glabrio and Publius Cornelius Scipio.

[113] On the meaning of *province,* see note 7 of Chapter XII.

[114] *the Roman people:* the voters voting in the Comitia Centuriata; see selections 225 and 226.

[115] Antiochus was king of Syria. In 192 B.C., he had invaded Greece, and thus the proposed war against him fell in the sphere of the consul whose province was Greece. Although Greece was not yet part of the Roman Empire, the Romans voted in favor of the war because they feared that if Antiochus conquered Greece, he might next invade Italy.

[116] *banquet tables of the gods:* Latin *lectisternium* (*lectus* = "couch"); see selection 389; on the days when the vow would be fulfilled, dining couches would be set up in public places and images of the gods would be placed on the couches. Expensive foods and other magnificent gifts would be offered (placed on the couches) to the gods attending the banquet. The Romans apparently borrowed this religious custom from the Greeks.

[117] *reciting after:* see selection 364.

to a conclusion deemed appropriate by the Roman Senate and people, then the Roman people will arrange for you, Jupiter, great games for ten consecutive days, and will offer at the banquet tables of the gods gifts of whatever monetary value the Senate shall decree. Whatever magistrate shall arrange these games, at whatever time and whatever place, let these games be duly celebrated and these gifts be duly presented." Then the period of prayer was proclaimed by both consuls to last for two days.

Divination: Augury and Auspicium

Communication with the gods through prayer and vow was essentially a one-way conversation; until one's wish was granted, one did not know whether the gods had committed themselves to the contractual arrangement. There were, however, ways to discern the will of the gods, because the gods sent men signs indicating their will. Divination was the art of interpreting these signs, which might take the form of thunder, lightning, or some unusual natural phenomenon; but more commonly the gods revealed their will in the internal organs of a sacrificial animal or by means of birds, that is, by making birds fly in a certain direction or eat in a certain way. The ability to interpret the divine message given by the flight pattern or eating habits of birds is called augury or *auspicium*.[118] The men who did the interpreting were called augurs, and they were elected to office. Once elected, they learned the secret, carefully formalized rules which enabled them to discern the meaning in the birds' actions. Since election to the position of augur was a political matter as much as a religious matter, the position was held by members of the senatorial class.[119] Augurs had a consultative role. An individual on behalf of his family or a magistrate[120] on behalf of the state would "take the auspices," that is, would observe the flight of eagles or vultures, or the eating habits of crows or chickens, would report to an augur what he had seen, and then would hear from him the interpretation of the birds' actions as a divine sign.[121] Most Romans considered divination a serious matter and would not start a project without taking the auspices,[122] or would abandon the project if the interpretation of the auspices indicated that the gods were not favorably disposed. On more than one occasion, however, the reporting of the auspices or their interpretation was influenced by military or political considerations. The following incident occurred in 293 B.C.

368 Livy, *A History of Rome* 10.40.1–5, 14

The soldiers were filled with confidence in both divine and human aid and, with one voice, demanded battle. It annoyed them that the battle had been postponed to the fol-

---

[118] *augury:* Latin = *augurium,* perhaps derived from *avis* = "bird." *auspicium: avis* = "bird," *spicio* = "look at."

[119] Cicero, for example, was an augur, although he admitted to being skeptical about divination. In selection 98, Cicero speaks of attending a banquet to celebrate a friend's election as augur.

[120] Usually a consul, but possibly a praetor.

[121] The augur did not himself look at the birds. In fact, if he were present during the "sighting," he kept his head covered.

[122] Auspices were always taken, for example, at weddings; see selection 50: "a good maiden will marry with good omens."

lowing day. They hated to wait a day and a night. In the middle of the night, the consul[123] quietly got up and sent the keeper of the sacred chickens to take auspices. There was not one group of men in that camp which had not been infected by the lust for battle. The highest and the lowest ranks were equally eager. The general[124] saw the flaming zeal in his soldiers; the soldiers saw it in their general. This zeal, which burned in everyone, reached even those men who handled the taking of auspices. For, although the sacred chickens would not eat, the chicken keeper dared to lie about the omen and announced to the consul a very favorable omen.[125] The consul was pleased and announced in public that the auspices were excellent and that they would be acting under the direction of the gods. He then gave the signal for battle.

[Just before the first charge of the battle, it was discovered that the chicken keeper had lied. He was killed, and the consul then declared that the Romans had done their best to correct the situation.]

Even as the consul was saying this, a crow cawed, right in front of him, with a loud, clear voice. The happy consul announced that the gods had never been more obviously involved in human affairs, and he ordered the trumpet signal to be played and the war cry to be shouted.

It did not pay to be too skeptical of augury. Publius Claudius Pulcher was consul in 249 B.C. and commander of the Roman fleet which blockaded Lilybaeum, Sicily, during the First Punic War.

369   Suetonius, *The Lives of the Caesars: Tiberius* 2.2

Claudius Pulcher showed his scorn of religion during a naval engagement off Sicily. When he took the auspices and discovered that the sacred chickens were not eating,[126] he threw them into the sea, saying, "If they don't want to eat, let them drink"; and then he engaged the enemy in a naval battle. He lost the battle.

Divination: Extispicium

Another form of divination was the interpretation of signs found in the entrails of sacrificial animals. This procedure is called *extispicium*.[127] The Romans themselves believed that they had borrowed this form of divination from the Etruscans.[128] Men skilled in this science were called *haruspices*. They learned the normal color, shape, and position of each internal organ, and then what every deviation from the norm meant in terms of signs from the gods. It was very common for anyone, private individual or state magistrate, who was offering a sacrifice to ask a *haruspex* to examine the entrails and determine whether the gods had looked favorably upon his prayer.

[123] The consul was the commander-in-chief of the army.
[124] *the general:* the consul.
[125] The chicken keeper announced that the chickens had eaten all their food, in the correct order.
[126] Roman military fleets obviously carried sacred chickens with them.
[127] *extispicium: exta* = "entrails," *spicio* = "look at."
[128] On the Etruscan domination of Rome, see notes 4 and 5 of Chapter I.

370   Livy, *A History of Rome* 8.9.1, 2

Before the Roman consuls led their troops into battle, they offered a sacrifice.[129] The *haruspex* reportedly pointed out to the consul Decius that the head of the liver was lying on the proper side and that the sacrificial victim had in any case been accepted by the gods. He said that the other consul, Manlius, had received very favorable omens. Decius replied, "It's fine with me, if my colleague has received favorable omens." They advanced into battle, with the troops arranged as described above; Manlius commanded the right wing, Decius the left.

The Sibylline Books

The Sibylline books were a collection of oracular responses. The original collection was believed to have been purchased by one of the last kings of Rome from a woman of prophetic power called (the) Sibyl who came to Italy from the east and settled at Cumae.[130]

371   Dionysius of Halicarnassus, *Roman Antiquities* 4.62.5, 6

After the expulsion of the kings,[131] the Roman people assumed responsibility for the Sibylline oracles and entrusted their care to distinguished citizens.[132] These priests have this responsibility for life, but are exempt from military service and other duties of a citizen. Public slaves[133] are assigned to them. No one is allowed to inspect the oracles if the priests are not present. In short, the Romans guard no other possession, whether sacred or profane, as they guard the Sibylline oracles. They consult them whenever the Senate decrees it—when civil disorder grips the city, or some great disaster has befallen them in a war, or some great prodigies or apparitions, which are difficult to understand, have been seen by them (this is the most frequent situation). Until the Social War,[134] these oracles remained underground in a stone chest beneath the temple of Capitoline Jupiter,[135] guarded by ten men. But when the temple was burned in 83 B.C. (either deliberately, as some people think, or by accident), the oracles, along with other objects consecrated to the god, were destroyed by the fire. The oracles which now exist[136] were collected from many different places, some from the cities of Italy, some from Erythrae

---

[129] This battle took place about 340 B.C.

[130] There were a number of different Sibyls who lived in different places at different times. The most famous Sibyl(s) lived in Cumae, a town near Naples which had been settled by the Greeks in the eighth century B.C.

[131] *expulsion of the kings:* see note 4 of Chapter I.

[132] Like the augurs, the fifteen priests who were responsible for the Sibylline books were political men.

[133] *Public slaves:* see selection 365.

[134] *Social War:* 91–89 B.C.; a war between Rome and her allies in Italy (Latin *socius* = "ally"); see note 2 of Chapter I.

[135] The temple of Jupiter Optimus Maximus situated on the Capitoline, one of Rome's Seven Hills. On the epithets Optimus Maximus, see note 89 of this chapter.

[136] Dionysius died in 8 B.C. (see Appendix I). Augustus transferred the new collection of oracles to the temple of Apollo on the Palatine, another of Rome's Seven Hills.

in Asia Minor (three envoys had been sent there by a decree of the Senate to copy the oracles), and some from other cities where they had been copied by private individuals.

Festivals

In addition to the prayers and vows which were made on particular occasions, by an individual wanting a divine favor, or by the state on behalf of its citizens, there were fixed dates or festivals during the year on which the Romans renewed their relationships with the various deities and once again asked for their benevolence. On festival days, there were prayers and sacrifices and usually some further ritual procedures whose meanings are often not clear today.[137] It was, of course, essential that every aspect of the ritual be performed with absolute correctness. And it was also essential that the festival not be neglected. Failure to celebrate the festival meant that the gods would no longer be benevolent; they would be disinterested or even hostile. Therefore, although many families celebrated the festivals with private prayers and sacrifices, the state assumed the responsibility of public prayers and sacrifices to ensure that no deity whose good will was necessary for the survival of the state was neglected. In time, as Rome grew from an agricultural community to a large city, these ancient festivals had little personal meaning for the urban dweller (although city folk would certainly be concerned about the success of the crops or herds which supplied them with food). Thus, the performance of the appropriate rites was left to state officials. Prayers and sacrifices took place outside the temple of the deity whose cooperation was being sought, and a citizen might, if he chose, attend the ceremony as a witness, but he was expected to remain silent as the priests intoned the prayers.[138] It was the correct performance of the ritual, and not the number of people attending it, which evidently mattered most to the gods. The ceremony would take place even without witnesses, although most ceremonies, since they were held outdoors, probably attracted curious bystanders.

In the country, the religious rites of the ancient festivals continued to be important to the individual farmer. In the passage translated here, Cato describes a *lustratio*[139] or purification ceremony which may have taken place during the Ambarvalia, a spring festival. A pig, a sheep, and a bull were led in a procession around the boundaries of one's property.

372   Cato the Elder, *On Agriculture* 141

It is necessary to purify your farmland in the following way. Have a pig-sheep-bull procession[140] led around the land, while the following words are spoken: "With the benev-

---

[137] For more on the activities during festival days, see the introduction to the section on spectacles in Chapter XIV.

[138] Temples were not designed to accommodate worshippers. The early Christians, therefore, adopted for the design of their churches not temples but instead basilicas; see note 81 of Chapter XI.

On the necessity of silence during public prayers, see selection 364.

[139] *lustratio:* the Latin verb *lustrare* means both "to travel around" and "to purify."

[140] A pig-sheep-bull procession was called a *suovetaurilia* (*sus* = "pig," *ovis* = "sheep," *taurus* = "bull").

olence of the gods, and hoping that everything may turn out well, I entrust to you the responsibility of having the pig-sheep-bull procession led around my farm, field, and land, wherever you decide the animals ought to be led or carried."

Invoke Janus and Jupiter with an offering of wine; then speak these words: "Father Mars,[141] I pray and entreat you to be benevolent and well disposed toward me and my home and my family. And for this reason I have ordered a pig-sheep-bull procession to be led around my field, land, and farm, so that you will hinder, ward off, and turn away diseases seen and unseen, barrenness and crop losses, disasters and storms; and so that you will allow the vegetable crops, the grain crops, the vineyards, and the orchards to grow and achieve a productive maturity; and so that you will protect the shepherds and the flocks and bestow safety and good health upon me and my home and my family. For these reasons, therefore, and because of the purifying of my farm, land, and field, and the offering of a sacrifice for purification, even as I have prayed, be honored by the sacrifice of the suckling pig-sheep-bull. For this reason, therefore, Father Mars, be honored by this suckling pig-sheep-bull sacrifice."

Slaughter the sacrificial animals with a knife. Bring forward sacrificial crackers and an oblation cracker, and offer them. When you slaughter the pig, lamb, and calf, you must use these words: "For this reason, therefore, be honored by the sacrifice of the pig-sheep-bull." . . . If all the sacrificial victims are not perfect,[142] speak these words: "Father Mars, if somehow the suckling pig-sheep-bull sacrifice was not satisfactory to you, I offer this new pig-sheep-bull sacrifice as atonement." If there is doubt about only one or two of the animals, speak these words: "Father Mars, since that pig was not satisfactory to you, I offer this pig as atonement."

Ambarvalia

The Ambarvalia was celebrated at the end of May.[143] In the countryside, farmers led the *suovetaurilia* along their property lines; in urban areas, the procession walked along the perimeter of the town or city.

In the poem translated here, Tibullus describes the same purification ceremony which Cato described in the previous passage. It is interesting to compare the two accounts. Tibullus concentrates on poetic effects, while Cato strives to give the most useful and practical advice to the farmer.[144]

141 In this prayer, Mars retains his agricultural sphere of influence; see selection 365.
On Janus, see selection 366.

142 That is, if the *haruspex*, when he examines the entrails of the sacrificed animals, finds one of the internal organs discolored or misshapen. If this happened, the practical Roman did not despair. He simply sacrificed another animal, and another, until a "perfect" victim was found.

143 *Ambarvalia: ambire* = "to go around," *arva* = "fields" (compare the term *Arval Brethren* in selection 365). This festival corresponds to the Christian custom of Beating-the-Bounds during Ascension-tide (Rogation-tide) in May.

144 On Tibullus's idealization of agricultural life, see selection 179. Compare also the poetic prayer of Catullus (selection 359) and practical prayers of Cato (selections 356 and 366).

373

Tibullus, Elegies 2.1.1–26

Let all present be silent.[145] We are here to purify the crops and the fields in accordance with the tradition handed down by our ancestors.

Come to us, Bacchus, with sweet grapes hanging from your horns. And Ceres, crown your forehead with a wreath of grain.[146] On this holy day, let the soil rest, let the plowman rest. Hang up the plowshare, and let hard labor cease. Undo the harness straps of the yokes; today the oxen should be decorated with garlands and left to rest at mangers full of hay. All activities must be devoted to the god. No woman should dare to use her hands today to make wool. I also order you to whom Venus brought pleasure last night to stand far off and move away from the altar.[147] Only the pure please the gods.[148] Therefore, come with clean clothing and draw the spring water with clean hands. Behold, the consecrated lamb approaches the shining altar, and behind him comes a procession of worshippers in white garments with olive leaves in their hair.

Gods of our fathers, we are cleansing the farms, we are cleansing the farmers. Drive away evils from our boundaries. Let not our grain fields mock the harvest with weeds. Let not the slow-moving lambs fear the swift-footed wolves. Then the sleek farmer, confident in his bountiful fields, will pile huge logs on the blazing hearth, while a crowd of young home-grown slaves,[149] sure proof of a prosperous farmer, will play in front of him, building toy houses out of twigs.

My prayers will be fulfilled. Do you see how the prophetic liver among the favorable entrails announces that the gods are propitious?[150]

Robigalia

The Robigalia was a festival celebrated on April 25. The purpose of this festival was to reach a *pax* with Robigus (sometimes spelled Robigo), the spirit of mildew or grain rust. (April 25 is now St. Mark's Day.)

374

Ovid, A Roman Calendar of Festivals 4.905–941

One day, as I was returning to Rome from Nomentum,[151] a crowd of people clad in white robes were blocking the middle of the road. A *flamen*[152] was proceeding to the

---

[145] The worshippers did not recite prayers or sing hymns; see selection 364.

[146] Bacchus was the god of grapes and wine production; Ceres was the goddess of grain crops.

[147] Venus was the goddess of sexual love. Since this festival was a purification ritual, only the pure were allowed to participate. Anyone who had not been sexually abstinent the night before the festival was forbidden to attend the ceremony.

[148] *the pure:* that is, ritually pure (clean clothes, clean body). Roman religion did not require that worshippers be morally pure.

[149] *home-grown slaves:* the children of slaves were the property of the slave-owner.

[150] Examination of the entrails of the sacrificed animal reveals that the gods will fulfill the requests of the prayer.

[151] *Nomentum:* about fourteen miles from Rome. Martial's villa was at Nomentum (selection 82). Robigus was worshipped outside the city limits because people did not want him in the city.

[152] *flamen:* a priest attached to the cult of a specific deity. The *flamen* of Ceres is mentioned in selection 358.

grove of ancient Mildew[153] in order to place in the flames[154] the entrails of a dog and of a sheep. I immediately moved closer so that I might learn about the ritual. The *flamen* of Quirinus[155] recited these words: "Cruel Mildew, spare the sprouts of the grain plants. Let their tender tips reach up above the surface of the ground. Allow the crops, which are nursed along by favoring stars in heaven, to grow until they become tall enough for the sickle. Your power is not trifling. A farmer sorrowfully considers as lost any crop on which you place your mark.[156] Neither the winds, nor the rain storms, nor the glistening frost which whitens the golden grain do as much harm to our crops as does the sun when it heats the wet stalks. Then, dread deity, comes your opportunity for wrath. Spare us, I pray, and keep your scabby hands away from our harvests. Do not harm our grain fields. Surely you can be satisfied just to know that you have the power to harm. Put your hands on hard iron, not tender crops.[157] First destroy objects which can destroy others. You will more profitably eat away at swords and harmful weapons. We have no need of them because the world is at peace. Let the hoes and the mattock and the curved plowshare, let all the farm equipment shine brightly, but let rust blemish weapons of war. And when someone tries to pull a sword from its scabbard, let him feel that it is sticky from lack of use. But you, Mildew, do not dishonor Ceres.[158] May the farmer always be able to offer prayers to you while you are absent."[159]

Thus spoke the *flamen*. In his right hand he held a loosely woven napkin. He also had a casket of incense and a bowl of wine. He placed on the altar fire the incense and wine and the viscera of the sheep and the foul entrails of the filthy dog. Then he spoke to me: "You have asked why so unusual a victim is sacrificed at these rites." (I had indeed asked that.) "Here is the explanation," the *flamen* said. "There is in heaven a Dog.[160] When this constellation rises, the earth is parched and thirsty, and the crops ripen too soon. This dog is put on the altar in place of the starry Dog."

Lupercalia

The Lupercalia, which was celebrated on February 15, was both a purification ceremony and a fertility rite. People swept clean their houses and then went outdoors to watch the young men, who were chosen to purify the city, run by. Large crowds of spectators gathered in the Forum, and the women present hoped not only to be purified, but also to be made very fertile. The occasion was one of merriment and revelry, and the Lupercalia was one of Rome's best-loved festivals. The early Christian church could not abolish completely so popular a holiday, but in A.D. 494, Pope Gelasius I declared February 15 the Festival of the Purification of the Virgin Mary.[161]

[153] *Mildew:* Robigus.
[154] *flames:* of the altar fire.
[155] *Quirinus:* a Roman deity closely associated with Jupiter and Mars.
[156] *mark:* the blemish of destructive mildew or grain rust.
[157] That is, rust iron, not grain crops.
[158] *Ceres:* that is, grain.
[159] Many prayers requested the presence of the deity. A person who prayed to Venus, for example, would hope that the goddess would come near and assist him in his sexual endeavors. Prayers to Mildew, however, specifically requested that the deity stay far away.
[160] The Dog-Star, Sirius.
[161] See comments about the Ambarvalia in note 143 and about the Saturnalia in note 172 of this chapter.

The Lupercalia would appear, because of its date, to be a purification ceremony since it is celebrated on the *dies nefasti*[162] of the month of February, a word which may be interpreted to mean "purifying";[163] indeed, the day on which this festival occurs used to be called *Februata* a long time ago. However, the name of the festival means the same as the Greek *Lukaia*,[164] and therefore the festival seems very ancient and to have been brought to Italy by the Arcadians under Evander.[165] And this is the widely accepted explanation, for the word can then be derived from the she-wolf of early Roman history.[166] In fact, the *Luperci*[167] begin their run around the city, as we see, at that spot where legend says Romulus was abandoned. However, the procedures at the festival offer no help in determining its origin. Goats are slaughtered. Then two young men of noble birth are brought before the priests. Some of the priests touch the boys' foreheads with the bloody knife, others immediately wipe clean their foreheads with wool soaked in milk. The young men must laugh after their foreheads are wiped. Then they[168] cut the hides of the goats into strips and run through the city, naked except for a loin covering, lashing anyone in their way with the strips of goathide.[169] However, women of child-bearing age do not avoid the lashings, since they think they aid in fertility, pregnancy, and childbirth. A peculiar feature of this festival is that the *Luperci* also sacrifice a dog.

Saturnalia

In the Roman year, as in the modern year, the winter solstice was the time for a festival of joy, optimism, and good will.[170] The Saturnalia was a festival honoring the god Saturn.[171] Originally it had occupied only one day, December 17, but by the late republican period, the merry spirit of Saturnalia extended over a number of days.[172] The holiday began on December 17 with a religious ceremony at the

[162] *dies nefasti:* days (*dies* = "days") on which law courts and legislative assemblies were forbidden to meet.

[163] The verb *februare* means "to purify."

[164] *Lukaia:* a Greek festival, which Plutarch suggests, perhaps incorrectly, means "Wolf Festival" (Greek *lukos* = "wolf"). *Lupercalia:* Latin *lupus* = "wolf."

[165] Evander is said to have brought a colony of Greek settlers from Arcadia (Greek *Lukaios* = "Arcadian") to Italy just before the Trojan War.

[166] *she-wolf:* the wolf who suckled the babies Romulus and Remus after they had been abandoned.

[167] *Luperci:* young men of noble families, chosen to participate in the purification ritual.

[168] The two young men were apparently joined in their run through the city by other *Luperci.*

[169] The *Luperci* lashed with the goathide strips the ground, buildings, objects, or people in their way in an attempt to drive evil out of the city. In British bound-beating rites of Ascension-tide (see note 143 of this chapter), peeled sticks are used to beat the boundaries.

[170] In addition to the state religion and to Christianity, other cults in the Roman world—the worship of Mithra, for example, and of the Sun (Sol Invictus)—celebrated a major festival at the end of December.

[171] *Saturn:* the god of seed sowing.

[172] Saturnalia was one of the most popular festivals of the whole year. Its place was conveniently taken in the Christian calendar by Christmas, but many of the festivities which sur-

temple of Saturn in the Forum. Often a free public banquet followed the religious ceremony. Stores and businesses were closed so that all workers could enjoy the celebration, and people greeted one another in the streets with shouts of "Io Saturnalia." There were no *ludi* presented during Saturnalia. Saturnalia was a time for family dinners, for parties, for gift giving, for wishing your friends and neighbors well. Slaves became masters for a day and were waited on by their owners. Generous owners gave their slaves gifts and allowed them a "day off." Even a miserly owner like Cato the Elder gave his slaves extra wine rations for the Saturnalia.[173]

In the passage translated here, the poet Statius urges the patron saints of learning and poetry, Phoebus, Pallas, and the Muses, to take a vacation and leave him alone during December. He doesn't want to work at poetry writing during the Saturnalia; he wants to go to parties![174]

376 Statius, *Silvae* 1.6.1–7

Father Phoebus and stern Pallas, go away! You, too, Muses, take a vacation and go far away! I will call you back on New Year's Day. But you, Saturn, cast off your fetters and come near. You, too, December, tipsy from so much wine, and laughing Good Cheer and wanton Joviality, come and be present.

Saturnalia Gifts

377 *Martial, Epigrams* 14.1, 28, 70, 71; 12.81

At this time of the year, when the equestrians and senators show off their party clothes, and even the emperor wears a freedman's cap,[175] and the home-bred slave is not afraid to look straight at the aedile and shake the dice box (even though he sees the icy tanks so nearby),[176] accept the gift you have drawn,[177] whether from a poor or a rich man. Let everyone give his guest an appropriate gift.

Accept this parasol which can block even the intense sunlight. Even when it is windy, you will be protected by your own awning.[178]

---

rounded the celebration of Saturn were absorbed into the celebration of Christ's birth. The Christians wisely absorbed what they could not eradicate.

[173] See selection 184.

[174] Contrast Seneca's abstinence (selection 424) or Pliny's indifference (selection 87).

[175] *freedman's cap:* see note 107 of Chapter VIII. It was customary for everyone to wear a freedman's cap during Saturnalia, perhaps to symbolize the general freedom of the season, or perhaps to emphasize that all men, slave or free, rich or poor, are equal. A spirit of compassion and good will prevailed during Saturnalia.

[176] Evidently a slave who was caught gambling during any other time of the year could be punished by the aedile (and perhaps thrown into a tank of cold water).

[177] At some Saturnalia parties, the gifts were distributed by lot.

[178] Many Roman theaters and amphitheaters had awnings which could be unfurled to shade spectators from the hot sun (see selection 337). On very windy days, however, the awnings were not unfurled.

This pig will make your Saturnalia merry. He was fed acorns and pastured with the foaming boars.

If your clothing has been soiled by yellow dust, this little oxtail brush will clean it with a light whisk.

On wintry cold days of Saturnalia, Umber used to give me, when he was poor, a cape as a gift. Now he gives me a drink, because he has become rich.

OFFICERS OF THE STATE RELIGION

It was the duty of the officers of the state religion to preserve the *pax deorum*. We have already noted that the secular and religious aspects of a Roman citizen's life were inseparable. And because religion was a function of the state, priesthoods were occupied by politicians. Men of wealth and education had an obligation to serve the state;[179] and being a priest was one way in which they could discharge this obligation. Most priests were elected to office,[180] and, once elected, they learned the very complicated religious procedures and rituals over which they now had charge.[181] Being a priest was a social distinction and therefore an office eagerly sought. As we have seen, Caesar was Pontifex Maximus, and Cicero was an augur. The Pontifex Maximus, who lived in a palace in the Forum (until the imperial period, when the emperor was Pontifex Maximus), supervised the other officers. The priests of Rome were the sixteen *pontifices,* whose duties are described below;[182] the fifteen *flamines,* who were in charge of the cults of specific deities;[183] and the six Vestal Virgins. There were also, among the officers, sixteen augurs and fifteen men whose task it was to care for the Sibylline books.[184]

Pontifices

378   Dionysius of Halicarnassus, *Roman Antiquities* 2.73.1, 2

The *pontifices* have authority over the most important matters in the Roman state. They serve as judges in all religious cases involving private citizens or magistrates or ministers

[179] For more on this obligation, see the introduction to the section on patronage in Chapter I, also the introduction to selection 147.

[180] Priests were elected in the Comitia Tributa.

[181] A priest had to learn the appropriate occasions for each prayer, vow, and sacrifice; the phrases and the order of each ritual; the names of all the deities, major and minor; and he had to know when to use which names.

[182] *pontifex:* English "pontiff." There were sixteen *pontifices* by the time of Julius Caesar. These *pontifices* were considered a "college"; Latin *collegium* = "association of people holding the same office or interest"; compare the English phrase "pontifical college." There was also a college of augurs. On funeral colleges, see selection 116.

[183] For example, the *flamen* of Ceres (selection 358) or the *flamen* of Quirinus (selection 374).

[184] On augurs and on the Sibylline books, see selections 368 and 371.

of the gods. They make laws concerning religious rituals which have not been recorded or handed down by tradition, but which they judge as appropriate to receive the sanction of law and custom.[185] They closely scrutinize all the magistracies which have duties involving any sacrifice or ministry of the gods;[186] they also scrutinize all the priesthoods, and watch carefully their servants and ministers whom they employ in the rituals to make sure that they commit no error in regard to the sacred laws. For private citizens who are not knowledgeable about religious matters concerning the gods and divine spirits, the *pontifices* are explainers and interpreters. And should they learn that some people are not obeying their injunctions, they punish them, examining each of the charges. They themselves are not liable to any prosecution or punishment, nor are they accountable to the Senate or people, at least concerning religious matters.

Vestal Virgins

Vesta was the deity of the hearth fire. Fire for cooking and heating was a necessity of life, and the Romans were therefore conscientious in their worship of Vesta. In private homes of early Rome, where the hearth was a central element, all family members[187] gathered once a day for a sacrifice to Vesta.[188] In a sense, then, every private home was a temple of Vesta. There was also, however, a city temple of Vesta, before which city residents could gather as one big "family." At this temple, religious officers assumed the responsibility, on behalf of the community for maintaining a good relationship with Vesta. Vesta was not represented by statues; instead, the eternal fire burning on her altar represented the deity, and it was the responsibility of her priestesses, the Vestal Virgins, to keep the fire burning at all times.

379   Aulus Gellius, *Attic Nights* 1.12.1–3, 5, 9, 14

A girl chosen to be a Vestal Virgin must, according to law, be no less than six and no more than ten years old. Both her father and her mother must be alive. She must not be handicapped by a speech or hearing problem or disfigured by some physical defect. . . . Neither one nor both of her parents may have been slaves or may engage in demeaning occupations.[189] . . .

As soon as a Vestal Virgin has been chosen, escorted to the House of Vesta,[190] and handed over to the *pontifices*, she immediately leaves the control of her father,[191]

---

[185] Religious law was public law. See selection 253. Pontiffs (*pontifices*) exerted a powerful influence on the early development of Roman law.

[186] Consuls or praetors, for example, made sacrifices or took auspices on behalf of the state.

[187] On the meaning of "family," see note 30 of this chapter.

[188] The sacrificial items were salt and flour.

[189] On "demeaning occupations," see Cicero's comments in selection 147. Most Vestal Virgins were of senatorial families.

[190] The sanctuary of Vesta, which included the temple and living quarters for the priestesses, was in the Forum. Much of it is still standing today.

[191] She will no longer be under *patria potestas* (see selection 14). Vestal Virgins were in some senses more liberated than the ordinary Roman woman, who could not, for example, make a will or be free of the power of a father or guardian.

without a ceremony of manumission or a loss of civil rights, and she acquires the right
to make a will. . . .

The words which the Pontifex Maximus should speak when he accepts a Vestal
Virgin are these: "I accept you, Amata,[192] as one who is legally suitable to be a priestess
of Vesta and to perform the sacred rites which it is lawful for a priestess of Vesta to
perform on behalf of the Roman people."

380   Dionysius of Halicarnassus, *Roman Antiquities* 2.67

The virgins who serve the goddess Vesta were originally four in number and chosen by
the king in accordance with the regulations which Numa established.[193] Later their
number was increased to six, because of the multitude of sacred duties which they perform, and it has remained at six up to our own time. They live in the sanctuary of the
goddess, which no one can be prevented from entering, if he wishes, during the day. It
is forbidden, however, for any man to stay there at night.

These priestesses must remain pure and unmarried for thirty years, offering sacrifices and performing other religious rites in accordance with the law. During the first
ten years they must learn these rites; during the second ten they perform them; and
during the remaining ten they must teach others. When the thirty years have been completed, there is no law which prohibits those who so wish from putting aside the head-
bands and other insignia of the priestly service and marrying. Only a few, however, do
so, and they have, during their remaining years, lives which are neither enviable nor
very happy. And therefore, taking the unhappy fates of these few as a warning, the rest
of the virgins remain in service to the goddess until their deaths, at which time another
virgin is appointed by the *pontifices* to take the place of the deceased.

The Vestal Virgins receive many fine honors from the city and do not therefore
yearn for children or marriage. In any case, the penalties imposed for misbehavior are
heavy. According to the law, the *pontifices* are the investigators and the punishers of the
misdeeds. They whip with rods those priestesses who have committed some lesser offense, but they sentence those who have lost their virginity to a most shameful and most
pitiable death. For while they are still alive they are carried on a bier in a funeral procession such as that arranged for dead men,[194] and their friends and relatives join the
procession and mourn for them. They are taken as far as the Colline Gate and placed
in an underground cell which has been constructed within the walls of the gate.[195] They
are dressed in funeral attire but do not receive a monument or funeral offerings or any
other customary rites.

There are apparently many clues which indicate that a priestess who is performing
holy rites is no longer a virgin, but the principal clue is the extinction of the fire, an occurrence which the Romans fear more than all catastrophes, since they believe that,
whatever the cause of the extinction, it is a sign warning of the destruction of the city.
They reintroduce fire into the temple with many rites of atonement.

---

[192] *Amata:* perhaps an adjective rather than a proper name; Latin *amata* = "beloved";
Greek *adamata* = "unwedded."

[193] *Numa:* the second king of Rome (after Romulus).

[194] On funeral biers and processions, see selection 115.

[195] *Colline Gate:* near the Quirinal Hill in the northeastern part of Rome. The priestess
is buried alive.

DEIFICATION

Although the conservative nature of the Roman people allowed them to retain religious rites which had lost meaning for most citizens, the religion was not static in all respects. It expanded to borrow, absorb, and incorporate new deities[196] and finally even to create deities. In the eastern part of the Mediterranean world, people had worshipped their kings as gods for hundreds of years. When these people were conquered by the Romans, they began naturally to look upon their new Roman rulers as divine figures. Since it appeared to Roman officials a dangerous precedent to have a man worshipped, while still alive, as a god, they encouraged the western provincials to worship instead Roma, the divine spirit of Rome. In Rome itself, a living ruler could not be considered a god, but when Julius Caesar died he was thought to have joined the ranks of the divinities,[197] to have been deified.[198] From that time on, it was common for an emperor to be deified after his death. The cult of the deified emperors was closely associated with the cult of Roma throughout the western part of the Empire. In the east, however, with its tradition of divine monarchs, attempts to prevent the worship of living emperors were unsuccessful, as the following passages indicate. All concern the emperor Tiberius, although he was by no means the only emperor to encounter this problem.

Tiberius and the City of Gythium

381   *SEG* 11.923 (Ehrenberg and Jones, *Documents* 102)

Tiberius Caesar Augustus, son of the deified Augustus, . . . to the directors and people of the city of Gythium:[199] Greetings. Decimus Tyrranius Nicanor, the envoy whom you sent to me and to my mother,[200] has delivered to me your letter in which you enclosed a copy of the resolutions passed by you to pay reverence to my father and honor to me. For these, I thank you, and I suppose that it is proper for all men in general, and your city in particular, to perpetuate special honors, suitable for the gods, in proportion to the magnitude of my father's great services to the whole world. But I myself am satisfied with the more modest honors suitable for mortal men. My mother, however, will answer you herself when she learns of your decision about honors to her.

---

[196] See selections 360, 361, and 362.
[197] The Julian family claimed that it was descended from the goddess Venus.
[198] *deified:* on the etymology of the word, see note 33 of Chapter IV.
[199] *Gythium:* a town in Greece.
[200] *my mother:* Livia, wife of Augustus; see selection 67.

Requests for Emperor-Worship

382   Tacitus, *Annals* 4.37, 38

At this time,[201] Farther Spain[202] sent a delegation to the Roman Senate asking permission to erect a shrine to Tiberius and his mother following the example of Asia.[203] On this occasion Caesar,[204] who was in any case very scornful of special honors and who thought, moreover, that he should reply to those critics who were spreading rumors that he had become insolent, began a speech which was like this: "I know, senators, that I have been found wanting in consistency by many of you because I recently did not reject the people of Asia when they made the same request. Therefore, I will defend my previous silence at the same time that I disclose what I have decided for the future. Since the deified Augustus had not forbidden the erection of a temple at Pergamum[205] to himself and the city of Rome,[206] so then I, who observe all his deeds and words as law, followed the example set by him, and all the more readily because veneration of the Senate was associated with worship of me. But although accepting such honors once can be excused, to be worshipped throughout all the provinces in the image of a god is insolent and arrogant. And the honor given to Augustus will fade if it is vulgarized by indiscriminate flattery and adulation. And so, senators, I ask you to be my witnesses of this, and I want posterity to remember this: I am a mortal, I perform the functions of a human being, and I am content to occupy the top position in the human world. Those who believe that I am worthy of my ancestors, prudent about your interest, firm in dangerous situations, and not afraid of incurring dislike if public welfare is at stake, will honor my memory enough, and more than enough. . . . And so I pray to our allies, citizens, and especially to the gods; to the gods I pray that to the end of my life they endow me with a mind which is free of anxiety and which understands human and divine law; to our allies and citizens I pray that, when I depart, they may honor my deeds and my reputation with praise and pleasant memories."

And from that time on he persisted in rejecting such worship of himself, even in private conversations.

Tiberius's Resistance to Emperor-Worship

383   Suetonius, *The Lives of the Caesars: Tiberius* 26

Tiberius forbade temples or priesthoods to be established in his name. He then forbade statues and busts to be set up without his permission, and he permitted them on this one condition alone, that they not be placed among statues of the gods but only as decorative ornaments in buildings. He vetoed a proposal that oaths be sworn to support his

---

[201] A.D. 25.

[202] The Iberian peninsula was divided by the Romans into two provinces: Nearer Spain and Farther Spain.

[203] The province of Asia.

[204] Each emperor was called Caesar; see note 39 of Chapter III.

[205] *Pergamum:* a city in the province of Asia.

[206] Note the association of the cult of the emperor with the cult of Roma. On the meaning of "cult," see the introduction to the section on ritual in this chapter.

actions, as well as a proposal that the months September and October be called instead Tiberius and Livius[207] respectively.

THE PERMANENCE OF THE STATE RELIGION

Neglect of the State Cult

The state religion had served Rome well from its first beginnings down through the republican period, as it evolved from a small village to a city which dominated the Mediterranean world. Rome had won all its major military confrontations and had only once suffered an enemy force within its gates.[208] The gods, whose benevolence had been won through the proper performance of ritual, had given success and prosperity to Rome. By the late republican period, however, many Romans did not feel quite so secure about their special relationship with the gods. The first half of the first century B.C. was a period of political chaos and civil disorder which all too often produced bloodshed.[209] Finally, in 49 B.C., when Caesar crossed the Rubicon River, the uneasy alliance between him and Pompey erupted into civil war, a war which dragged on long after the death of Caesar, after the death of Antony, until Augustus consolidated his powers about 30 B.C. and the republic became a dictatorship.[210] Internal turmoil, moreover, made Rome vulnerable to external attacks, and the crushing defeat by the Parthians at Carrhae in 53 B.C. of the army under Crassus was a blow to Roman confidence.[211] In this period of gloom and desperation, many people began to attribute Rome's problems to neglect of the state cult. The following passage, a translation of a poem by Horace,[212] expresses well the uneasiness of the Roman people about their relationship with the gods.

384   Horace, *Odes* 3.6.1–20, 33–43

You will continue to pay for your fathers' sins, O Roman, although you yourself are guiltless, until you have restored the temples and crumbling shrines of the gods and their statues, filthy with black smoke.[213]

   You rule an empire because you acknowledge that you are subordinate to the gods.

---

[207] The month Quintilis had had its name changed to Julius (July) in honor of Julius Caesar; and the month Sextilis had been changed to Augustus (August) in honor of the emperor Augustus. This new proposal was meant to honor Tiberius and his mother, Livia.

[208] On the Gallic invasion, see note 27 of Chapter XIV.

[209] For example, the Social War, the proscriptions of Sulla (see note 114 of Chapter VII), and the conspiracy of Catiline (see selection 291).

[210] See selection 241.

[211] See note 113 of Chapter VII.

[212] Horace, who was born in 65 B.C. and died in 8 B.C., witnessed the Civil War, the defeat of Antony, and Octavian's consolidation of imperial power.

[213] Temples which had caught fire and burned had not been restored. The statues of the gods were discolored by the smoke from these fires and had not been cleaned.

From them comes every beginning; attribute to them also every outcome. You neglected the gods, and they heaped on Italy many grievous calamities.

Twice now the Parthians have crushed our inauspicious assaults.[214] . . .

Dacia and Egypt almost destroyed Rome when it was paralyzed by civil war.[215] . . .

Our age has blossomed with vice and polluted our homes and marriages and families first; then, rising from these sources, a river of disaster has flooded our country and our people. . . .

Not from such parents were those young men born who stained the sea with Punic blood and cut down Pyrrhus and mighty Antiochus and dire Hannibal.[216]

On the contrary, they were the manly offspring of peasant soldiers, who knew how to turn the clods of earth with Sabine hoes, and to chop and carry in firewood at their stern mother's command, when the sun had lengthened the shadows on the mountains and removed the yoke from the weary oxen.[217]

Resistance to Intolerance

Augustus devoted much energy to the revitalization of the state religion; he rebuilt temples, revived rituals, and encouraged people to attend the public religious ceremonies. More importantly, he brought peace and prosperity to Rome and thus restored the confidence of the Roman people in the efficacy of their religion. During the imperial period, when crises arose, many people sought assistance also from foreign deities such as Isis, Mithra, and Christ, but the state religion remained a strong influence in Roman life. By the fourth century A.D., however, Christianity began to win the support of the emperors, and in A.D. 392, the emperor Theodosius I banned all non-Christian rites. Christianity became the official state religion.

The author of the passage translated here, Quintus Aurelius Symmachus (about A.D. 340–402) was an "old" Roman. He "belonged to a society ennobled by public office, and to an inner circle of that society held together by intermarriage and a shared refusal to abandon the institutions, traditions, literature, and outlook of the past. Backward-looking, defensive, proud, they believed that Rome had grown great under divine guidance. . . . There was a reticence, an inarticulate feeling, at any rate among the older and prouder families, that Emperors came and went, wars or famines occurred or did not, but Rome and the senate and a way of life were permanent and important above all else."[218] Symmachus was prefect of the city in A.D. 384–385, a position of immense power and prestige, and consul in A.D. 391.[219] He fought a valiant but ultimately unsuccessful battle against the tightening stranglehold of Christianity. In A.D. 382, the emperor Gratian removed

[214] *twice:* in 53 B.C., at Carrhae, and in 40 B.C.
inauspicious: undertaken without good auspices.

[215] Dacia (a Roman province north of the Danube) assisted Antony in his struggle against Octavian (Augustus). Similarly Egypt, under Cleopatra, supported Antony.

[216] Pyrrhus: see note 198 of Chapter VII. Antiochus: see note 115 of this chapter; Spurius Ligustinus (selection 266) fought against Antiochus's army. Hannibal: see note 87 of Chapter VII.

[217] Even after they had finished a hard day's work in the field, the young men still had to chop and carry firewood. On the Roman ideals of the sober peasant soldier, see selections 1 and 266; on the stern mother, see selection 17; and on obedient children, see selection 38.

[218] R. H. Barrow, *Prefect and Emperor* (Oxford, 1973), pp. 13–14.

[219] On these offices, see selections 232 and 242.

from the Senate house the altar of Victory which Augustus had placed there about 30 B.C. For four centuries the altar had symbolized the successful relationship between the Romans and the gods of the state cult. Gratian's removal of the altar was an attempt to eradicate the state cult. He also refused to be Pontifex Maximus, and he deprived the priests of various revenues and privileges. Symmachus was sent by the Senate to plead with Gratian but was not granted a hearing. In A.D. 384, after Gratian's death, Symmachus attempted to persuade the emperor Valentinian II to restore the altar, but again he was unsuccessful. The following poignant plea for tolerance is taken from Symmachus's petition of A.D. 384.

Once Christianity became the official religion, its followers did not hesitate to ban other religions, to destroy temples, and even to persecute non-Christians. The rites of the old state cult were forbidden, but many people who adopted Christianity preserved some of the traditions of their ancestors' religion; more than a few elements of the Roman cult were absorbed by the new religion and have been passed down to modern Christianity.

385   Symmachus, *Dispatches to the Emperor* 3.8–10

Every man has his own customs and his own religious practices. Similarly, the divine mind has given to different cities different religious rites which protect them. And, just as each man receives at birth his own soul, so, too, does each nation receive a *genius*[220] which guides its destiny. We should also take into account the bestowal of favors, which, more than anything else, proves to man the existence of gods.[221] For, since no human reasoning can illuminate this matter, from where else can knowledge of the gods come, and come more correctly, than from the recollection and evidences of prosperity? If the long passage of time gives validity to religious rites, we must keep faith with so many centuries and we must follow our fathers, who followed their fathers and therefore prospered.[222]

Let us imagine that Rome herself is standing before us now and addressing these words to you: "Best of emperors, fathers of the fatherland,[223] respect my age! The dutiful performance of religious rites has carried me through many years. Let me enjoy the ancient ceremonies, for I do not regret them. Let me live in my own way, for I am free. This is the religion which made the whole world obedient to my laws. These are the rites which drove back Hannibal from my walls and the Senones from my Capitol.[224] Have I been preserved only for this—to be rebuked in my old age? I will consider the changes which people think must be instituted, but modification, in old age, is humiliating and too late."

[220] *genius:* guardian spirit.

[221] Compare Cicero's comments, quoted in the introduction to the section on ritual in this chapter.

[222] When Rome fell victim to the barbarian invasions of the fifth century A.D., some people suggested that Rome was being punished for its neglect of the old religion. See note 31 of this chapter.

[223] *fathers of the fatherland: patres patriae;* see notes 122 and 170 of Chapter X. On paternalism in Roman society, see the introduction to the section on patronage in Chapter I.

[224] *Senones:* a tribe of Gauls.

Capitol: one of Rome's Seven Hills (the Capitoline).

For the assault on Rome by the Gauls in 390 B.C., see note 27 of Chapter XIV.

And so we are asking for amnesty for the gods of our fathers, the gods of our homeland. It is reasonable to assume that whatever each of us worships can be considered one and the same. We look up at the same stars, the same sky is above us all, the same universe encompasses us. What difference does it make which system each of us uses to find the truth? It is not by just one route that man can arrive at so great a mystery.

RELIGIONS FROM THE EAST

By the late republican period, the people of Rome had become acquainted with several religions which were quite unlike their own state religion. These religions had their origins in areas east of Rome and hence are called eastern or oriental religions.[225] They shared certain characteristics; for example, they allowed, even encouraged, the emotional involvement of the worshipper, a novelty for the Romans whose state religion was impersonal and unemotional.[226] More importantly, most of these eastern religions had a central myth which explored the death and resurrection of a deity or a figure closely associated with a deity. This victory over death served as a promise to the adherents that they, too, could achieve immortality and a blessed life after death. Assurance of an afterlife could be granted, however, only to people who had been initiated into the mysteries of the religion. Most of the eastern religions were therefore mystery religions, that is, religions which could illuminate the mystery of achieving immortality and which kept their teachings a mystery or secret to all but the initiates. Initiation, which often involved a cleansing rite such as baptism, was a joyous occasion; the initiate had been redeemed by a savior god from his former life; he had learned the mysteries of immortality and was assured of a blessed afterlife; and he was now welcomed into a supportive group of fellow initiates.[227]

Eastern religions gained many adherents in Rome and Italy during the late republican period and throughout the imperial period. One of these religions, Christianity, has survived to our own time.[228] Most Romans did not renounce the state cult when they were initiated into another religion;[229] they felt no conflict between the demands of the state cult and those of an eastern religion. The former was public and impersonal, the latter private and personal. It was easy enough to stand silently at an occasional ceremony conducted for the welfare of the state,[230]

[225] *oriental:* from Latin *oriens* = "rising (sun)"; the orient was the place of the rising sun, the east. These religions originated in areas which we today consider the Near and Mideast, not the Far East.

[226] On personal experience as one of the dimensions of religion, see the introduction to this chapter.

[227] The feeling of belonging is an important element in human institutions. On this dimension of religion, see the introduction to this chapter.

[228] Unlike some of the other eastern religions, Christianity did not keep its teachings about immortality a mystery. Initiation, or baptism, was, however, a requirement for a blessed afterlife.

[229] Only Christianity demanded that its converts renounce all other beliefs. The other eastern religions were willing to coexist.

[230] On the requirement that the audience at a state ritual maintain absolute silence, see selection 364.

and thus to fulfil one's public obligations. Personal salvation, however, was a matter for the eastern religions. In other words, the eastern religions were not competing with the state cult; they satisfied needs which the state cult could not. The rigid formalism of the latter, with its remarkable emphasis on the ritual dimension, allowed no outlets for emotionalism, no communion with the deities, no ecstasy of faith. There was no promise of salvation and redemption and a blessed afterlife, no code of ethics to provide guidance for the conduct of one's life.[231] The popular appeal of the eastern religions must be seen in the context of the political, economic, and social expansion of Rome. The religion which had served the Romans well when their community was small, cohesive, and homogeneous did not provide sufficient comfort for the cosmopolitan population of imperial Rome.

The passages below contain accounts of some of the more popular eastern religions. An account of Mithraism, the soldiers' religion, unfortunately is lacking because we have very few literary references to this Persian religion, although an abundance of archeological evidence indicates that it won adherents among Roman soldiers throughout the Empire.

Turning to Other Religions

As early as the third century B.C., eastern cults were finding eager disciples among the people of Rome. The population of Rome included, of course, many people of non-Roman birth—slaves, freedmen, foreign businessmen—for whom the eastern cults were "native" religions; but Roman citizens, too, were attracted to these cults, especially in times of crisis and despair when the state religion seemed unable to provide hope and comfort. Such a time was the Second Punic War, when Hannibal's troops were ravishing Italy, and the traditional gods and ancestral rituals had not been able to secure a military victory for the Romans.[232] The passage translated here describes the situation in Rome in 213 B.C.

386   Livy, *A History of Rome* 25.1.6–8

The longer the war dragged on, and the alternation of success and defeat affected both the prosperity and the attitudes of men, an increasing number of religious cults, most of them foreign, invaded the city with the result that either the men or the gods seemed to have changed rather suddenly. No longer did people keep their disaffection with the state religion a secret, voiced only in private homes. In public places, in the Forum, on the Capitoline, was seen a crowd of women who did not pray or sacrifice to the gods in accordance with ancestral ritual. Priestlings and prophets had captured the minds of the men as well as the women.

---

[231] Not all eastern religions contained an ethical dimension, but the more popular ones (Christianity, Mithraism, Isis worship) apparently did. On the teaching of ethics in Roman society, see the introduction to the section on ritual in this chapter. Morality and ethical behavior were a function of family and civic responsibility (*pietas*) rather than of religion. In fact, religion, devotion to the gods, was but one aspect of *pietas*.

[232] In the end, of course, the Romans did defeat Hannibal and win the war. See Appendix III.

BACCHUS

Most foreign religions entered Rome quite imperceptibly; introduced to the city by natives of the east who brought their religions with them, these cults gradually attracted the support of some Romans. One such religion was the worship of Bacchus.[233] We do not know when this cult was first introduced to the city,[234] but by the early second century B.C. it had acquired wide popularity. Bacchus was a savior god who offered his followers salvation and blessed afterlife. He was particularly interested in the growth of grapevines (their death each autumn and rebirth each spring provided for mankind a promise of immortality); and therefore wine, the product of the grapevine, was used in the celebration of Bacchic rites. Drinking wine was a form of communion with the god, and intoxication was apparently thought to provide ecstatic religious experiences.[235] Undoubtedly some initiates were more excessive than others in their use of wine. In the Greek world, frightening tales were told about Bacchae, female worshippers of Bacchus, who drank large quantities of wine, became enthusiastic, and entered a frenzied state in which they lost all recognition of moral values.[236] In Rome, by the early second century B.C., Bacchic rites had acquired a reputation of being drunken orgies which were breeding grounds for all forms of corruption and immorality. Before accepting this reputation as valid and truthful, we should remember that similar charges were later made against another eastern cult which used wine in its rituals: Christianity.

Suppression of the Bacchanalia

In 186 B.C., the consuls, responding to complaints about moral and criminal offenses by Bacchic initiates, urged the Senate to take measures to restrict cult activities. The passage translated here is a description of these measures. It is important to notice that the matter was not a case of religious persecution of the type later practiced by Christian denominations, who tortured and killed anyone who disagreed with them on religious issues. The suppression of Bacchanalia[237] was a political rather than a religious matter. The very aspect which made Bacchus worship appealing to some Romans—its emotionalism—made it frightening to others. The ruling class, in particular, was suspicious of any gathering which occurred

---

[233] *Bacchus:* also known as Dionysus.

[234] It was perhaps introduced by slaves brought from the Greek colonies of southern Italy. It appealed more to the lower classes than to the upper classes of Roman society.

[235] *apparently:* since the cult of Bacchus was a mystery religion, we know very little about the meaning of its rituals.

[236] *Bacchae:* also called Bacchants or Maenads. In Euripides' play, *Bacchae,* Pentheus, king of Thebes, was torn to pieces by his mother and aunts who were in a Bacchic frenzy and thought he was a wild animal.

enthusiastic: from the Greek *entheos* = "to have the god within oneself" (*en* = "in," *theos* = "god").

[237] *Bacchanalia:* celebrations in honor of Bacchus.

without the official sanction of the magistrates, and a gathering whose activities were a mystery and which promoted emotional frenzy was especially alarming.[238] When rumors spread about lewd behavior, kidnappings, forgeries, and murders by cult initiates, state officials felt that the activities of the cult, which appealed largely to the lower classes, posed a threat to the public safety of Rome and the rest of Italy. Because initiates would not reveal the mysteries of their religion to noninitiates, they were accused of conspiring to subvert Roman society and to overthrow the government. It was therefore state officials who took measures to restrict the cult. Punishment for assembling or conspiring to assemble was severe, and crippling restrictions were placed on future cult activities, but the state did not interfere with individual worship of Bacchus. An individual was free to worship the god of his choice but forbidden to participate in disorderly assemblies. The measure of 186 B.C. restricted but by no means destroyed the worship of Bacchus. This religion remained popular in Italy for many centuries.[239]

The rumors about lewd behavior, kidnappings, forgeries, and murders were probably just that—rumors based on a misinterpretation of mysterious cult activities. Similar stories were later spread about the Christians. Livy, the author of the passage translated here, has, however, reported these rumors as historical fact; his exaggeration of the danger of the situation probably reflects the perceptions of the upper class.

387   Livy, *A History of Rome* 39.8, 9, 14, 17, 18

The consuls, Spurius Postumius Albinus and Quintus Marcius Philippus, were diverted from the army and from the management of wars and provinces to the crushing of an internal conspiracy. . . . An obscure Greek had arrived in Etruria, a man with none of those many skills which the highly educated Greek race has introduced to us for the care of our minds and bodies. He was instead a fortune teller and a sacrifice maker. Nor was he the kind of evangelist who taints minds with fallacies by openly disclosing his religious system and announcing publicly both his intentions and his creed. No—he was a practitioner of occult and nocturnal rites. The secrets of the mystery religion were at first revealed to only a few people, but soon began to be taught widely to both men and women. The pleasures of wine and banquets were added to the religious ceremonies in order to attract the minds of a larger number of people. When the wine had inflamed their minds, and the dark night and the intermingling of men and women, young and old, had smothered every feeling of modesty, depravities of every kind began to take place because each person had ready access to whatever perversion his mind so inclined him. There was not just one kind of immorality, not just promiscuous and deviant sex between freeborn men and women, but false witnesses and forged seals, wills and documents of evidence also issued from this same "office." And poisonings and murders, too, murders so secret that sometimes the bodies

---

[238] On the Roman aristocracy's fear of crowds or assemblies, see selections 228 and 334, especially note 186.

[239] At Pompeii, for example, where grape growing and wine production were major industries, Bacchus had many worshippers. Excavations have revealed a villa (called by archeologists "The Villa of the Mysteries") in which there are painted on the walls of one room scenes depicting central elements of the Bacchic mysteries.

were not even located for burial. Many outrages were attempted through fraud, more through violence. The violence was concealed, however, because the shrieks of those tortured by deviant sex or murder could not be heard over the loud wails[240] and the crash of drums and cymbals.[241]

This evil pollution spread from Etruria to Rome like the contagion of a plague. At first the size of the city, which was quite large and therefore able to tolerate such evils, concealed them; but finally information reached the consul Postumius.

[Postumius interviewed a freedwoman who had, while still a slave, accompanied her mistress to Bacchanalia. She described the frenzied behavior of the initiates and spoke of human sacrifices, kidnappings, and the sexual abuse of boys.]

When Postumius had witnesses ready to testify, he brought the matter before the Senate, disclosing everything in detail, starting with information reported to him and then moving to what he himself had discovered through his investigations. A great panic seized the senators, who feared both for the public safety, lest these nocturnal conspiracies and cabals might produce some hidden treachery or danger, and privately, each for reasons of his own, lest one of his family be involved in this malignity. The Senate proposed that the consul be thanked for having investigated this matter both with remarkable diligence and without any commotion. They then entrusted to the consuls a special investigation of the Bacchanalia and the nocturnal rites. They ordered them to make sure that the witnesses Aebutius and Faecenia not be endangered by their giving testimony, and to solicit other witnesses by offers of rewards. The priests of this cult, whether they were men or women, were to be searched for not only in Rome but in every town square or village green so that they might be in the custody of the consuls. Edicts were to be read out in the city of Rome and sent through all of Italy, forbidding any initiates of the Bacchic rites to meet or assemble for the purpose of celebrating these rites, or to perform any such ritual. Above all, they recommended that an inquiry should be conducted about those people who had assembled or conspired for the purpose of promoting debauchery or crime.

The consuls ordered the curule aediles to search out all the priests of this cult, to apprehend them, and to keep them under house arrest until the hearing. The plebeian aediles were to see that no rites were held in secret. Three city commissioners were entrusted with the task of placing guards throughout the city and of making sure that no nocturnal meetings took place and that no fires broke out. Assigned as assistants to the commissioners were five men on each side of the Tiber. Each was to keep watch over the buildings in his own district.

[The consuls then summoned an open meeting of the people of Rome[242] where they revealed the dangers posed by gatherings of Bacchic initiates and explained the measures they were enacting. They tried to make the people see that gatherings held in secret, at night, with no government official present as moderator, threatened the security of the city. They suggested that the followers of Bacchus might be conspiring to take control of the city.]

Then the consuls ordered the decree of the Senate to be read aloud, and announced that a reward would be paid to anyone who brought anyone into their custody or even reported the name of anyone in his absence. They announced that they

---

[240] *wails:* the frenzied initiates made a sound which resembled "ululul . . ."

[241] Roman writers frequently mention the strange (to the Roman ear) sound of the musical instruments used by the eastern religions; see selection 212.

[242] *open meeting: contio;* see selection 228.

would set a specific day on which anyone who had been named and therefore had fled would be summoned before them. If he did not appear to answer the charges, he would be condemned *in absentia*. If anyone named by an informer was among those who were at that time outside the boundaries of Italy, he would be given a date of more latitude if he wished to come to Rome to plead his case. Then they proclaimed that no one should try to sell or buy anything useful for flight, and that no one should harbor, conceal, or in any way aid fugitives.

When the public meeting was adjourned, a great panic seized the whole city, and it was not confined within the walls of the city or the boundaries of Rome. Once people received letters from their friends about the decree of the Senate and the public meeting and the edict of the consuls, alarm grew. During the night which followed the day on which the matter had been publicly disclosed at the meeting, the guards who had been posted at the city gates by the three commissioners apprehended many people who were trying to escape and brought them back. In addition, the names of many people were reported. Some of them, both men and women, committed suicide. Over 7000 men and women were said to have been involved in the conspiracy. . . . The consuls traveled around to towns and villages to make investigations and hold trials there.[243] People who had merely been initiated into the mysteries and had made prayers in accordance with the ritual of the cult, repeating after the priest words which confirmed the abominable conspiracy to every wicked and foul deed, but had not perpetrated against themselves or others any of the deeds to which they were bound by oath—these people were left in chains. Those who had defiled themselves by debauchery or murder, who had polluted themselves by false testimony, forged seals, substitution of wills, or other fraudulent acts, were sentenced to capital punishment. More people were executed than were put in chains, although there was a large number of men and women in each category. Convicted women were handed over to their relatives or to their guardians, who would punish them in private.[244] If the woman had no one who might serve as a suitable punisher, she was punished in public by the state.

Next the consuls were assigned the task of destroying all Bacchic sanctuaries, first in Rome, and then through all of Italy, except where there was an ancient altar or a consecrated statue. The Senate then advised for the future that there be no Bacchic ceremonies at Rome or in Italy. If anyone considered such rites necessary and traditional and believed that he could not neglect them without committing sacrilege and sin, he was to appeal to the *praetor urbanus* who would then consult the Senate. If he received permission, when no fewer than 100 senators were present at the meeting, he could perform that rite provided that no more than five people took part in the ritual and there was no common fund or deacon or priest.

The Decree of the Senate

In the previous passage we learned that the Senate had recommended that "edicts were to be read out in the city of Rome and sent through all of Italy, forbidding

---

[243] The consuls of Rome had jurisdiction over the whole Empire, although they usually delegated their authority to lesser officials. The situation described here, however, was extraordinary, and the consuls therefore dealt with it personally.

[244] The *paterfamilias* had it within his legal power to punish his children by death; see selection 14.

any initiates of the Bacchic rites to meet or assemble for the purpose of celebrating these rites." The following passage is a translation of that edict. The copy sent by the Senate to the people of Ager Teuranus (now Tiriolo) in southern Italy was inscribed on bronze and set up in a public place. The Senate of Rome, like the consuls of Rome, could make policy for the whole Empire, although its decisions were referred to as "advice" or "recommendations" rather than laws.[245]

388   *CIL* 1.2.581 (*ILS* 18)

Quintus Marcius, son of Lucius, and Spurius Postumius, son of Lucius, consuls for that year, consulted the Senate on October 7 in the temple of Bellona.[246] Marcus Claudius, son of Marcus, Lucius Valerius, son of Publius, and Quintus Minucius, son of Gaius, were witnesses to the recording of this decree.

With reference to Bacchanalia, the senators advised that the following be proclaimed to those who are confederated with Rome:[247] "Let no one of them plan to hold Bacchanalia in his home. If there are any who maintain that it is necessary for them to hold Bacchanalia, they should come before the *praetor urbanus* at Rome. And then, when their arguments have been heard, our Senate should make the final decision about these matters, as long as there are no fewer than 100 senators present when the matter is discussed. Let no man, whether a Roman citizen or a Latin or one of the allies, plan to associate with Bacchant women unless he has come before the *praetor urbanus,* who should then make a decision in accordance with the recommendation of the Senate, as long as there are no fewer than 100 senators present when the matter is discussed." The Senate so advised.

"Let no man be a priest. Let no man or woman be a deacon. Let no one plan to establish a common fund.[248] Let no one plan to make either a man or a woman a deacon or a vice-deacon, or plan henceforth to swear mutual oaths, vows, pledges, or promises with others, or plan to exchange guarantees of good faith with others. Let no one plan to hold cult ceremonies in secret. Let no one plan to hold cult ceremonies in public or in private or outside the city unless he has come before the *praetor urbanus,* who should then make a decision in accordance with the recommendation of the Senate, as long as there are no fewer than 100 senators present when the matter is discussed." The Senate so advised.

"Let no one plan to hold cult ceremonies with more than five men and women present as participants. And let those who plan to attend as participants be no more than two men and three women, unless authorization is given by the *praetor urbanus* and the Senate, as recorded above."

You should proclaim these decisions at a public meeting no less than three weeks

---

[245] See selection 238.

[246] The Senate frequently met in places other than the Senate house (or Curia), which was situated in the north end of the Forum. Bellona was a goddess of war (see note 52 of Chapter IV). There was a temple of Bellona in the Campus Martius.

[247] *confederated with Rome:* as allies or *socii.* This decree was written almost 100 years before the Italian allies were granted Roman citizenship.

[248] *common fund:* The Roman aristocracy was afraid that such a fund might be used not for religious purposes but for the promotion of civil unrest and rebellion. The Senate carefully regulated the size of the treasury even of funeral colleges; see selection 116.

before their implementation.[249] In order that you be fully aware of the recommendation of the Senate, their recommendation was as follows: "If there are any who act contrary to the restrictions recorded above, they advise that capital charges be brought against them."[250] And you should engrave this on a bronze tablet, for the Senate so advises that this is proper. And you should order the tablet to be hung up where it can be most easily read. And within ten days from the time that this letter is delivered to you, you should see to it that those places of Bacchic worship, if there are any in your region, are destroyed, as recorded above, unless there exists in them anything sacred to our own religion.

CYBELE, MAGNA MATER

Bringing the Goddess to Rome

Unlike the other eastern cults, which gained supporters in Rome only gradually, the cult of Cybele, Magna Mater, was introduced to Rome by government leaders and immediately given an official position in Roman society. Magna Mater was a goddess whose name means "Great Mother";[251] she was considered the mother of men, of animals, indeed of all living things, a universal Mother Earth deity. Her worship was prominent in Asia Minor, where she was also called Cybele. The death and resurrection of her young consort, Attis, which was commemorated by an annual celebration, gave promise of immortality to those initiated into her cult. In 205 B.C., when the Romans were distressed by their inability to defeat the Carthaginians,[252] government leaders consulted the Sibylline books[253] and were told that the Romans would drive enemy forces out of Italy if Magna Mater were brought to Rome. A delegation of high-ranking diplomats was at once sent to Phrygia to obtain a black meteoric stone which was the symbol of the goddess. On April 4, 204 B.C., the stone was carried into Rome, attended by throngs of happy people.

This passage describes the dramatic arrival of Magna Mater to Italy.

389   Livy, *A History of Rome* 29.14.10–14

Publius Cornelius Scipio was ordered to go to Ostia[254] with all the matrons of Rome to meet the goddess. He personally was to receive her[255] from the ship and then en-

---

[249] Market days were held once a week. The senatorial decree would be read out by a herald on three successive market days. Compare the publishing of banns in Christian churches. Decrees were read out for the benefit of the illiterate, who could not read the posted bronze tablet. On heralds, see selection 194.

[250] Treason was a capital offense. Since Bacchanalia were thought to be conspiracies, attendants at Bacchanalia were charged with treason.

[251] Latin *mater* = "mother"; *cf.* English "maternal."

[252] See selection 386.

[253] See selection 371.

[254] *Ostia:* the harbor of Rome; see note 71 of Chapter IV.

[255] *her:* the black stone which symbolized Magna Mater.

trust her, once she was on land, to the matrons who would carry her into the city. Once the ship had arrived at the mouth of the Tiber, he did as he had been ordered, that is, he rowed out to sea, received the goddess from her priests, and brought her to land. The foremost matrons of the city (among whom only the name of Claudia Quinta is remembered) received her. (Claudia's reputation, which had earlier been in question, as the story goes, made her modesty, proved by her religious devotion on this occasion, more memorable to later generations.[256] The matrons took turns carrying the goddess, passing her from hand to hand. The whole city had turned out to meet her, and incense burners had been placed in front of the doorways along the route, and, as people lit the incense, they prayed that the goddess would enter the city of Rome willingly and propitiously. The matrons carried her into the temple of Victory which is on the Palatine.[257] That day, April 4, was declared a festival.[258] Crowds of people brought gifts to the goddess on the Palatine, and there was a *lectisternium*,[259] and games were held, called the Megalesia.

A Religious Procession

When Roman officials first welcomed Cybele, Magna Mater, to their city, they knew little about the cult activities. What they soon learned shocked them because rites in honor of this goddess were quite unlike the calm, orderly, and methodical ceremonies of the state religion. Initiates to the cult of Cybele seemed to act in a state of emotional frenzy; their music was shrill and raucous. And the priests of the cult, called *Galli,* were particularly offensive to the staid and sober Roman temperament. *Galli* were eunuchs who had castrated themselves upon entering the service of the goddess. Nor was this self-mutilation a unique experience in the priest's life. Apparently the *Galli* slashed their arms and shed their own blood during the annual celebration of Attis's death and resurrection.[260] As soon as Roman officials realized the nature of the cult activities, they took immediate measures to keep the cult tightly restricted. It was placed under the close supervision of the priests who dealt with the Sibylline books, and no Roman citizens were allowed to become *Galli.* We might contrast the Roman attitude toward Cybele, Magna Mater, with that toward the cult of Bacchus twenty years later. The former was brought to the city by government officials and, from the beginning, its organization remained under the control of government officials who made sure that the cult did not endanger public order. The latter had spread to Rome gradually, and the gov-

---

[256] Some people had suggested that Claudia Quinta was less modest and less virtuous than a Roman matron should be. When the ship carrying Magna Mater reached the mouth of the Tiber, it stuck on a sandbar, and soothsayers announced that it could be moved only by a matron whose virtue was beyond reproach. Claudia took hold of the rope and pulled the ship off the sandbar, thus proving her modesty and innocence.

[257] In 191 B.C., Magna Mater was moved into her own temple.

[258] The day was marked in the Roman calendar as the Megalesia (Greek *megala =* "great") and celebrated each year as a holiday with state-financed games. By the late republican period, the days of games had been extended to April 10 (seven days of games); see the introduction to the section on spectacles in Chapter XIV.

[259] *lectisternium:* see note 116 of this chapter.

[260] It was, in the past, not unusual for some Christian monastic orders to practice self-flagellation and mortification of the flesh.

ernment imposed no regulations on it until it seemed to pose a threat to the state, whereupon the magistrates immediately crushed its organization (though not the individual worship of Bacchus). In this passage, the poet Lucretius describes a procession in honor of Cybele, Magna Mater.

390   Lucretius, *About the Nature of the Universe*
                                                              2.594–601, 606–614, 618–632

The earth contains the material from which it can produce shining grain crops and fruitful orchards for the use of the human race and from which it can provide streams and forests and lush meadows for the wild animals that roam the mountains. And therefore it is called "Mother Earth," Great Mother of the Gods and Mother of Wild Animals and Progenitor of the Human Race. The ancient Greek poets sang hymns to Mother Earth, and portrayed her as seated in a chariot driving a team of lions. . . . They placed on the top of her head a crown resembling the battlements of a city, because in select locations Earth is fortified by cities and bears their weight. And even now the image of the Divine Mother, clothed in such regalia, is carried throughout the world and inspires awe. In adherence with the time-honored rites of her cult, various nations call her Mother of Mount Ida[261] and appoint as her attendants groups of Phrygians because, according to tradition, it was that land, Phrygia, which first, of all the earth, began to produce crops. Her attendants are *Galli,* mad eunuch priests. . . . In processions, tightly stretched drums thunder out as they are struck by the hands of her attendants. Curved cymbals clash, and horns threaten with their harsh wailing. And the hollow flute stirs the heart with Phrygian tune. Attendants precede her, carrying weapons as symbols of violent frenzy, to fill the ungrateful minds and irreverent hearts of the crowd with fear of the power of her divinity. Therefore, when she is first carried into a large city and voicelessly bestows wordless blessings upon mortals,[262] people freely strew her path along the whole route with lavish quantities of copper and silver coins and scatter on the Great Mother and her bands of attendants a snowy shower of roses. An armed group of attendants, called Phrygian Curetes by the Greeks, follow her. They stage mock battles among themselves and dance in frenzied rhythm,[263] exhilarated by the bloodshed. They wear terrifying crests on their heads which quiver as they shake their heads in dance.

ISIS

Worship of the Goddess

Isis was a goddess whose worship originated in Egypt and was already of great antiquity by the time the Romans became acquainted with it. Isis was a loving and

---

[261] Mount Ida is in Phrygia.

[262] The silence of the mute symbol or statue of the goddess is a striking contrast to the loud, shrill music and wailing. For Roman reaction to eastern music, see note 241 of this chapter.

[263] For the dancing of the Arval Brethren, another group of priests who worshipped a deity of fertility and crop production, see selection 365.

compassionate deity who showed concern for each individual suppliant. She had herself suffered the loss of a beloved family member and could therefore understand and sympathize with human grief. Each year, when she saw the land of Egypt dry and unproductive, and the people sad and hungry, she was filled with sorrow, and her tears would cause the Nile to flood. The annual flood, of course, made the land once more alive and productive and the people happy. Like the death and rebirth of Bacchus's grapevines, the death and rebirth of the land provided evidence of immortality. In addition, the central myth of this religion involved the death and resurrection of Isis's husband, Osiris, and thus a promise to initiates of resurrection after death and a blessed afterlife. Isis was a goddess of fertility, and also of marriage and of sailing. She became, in fact, a universal goddess, since she was concerned about any problem of suffering mankind. She was frequently portrayed as a loving mother nursing her son, Horus, and these depictions often bear a striking resemblance to depictions of the Virgin Mary. The worship of Isis reached Rome early in the first century B.C. and acquired a strong following. In the 30s, however, it was harshly oppressed in Rome by Octavian because it was the religion of his enemy, the Egyptian queen, Cleopatra.[264] It could not, however, be crushed because its followers were so numerous and devoted. By the early first century A.D., the worship of Isis was again flourishing in Rome, and throughout the Roman Empire. The compassionate goddess and loving mother who listened to the prayers of the lowliest individual and who grieved for the suffering of mankind won the personal devotion of Roman citizens as the stern, inaccessible deities of the state religion could not. The following passage is from the story of Lucius, a man who had been changed into an ass.[265] He finally prayed to Isis, who took pity and changed him back into human form. The first part of the passage describes an annual procession in honor of Isis, goddess of sailing, which took place at the beginning of every sailing season. The passage continues with an account of Lucius's initiation into the cult of Isis.

391   Apuleius, *The Golden Ass* 11.7, 9–11, 16, 17, 22–24

Lo, a throng of people filled the streets, wending their way in a triumphal religious procession. Not only I,[266] but everyone and everything seemed bursting with joy; every animal, all the houses, even the day itself, with its serene weather, seemed to be rejoicing. For a calm, sunny day had driven out the nighttime frost, and the little songbirds, enticed by the spring warmth, sang sweet melodies to delight the mother of the stars, the parent of the seasons, and the queen of the universe[267] with their pleasant warbling. And the trees, too, both those which provided fruit and those which were content to provide shade, were released from their winter stiffness by the warm south wind; they smiled at the buds of their new leaves and made a soft rustling sound as they moved their branches. And, now that the howling winds had been stilled and

---

[264] Cleopatra was Octavian's enemy because she had allied herself with his enemy Antony; see note 215 of this chapter and also note 81 of Chapter III.

[265] See selection 187.

[266] *I:* Lucius, who was still in asinine form. When he prayed to Isis, he was told to attend this procession and eat roses carried by one of the priests.

[267] That is, Isis.

the raging, crashing waves had been calmed, the sea was an unruffled lake. Dark clouds had scattered, and the sky was radiant with the bright, clear light of the sun. . . . And now the procession of the divine Savior moved forward. The women were a splendid sight, in their white garments, accented by various kinds of finery. On their heads they wore garlands of spring flowers, and, from bouquets in their arms, they scattered flowers on the pavement of the streets where the sacred procession was passing. . . . Some sprinkled the streets with drops of fragrant balsam and other perfumes. Then came a large contingent of both men and women with lamps, torches, candles, and other kinds of light in honor of the goddess who was born from the heavenly stars. Next, flutes and pipes and piccolos sounded a very soothing harmony. An attractive choir of carefully chosen boys, radiant in their white vestments, followed, singing a hymn which had been composed by a skillful poet, inspired by the Muses, and which explained the precessional rites of this important ceremony. Then came the pipe players dedicated to the cult of mighty Serapis.[268] Holding their pipes out to the side, toward their right ears, they played a tune usually heard in a temple, by the god. A large number of monitors warned people to provide a clear passage for the sacred procession. Then there appeared streaming crowds of people who had been initiated into the divine mysteries, both men and women, of every social class and of all ages, dazzling in their linen vestments of pure white.[269] The women's hair had been anointed and covered with sheer kerchiefs. The men had shaved off all their hair and had shiny bald heads, representing the earthly "stars" of this great religion. They carried *sistra*[270] of bronze and silver and even gold with which they made stridulant sounds. The priests or ministers of the sacred rites, who wore shiny white linen garments wrapped tightly around their chests and hanging down to their feet, held out in front of them the insignia and emblems of the most powerful gods. The first priest stretched out in front of him a lamp shining with a clear light (not like those we use to illuminate our evening banquets, because it had a golden bowl which produced from its center opening a quite large flame). The second priest wore a similar vestment but carried in both hands sacrifice pots or *auxilla* which had received their names from the helpful aid [*auxilium*] of the distinguished goddess. A third priest held up a *caduceus,* or staff of Mercury,[271] and a model of a palm tree with leaves of delicate gold work. A fourth displayed the symbol of impartiality, which is a model of a left hand with outstretched palm; because the left hand is naturally slow and not endowed with craftiness and cleverness, it seemed more suited to impartiality than the right hand.[272] The same priest also carried a round gold vessel in the shape of a breast from which milk flowed. A fifth carried a gold winnowing fan woven of slender gold reeds; another carried a wine jug.

Immediately behind the priests came the gods who deigned to walk on human feet.[273] Here was Anubis, the awesome messenger of the gods, both those above the earth and those below it;[274] his face was half black and half gold, and clearly visible

---

[268] *Serapis:* another Egyptian deity, closely associated with Isis; see note 119 of Chapter VII.

[269] Initiates wore linen, a product of Egypt.

[270] *sistra: sistrum* was a rattle carried by worshippers of Isis. On eastern music, see notes 241 and 262 of this chapter.

[271] On the staff of Mercury, see note 203 of Chapter XIV.

[272] For a different view of left hands, see note 54 of Chapter XIV.

[273] People dressed as the gods walk in the procession as representatives of the gods.

[274] Gods of the upperworld (i.e., gold faces) and gods of the underworld (i.e., black faces).

because of his height; his canine shoulders[275] were raised high above the crowd, and in his left hand he brandished a *caduceus,* in his right a green palm branch. A cow followed closely on his footsteps, portrayed in an upright position; it represented the fecundity of the goddess who is mother of us all, and it was carried on the shoulders of a priestly assistant who moved with animated and happy steps. Another man carried a box filled with secrets and concealing the mysteries of the glorious religion. Still another held close to his blessed breast a venerated representation of the most exalted deity. It was not made in the shape of a farm animal or a bird or a wild animal or even a human; but it inspired reverence by its very novelty and its cleverly innovative design, and bore mute evidence of a religion which was sublime and whose mysteries had to remain veiled in deep silence. This small vessel, wrought of shiny gold, was a masterpiece of skilled artistry. It was hollow, had a round base, and was decorated on the outside with wonderful Egyptian hieroglyphics. The mouth of the vessel was raised up on a long neck which resembled a long water pipe. On either side was a handle which stuck out a considerable distance; and coiled around each handle was an asp arching its scaly, wrinkled, and swollen neck.

[At this point in the story, Lucius, in the form of an ass, eats roses carried by one of the priests in the procession and is miraculously transformed back into human shape. The priest declares to the crowd that the transformation was the work of Isis, the kindly and compassionate goddess. Lucius then joins the crowd as it continues its way to the harbor.]

I followed the religious procession, mingling with the crowd; but I attracted attention, and everyone in the town recognized me, and people pointed at me with their fingers or nodded their heads. Everyone was saying, "That's the man who was today changed back into human form by the glorious power of the almighty goddess. He was certainly lucky and three times blessed to have earned such enormous help from heaven because of the purity and honesty of his former life.[276] And now he has been reborn, as it were, and dedicated to the service of the goddess." Surrounded by such comments and shouts of happy prayers, we advanced slowly, but finally approached the seashore and arrived at the very same spot where I had, as an ass, lain down just the night before. There, after the religious statues and objects had been set down with proper ritual, the high priest vowed and dedicated to the goddess a ship which had been very carefully crafted and decorated on all sides with wonderful Egyptian hieroglyphics. He purified it with a glowing torch and an egg and sulfur, uttering very solemn prayers from his pure mouth. The shiny white sail of this blessed ship bore the words of a prayer offered for the successful conduct of a new sailing season. The pinewood mast, tall, straight, and smooth, rose so high that the masthead could be seen by everyone. The stern was shaped like a gooseneck and covered with shiny gold leaf. The whole ship was a fine sight with its highly polished citrus wood. Then everyone, both priests and laymen, began to pile on board winnowing fans heaped with spices and other offerings of this type, and to pour into the sea libations made of milk, until the ship was loaded with generous gifts and prayers for favor. Then the anchor ropes were untied and the ship was released into the sea, driven by a serene breeze which moved

---

[275] The Egyptian god Anubis was portrayed as having the head of a dog. Since he, like the Greek god Mercury, was a messenger, he brandished a *caduceus* in his hand.

[276] There was apparently an ethical dimension in the religion of Isis. The goddess demanded moral purity, not just ritual purity. On ritual purity in the Roman state religion, see selection 373.

only that ship. And after it had traveled far enough that we could no longer see it, the priestly assistants picked up the holy objects which they had each carried down to the shore and joyously returned to the temple, maintaining the same place in the procession which they had before.

When we arrived at the temple, the high priest and the assistants who had carried the images of the gods, and the people who had already been initiated into the mysteries of the religion were received into the sanctuary of the goddess and returned the lifelike statues to their proper places there. Then one man, whom all the others called the "secretary," stood in front of the doors of the sanctuary and addressed a gathering of the Pastophori (which is the name given to the highest priests of the holy college of Isis) who had been summoned to an assembly meeting as it were. Then, from a high pulpit, he read out from a book words of prayer for the emperor, the Senate, the equestrians, and all the Roman people, and for the sailors and ships which acknowledge the sovereignty of our Empire. He then proclaimed in Greek a Greek formula, "Ploiaphesia," which means, "The ships may now sail." When the people heard this word, they responded with a cry of joy. Brimming with happiness, they left the temple, kissed the feet of the silver statue of Isis which stood on the steps, and departed for home carrying green boughs, leafy branches, and flower garlands.

[Lucius was later accepted for ordination as a priest of Isis.]

The high priest took my right hand and led me courteously to the doors of the spacious temple. After the ritual of opening them had been duly performed and the morning sacrifice had been celebrated, he brought out from the sanctuary of the temple certain books written in characters unknown to me. These books used, for the words of their texts, characters of two kinds: some were abridged words, or hieroglyphics of animals; others were letters concealed from the prying eyes of profane readers by having the tops of the letters knotted and curled into the shape of a wheel and intertwined like the tendrils of a vine. Reading from the books, the priest told me what materials I needed to obtain for my initiation. At once I set out to obtain these necessities, diligently and with little worry about cost. Some I bought myself; others I asked my friends to purchase. And then, at the time deemed appropriate by the priest, he led me to the nearest public baths, accompanied by a crowd of priests. After I had been allowed my ordinary bath, he himself washed me and poured holy water over me and prayed to the gods for my purification. Then we returned to the temple in the afternoon, and he placed me at the feet of Isis[277] and privately entrusted to me certain secrets which are too sacred to be revealed. But openly, with everyone else serving as a witness, he ordered me to abstain from the pleasure of food for ten consecutive days, to eat no meat, and to drink no wine. I maintained this fast with admirable self-restraint, and finally that day arrived which had been set for my appearance before the goddess. The setting sun made way for the evening star. At dusk, throngs of initiates poured in from all directions, each one honoring me with various gifts, according to their ancient custom. Then, when all the laymen had been ordered to leave, the priest dressed me in a garment of new linen, took my hand, and led me into the most sacred recess of the holy sanctuary.

O curious reader, perhaps you are very anxious to find out what was said and what was done there. I would tell you if I were allowed to, and you would learn the answers, if you were allowed to hear them. But your ears and my tongue would then

---

[277] That is, the statue of Isis.

both be guilty of indiscreet curiosity. I will not, however, torture you by keeping you in suspense for a long time, particularly since your interest is of a religious nature. Listen then, and believe what follows, for it is true. I approached the borders of death, I stepped upon the threshold of Proserpina,[278] I was borne along through all the elements, and then I returned. At midnight I saw the sun blazing with bright light. I came into the presence of the gods who dwell above the earth and those who dwell below, and I paid them honor as I stood before them. And so, I have revealed to you things which you must forget you have heard. From now on, let me tell you only those things which can be made available for the information of the profane without risking impiety.

When it was morning and the solemn rites had been concluded, I came out of the sanctuary as an ordained priest. I wore twelve different shawls, which were my religious vestments certainly, but I am not forbidden to mention them because many people who were present on that occasion saw them. I was ordered to mount into a wooden pulpit which stood in the very middle of the temple, right in front of the statue of Isis. I was splendidly garbed in a vestment of finest linen embroidered with flowers. Around my shoulders was a priceless shawl which hung down my back right to my ankles. All over it were embroidered animals in different colors, Indian dragons, for example, and Hyperborean griffins, which are winged creatures generated in another part of the world. The initiated call this shawl an "Olympian stole." In my right hand I carried a blazing torch and around my head was a garland of white palm leaves, which projected outward like the rays of the sun. And thus I was costumed to resemble the sun, and I stood there like a statue. The curtains were opened, and people wandered in to gaze at me. Later I celebrated this very happy day, this day of my rebirth and initiation into the holy order, with a magnificent banquet with charming dining companions. And the third day, too, was devoted to similar religious ceremonies, breakfast with the priests, and the final rites of ordination.[279]

Christian Skepticism

Minucius Felix was a Christian writer of the third century A.D. Although he probably participated in the rites of Easter, the annual celebration of the death and resurrection of Jesus, he criticized similar celebrations by worshippers of other religions.

392   Minucius Felix, *Octavius* 22.1

Consider the various rites of the mystery religions. You will find sorrowful deaths, sad fates, funerals, grief, and lamentation for the poor gods. Isis, along with Anubis and

---

[278] *Proserpina:* the Roman goddess who, as wife of Pluto, god of the underworld, rules over the spirits of the dead. When Lucius is initiated into the mysteries of the religion, he experiences a spiritual death and rebirth.

Some readers view Lucius's transformation into an ass as an allegory of the descent into bestiality and of the sensual abasement of the soul.

[279] Communal dinners played a significant role in the cult of Isis. In the temple of Isis at Pompeii (see note 119 of Chapter VII), the priests were preparing dinner when Vesuvius erupted. Remains of their dinner, which had been buried for almost 2000 years, were found by excavators.

the bald priests,[280] mourns for her dead son. She grieves and searches for him, and her sad worshippers beat their breasts and share the sorrows of the very unhappy mother. When the boy is found, Isis rejoices, the priests exult, and Anubis swells with pride. Year after year, without fail, they lose what they will find, and they find what they have lost. Isn't that ridiculous, either to mourn for the thing which you worship, or to worship the thing which you mourn for? Yet these Egyptian rites have now become Roman as well.

JUDAISM

Tolerance

The eastern religions discussed above welcomed people of all races and social classes as new members. In contrast, Judaism was a racially exclusive religion whose members did not attempt to make converts among non-Jews. They could not, therefore, be accused, as were the worshippers of Bacchus, for example, of trying to subvert the masses and foment revolution. There were Jews living in all parts of the Roman Empire, but they did not involve themselves with the religious life of the people around them. And they hoped, in turn, that no one would interfere with their religious life; they wanted only to be left alone to worship their own god in their own way.

This passage, written by a Jew who was born in Alexandria, is taken from an appeal for tolerance made to the emperor Caligula. The author describes the emperor Augustus's tolerant attitude toward Jews, which he hopes will be a precedent for Caligula.

393   Philo, *The Embassy to Gaius*[281] 155–158

Augustus knew that a large part of Rome on the far side of the Tiber was occupied and inhabited by Jews. Most of them were freedmen who were now Roman citizens; they had been brought to Italy as captives and then manumitted by their owners. They were not forced to violate their ancestral traditions. Augustus knew that they have places for prayer meetings and that they meet together in these places, especially on the holy sabbaths when they come together as a group to learn their ancestral philosophy. He also knew that they take a first-fruit collection to raise money for religious purposes,[282] and that they send this money to Jerusalem with people who will offer sacrifices. However, he did not banish them from Rome[283] or deprive them of their Roman citizenship just because they were careful to maintain their identities

---

[280] *bald priests:* the men in the procession described by Apuleius (selection 391) "had shaved off all their hair and had shiny bald heads."

[281] Gaius (Caesar): the emperor Caligula.

[282] Roman officials did not like organizations with an established treasury (see note 248 of this chapter), perhaps fearing that the money might be used in Rome to foment civil unrest. The money collected by the Jews, however, was sent to the temple in Jerusalem.

[283] Contrast the later policy of Tiberius, described in selection 394.

as Jews. He did not force them to abandon their places for prayer meetings,[284] or forbid them to gather to receive instruction in the laws, or oppose their first-fruit collections. . . .

In regard to the monthly grain doles,[285] when everyone receives his share of money or grain, Augustus never deprived the Jews of this charity. In fact, if the distributions happened to occur on the holy sabbath, when no Jew is allowed to receive or to give anything or to do any regular business at all, particularly financial business, he ordered the officials in charge of the distribution to set aside until the next day the portion of the welfare which belonged to the Jews.

Persecution

The Romans were quite tolerant of other religions, but, since they equated the health of the state with scrupulous worship of the state gods,[286] the wish of the Jews to remain a separate community and their refusal to worship any god but their own frequently made them targets of suspicion and hatred.[287] We have earlier seen examples of the prejudice of individuals,[288] but sometimes the state instituted a policy of persecution.

394   Suetonius, *The Lives of the Caesars: Tiberius* 36

The emperor Tiberius suppressed foreign cults, such as the Egyptian and Jewish religions, by forcing those who embraced such superstitions to burn their religious vestments and all their holy objects. Using required military service as a pretext, he assigned young Jews to provinces with harsher climates. Other men of that same race or belonging to similar cults he banished from the city under penalty of lifelong slavery if they did not obey. He also expelled astrologers, although he granted pardon to those who begged for it and promised to give up their practice.

Compromise

In a letter written in A.D. 41 to the people of Alexandria, Egypt, the emperor Claudius urges on them a more generous and tolerant attitude toward the Jews of that city.

395   *Greek Papyri in the British Museum* 1912 (lines 73–103)

With regard to which side was responsible for the violence and uprising, or I should say, if the truth must be told, the war against the Jews, although your envoys, and Dionysius, son of Theon, in particular, argued earnestly and at length to contradict

---

[284] Contrast the destruction of Bacchic sanctuaries almost 200 years before Augustus's time (selection 387).

[285] *grain doles:* see selection 153.

[286] Horace voices this belief in selection 384.

[287] Most eastern religions allowed their initiates to continue participation in the state cult.

[288] See Juvenal's comments in selection 81.

the other side, I was nevertheless not willing to assign any specific blame; but I have stored up implacable anger against anyone who begins fighting again. And I will say, simply and clearly, that, if you do not end this deadly and willful anger against one another, I will be forced to show you what even a benevolent leader is like when turned to righteous anger. Therefore, I entreat you, the Alexandrians, to behave tolerantly and benevolently toward the Jews, since they have lived in the same city as you for many years, and not to abuse the religious rites which they practice in the worship of their god, but to allow them to observe their own customs which they observed also in the time of the deified Augustus. For I, having heard both sides, have approved these customs. But without reservation I order the Jews not to agitate for more indulgence than they enjoyed in the past, and not to send in the future a second, separate delegation, as if they lived in a separate city; for such a thing has never been done before. . . . Otherwise I will prosecute them in every way as transmitters of a general disease infecting the whole world. If, however, both sides leave behind their quarrels and indicate a willingness to live together in tolerance and benevolence, then I will show the utmost care for the city.

CHRISTIANITY

The Promises of Christianity

Christianity arose from within Judaism, and the earliest believers that Christ was the Messiah were devout Jews. However, they soon quarreled with their fellow Jews on the issue of proselytism, or acceptance of non-Jews as converts to belief in the Messiah. The followers of Christ felt that they had a sacred mission to spread the "good news" to all people, whether Jew or Gentile.[289] Within a short time after Christ's death, Christianity became identified as a cult quite separate and distinct from Judaism. Non-Jewish converts often brought to the new cult ideas and rhetoric from their former religions or philosophies, and we frequently find in Christianity reminiscences of other eastern cults. Certainly the promises made by Christianity were similar to those made by the religions of Cybele, Bacchus, Isis, and Mithra: revelation of mysteries, redemption, resurrection, and life after death. And, in describing the existence of the spirit, Christian writers often used images familiar also in other religions, for example, metaphors of darkness and light, plant growth, and military life. Compare the images in the following passages from the New Testament with images found above in passages about oriental religions.

396   *New Testament:* I Corinthians 4.1; 1 Corinthians 15.51;
Romans 6.3, 4; John 12.46; 2 Corinthians 4.6; John 12.24, 25;
John 15.1; Ephesians 6.10, 11

Let a man so account of us, as of the ministers of Christ, and stewards of the mysteries of God.

[289] The word evangelism comes from the Greek *euangelos* = "bringing good news" (*eu* = "good," *angelos* = "messenger"; compare "angel").

Behold, I shew you a mystery; we shall not all sleep, but we shall all be changed.

Know ye not, that so many of us as were baptized into Jesus Christ were baptized into his death?

Therefore we are buried with him by baptism into death: that like as Christ was raised up from the dead by the glory of the Father, even so we also should walk in newness of life.

I am come a light into the world, that whosoever believeth on me should not abide in darkness.

For God, who commanded the light to shine out of darkness, hath shined in our hearts, to give the light of the knowledge of the glory of God in the face of Jesus Christ.

Verily, verily, I say unto you, except a corn of wheat fall into the ground and die, it abideth alone: but if it die, it bringeth forth much fruit.

He that loveth his life shall lose it; and he that hateth his life in this world shall keep it unto life eternal.

I am the true vine, and my Father is the husbandman.

Finally, my brethren, be strong in the Lord, and in the power of his might.

Put on the whole armor of God, that ye may be able to stand against the wiles of the devil.

First Christians in Rome

The following passage indicates that not too long after Christ's death, when people who believed that Christ was the Messiah were still regarded as Jews, Roman officials had already begun to worry about the unrest caused by this new belief.

397   Suetonius, *The Lives of the Caesars: Claudius* 25.4

Because the Jews were continually causing disturbances at the instigation of Chrestus,[290] Claudius expelled them from Rome.

An Early Instance of Persecution

Christianity was regarded by Roman officials with the same suspicions that the cults of Bacchus, Cybele, and Isis encountered, and for the same reasons: it was a cult which attracted large numbers of lower-class people and encouraged them to participate in secret rites and emotional outbursts. In addition, Christianity, with its roots in Judaism, was a monotheistic cult,[291] and its one god would tolerate no

---

[290] The name is spelled thus in the Latin text.
[291] *monotheistic:* from the Greek *monos* = "one," *theos* = "god."

rivals. Unlike the Jews, however, the Christians were aggressively, sometimes offensively monotheistic, and their denial of the existence of any god but their own angered polytheists[292] whose policy had been one of tolerance and peaceful coexistence among all cults.[293] Thus, Christians set themselves apart from the rest of Roman society and angered Roman officials by refusing to acknowledge or worship the state gods. Their self-imposed segregation made them easy scapegoats to which could be attached the blame for disasters which befell the state. In A.D. 64, when Nero was emperor, a great fire destroyed a large part of Rome. A rumor spread that the emperor himself was responsible for setting the destructive fire, and so Nero looked quickly for a scapegoat. He found it in the Christians, who, just thirty or so years after the death of Christ, had already attracted the attention of Roman officials. Many people would believe that the Christians were indirectly responsible for the fire because they had angered the state gods by refusing to worship them. Fortunately, this early persecution was an isolated incident and did not give rise to widespread persecution.

398 Tacitus, *Annals* 15.44

To put an end to the rumor that he had ordered the fire, Nero invented charges of guilt and inflicted the most exquisite tortures on a group of people whom the Roman mob called "Christians" and hated because of their shameless activities.[294] During the reign of Tiberius, Christus, who gave his name to this group, had suffered crucifixion under the procurator Pontius Pilatus; and a dangerous cult, which had been kept in check for the moment, burst forth again, not only throughout Judaea, the origin of the evil, but even in Rome, where all the hideous and shameful things from all over the world flow together and swarm. Therefore, first of all, people who admitted their belief were arrested, and then later, through their information, a huge crowd was convicted not so much of the crime of setting the fire, as of hating mankind. Mockery was heaped upon them as they were killed: wrapped in the skins of wild animals, they were torn apart by dogs, or nailed to crosses, or set on fire and burned alive to provide light at night, when they daylight had faded.

Nero offered his garden for this spectacle and provided circus entertainment where he put on a chariot driver's outfit and mingled with the crowd or stood in a chariot. And so pity arose, even for those who were guilty and deserved the most extreme punishment, since they seemed to have been slaughtered not for public good but to satisfy the cruelty of one man.

292 *polytheist:* Greek *poly* = "much," "many."

293 See Symmachus (selection 385): "It is reasonable to assume that whatever each of us worships can be considered one and the same. We look up at the same stars, the same sky is above us all, the same universe encompasses us. What difference does it make which system each of us uses to find the truth? It is not by just one route that man can arrive at so great a mystery."

294 For the details of these "shameless activities," see selection 401.

Imperial Advice about Dealing with Christians

In A.D. 111, the emperor Trajan appointed Pliny governor of the province of Bithynia.[295] Pliny was apparently a conscientious administrator who wanted to enforce Roman rule but also to treat the Bithynians as fairly as possible. One problem which demanded his attention as governor was the adoption of an official policy toward the Christians. Trajan had forbidden the existence of secret societies,[296] and Christians could therefore be legally prosecuted for disobeying this edict. Some Christians were also charged with treason because they refused to pay reverence to statues of the gods and the emperor. Pliny suspected, however, that court actions against the Christians were often motivated by personal hostility rather than legal scrupulousness. He wrote to Trajan, asking his advice on establishing an official policy for dealing with the Christians. Trajan's reply was a *rescriptum*,[297] and thus had the authority of a law; while it was not, as Trajan himself stated, a recommendation meant to "establish a general law" or "provide a fixed standard," since Trajan suggested that each case be reviewed individually, yet it unfortunately set a precedent for later officials to execute anyone who confessed to being a Christian.

The exchange of letters between the emperor and his governor offers a valuable insight into the Roman attitude toward provincial administration: be fair and tolerant, do not interfere needlessly with local customs, but maintain law and order firmly and strictly.[298] The Christian "question," however, had no solution. Roman officials believed that the Christian refusal to acknowledge the state gods was a matter of civil disobedience, while the Christians feared that they would anger their own god if they attended state rituals. They could not obey both the state and their own god. Roman officials thought that punishment of Christians was a matter of maintaining law and order, but the Christians believed that they were being persecuted for practicing their religion.

399   Pliny the Younger, *Letters* 10.96, 97

Dear Trajan:

It is my regular practice, my lord, to refer to you all matters about which I am in doubt; for who can better guide me in my hesitation or instruct me in my ignorance? I have never dealt with investigations about Christians, and therefore I don't know what is usually either punished or investigated, or to what extent. I have hesitated no small amount about whether there should be some distinction in respect to age, or whether young people, however young, should be considered not at all different from more mature people; whether pardon should be given to those who repent, or whether it should be of no use to someone who was once a Christian that he has ceased to be

[295] Pliny died in his province in A.D. 113. This letter is an example of his official correspondence. Many of Pliny's personal letters appear in this book; consult the index.

[296] Membership in a secret society was considered a treasonous offense and was punished as severely as armed riot, that is, by death. On *collegia* and Senate restrictions, see note 102 of Chapter V.

[297] *rescriptum:* official imperial correspondence; see selection 252.

[298] On *pax Romana,* see selections 251 and 282.

one; whether the name itself, even if there are no criminal offenses, should be punished,[299] or whether only the criminal offenses associated with the name should be punished.[300] In the meantime, among those who were brought before me as Christians, I have used the following method. I asked them whether they were Christians. If they admitted it, I asked them a second and even a third time, threatening them with punishment. I ordered those who persisted to be led away for execution, for I had no doubt that, whatever the nature of their belief, their stubbornness and inflexible obstinacy surely should be punished. There were others who were afflicted by a similar madness, but I wrote in the recordbook that they should be sent to Rome because they were Roman citizens.[301]

Soon, as a result of this investigation, as usually happens, accusations became widespread and more incidences were reported. An anonymous pamphlet was published which contained the names of many people. I thought that those who denied that they were or had been Christians should be dismissed, if they prayed to our gods, repeating the words after me, and if they dedicated incense and wine to your image, which I had ordered to be brought in for this purpose with the statues of the gods,[302] and if, moreover, they cursed Christ. It is said that those who are truly Christians cannot be forced to do any of these things. Others who were named by the informer said that they were Christians, but then soon denied it, and said that they had indeed been Christians, but had now ceased to be, some three years ago, some many years ago, a few even twenty years ago. All of these people also venerated both your image and the statues of the gods, and cursed Christ. They asserted, however, that this had been the sum total of their offense or error: they were accustomed to meet on a fixed day before dawn and to sing in responsion a hymn to Christ as if to a god, and to bind themselves by an oath—not an oath to commit some crime, but an oath not to commit theft, robbery, or adultery, not to break their word, and not to refuse to return a deposit when called upon.[303] When these things had been done, it had been their custom, they said, to depart, and then meet again later to dine together, on food that was ordinary and innocent.[304] They had ceased to do even this, they said, after my edict by which I had forbidden the existence of secret societies in accordance with your instructions. And so I believed that it was necessary to search out the truth

---

[299] That is, whether Christians should be punished for belonging to a secret society (Trajan had forbidden their existence). The Romans were tolerant of differing religious beliefs, but intolerant of groups which might threaten the security of the state.

[300] Christians were accused, for example, of cannibalism. See selection 401.

[301] The power of a Roman governor over non-Romans in his province was virtually supreme, but he was strictly forbidden to punish a Roman citizen, even by imprisonment or corporal punishment. See selection 281; also *Acts* 22.25–27: "And as they bound him with thongs, Paul said unto the centurion that stood by, Is it lawful for you to scourge a man that is a Roman, and uncondemned? When the centurion heard that, he went and told the chief captain, saying, Take heed what thou doest: for this man is a Roman. Then the chief captain came, and said unto him, Tell me, art thou a Roman? He said, Yea."

[302] On emperor-worship in the eastern part of the Roman Empire, see selections 381 and 382.

[303] Since there were no bank buildings in the Roman world where people could deposit their savings, an individual might give his money for safekeeping to an acquaintance with a secure home. An unscrupulous acquaintance might later refuse to return the money.

[304] *ordinary and innocent:* that is, not human flesh. For more on the Christian communal dinner, *agape,* see selection 402. Non-Christians who heard Christians speak of eating the flesh and drinking the blood of Christ thought that the Christians engaged in cannibalism at their dinners.

of this matter by torturing two female slaves who were called deaconesses.[305] However, I found nothing other than depraved, excessive superstition.

Therefore, I delayed the investigation and hastened to consult you, for the matter seemed to me worth a consultation, especially because of the number of those involved. Many people of every age, of every rank, and of both sexes are put, and will be put, in a dangerous position. The contagion of this superstition has spread not only to the cities, but also to the villages and even to the farms. It seems possible, however, that it can be arrested and cured. Indeed, it is certainly quite well known that temples which had been until recently almost deserted have begun to be frequented again, and that sacred rites which had been neglected for a long time have been resumed, and that sacrificial animals, for which, until now, very few buyers could be found, are selling again.[306] From this it is easy to infer what a large number of people can be reformed if an opportunity for repentance is given.

Dear Pliny:

You have followed the procedure which you ought to have, my dear Pliny, in investigating the cases of those who had been brought before you as Christians. It is not possible to establish a general law which will provide a fixed standard. However, these people are not to be searched out. If they should be brought before you and proved guilty, they must be punished, with this proviso, however, that anyone who denies that he is a Christian and proves this by his action, that is, by worshipping our gods, even if he has been suspected in the past, should obtain pardon because of his repentance. But pamphlets published anonymously should have no place in a criminal proceeding, for this is a very bad precedent and not in keeping with the spirit of our age.

Christian Reaction to Trajan's Rescriptum

Most modern scholars have recognized that Trajan viewed the Christians as a potential threat to civil order and that his reply to Pliny reflects an honest desire to be fair but firm in eradicating this threat. The Christians, of course, had a different interpretation of the situation and felt they were innocent people being unfairly persecuted because of their religious beliefs. Tertullian lived from about A.D. 160 to about A.D. 230, that is, about 120 years after Trajan and Pliny.

400 Tertullian, *Apology*[307] 2.7–9

Trajan replied to Pliny that Christians should certainly not be hunted down, but, if they were brought into court, they should be punished. What a confused and confusing decision! He says that they should not be hunted down, implying that they are in-

---

[305] On the torture of slaves who were to give evidence in court, see selections 200 and 206.

deaconesses: the Latin here is *ministrae* (see note 190 of Chapter VII.) Pliny used the Latin word *ministrae* to translate the Greek word *diakonissai*. Greek was the language spoken by the Bithynians.

[306] That is, the rites of the Roman state cult are receiving proper attention.

[307] *Apology:* Greek *apologia* = "a defense," "a statement defending oneself" (not an apology in the modern English usage).

nocent, and yet he insists that they should be punished, implying that they are guilty. He pardons them, he persecutes them; he ignores them, he notices them. Why deceive yourself with your decision? If you condemn them, why not also hunt them down? If you don't hunt them down, why not also acquit them? . . . As it is, you condemn a man who is brought into court although no one wanted him hunted down, a man who has not, I think, deserved punishment because he is guilty, but because he was found, although it was forbidden to hunt him down.

Accusations against the Christians

In the passage translated here, Minucius Felix, a Christian,[308] plays devil's advocate and lists the accusations against the Christians from a non-Christian point of view. (Later in his work, he refutes the charges.) Compare the accusations made against the worshippers of Christ with those made against the worshippers of Bacchus.[309]

401   Minucius Felix, *Octavius* 8.4, 5; 9.2, 4–7; 10.2, 5; 12.5

These people gather together illiterates from the very dregs of society and credulous women who easily fall prey because of the natural weakness of their sex. They organize a mob of wicked conspirators who join together at nocturnal assemblies and ritual fasts and inhuman dinners,[310] not for a particular religious ceremony, but for sacrilegious sacrifice; a secret and light-fearing tribe, silent in public, garrulous in dark corners. They despise temples as if they were tombs, they spit on the gods, they laugh at our sacred rites. Although they themselves are pitiful, they irreverently express pity for our priests. They despise political offices and regalia, and wander about half-naked. What amazing stupidity and incredible audacity! They scoff at present tortures, but fear those uncertain ones in the future, and they fear a death after death, but do not fear death now! And so for them, a deceptive hope of a comforting afterlife assuages terror. . . . Everywhere they share a kind of religion of lust, and promiscuously call one another brothers and sisters so that even ordinary sexual intercourse becomes incest by the use of a sacred name.[311] . . . Anyone who says that the items they venerate are an ordinary man who was punished by execution for a criminal act and the deadly wood of a cross, anyone who says this attributes to these irredeemable and wicked people very appropriate religious objects, so they worship just what they deserve to. Tales about their initiation of converts are as disgusting as they are notorious. An infant is wrapped in bread dough so as to deceive the unsuspecting and is placed beside the person being initiated into the rites. The initiate is required to strike the surface of the bread with blows he presumes are harmless, but he thus kills the infant with wounds not seen by him. And then what an abomination! They voraciously lick up the blood of the infant and greedily tear apart its limbs, and swear alliance over this sacrificial victim and pledge themselves to mutual silence by complicity in this crime. . . . On

---

308 *Minucius Felix:* see selection 392.
309 See selection 387.
310 On charges of cannibalism, see selection 399.
311 Christians, who called one another brother or sister, were accused of incest.

holy days, they gather for a banquet with all their children, sisters, and mothers, people of both sexes and all ages. There, after many courses of food, the party heats up and the passion of incestuous lust inflames those who are drunk. . . . In the shameless darkness they are indiscriminately wrapped in shocking embraces. . . . Why do they struggle to hide and conceal whatever it is they worship, if decent things always welcome publicity, and only wicked things are secretive? Why have they no altars, no temples, no recognizable statues? Why do they never speak in public or assemble openly, unless that which they worship and conceal is something illegal or shameful? . . . And what great prodigies and what marvels the Christians invent! That god of theirs, whom they can neither show to us nor see themselves, inquires carefully into the behavior of all men, and into the deeds of all men, and even into their words and hidden thoughts, dashing about and being present everywhere. They claim he is troublesome, restless, and even shamelessly nosey, that he hovers over every action and prowls in every place. . . . You apprehensive and anxiety-ridden Christians abstain from innocent pleasures. You don't watch the public spectacles, you don't take part in the processions, you absent yourselves from the public banquets, you shrink away from sacred games, sacrificial meat,[312] and altar libations. That's how frightened you are of the gods whose existence you deny!

A Christian's Reply to the Accusations

402   Tertullian, *Apology* 7.1; 10.1, 2; 17.1; 21.10, 11;
                           30.1, 4; 31.3; 32.2; 35.1; 39.1–3, 5, 16–19

We are said to be the most depraved of men because of our alleged ritual of baby killing and baby eating and then incest after the baby banquet. . . .

You say, "You do not worship the gods and you do not offer sacrifices on behalf of the emperors." It logically follows that we do not sacrifice on behalf of others, because we do not sacrifice on behalf of ourselves. And this follows from our not worshipping the gods. Therefore, we encounter a charge of sacrilege and treason. And that is the chief case against us, or rather, the whole case, and so it is worth investigating it, unless prejudice or injustice will decide the case (the former ignores the truth, the latter rejects it). We stop worshipping your gods as soon as we recognize that they are not gods. You should therefore force us to prove our case, that those gods are not really gods, and ought not to be worshipped; because if they were gods, then they should be worshipped. Christians would certainly then deserve punishment if it were established that those gods, whom they are not worshipping because they do not think they are gods, in fact really are gods. . . .

We worship the one God, who formed this whole mass out of nothing, who formed it with its entire supply of elements, bodies, and spirits, who formed it in the glory of his majesty by the Word with which he commands, by the Logic with which he arranges, and by the Might with which he has power. . . .

We have already said that God created the whole universe by Word, by Logic, and by Might. Among your philosophers, too, it is believed the *logos* (that is, word

---

[312] At public sacrifices, the meat of the sacrificed animal was offered to the public. Christians refused to eat this meat.

and reason) seems to be the creator of the universe.[313] Zeno defines *logos* as the maker who formed and arranged all things. He says that *logos* can be called fate and God and the mind of Jupiter and the inevitability of the universe. Cleanthes[314] collects all these under the title "spirit" and affirms that spirit permeates the universe. We, too, ascribe "spirit" as the appropriate nature of Word, Logic, and Might (by which God formed all things, as we said above). When the Spirit speaks, Word is present in it. When the Spirit arranges, Logic is present in it. When the Spirit accomplishes, Might is present in it.[315] . . .

On behalf of the safety of the emperors, we invoke the eternal God, the true God, the living God. . . . We Christians are continually praying for all the emperors; we pray looking upward, with our hands spread, because innocent, with our heads bare,[316] because we do not blush, and without a prompter,[317] because we pray from the heart. We pray for the emperors a long life, a secure reign, a safe home, strong armies, a faithful Senate, honest subjects, and a world at peace. . . . God has said clearly and explicitly, "Pray for kings and princes and worldly powers so that your lives may be tranquil."[318] For when the Empire is shaken, and all the other members of it are shaken, we, too, of course, although we are considered aliens by the crowds, find ourselves sharing some part of the disaster. . . .

But we make our oaths not by the *genius* of the emperor, but by his health, which is more sacred than any *genius*.[319] . . .

So therefore the Christians are considered public enemies because they do not bestow empty or false or rash praise on the emperors, because they celebrate the emperors' festivals, since they are men of true religion, in good conscience rather than in good spirits.[320] . . .

I will now disclose the affairs of a Christian association so that I may show you that they are honorable (I have already proved that they are not evil). We are a society with a common religious belief, a common body of teachings, and a common bond of hope. We gather in meeting and congregation so that we may join together in our own prayers toward God, like a regiment of supplicants. . . . We nourish our faith on the sacred words of holy books, we rouse our hope, we strengthen our confidence, but we also substantiate our teachings by the inculcation of divine precepts. . . .

---

[313] *Logos* is a Greek word which means "word," but which can also mean "reason," "rational thought," "calculation," "account," or "system." Stoic philosophers, such as Zeno, believed that *logos* was the rational system or reason of the universe.

[314] *Cleanthes:* also a Stoic philosopher. Both Zeno and Cleanthes lived in the third century B.C.

[315] See John 1.1: "In the beginning was the Word, and the Word was with God, and the Word was God." In this passage the English *word* is used to translate the New Testament Greek *logos*.

[316] Roman priests covered their heads with a veil or shawl when praying.

[317] *prompter:* see selection 364 on the use of prompters in Roman rituals.

[318] 1 Timothy 2.1 and 2: "I exhort therefore, that, first of all, supplications, prayers, intercessions, and giving of thanks, be made for all men; for kings, and for all that are in authority; that we may lead a quiet and peaceable life in all godliness and honesty." The early Christians were not actively resistant to Roman rule. Indeed, *pax Romana* made it much easier for the Christian evangelists to travel quickly and safely throughout the civilized world to spread the "good news."

[319] *genius:* guardian spirit.

[320] The Christians disapproved of the drunken behavior which some people exhibited on festival days.

Even if there is a kind of treasury, it is not built up from money paid as an entrance fee to a religious belief which one could buy, as it were.[321] Once a month, or whenever he wishes, each member gives a small coin, but only if he wishes and only if he can. For no one is compelled; the offering is voluntary. . . .

The name we give to our communal dinners reveals their purpose, for such a dinner is called by the Greek word for love.[322] Whatever the cost of the dinner, we consider it profitable to incur expenses in the name of charity, if we can help some less fortunate people with the refreshments we provide. We do this, not under the authority of your system, whereby parasites aspire to win the freedom to be a slave and pay for fattening their bellies by swallowing insults.[323] No, we do this under the authority of God, whereby consideration for people of humble means is a major concern. If the purpose of our communal dinner is honest, then judge the other aspects of our dinner with the purpose in mind. Because the dinner is a matter of religious duty, nothing shameful, nothing disgraceful is allowed. Christians do not take their places at the table to eat until they have first "tasted" a prayer to God. They eat only enough to satisfy their hunger and drink only an amount suitable to modest people.[324] They satisfy their needs as people who remember that they must praise God even during the night, and they converse as people who know that the Lord hears them.[325] After they wash their hands and light the lamps, each person in turn is called into the middle of the room to sing to God as best he can either from the Holy Scriptures or from his own heart. And here it becomes evident how much wine he has drunk. Prayer, done in the same way, brings the dinner to a close. Then they divide up, not into bands of muggers or crews of rioters or instigators of debauchery; they maintain the same concern for decency and purity as people who have dined not so much on dinner as on moral instruction.

Martyrs

The following passage, written by a Christian, describes the persecution of Christians in Gaul in A.D. 177. The tortures and executions had been approved by the emperor Marcus Aurelius.[326]

403   Eusebius, *Ecclesiastical History* 5.1.6–9, 11, 13–16

The Christians gathered together and endured every kind of insult and punishment. In their zeal for Christ, they considered many things to be but few, and they truly proved

---

[321] The worshippers of Bacchus and the Jews were similarly accused of establishing a treasury; see selections 388 and 393. To Roman officials, establishing a treasury and charging entrance fees or initiation fees were indications of the formation of a secret (hence dangerous) society. Tertullian is careful to explain that no Christian is required to pay money into a treasury.

[322] *the Greek word for love: agape* = "love," "affection" ("sexual love" = *eros*).

[323] On Roman patron-client relationships, see Chapter I.

[324] The worshippers of Christ, like the worshippers of Bacchus who also used wine in their religious rites, were accused of drunkenness and of shameless behavior while drunk.

[325] Christians called their god *dominus*, "lord," "master." The word *dominus* was also used by the Romans to refer to the emperor; see Pliny's letter to Trajan (selection 399).

[326] *Marcus Aurelius:* see selections 18, 176, and 322.

that "the sufferings of this present time are not worthy to be compared with the glory which shall be revealed in us."[327] First they courageously endured every attack mounted by the tumultuous mob: verbal abuse and beatings and draggings and pillage and stoning and imprisonment and all those things which an enraged group of people likes to do to its supposed foes and enemies. The Christians were dragged into the marketplace by the tribune and the city officials in charge of all the people; they were indicted and they confessed,[328] and they were imprisoned until the arrival of the governor. When he arrived, they were led before him, and he employed all his cruelty against them. . . .

The first martyrs[329] were ready and waiting, and they completed their confession of martyrdom with all eagerness. But others were not ready, were not prepared, and were not strong; they were not able to endure the stress of a valiant resistance, and about ten in number failed to become martyrs.[330] They caused us great grief and immeasurable sorrow, and they blunted the zeal of the others who had not been arrested. . . . Day after day, however, those who were worthy continued to be arrested. . . . Some foreign slaves who belonged to our church were also arrested because the governor had issued a public order that we were all to be questioned. These slaves were caught in the snare of Satan. Because they were terrified of the tortures which they saw the saints suffering, when the soldiers urged them, they falsely accused us of Thyestean banquets and Oedipodean intercourse,[331] and things which it is wrong for us either to speak of or think of or even to believe could ever possibly happen among men. When these accusations were heard, everyone acted like a wild animal toward us, with the result that even people who had formerly been restrained because of personal friendship now became intensely angry and furious at us. And the words of the Lord to us were fulfilled: "Yea, the time cometh, that whosoever killeth you will think that he doeth God service."[332] Then at last the holy martyrs suffered tortures beyond all description.

Toleration

The most systematic and brutal persecutions of Christians did not take place until the late third and early fourth centuries A.D. Many were initiated by the emperor Galerius. In A.D. 311, however, when Galerius was critically ill, he repented of his cruelty and issued an edict of toleration which canceled his earlier orders for persecution and which allowed Christians freedom of worship. Galerius died shortly afterward.

[327] Romans 8.18.

[328] *confessed:* to being Christians; see selection 399.

[329] *martyrs:* the Greek word *martys* means "witness."

[330] *failed to become martyrs:* that is, they did not die; under torture, they recanted and claimed that they were not Christians. Marcus Aurelius had ordered any who recanted to be set free.

[331] Thyestes, a figure from Greek mythology, partook of a banquet at which his sons were dismembered, cooked, and eaten. Oedipus, also of Greek mythology, had intercourse with his mother. On the charges of cannibalism and incest against the Christians, see selection 401.

[332] John 16.2.

404   Eusebius, *Ecclesiastical History* 8.17.1

While the emperor Galerius was wrestling with many misfortunes, he began to regret the cruelties he had perpetrated against the God-fearing. He pondered this matter, and first confessed to the God of the universe and then summoned those around him and ordered them without delay to halt the persecution against the Christians, and to urge them by law and imperial decree to build their churches and observe their customary rites, and to offer prayers on behalf of the emperor.

Christian Intolerance

In A.D. 312, Constantine was engaged in a battle near Rome against Maxentius, a rival for the position of emperor. Constantine put his fate in the hands of the Christian god and won the battle and the throne. In A.D. 313, Constantine, now a convert to Christianity, established a new official policy toward the Christians: they were free to worship as they pleased, and they would not be required to participate in the rites of the state cult.

Constantine and succeeding emperors enacted much legislation that provided tolerance for the Christians but which, unfortunately, suppressed the religious freedom of other groups. The law translated below, which was enacted in A.D. 326, is an example of such discriminatory legislation. The Christians had never intended to live in peaceful coexistence with people of other religious beliefs. Once they gained power, they ruthlessly and systematically set out to destroy other cults; we earlier saw their success in the persecution of followers of the state cult.

405   *The Law Code of Theodosius*[333] 16.5.1

The privileges which have been granted upon consideration of religious belief must be enjoyed only by adherents of the catholic rite.[334] We require that heretics and schismatics not only be excluded from these privileges, but also be bound and subject to various compulsory public services.

SYNCRETISM

A Roman Virtue

One of the most noble aspects of the Roman character was its ability to adopt the customs and beliefs of other cultures and to incorporate them into Roman culture.

---

[333] *The Law Code of Theodosius:* a compilation of laws which was done in A.D. 438 under the auspices of the emperor Theodosius II. It was superseded in the Eastern Empire by the *Corpus Iuris Civilis* of Justinian's time, but it continued to be used in the west; see Appendix I.

[334] *catholic:* from Greek *katholikos* = "general," "universal." The term was used by the early Christians to denote (1) the whole body of Christian believers, and (2) writings intended for wide circulation.

Many scholars, both ancient and modern, believe that this ability was the source of Rome's greatness. And until the triumph of Christianity, which was fanatically intolerant and whose growth coincided with the sharp decline of Roman power, Roman open-mindedness had been rewarded by success in building and maintaining an empire.

406   Minucius Felix, *Octavius* 6

Throughout the whole far-flung empire, in provinces, in towns, we see that each local group of people has its own religious rituals and worships local gods. The Eleusinians, for example, worship Ceres, the Phrygians worship Great Mother, the Epidaurians Aesculapius, the Chaldaeans Baal, the Syrians Astarte, the Taurians Diana, and the Gauls Mercury. The Romans, however, worship all the gods in the world. Their power and authority have occupied the farthest limits of the whole world, and extended their empire beyond the paths of the sun and the borders of the very ocean. . . . And after they have captured a town, when brutality in victory might be expected, the Romans pay honor to the deities of the conquered people. They invite to Rome gods from all over the world, and they make them their own.[335] . . . And thus, while the Romans were adopting the religious rites of all nations, they also won for themselves an empire.

MAGIC AND SUPERSTITION

Like religion, magic and superstition have their origin in a belief in mysterious forces which can affect man's life. Superstition usually involves an unreasoning fear of the unknown and a false concept of causation (that a black cat, for example, may be the cause of bad luck). Superstitious people often depend on magic to ward off misfortune. In using magic, man utilizes words or ritual actions or the assumed potency of some object to cause the mysterious forces to produce a certain result. When a man recites or sings a magical charm,[336] he is utilizing the sound of the words and is assuming for himself the power to control nature and the course of events. In religion, man uses words or ritual actions only as the method of propitiating the mysterious forces and persuading them to produce the desired result. When a man recites a religious prayer or sings a hymn, he is adopting an attitude of dependence toward superhuman powers; he is appealing to them, through the words of the prayer or through the ritual action, to influence the course of events. In magic, man thinks he can control events directly. There is obviously a close relationship between magic and religion, and in ancient Roman religion,[337] as in modern Christianity, elements of magical practice can be observed. However, one

---

[335] See selection 361.

[336] *charm:* from the Latin *carmen* = "song," "poem," "ritual formula." Compare *chant,* from the Latin *cantum* = "sung," and *enchant,* from the Latin *incantatus* = "sung over," "enchanted."

[337] See, for example, the account of procedures at the Lupercalia (selection 375), or the insistence on strict wording of prayers (selection 364), or the emphasis on three in the prayer of the Arval Brethren (selection 365).

might argue that the distinction between magic and religion rests not in the nature of the practices (the use of prayers, charms, rites, ceremonies), but in the intention of the practices (whether one wishes to control or to propitiate mysterious forces).

Superstitions

407   Pliny the Elder, *Natural History* 28.5.23–29

Why, whenever we mention the dead, do we quickly add: "May they rest in peace"?[338] Why do we believe that odd numbers are more powerful in all matters than even numbers? . . . Why do we say "Bless you"[339] to someone who sneezes? . . . And it is an accepted belief that people who are not present at a conversation can know by the ringing in their ears that the conversation is about them. . . . It is considered very unlucky to sweep the floor when a dinner guest is leaving the banquet, or to remove a table or serving tray while a guest is drinking. . . . Cutting your hair on the seventeenth or the twenty-ninth day of the month prevents baldness as well as headaches. Marcus Servilius Nonianus,[340] a leading citizen, not so long ago feared inflammation of the eyes. And he used to tie around his neck with a linen thread a piece of papyrus on which were written two Greek letters, P [rho] and A [alpha]. Mucianus,[341] who has been consul three times, employed a similar practice, but used a living fly in a small white linen cloth. Both men claimed that they were free of eye inflammation because of these practices.

The Potency of Words

Although the state officially always frowned on the practice of magic, it was widely used in private life. The passage below offers a chant which may be sung to aid healing of fractures or dislocations. The "words" used are nonsense syllables, but their sound has the power to effect a cure.

408   Cato the Elder, *On Agriculture* 160

A dislocation can be remedied with this chant. Take a green reed, about four or five feet long, split it down the middle, and have two men hold it against their hips. Begin to chant: motas vaeta daries dardares astataries dissunapiter. Continue until the two halves of the reed come together. Wave an iron knife over the reed. When the halves have joined and are touching one another, take the reed in your hand and cut it on the right and on the left. Fasten it to the dislocation or fracture, which will then heal. Continue to chant every day: huat hauat huat ista pista sista dannabo dannaustra. Or: huat haut haut istasis tarsis ardannabou dannaustra.

338 A more literal translation of the Latin is "Let us not disturb the memory of them."
339 More literally: "Good health."
340 *Marcus Servilius Nonianus:* consul in A.D. 35; he died in A.D. 59.
341 *Gaius Licinius Mucianus:* consul for the third time in A.D. 72.

The Potency of Objects

Certain objects had the power to influence events. Objects struck by lightning or taken from the dead were particularly potent.

409 Pliny the Elder, *Natural History* 28.11.45, 46

It is said that if a person who has put his hands behind his back bites off a piece from some wood that has been struck by lightning, and if the piece is applied to the tooth of someone with a toothache, it will serve as a remedy. . . . Some people wrap up in wool a piece of a nail taken from a cross,[342] and tie it around the neck of those suffering from quartan fever. Or they may take a rope used in a crucifixion. Once the person has been cured, they bury the rope in a hole or cave which the sun cannot reach.

The Potency of Rituals

There are many descriptions in Roman literature of witches. Like the witches of *Macbeth,* their Roman counterparts performed rituals, cast spells, and concocted foul brews. This passage describes a ritual which was effective for shutting the mouths of one's detractors. This is imitative or homeopathic magic; one produces a certain result (sealing shut the enemy's mouth) by imitating this result (sealing shut a fish's mouth).[343]

410 Ovid, *A Roman Calendar of Festivals* 2.571–582

An aged old hag sits in a circle of young girls and performs rites in honor of Tacita, the Silent One[344] (although the hag is certainly not silent). With three fingers she places three pieces of incense under the threshold[345] where a tiny mouse has made a secret passageway for itself. Then she ties enchanted threads onto dark gray lead and rolls seven black beans around in her mouth.[346] She roasts over a fire the head of a small fish which she has sealed shut with pitch and sewn up with a bronze needle. She also drizzles wine on it. She and her companions drink whatever wine is left over, although she drinks the most. And, as she leaves, she says, "We have tightly bound hostile tongues and unfriendly mouths." Then the drunk old hag departs.

[342] *from a cross:* that is, a cross used in a crucifixion.
[343] See selection 365 on the procession of the Arval Brethren whose high leaps were meant to imitate the action of crops leaping up and growing high.
[344] *Silent One:* Latin *tacere* = "to be silent"; *tacita* is a feminine form of the adjective "silent," "mute."
[345] Thresholds were favorite haunts of spirits. Roman brides were carried across the thresholds of their new homes to protect them from unwelcome interference from the spirits.
[346] Black beans had a chthonic association in Roman ritual.

Curse Tablets

People frequently put curses on their enemies and consecrated them to the spirits of the underworld. The procedure was to write the name of the intended victim on a tablet (usually a lead tablet), to make the consecration, and then to stick a long nail through the name on the tablet. Sometimes a rough sketch of the hated person was also included on the tablet and was pierced by many long nails. We have already seen one example of a curse tablet in the section on chariot racing.[347] These tablets were usually placed in tombs so that they might be close to the underworld spirits. The consecration translated here, found at Minturna, was written in Latin but has many misspellings. It is probably the work of someone in the lower class, as is true of most curse tablets.

411   *CIL* 10.8249

Spirits of the netherworld, I consecrate and hand over to you, if you have any power, Ticene of Carisius. Whatever she does, may it all turn out wrong. Spirits of the netherworld, I consecrate to you her limbs, her complexion, her figure, her head, her hair, her shadow, her brain, her forehead, her eyebrows, her mouth, her nose, her chin, her cheeks, her lips, her speech, her breath, her neck, her liver, her shoulders, her heart, her lungs, her intestines, her stomach, her arms, her fingers, her hands, her navel, her entrails, her thighs, her knees, her calves, her heels, her soles, her toes. Spirits of the netherworld, if I see her wasting away, I swear that I will be delighted to offer a sacrifice to you every year.

EPICUREANISM

The practical-minded Romans of the early and middle republican periods had frowned upon the Greeks' interest in philosophic speculation and had considered it an unprofitable pursuit. As late as 161 B.C., the Senate authorized the praetors to expel philosophers from Rome, apparently because it was felt that people's time could be better spent in more practical pursuits.[348] By the end of the second century B.C., however, Greek philosophers had won a limited but devoted audience among members of the educated upper class. In the late republican period, when the social, political, and economic changes produced by the expansion of the Roman Empire had complicated and confused people's lives, many turned for solace to oriental religions; a few looked to philosophy for comfort. Two of the schools of Greek philosophy which won supporters among thoughtful and educated Romans were Stoicism and Epicureanism.

The Epicureans were disciples of Epicurus, a Greek philosopher who taught

[347] See selection 350.

[348] Even in the imperial period many Romans insisted that education should be practical in nature; see selections 134 and 210.

in Athens until his death in 270 B.C. Much of our knowledge about Epicurus's teachings comes from the work of a Roman disciple, Lucretius. Titus Lucretius Carus lived in Rome from about 99 to 55 B.C. He wrote six books of dactylic hexameter verse in which he expounded the doctrines of Epicurus. His didactic poem is called *About the Nature of the Universe*. The passages translated here are taken from this poem.

The Reasons for Studying Philosophy

Epicurus believed that the *summmum bonum*[349] of life (that which made man truly happy) was pleasure, but he defined pleasure not as sensual enjoyment, but as peace of mind, freedom from anxiety. He taught that the body needed only a few simple things to alleviate mental and physical distress: just enough food to prevent hunger, just enough water to prevent thirst, just enough clothing to prevent chill. Anything else was superfluous, and even dangerous, because luxuries cause pain, either of anticipation or of reaction. The true Epicurean therefore restricted his physical desires within very narrow limits.[350] Although Epicurus believed in the existence of gods, he did not think that the gods influenced human life in any way. He believed, moreover, that the human soul was both mortal and material, and perished along with the body at death. He therefore denounced religion because he thought that fear of the gods and of the afterlife created anxiety and prevented people from achieving real pleasure (peace of mind). He thought that human fears could best be allayed by scientific knowledge about the composition of the universe and about natural phenomena.[351]

412   Lucretius, *About the Nature of the Universe*
                                                      1.107–115, 127–135, 146–148

If men could see that there is a definite termination point for their troubles,[352] they would in some way have the strength to withstand religious superstitions and the threats of prophets. But as it is now, they have no plan or power of resistance, because they fear eternal punishment after death. For they don't know what the soul is, and whether it is born with a person, or implanted in him at birth, and whether it is destroyed at the moment of death and perishes along with the rest of us, or whether it travels to the desolate swamps and dark shadows of Orcus.[353] . . . And therefore I must first provide a full explanation of celestial phenomena, such as the regular movements of the sun and moon, and of how and why things happen on earth. And then

[349] *summum bonum:* literally, "the highest good."

[350] The modern definition of *epicurean,* as a person devoted only to sensual enjoyment, is thus a gross distortion of Epicurus's doctrine.

[351] The study of ancient philosophy was divided into three branches: ethics (moral philosophy, the study of human behavior and conduct), physics (natural philosophy, the study of nature and the universe), and logic (rational philosophy, the study of arrangement of arguments and proofs).

[352] That is, that death brings an end to man's troubles because there is no afterlife. (Conversely, the oriental religions appealed to people because they promised a happy afterlife.)

[353] *Orcus:* the underworld.

with careful thought I must investigate in particular the composition of the soul and the mind, and the nature of those things which enter our minds and terrify us when we are buried in sleep or are awake but ill; for then we seem to hear and to see right in front of us those who are dead and whose bones are embraced by the earth. . . . The terror and darkness of the mind cannot be dispelled by the rays of the sun and the shining shafts of the day, but only by a scientific explanation of how nature works.

The First Principle

Epicurus taught that the universe was material, and was composed of indestructible matter called atoms and of void.[354] All objects, including the human body and soul, are but compounds of atoms and void. All compounds are perishable, and death is simply a dissolution of the assemblage of atoms. The atoms, however, are eternal and, upon dissolution of the compound, move on to form another compound. Epicurus hoped with this scientific theory to relieve men's anxieties by showing that the gods play no role in creation or destruction, that they do not intervene in human life, that death is simply nonexistence, the dissolution of the compounds into individual atoms, and that every phenomenon is the result of natural causes.

413   Lucretius, *About the Nature of the Universe* 1.149–158

We will begin our task with an explication of nature's first principle: nothing is ever created by divine power out of nothing. For fear paralyzes all mortals when they cannot find a rational explanation for the causes of many things happening in heaven and on earth. And so they think these things happen through some divine agency. But when we have seen that nothing can be created out of nothing, we will then perceive more accurately the answers we are pursuing, and we will learn where and how things can be created and how they come into existence without the agency of the gods.

The Second Principle

414   Lucretius, *About the Nature of the Universe* 1.215–237, 250–264

And this is the second principle: nature dissolves all things in turn into their constituent atoms and never reduces anything to nothing. For if anything were totally perishable, such a thing might suddenly be snatched from our sight and vanish. No force would be needed to cause the separation into smaller parts or to unravel the compound. But in fact, since all things are composed of imperishable particles, nature does not allow any compound to disintegrate until it meets a force that shatters it with an external blow or penetrates the spaces between the atoms and unravels it from within.

Moreover, if time, which removes compounds from our sight when they get old, annihilated these compounds by destroying all their matter completely, from what

---

[354] *atoms:* from the Greek adjective *atomos* = "indivisible" (only recently have scientists learned that the atom can be split). The atomic theory had been first expounded by the fifth-century Greek philosophers Leucippus and Democritus.

matter does the power of procreation continue to bring the various species of animals into the light of life? And from what matter does the inventive earth nourish the animals it has brought to life, or provide the food needed to sustain each species? From what matter do the native springs and far-off rivers continue to replenish the sea? From what matter does the ether find fuel for the stars? For if matter were perishable in nature, then infinite time and the days that have passed should have used up all the matter. On the other hand, if, during the passage of this infinite time, there have existed particles from which the universe has been continually renewed, surely these particles are imperishable in nature. And therefore things cannot be reduced to nothing. . . .

Rainwater, which Father Sky has thrown down into the lap of Mother Earth, vanishes. But shining crops rise up and branches grow green, and the trees grow taller and become heavy with fruit. And because of this, the species of animals and our own human race are nourished. Because of this, we see flourishing cities blossom forth with children, and all the leafy forests resound with the songs of young birds. Because of this, fat cattle heave their heavy bodies down in lush pastures, and white milk flows from their stretched udders. Because of this, a new generation frolics playfully on wobbly legs in the tender grass, their young minds intoxicated with pure milk. And therefore, things which we see now do not ever perish completely, because nature builds up one thing from another thing, and does not allow one compound to be born unless aided by the death of another compound.

Proof of the Existence of Atoms

415   Lucretius, *About the Nature of the Universe*
1.265–279, 305–316, 319–328

I have explained that things cannot be created out of nothing and that things cannot be reduced to nothing. Nevertheless, you are perhaps beginning to distrust my words because the atoms cannot be seen with your eyes. Think, however, about the particles which you cannot see, but which you must admit do exist. First of all, the force of the raging wind whips up the sea, overturns ships, and scatters clouds. Sometimes it races across the open plains in a whirling tornado and knocks flat huge trees and shakes the mountaintops with gusts that shatter forests. Thus does the wind rage with a furious howl and churn with a menacing roar. Surely there are invisible particles of wind which sweep the sea and the land and the clouds. . . .

Another example: clothes hung out on a surf-beaten shore grow damp. The same clothes, spread out in the sun, become dry. But we do not see how the water has soaked in, nor again how it has departed as a result of the sun's heat. Surely the water is distributed into tiny particles which the eyes cannot possibly see.

Another example: after many annual revolutions of the sun, the inside of a ring on a finger becomes thin because of the constant contact. Dripping water hollows a rock. A curved plowshare, even though it is iron, imperceptibly becomes thinner when used in the fields. We see that the pavement of roads, although cobblestone, is worn down by the feet of the crowds. . . . And thus we see that these things are being diminished as they are worn away, but our human sense of sight begrudges us a glimpse of what particles leave at what particular time. In conclusion, no scrutiny by our eyes, however close, can perceive the particles which time and nature gradually add to things, causing them to increase little by little. Neither can you perceive the particles which things lose because of wasting old age (rocks hanging over the sea, for example, crumbling because of erosive salt water), nor the time at which they lose them. Therefore, nature works through invisible but material particles.

Void

416   Lucretius, *About the Nature of the Universe*
1.329–330, 334–343, 346–357

Things are not, however, held closely packed together by a mass of matter. And this is the reason: void exists in all things. . . . Void is an intangible and empty space. If void did not exist, things could not possibly move. For it is the function of matter to obstruct and offer resistance, but if only matter existed, obstruction and resistance would be present everywhere, all the time. Nothing could move forward, because nothing could begin to yield. But as it is now, we see with our own eyes that many different things on earth, on the sea, and in the sky move in many different ways. If void did not exist, these things would be deprived of the circumstance for restless movement. . . .

Furthermore, although we may think that things are solid, nevertheless you can learn from the following examples that they have a porous composition. In rocky caves, for example, water seeps through, and all the surfaces are moist with plentiful drops of water. Food trickles through every part of an animal's body. Trees grow and in time produce fruit because their food is dispersed into every part of the tree, from the deepest part of the root, up through the trunk, and up into every branch. Voices pass through walls and fly through closed doors. Freezing cold penetrates right to the bone. If void did not exist, through which matter can move, none of this could possibly happen.

Life and Death

417   Lucretius, *About the Nature of the Universe*
2.1002–1004, 72–79, 575–580

Death does not destroy compounds by annihilating the individual atoms; it simply breaks up the compound and releases the atoms. Then it joins each atom to some other atoms. . . .

Atoms which leave one compound diminish it when they depart, but, on the other hand, they bring an increase in size to the compound to which they add themselves. For some compounds, they produce waning, but for others they produce growth, although they never remain permanently in one spot. And thus the universe is continually being renewed; and mortals exist through successive exchanges of atoms. One race grows up even as another wastes away, and the generations of living things come and go in brief spans of time; and like runners, they pass on the torch of life.[355] . . .

[355] In Athens there was an annual relay race in which the contestants carried lighted torches.

Now here, now there, the forces which give life conquer and then in turn are conquered. Mingled with a funeral lament is a wail which a baby raises when it first sees the bright shores of life. Every night which follows day, every dawn which follows night hears cries of mourning mixed with an infant's howl.

STOICISM

Like Epicureanism, Stoicism had its origin in the troubled Hellenistic period, when Athens was in decline. The founder of the Stoic school of philosophy was Zeno, who taught in Athens until his death in 263 B.C.[356] Zeno met with his disciples in a large *stoa* in Athens, called the *Stoa Poikile*,[357] and they were therefore called Stoics. Stoic and Epicurean philosophers, and philosophers of other schools as well,[358] first came to Rome in the second century B.C. Although none of the schools had much appeal outside of the educated upper class, Stoic ethics became widely known and were frequently adopted as popular philosophy by people with no interest in or knowledge of Stoic logic and physics.[359] Stoic ethics were, in fact, easily assimilated into traditional Roman culture. The Stoics preached self-discipline, perseverance, and steadfastness, qualities which had also defined the Roman code of behavior from Rome's earliest history.[360] Stoicism influenced the Romans, but the Romans also influenced Stoicism. Roman adherents were less concerned with speculation and more concerned with practical ethics; and a type of Stoicism developed whose emphasis on duty and discipline made it uniquely Roman. Our best source of information about Roman Stoicism is Seneca the Younger, who lived in the early imperial period and wrote treatises as well as letters in which he explained Stoic ideas.[361]

The Promise of Philosophy

Like Epicureanism, Stoicism offered to guide its adherents to a life free of anxiety, fear, and inner turmoil.

418   Seneca the Younger, *Letters* 48.7, 8

Do you want to know what promise philosophy can offer to mankind? Guidance for life. One man hears death calling him, another is stung by poverty, yet another is tor-

[356] Neither Zeno nor Epicurus was a native of Athens. Zeno was born in Cyprus, Epicurus in Samos.

[357] *Stoa:* a meeting hall with a covered colonnade. *Poikile:* "painted." The *Stoa Poikile* was a meeting hall decorated with frescoes.

[358] Platonists and Academics, for example.

[359] On the three branches of ancient philosophy, see note 351 of this chapter.

[360] Consider the story of Horatius at the bridge in selection 1 and the description of the ideal centurion in selection 265.

[361] See Appendix I. Seneca is the author of many other selections in this book; consult the index.

mented by wealth (fear for his own or envy of another's). That man trembles at his bad luck, this man longs to free himself from his good fortune. This man is unhappy because of other men, that man because of the gods. . . . Lives that are in ruins, lives that will be in ruins, are begging for help.

Stoic Definition of Happiness

According to Stoic physics, the universe was material, but the matter was not Epicurean atoms. The matter of the universe was a single substance whose quality could range from coarse to very refined. The most refined form of matter was variously identified as fire, fiery ether, breath, or embodied spirit. This fiery spirit was the active, creative force in the universe, the spirit or soul of the universe, as it were, acting on the coarser and passive forms of the matter. The spirit of the universe, which permeated the body of the universe, was thus as material as the body; the body was like a honeycomb, and the spirit was like the honey which flowed through the comb.

This material spirit was rational, and was in fact sometimes called Reason.[362] It was the plan or purpose of the universe. It is important to note that the material spirit did not *provide* the plan, but rather it *was* the plan. It was identified variously as Nature, Fate, God, Destiny, Providence, or the Mind of the Universe. God (Fate, Nature, etc.) therefore dwells throughout the universe, like honey in a honeycomb. The human body was a microcosm or miniature version of the universe, the macrocosm.[363] The body of man was the same substance as the body of the universe, and the soul of man was part of the spirit of the universe.

Like the Epicureans, the Stoics believed that man could be truly happy only if he were free of anxiety. The Epicureans, however, believed that man's whole life was merely a random or chance convergence of atoms, and his death was but the dispersion of the atoms. For the Stoics, on the other hand, the plan in the universe—called Nature, God, Fate, Providence and so on—was rational and was, in fact, Reason (*ratio*) itself. Since man's soul was part of this Reason or plan, he would be truly happy only when he allowed Reason to govern his life. He would then be in harmony with the spirit of the universe (with Nature, God, Fate, etc.). The *summum bonum* of Stoic philosophy therefore is life in harmony with Nature.[364]

419   Seneca the Younger, *Letters* 124.7, 14

We Stoics maintain that happiness is living in accordance with Nature. . . . Only that which is perfectly in accordance with Nature as a whole is truly perfect. And Nature as a whole is rational.

---

[362] *Reason:* Latin *ratio*, Greek *logos*. For a Christian interpretation of *logos* or *ratio* in the universe, see selection 402.

[363] *microcosm, macrocosm:* from the Greek *cosmos* = "world," "universe"; *micros* = "small"; *macros* = "large."

[364] *summum bonum:* see note 349 of this chapter.

Fate and Free Will

For the man who is in perfect harmony with Nature, his every plan will coincide with the plan of Nature (Fate or Providence).[365] He will choose of his free will to do what Fate had planned for him to do. He will thus never suffer anxiety or distress.

420 Seneca the Younger, *An Essay about Providence* 5.4, 6

Good men are not dragged by Fate; they follow it and keep in step.[366] . . . Demetrius said: "I am not being forced into anything and I am not putting up with anything against my will. I do not submit to God, I agree with him, and I strongly agree with him because I know that all things happen according to a law which is valid and established for eternity."

Emotions

Emotions were considered harmful because they produced irrational responses, and true happiness could be obtained, as we have seen, only if one were totally rational and thus in harmony with the rational universe. The Stoic was advised therefore to avoid emotional responses to situations.[367] Emotions, however, were powerful, and the aspiring Stoic had to wage constant battle to keep emotions from the borders of his soul lest they enter, drive out Reason, take control, and thus make him a slave to his passions. The only truly free man was the man free of passions, whose soul was occupied by perfect Reason.[368]

421 Seneca the Younger, *An Essay about Anger* 1.7.2, 3

It is easier to prevent harmful emotions from entering the soul than it is to control them once they have entered, and it is easier not to admit them than to restrain them when they have been admitted. For once they have occupied a position, they are more powerful than their ruler[369] and do not allow themselves to be curtailed or reduced. Moreover, Reason itself, to whom the reins have been given, is dominant only as long as it remains separated from the emotions. If it mingles with them and is contaminated, it can no longer even keep within bounds those emotions which it previously could

[365] For more on Stoic theory of fate and free will, see selection 99 and 345.

[366] As a dog, who is in "harmony" with his master, willingly follows on the leash. It is the dog who is unwilling who is dragged on the leash and suffers. Man, like the unwilling dog, causes his own suffering when he does not lead a life of perfect reason; on the dog image, see selection 99.

[367] For Seneca's views on the dangers of anger, see selection 198. On the dangers of watching arena events, see selection 344.

[368] For Stoic views on slavery and freedom, see selection 198.

[369] Reason should be the ruler.

have dislodged altogether. Once the mind has been agitated and shaken, it becomes a slave to that which disturbed it.

The Invulnerability of the Wise Man

Many of man's anxieties are caused by his fear of apparently chance events; he feels helpless against the whims of Fortune (Latin *Fortuna*). The Stoic, therefore, strove to make himself self-sufficient so that he would not fear any (mis)fortune because he would have nothing to lose. His only "possession" would be *virtus*, which Seneca elsewhere defines as "perfect Reason."[370]

422   Seneca the Younger, *An Essay about Constancy* 5.4, 5; 8.3

The wise man cannot suffer injury or loss, because he keeps all his "valuables" within himself and trusts nothing to Fortune. He has "goods" which are safe and secure because he finds satisfaction in *virtus*, which does not depend on chance occurrences and can therefore be neither enlarged nor diminished. . . . Fortune does not snatch away what she herself has not given; and certainly *virtus* is not a gift of Fortune, so it cannot be taken from us. *Virtus* is free, inviolable, immovable, unshaken, and so steeled against the blows of chance that it cannot even be bent, much less toppled. It looks straight at instruments of torture and does not flinch; its expression never changes, whether adversity or prosperity[371] comes into its view. The wise man therefore will lose nothing which he might perceive as a loss, for his only possession is *virtus*, and he can never be separated from it. He treats everything else like someone else's property, and who can be distresssed by the loss of things which are not yours? And so it follows that if injury can do no harm to the things which truly belong to the wise man, and if his things are secure because his *virtus* is secure, then injury cannot harm the wise man. . . .

Death is the ultimate threat, and injustice and the most cruel tyrants have nothing beyond death with which to threaten us. Death is Fortune's final expenditure of energy. And so if we accept death with a calm and steadfast mind, and we realize that death is not an evil and therefore not even an injury, we will much more easily endure other things—losses and insults, humiliations, exiles, bereavements, and separations. These things cannot overwhelm the wise man even if they all beset him at one time, and still less does he complain when they attack him singly.

Death as True Freedom

Although the Stoic tried to remain rational and unperturbed by the events of his life, circumstances sometimes made it impossible for him to live as he wished, in harmony with Nature (Fate, God, Reason, etc.). If a Stoic felt that he was under

[370] *Letter* 76.10. There is no one word in English which will provide a satisfactory translation of *virtus*. In other contexts, it can mean "excellence," "courage," or "valor."

[371] The Stoic must respond rationally, unemotionally to both bad fortune and good fortune. He must neither despair in adversity nor rejoice in prosperity. He must neither fear nor hope.

constraint and forced to live in a manner which he judged wrong, he might commit suicide. Death was a blessing, for it removed one from constraint and liberated the soul from the coarser matter of the body; and suicide was thus the ultimate freedom.

We have already read Seneca's account of brave men who chose suicide rather than the forced combats of the arena.[372] Seneca himself, who could no longer endure the demands of the emperor Nero, committed suicide in A.D. 65.

---

423 Seneca the Younger, *Letters* 65.21, 22

I was born for a greater destiny than to be the slave of my body. I consider my body as nothing else but a chain which restricts my freedom. And therefore I set my body as an obstacle to Fortune; on it she may make assaults; but I will not allow any wound to penetrate through the body to the real me. My body is that part of me which can be injured; but within this fragile dwelling-place lives a soul which is free. And never will that flesh drive me to fear, never to a role which is unworthy of a good man. Never will I tell lies for the sake of this silly little body. Whenever it seems the right time, I will end my partnership with the body. Even now, while we are still associated, we will not be partners on equal terms, because the soul will assume all authority. Contempt for one's body is absolute freedom.[373]

Training and Preparation

Seneca was a very wealthy person with many slaves to attend to his needs;[374] he had no experience with the physical suffering which poverty can bring.[375] He advised other wealthy Stoics like himself to create "test situations" and to welcome minor misfortunes in order to prepare themselves for serious hardships. If you trained yourself to endure discomforts calmly, he advised, you would free yourself of your anxiety about them.

Many scholars have noted that this emphasis on self-imposed deprivation is peculiarly Senecan. Other Stoic authors rarely mention this type of "testing," but Seneca stresses again and again its benefits. Although some scholars have suggested that Seneca was neurotically anxious about anxiety itself, we can nonetheless understand how a wealthy and talented man living close to the court of a fickle and cruel emperor might well worry about a sudden change in fortune.[376]

---

[372] See selection 345.

[373] Compare Seneca's comments in selection 99.

[374] For Seneca's advice on the humane treatment of slaves, see selection 198.

[375] Seneca did, however, experience the physical afflictions of illness; on Seneca's asthma, see selection 99.

[376] Seneca had been sent into exile by the emperor Claudius, recalled to serve as tutor to the young Nero, appointed as advisor when Nero became emperor in A.D. 54, and then was forced to suicide by Nero in A.D. 65.

424   Seneca the Younger, *Letters* 18.1, 3, 5, 6

This is the month of December, when the whole city is aglow with excitement.[377] License has been given for intemperate behavior by the general public. Everywhere you can hear the sound of elaborate preparations, as if there were some difference between the Saturnalia and regular business days. The distinction is fading. I think that man was quite right who said, "December used to be a month; now it's a whole year."[378] . . . But perhaps it is on these days in particular that we should force the soul to abstain from pleasures when the whole crowd is wallowing in them. For this is the most definite proof of one's strength of mind: neither to approach nor to be drawn toward pleasant pastimes which lure you into self-indulgence. . . . The topic of testing the strength of one's mind is so satisfying that I will offer you instructions from the teaching of great men. For example, allow yourself a certain number of days on which you will be content with small portions of very plain food and with ill-fitting, coarse clothing. And then say to yourself, "Is this what I was so worried about?" The soul should use times of security to prepare itself for harsh circumstances. It should fortify itself, when enjoying the blessings of Fortune, against the blows of Fortune. A soldier practices maneuvers during peacetime and constructs defensive ramparts, although no enemy is near, and wearies himself with nonessential exertion so that he can be ready for necessary exertion. If you don't want someone to panic in a crisis, you must train him before the crisis. And people who simulate poverty every month and come close to real need are following the same plan as the soldier, so that they will never panic at what they have often learned to deal with.[379]

Self-Discipline and Steadfastness

425   Seneca the Younger, *An Essay about Providence*
                                                             2.1–4; 4.1, 3, 6, 11–13

You may ask, "Why is it that misfortunes often befall good men?"

Learn this: nothing that is truly evil can happen to a good man. Opposites do not mix. Just as the flood of freshwater streams, rain falling from heaven, and mineral springs does not alter the salty taste of the sea, or even dilute it, so, too, the onslaught of misfortunes does not affect the mind of the brave man. He remains firm, and, whatever happens, he adapts it to his own advantage, for he is more powerful than all external events. I am not saying that he is insensible to these events, but he prevails over them and remains serene and unruffled as he rises up to meet every assault. He regards every misfortune as a training exercise. . . . We see that athletes, whose concern is physical strength, have practice sessions with very brawny men and demand that their sparring partners use all their strength against them. They endure cuts and beatings, and if they can't find one individual who is an equal match, they engage several men at

---

[377] On the Saturnalia, see selection 376.

[378] The Saturnalia, like Christmas, was originally a one-day festival, but the merriment and parties gradually spread over all of December. Seneca thinks that the self-indulgence allowed in December is now allowed all year long.

[379] See selections 265 and 268 on training and discipline in the Roman army.

the same time. Physical strength withers away if it has no opponent. Its extent and its potential can be seen only when it displays its capabilities in a test of endurance. You should realize that good men must follow a similar plan. They should not shrink from hardships or difficulties, or complain about fate. They should welcome whatever happens and turn it to their own advantage. It is not what you endure, but how you endure it that is important. . . .

Even common and vulgar personalities can enjoy prosperity, but it is the special characteristic of the great man to prevail over the disasters and terrors of mortal life. . . . I would say this to a good man who has never had the opportunity which adverse Fortune provides to display the strength of one's mind: "I consider you unfortunate because you have never been unfortunate. You have passed through life without an adversary. No one will ever know your potential, not even you." To gain self-knowledge, you must undergo testing. . . . Do not, therefore, I implore you, be anxious about the things which the immortal gods apply to our minds like spurs. Disaster provides an opportunity for *virtus*. . . . And, in dealing with good men, the gods follow the same plan that teachers follow in dealing with their students: they demand more work from those in whom they have the most confidence and hope. . . . Why are you surprised if God tests noble spirits harshly? The demonstration of one's *virtus* is never an easy thing. Fortune beats and lashes us, but we should patiently endure. This is not cruelty, but a contest, and the more often we enter, the stronger we will be. . . . By enduring misfortunes, the mind acquires the ability to scorn the power of evil Fortune.

His ego nec metas rerum nec tempora pono:
imperium sine fine dedi.

For the achievements of these people I fix neither spatial boundaries
nor temporal limits: I have given them empire without end.

VERGIL, *Aeneid* I.278, 279

We are all, so far as we inherit the civilization of Europe, still citizens
of the Roman Empire, and time has not yet proved Virgil wrong when
he wrote *nec tempora pono: imperium sine fine dedi.*

T. S. ELIOT, *Virgil and the Christian World*

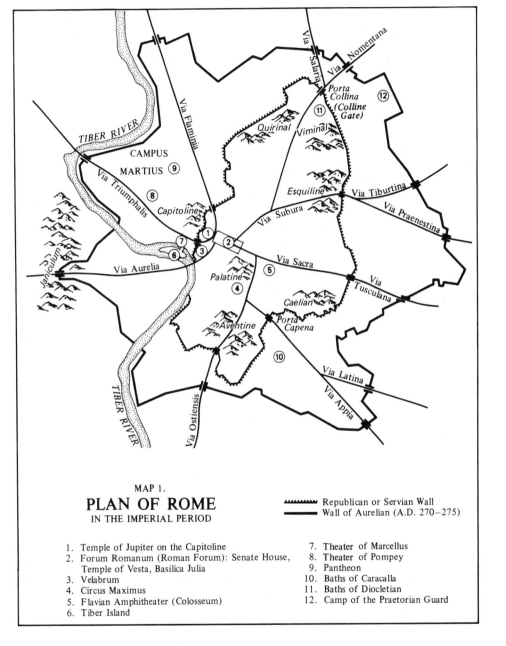

MAP 1.

PLAN OF ROME
IN THE IMPERIAL PERIOD

━━━━━ Republican or Servian Wall
━━━━━ Wall of Aurelian (A.D. 270–275)

1. Temple of Jupiter on the Capitoline
2. Forum Romanum (Roman Forum): Senate House,
   Temple of Vesta, Basilica Julia
3. Velabrum
4. Circus Maximus
5. Flavian Amphitheater (Colosseum)
6. Tiber Island
7. Theater of Marcellus
8. Theater of Pompey
9. Pantheon
10. Baths of Caracalla
11. Baths of Diocletian
12. Camp of the Praetorian Guard

439

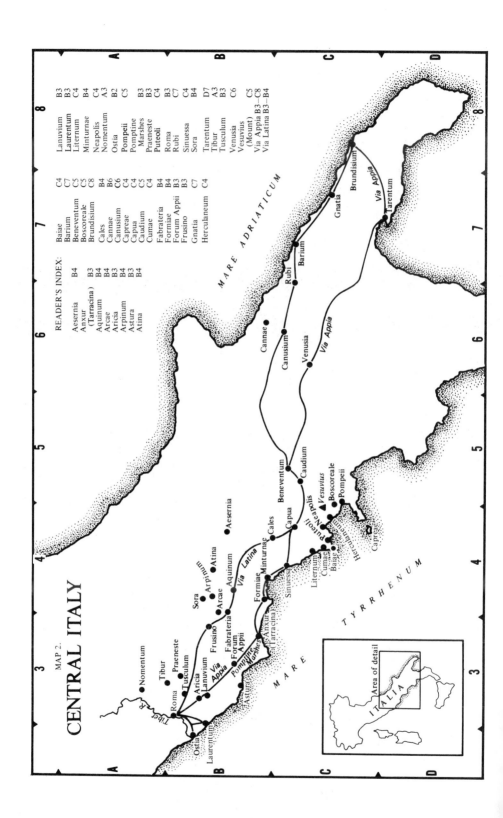

MAP 2.

CENTRAL ITALY

READER'S INDEX:

Aesernia	B4	Baiae	C4
Anxur		Barium	C7
(Tarracina)	B3	Beneventum	C5
Aquinum	B4	Boscoreale	C5
Arcae	B4	Brundisium	C8
Aricia	B3	Cales	B4
Arpinum	B4	Cannae	B6
Astura	B3	Canusium	C6
Atina	B4	Capreae	C4
		Capua	C4
		Caudium	C5
		Cumae	C4
		Fabrateria	B4
		Formiae	B4
		Forum Appii	B3
		Frusino	B3
		Gnatia	C7
		Herculaneum	C4

Lanuvium	B3	Venusia	C6
Laurentum	B3	Vesuvius	C5
Liternum	C4	(Mount)	
Minturnae	B4	Via Appia B3—C8	
Neapolis	C4	Via Latina B3—B4	
Nomentum	A3		
Ostia	B2		
Pompeii	C5		
Pomptine			
Marshes	B3		
Praeneste	B3		
Puteoli	C4		
Roma	B3		
Rubi	C7		
Sinuessa	C4		
Sora	B4		
Tarentum	D7		
Tibur	A3		
Tusculum	B3		

MAP 3.

ITALY AND SICILY

Comum

Mediolanum •   • Brixia   Patavium

Padus (Po) River

Ravenna

Luca   Ariminum

Florentia

Pisae   *Arno R.*

MARE ADRIATICUM

Ancona

ETRURIA

CORSICA

Clanius

Tiber   *UMBRIA*   *River*

PICENUM   *SAMNIUM*

SABINI

Roma

Ostia   *LATIUM*

Beneventum

Cannae   *APULIA*

CAMPANIA

Neapolis

Pompeii

Brundisium

Tarentum   *CALABRIA*

LUCANIA

SARDINIA

MARE   TYRRHENUM

BRUTTIUM

Messana

Rhegium

Tauromenium

Lilybaeum   Halicyae   Imachara   ▲ *Aetna*

SICILIA   Centuripa

Enna

Murgantia

Mutyca   Syracuse

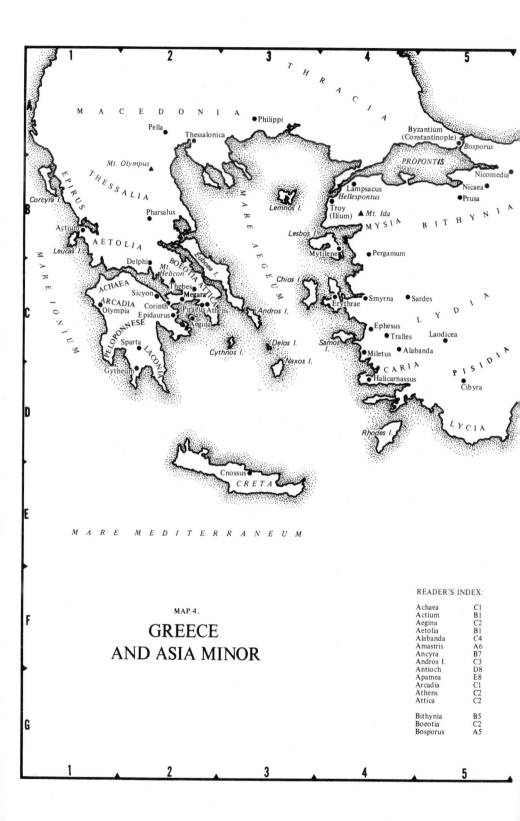

MAP 4.

GREECE
AND ASIA MINOR

READER'S INDEX:

Achaea	C1
Actium	B1
Aegina	C2
Aetolia	B1
Alabanda	C4
Amastris	A6
Ancyra	B7
Andros I.	C3
Antioch	D8
Apamea	E8
Arcadia	C1
Athens	C2
Attica	C2
Bithynia	B5
Boeotia	C2
Bosporus	A5

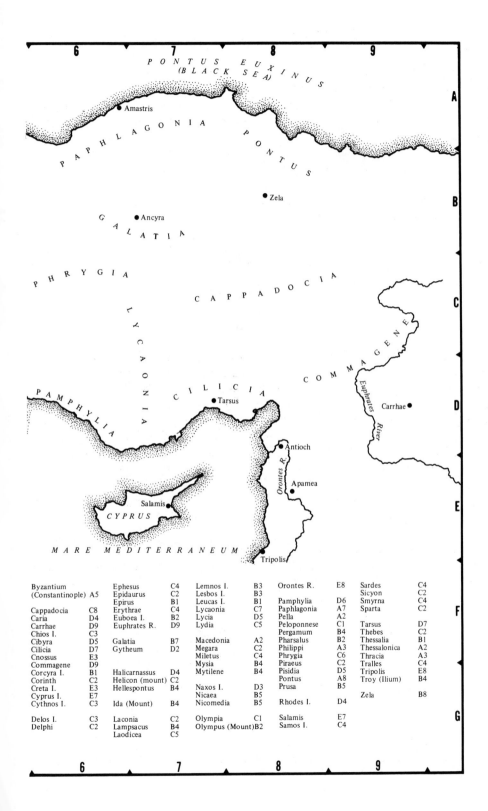

P O N T U S   E U X I N U S
(B L A C K   S E A)

A

● Amastris

P A P H L A G O N I A

P O N T U S

● Zela

B

G
A
L
A
T
I
A
● Ancyra

P H R Y G I A

C A P P A D O C I A

C

L
Y
C
A
O
N
I
A

C O M M A G E N E

P A M P H Y L I A

C I L I C I A

● Tarsus

Euphrates River

Carrhae ●

D

● Antioch

Orontes R.

Apamea ●

Salamis ●

C Y P R U S

E

M A R E   M E D I T E R R A N E U M

Tripolis

Byzantium		Ephesus	C4	Lemnos I.	B3	Orontes R.	E8	Sardes	C4
(Constantinople)	A5	Epidaurus	C2	Lesbos I.	B3			Sicyon	C2
		Epirus	B1	Leucas I.	B1	Pamphylia	D6	Smyrna	C4
Cappadocia	C8	Erythrae	C4	Lycaonia	C7	Paphlagonia	A7	Sparta	C2
Caria	D4	Euboea I.	B2	Lycia	D5	Pella	A2		
Carrhae	D9	Euphrates R.	D9	Lydia	C5	Peloponnese	C1	Tarsus	D7
Chios I.	C3					Pergamum	B4	Thebes	C2
Cibyra	D5	Galatia	B7	Macedonia	A2	Pharsalus	B2	Thessalia	B1
Cilicia	D7	Gytheum	D2	Megara	C2	Philippi	A3	Thessalonica	A2
Cnossus	E3			Miletus	C4	Phrygia	C6	Thracia	A3
Commagene	D9			Mysia	B4	Piraeus	C2	Tralles	C4
Corcyra I.	B1	Halicarnassus	D4	Mytilene	B4	Pisidia	D5	Tripolis	E8
Corinth	C2	Helicon (mount)	C2			Pontus	A8	Troy (Ilium)	B4
Creta I.	E3	Hellespontus	B4	Naxos I.	D3	Prusa	B5		
Cyprus I.	E7			Nicaea	B5			Zela	B8
Cythnos I.	C3	Ida (Mount)	B4	Nicomedia	B5	Rhodes I.	D4		
						Salamis	E7		
Delos I.	C3	Laconia	C2	Olympia	C1	Samos I.	C4		
Delphi	C2	Lampsacus	B4	Olympus (Mount)	B2				
		Laodicea	C5						

F

G

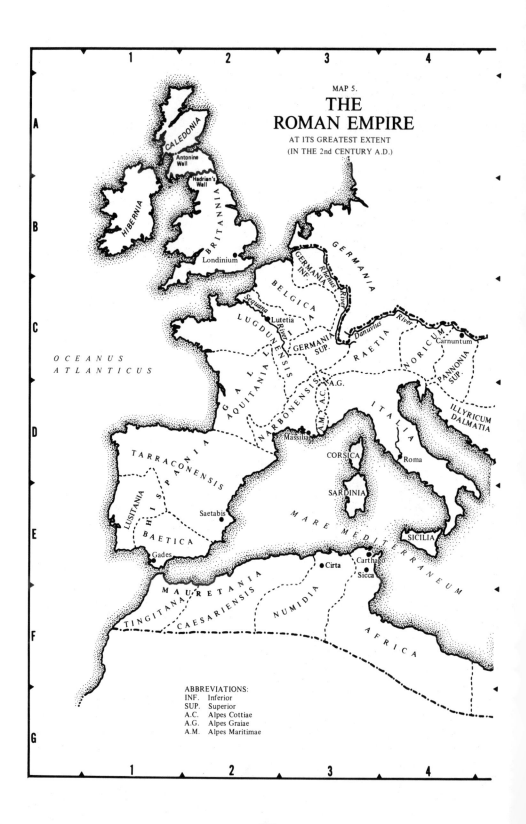

MAP 5.

THE
ROMAN EMPIRE
AT ITS GREATEST EXTENT
(IN THE 2nd CENTURY A.D.)

CALEDONIA

Antonine
Wall

Hadrian's
Wall

HIBERNIA

BRITANNIA

Londinium

GERMANIA

GERMANIA
INF.

Rhenus River

BELGICA

LUGDUNENSIS

Sequana River

Lutetia

GERMANIA
SUP.

RAETIA

Danuvius River

NORICUM

Carnuntum

PANNONIA
SUP.

OCEANUS
ATLANTICUS

GALLIA

AQUITANIA

NARBONENSIS

A.M.
A.C.
A.G.

ITALIA

ILLYRICUM
DALMATIA

Massilia

CORSICA

Roma

TARRACONENSIS

HISPANIA

LUSITANIA

Saetabis

SARDINIA

BAETICA

Gades

MARE   MEDITERRANEUM

SICILIA

Cirta

Carthago

Sicca

MAURETANIA

TINGITANA

CAESARIENSIS

NUMIDIA

AFRICA

ABBREVIATIONS:
INF.   Inferior
SUP.   Superior
A.C.   Alpes Cottiae
A.G.   Alpes Graiae
A.M.   Alpes Maritimae

444

READER'S INDEX:

	Britannia	B2	Gades	E1	Lutetia	C2
			Galatia	E7	Lycia	E6
Achaea	E5	Caesariensis		Gallia	C2		
Aegyptus	F6	(Mauretania)	F2	Germania	B3	Macedonia	D5
Africa	F3	Caledonia	A1	Germania		Massilia	D3
Alexandria	F6	Cappadocia	E7	Inferior	B3	Mauretania	F2
Antioch	E7	Carnuntum	C4	Germania		Mesopotamia	E7
Antonine Wall	A2	Carrhae	E7	Superior	C3	Moesia	D5
Aquitania		Carthago	E3				
(Gallia)	D2	Cilicia	E7	Hadrian's Wall	A2	Narbonensis	
Arabia	F7	Cirta	E3	Hibernia	B1	(Gallia)	D3
Armenia	E8	Corsica	D3	Hispania	E1	Nile R.	G6
Asia	E6	Creta	E5	Illyricum		Noricum	C4
Assyria	E8	Cyprus	F6	Dalmatia	D4	Numidia	F3
Athens	E5	Cyrenaica		Italia	D4		
		(Libya)	F5			Oxyrhynchus	F6
Babylon	F8			Jerusalem	F7		
Babylonia	F8	Dacia	C5			Palestina	F7
Baetica		Damascus	F7	Londinium	B2	Pamphylia	E6
(Hispania)	E1	Danuvius R.	C4	Lugdunensis		Pannonia	
Belgica				(Gallia)	C2	Inferior	C5
(Gallia)	C3	Epirus	E5	Lusitania		Pannonia	
Bithynia et		Euphrates R.	E7	(Hispania)	E1	Superior	C4
Pontus	D6					Parthia	E8

Philadelphia	F6
Raetia	C3
Rhenus R.	B3
Roma	D4
Saetabis	E2
Sardinia	E3
Sicca	E3
Sicilia	E4
Sequana R.	C2
Syene	G7
Syria	E7
Tarraconensis	
(Hispania)	D1
Tebtunis	F6
Thebes	G6
Thracia	D5
Tigris R.	E8
Tingitana	
(Mauretania)	F1
Tomis	D6
Tyre	F7

Appendix I: Sources

Information about the ancient Roman world is found in a variety of sources.

ANCIENT AUTHORS

The works of authors who lived in the ancient Roman period were copied and recopied through the centuries and have been preserved for us mainly in the form of copies produced during the medieval period. Although the author himself wrote on papyrus or waxed tablets, our earliest extant copies, which may postdate the author by 1000 years, were made on parchment. These literary sources include history books, speeches, poems, plays, practical manuals, law books, biographies, treatises, and personal letters. The authors were well educated; many were very wealthy; their opinions therefore frequently reflect the attitudes of the upper class.

Below is a list of ancient authors whose work appears in this book. The name by which the author is commonly known today in the English-speaking world is printed in upper-case letters. Unless it is specified that the author wrote in Greek, he wrote in Latin.

APICIUS is the name of a proverbial gourmand who lived in the early imperial period. The cookbook which is ascribed to him was probably written at a later time.
Cookbook = De Re Coquinaria

APPIAN, a historian, was born in Alexandria, Egypt, in the early second century A.D., but lived much of his life in Rome. He wrote, in Greek, a twenty-four-volume history of Rome, only parts of which are now extant.
The Civil Wars = Bella Civilia

Lucius AP(P)ULEIUS was born about A.D. 124 in Madauros, Numidia (province in North Africa); the date of his death is unknown. He was educated in Carthage and Athens and traveled extensively. After returning to Africa, he enjoyed renown as a philosopher and rhetorician. His best-known extant work is *The Golden Ass,* a narrative about a man named Lucius who assumed the body of a donkey or ass (although retaining his human intelligence) when he used a magic ointment. He was finally returned from bestial to human form by the intervention of the goddess Isis.
The Golden Ass = Metamorphoses

AQUILIUS was a Latin writer of comedy who lived in the second century B.C. Only fragments of his work remain.
Scaenicorum Romanorum Fragmenta, ed. O. Ribbeck

ARETAEUS of Cappadocia (province in Asia Minor) was a medical writer who lived in the second century A.D. and wrote in Greek.
Medical Writings = Medici Libri

Aelius ARISTIDES was a Greek rhetorician who lived from about A.D. 117 to about A.D. 189. He traveled and lectured in Asia Minor, Egypt, and Italy. Among his fifty-five extant speeches, written in Greek, is one praising Rome.
In Praise of Rome = Romes Encomium

Aurelius Augustinus (AUGUSTINE) was born in Thagaste, Numidia (province in

446

North Africa), in A.D. 354; he died in 430. He studied rhetoric at Carthage and, in 383, traveled to Rome. In 384, he was appointed professor of rhetoric at Milan. While in Milan, Augustine was converted to Christianity and was baptized in 387. In 388, he returned to Numidia; in 391, he was ordained as priest; and in 395, he became bishop of Hippo. He died in 430, when Vandals besieged that city. He was a prolific writer, and many of his works are extant.

City of God = De Civitate Dei

MARCUS AURELIUS, who was emperor A.D. 161 to 180, was born in Rome in A.D. 121. While still a boy, he attracted the attention of Hadrian (emperor 117–138), who retained for him the best teachers of rhetoric, law, and philosophy. Marcus Aurelius was the adopted son, and also the son-in-law, of Antoninus Pius (emperor 138–161). Aurelius's reign as emperor was troubled by incursions on the eastern and northeastern frontiers of the Empire, and much of his time was occupied by military considerations.

Aurelius was devoted to Stoic philosophy. Extant is a personally reflective philosophic work, entitled *Meditations,* which he wrote, in Greek, during his military campaigns. We also possess a collection of correspondence, in Latin, between Aurelius and his former teacher, Fronto.

Fronto's Letters = M. Cornelius Fronto: Epistulae ad M. Aurelium

Marcus Porcius CATO was born in Tusculum, Italy, in 234 B.C.; he died in 149 B.C. He had a distinguished military and political career and was *quaestor* in 204 B.C., *plebeian aedile* in 199 B.C., praetor in 198 B.C., *consul* in 195 B.C., and *censor* in 184 B.C. He was a vigorous opponent of the introduction to Rome of Greek culture, learning, and luxury, which he believed would weaken the social stability of the Roman state. He was idealized by later generations as a man of uncompromising morality, a stern conservator of traditional Roman virtues. Although he was the author of several prose works, only *On Agriculture,* a treatise on how to run a profitable farming operation, is now extant.

On Agriculture = De Agri Cultura

Gaius Valerius CATULLUS, one of Rome's best-known and best-loved poets, was born in Verona, Italy, about 84 B.C.; he died about 54 B.C. His family was wealthy, and he was well educated. As a young man, he settled in Rome and became a member of the fashionably elegant set. He was infatuated with a woman whom he calls Lesbia in his poems, but who may have been Clodia, a woman denounced by Cicero as a notorious seducer of fine young men. Extant are 113 of Catullus's poems; they reveal a wide range of topics, styles, tones, and meters. Catullus was equally comfortable with and skillful at writing erotic or satiric lyrics, witty or abusive epigrams, polished hymns and learned epyllia ("little epics").

Poems = Carmina

Marcus Tullius CICERO was born in Arpinum, Italy, in 106 B.C., to a wealthy equestrian family; he died in 43 B.C. He was educated in Rome, and as a young man he soon gained an impressive reputation as a persuasive orator and a successful pleader of court cases. In 76 B.C., he was elected to the office of *quaestor,* and he spent his term as *quaestor* (75 B.C.) in Sicily on the staff of the governor. In 70 B.C., he successfully prosecuted Verres, an unscrupulous governor of Sicily (73–71 B.C.), on behalf of the Sicilians; Cicero's victory in this case established him as the leading advocate in Rome. He was *curule aedile* in 69 B.C., *praetor* in 66 B.C., and *consul* in 63 B.C. During his consulship, Cicero discovered and frustrated a conspiracy organized by Catiline to subvert the state, and he implemented the Senate's decision to execute the conspirators. In 59 B.C., Cicero was invited but declined to join a political alliance formed by Caesar, Pompey, and Crassus (later called the First Triumvirate). In 58 B.C., Cicero's political enemies accused him of putting to death Roman citizens because he had executed the Catilinarian conspirators, and they obtained a sentence of banishment. Cicero lived in Greece until his recall from banishment in 57 B.C. In 51 B.C., he went, quite reluctantly, to Cilicia (province in Asia Minor) as governor. He returned from Cilicia to Rome in early 49 B.C., just as the civil war between Caesar and Pompey erupted. After hesitating for a long time about which side to support, he sailed to Greece to join Pompey. After the battle of Pharsalus in 48 B.C., in which the forces of Caesar defeated those of Pompey, Caesar pardoned Cicero; but Cicero retired from public life until after the assassination of Caesar in 44 B.C. Then he vehemently denounced Caesar's successor, Marcus Antonius (Mark Antony), in a series of speeches called *Philippics*. When the Second Triumvirate published its proscription lists, Cicero's name appeared among those of the proscribed. He tried to escape from Italy, but was captured at Formiae and beheaded (43 B.C.). His head and hands were put on display in the Roman Forum by his enemies.

Cicero had a son, Marcus, and a daughter, Tullia, by his wife Terentia, whom he divorced after thirty years of marriage. He had a brief second marriage to a wealthy young woman whose guardian he was.

Cicero was a prolific writer. Extant are some of his forensic and political orations, treatises on rhetoric and on political and ethical philosophy, and about 800 letters to various people. He has a well-deserved reputation as a master of Latin prose style.

About the Orator = De Oratore
About the Republic = De Re Publica
A Book about Constitutions = De Legibus
Correspondence with Family and Friends = Epistulae ad Familiares
An Essay about Duties = De Officiis
An Essay about Friendship = De Amicitia
An Essay on Old Age = De Senectute
Letters to Atticus = Epistulae ad Atticum
Letters to His Brother Quintus = Epistulae ad Quintum Fratrem
The Prosecution of Verres = Actiones in Verrem
Speech in Defense of Caelius = Pro Caelio
Speech in Defense of Flaccus = Pro Flacco
Speech in Defense of Fonteius = Pro Fonteio
Speech in Defense of Milo = Pro Milone
Speech in Defense of Rabirius Postumus = Pro Rabirio Postumo
Speech in Defense of Sestius = Pro Sestio

Quintus Tullius CICERO, the younger brother of Marcus, was born in Arpinum about 102 B.C. He was *aedile* in 65 B.C., *praetor* in 62 B.C., and then spent three years in the province of Asia as *propraetor*. He was married for a time to Pomponia, sister of Pomponius Atticus, Marcus Cicero's good friend. Quintus was, like his brother, proscribed by the Second Triumvirate and executed in 43 B.C. He is considered by many scholars to be the author of a treatise on campaigning for the consulship.

Some Thoughts about Political Campaigns = Commentariolum Petitionis

Lucius Junius Moderatus COLUMELLA lived in the first century A.D.; he was a native of Gades (modern Cádiz), Spain. His extant work is a treatise on farming.

On Agriculture = De Re Rustica

DIO CASSIUS, a historian, was born about A.D. 155 in Nicaea, Bithynia (province in Asia Minor). He held public offices in Rome under the emperors Commodus (A.D. 180–192), Caracalla (211–217), and Alexander Severus (222–235), but retired to Nicaea where he died. He wrote, in Greek, an eighty-volume history of Rome from its beginning to A.D. 229; only volumes 36–60 and 79 (68 B.C.–A.D. 46) are extant, although we have epitomes, or summaries, of other volumes by Byzantine writers such as Zonaras.

Roman History = Historiae Romanae

DIODORUS SICULUS, a historian, was a native of Sicily who lived in the first century B.C. He wrote, in Greek, a "world history" from mythical times to Caesar's Gallic War. Of the original forty volumes, only fifteen are fully extant.

History of the World = Bibliotheca Historika

DIONYSIUS of Halicarnassus (a city in Asia Minor) was a Greek rhetorician and historian who lived and taught in Rome about 30 B.C. to his death about 8 B.C. He wrote treatises on rhetoric and literary criticism. He also wrote, in Greek, a history of Rome from its legendary beginnings down to the First Punic War (264–241 B.C.). Only the first half of this history is now extant.

Roman Antiquities = Antiquitates Romanae

EPICTETUS, a philosopher, lived from about A.D. 55 to about 135. He was a Phrygian by birth, brought to Rome as a slave. He was later manumitted and taught Stoic philosophy in Rome until A.D. 89, when he was expelled from the city in a general expulsion of philosophers ordered by the emperor Domitian. He then taught in Epirus, Greece, until his death. One of his students, the Greek historian Arrian, collected and published Epictetus's lectures.

Lectures Collected by Arrian = Arrianus: Epicteti Dissertationes

EUSEBIUS, a historian, was born in Palestine about A.D. 264; he was appointed bishop of Caesarea about 311; he died about 340. Among his extant works is *Ecclesiastical History,* an account, in Greek, of the rise of the Christian church.

Ecclesiastical History = Historia Ecclesiastica

Sextus Julius FRONTINUS was born about A.D. 30 and died about 104. He was *praetor urbanus* in A.D. 70, *consul suffectus* in 73, governor of Britain 74–78, and *curator aquarum* (commissioner of the water supply for Rome) in 97. His extant writings are *Strategemata,* a treatise on military science, and *The Aqueducts of Rome,* a treatise about the water supply of Rome.

The Aqueducts of Rome = De Aquis Urbis Romae

Marcus Cornelius FRONTO, an orator and rhetorician, was born in Cirta, Numidia (province in North Africa), about A.D. 100, but spent much of his life in Rome; he died about A.D. 166. In 143 he was *consul suffectus.* Earlier he had been tutor to Marcus Aurelius, the future emperor. Their extant correspondence reveals a deep affection between the two men.

Elements of History = Principia Historiae

Fronto's Letters = M. Cornelius Fronto: Epistulae ad M. Aurelium

GAIUS lived in the second century A.D. Although he was one of Rome's most renowned jurists, little is known about him, not even his *nomen* (family name). Extant is a treatise on Roman law and jurisprudence.

Institutes = Institutiones

Aulus GELLIUS was born about A.D. 123; he lived most of his life in Rome, where he practiced law, and died about A.D. 165. His extant work is *Attic Nights,* which he composed during the winter nights on an extended visit to Attica, Greece. This twenty-volume work contains essays by Gellius on curious points of grammar, language, history, criticism, and other topics. For illustration Gellius uses passages from a large number of Greek and Roman writers; he thus preserves for us at least extracts of many works which are otherwise lost.

Attic Nights = Noctes Atticae

Quintus Horatius Flaccus (HORACE), Rome's great lyric poet and satirist, was born in Venusia, Italy, in 65 B.C. and died in 8 B.C. His father was a freedman of modest means, though not poor, who apparently devoted his life to his son's education and advancement. He took Horace to Rome to attend the best schools and to be educated with the sons of senatorial and equestrian families. When Horace was eighteen years old, he went to Athens to further his education. After the assassination of Caesar in 44 B.C., the assassins and their supporters fled to Athens; Horace joined their cause and fought in the Battle of Philippi in 42 B.C., where the republican forces (the assassins) were defeated by the forces of the Second Triumvirate. Horace was pardoned by the triumvirs and returned to Rome, where he worked as a clerk in the quaestor's office. About 39 B.C., his poems attracted the attention of the poet Vergil, who introduced Horace to Maecenas, a statesman, a friend of Augustus, and a wealthy patron of the arts. In time, Maecenas introduced Horace to Augustus, and Horace became a member of an illustrious and powerful circle of poets, patrons, and statesmen.

Horace's earliest poems, the *Epodes,* are sometimes bitter in tone. His later poems, however, the *Satires* and the *Epistles,* are filled with good humor and good sense. The tone is frequently philosophic, as Horace reflects on human manners and conduct. The topics are widely diverse, and the poems thus provide a broad but intimate picture of the Romans of his day. Many scholars consider Horace's *Odes* to be his masterpieces; these are lyric poems on themes such as love, the human condition and the glory of Rome.

Epistles = Epistulae
Epodes = Epodi
Odes = Carmina
Satires = Sermones

Flavius JOSEPHUS, a historian, was born in Jerusalem in A.D. 37; he died about A.D. 100. In 63, he traveled to Rome, became a friend of the emperor Nero's second wife, and apparently formed the opinion that Rome's military might was irresistible. He returned to Jerusalem and at first tried to dissuade his fellow countrymen from opposing Roman rule. When, however, rebellion broke out in A.D. 66 (the "Jewish War"), Josephus was an officer of the Jewish forces; he was captured in 67. After the fall of Jerusalem in 70, he was taken to Rome, where he became a friend of Vespasian (emperor 69–79) and his two sons, Titus (emperor 79–81) and Domitian (emperor 81–96). Josephus was granted Roman citizenship and died in Rome. Among his extant works is an account, in Greek, of the Jewish War or rebellion of A.D. 66–70.

A History of the Jewish War = De Bello Judaico

Decimus Junius Juvenalis (JUVENAL) lived at the end of the first century A.D. and the beginning of the second century. Little is known about his life. Extant are sixteen satires, ranging in length from 130 to 660 lines, in which he rails at the vices and follies of Roman society. The satires are filled with biting invective and relentless moral indignation.

Satires = Saturae

Titus Livius (LIVY) was born in Patavium (modern Padua), Italy, in 59 B.C. and died in A.D. 17. He spent much of his life in Rome and was a member of the elite literary circle patronized by Augustus. He wrote a history of Rome in 142 volumes which extended from the foundation of the city to 9 B.C. Of the original 142 volumes, only 35 are now extant, but abridgments made in later centuries exist for most of the volumes. His patriotically inspired work has been called a prose epic because it glorifies the achievements of the Romans and exalts the rise of Rome to imperial greatness.

A History of Rome = Ab Urbe Condita Libri

LUCIAN, a Greek writer, was born in Samosata, Syria, and lived in the second century A.D. He traveled in Greece and Italy, teaching rhetoric, and once held a position in the Roman administration of Egypt. Extant are eighty literary pieces in Greek, many written in dialogue form, on a variety of topics.

The Baths = Hippias

Titus LUCRETIUS Carus, a poet, was born about 99 B.C. and died about 55 B.C.; little is known of his life. Extant is one work, *About the Nature of the Universe,* a didactic poem which provides an exposition of the philosophy of Epicurus, a Greek philosopher of the late fourth and early third centuries B.C. Much of the poem is devoted to the Epicurean theory that the universe is material and is composed of tiny imperishable particles (atoms). Epicurus and Lucretius hoped to abolish fears of death and of an afterlife by persuading men that the human soul was material and mortal. Lucretius was a keen observer, and his poetry is admired for the vivid imagery drawn from the natural world.

About the Nature of the Universe = De Rerum Natura

Ambrosius Theodosius MACROBIUS, a grammarian, lived around A.D. 400; he was perhaps African by birth. Among his extant writings is a seven-volume work, *Saturnalia Conversations,* a miscellany of historical, philological, and critical information.

Saturnalia Conversations = Saturnalia

Marcus Valerius Martialis (MARTIAL), a poet, was born in Bilbilis, Spain, about A.D. 40; he traveled to Rome in 64 and lived there until about 100, when he returned to Spain where he died about 104. Extant are fourteen books of epigrams, containing over 1500 poems, many of them satiric, on a wide range of topics. Martial is renowned as a poet of brevity and wit.

Epigrams = Epigrammata

MINUCIUS FELIX lived from the mid-second century to the mid-third century A.D. He was a Christian and perhaps a native of Africa. His extant work, *Octavius,* is an apology, or defense, of Christianity.

Octavius

Publius Ovidius Naso (OVID) was born in Sulmo, Italy, in 43 B.C., of an equestrian family; he died about A.D. 17. He studied law and rhetoric in Rome and Athens and traveled in Asia Minor. He decided, however, to devote himself to poetry rather than law. He lived most of his life in Rome and apparently enjoyed the support of Augustus until A.D. 8, when he was suddenly sentenced by imperial edict to banishment at Tomis, a small town on the Black Sea, far from the cultural refinement of Rome; he lived in Tomis until his death. The reason for his banishment has never been clearly revealed, but he had obviously offended Augustus gravely.

Ovid was a prolific, talented, and sophisticated poet. Extant are amatory poems; *Metamorphoses,* a collection of stories in epic style about changes of shape; a poetical calendar explaining month by month the origins of Roman religious festivals (only the explanations for six months are extant); and poetical letters which he wrote while in Tomis.

The Art of Love = Ars Amatoria

A Book about Facial Cosmetics = Medicamina Faciei

Love Affairs = Amores

A Roman Calendar of Festivals = Fasti

Julius PAULUS lived at the end of the second century A.D. and the beginning of the third century. He was a jurist and teacher, as well as a prolific writer who published about 320 books on laws, constitutions, and jurisprudence. Extracts from the works of Paulus constitute about one-sixth of the *Digest,* a collection of Roman laws compiled by legal scholars under commission by Justinian (emperor A.D. 527–565).

Opinions = Sententiae

PETRONIUS lived in the first century A.D. He was a member of the emperor Nero's intimate circle of self-indulgent friends and received the title *elegantiae arbiter* ("judge of taste," or "director of imperial pleasures"). In A.D. 66, he was accused of treason and committed suicide. He wrote a comic picaresque novel, known as the *Satyricon,* only fragments of which survive. One of the lengthy surviving fragments is an episode known as *The Banquet of Trimalchio.*

The Banquet of Trimalchio = Cena Trimalchionis

PHILO lived from about 30 B.C. to about A.D. 45. He was born and lived in Alexandria, Egypt, and was a prominent member of the Jewish community there. In A.D. 39, he traveled to Rome as a delegate of this community to ask the emperor Caligula to exempt the Jews of Alexandria from worshipping the emperor. Several of Philo's works, in Greek, are extant; in some he tries to reconcile Jewish scriptures with the doctrines of Greek philosophy.

The Embassy to Gaius = Legatio ad Gaium

Titus Maccius PLAUTUS, a writer of verse comedy, was born about 254 B.C. in Sarsina, Italy; he died in 184 B.C. Extant are twenty of his comedies, which were based on plots used in Greek New Comedy and which, in turn, influenced later playwrights such as Shakespeare. His plays are among the earliest specimens of Latin literature.

The Pot of Gold = Aulularia

Gaius Plinius Secundus (PLINY THE ELDER) was born in Comum (modern Como), Italy, in A.D. 23; he died in 79. He was educated in Rome, served in the military, had a career as a pleader of court cases, and held a number of provincial procuratorships. He was commander of the Roman fleet stationed at Misenum, on the Bay of Naples, in A.D. 79 when Mount Vesuvius erupted. He died while attempting to rescue people in the eruption area.

Pliny the Elder had an inquisitive mind and a thirst for knowledge; he was an avid reader, an industrious note taker, and a diligent cataloguer. He wrote histories, biographies, and treatises on oratory, grammar, and military science. There remains extant only his *Natural History,* a thirty-seven volume encyclopedia of natural science.

Natural History = Naturalis Historia

Gaius Plinius Caecilius Secundus (PLINY THE YOUNGER), nephew of the above-mentioned Pliny, by whom he was adopted after his father died, was born in Comum (modern Como), Italy, about A.D. 61; he died about 113. He studied in Rome, and, when only eighteen years old, he appeared in court to plead his first case. He became a noted pleader and orator. He had a successful public career and advanced politically under the emperors Domitian, Nerva, and Trajan. He was *consul suffectus* in A.D. 100. In 111, Trajan sent Pliny to the province of Bithynia (in Asia Minor) as imperial legate or governor. Pliny died in the province.

Although Pliny published many of his forensic orations, none is extant today. We have one *Panegyricus,* written for Trajan, and ten books of correspondence. The first nine are addressed to various family members and friends; the tenth book contains correspondence between Pliny and Trajan, mainly about the administration of Bithynia. The letters offer a broad and interesting portrait of the life of the Roman upper class in the early imperial period; they provide a counterbalance to the negative impressions left by the biting invective of Juvenal and the brooding pessimism of Tacitus.

Letters = Epistulae

PLUTARCH, a Greek biographer and philosopher, was born in Chaeronea, Greece, about A.D. 45; he died about 125. He lived for some time in Rome but returned to Chaeronea before his death. He was the author of many philosophical works, most of them now lost. His best-known extant works, in Greek, are his biographies of famous historical figures. Most of the biographies are arranged in pairs—a Greek life and a Roman life—followed by a comparison of the two.

Lives = Vitae

POLYBIUS, a Greek historian, was born in Megalopolis, Greece, about 204 B.C.; he died about 122 B.C. As a young man, he enjoyed a promising political career. After the conquest of Macedonia by Rome in 168 B.C., Polybius was one of 1000 hostages taken to Rome. He lived in Rome for seventeen years and gained the friendship of Scipio Aemilianus, a wealthy senator, respected military figure, and generous literary patron. In 150 B.C. Polybius was allowed to return to Greece. He traveled extensively in the

Mediterranean world to visit places which he described in his historical work. He wrote, in Greek, a forty-volume history, from 220 B.C. to 146 B.C., the year Corinth was destroyed by the Romans. His work recorded the rapid rise of Rome to supremacy in the Mediterranean area. Only the first five volumes are now fully extant; we have fragments of the other volumes.

History of the World = Historiae

Marcus Fabius Quintilianus (QUINTILIAN) was born in Calagurris, Spain, about A.D. 40, but was sent to Rome for his education. He died about 118. He was a pleader of court cases, but is best known as a teacher of rhetoric and oratory. One of his pupils was Pliny the Younger. Quintilian was appointed by the emperor Vespasian to the first state-financed professorship of rhetoric. Extant is a twelve-volume work, entitled *The Elements of Oratory*, which deals with the proper education of an orator.

The Elements of Oratory = Institutiones Oratoriae

Gaius Sallustius Crispus (SALLUST), a historian, was born in Amiternum, Italy, in 86 B.C.; he died about 34 B.C. He was tribune of the plebs in 52 B.C., and a supporter of *popularis* politicians, such as Julius Caesar. In 50 B.C., Sallust was expelled from the Senate by the censors for alleged immorality, but he was reinstated the next year, 49 B.C., when Caesar marched on Rome. In 46 B.C., he was appointed governor of Numidia (province in North Africa) by Caesar and reportedly became a very wealthy man during his term as governor. Extant are two of his historical monographs, *The Catilinarean Conspiracy*, an account of the conspiracy of Catiline in 63 B.C. to subvert the Roman state, and *The Jugurthine War*, an account of the war of the Romans against Jugurtha, king of Numidia (111–106 B.C.).

The Catilinarean Conspiracy = Bellum Catilinae
The Jugurthine War = Bellum Jugurthinum

Marcus Annaeus Seneca (SENECA THE ELDER), a rhetorician, was born in Corduba (modern Córdoba), Spain, about 55 B.C. Although educated in Rome, he later returned to Spain, but then journeyed back to Rome, where he resided until his death about A.D. 40. Extant are portions of two of his books, *Controversiae* and *Suasoriae*, which provide us with examples of topics assigned as classroom exercises by teachers of rhetoric, and with information about public speakers whom Seneca had heard.

Controversiae
Suasoriae

Lucius Annaeus Seneca (SENECA THE YOUNGER), son of the above-mentioned, was born in Corduba (modern Córdoba), Spain, about 4 B.C.; he died in A.D. 65. He was taken to Rome as a child, where he received an education in rhetoric and philosophy. As a young man, Seneca won admiration as a pleader of cases. In A.D. 41, however, he was banished to Corsica by the emperor Claudius for alleged intimacy with Claudius's niece. In A.D. 49, he was recalled to Rome at the prompting of Claudius's fourth wife, Agrippina, and was appointed tutor for Agrippina's son, the future emperor Nero. When Nero acceded to the imperial throne in A.D. 54, Seneca became his chief advisor, but failed to curb the immoderate behavior of the young emperor. In A.D. 62, Seneca tried to retire from the court; in 65 he was accused of complicity in a plot to assassinate Nero and was sentenced to death. Seneca chose suicide rather than the humiliation of a public execution.

Seneca was devoted to Stoic philosophy, and most of his extant writings have ethical and philosophical themes. We have 12 ethical essays or treatises, 124 "moral" letters, 9 verse tragedies, and a scientific work, *Investigations in Natural Science*.

An Essay about Anger = De Ira
An Essay about the Brevity of Life = De Brevitate Vitae
An Essay about Constancy = De Constantia Sapientis
An Essay about Kindness = De Beneficiis

An Essay about Peace of Mind = De Tranquillitate Animi
An Essay about Providence = De Providentia
Investigations in Natural Science = Naturales Quaestiones
Letters = Epistulae

SERVIUS Honoratus was a grammarian and commentator who lived in the fourth century A.D. He is best known for his commentary on the works of the Latin poet Vergil.

On Vergil's Georgics = In Vergilii Carmina Commentarii

SIDONIUS APOLLINARIS was born in Lugdunum (modern Lyons), Gaul, about A.D. 430; he died about 479. He held a number of government offices in Rome, including *praefectus urbi*. In 469 he became bishop of Auvergne. Extant are twenty-four poems and nine books of letters to friends and family which offer valuable information about the fifth century A.D.

Poems = Carmina

SORANUS was a Greek physician born in Ephesus who practiced medicine in Alexandria, Egypt, and then in Rome during the first part of the second century A.D. Extant are several of his medical works, in Greek, including a four-volume work on gynecology.

Gynecology = Gynaecia

AELIUS SPARTIANUS, who lived probably in the fourth century A.D., was one of the authors of the *Historia Augusta,* a collection of the biographies of thirty Roman emperors from Hadrian to Numerian (A.D. 117–284).

Historia Augusta

Publius Papinius STATIUS, a poet, was born about A.D. 45 in Neapolis (modern Naples), where he died about 96. He was the son of a prominent schoolteacher who encouraged his literary interests. He lived in Rome during the reign of Domitian and won many prizes for the recitation of his poetry. Extant are *Thebais,* a twelve-book epic poem recounting the expedition of the Seven against Thebes, and *Silvae,* a five-volume collection of miscellaneous poems.

Silvae
Thebais

STRABO was a Greek geographer and historian who was born in Amasia, Pontus (province in Asia Minor), about 60 B.C. and died there about A.D. 24. He traveled widely and lived some years in Rome. His forty-seven-volume history is lost. Extant is a seventeen-volume geography, in Greek, of the countries in the Roman world.

Geography Book = Geographica

Gaius SUETONIUS Tranquillus was born about A.D. 69 and died about 140. He practiced law in Rome but is best remembered as a biographer. He wrote the biographies of Julius Caesar and the first eleven emperors of Rome, as well as the biographies of well-known teachers. The biographies of the emperors show little interest in historical methodology, but are an entertaining source of gossip and scandal.

A Book about Schoolteachers = De Grammaticis et Rhetoribus
The Lives of the Caesars = De Vita Caesarum

Quintus Aurelius SYMMACHUS was born about A.D. 340 and died about 402. He came from a distinguished senatorial family and won fame as an orator. In A.D. 373, he was appointed proconsul of Africa; in 384, he was prefect of Rome; and in 391, he became *consul.* He was an ardent and eloquent supporter of the state religion at a time when Christianity was gaining dominance. Extant are ten books of letters and fragments of his speeches.

Dispatches to the Emperor = Relationes

Cornelius TACITUS, a historian, was born in north-central Italy, about A.D. 55, and died about 118. In A.D. 77, he married the daughter of Agricola, who was governor of Britain for seven years, beginning in 78. Tacitus advanced politically under Vespasian and Domitian. He was *praetor* in 88 and *consul suffectus* in 97. He was proconsul of Asia, probably 112–113.

Among his extant works are *A Dialogue on Orators*, which is a discussion of the decline of oratory, and a biography of his father-in-law, Agricola. Tacitus is best known for his historical works, *Annals*, in at least sixteen volumes, covering the period from the death of Augustus in A.D. 14 to the death of Nero in 68 (volumes 7–10 and the last part of 16 are missing), and *Histories*, covering the period from the death of Nero to (probably) the death of Domitian in A.D. 96 (only the first four and a half volumes are extant). Tacitus is noted for his epigrammatic style—concise, intense, and pregnant with meaning. As a historian he was particularly interested in human motivation and had penetrating insight into character. He was an unremitting critic of the principate or imperial form of government and a pessimistic commentator on the decline of the Roman character.

Annals = Annales
A Biography of Agricola = De Vita Agricolae
A Dialogue on Orators = Dialogus de Oratoribus
Histories = Historiae

Publius Terentius Afer (TERENCE), a writer of verse comedy, was born at Carthage, in the province of Africa, about 195 B.C. and died about 159 B.C. He arrived in Rome as a slave and was owned by a Roman senator who educated and finally manumitted him. Terence's literary talents earned him the support of Scipio Aemilianus, statesman, military figure, and wealthy patron of the arts. Terence produced his first play for the Roman stage in 166 B.C. His plays were adaptations of Greek New Comedies. He spent his last years in Greece, where he died. Only six of his plays are extant.

The Mother-in-law = Hecyra

Quintus Septimius Florens Tertullianus (TERTULLIAN) was born in the province of Africa about A.D. 160. He was trained as a lawyer, spent most of his life in Carthage, and died about 230. He was converted to Christianity and composed many works about the history and character of the church. Among Tertullian's extant works is *Apology*, in which he refutes charges made against the Christians.

Apology = Apologeticum

Albius TIBULLUS, a poet, was born about 48 B.C. and died about 19 B.C. Little is known of his life. His family was of equestrian rank, and he spent most of his life in Rome or on his ancestral estate near Rome. He wrote elegiac poems; two themes dominate: love and an idyllic dream of the simplicity of rural life.

Elegies = Carmina

Domitius Ulpianus (ULPIAN), a jurist, was born in Tyre at the end of the second century A.D. He became chief advisor for Alexander Severus (emperor A.D. 222–235). He was killed in A.D. 228 by mutinous soldiers. He was a voluminous writer and published about 280 books on laws, legislation, and constitutions. He became the main source for the legal scholars who, under commission by Justinian (emperor A.D. 527–565), compiled the *Digest*, a collection of Roman laws. One-third of the whole collection is taken from Ulpian's work.

Rules = Regulae

VALERIUS MAXIMUS lived during the reign of the emperor Tiberius (A.D. 14–37). His extant work, *Memorable Deeds and Words*, is a compilation of historical anecdotes intended to illustrate aspects of human character. The work has a strong moral and philosophical tone.

Memorable Deeds and Words = Facta et Dicta Memorabilia

Marcus Terentius VARRO was born in Reate, Italy, in 116 B.C. and died in 27 B.C. He studied rhetoric and philosophy in both Rome and Athens. In his political career he advanced to the rank of *praetor*. In the Civil War, he supported Pompey but was later pardoned by Caesar and appointed to superintend the public library at Rome. Varro is said to have produced 490 books; only two now survive, a book about farming and a treatise on Latin grammar and etymology, which is extant only in part.

A Book about the Latin Language = De Lingua Latina

On Agriculture = De Re Rustica

Flavius Renatus VEGETIUS, who lived in the last part of the fourth century A.D., was author of a treatise on the Roman military system.

A Book about Military Affairs = De Re Militari

Gaius VELLEIUS PATERCULUS, a historian, was born in Campania, Italy, about 19 B.C. and died later than A.D. 30. During the reign of Augustus, Velleius did military service in Germany under the future emperor, Tiberius. He was *quaestor* in A.D. 6 and *praetor* in 15. His extant work recounts the history of Rome from the legendary period down to A.D. 30. Velleius was an admirer of Tiberius, and his favorable account of Tiberius's reign provides a valuable corrective to the very negative accounts of Tacitus and Suetonius.

A History of Rome = Historiae Romanae

Publius Vergilius Maro (VERGIL), a poet, was born near Mantua, in northern Italy, in 70 B.C.; he died in 19 B.C. He was educated at Cremona, Mediolanum (modern Milan), and Rome. By 37 B.C. he had published ten *Eclogues* (or *Bucolics*), poems with idyllic or pastoral themes. During this time, he gained the attention and then patronage of Maecenas, a chief advisor of Octavian (later called Augustus). By about 30 B.C., Vergil had published four *Georgics*, didactic poems about the life and tasks of a farmer. He spent the last ten years of his life in or near Naples, working on the *Aeneid,* an epic poem about the journey to Italy of Aeneas, a Trojan hero who survived the fall of Troy, traveled to Italy, and established a race of people who were destined to found Rome. Vergil wanted it burned when he died, but the emperor Augustus disregarded his will and had the poem published. Although the *Aeneid* is a poem about the achievements of people who lived long before the time of Vergil, the prevailing theme is the greatness of Rome, and the prevailing mood is an optimism in the new era inaugurated by Augustus. Vergil is considered Rome's greatest epic poet, and he is certainly one of the greatest epic poets of world literature.

Aeneid = Aeneis

VITRUVIUS Pollio lived in the first century B.C. He wrote a ten-volume treatise on architecture and engineering which he dedicated to Augustus.

On Architecture = De Architectura

ZONARAS, a historian, lived in Constantinople in the late eleventh and early twelfth centuries A.D. He wrote, in Greek, a history of the world down to A.D. 1118. His work preserves for us epitomes or summaries of some of the lost volumes of Dio Cassius.

INSCRIPTIONS

Inscriptions (Latin *in + scriptum* = "written on") are words carved into or written on durable materials such as stone and metal. The study of inscriptions is called epigraphy (Greek *epi + graphein* = "to write on"). Many thousands of inscriptions from the ancient Roman period have been discovered, in all parts of the Roman Empire. These inscriptions preserve laws, edicts, government records, and commemorative documents, and serve as a valuable source of information about Roman administration both in Italy and in the provinces. Inscriptions also preserve information of a more private nature in epitaphs and graffiti. Graffiti, in particular, provide us with subjective responses to a variety of events and situations. The following collections of inscriptions have been consulted.

CIL = Corpus Inscriptionum Latinarum
ILS = Inscriptiones Latinae Selectae, ed. H. Dessau
ROL = Remains of Old Latin, ed. E. H. Warmington, Loeb Classical Library
SEG = Supplementum Epigraphicum Graecum

PAPYRI

Papyrus was a writing material produced in Egypt from the papyrus plant and widely used throughout the Roman world. Because of the perishable nature of the material, very few papyrus documents have survived, except in the dry areas of Egypt. There, large quantities of papyri have been discovered, often during the excavation of ancient garbage dumps, at the sites of ancient towns such as Oxyrhynchus, Tebtunis, and Karanis. Papyri were used for administrative and business records, for contracts and legal documents, and for personal letters and memoranda. They record the many and various transactions and concerns of everyday life, and thus provide one of the best sources of information about the activities and thoughts of the "average man" in a Roman province. Papyrus letters offer an interesting point of comparison, both in content and style, with the more literary letters of upper-class Roman authors such as Cicero, Seneca, and Pliny.

Egypt had been conquered in 332 B.C. by the Macedonians under Alexander the Great and was subsequently ruled by a dynasty of Macedonian kings until it was annexed by the Romans as a Roman province in 30 B.C. Almost all the papyri, therefore, even those composed during the period of Roman domination, are written in Greek.

Papyrology, the study of papyri, also includes the study of waxed tablets.

The following collections of papyri have been consulted:

BGU = Berliner griechische Urkunden (Aegyptische Urkunden aus den Staatlichen Museen Berlin)
P. Bour. = Les Papyrus Bouriant
P. Lond. = Greek Papyri in the British Museum
P. Mich. = Papyri in the University of Michigan Collection
P. Oxy. = The Oxyrhynchus Papyri
P. Tebt. = The Tebtunis Papyri
P. Wisc. = The Wisconsin Papyri
Sammelbuch = Sammelbuch griechischer Urkunden aus Aegypten
Select Papyri, eds. A. S. Hunt and C. C. Edgar, Loeb Classical Library

LEGAL SOURCES

Roman laws have been preserved in the works of ancient authors, in inscriptions, and on papyri. The earliest written code of Roman laws was the Twelve Tables, published about 450 B.C. Other sources of laws were the legislation of popular assemblies, edicts of magistrates, decrees of the Senate, and, in the imperial period, the *constitutiones* or regulations of the emperor. Legal procedure was influenced also by the opinions of jurists. A jurist (Latin *jurisconsultus* or *jurisprudens*) was a man with special learning and experience who was consulted about the interpretation of a law. There are extant today the commentaries of three jurists who lived in the imperial period: the *Institutes* of Gaius (about A.D. 161), the *Opinions* of Paulus (about A.D. 200), and the *Rules* of Ulpian (about A.D. 320–342). Biographies of these men appear in the list of ancient authors above.

In A.D. 438, the *Law Code of Theodosius* (*Codex Theodosianus*) was published. It was a codification ordered by the emperor Theodosius II of all *constitutiones* of the emperors from Constantine on.

About A.D. 540, the emperor Justinian appointed a commission of jurists to publish a complete body of law. These jurists published (1) the *Digest* (a collection of legislation and commentaries by earlier jurists),* (2) the *Justinian Code* (a collection of the imperial *constitutiones*), (3) the *Institutes* (a legal textbook, and (4) the *New Constitutions*. These four legal works are known by the collective title *Corpus Iuris Civilis* (Body of Civil Law) and form the code of Roman law which was inherited by modern Europe.

The following collections of laws and legal documents have been consulted:

ADA = *Acta Divi Augusti* (Rome, 1945)

Documents Illustrating the Reigns of Augustus and Tiberius (eds. V. Ehrenberg and A. H. M. Jones, 2nd ed., Oxford, 1955)

FIRA = *Fontes Iuris Romani Antejustiniani* (2nd ed., Florence, 1940–1943)

---

* The *Digest* contains interpretations by the jurists Gaius, Paulus, and Ulpian, as well as by the jurists Celsus, Julian, Marcianus, Modestinus, Papinianus, and Pomponius.

Appendix II: Roman Money

Three different coins were in common use in ancient Rome:
  as (pl.: *asses*), a bronze coin
  sestertius (pl.: *sestertii;* English "sesterce"), a silver coin
  denarius (pl.: *denarii*), a silver coin
Before the Second Punic War (218–201 B.C.):
  2½ *asses* = 1 *sestertius*
  10 *asses* = 1 *denarius*
  4 *sestertii* = 1 *denarius*
After the Second Punic War:
  4 *asses* = 1 *sestertius*
  16 *asses* = 1 *denarius*
  4 *sestertii* = 1 *denarius*
Another, smaller bronze coin, the *quadrans,* was worth about one-quarter of an *as.*

It is fruitless to give a modern dollar equivalent for the values of ancient money; inflation would make any suggested equivalents out of date almost as soon as they were published. In addition, direct comparisons between prices or wages in ancient Roman and modern American societies are not valid because the two societies differ so radically. Technology and industrialization have altered the location and nature of employment, the distribution of wealth, the availability and variety of consumer items, and the "buying power" of the "average" person. The standard of living of the "average" modern American is much higher than that of the "average" inhabitant of the Roman world (or any preindustrial society). Comparing prices and incomes within Roman society (and within the same time period) is a more helpful indication of standard of living than trying to give dollar equivalents for the values of ancient money. In A.D. 301, for example, sewer cleaners were paid 25 *denarii* a day, and carpenters and bakers were paid 60 *denarii* a day. Pork cost 12 *denarii* a pound. Thus, a sewer cleaner had to work a full day, a carpenter or baker a half-day, in order to earn the money to purchase two pounds of pork. Today, even workers at minimum wage can purchase the same amount of pork after about one hour of work. A very small number of people were enormously wealthy, while the vast majority could afford only basic necessities. At the time of Caesar (about 50 B.C.), for example, a senator had a property value of at least 800,000 sesterces (most had considerably more), while a rank-and-file soldier was paid 900 sesterces a year, and a laborer earned about 1000 sesterces. At the time of Pliny the Younger (A.D. 100), who purchased one piece of property for 3,000,000 sesterces, collected an income of 400,000 sesterces from another piece of property, and bequeathed almost 2,000,000 sesterces to support 100 of his freedmen, a soldier was paid 1200 sesterces a year. About A.D. 180, in the Roman province of Numidia (North Africa), 5 percent interest on 1,300,000 sesterces could support 600 children.

Appendix III: Important Dates and Events

B.C.

753	Romulus founds Rome (traditional date).
6th c.	Etruscan domination of Rome.
509	Seventh and last king, Tarquin the Arrogant, expelled from Rome.

BEGINNING OF THE REPUBLICAN PERIOD

508	Horatius Cocles wards off the Etruscan army at the bridge.
494	Office of *tribunus plebis* established.
458	Cincinnatus summoned from his plowing to the dictatorship.
451–449	Publication of the Twelve Tables of laws.
390	Gauls sack Rome.
367	After passage of *Lex Licinia-Sextia,* first plebeian elected to consulship.
340–338	Rome defeats and dissolves the Latin League.
339	*Plebiscita* become binding on the whole community, subject to the consent of the Senate.
312	Appius Claudius is censor; construction begins on the Via Appia, a major highway, and the Aqua Appia, Rome's first aqueduct.
293	Cult of Aesculapius introduced into Rome.
c. 290	Rome's victory over the Samnites completes Roman domination of central Italy.
287	After passage of *Lex Hortensia,* Senate's right of veto on *plebiscita* abolished.
280–275	Pyrrhus invades Italy but wins only a "Pyrrhic victory."
270	Greek philosopher Epicurus dies in Athens.
264	Outbreak of First Punic (Carthaginian) War.
263	First sundial brought to Rome. Zeno, Greek philosopher, founder of the Stoic school, dies in Athens.
241	End of First Punic War: Rome acquires Sicily as first province or overseas territorial possession. Office of *praetor peregrinus* established.
238	Sardinia and Corsica become Roman province.
218	Outbreak of Second Punic War: battle at Trebia River, Roman defeat by Hannibal. Law passed limiting size of cargo ships which could be owned by senators.
217	Battle at Lake Trasimene, Roman defeat.
216	Battle at Cannae, Roman defeat.
215	*Lex Oppia* restricts amount of jewelry and expensive clothing which women could own and wear.
204	Cult of Cybele, Magna Mater, introduced to Rome.
201	End of Second Punic War.
200–146	Intermittent wars in Greece, Macedonia, and Asia Minor.
197	Spain annexed as two provinces; campaign to "pacify" Spain begins.
195	Repeal of *Lex Oppia.*

191 Outbreak of war against Antiochus III of Syria.

188 Citizens of Arpinum, town in Latium, birthplace of Marius and Cicero, granted Roman citizenship.

186 *Senatus Consultum Ultimum* suppresses Bacchic rites throughout Italy.

184 Cato the Elder elected censor.

173 Greek philosophers expelled from Rome.

171–168 Third Macedonian War: Roman victory at Pydna in 168. Deportation of 1000 hostages, including historian Polybius, to Rome.

161 Greek philosophers expelled from Rome.

156–155 Embassy to Rome of three Greek philosophers (a Stoic, an Academic, a Peripatetic) favorably received.

149 Establishment of first permanent court or standing tribunal (*quaestio perpetua*). First *quaestio* established to hear cases of provincial administrators charged with extortion.

149–146 Third Punic War: victorious Romans burn Carthage to the ground.

146 Rebellion in Greece against Roman authority; Romans burn Corinth to the ground as punishment. Annexation of Macedonia and (North) Africa as provinces.

135–132 Slave revolt in Sicily.

133 Tribunate of Tiberius Sempronius Gracchus, who promotes distribution of public land.

129 Annexation of Asia (western Asia Minor) as province.

123–121 Tribunates of Gaius Sempronius Gracchus, who promotes a law guaranteeing fixed low price of grain for Roman citizens; also promotes legislation switching the composition of *quaestiones perpetuae* from men of senatorial rank to men of equestrian rank.

120 Gallia Narbonensis annexed as province.

111–106 Wars in North Africa against Jugurtha, king of Numidia.

107 Marius is consul for the first of seven times; he is sent to Africa to fight Jugurtha; in recruiting his soldiers he disregards the property qualification, thus converting the citizen militia into a professional army.

104–101 Slave revolt in Sicily.

90–88 Social War: Rome's Italian allies rebel and demand citizenship.

89 Roman citizenship granted to all Italians.

88–85 First Mithridatic War: Mithridates, king of Pontus, invades Roman territory in Asia Minor. Sulla imposes very heavy war indemnity on province of Asia.

87–81 Civil wars in Rome.

81–79 Sulla appointed dictator, posts proscription lists.

73–71 Slave revolt in Italy led by Spartacus. Verres is governor of Sicily.

70 Trial of Verres for extortion in Sicily; Cicero speaks for the prosecution. Pompey and Crassus are consuls.

63 Cicero is consul. Conspiracy of Catiline. Syria annexed.

60 Formation of First Triumvirate (Julius Caesar, Pompey, Crassus).

59 Julius Caesar is consul. Pompey marries Caesar's daughter Julia.

58 Caesar begins campaign to pacify all of Gaul. Tribunate of Clodius, who promotes legislation for free distribution of grain to citizens.

55 Theater of Pompey, first permanent theater in Rome, built.

54 Death of Julia, Caesar's daughter, Pompey's wife.

53 Death of Crassus (a triumvir) at Carrhae, Mesopotamia, while on campaign.

52 Milo kills Clodius, as civil unrest in Rome increases.

51–50 Cicero goes as governor to Cilicia (annexed as province in 66).

51	All of Gaul annexed.
49	Caesar crosses Rubicon River and marches toward Rome. Pompey and his supporters (the republicans) flee to Greece.
48	Battle of Pharsalus: Caesar defeats Pompey.
48–44	Caesar appointed dictator.
44	Caesar assassinated. Outbreak of civil wars between Caesar's assassins (the republicans) and Caesar's successors (Mark Antony and Octavian).
43	Formation of Second Triumvirate (Mark Antony, Octavian, and Lepidus). Cicero proscribed and executed.
42	Battle of Philippi: victory of Second Triumvirate crushes republican opposition.
40	Octavian and Antony partition Roman Empire, the former controlling the western provinces, the latter the eastern provinces.
40–31	Tension between Mark Antony and Octavian develops and increases. Period of civil unrest.
31	Battle of Actium: Octavian's victory over Antony and Cleopatra gives him supreme control over Roman Empire.
30	Suicide of Antony and Cleopatra. Annexation of Egypt.
27	Octavian assumes name Augustus and receives from Senate a package of powers making him ruler of Roman Empire.

BEGINNING OF THE IMPERIAL PERIOD

18	Publication of *Lex Julia* regulating marriage and adultery.
A.D.	
14	Death of Augustus. Mutiny of legions in Rhine and Danube areas.
14–37	Tiberius, Augustus's stepson, is second emperor of Roman world. End of elections for magistrates in popular assemblies.
c. 30	Crucifixion of Jesus.
32	Public protests in Rome about shortage of free grain.
37–41	Caligula, grandnephew of Tiberius, is emperor.
41–54	Claudius, nephew of Tiberius, uncle of Caligula, is emperor.
43	Invasion of Britain by Claudius.
51	Public protests in Rome about shortage of free grain.
54–68	Nero, stepson of Claudius, last of the Julio-Claudian emperors.
64	Great fire in Rome.
65	Conspiracy to assassinate Nero; suicides of Seneca and Petronius.
69	Year of the Four Emperors: Galba, Otho, Vitellius, Vespasian.
69–79	Vespasian is emperor.
70	Capture and destruction of Jerusalem.
79	Eruption of Mount Vesuvius and burial of Pompeii and Herculaneum.
79–81	Titus is emperor.
80	Dedication of Flavian Amphitheater (Colosseum).
81–96	Domitian, younger son of Vespasian, is emperor.
93	Expulsion and execution of Stoic opponents to emperor.
97–98	Nerva is emperor.
97	Last recorded legislation by popular assemblies.
98–117	Trajan is emperor.
106	Annexation of Dacia.
111	Pliny sent to Bithynia as governor.
112	Dedication of Trajan's Forum.
117–138	Hadrian is emperor.

131–135	Uprising of Jews in Palestine suppressed. Hadrian forbids Jews henceforth to enter Jerusalem.
138–161	Antoninus Pius is emperor.
161–180	Marcus Aurelius is emperor.
166	Great plague sweeps through Roman Empire.
167	Invasions by barbarian tribes along northeastern and eastern frontiers of Roman Empire.
180–192	Commodus is emperor.
193–211	Septimius Severus is emperor.
197	Prohibition of marriage for soldiers lifted.
212–217	Caracalla is emperor.
212	Roman citizenship extended to every free person within the borders of the Empire.
218–222	Elagabalus is emperor.
222–235	Alexander Severus is emperor.
235–270	Period of civil disorder; thirteen emperors.
251	Invasions of the Empire by the Goths and other barbarians begin.
270–275	Aurelian is emperor; builds a wall around city of Rome for protection from invaders.
275–284	Civil disorder; six emperors.
284–305	Diocletian is emperor.
286	Diocletian chooses Maximian as colleague and shares with him imperial power. Both men are called Augustus. Diocletian rules the eastern provinces, Maximian the western.
286–305	Maximian is Augustus of western provinces.
293	Tetrarchy established: Diocletian further divides imperial power and appoints two younger subordinates to be Caesars.
301	Diocletian publishes edict on wage and price controls.
305–311	Galerius is Augustus of eastern provinces. Persecution of Christians.
306	Constantine becomes Augustus of western provinces.
311–323	Licinius is Augustus of eastern provinces.
312	Battle of Milvian Bridge: Constantine consolidates position as Augustus in western provinces.
313	Edict of Milan.
315	Arch of Constantine built.
323	Constantine defeats Licinius in battle, executes him, and becomes sole ruler of Roman Empire.
323–337	Roman Empire ruled by one emperor, Constantine.
325	Council of Nicaea.
330	Constantine transfers seat of Roman Empire from Rome to Byzantium, which he renames Constantinople.
361–363	Julian (the Apostate) is emperor; tries to revive Roman state religion.
367–383	Gratian is emperor in western part of Roman Empire.
379–395	Theodosius I is emperor in eastern part of Roman Empire; bans all non-Christian rites.
395	Roman Empire permanently divided into an eastern half and a western half.
410	Visigoths, under Alaric, sack Rome.
451	Attila the Hun defeated by a Roman army.
455	Vandals sack Rome.
476	Odoacer, a Germanic chieftain, deposes Romulus Augustulus, last emperor of western Roman Empire.
527–565	Justinian is emperor of eastern Roman Empire; appoints commission of jurists to produce codification of Roman laws.

Bibliography

GENERAL REFERENCE WORKS

Bowder, D., ed. *Who Was Who in the Roman World*. Oxford, 1980.

The Cambridge Ancient History, 1961–

Cary, M. *The Geographic Background of Greek and Roman History*. Oxford, 1949.

Grant, M. *Myths of the Greeks and Romans*. Cleveland, 1962.

Hamilton, E. *Mythology*. Boston, 1942.

Hammond, N. G. L., ed. *Atlas of the Greek and Roman World in Antiquity*. Park Ridge, N.J., 1981.

Jones, H. S. *Companion to Roman History*. Oxford, 1912.

Nash, E. *Pictorial Dictionary of Ancient Rome*, 2d ed. 2 vols. New York, 1968.

The Oxford Classical Dictionary, 2d ed. Oxford, 1970.

Petrie, A. *An Introduction to Roman History, Literature and Antiquities*, 3d ed. London, 1963.

Radice, B. *Who's Who in the Ancient World*. New York, 1971.

Scullard, H. H., and A. A. M. Van Der Heyden, eds. *Atlas of the Classical World*. London and New York, 1959.

Smith, W. *Smaller Classical Dictionary*, eds. E. H. Blakeney and J. Warrington. New York, 1958.

Thomas, J. O. *Everyman's Classical Atlas*, 3d ed. London, 1961.

Zimmerman, J. E. *Dictionary of Classical Mythology*. New York, 1964.

SOURCE COLLECTIONS

Lewis, N., and M. Reinhold. *Roman Civilization, Sourcebook I, The Republic*, 2d ed. New York, 1966.

———. *Roman Civilization, Sourcebook II, The Empire*, 2d ed. New York, 1966.

READING THE PAST

Gordon, A. E. *Illustrated Introduction to Latin Epigraphy*. Berkeley, 1983.

MacKendrick, P. L. *The Mute Stones Speak: The Story of Archaeology in Italy*, 2d ed. New York, 1983.

Sandys, J. E. *Latin Epigraphy*. Cambridge, 1919.

Sutherland, C. H. V. *Roman Coins*. London, 1974.

Turner, E. G. *The Papyrologist at Work*. Durham, N.C., 1973.

HISTORY: GENERAL

Africa, T. W. *The Immense Majesty: A History of Rome and the Roman Empire*. New York, 1974.

Boak, A. E. R., and W. G. Sinnigen. *A History of Rome to* A.D. *565,* 5th ed. New York, 1965.
Cary, M., and H. H. Scullard. *A History of Rome,* 3d ed. New York, 1975.
Grant, M. *History of Rome.* London, 1978.
Jones, A. H. M. *History of Rome through the Fifth Century.* New York, 1968.
Mommsen, T. *The History of Rome.* New York, 1895.
Rostovtzeff, M. *Rome.* New York, 1961.
———. *Social and Economic History of the Roman Empire,* 2d ed. Oxford, 1957.
Scullard, H. H. *From the Gracchi to Nero,* 5th ed. London, 1982.

HISTORY: REPUBLICAN PERIOD

Badian, E. *Roman Imperialism in the Late Republic,* 2d ed. Ithaca, N.Y., 1968.
Crawford, M. *The Roman Republic.* Atlantic Highlands, N.J., 1978.
Gruen, E. S. *The Last Generation of the Roman Republic.* Berkeley, 1974.
Harris, W. V. *War and Imperialism in Republican Rome, 327–70* B.C. Oxford, 1979.
Holmes, T. Rice. *The Roman Republic.* Oxford, 1923.
Marsh, F. B. *History of the Roman World 146–30* B.C. London, 1953.
Scullard, H. H. *History of the Roman World from 753–146* B.C., 4th ed. London, 1980.
Smith, R. E. *The Failure of the Roman Republic.* Cambridge, 1955.
Syme, R. *The Roman Revolution.* Oxford, 1939.

HISTORY: IMPERIAL PERIOD

Earl, D. C. *The Age of Augustus.* New York, 1968.
Garnsey, P. D. A., and R. Saller. *The Early Principate.* Oxford, 1982.
Grant, M. *The Fall of the Roman Empire.* New York, 1976.
———. *From Imperium to Auctoritas.* London, 1969.
———. *The Twelve Caesars.* London, 1975.
Hammond, M. *The Augustan Principate in Theory and Practice,* 2d ed. New York, 1968.
Holmes, T. Rice. *The Architect of the Roman Empire.* Oxford, 1928–31.
Jones, A. H. M. *The Later Roman Empire, 284–602.* Oxford, 1964.
Kagan, D., ed. *Decline and Fall of the Roman Empire: Why Did It Collapse?* 2d ed. Lexington, Mass., 1978.
Luttwak, E. N. *The Grand Strategy of the Roman Empire.* Baltimore, 1976.
Marsh, F. B. *The Founding of the Roman Empire,* 2d ed. Cambridge, 1959.
Millar, F. *The Emperor in the Roman World.* Ithaca, N.Y., 1977.
———, ed. *The Roman Empire and Its Neighbours,* 2d ed. London, 1981.
Parker, H. M. D. *History of the Roman World from* A.D. *138 to 337.* London, 1935.
Salmon, E. T. *A History of the Roman World from 30* B.C. *to* A.D. *138,* 3d ed. London, 1957.
Starr, C. G. *The Roman Empire.* New York, 1982.
Wells, C. *The Roman Empire.* Stanford, 1984.
Yavetz, Z. *Plebs and Princeps.* Oxford, 1969.

ANIMALS

Jennison, G. *Animals for Show and Pleasure in Ancient Rome.* Manchester, 1937.
Toynbee, J. M. C. *Animals in Roman Life and Art.* London, 1973.

ART AND ARCHITECTURE

Andreae, B. *The Art of Rome.* New York, 1977.

Boethius, A., and J. B. Ward-Perkins. *Etruscan and Roman Architecture.* Harmondsworth, 1970.

Brendel, O. *Prolegomena to the Study of Roman Art.* New Haven, 1979.

Brilliant, R. *Roman Art from the Republic to Constantine.* London, 1974.

Brown, F. E. *Roman Architecture.* New York, 1961.

Hanfmann, G. M. A. *Roman Art: A Modern Survey of the Art of Imperial Rome.* Greenwich, Conn., 1964.

Harte, G. B. *The Villas of Pliny.* New York, 1928.

Henig, M. *A Handbook of Roman Art.* Ithaca, N.Y., 1983.

Kaehler, H. *The Art of Rome and Her Empire,* 2d ed. New York, 1965.

L'Orange, H. P. *Art Forms and Civil Life in the Late Roman Empire.* Princeton, 1965.

MacDonald, W. L. *The Architecture of the Roman Empire.* New Haven, 1965.

McKay, A. G. *Houses, Villas and Palaces in the Roman World.* Ithaca, N.Y., 1975.

Percival, J. *The Roman Villa.* Berkeley, 1976.

Richardson, E. *The Etruscans, Their Art and Civilization.* Chicago, 1964.

Richter, G. M. A. *Ancient Italy: A Study of the Interrelations of Its People as Shown in Their Arts.* Ann Arbor, 1955.

Rivoira, G. T. *Roman Architecture and Its Principles of Construction under the Empire.* Oxford, 1925.

Robathan, D. M. *The Monuments of Ancient Rome.* Rome, 1950.

Robertson, D. S. *Handbook of Roman and Greek Architecture,* 2d ed. Cambridge, 1969.

Sear, F. *Roman Architecture.* Ithaca, N.Y., 1983.

Strong, D. E. *Roman Art.* Harmondsworth, 1976.

———. *Roman Imperial Sculpture.* London, 1961.

Strong, E. S. *Art in Ancient Rome.* New York, 1928.

Tanzer, H. H. *The Villas of Pliny the Younger.* New York, 1924.

Toynbee, J. M. C. *The Art of the Romans.* New York, 1965.

———. *Roman Historical Portraits.* Ithaca, N.Y., 1978.

Ward-Perkins, J. B. *Roman Imperial Architecture,* 2d ed. New York, 1981.

Wheeler, R. E. M. *Roman Art and Architecture.* New York, 1964.

CHARACTER AND CUSTOMS

Arnott, P. D. *The Romans and Their World.* New York, 1970.

Balsdon, J. P. V. D., ed. *The Romans.* London, 1965.

Barrow, R. H. *The Romans.* Harmondsworth, 1949.

Brown, P. *The World of Late Antiquity.* New York, 1971.

Carcopino, J. *Daily Life in Ancient Rome.* London, 1941.

Cary, M., and T. J. Haarhoff. *Life and Thought in the Greek and Roman World,* 6th ed. New York, 1959.

Christ, K. *The Romans.* Berkeley, 1983.

Clarke, M. L. *The Roman Mind.* London, 1956.

Cowell, F. R. *Everyday Life in Ancient Rome.* London, 1961.

Dilke, O. A. W. *The Ancient Romans: How They Lived and Worked.* Newton Abbot, 1975.

Dill, S. *Roman Society from Nero to Marcus Aurelius,* 2d ed. London, 1905.

Dudley, D. R. *The Romans*. New York, 1970.
Friedlander, L. *Roman Life and Manners under the Early Empire*. 4 vols. New York, 1908–1913.
Grant, M. *The World of Rome*. 3d ed. London, 1974.
Grimal, P. *The Civilization of Rome*. London, 1963.
————. *Rome of the Caesars*. London, 1956.
Hamilton, E. *The Roman Way*. New York, 1932.
Hooper, F. *Roman Realities*. Detroit, 1979.
Mattingly, H. *Man in the Roman Street*. New York, 1947.
Nichols, R., and K. McLeish. *Through Roman Eyes*. Cambridge, 1974.
Nicolet, C. *The World of the Citizen in Republican Rome*. Berkeley, 1980.
Paoli, U. E. *Rome, Its People, Life and Customs*. New York, 1963.
Rowell, H. T. *Rome in the Augustan Age*. Norman, Okla., 1962.
Showerman, G. *Rome and the Romans*. New York, 1933.
Starr, C. G. *The Ancient Romans*. Oxford, 1971.
————. *Civilization and the Caesars*. Ithaca, N.Y., 1954.
Tingay, G. I. F., and J. Badcock. *These Were the Romans*. Amersham, 1972.
Wilkinson, L. P. *The Roman Experience*. New York, 1974.

COMMERCE AND TRADE

Casson, L. *Ancient Trade and Society*. Detroit, 1984.
Charlesworth, M. P. *Trade-Routes and Commerce of the Roman Empire*, 2d ed. Chicago, 1974.
Crawford, M. *Coinage and Money under the Roman Republic*. Berkeley, 1984.
D'Arms, J. H., and E. C. Kopff, eds. *The Seabourne Commerce of Ancient Rome*. Rome, 1980.
Garnsey, P. D. A., K. Hopkins, C. R. Whittaker, eds. *Trade in the Ancient Economy*. Berkeley, 1983.
Loane, H. J. *Industry and Commerce of the City of Rome, 50 B.C.–200 A.D.* Baltimore, 1938.
Rickman, G. *The Corn Supply of Ancient Rome*. Oxford, 1980.

DEATH

Hopkins, K. *Death and Renewal* (*Sociological Studies in Roman History*, Vol. 2). Cambridge, 1983.
Toynbee, J. M. C. *Death and Burial in the Roman World*. Ithaca, N.Y., 1971.

ECONOMY

Duncan-Jones, R. *The Economy of the Roman Empire: Quantitative Studies*, 2d. ed. Cambridge, 1982.
Finley, M. I. *The Ancient Economy*. Berkeley, 1973.
Frank, T., ed. *An Economic Survey of Ancient Rome*. Baltimore, 1933.
Jones, A. H. M. *The Roman Economy: Studies in Ancient Economic and Administrative History*, ed. P. A. Brunt. Totowa, N.J., 1974.

EDUCATION, RHETORIC, AND INTELLECTUAL LIFE

Bonner, S. F. *Education in Ancient Rome.* Berkeley, 1977.
―――. *Roman Declamation in the Late Republic and Early Empire.* Berkeley, 1949.
Clark, D. L. *Rhetoric in Greco-Roman Education.* New York, 1957.
Clarke, M. L. *Rhetoric at Rome: A Historical Survey.* London, 1953.
Gwynn, A. O. *Roman Education from Cicero to Quintilian.* New York, 1926.
Kennedy, G. *The Art of Rhetoric in the Roman World.* Princeton, 1972.
Kenyon, F. G. *Books and Readers in Ancient Greece and Rome,* 2d ed. Oxford, 1951.
Marrou, H. I. *A History of Education in Antiquity.* New York, 1956.
Pinner, H. L. *The World of Books in Classical Antiquity.* Leiden, 1948.
Rawson, E. *Intellectual Life in the Late Roman Republic.* Baltimore, 1985.
Smith, W. A. *Ancient Education.* New York, 1955.

ENTERTAINMENT

Arnott, P. D. *The Ancient Greek and Roman Theatre.* New York, 1971.
Auguet, R. *Cruelty and Civilization: The Roman Games.* London, 1972.
Beare, W. *The Roman Stage.* London, 1950.
Bieber, M. *The History of the Greek and Roman Theater,* 2d ed. Princeton, 1961.
Cameron, A. *Circus Factions: Blues and Greens at Rome and Byzantium.* Oxford, 1976.
Grant, M. *Gladiators.* New York, 1968.
Humphrey, J. *Roman Circuses.* Berkeley, 1985.

FARMING

Heitland, W. E. *Agricola: A Study of Agriculture and Rustic Life in the Greco-Roman World.* Cambridge, 1921.
White, K. D. *Agricultural Implements of the Roman World.* London, 1967.
―――. *Country Life in Classical Times.* Ithaca, N.Y., 1977.
―――. *Farm Equipment of the Roman World.* Cambridge and New York, 1975.
―――. *Roman Farming.* Ithaca, N.Y., 1970.

FOOD, DRINK, AND CLOTHING

Edwards, J. *The Roman Cookery of Apicius.* Point Roberts, Wash., 1985.
Flower, B., and E. Rosenbaum. *Apicius, the Roman Cookery Book.* London, 1958.
Houston, M. G. *Ancient Greek, Roman and Byzantine Costume and Decoration,* 2d ed. London, 1947.
Seltman, C. *Wine in the Ancient World.* London, 1957.
Wilson, L. M. *The Clothing of the Ancient Romans.* Baltimore, 1938.

FREEDMEN

Duff, A. M. *Freedmen in the Early Roman Empire.* Oxford, 1928.
Treggiari, S. M. *Roman Freedmen during the Late Republic.* Oxford, 1969.

GOVERNMENT AND POLITICS

Abbott, F. F. *A History and Description of Roman Political Institutions,* 3d ed. New York, 1963.
———. *Roman Politics.* Boston, 1923.
Adcock, F. E. *Roman Political Ideas and Practice.* Ann Arbor, 1959.
Botsford, G. W. *The Roman Assemblies from Their Origin to the End of the Republic.* New York, 1909.
Dickinson, J. *Death of a Republic: Politics and Political Thought of Rome 59–44* B.C. New York, 1963.
Earl, D. C. *The Moral and Political Tradition of Rome.* Ithaca, N.Y., 1967.
Greenidge, A. H. J. *Roman Public Life.* New York, 1901.
Gruen, E. S. *Roman Politics and the Criminal Courts, 149–78* B.C. Cambridge, Mass., 1968.
Hawthorn, J. R. and C. Macdonald. *Roman Politics 80–44* B.C. London, 1960.
Homo, L. P. *Roman Political Institutions.* London, 1929.
Jones, A. H. M. *Studies in Roman Government and Law.* New York, 1960.
Kunkel, W. *An Introduction to Roman Legal and Constitutional History,* 2d ed., Oxford, 1973.
Scullard, H. H. *Roman Politics 220–150* B.C., 2d ed. Oxford, 1973.
Stavely, E. S. *Greek and Roman Voting and Elections.* Ithaca, N.Y., 1972.
Taylor, L. R. *Party Politics in the Age of Caesar.* Berkeley, 1949.
———. *Roman Voting Assemblies.* Ann Arbor, 1966.
Wirszubski, C. *Libertas as a Political Idea at Rome.* Cambridge, 1950.
Wylie, J. K. *Roman Constitutional History from Earliest Times to the Death of Justinian.* Cape Town, 1948.

LAW

Berger, A. *Encyclopedic Dictionary of Roman Law.* Philadelphia, 1953. (Transactions of the American Philosophical Society XLIII, Part 2.)
Buckland, W. W. *A Text-Book of Roman Law from Augustus to Justinian,* 3d ed. Cambridge, 1966.
Crook, J. A. *Law and Life of Rome.* Ithaca, N.Y., 1967.
Daube, D. *Forms of Roman Legislation.* Oxford, 1956.
———. *Roman Law.* Edinburgh, 1969.
Jolowicz, H. F. and B. Nicholas. *Historical Introduction to the Study of Roman Law,* 2d ed. Cambridge, 1972.
Jones, A. H. M. *The Criminal Courts of the Roman Republic and Principate.* Oxford, 1972.
Kelly, J. M. *Roman Litigation.* Oxford, 1966.
Leage, R. W. *Roman Private Law,* 3d ed. London, 1961.
Nicholas, B. *An Introduction to Roman Law.* Oxford, 1962.
Schulz, F. *History of Roman Legal Science.* Oxford, 1953.
———. *Principles of Roman Law.* Oxford, 1936.
Thomas, J. A. C. *Textbook of Roman Law.* Amsterdam, 1976.
Turner, J. W. C. *Introduction to the Study of Roman Private Law.* Cambridge, 1953.
Watson, A. *Rome of the Twelve Tables.* Princeton, 1975.
Wolff, H. J. *Roman Law: An Historical Introduction.* Norman, Okla., 1951.

LEISURE

Anderson, J. K., *Hunting in the Ancient World*. Berkeley, 1985.
Balsdon, J. P. V. D. *Life and Leisure in Ancient Rome*. London, 1969.
Gardiner, E. N. *Athletics of the Ancient World*. Oxford, 1930.
Harris, H. A. *Sport in Greece and Rome*. Ithaca, N.Y., 1972.

LITERATURE

The Cambridge History of Classical Literature, Vol. 2, *Latin Literature*.
Copley, F. O. *Latin Literature from the Beginnings to the Close of the Second Century* A.D. Ann Arbor, 1969.
Duff, J. W. *A Literary History of Rome from the Origins to the Close of the Golden Age*, 3d ed. New York, 1960.
———. *A Literary History of Rome in the Silver Age*, 3d ed. New York, 1964.
Grant, M. *Roman Literature*, 3d ed. Harmondsworth, 1964.
Ogilvie, R. M. *Roman Literature and Society*. Totowa, N.J., 1980.

MANPOWER AND LABOR

Boak, A. E. R. *Manpower Shortage and the Fall of the Roman Empire in the West*. Ann Arbor, 1955.
Brewster, E. H. *Roman Craftsmen and Tradesmen of the Early Roman Empire*. Philadelphia, 1917.
Brown, D. *Roman Craftsmen and Their Techniques*. London, 1974.
Brunt, P. A. *Italian Manpower 225* B.C.–A.D. *14*. Oxford, 1971.
Burford, A. *Craftsmen in Greek and Roman Society*. Ithaca, N.Y., 1972.
Garnsey, P. D. A., ed. *Non-Slave Labour in the Greco-Roman World*. Cambridge, 1980.
Mossé, C. *The Ancient World at Work*. New York, 1969.

MEDICINE

Allbutt, T. C. *Greek Medicine in Rome*. London, 1921.
Scarborough, J. *Roman Medicine*. Ithaca, N.Y., 1969.

MILITARY

Adcock, F. E. *The Roman Art of War under the Republic*. Cambridge, Mass., 1940.
Gabba, E. *Republican Rome, the Army and the Allies*. Berkeley, 1976.
Grant, M. *The Army of the Caesars*. London, 1974.
Parker, H. M. D. *The Roman Legions*. New York, 1958.
Smith, R. D. *Service in the Post-Marian Army*. Manchester, 1958.
Watson, G. R. *The Roman Soldier*. Ithaca, N.Y., 1969.
Webster, G. *The Roman Imperial Army of the First and Second Centuries*. London, 1969.

PHILOSOPHY

Armstrong, A. H. *An Introduction to Ancient Philosophy,* 3d ed. London, 1957.
Arnold, E. V. *Roman Stoicism.* Cambridge, 1911.
Bréhier, E. *The History of Philosophy,* Vol. 2, *The Hellenistic and the Roman Age.* Chicago, 1965.
Clay, D. *Lucretius and Epicurus.* Ithaca, N.Y., 1984.
Festugière, A. J. *Epicurus and His Gods.* New York, 1969.
Hicks, R. D. *Stoic and Epicurean.* London, 1910.
Long, A. A. *Hellenistic Philosophy. Stoics, Epicureans, Sceptics,* 2d ed. London, 1974.
Sandbach, F. H. *The Stoics.* New York, 1975.
Wenley, R. M. *Stoicism and Its Influence.* Boston, 1924.
Winspear, A. D. *Lucretius and Scientific Thought.* Montreal, 1963.

POMPEII, HERCULANEUM, AND OSTIA

Corti, E. C. *The Destruction and Resurrection of Pompeii and Herculaneum.* London, 1951.
D'Arms, J. H. *Romans on the Bay of Naples.* Cambridge, Mass., 1970.
Deiss, J. J. *Herculaneum: Italy's Buried Treasure.* New York, 1966.
Grant, M. *Cities of Vesuvius: Pompeii and Herculaneum.* London, 1971.
Hermansen, G. *Ostia: Aspects of Roman City Life.* Edmonton, 1981.
Jashemski, W. F. *The Gardens of Pompeii, Herculaneum, and the Villas Destroyed by Vesuvius.* New Rochelle, N.Y., 1979.
Mau, A. *Pompeii: Its Life and Art.* New York, 1902.
Meiggs, R. *Roman Ostia,* 2d ed. Oxford, 1973.

PROVINCES

Abbott, F. F., and A. C. Johnson. *Municipal Administration in the Roman Empire.* Princeton, 1926.
Arnold, W. T. *The Roman System of Provincial Administration,* 3d ed. Oxford, 1914.
Frank, T. *Roman Imperialism.* New York, 1972.
Jones, A. H. M. *The Cities of the Eastern Roman Provinces,* 2d. ed. Oxford, 1971.
Lewis, N. *Life in Egypt under Roman Rule.* Oxford, 1983.
Lindsay, J. *Daily Life in Roman Egypt.* London, 1963.
Magie, D. *The Roman Rule in Asia Minor.* Princeton, 1950.
Mommsen, T. *The Provinces of the Roman Empire.* Chicago, 1968.
Petit, P. *Pax Romana.* Berkeley, 1976.
Richardson, J. *Roman Provincial Administration 227* B.C. *to* A.D. *117.* Basingstoke, 1976.
Rivet, A. L. F. *Town and Country in Roman Britain,* 2d ed. London, 1964.
Salway, P. *Roman Britain.* Oxford, 1981.
Sherwin-White, A. N. *Roman Foreign Policy in the East, 168* B.C. *to* A.D. *1.* Norman, Okla., 1984.
———. *Roman Society and Roman Law in the New Testament.* Oxford, 1963.
Smallwood, E. M. *The Jews under Roman Rule from Pompey to Diocletian.* Leiden, 1976.
Stevenson, G. H. *Roman Provincial Administration.* New York, 1939.

RELIGION

Altheim, F. *A History of Roman Religion*. London, 1938.
Bailey, C. *Phases in the Religion of Ancient Rome*. Berkeley, 1932.
Barnes, E. W. *The Rise of Christianity*. London and New York, 1947.
Chadwick, H. *The Early Church*. Grand Rapids, Mich., 1967.
Cumont, F. *Afterlife in Roman Paganism*. New Haven, 1922.
––––––. *Oriental Religions in Roman Paganism*. Chicago, 1911.
Dodds, E. R. *Pagan and Christian in an Age of Anxiety*. Cambridge, 1965.
Dumézil, G. *Archaic Roman Religion*. Chicago, 1970.
Ferguson, J. *Greek and Roman Religion: A Source Book*. Park Ridge, N.J., 1980.
––––––. *The Religions of the Roman Empire*. Ithaca, N.Y., 1970.
Fowler, W. W. *The Religious Experience of the Roman People*. London, 1911.
––––––. *The Roman Festivals*. London, 1908.
Glover, T. R. *The Conflict of Religions in the Early Roman Empire*. London, 1909.
Gough, M. *The Early Christians*. New York, 1961.
Grant, M. *Jesus*. London, 1977.
––––––. *The Jews in the Roman World*. New York, 1973.
Heyob, S. K. *The Cult of Isis among Women in the Graeco-Roman World*. Leiden, 1975.
Laistner, M. L. W. *Christianity and Pagan Culture in the Later Roman Empire*. Ithaca, N.Y., 1951.
Leon, H. J. *The Jews of Ancient Rome*. Philadelphia, 1960.
Liebeschuetz, J. H. W. G. *Continuity and Change in Roman Religion*. Oxford, 1979.
Luck, G. *Arcana Mundi: Magic and the Occult in the Greek and Roman Worlds*. Baltimore, 1985.
MacMullen, R. *Paganism in the Roman Empire*. New Haven, 1981.
Markus, R. A. *Christianity in the Roman World*. London, 1974.
Meeks, W. A. *The First Urban Christians*. New Haven, 1983.
Michels, A. K. *The Calendar of the Roman Republic*. Princeton, 1967.
Momigliano, A., ed. *The Conflict between Paganism and Christianity in the Fourth Century*. Oxford, 1963.
Ogilvie, R. M. *The Romans and Their Gods in the Age of Augustus*. London, 1969.
Radin, M. *The Jews among the Greeks and Romans*. Philadelphia, 1915.
Ramsay, W. M. *The Church in the Roman Empire*. New York and London, 1893.
Rose, H. J. *Ancient Roman Religion*. London, 1948.
Scullard, H. H. *Festivals and Ceremonies of the Roman Republic*. London, 1981.
Solmsen, F. *Isis among the Greeks and Romans*. Cambridge, Mass., 1979.
Speidel, M. P. *Mithras-Orion: Greek Hero and Roman Army God*. Leiden, 1980.
Taylor, L. R. *The Divinity of the Roman Emperor*. Middletown, Conn., 1931.
Teixidor, J. *The Pagan God: Popular Religions in the Greco-Roman Near East*. Princeton, 1977.
Vermaseren, M. J. *Cybele and Attis: The Myth and the Cult*. London, 1977.
––––––. *Mithras, the Secret God*. London, 1963.
Wagenvoort, H. *Pietas: Selected Studies in Roman Religion*. Leiden, 1980.
Wardman, A. *Religion and Statecraft among the Romans*. Baltimore, 1982.
Wilken, R. L. *The Christians as the Romans Saw Them*. New Haven, 1984.
Witt, R. E. *Isis in the Graeco-Roman World*. Ithaca, 1971.

SCIENCE AND TECHNOLOGY

Ashby, T. *The Aqueducts of Ancient Rome*, ed. I. A. Richmond. Oxford, 1935.
Bernal, J. D. *Science in History*, 3d ed. London, 1965.
Blake, M. E. *Ancient Roman Construction in Italy*. 3 vols. Washington and Philadelphia, 1947–73.
Claggett, M. *Greek Science in Antiquity*, 2d ed. London, 1963.
Farrington, B. *Science in Antiquity*, 2d ed. Oxford, 1969.
Forbes, R. J. *Studies in Ancient Technology*, 2d ed. Leiden, 1964–72.
Landels, J. G. *Engineering in the Ancient World*. Berkeley, 1978.
Stahl, W. H. *Roman Science: Origins, Development and Influence to the Later Middle Ages*. Madison, 1962.
Van Deman, E. B. *The Building of the Roman Aqueducts*. Washington, 1934.
White, K. D. *Greek and Roman Technology*. Ithaca, N.Y. 1984.

SEXUAL ACTIVITY

Foucault, M. *The Care of the Self*. Vol. 3 of *The History of Sexuality*. New York, 1986.
Kiefer, O. *Sexual Life in Ancient Rome*. New York, 1953.
Richlin, A. *The Garden of Priapus: Sexuality and Aggression in Roman Humor*. New Haven, 1983.

SLAVERY

Barrow, R. H. *Slavery in the Roman Empire*. New York, 1928.
Bradley, K. R. *Slaves and Masters in the Roman Empire: A Study in Social Control*. Brussels, 1984.
Finley, M. I. *Ancient Slavery and Modern Ideology*. London, 1980.
————, ed. *Slavery in Classical Antiquity*. Cambridge, 1960.
Vogt, J. *Ancient Slavery and the Ideal of Man*. Oxford, 1974.
Westermann, W. L. *The Slave Systems of Greek and Roman Antiquity*. Philadelphia, 1955.
Wiedemann, T. *Greek and Roman Slavery*. Baltimore, 1981.

SOCIAL AND FAMILY STRUCTURES

Arnheim, M. T. W. *The Senatorial Aristocracy of the Later Roman Empire*. Oxford, 1972.
Badian, E. *Foreign Clientelae*. Oxford, 1958.
————. *Publicans and Sinners*. Oxford, 1972.
Balsdon, J. P. V. D. *Roman Women: Their History and Habits*. London, 1962.
————. *Romans and Aliens*. Chapel Hill, 1979.
Bertman, S., ed. *The Conflict of Generations in Ancient Greece and Rome*. Amsterdam, 1976.
Brunt, P. A. *Social Conflicts in the Roman Republic*. New York, 1971.
D'Arms, J. H. *Commerce and Social Standing in Ancient Rome*. Cambridge, Mass., 1981.
Frier, B. W. *Landlords and Tenants in Imperial Rome*. Princeton, 1980.

Gardner, J. *Women in Roman Society and Law.* London, 1986.

Garnsey, P. D. A. *Social Status and Legal Privilege in the Roman Empire.* Oxford, 1970.

Gelzer, M. *The Roman Nobility.* Oxford, 1969.

Hallet, J. *Fathers and Daughters in Roman Society.* Princeton, 1984.

Hill, H. *The Roman Middle Class in the Republican Period.* Oxford, 1952.

Hopkins, K. *Conquerors and Slaves: Sociological Studies in Roman History I.* Cambridge, 1978.

Kampen, N. *Image and Status: Roman Working Women in Ostia.* Berlin, 1981.

Lefkowitz, M. R., and M. B. Fant, eds. *Women's Life in Greece and Rome.* Baltimore, 1982.

Lintott, A. W. *Violence in Republican Rome.* Oxford, 1968.

MacMullen, R. *Roman Social Relations 50 B.C.–A.D. 284.* New Haven, 1974.

————. *Soldier and Civilian in the Later Roman Empire.* Cambridge, Mass., 1963.

Nicolet, C. *The World of the Citizen in Republican Rome.* Berkeley, 1980.

Pomeroy, S. B. *Goddesses, Whores, Wives and Slaves: Women in Classical Antiquity.* New York, 1975.

Rawson, B., ed. *The Family in Ancient Rome.* Ithaca, N.Y., 1986.

Saller, R. P. *Personal Patronage under the Early Empire.* Cambridge, 1982.

Sherwin-White, A. N. *Racial Prejudice in Imperial Rome.* Cambridge, 1967.

————. *The Roman Citizenship,* 2d ed. Oxford, 1973.

TOPOGRAPHY AND CITY PLANS

Dudley, D. R. *Urbs Roma.* London, 1967.

Grimal, P. *Roman Cities,* ed. G. M. Woloch. Madison, 1983.

Mazzolani, L. S. *The Idea of the City in Roman Thought.* Bloomington, 1970.

Platner, S. B. *Topography and Monuments of Ancient Rome.* Boston, 1904.

Platner, S. B., and T. Ashby. *A Topographical Dictionary of Ancient Rome.* Oxford, 1929.

Ward-Perkins, J. B. *Cities of Ancient Greece and Italy: Planning in Classical Antiquity.* New York, 1974.

TRAVEL

Casson, L. *Ships and Seamanship in the Ancient World.* Princeton, 1971.

————. *Travel in the Ancient World.* London, 1974.

Chevallier, R. *Roman Roads.* Berkeley, 1976.

Von Hagen, V. W. *The Roads That Led to Rome.* Cleveland and New York, 1967.

Index

This index includes only names of general importance.
Translations from Latin or Greek appear in *italics*.

Abortion, 27
Abstinence, 382 *n* 147, 407, 436
Accius, L., 212
Accountant, 109
Achilles, 4 *n* 4
Acilius Glabrio, M'., 257, 376
Acre. *See* Measurement
Acta Divi Augusti, 29, 54–55, 458
Actium, 55 *n* 80, 442, 462
Actor, 55, 85, 124, 334–35, 337, 340, 345
Actress, 187, 340
Adoption, 29–30, 35, 120, 192, 193–94
Adultery, 50–58, 319, 415
Advertisement on wall, 64–65, 71, 224–25, 329, 344
Aedile, 132, 211, 212, 217–18, 280, 333, 334, 347, 348
  curule, 98, 218
  curule and plebeian, 207, 214, 333 *n* 158, 398
Aelius Aristides, *139–40,* 446
Aemilius Celer, 102, 225, 344
Aeneas, 300 *nn* 37–38, 372 *n* 88
Aeneid, 300 *nn* 37–38, 363 *n* 20, 372 *n* 88
Aesculapius, 188, 369, 423, 460
Afranius, L., 334
Africa, 36, 69, 136 *n* 56, 142 *n* 87, 293, 309, 444, 461
Agamemnon, 119, 347 *n* 227
Agent, business, 9, 140, 141, 143, 203, 274 *n* 24, 283
Agricola, Cn. Julius, 21, 288
Agriculture. *See* Farming
Agrippa, M. Vipsanius, 56–58
Ajax, 4 *n* 4
Ala, 60
Alaric, 365 *n* 31, 463
Alexander Severus (emperor), 463
Alexandria, 28, 150, 410–11, 445
Alliance, political, 144 *n* 104, 219, 221 *n* 96, 229 *n* 139, 277, 294 *n* 18, 295 *n* 20, 326, 391
Ally, Italian, 6 *n* 2, 155, 156 *n* 166, 270

military, 249, 250, 251, 253
  provincial, 273
Ambarvalia, 380, 381
Amphitheater, Flavian. *See* Colosseum (Flavian Amphitheater)
Amphitheater event, 332–35, 342–50. *See also* Arena event
Ancestors. *See* Conservatism, Roman; Wax image
Animal
  for arena event, 12–13, 188, 343–44, 347–48
  for sacrifice, 202, 375, 378–79, 380–84, 416
Animism, 362–63
Annee Epigraphique, 69
Ante meridiem, 127
Anthropomorphism, 362, 367
Antinous, 100–101
Antiochus III, 257, 376, 392, 461
Antoninus Pius (emperor), 69, 463
Antonius, M., 55–58, 68 *n* 35, 119–20, 144 *n* 104, 231, 294 *n* 18, 326, 392 *n* 215, 462
Anubis, 405, 408–9
Apamea, 35, 265 *n* 88, 443
Aphrodite, 374 *n* 98
Apicius, *86–88,* 446
Apollo, 40 *nn* 20–21, 362, 367, 370 *n* 136
Appeal, right of, 213
Appian, *155–58,* 446
Appian Way, 183, 193, 203, 204, 326–29, 460
Appius Claudius Caecus (censor), 327 *n* 106, 460
Appius Claudius Pulcher, 150 *n* 133, 273–76
Apprenticeship, 104, 115–16, 118
Apuleius, L., *176, 217–18, 341–42, 404–8,* 446
Aqueduct, 65–67, 211
Aquilius, *128,* 446
Architect, 130, 145
Architecture, 59–62, 76–80, 315
  teacher of, 136
Arena, 317 *n* 46

Arena event, 109, 188, 316, 317 *n* 46, 323
  n 81. *See also* Amphitheater event
Ares, 370, 371 *n* 80, 374
Aretaeus, *303–4,* 446
Ariobarzanes, 275–76
Aristocracy
  definition, 10 *n* 25
  government by, 10–11
Aristocracy, Roman
  composition, 7
  power of, 96 *n* 81, 207, 231, 241
Arithmetic, 104, 115, 197
  teacher of, 135
Army
  auxiliary unit, 249 *n* 2, 250, 261 *n* 70, 270,
    292
  billeting, 274
  camp, 253, 260, 264
  campaign, 142, 145 *n* 113, 147, 168 *n* 1,
    256–57, 288, 376, 377–78
  cavalry, 8, 211, 251, 253 *n* 31, 261, 268,
    274, 276
  century, 251, 252 *n* 27, 257, 265
  cohort, 236, 251, 252 *n* 27, 262, 265, 268,
    370
  commander-in-chief (consul), 142 *n* 189,
    211, 214–15, 227, 251, 271, 378
  commander-in-chief (emperor), 233
  commissions, 215, 236 *n* 181, 265
  conscription, 215, 268–69, 288, 410
  construction work, 250, 261, 264 *n* 82, 267
  decoration, 255, 257, 258
  discipline, 254–55, 260–61, 263
  duties, 139, 182, 184, 260–61, 267
  early and middle republican, 154, 156, 208
    n 19, 249–57, 310
  enlistment, 107, 256–57, 262, 268
  imperial, 249, 259–69
  legion, 214, 236, 250–51, 257, 292
  maniple, 251, 252, 253, 254, 256, 257, 267
  Marius's reform, 249–50, 461
  mutiny, 266–67
  officer, 236, 251–55, 257, 260. *See also*
    specific title
  pay, 255–56, 266, 289
  in provinces, 270–71, 276, 289
  provisions for, 142, 147, 227
  punishment, 179 *n* 67, 215, 254–55, 266
  standardbearer, 252
  term of service, 208 *n* 19, 249–50, 266–67
  training, 260, 262–64, 310
  triumph, 144, 227, 237, 257, 258–59
  veteran, 19 *n* 6, 155 *n* 160, 266, 267
  weapons, 208 *n* 19, 251–52, 261, 266
Arpinum, 49, 220, 250 *n* 5, 270 *n* 3, 440
Arria, 296, 297, 298, 303 *n* 52
Artemis, 367–68, 371 *n* 80
Arulenus Rusticus, Q. Junius, 38

Arval Brethren, 373–74, 423 *n* 337, 425 *n* 343
As. *See* Appendix II
Asia, 95, 149, 198, 231, 272–73, 281–82, 390,
  445, 461
Asinius Marrucinus, 318
Asinius Pollio, C., 318
Assembly, popular, 118–19, 147, 148, 156,
  206–10, 224, 226, 228, 237–38, 299, 384
  n 162
Association (Club), 99–101, 132, 225 *n* 121,
  414 *n* 296, 420 *n* 321
Asthma, 89
Astrology, 410
Astronomy, 116, 117, 119, 244
  muse of, 40 *n* 21
Athena, 367
Athens, 125, 183, 431, 442
Athlete, 336 *n* 180, 436, 437
Athletics, 105, 310, 334
  Roman attitude toward, 310, 336–37, 339
Atomic theory, 428–31
Atrium, 17, 59–62, 76
Atticus, T. Pomponius, 20, 48–49, 63, 94,
  150, 273–76
Attila, 463
Attis, 401, 402
Auctioneer, 197, 201, 301
Augur, 88 *n* 50, 377, 386
Augury, 377–78
  god of, 353 *n* 261
Augustine, *365–66, 446–47*
Augustus
  adultery, 54–55, 58
  and Antony, 55, 294 *n* 18, 326
  assumption of power, 216 *n* 72, 231–35,
    391, 462
  deification, 237 *n* 191, 389–90
  distribution of provinces, 232, 262 *n* 74
  and equestrians, 236
  family, 55–58
  legislation, 28–29, 54–55
  life span, 93
  opposition to, 10 *n* 24, 235, 240 *n* 211
  and religion, 392, 404, 409–10
  restoration of peace, 241–42, 392
  Second Triumvirate, 55 *n* 80
  and Senate, 235, 257
  title, 55 *n* 79, 232–33
Aulus Gellius, *208–9, 218, 387–88,* 449
Aurelian (emperor), 463
Auspices, 41 *n* 24, 377–78, 387 *n* 186
Aventine Hill, 200, 439
Awning, amphitheater, 344, 385

Bacchanalia, suppression of, 396–401, 461
Bacchus, 353, 382, 396–401, 404, 409, 411,
  412

Baker, 71, 132, 135, 306
Bakery, 60
Baldness, 306, 424
Ball court, 78
  game, 310, 311, 316, 328
  player, 102, 225, 314
Banker, 62, 165
Banking, 8–9, 140–50, 196
Banquet. *See also* Dinner party
  for gods, 376–77
  of oriental religions, 397, 408, 418
  public, 145, 385
Baptism, 394, 407, 412
Bar, 171, 308, 314, 329
Barbarian invasion, 243 *n* 227, 393 *n* 222, 463
Barber, 33, 132, 135, 180, 197
Barrow, R. H., 392
Basilica, 62, 128 *n* 8, 264 *n* 81, 380 *n* 138
Bath
  attendant, 136, 315
  heating, 61, 78, 182, 312–13, 315
  lighting, 61, 73, 312–13, 315
  oil, 78, 101, 129 *n* 13, 132 *n* 40, 315
  private, 73, 74, 78, 182, 312–14
  public, 80, 84, 101, 129 *n* 13, 132 *n* 40,
    311, 313, 314, 315, 316, 320, 407
  scraper (strigil), 132 *n* 40
Bathing
  leisure activity, 311–15
  slaves, 75, 317
  time of day, 129, 311
Bellona, 71, 400
Beneventum, 107–8, 201, 328, 440
Benevolence of gods, 371, 375, 380–81, 391
Bequest. *See* Will (Testament)
*Berliner griechische Urkunden, 22, 44, 50,
  240, 264–65,* 457
Bethlehem, 149
Bibulus, M. Calpurnius, 333
Birth announcement, 25
Birth control, 26–28
Bithynia, 86, 414–16, 442
Boatman, 327
Book
  account, 139, 160, 173, 177, 284–85
  burning, 298
  case, 78, 108 *n* 20
  composition, 105, 108, 322–23
  damage, 61–62, 109
  grammar, 301
  hymn, 374
  law, 197
  papyrus, 83, 321 *n* 70
  prayer, 373
  as prize, 110
  sacred, 407, 419
  text, 105, 108 *n* 23, 109–10
Booty, distribution of, 258, 370 *n* 73

Boreas, 63
Boscoreale, 74, 440
Boxer, 340, 353
Boxing, 105, 339, 340
  god of, 353 *n* 261
Bread, 17, 101, 114, 174, 225, 328, 330
Bread and circuses, 137, 336 *n* 176
Breadmaking, 81, 102, 162
Bribery
  in army, 265–66, 267
  of court, 278 *n* 46, 279, 283
  election, 219, 238, 280
  of paedagogue, 109
  prosecution for, 150
  in province, 272, 274 *n* 22, 275 *n* 30
Britain (Britannia), 21 *n* 18, 264 *n* 83, 288–
    89, 370, 444, 462
Brothel, 171, 180 *n* 72, 188
Brundisium (Brindisi), 326, 329, 440
Brutus, M. Junius, 95, 202, 274–76
Building collapse, 63, 64, 145
Bulla, 152 *n* 145
Burglar, 62, 70, 72, 102, 194
Burial. *See* Funerary law
Business and investment, 8–9, 137–51, 196,
    198–99, 228, 350
Businessman
  promotion of peace, 139, 224
  in province, 230, 271, 274, 276
Butcher, 47, 130
Byzantine period, 243 *n* 227, 350 *n* 245

Caelius Rufus, M., 53–54, *347–48*
Caesar. *See* Julius Caesar, C.
Caesar, name as title, 44 *n* 39, 234
Caldarium, 313, 315 *n* 36
Calendar, Roman, 361, 391 *n* 207
Calgacus, 288–89
Caligula, Gaius (emperor), 57, 267 *n* 101,
    351 *n* 251, 359, 409, 462
Calpurnia Hispulla, 24–25, 45–46, 298 *n* 29
Camel driver, 135
Camp. *See* Army
Campaign, political
  advice, 219–24
  bribery, 219, 238, 280
  end of, 237–38, 242
  endorsement, 132, 224–25
  role of client, 14–15, 221, 222–23
  role of family, 39, 218–19
Campus, 68 *n* 36
Campus Martius, 68, 171, 207, 208, 238, 242,
    279, 310, 439
Candidate, political
  imperial period, 237–38, 240
  republican period, 219–24
Cannae, 299, 440, 460

Cannibalism, 184, 417, 418, 421
Capital offence and punishment
  adulterer, 55
  honestior and *humilior,* 12–13, 97, 349
  non-Roman, 6, 282, 349
  Roman citizen, 6, 213, 277 *n* 44, 287
  slave, 178, 182, 183, 188–89
  soldier, 179, 254–55
  for treason, 398–99, 413, 415
  Vestal Virgin, 388
Capitoline Hill, 379 *n* 135, 393 *n* 224, 395, 439
Cappadocia, 199, 275 *n* 35, 443
Capua, 202, 328, 440
Caracalla (emperor), 250 *n* 10, 255 *n* 39, 463
Carpenter, 132, 135
Carrhae, 145 *n* 113, 391, 443, 461
Carthage (Carthago), 142 *n* 87, 147 *n* 121, 270, 300 *n* 38, 311–12, 369, 444, 461
Cassius Longinus, C., 202
Castor, 353
Castration, 402
Catholic rite, 422
Catilina, L. Sergius, 230 *n* 145, 289, 299, 461
Cato, M. Porcius (the Elder), 34, 93, 104–5, 130, 143, 164, 172, *173–74,* 189, 257, 299–300, 324 *n* 89, 325, *364–65, 375, 380–81, 424,* 447, 461
Cato, M. Porcius (the Younger), 219 *n* 87
Catullus, C. Valerius, *40–43, 52, 53, 239, 291–92, 318–19, 368,* 447
Censor, 144 *n* 105, 207, 210 *n* 33, 211, 212, 227, 228, 233
Census, 138 *n* 64, 144 *n* 105, 149, 211, 233
Centurion, 19 *n* 6, 251, 252–54, 257, 266, 267
Century
  electoral, 207, 210, 221, 222
  military, 208 *n* 19, 251
Cerealia, 366 *n* 52
Ceres, 332, 353, 362, 366, 367, 375, 382, 383
Chamberpot, 68, 70 *n* 46
Character, Roman. *See* Virtue, Roman
Chariot
  funeral, 99
  racing, 350, 351–52, 357
  triumphal, 258–59
Chariot racing
  driver, 90, 110, 333 *n* 156, 350–59
  financing, 332–33, 335, 350
  imperial involvement, 334, 335, 339 *n* 190, 351
  origin, 337 *n* 184
  popularity, 350, 354–55
  team (faction), 350, 351–52, 355–59
  track, 51 *n* 67, 344, 350 *n* 245, 351
Charm, good-luck. *See* Bulla
Chicken, sacred, 377–78

Chicken seller, 132
Child
  disown, 18, 120
  raise, 31–36, 291
  relinquish, 30
Childbirth, 93, 292–93, 368, 384
Childlessness, 24–25, 29, 295, 304 *n* 58
Child-parent relationship, 18–23, 30, 31–32, 94–95, 105, 125, 197, 205, 264–65, 291
Christ, 411, 412, 413, 415, 462
Christianity
  absorption of Roman elements, 367 *n* 57, 383, 384 *n* 172
  accusations against, 417–18
  becomes state religion, 392, 422
  blame for Rome's decline, 365 *n* 31
  charge of civil disobedience, 414–16
  church design, 264 *n* 81, 380 *n* 138
  evangelism, 411
  intolerance to other religions, 393, 396, 408–9, 422
  otherworldly, 360–61
  persecution of, 412–13, 420–21
  rite, 415, 419–20
Christmas, 384 *n* 172
Cicero, M. Tullius
  and Antony, 119–20, 462
  and brother, 48, *49, 107,* 192, 219, 272
  and businessmen, *139, 150–51, 230–31, 272–73*
  and Caelius Rufus, 53, *54,* 347, *348*
  career of, 219–24, 277, 447–48, 461
  and Catiline, 298
  on class structure, *10–11, 129–30,* 209, *210,* 215
  and daughter, 19–20, *20,* 94–96, *95*
  on education, *33, 124*
  on farming, *164–65*
  on government, *211–12,* 215, *216–17, 229–30*
  as governor, *273–77*
  on illness, *88*
  as landlord, *64*
  and manumission, *193*
  and public spectacles, *346–47*
  and religion, 372, 377 *n* 119
  and son, 125–26, 216
  and Verres, *278–87*
Cicero, M. Tullius (son of above), 106, *125–26,* 192, 216
Cicero, Q. Tullius, 48–49, 106–7, *192–93,* 219, *220–24,* 272, 333 *n* 158, 448
Cilicia, 150, 273–77, 281 *n* 64, 347–48, 443, 461
Cincinnatus, L. Quinctius, 165, 460
Circus, 51 *n* 67
Circus, Ovid at, 51, 352–54
Circus event. *See* Chariot racing

Circus Maximus, 51 *n* 67, 171, 337 *n* 184, 344, 351, 354

Citizenship, Roman
grant of, 3, 6, 190, 195, 250, 270
right and privilege, 6, 12, 206, 222 *n* 102, 286–87, 461, 463

Civil service, imperial period, 236, 241

Civil war, Roman, 96 *n* 81, 153 *n* 150, 216 *n* 72, 230–31, 232, 241, 273 *n* 18, 391, 461, 462

Class structure, 6–17, 129–30, 138, 151 *n* 137, 277 *n* 44

Claudius (emperor), 56–57, 137, 188, 240, 296, 321, 410–11, 412, 435 *n* 376, 462

Claudius Pulcher, P., 378

Cleanthes, 419

Cleopatra, 55 *n* 80, 58 *n* 81, 231, 259 *n* 67, 404, 462

Client, 14–17, 111 *n* 40, 136, 166 *n* 206, 191, 317–18, 319, 320

Clitumnus River, 363–64, 441

Clock, 127, 128, 196, 315

Clodia, 52–54

Clodius Pulcher, P., 52 *n* 72, 58, 81, 137, 193, 230 *n* 145, 461

Cloth dyer, 131, 132

Clothing, 131, 135–36, 162–63, 172, 174, 176, 196, 324, 405. *See also* Toga; Tunic

Club. *See* Association (Club)

Clytemnestra, 347

Cognomen, 203 *n* 78

Coin. *See* Money

Coin in fountain, 364

Collar, identification, 180

College, priestly, 373, 386, 407

Collegium, 99 *n* 99

Colony
Greek, 21 *n* 19, 331 *n* 143, 362
Roman, 19 *n* 6, 155, 237

Colosseum (Flavian Amphitheater), 109, 334 *n* 167, 335, 344, 462

Columella, L. Junius Moderatus, *73–76, 171–72,* 448

Coming of age, 152 *n* 145

Comitia Centuriata, 207, 208, 211 *n* 40, 251, 279 *n* 55

Comitia Curiata, 207 *n* 6

Comitia Tributa, 207, 208, 211 *n* 40, 280 *n* 61, 386 *n* 180

Commodus (emperor), 237 *n* 186, 463

Compitalia, 174

Compluvium, 61

Composition, literary. *See* Literary study; Poetry

Comum (Como), 111, 441

Concilium Plebis, 207, 208–9, 212, 215 *n* 64, 226 *n* 123

Concubine, 182

Conservatism, Roman, 3, 178, 210, 300, 361, 372, 374

Conspiracy, Catilinarian, 18, 298, 461

Constantine (emperor), 422, 463

Constantinople, 243 *n* 227, 463

Constitution. *See* Government

Construction, public, 66–68, 146, 211, 228
as punishment, 13, 97, 422

Construction worker, 170, 201, 228 *n* 133

Consul, 141 *n* 81, 142–43, 190, 207, 208 *n* 19, 209, 211–15, 219–20, 227, 233, 251, 271, 279–80, 339, 376, 379, 396–401, 460

Contio, 209–10, 398 *n* 242

Contraception, 26

Contract, government
aqueduct repair, 66
distribution, 8, 211, 228, 271
fraud, 148
military provisions, 146–47
public construction, 146
public revenue, 148–49, 230, 271, 273, 284, 285–86

Contract, legal
apprenticeship, 116
construction, 146
interpretation of, 141 *n* 83, 247
loan, 140–41
slave purchase, 168–69
slave rental, 169–70

Controversia, 119–22

Cook, 130, 177

Cook book, 85–88

Coppersmith, 71

Corinna, 27

Corinth, 95, 442, 461

Cornelia, 24, 105–6

Cornelius Lentulus Spinther, P., 88

Cornelius Scipio, P., 147, 157

Cornelius Scipio Aemilianus, P., 157, 250

Cornelius Scipio Africanus, P., 157, 311–14

Cornelius Scipio Calvus, Cn., 147

Cornelius Scipio Nasica, P., 376, 401

Corporal punishment. *See also* Army; Slave
of child, 33, 105
of criminal, 12–13, 55, 269, 335, 343, 349
of student, 108, 109
of Vestal Virgin, 388

Corpus Glossariorum Latinorum, 113–14

Corpus Inscriptionum Latinarum
death, *94, 98, 100–103*
families, *23, 25, 36, 37*
freedmen, *193–94, 201–5*
housing, *64–65, 68, 69, 71*
leisure, *309, 319, 329–30, 344–45, 356–59*
marriage, *45, 47, 48*
occupations, *132, 133, 134–36, 138, 140, 141, 146*
politics, *224–25, 236–37*

Corpus Inscriptionum Latinarum (Cont.)
  religion, *370, 374, 400–401, 426*
  slaves, *180*
  women, *292, 293–96, 306–7*
Corpus Iuris Civilis, 243, 458
Cosmetics, 305
Council of Nicaea, 463
Court, standing (tribunal), 151 *n* 137, 188,
  228 *n* 135, 277 *n* 43, 278 *n* 46, 461
  corruption, 278
  procedure, 277, 278, 279 *n* 54
  recess, 322 *n* 78, 384 *n* 162
Court case, 53, 150, 193, 277–87
Cowherd, 74, 163, 187
Craftsman, 130, 131, 133
  patron deity of, 353 *n* 261
Crassus, M. Licinius, 144–45, 231, 391, 461
Crucifixion, 13 *n* 36, 131 *n* 26, 183, 287, 413,
  417
Cubiculum, 60, 61, 77–79
Cultus, 372
Curia, 400 *n* 246
Curio, C. Scribonius (cos. 76), 279
Curio, C. Scribonius (trib. 50), 347, 348
Curling iron, 178, 305
Curse, 98, 357, 426
Cursus Honorum, 210 *n* 34
Curule seat, 99 *n* 98
Cybele, 348 *n* 238, 401–3, 411, 412, 460
Cymbal, 398, 403
Cyprus, 150, 274–75, 443
Czar, 44 *n* 39

Dacia, 140, 335, 392, 445, 462
Daedalus, 335 *nn* 169–70
Dancing, 84, 85, 130, 299, 335, 341–42
Danube (Danuvius) River, 266 *n* 92, 444–
  45
Daughter, 19–20, 27–28, 30, 58, 94–95, 203,
  205, 291–92
Debt
  enslavement for, 159, 168
  of a province, 149, 275–76
  remission of, 216–17
Decimation, 179 *n* 67, 255 *n* 37
Decius Mus, P., 379
Declamation, 121, 122, 126
Deification, 39 *n* 12, 67 *n* 33, 389–91
Deity. *See also specific name*
  eastern religion, 394–423
  Epicurean, 427, 428
  of hearth, 363, 387
  of household, 112, 152 *n* 145, 173, 174,
    330, 363
  state religion, 361–94
  Stoic, 432, 433
  of underworld, 98, 194, 205
  of wedding, 40–43

Demeter, 366 *n* 52
Democracy
  definition of, 10 *n* 25
  of republican Rome, 206–7, 226
Democritus, 428 *n* 354
Dentatus, M'. Curius, 164–65
Diana, 100, 324, 362, 367–68
Dictator, 165, 213, 232, 233
Dido, 300
Digesta, 12, 188–89, 213–14, 235, 243 *n* 228,
  245–48, 458
Dinner party, 17, 51–52, 58, 83–84, 88, 186,
  196–99, 308, 315–19
Dio Cassius, *29, 232–35,* 448
Diocletian, 133, 463
Diodorus Siculus, *175, 183–84,* 449
Dionysius of Halicarnassus, *14, 194–95, 379–
  80, 386–87, 388,* 449
Dionysus, 396 *n* 233
Divination, 375 *n* 106, 377–79, 382
Divorce, 18, 21, 49–50, 55, 58, 219, 295
Doctor, 91–93, 130, 200, 205. *See also* Medi-
  cine
Dog star, 383
Dominus, 420 *n* 325
Domitian (emperor), 38 *n* 7, 239, 255 *n* 39,
  462
Domus, 59 *n* 1
Donative, 258 *n* 62
Door, 181 *n* 77
  deity of, 366, 375 *n* 102
Doorman, 16, 192, 197
Dowry, 34, 44, 50, 55, 97, 203, 294, 295 *n* 23
Drachma. *See* Money, Greek
Dressmaker, 306
Duovir, 36, 132, 146, 225, 237

Easter, 35, 408
Eastern religion. *See* Religion, foreign
Edict
  imperial, 133–36
  praetor's, 245, 275
Edict of Milan, 463
Education, 19, 71, 104–26, 135–36, 197,
  201–2, 300–301, 426
Egypt (Aegyptus), 22, 44, 140, 150, 171, 236,
  392, 403–4, 410–11, 445, 462
  documents from, 22, 23, 28, 30, 35, 44, 50,
    72, 112, 114, 116, 149, 169–70, 240, 262,
    264–65, 266, 410–11
Election, popular
  abolition of, 237–38, 242, 462
  campaign for, 132, 219–25, 279–80
  voting in, 206–7
Empedocles, 117
Emperor
  and Christianity, 412–16, 420, 421–22

and grain supply, 137
last in western empire, 243 *n* 227
and military, 255 *n* 39, 257, 258 *n* 62
obliteration of, 237 *n* 186
opposition to, 240 *n* 211, 297
as Pontifex Maximus, 386, 393
power and privilege of, 231–35
and public entertainment, 334–36, 339, 351
residence of, 221 *n* 94
and senatorial class, 235–38, 240
worship of, 389–91
Empire, Roman
administration, 226, 230, 232, 236–37, 248,
270–89
border defense, 249, 268, 270–71
decline, 361 *n* 3, 463
division, 243 *n* 227, 463
extent, 3, 139–40, 249, 423
growth, 270–71, 460–62
as reward for valor, 249, 260, 391, 393
Engagement, marriage, 20, 152, 291
Engineer, army, 236, 264 *n* 82
Engineering, 65–69
Entertainer, Roman attitude toward, 55, 124,
299 *n* 31, 337, 340, 345, 359
Entertainment, private. *See* Dinner party;
Recitation
Entertainment, public, 331–59. *See also* Amphitheater event; Arena event; Chariot
racing; Theater
Epictetus, *239,* 449
Epicureanism, 426–31, 432
Epicurus, 426–27, 428, 431 *n* 356, 460
Epidaurus, 369, 442
Epilepsy, 169, 302, 303
Eques (equites), 8
Equestrian class. *See also* Business and in-
vestment; Businessman
in imperial period, 236–37
and juries, 228 *n* 135
in republican politics, 130 *n* 21, 144, 215,
220, 222, 230–31
rise of, 8–9
Equity under law, 247–48
Erebus, 94
Esquiline Hill, 16, 200, 439
Ethics
in philosophy, 427 *n* 351, 431
in religion, 360, 372–73, 395
Etruscan, 5, 6 *n* 4, 7 *n* 5, 342, 362, 378, 460
Euripides, 396 *n* 236
Eusebius, *420–22,* 449
Execution. *See* Capital offence and punish-
ment
Exedra, 61
Exercise, physical, 152, 263–64, 310, 311, 314
Exile, as punishment, 12–13, 51, 55, 58 *n* 83,
97, 133, 277 *n* 44, 298, 410, 435 *n* 376

Exposure of child, 18, 19, 27–28, 35–36, 168,
203, 290
Expulsion of monarchy, 6 *n* 4, 7, 460
Extispicium, 378
Eye inflammation, 109 *n* 30, 176, 327, 328,
424

Fabius Pictor, 366
Factio, 350
Faction, circus. *See* Chariot racing
Factory, 133, 137–38, 170 *n* 12
Familia, 59 *n* 1
Family, Roman, 13, 18–36, 59 *n* 1, 144
Fannia, 296–98
Farm
housing, 72–76, 82, 256
product, 73–76, 134–35, 163, 166, 173–74,
285, 381–83
size, 156 *n* 168, 256, 285
Farmer, idealization of, 4–5, 152–53, 164–67,
215 *n* 68, 256, 314, 338 *n* 186, 392
Farming
operation, 72–76, 161–63, 173
and religion, 364–65, 370–71, 380–83
Farmland
distribution reform, 154–58, 215–17, 249,
461
ownership, 7, 72–73, 129, 130, 153–54,
164, 215–17
sharecropping, 161–62
for soldier, 266
tenancy, 75, 159–61
Farmworker, 7, 73–74, 135, 159–63, 172–74
Fasces, 217 *n* 80
Fascist, 217 *n* 80
Fates, Three, 359 *n* 290
Father of family, 13, 18–20, 32, 104–5, 111–
12, 120–21, 298 *n* 30
Father of Fatherland (title), 13, 234
Father of the state, 7, 13, 226 *n* 122, 241,
393
Fauces, 60–61
Fertility, human, 24, 28–29, 256
rite, 383–84
Fescennine joke, 42
Festival, 173 *n* 37, 331–32, 380–86, 402. *See
also specific festival*
Fine, as punishment, 13, 67, 148, 254
Finley, M. I., 195 *n* 24
Fish sauce, 85–86, 135 *n* 50, 138
Fish seller, 130, 217, 307
Fisherman, 130, 132
Flamen, 382–83, 386
Flamininus, T. Quinctius, 256
Flogging. *See* Corporal punishment
Flora, 16, 180, 316, 371
Floralia, 317 *n* 46

Fontes Iuris Romani Antejustiniani, 12–13, 14, 97, 140–41, 240, 458

Food, 70, 81–88, 101, 114, 134–35, 161–62, 174, 177, 217, 255, 316 *n* 40, 317, 318, 321

Foreigner, resentment toward, 70 *n* 48, 92 *n* 68, 200–201

Formiae, 182, 239, 327, 440

Fortunata, 196–99

Forum, Roman, 66 *n* 29, 122, 127, 128 *n* 8, 152 *n* 145, 166 *n* 205, 207, 221, 334 *n* 167, 340 *n* 194, 386, 387 *n* 190, 439

Fraud
  contract, 148
  insurance, 65

Free worker, 131–32, 136, 138 *n* 66, 158, 159

Freedman
  cap, 187, 191, 385
  as client, 15, 202–4
  family life, 193–94, 204–5
  occupation, 131–32, 201–2, 345
  resentment of, 195–201
  social status, 190–91, 195, 203 *n* 79
  son of, 19, 182

Freedom of speech, 83 *n* 19, 238–39

Freedwoman, 29, 182 *n* 83, 194, 307

Friendship, 95–96, 204–5, 221 *n* 96, 265, 318–19, 328

Frigidarium, 315 *n* 38

Frontinus, Sex. Julius, *66–67,* 449

Fronto, M. Cornelius, 21, 164, 324, *336,* 449

Fruit seller, 132

Fuller, 132, 143

Fulvia, 58

Fulvius Flaccus, Q. (praet. 215), 147

Fulvius Flaccus, Q. (cos. 180), 257

Fundanus, Minicius, 152, 291

Funeral
  club, 99–101
  oration, 99, 293–96
  procession, 98–99, 195, 388

Funerary law, 97

Gabinius, A., 150

Gades (Cadiz), 84, 85, 444

Gaius (jurist), 243, *245, 246,* 449

Galba (emperor), 462

Galerius (emperor), 421–22, 463

Game
  board, 302, 309
  dice, 385

Game (Ludus), 235, 237, 331–59, 370, 377, 402

Garum, 85–86

Gaul (Gallia), 139, 168 *n* 1, 273 *n* 18, 289, 420, 444, 461, 462

Gauls, sack of Rome by, 312 *n* 27, 460

Gellius. *See* Aulus Gellius

Genius, 393, 419

Geometry, 115, 136

Geoponica, 86

Germanicus Caesar, 56–57, 241, 267

Germany (Germania), 171, 267, 306, 444

Gladiator, 55, 91, 109, 182, 188, 332, 333, 334–35, 341, 342–46

Glass, 77 *n* 63, 79, 312

God. *See* Deity

Goldsmith, 131, 132

Good old days, 38 *n* 10, 45, 54, 71, 98, 118, 301, 312–14, 321 *n* 71, 338 *n* 187

Goth, 243 *n* 227, 463

Government
  form and definition, 10–11
  Roman, 7–8, 147, 206–42, 398–99

Governor. *See* Province, administration of

Gracchus, C. Sempronius, 24 *n* 32, 81, 136, 156, 157, 228 *n* 135, 229, 461

Gracchus, Ti. Sempronius, 155–58, 216 *n* 74, 226 *n* 123, 229, 230 *n* 145, 257 *n* 52, 292 *n* 6, 461

Grain dole, 81, 136–37, 140 *n* 74, 154, 229–30, 286 *n* 77, 336, 410, 461
  supply officer, 180, 237

Grammaticus, 107, 109, 116–17, 136

Grant, M., 199 *n* 66

Grape picker, 132

Gratian (emperor), 392–93, 463

Greece
  education in, 125–26
  governor of, 95 *n* 78
  hostage from, 250
  influence on Roman culture, 335, 339, 340, 362, 367–68, 369, 426
  slave from, 171

Greek language, 107, 113–14, 117, 126, 197, 199

Greek Papyri in British Museum, 114, 149, 410–11, 457

Greek people
  their perception of Romans, 255 *n* 38, 261 *n* 73
  Roman perception of, 92, 104, 200–201, 209–10, 338 *n* 188

Guardian, 34, 290, 300, 387 *n* 191, 399

Guardian spirit. *See* Genius; Spirit, protective

Gymnasium, 129, 337, 339

Hadrian (emperor), 100 *n* 101, 188, 462

Hair
  dresser, 178–79, 305–6
  plucker, 314

Hamilton, E., 119 *n* 66

Hand, left, 318, 405

Hannibal, 142, 299, 301, 311, 393, 395, 460

Haruspex, 378–79

Headache, 424
Heating, 75, 78, 79, 182 *n* 81, 315
Heir, desire for, 24, 25, 41, 43, 192
Helen of Troy, 40 *n* 23, 341
Helicon, Mount, 40, 442
Helvidia, 292–93, 297
Helvidius Priscus, C., 297
Hera, 367
Herald, 19 *n* 11, 180–81, 201, 261, 401 *n* 249
Herculaneum, 26 *n* 37, 59, 440, 462
Hercules, 145, 205, 217
Herdsman, 74, 155, 163–64, 183
Herod, 262 *n* 74
Heroism, Roman concept of, 4–5, 153, 164–65, 296, 298, 312, 372 *n* 88
Hieroglyphic, 406, 407
Hilarion, 28
Hills, Seven (of Rome), 16 *n* 46, 200 *n* 61, 439. See also specific name
Hired worker, 129–33, 138, 159
History, study of, 119, 124, 301
Holiday, 75, 170, 173 *n* 37. See also Festival
Homer, 4 *n* 4, 300
Homesickness, 330
Homosexuality, 178, 186, 198, 239
Honestior, 12–13, 97
Honor, 11 *n* 28
Horace, *19,* 108, 109, *110, 115, 165–66, 167, 326–29, 391–92,* 449–50
Horatius Cocles, 3–5, 460
Horse race. See Chariot racing
Hortensius, Q., 209
Hortensius Hortalus, Q., 219 *n* 87, 277, 279
Horus, 404
Hostage, 250
Hot tub, 78, 311, 312–13, 315
Hotel, 180–81, 326, 327 *n* 116, 328, 329–30
Hour, Roman, 127–29, 316
House, rural. See Farm; Villa
House, urban, 59–62, 199, 200 *n* 61, 221 *n* 94
House of Pansa, 60
House of the Moralist, 319
House of the Surgeon, 60
Household god. See Deity
Housing, cost of, 59, 64
Humilior, 12–13, 97
Hun, 243 *n* 227, 463
Hunting, 309, 323–25, 348
  god of, 353 *n* 261
Husband, recommendation for, 38–40
Hymen Hymenaeus, 40–43
Hymn, 40–43, 368
Hysteria, 97 *n* 90, **302–4**

Icarus, 335
Icon, 98
Ida, Mount, 403, 442

Ides, 19 *n* 8
Iliad, 4 *n* 4, 300 *n* 39
Illiteracy, 19 *n* 11, 116, 401 *n* 249
Illness, 69, 88–89, 90, 102, 291, 296, 298, 302–4, 325, 369, 424, 425
Imago, 98
Imperator, 233, 258
Imperial period
  army, 259–69
  definition of, 9 *n* 21, 462–63
  education, 121–23
  form of government, 231–42
  freedom of speech, 83 *n* 19, 238–39
  politics, 39 *n* 14, 151–52
  population decline, 268
  public entertainment, 334–39
  social division, 12
  social reform, 35–36, 188–89
Imperium, 233 *n* 164
Impluvium, 60, 61 *n* 10
Indemnity, war, 142 *n* 91, 148, 149, 271
Indentureship, 158 *n* 175, 168 *n* 4
Infant mortality, 24, 25, 45, 93, 292
Infertility. See Childlessness
Initiation, religious, 394, 396–97, 407–8
Inn. See Hotel
Innkeeper, 132, 181, 327, 328, 330
Inscriptiones Latinae Selectae. See Corpus Inscriptionum Latinarum
Institutes, 243, 458
Insurance, 65, 147, 148
Interest on loan, 115, 141, 216 *n* 75, 275–77
Iphigenia, 119
Iphis, 28
Isis, 146 *n* 119, 225, 403–9
Italian people
  allies of Rome, 270
  confiscation of land, 155
  governed from Rome, 227, 228, 235
  granted Roman citizenship, 6, 287
  solicitation of votes of, 222
  virtue of, 38–39
Iunior, 207 *n* 10
Iurisconsultus, 243 *n* 225
Iurisprudens, 243 *n* 225
Ius gentium, 246 *n* 248

Janiculum Hill, 4
Janus, 375, 381
Jerusalem, 259, 409, 445, 462
Jew, 70, 71, 409–11, 412, 463
Jewelry, 44, 50, 97, 291, 294, 299
Josephus, Flavius, 259, *260–61,* 450
Judaea, 149, 413
Judaism, 409–11
Judge, court, 211, 244, 271, 273 *n* 21, 278 *n* 45

Jugurtha, 461
Julia (daughter of Augustus), 55, 56, 58
Julia (daughter of Caesar), 219 *n* 86, 461
Julia Procilla, 21
Julian the Apostate (emperor), 463
Julius Caesar, C.
  assassination of, 10 *n* 24, 231, 232, 338
    n 185, 462
  and Catullus, 239
  deification of, 67, 389
  family of, 56–57, 219 *n* 86, 461
  and First Triumvirate, 144 *n* 104, 230
    n 149, 461
  games of, 333
  in Gaul, 168 *n* 1, 461
  kidnapped, 279 *n* **53**
  legislation of, 69 *n* 43, 216 *n* 75, 273 *n* 21
  name of, 44 *n* 39
  and patricians, 7 *n* 8
  and Pompey, 96 *n* 81, 219 *n* 86, 391, 461
  as Pontifex Maximus, 361
  as *popularis*, 229 *n* 138
Junius Mauricus, 38
Juno, 332, 341, 342, 362, 367, 375
Jupiter, 16, 82, 152 *n* 145, 332, 362, 367, 372,
  375–77, 379, 381
Jurist, 243 *n* 225, 245, 247
Jury, 151 *n* 137, 228 *n* 135, 277 *n* 43, 278
  n 46, 461
Justice
  administration of, 12–13, 211, 214, 235,
    243–44, 245, 271, 282, 283
  definition of, 11–12, 247–48
Justinian (emperor), 11, 243, 463
Juvenal, *17, 63, 64, 69–71, 109–10, 121, 177–*
  78, 200–201, 300–301, 336 *n* 176, 450

Kaiser, 44 *n* 39
Kalends, 160
Kidnap, 168, 172 *n* 29, 397, 398
King, eastern, 150–51, 275–76, 389
King of Rome, 6–7, 14, 47, 199 *n* 55, 211
  n 41, 213, 226, 233, 388, 460

Lamp, 65, 70, 75, 109, 162
Land distribution reform. *See* Farmland
Lar, 173, 174 *n* 47, 330, 363, 374. *See also*
  Deity
Lararium, 363
Larcius Macedo, 181–82, 311 *n* 18
Latin language, study of, 104–6, 109, 113–14,
  136, 197
Latin League, 460
Laurentum, 76, 152, 440
Law, Roman
  application, 243–44

categories, 245–46, 387
codification, 242–43, 457–58, 463
definition, 11–12, 247
interpretation, 189, 243 *n* 225, 247–48
sources, 207, 208–9, 226, 234, 245, 275
  n 31, 387
study of, 118–21, 124, 197
Twelve Tables, 214 *n* 56, 242–43, 460
Law Code of Theodosius, 36, 189, 268, 269,
  422, 458
Lawyer, 118–19, 128, 151, 152, 220, 221
  n 98, 223, 243 *n* 225, 277
Laxative, 84
Lectisternium, 376 *n* 116, 402
Legacy. *See* Will (Testament)
Legislation, 12–13, 28–29, 54–55, 66–67, 69
  n 43, 97, 136–37, 156, 168 *n* 4, 178–79,
  188–89, 194, 273 *n* 21, 299, 414–16
Leisure activity, 129, 152, 302, 308–59, 385
Lepidus, M. Aemilius, 55 *n* 80, 144 *n* 104,
  295, 462
Lesbia, 52–53
Lesbos, 52 *n* 72, 442
Leto, 368
Leucippus, 428 *n* 354
Lex, 208 *n* 24
Liberalia, 152 *n* 145
Library, 61–62, 325
Libya, 140, 305, 445
Life expectancy, 93–94, 292–93, 306
Lighting, 70, 109, 128, 162, 180, 312, 316
  n 42, 405
Liquamen, 85–88, 135
Literary study, 115, 152, 197, 299, 300, 314,
  319–25, 346
Litter bearer, 69
Litterator, 107, 113–15
Livia, 56, 58, 68 *n* 34, 93, 389 *n* 200, 391
  n 207
Livy, *4–5, 142–43, 147, 148, 256–57, 299–*
  300, 376–77, 377–78, 379, 395, 397–99,
  401–2, 450
Logos, 419, 432 *n* 362
Lower class, 12, 129–32, 136–37, 138 *n* 66,
  158, 228, 240 *n* 211, 241, 308, 338
Lucian, *315,* 450
Lucilius, C., 212
Lucretius Carus, T., 117, *403, 427–31,* 450–
  51
Ludi, 332, 339, 342
  Apollinares, 332 *n* 151
  Cereales, 332 *n* 151, 366 *n* 52
  Florales, 317 *n* 46, 332 *n* 151
  Megalenses, 332 *n* 151, 348, 402
  Plebeii, 332 *n* 151
  Romani, 332 *n* 151, 350 *n* 247
Ludus, 332 *n* 147
Lupercalia, 383–84

Macedonia, 193, 250, 256, 293, 442, 461
Macrobius, *369–70*, 451
Maecenas, C., 326–28
Magic, 423–26
Magister, 107
Magister equitum, 213
Magister populi, 213
Magistrate, 11 *n* 28, 129, 132, 207, 210–18, 220, 225–26, 232–38, 245, 270–71. *See also specific title*
Magna Mater. *See* Cybele
Maid, 202
Mail service, 125
Manes, 48, 296
Manlius Torquatus, T., 379
Manufacture, 137 *n* 63
Manumission
    from *patria potestas,* 388
    from slavery, 101, 172, 178, 185–86, 188, 190–95, 198, 205
Manus, 129 *n* 16, 137 *n* 63, 185 *n* 93
Marcellus, M. Claudius, 56, 58
Marcius Philippus, Q., 397, 400
Marcus Aurelius, 21, *22, 164, 324–25,* 420, 447, 463
Marius, C., 220 *n* 91, 249–50, 261 *n* 72, 461
Mark Antony. *See* Antonius, M.
Market, 172, 211, 217, 235, 401 *n* 249
Marriage
    age at, 37, 45, 46–47
    arranged, 18, 20, 38–39, 50, 58, 120, 256
    contract, 44
    function of, 24, 43, 44
    husband and wife, 28, 37, 44–49, 58, 144, 177, 196–97, 198, 256, 293–301
    remarriage, 29, 45, 55, 58, 219
    restriction, 6, 7, 29, 194, 388
    of soldier, 250 *n* 9
Mars, 68 *n* 36, 362, 370, 374, 381
Martial, *16, 33–34, 63, 65, 71, 72, 83–84, 91, 109, 128–29, 177, 199, 316–18, 319, 320–21, 359, 370–71, 385–86,* 451
Martyr, 420–21
Mary, mother of Christ, 149, 383, 404
Massage, 132 *n* 40, 314, 315
Massilia (Marseilles), 21, 277 *n* 44, 444
Mat maker, 132
Mater, 401 *n* 251
Matrona, 20, 290
Maximian (emperor), 463
Maximus, 51 *n* 67, 361 *n* 4, 372 *n* 89
Meal, 81–88. *See also* Dinner party
Measurement
    land, 156 *n* 168
    length, 60 *n* 6, 66 *n* 29, 251–52, 268 *n* 103
    time, 100 *n* 100, 127–29
    weight and volume, 133 *n* 45, 134 *n* 49
Medicine, 24, 26–27, 88, 90–93, 302–4, 369,

424. *See also* Doctor; Eye inflammation; Illness
Megalesia, 402
Menander, 114
Menelaos, 341
Menopause, 304
Menstruation, 24, 304
Mercury, 82, 341, 362, 405
Metamorphosis, 82, 176, 217, 404, 406, 408 *n* 278
Michigan Papyri, University of, 266, 457
Middle class, 9–10, 137–38
Midwife, 92–93
Milan (Mediolanum), 111, 441
Mildew, spirit of, 382–83
Mile, 66 *n* 29
Milestone, 66, 69, 76, 100, 143
Military service. *See* Army
Military tribune, 203, 211, 215, 236, 251, 253–55, 265
Miller, 132
Millstone, 162, 176, 305
Milo, T. Annius, 193, 461
Milvian Bridge, battle of, 463
Mime, 340, 346–47
Mine, 12–13, 97, 171, 175, 237
Minerva, 324, 332, 341–42, 353, 362, 367
Minicius Acilianus, 38–40
Ministra, 416 *n* 305
Minos, King, 335 *n* 169
Minotaur, 335 *n* 169
Minucius Felix, *408–9, 417–18, 423,* 451
Miscarriage, 24–25, 304
Mithra, 384 *n* 170, 392, 395
Mithridates, 461
Mock heroic style, 162, 167 *n* 214, 327 *n* 108
Monarchy. *See also* King of Rome
    definition of, 10
    imperial power as, 232–33, 241
    period of, 206, 460
Money
    Greek, 50, 116, 169, 252, 255, 274 *n* 22
    Roman. *See* Appendix II
Moneychanger, 71
Moneycollector, 19
Moneylending, 129–30, 140–43, 147, 149–51, 166, 199, 216, 271, 274–77, 284
Monotheism, 410, 412
Month, name of, 384, 391
Moon, deity of, 368
Moral decline, fear of, 54, 92 *n* 68, 200, 210, 301, 338 *n* 188, 339, 391–92
Morality, as function of religion, 372–73, 395 *n* 231
Moretum, 161–62
Mosaic, 138, 309
Mother, 20–23, 28, 30, 105–6, 205, 293 *n* 10, 296, 404, 408–9

Mother earth deity, 366, 401, 403, 429
Mourning, restriction on. *See* Funerary law
Mug (Assault), 70, 420
Mule driver, 132, 135, 136, 186, 199
Muse, 40 *nn* 20–21, 385
Music, 46, 84, 85, 196, 340, 341
    oriental, 200, 398, 403, 405
Mutilation of self, 71 *n* 52, 269, 402
Mutiny, 266–67
Myth, 82–83, 119, 335 *nn* 169–70, 341–42,
    347, 367, 394, 404, 421 *n* 331

Name
    family, 7
    of freedman, 203 *n* 78
    obliteration of, 237 *n* 186
    prompter, 223 *n* 111
    of woman, 157 *n* 4
Napkin, 196, 317, 318–19
Naples (Neapolis), 182, 331, 440
Navy, 142, 147, 279, 288, 378
Neptune, 199, 353, 362
Nero (emperor), 57, 90, 179, 259, 334–35,
    336, 339, 344, 351 *n* 251, 413, 435, 462
Nerva (emperor), 462
Net fighter (gladiator), 343, 345
New man, 215, 220, 221, 277
New Testament, 149, 411–12
Nile River, 28 *n* 38, 404, 445
Nobiles, 7
Nomen, 203 *n* 78
Nomenclator, 223 *n* 111
Nomentum, 71, 382, 440
Norbanus, 197, 346
Novus homo, 215 *n* 67, 220
Numa, 199, 388
Nurse, 21, 32–33, 105, 113, 291

Occupation, 131–32, 135–36, 170. *See also*
    specific title
Octavia, 56, 58, 68 *n* 35
Octavian, 55 *n* 79. *See also* Augustus
Oculist, 205
Odoacer, 463
Odyssey, 181 *n* 76, 300 *n* 39
Oecus, 60–61
Oedipus, 421 *n* 331
Officer
    military. *See* Army
    religious. *See* Religion
    state. *See* Magistrate
Oil. *See* Bath; Lamp
Olympic Games, 310, 336, 339 *n* 190
Olympus, Mount, 362, 442
Omen, 41, 373, 377, 378, 379

Ophthalmologist, 91
Optimates, 221, 229
Oracle, 379
Oratory, 117, 119, 122–24
Orbilius Pupillus, L., 107–8, 110
Orcus, 427
Ordo, 8 *n* 11
Oriens, 394 *n* 225
Orphan, 34–35, 293, 294 *n* 17
Ostia, 76, 80, 136, 203, 401, 440
Otho (emperor), 462
Ovid, *27, 28, 50–51, 51–52, 82–83, 305–6,
    352–54, 382–83, 425,* 451
Oxyrhynchus, 28, 30, 116, 169, 445
Oxyrhynchus Papryi, 28, 30, 169, 262, 457

Paedagogue, 33–34, 106, 108 *n* 24, 109,
    113, 291
Paetus, Caecina, 296, 297
Painter, 135
Palace, 221 *n* 94
Palaemon, Q. Remmius, 109, 301
Palatine Hill, 221 *n* 94, 321, 402, 439
Pallas, 385
Panem et circenses, 336 *n* 176
Pannonia, 266, 292, 444–45
Panoply, 252
Pantomime, 302, 340, 341–42
Papyrus, 22, 62, 84 *n* 20, 113 *n* 50, 321
    n 70
Parilia, 331 *n* 145
Paris of Troy, 40, 341–42
Parthia, 145, 199, 204, 391, 392, 445
Pasiphae, 335
Pastor, 163
Pastoral poetry, 163
Patavium (Padua), 39, 441
Pater, 7 *n* 6, 13
Pater Patriae, 13, 234 *n* 170
Paterfamilias, 18 *n* 1, 290 *n* 2, 361, 363, 373,
    399 *n* 244
Paternalism, 13–14
Patria potestas, 18, 23, 120 *n* 70, 121 *n* 72,
    387 *n* 191
Patrician
    consul, 213 *n* 50, 214
    definition of, 7, 14
    emperor, 233–34
    voter, 207, 208, 209
Patron, community, 36, 111–12
Patron, literary, 326
Patron deity, 353, 362–63, 385
Patronage, 13–17, 111, 136, 191, 194, 195,
    203, 317–18
Paul, Saint, 415 *n* 301
Paulus, *12, 13, 97, 247, 248,* 451, 457
Pax, 287–88, 371, 382

Pax deorum, 371, 386
Pax Romana, 249, 287, 419 *n* 318
Peace, Roman, 139 *n* 69, 224, 236, 241–42, 244, 249, 273, 287–89
Peculium, 170, 171, 175, 185 *n* 95
Pedanius Secundus, 178–79
Penates, 363 *n* 14
Pentheus, 396 *n* 236
Perfume maker, 130
Peristylium, 60–62
Persecution, 392–93, 396–97, 410, 412–13, 420–21, 422
Persephone, 366 *n* 40
Petilius Cerialis, 289
Petronius, *115, 133, 180–81, 196–99, 346,* 451, 462
Pharsalus, 442, 462
Philemon and Baucis, 82–83
Philip of Macedon, 142 *n* 91, 256
Philippi, 442, 462
Philo, *409–10,* 452
Philosophy, 21, 117, 125–26, 297, 426–37, 461, 462. *See also* Epicureanism; Stoicism
Phoebe, 353
Phoebus, 353, 385
Phrygia, 401, 403, 423, 443
Physician, 205
Physics, 427 *n* 351, 428, 432
Pietas, 4, 13, 293, 300 *n* 38, 372, 395 *n* 231
Pimp, 55, 120, 188, 280
Pirate, 120, 168, 279, 326
Plague, 369, 374, 463
Plasterer, 47
Plautus, *131,* 452
Playwright, 340–41
Plebeian
  agitation by, 7, 208 *n* 23, 211 *n* 42, 214, 242
  assembly, 207, 208–9, 212
  client, 14
  consul, 213 *n* 50, 214
  definition of, 7
  officer. *See* Aedile; Tribune, plebeian (of plebs)
Plebiscite, 208, 209, 214, 245, 460
Plebs, 7 *n* 7, 209, 245
Pliny the Elder, *26, 90, 92, 177, 373, 424, 425,* 452
Pliny the Younger, 24, 151, 325 *n* 91, 354, 452, 462
  army recommendation, *265*
  chariot racing, *355*
  Christians, *414–16*
  dinner invitation, *85*
  families, *25, 32*
  hunting, *323–24*
  marriage, *38–40, 45–46*

recitation, *321–23*
river spirit, *363–64*
school endowment, *111–12*
senatorial activities, *152*
sharecroppers, *160–61*
slavery, *181–82, 184–85*
villa, *76–80*
women, *291, 292–93, 296, 298, 302*
Plutarch, *105, 143–45, 384,* 452
Pluto, 408 *n* 278
Poetry
  analysis of, 116–17, 300
  composition of, 110 *n* 35, 199, 299, 318, 322, 326, 385
  recitation of, 84, 320–21
Poisoning, 167 *n* 215, 194, 227, 264 *n* 82, 397
Politics. *See also* Alliance, political; Campaign, political
  career in, 7–8, 11 *n* 28, 39, 151, 210, 218–20, 228, 271, 272, 333, 386
  in imperial period, 38–39, 231–39
Pollux, 353
Polybius, *98–99, 214–15, 226–28,* 250, *251–56,* 259, 452–53, 461
Polytheism, 413
Pompa, 353 *n* 261
Pompeii, 25, 59, 60, 85, 162 *n* 188, 238 *n* 195, 440, 462
  leisure activity, 308, 311 *n* 20, 312 *n* 30, 313, 338 *n* 185, 343 *n* 214, 344 *n* 216
  religion, 397 *n* 239, 408 *n* 279
  sources from, 25, 64–65, 68, 71, 102–3, 138, 224–25, 319, 329, 330, 344–45
Pompey (Cn. Pompeius Magnus), 56, 67, 96 *n* 81, 144 *n* 104, 145 *n* 111, 219 *n* 86, 273 *n* 18, 275–76, 338, 339, 346, 347, 461, 462
Pomponia, 48–49
Pomptine Marsh, 70, 327 *n* 106, 440
Pontifex, 386–87, 388
Pontifex Maximus, 233 *n* 166, 361, 376, 386, 388, 393
Pontifical college. *See* College, priestly
Pontius Pilatus, 413
Poppaea, 259
Populares, 216, 221, 229
Population
  Pompeii, 311 *n* 20
  Rome, 3 *n* 1, 268
Populus, 206 *n* 4, 208 *n* 21, 209
Porter, 132, 133, 197
Portico, 60–61, 76–77
Post meridiem, 127
Postumius Albinus, Sp., 397, 398, 400
Poultry raiser, 130
Praenomen, 203 *n* 78
Praeteritio, 280 *n* 62

Praetor, 147, 148, 190, 207, 211, 212, 214, 220, 235, 271, 275, 278, 280, 373 *n* 91, 387 *n* 186
Praetor peregrinus, 214, 245
Praetor urbanus, 214, 245, 399, 400
Praetorian guard, 236
Prayer, Roman, 364–65, 368, 373–76, 380–83
Prefect
  city, 178, 235, 392
  of Egypt, 149, 236, 262
  military, 236, 251, 253, 254, 262, 267, 274–75, 276
  of praetorian guard, 236
Priapus, 371
Price
  food, 134–35
  manumission, 198, 205
Priest, 71, 237, 344, 373–74, 379, 384, 398, 400, 402–3, 405–8
Priesthood, 129, 233, 344 *n* 217, 360–61, 386–87, 390, 393, 419 *n* 316
Prince, 238 *n* 199
Princeps, 238
Principate, 231–35, 238, 240–42
Prison, private, 73, 172, 188
Prison, public, 71, 120, 184, 259, 286
Procession, 40, 98–99, 257–59, 308, 353, 380, 381, 402, 403, 404–7
Proconsul, 227, 233, 271, 273
Procurator, 236–37, 413
Property
  confiscation of, 13, 55, 145, 155, 254, 298
  ownership and military service, 154, 156, 249–50
  qualification, equestrian, 9, 224 *n* 113
  qualification, senatorial, 8 *n* 11, 9
  rights defended, 215–17
  value and military units, 252
  value and voting groups, 207, 208, 211, 222 *n* 104
Propraetor, 227 *n* 131, 271
Proscription, 145, 202, 294 *n* 18, 461
Proserpina, 366, 408
Prostitution, 54, 120, 170, 188, 197, 200, 218, 329–30
Protest, public. *See* Riot
Province
  administration of, 226, 227 *n* 131, 232, 245, 270–77, 414–16
  definition of, 147 *n* 121
  exploitation of, 272, 277–87, 333 *n* 157, 347–48
  hatred of Romans, 287–89
  rebellion in, 149, 259, 261 *n* 73, 270, 289
  tax collection and moneylending in, 148–50, 230, 271, 272–77, 285–86
Provincia, 147 *n* 121, 271 *n* 7

Ptolemy Auletes, 150–51
Public (State)
  land, 155, 156, 158, 216 *n* 74, 284
  office. *See* Magistrate
  revenue and expenditure, 136–37, 147, 148, 155, 211, 212, 214, 215, 226–28, 236–37, 271, 272–73, 285–86
  service, 7–8, 12, 13, 129, 151
  slave, 170, 259, 374, 379
  works, 13, 65–69, 146, 211, 227, 228, 237
Public speaker, 117–19, 123–24, 220, 224, 277, 320. *See also* Oratory
Publican, 8, 62, 148, 149, 228, 230–31, 271–72, 276–77, 284 *n* 69
Puls, 81
Punic War, First, 270, 378, 460
Punic War, Second, 142, 147, 299, 311–12, 395, 460
Punic War, Third, 461
Punishment. *See* Capital offence and punishment; Corporal punishment
Puteoli (Pozzuoli), 146, 440
Pyrrhus, 165, 392, 460

Quaestor, 207, 210, 211, 212, 214, 215, 220, 235, 273 *n* 20, 277, 280
Quintilian, *32–33, 105–6,* 111 *n* 45, *117, 122–23,* 453
Quirinal Hill, 16, 439
Quirinus, 383

Rabirius Postumus, C., 150–51
Race. *See* Chariot racing
Ratio, 432
Reading. *See* Education; Library; Literary study; Recitation.
Real estate investment, 130, 138, 142 *n* 93, 144–45
Recipe, 85–88
Recitation, 46, 83–84, 319–23
Religion, family, 112, 152 *n* 145, 173, 294, 330, 361, 362–63, 387
Religion, foreign
  appeal of, 394–95, 404, 411
  of Bacchus, 396–401
  Christianity, 411–22
  of Cybele, 401–3
  of Isis, 403–9
  Judaism, 409–11
  mystery of, 394, 406, 407–8, 412
  other, 422–23
Religion, six dimensions of, 360
Religion, state (Roman)
  afterlife, 98 *n* 91
  deification, 39 *n* 12, 67 *n* 33, 389–91

deity, 361–71, 374, 375, 381–85, 387, 423.
    See also specific name
efficacy of, 360, 372, 391, 393, 423
ethics in, 372–73
festival, 80, 152 *n* 145, 173 *n* 37, 174, 317
    n 46, 331–32, 366 *n* 52, 380–86, 402
formalism, 364 *n* 25, 368 *n* 60, 372, 376,
    380, 394–95
Greek and Etruscan influence, 362, 367–68,
    376 *n* 116
materialistic, 361 *n* 3, 372
officer, 71, 129, 233, 237, 344, 360–61,
    373–74, 379, 384, 386–88
permanence, 383, 384 *n* 172, 392–94
ritual, 364–65, 369–70, 371–80
syncretism, 422–23
Remus, 384 *n* 166
Republican period
    definition of, 9 *n* 21, 460–62
    end of, 10 *n* 24, 96, 202 *n* 72, 216 *n* 72,
        231–32, 391
    establishment of, 7
    form of government, 7, 10–11, 206–31,
        241, 270–72
    freedom of speech, 238–39
    territorial expansion, 249, 270–71
Res publica, 10 *n* 23
Rhetor, 107, 109, 111 *n* 45, 117–23, 136,
    192
Rhetoric, 118, 119, 122–23, 280 *n* 62, 283
    n 68, 320
Rhine (Rhenus) River, 266, 444
Riding, horse, 76, 105, 164, 310, 325
Ring, 52, 196, 237 *n* 194
Riot, 137, 178–79, 242, 299–300
Road, 67, 68–69, 76, 139, 205, 211, 261
    n 72, 267, 325–26, 330, 429
Robigalia, 382–83
Robigus, 382–83
Roma, cult of, 389
Romanization, 3, 242, 264 *n* 83, 266 *n* 94,
    311 *n* 20
Rome
    city planning, 67–68
    development and change, 3, 139–40, 200,
        231, 301, 336 *n* 176, 361, 391, 395
    extension of power, 3, 6, 8, 249, 270–71,
        287–88
    fall of, 365 *n* 31, 393 *n* 222, 463
    fire in, 63, 145, 413, 462
    founding of, 6 *n* 4, 337 *n* 184, 460
    sack of, 243 *n* 227, 312 *n* 27, 365 *n* 31,
        391, 460, 463
    traffic, 69–70, 131 *n* 25
Romulus, 6 *n* 4, 14, 18, 199, 232, 337 *n* 184,
    384, 460
Romulus Augustulus, 463

Rostra, 98
Rubicon River, 391, 441

Sabine, 134, 165 *n* 198, 200, 256, 337 *n* 184,
    392, 441
Sacrifice, religious, 173 *n* 34, 202, 364–65,
    371, 373, 375, 379, 381, 383, 387
Sacrosanct, 212, 233 *n* 167
Sailing festival, 404, 406–7
Sailor, 71, 148
Saint Peter's Basilica, 374
Salamis, 274–76, 443
Salesman, 109, 131, 193
Sallust, 210 *n* 33, *298–99,* 453
Salutatio, 15 *n* 44, 16, 111 *n* 40
Salute, morning, 15–17, 111 *n* 40, 128, 222
Sammelbuch, 23, 112, 457
Samnite, 164 *n* 197, 165 *n* 198, 441, 460
Sappho, 52 *n* 72
Satan, 421
Saturn, 384–85
Saturnalia, 80, 174, 384–86, 436
School. *See* Education
Science, natural, 117
Scipio. *See* Cornelius Scipio
Scorpus, 359
Scribe, 105 *n* 7
Scribonia, 56, 58
Scriptores Historiae Augustae, 188
Sculptor, 109, 110, 244
Secretary, 105 *n* 7, 125–26, 177, 192
*Select Papyri, 23, 28, 30, 35, 44, 50, 112,
    149, 262,* 457
Self-image, Roman, 4–5, 152–53, 164–66,
    256–57, 314–15, 337–38, 392
Sempronia, 298–99
Senate of Rome
    administration of provinces, 226, 232, 271
    awarding of military triumph, 227, 258
    control of assemblies, 207, 226, 228–29
    control of public finances, 142–43, 147,
        226–27, 228, 333
    decree of, 66–67, 100, 226, 245, 275, 376,
        399–401
    development of, 6–8, 226
    duties, 226
    and equestrians, 142–43, 147, 148, 230–
        31, 272
    expulsion from, 210 *n* 33, 211
    house, 178, 393, 400 *n* 246, 439
    in imperial period, 39 *n* 14, 231, 232,
        238, 240, 320 *n* 63
    maintain public order, 178–79, 227, 396–
        401
    membership, 210, 219, 221 *n* 100, 225–26,
        240

Senate of Rome (*Cont.*)
  plea for religious tolerance, 393
  sends and receives embassies, 214, 227, 234, 390
Senator, 151–52, 153, 165, 209, 225–26, 230, 231, 361 *n* 5
Senatorial order (class), 7–9, 13, 99 *n* 95, 195, 198 *n* 49, 215, 218–19, 220, 235, 238, 274, 277 *n* 43, 278, 377
Senatus consultum, 226
Seneca, L. Annaeus, (the Younger), *15–16, 17, 31–32, 89,* 185, *186–87, 312–14, 331, 348–50, 363, 431–37,* 453–54, 462
Seneca, M. Annaeus, (the Elder), *119–21,* 453
Senior, 207 *n* 10
Septimius Severus (emperor), 250 *n* 9, 255 *n* 39, 463
Serapis, 146, 264, 405
Servilius Nonianus, M., 321, 424
Servius, *366,* 454
Sesterce. *See* Appendix II
Sewer, 67–68
Sewer cleaner, 135
Sharecrop, 159–61, 166 *n* 211
Shave. *See* Barber
Shepherd, 74, 135, 163–64, 183, 331 *n* 145, 381
Shipping, 8–9, 139–40, 143, 147, 148, 198–99
Shipwreck, 71, 199, 326
Shoemaker, 70, 131, 137–38
Shop, 60, 64–65, 70, 71, 137–38, 193–94, 217, 313
Sibyl, 379
Sibylline books, 369, 379–80, 386, 401, 402
Sicily, 136 *n* 56, 140, 182–84, 270–71, 277–78, 283–87, 441, 460
Sidonius Apollinaris, *351–52,* 454
Siege, 184, 264 *n* 82, 276, 369–70
Sign painter, 102, 225, 344
Sing, 46, 314
Sirius, 383
Sistrum, 405
Slaughterer, 202
Slave
  cruelty to, 176–78, 305–6
  dealing, 106 *n* 12, 143, 168–70, 199, 202
  execution of, 178–79, 188
  family separation, 189
  freedom, 185. *See also* Manumission
  funeral of, 101
  home-bred, 155, 171, 172 *n* 30, 175, 179, 192, 193, 382
  housing, 73–74
  kindness to, 184–89
  public, 170, 259, 374, 379
  revolt, 156, 181–84, 333 *n* 160, 461
  runaway, 180–81

at Saturnalia, 174, 385
  sexual exploitation of, 42, 50, 177, 178, 186
  source of, 30, 35, 168
  tortured for evidence, 192, 193, 416
  treatment of, 170–76
Smart, N., 360
Social mobility, 9–10
Social stratification. *See* Class structure
Social War, 6 *n* 2, 270, 461
Society, secret. *See* Association (club)
Socius, 6 *n* 2
Soldier. *See* Army
Solstice celebration, 384
Son, 18–19, 21, 30, 32, 105, 125–26, 264–65
Soranus, *24, 26, 27, 93, 304,* 454
Spain (Hispania), 147, 175, 257, 271, 319, 390, 444, 460
Span. *See* Measurement
Spartacus, 182–83, 333 *n* 160, 342 *n* 209, 461
Spectacle, 331–59. *See also* Amphitheater event; Arena event; Chariot racing; Theater
Spirit, protective, 48 *n* 55, 173 *n* 34, 419 *n* 319
Spoils. *See* Booty, distribution of
Spurius Ligustinus, 256–57
Stabian Baths, 312 *n* 30, 313
Staff, herald's, 341, 405
State. *See* Public (State)
State as family, 13, 234, 361 *n* 5, 387
Statius, *385,* 454
Stilus, 114 *n* 54
Stoa Poikile, 431
Stoicism, 21, 89, 185–87, 239, 297, 348–50, 431–37
Stola, 301 *n* 43
Strabo, *67–68, 241, 310,* 454
Strigil, 132 *n* 40
Student. *See* Education
Suasoria, 119–20, 122
Suetonius, *55, 58, 107–8, 110,* 188, *192, 202, 333, 334–35, 378, 390–91, 410, 412,* 454
Suicide, 184, 296, 300, 349–50, 399, 435
Sulla, L. Cornelius, 145, 149, 202, 213 *n* 52, 219 *n* 87, 228 *n* 135, 332, 461
Sulpicius Rufus, Servius, *95–96*
Summum bonum, 427, 432
Sundial, 127, 128, 196 *n* 30, 315, 460
Suovetaurilia, 380 *n* 140, 381
Superstition, 42 *nn* 30–31, 93, 416, 423–26, 427
Supplementum Epigraphicum Graecum, 389, 457
Surgeon, 205
Swim, 78, 105, 263, 310, 314, 320
Syme, Sir R., 238 *n* 201
Symmachus, 392, *393–94,* 454

Syria, 35, 145 *n* 113, 150, 200, 262 *n* 74, 376 *n* 115, 461

Tablet
  bronze, 36, 400, 401
  lead, 426
  marble, 100, 146, 373
  waxed, 36, 113–14, 140, 141, 284, 285, 323
Tablinum, 60–62
Tacitus, *15, 21, 29,* 111–12, *118–19, 122, 137, 178–79, 238, 266–67, 288–89,* 323, 336, 338, *339, 390, 413,* 454–55
Tailor, 131, 135
Talent (weight), 145, 274
Tarquin the Arrogant (Tarquinius Superbus), 6 *n* 4, 208 *n* 23, 460
Taxation, 148–49, 150, 169, 198, 231, 236–37, 271, 272–73, 285, 288, 289
Teacher, 71, 130, 192, 200. *See also* Education
Tebtunis, 72, 445
Tebtunis Papyri, 72, 457
Temple, 12, 211, 214, 360, 370, 380, 387, 400, 407–8
Tenant farmer. *See* Farmland
Tent, 253, 260, 266, 274
Tepidarium, 315 *n* 37
Terence, 130 *n* 19, *340–41,* 455
Tertullian, *416–17, 418–20,* 455
Theater, 128, 137, 210, 242, 302, 332–42, 385 *n* 178
Theater of Pompey, 338, 346–47, 461
Theft, 70, 71, 102, 163, 180, 194, 254, 314, 318
Theodosius I (emperor), 392, 463
Theodosius II (emperor), 422, 458
Thessaly (Thessalia), 217–18, 442
Thrace (Thracia), 202, 342 *n* 209, 442, 445
Thyestes, 421
Tiber River, 3, 4–5, 310, 363 *n* 20, 369, 409, 439
Tiberius (emperor), 56, 58, 93, 137 *n* 61, 237–38, 240, 241, 242 *n* 223, 389–91, 410, 462
Tibullus, *166,* 381, *382,* 455
Tightrope walker, 200, 340
Time. *See* Clock; Measurement
Tiro, M. Tullius, 125–26, 192–93
Titus (emperor), 259, 335, 461
Toga, 16, 33 *n* 49, 99, 111 *n* 39, 152 *n* 145, 237 *n* 194, 256, 318, 354, 364
Toilet, 68, 350
Tolerance, religious, 393–94, 409–10, 412–13, 421–22
Tomb. *See* Funerary law
Tomb, speaking from, 37 *n* 2, 194, 201, 205
Toothache, 425

Torch, 40–42, 70, 179, 180, 430
Trade, 85, 130, 139–40, 199, 288
Traffic, 69–70, 131 *n* 25
Trajan (emperor), 69, 248, 335, 336 *n* 175, 344, 414–16, 462
Transformation. *See* Metamorphosis
Transportation industry, 68, 133, 138, 140, 197
Travel, 76, 133, 149, 172 *n* 29, 206, 288, 325–31
Treason, 13, 227, 401 *n* 250, 414
Treggiari, S., 191
Trial. *See* Court case
Tribe, 207, 211, 212, 222, 238
Tribune, plebeian (of plebs), 136–37, 148, 155, 207, 208, 211–12, 213, 214, 218, 228 *n* 136, 233–34, 299, 460
Tribute, provincial, 136 *n* 56, 140 *n* 74, 270, 285–86, 288, 289
Triclinium, 60–61, 319, 329
Trimalchio, 115, 196–99, 316 *n* 40
Triumph. *See* Army
Triumvirate, First, 56–57, 144, 230 *n* 149, 231 *n* 152, 239, 276 *n* 36, 461
Triumvirate, Second, 55 *n* 80, 56–57, 144 *n* 104, 153 *n* 150, 294 *n* 18, 326, 462
Trivia, 368
Trojan War, 40 *n* 23, 300 *n* 37, 341, 347 *n* 227
Tullia, 20, 94–96, 192
Tunic, 113, 172, 174, 301, 351 *n* 252, 355
Turia, 293–96, 298
Turner, J.W.C., 243 *n* 225
Tusculum, 20, 49, 88, 440
Twelve Tables, 214, 242–43, 460
Tyrant, 121, 122, 187

Ulpian, *34,* 455, 458
Ulysses, 4, 181
Ummidia Quadratilla, 302
Undertaker, 91
Underworld, 94, 98, 205, 408 *n* 278
Upper class, 7–11, 12–17, 129–30, 138 *n* 66, 215, 244, 308, 324, 338, 340, 396–97, 426
Urania, 40

Valentinian II (emperor), 393
Valerius Maximus, *48,* 455
Vandal, 243 *n* 227, 463
Varro, 117, *163, 175, 212–13,* 455–56
Vedius Pollio, P., 177
Vegetius, *263–64, 268,* 456
Veith, I., 303
Velabrum Street, 84, 439
Velleius Paterculus, *242,* 456

Vellum, 22 *n* 25
Venereal disease, 239
Venus, 40, 341–42, 353, 362, 367, 382
Vergil, 84, 109, *244,* 300, 326, 327–28, 363
    n 20, 372 *n* 88, *438,* 456
Verres, C., 238, 277–87, 461
Verrius Flaccus, M., 110
Vespasian (emperor), 39, 259, 297, 462
Vesta, 363 *n* 14, 387–88
Vestal Virgin, 105, 144, 386, 387–88
Vestibulum, 60, 62, 77, 79
Vesuvius, Mount, 26 *n* 37, 102, 440, 462
Veteran. *See* Army
Veterinary, 135
Veto, 211, 218 *n* 85
Via, 165 *n* 200
Via Appia. *See* Appian Way
Victim. *See* Sacrifice, religious
Villa, 20, 49, 71, 72–80, 152, 163, 173, 182,
    312, 327 *n* 116, 331. *See also* Farmland
Villa of the Mysteries, 397 *n* 239
Viminal Hill, 47, 200, 439
Vir, 36 *n* 60, 144 *n* 104
Virginity, 292, 304 *n* 58, 388
Virtue, Roman, 3–5, 38–39, 45–46, 104, 153,
    242, 244, 253, 265, 293–94, 296, 298,
    324, 338, 361, 372, 422–23, 431
Virtus, 10 *n* 25, 434, 437
Visigoth, 312 *n* 27, 463
Vitellius (emperor), 462
Vitruvius, *59–62,* 456
Vocational training, 115–16
Von Hagen, V. W., 68 *n* 37
Voter, 6, 195, 206–11, 221–22, 237–38
Votive offering, 370 *n* 74, 376 *n* 109
Vow, 332, 370, 376–77
Vulcan, 362
Vulgus, 129 *n* 16

Wage and price control, 133–36, 463
Wall message, 25, 102–3, 132, 319, 330, 345.
    See also Advertisement on wall

War, Macedonian, 142 *n* 91, 461
War bond, 142–43
War captive, 143, 154, 168, 204, 259, 342,
    343, 409
War declaration, 208 *n* 19, 233
War with Allies. *See* Social War
Water clock, 315
Water supply, 65–67, 80, 317
Wax image, 61, 98, 99, 110
Weaver, 116, 131, 169
Wedding, 40–43, 152, 291, 308
Welfare assistance, 35–36, 136–37, 237
White, K. D., 153 *n* 148, 161
Widow, 23, 29, 30, 54, 304
Wife, battered, 47–48
Wig, 306
Wild animal hunt. *See* Amphitheater event
Will (Testament), 16, 70, 101, 120, 152, 185,
    190, 194, 198, 388
Window, 77, 79
Wine, 47–48, 82, 85–88, 134, 174, 198–99,
    308, 309, 319, 329, 373, 375, 396
Wine production, 74, 75, 397 *n* 239
    deity of, 382 *n* 146, 396
Wisconsin Papyri, 116, 169–70, 457
Witch, 425
Woman, Roman, 34, 106, 109 *n* 26, 151
    n 137, 208 *n* 21, 290–307, 384, 387–88,
    399, 417. *See also separate listings such
    as* Birth control; Childlessness; Daughter;
    Guardian; Marriage; Mother; Widow
Wool-working, 45, 109, 294, 301, 382
Worcestershire sauce, 85
Wrestler, 200, 310
Writing. *See* Education; Literary study;
    Poetry
Writing instrument, 113–14

Zeno, 419, 431, 460
Zeus, 367, 368 *n* 60, 371 *n* 80
Zonaras, *258–59,* 456